Tom Harmon
869-8324
870-6296

Pirsig & Kirwin-Pro.Respon. 4th Ed.—1

# *American Casebook Series*
# *Hornbook Series and Basic Legal Texts*
# *Nutshell Series*

of

## WEST PUBLISHING COMPANY

P.O. Box 43526
St. Paul, Minnesota 55164
June, 1984

---

### ACCOUNTING

Faris' Law and Accounting in a Nutshell, 377 pages, 1984 (Text)

Fiflis, Kripke and Foster's Teaching Materials on Accounting for Business Lawyers, 3rd Ed., 838 pages, 1984 (Casebook)

Siegel and Siegel's Accounting and Financial Disclosure: A Guide to Basic Concepts, 259 pages, 1983 (Text)

### ADMINISTRATIVE LAW

Davis' Cases, Text and Problems on Administrative Law, 6th Ed., 683 pages, 1977 (Casebook)

Davis' Basic Text on Administrative Law, 3rd Ed., 617 pages, 1972 (Text)

Davis' Police Discretion, 176 pages, 1975 (Text)

Gellhorn and Boyer's Administrative Law and Process in a Nutshell, 2nd Ed., 445 pages, 1981 (Text)

Mashaw and Merrill's Introduction to the American Public Law System, 1095 pages, 1975, with 1980 Supplement (Casebook)

Robinson, Gellhorn and Bruff's The Administrative Process, 2nd Ed., 959 pages, 1980, with 1983 Supplement (Casebook)

### ADMIRALTY

Healy and Sharpe's Cases and Materials on Admiralty, 875 pages, 1974 (Casebook)

Maraist's Admiralty in a Nutshell, 390 pages, 1983 (Text)

Sohn and Gustafson's Law of the Sea in a Nutshell, 264 pages, 1984 (Text)

### AGENCY—PARTNERSHIP

Fessler's Alternatives to Incorporation for Persons in Quest of Profit, 258 pages, 1980 (Casebook)

AGENCY—PARTNERSHIP—Continued

Henn's Cases and Materials on Agency, Partnership and Other Unincorporated Business Enterprises, 2nd Ed., approximately 400 pages, 1985 (Casebook)

Reuschlein and Gregory's Hornbook on the Law of Agency and Partnership, 625 pages, 1979, with 1981 pocket part (Text)

Seavey, Reuschlein and Hall's Cases on Agency and Partnership, 599 pages, 1962 (Casebook)

Selected Corporation and Partnership Statutes and Forms, 556 pages, 1982

Steffen and Kerr's Cases and Materials on Agency-Partnership, 4th Ed., 859 pages, 1980 (Casebook)

Steffen's Agency-Partnership in a Nutshell, 364 pages, 1977 (Text)

### AMERICAN INDIAN LAW

Canby's American Indian Law in a Nutshell, 288 pages, 1981 (Text)

Getches, Rosenfelt and Wilkinson's Cases on Federal Indian Law, 660 pages, 1979, with 1983 Supplement (Casebook)

### ANTITRUST LAW

Gellhorn's Antitrust Law and Economics in a Nutshell, 2nd Ed., 425 pages, 1981 (Text)

Gifford and Raskind's Cases and Materials on Antitrust, 694 pages, 1983 (Casebook)

Hovenkamp's Economics and Federal Antitrust Law, Student Ed., approximately 375 pages, 1985 (Text)

Oppenheim, Weston and McCarthy's Cases and Comments on Federal Antitrust Laws, 4th Ed., 1168 pages, 1981 (Casebook)

Posner and Easterbrook's Cases and Economic Notes on Antitrust, 2nd Ed., 1077 pages, 1981, with 1984–85 Supplement (Casebook)

### ANTITRUST LAW—Continued

Sullivan's Hornbook of the Law of Antitrust, 886 pages, 1977 (Text)

See also Regulated Industries, Trade Regulation

### ART LAW

DuBoff's Art Law in a Nutshell, 335 pages, 1984 (Text)

### BANKING LAW

Lovett's Banking and Financial Institutions in a Nutshell, 409 pages, 1984 (Text)

Symons and White's Teaching Materials on Banking Law, 2nd Ed., approximately 943 pages, 1984 (Casebook)

### BUSINESS PLANNING

Epstein and Scheinfeld's Teaching Materials on Business Reorganization Under the Bankruptcy Code, 216 pages, 1980 (Casebook)

Painter's Problems and Materials in Business Planning, 2nd Ed., 1008 pages, 1984 (Casebook)

Selected Securities and Business Planning Statutes, Rules and Forms, 485 pages, 1982

### CIVIL PROCEDURE

Casad's Res Judicata in a Nutshell, 310 pages, 1976 (text)

Cound, Friedenthal and Miller's Cases and Materials on Civil Procedure, 3rd Ed., 1147 pages, 1980 with 1984 Supplement (Casebook)

Ehrenzweig, Louisell and Hazard's Jurisdiction in a Nutshell, 4th Ed., 232 pages, 1980 (Text)

Federal Rules of Civil-Appellate-Criminal Procedure—West Law School Edition, approximately 477 pages, 1984

Hodges, Jones and Elliott's Cases and Materials on Texas Trial and Appellate Procedure, 2nd Ed., 745 pages, 1974 (Casebook)

Hodges, Jones and Elliott's Cases and Materials on the Judicial Process Prior to Trial in Texas, 2nd Ed., 871 pages, 1977 (Casebook)

Kane's Civil Procedure in a Nutshell, 271 pages, 1979 (Text)

Karlen's Procedure Before Trial in a Nutshell, 258 pages, 1972 (Text)

Karlen, Meisenholder, Stevens and Vestal's Cases on Civil Procedure, 923 pages, 1975 (Casebook)

Koffler and Reppy's Hornbook on Common Law Pleading, 663 pages, 1969 (Text)

Park's Computer-Aided Exercises on Civil Procedure, 2nd Ed., 167 pages, 1983 (Coursebook)

### CIVIL PROCEDURE—Continued

Siegel's Hornbook on New York Practice, 1011 pages, 1978 with 1981–82 Pocket Part (Text)

See also Federal Jurisdiction and Procedure

### CIVIL RIGHTS

Abernathy's Cases and Materials on Civil Rights, 660 pages, 1980 (Casebook)

Cohen's Cases on the Law of Deprivation of Liberty: A Study in Social Control, 755 pages, 1980 (Casebook)

Lockhart, Kamisar and Choper's Cases on Constitutional Rights and Liberties, 5th Ed., 1298 pages plus Appendix, 1981, with 1984 Supplement (Casebook)—reprint from Lockhart, et al. Cases on Constitutional Law, 5th Ed., 1980

Vieira's Civil Rights in a Nutshell, 279 pages, 1978 (Text)

### COMMERCIAL LAW

Bailey's Secured Transactions in a Nutshell, 2nd Ed., 391 pages, 1981 (Text)

Epstein and Martin's Basic Uniform Commercial Code Teaching Materials, 2nd Ed., 667 pages, 1983 (Casebook)

Henson's Hornbook on Secured Transactions Under the U.C.C., 2nd Ed., 504 pages, 1979 with 1979 P.P. (Text)

Murray's Commercial Law, Problems and Materials, 366 pages, 1975 (Coursebook)

Nordstrom and Clovis' Problems and Materials on Commercial Paper, 458 pages, 1972 (Casebook)

Nordstrom and Lattin's Problems and Materials on Sales and Secured Transactions, 809 pages, 1968 (Casebook)

Nordstrom, Murray and Clovis' Problems and Materials on Sales, 515 pages, 1982 (Casebook)

Nordstrom's Hornbook on Sales, 600 pages, 1970 (Text)

Selected Commercial Statutes, 1379 pages, 1983

Speidel, Summers and White's Teaching Materials on Commercial and Consumer Law, 3rd Ed., 1490 pages, 1981 (Casebook)

Stockton's Sales in a Nutshell, 2nd Ed., 370 pages, 1981 (Text)

Stone's Uniform Commercial Code in a Nutshell, 2nd Ed., approximately 500 pages, 1984 (Text)

Uniform Commercial Code, Official Text with Comments, 994 pages, 1978

UCC Article 9, Reprint from 1962 Code, 128 pages, 1976

UCC Article 9, 1972 Amendments, 304 pages, 1978

Weber and Speidel's Commercial Paper in a Nutshell, 3rd Ed., 404 pages, 1982 (Text)

**COMMERCIAL LAW**—Continued

White and Summers' Hornbook on the Uniform Commercial Code, 2nd Ed., 1250 pages, 1980 (Text)

**COMMUNITY PROPERTY**

Mennell's Community Property in a Nutshell, 447 pages, 1982 (Text)

Verrall and Bird's Cases and Materials on California Community Property, 4th Ed., 549 pages, 1983 (Casebook)

**COMPARATIVE LAW**

Barton, Gibbs, Li and Merryman's Law in Radically Different Cultures, 960 pages, 1983 (Casebook)

Glendon, Gordon, and Osakwe's Comparative Legal Traditions in a Nutshell, 402 pages, 1982 (Text)

Langbein's Comparative Criminal Procedure: Germany, 172 pages, 1977 (Casebook)

**COMPUTERS AND LAW**

Mason's An Introduction to the Use of Computers in Law, 223 pages, 1984 (Text)

**CONFLICT OF LAWS**

Cramton, Currie and Kay's Cases-Comments-Questions on Conflict of Laws, 3rd Ed., 1026 pages, 1981 (Casebook)

Scoles and Hay's Hornbook on Conflict of Laws, Student Ed., 1085 pages, 1982 (Text)

Scoles and Weintraub's Cases and Materials on Conflict of Laws, 2nd Ed., 966 pages, 1972, with 1978 Supplement (Casebook)

Siegel's Conflicts in a Nutshell, 469 pages, 1982 (Text)

**CONSTITUTIONAL LAW**

Engdahl's Constitutional Power in a Nutshell: Federal and State, 411 pages, 1974 (Text)

Lockhart, Kamisar and Choper's Cases-Comments-Questions on Constitutional Law, 5th Ed., 1705 pages plus Appendix, 1980, with 1984 Supplement (Casebook)

Lockhart, Kamisar and Choper's Cases-Comments-Questions on the American Constitution, 5th Ed., 1185 pages plus Appendix, 1981, with 1984 Supplement (Casebook)—reprint from Lockhart, et al. Cases on Constitutional Law, 5th Ed., 1980

Manning's The Law of Church-State Relations in a Nutshell, 305 pages, 1981 (Text)

Miller's Presidential Power in a Nutshell, 328 pages, 1977 (Text)

**CONSTITUTIONAL LAW**—Continued

Nowak, Rotunda and Young's Hornbook on Constitutional Law, 2nd Ed., Student Ed., 1172 pages, 1983 (Text)

Rotunda's Modern Constitutional Law: Cases and Notes, 1034 pages, 1981, with 1984 Supplement (Casebook)

Williams' Constitutional Analysis in a Nutshell, 388 pages, 1979 (Text)

See also Civil Rights

**CONSUMER LAW**

Epstein and Nickles' Consumer Law in a Nutshell, 2nd Ed., 418 pages, 1981 (Text)

McCall's Consumer Protection, Cases, Notes and Materials, 594 pages, 1977, with 1977 Statutory Supplement (Casebook)

Selected Commercial Statutes, 1379 pages, 1983

Spanogle and Rohner's Cases and Materials on Consumer Law, 693 pages, 1979, with 1982 Supplement (Casebook)

See also Commercial Law

**CONTRACTS**

Calamari & Perillo's Cases and Problems on Contracts, 1061 pages, 1978 (Casebook)

Calamari and Perillo's Hornbook on Contracts, 2nd Ed., 878 pages, 1977 (Text)

Corbin's Text on Contracts, One Volume Student Edition, 1224 pages, 1952 (Text)

Fessler and Loiseaux's Cases and Materials on Contracts, 837 pages, 1982 (Casebook)

Freedman's Cases and Materials on Contracts, 658 pages, 1973 (Casebook)

Friedman's Contract Remedies in a Nutshell, 323 pages, 1981 (Text)

Fuller and Eisenberg's Cases on Basic Contract Law, 4th Ed., 1203 pages, 1981 (Casebook)

Hamilton, Rau and Weintraub's Cases and Materials on Contracts, 830 pages, 1984 (Casebook)

Jackson and Bollinger's Cases on Contract Law in Modern Society, 2nd Ed., 1329 pages, 1980 (Casebook)

Keyes' Government Contracts in a Nutshell, 423 pages, 1979 (Text)

Reitz's Cases on Contracts as Basic Commercial Law, 763 pages, 1975 (Casebook)

Schaber and Rohwer's Contracts in a Nutshell, 2nd Ed., 425 pages, 1984 (Text)

**COPYRIGHT**

See Patent and Copyright Law

**CORPORATIONS**

Hamilton's Cases on Corporations—Including Partnerships and Limited Partnerships, 2nd Ed., 1108 pages, 1981, with 1981 Statutory Supplement and 1984 Supplement (Casebook)

**CORPORATIONS**—Continued

Hamilton's Law of Corporations in a Nutshell, 379 pages, 1980 (Text)

Henn's Cases on Corporations, 1279 pages, 1974, with 1980 Supplement (Casebook)

Henn and Alexander's Hornbook on Corporations, 3rd Ed., Student Ed., 1371 pages, 1983 (Text)

Jennings and Buxbaum's Cases and Materials on Corporations, 5th Ed., 1180 pages, 1979 (Casebook)

Selected Corporation and Partnership Statutes, Regulations and Forms, 556 pages, 1982

Solomon, Stevenson and Schwartz' Materials and Problems on the Law and Policies on Corporations, 1172 pages, 1982 with 1984 Supplement (Casebook)

**CORPORATE FINANCE**

Hamilton's Cases and Materials on Corporate Finance, 895 pages, 1984 (Casebook)

**CORRECTIONS**

Krantz's Cases and Materials on the Law of Corrections and Prisoners' Rights, 2nd Ed., 735 pages, 1981, with 1982 Supplement (Casebook)

Krantz's Law of Corrections and Prisoners' Rights in a Nutshell, 2nd Ed., 384 pages, 1983 (Text)

Popper's Post-Conviction Remedies in a Nutshell, 360 pages, 1978 (Text)

Robbins' Cases and Materials on Post Conviction Remedies, 506 pages, 1982 (Casebook)

Rubin's Law of Criminal Corrections, 2nd Ed., 873 pages, 1973, with 1978 Supplement (Text)

**CREDITOR'S RIGHTS**

Bankruptcy Code and Rules, Law School Ed., 438 pages, 1984

Epstein's Debtor-Creditor Law in a Nutshell, 2nd Ed., 324 pages, 1980 (Text)

Epstein and Landers' Debtors and Creditors: Cases and Materials, 2nd Ed., 689 pages, 1982 (Casebook)

Epstein and Sheinfeld's Teaching Materials on Business Reorganization Under the Bankruptcy Code, 216 pages, 1980 (Casebook)

Riesenfeld's Cases and Materials on Creditors' Remedies and Debtors' Protection, 3rd Ed., 810 pages, 1979 with 1979 Statutory Supplement and 1981 Case Supplement (Casebook)

**CRIMINAL LAW AND CRIMINAL PROCEDURE**

Cohen and Gobert's Problems in Criminal Law, 297 pages, 1976 (Problem book)

**CRIMINAL LAW AND CRIMINAL PROCEDURE**—Continued

Davis' Police Discretion, 176 pages, 1975 (Text)

Dix and Sharlot's Cases and Materials on Criminal Law, 2nd Ed., 771 pages, 1979 (Casebook)

Federal Rules of Civil-Appellate-Criminal Procedure—West Law School Edition, approximately 477 pages, 1984

Grano's Problems in Criminal Procedure, 2nd Ed., 176 pages, 1981 (Problem book)

Israel and LaFave's Criminal Procedure in a Nutshell, 3rd Ed., 438 pages, 1980 (Text)

Johnson's Cases, Materials and Text on Substantive Criminal Law in its Procedural Context, 2nd Ed., 956 pages, 1980 (Casebook)

Kamisar, LaFave and Israel's Cases, Comments and Questions on Modern Criminal Procedure, 5th ed., 1635 pages plus Appendix, 1980 with 1984 Supplement (Casebook)

Kamisar, LaFave and Israel's Cases, Comments and Questions on Basic Criminal Procedure, 5th Ed., 869 pages, 1980 with 1984 Supplement (Casebook)—reprint from Kamisar, et al. Modern Criminal Procedure, 5th ed., 1980

LaFave's Modern Criminal Law: Cases, Comments and Questions, 789 pages, 1978 (Casebook)

LaFave and Israel's Hornbook on Criminal Procedure, Student Ed., approximately 1300 pages, 1985 (Text)

LaFave and Scott's Hornbook on Criminal Law, 763 pages, 1972 (Text)

Langbein's Comparative Criminal Procedure: Germany, 172 pages, 1977 (Casebook)

Loewy's Criminal Law in a Nutshell, 302 pages, 1975 (Text)

Saltzburg's American Criminal Procedure, Cases and Commentary, 2nd Ed., 1193 pages, 1984 with 1984 Supplement (Casebook)

Uviller's The Processes of Criminal Justice: Investigation and Adjudication, 2nd Ed., 1384 pages, 1979 with 1979 Statutory Supplement and 1983 Update (Casebook)

Uviller's The Processes of Criminal Justice: Adjudication, 2nd Ed., 730 pages, 1979. Soft-cover reprint from Uviller's The Processes of Criminal Justice: Investigation and Adjudication, 2nd Ed. (Casebook)

Uviller's The Processes of Criminal Justice: Investigation, 2nd Ed., 655 pages, 1979. Soft-cover reprint from Uviller's The Processes of Criminal Justice: Investigation and Adjudication, 2nd Ed. (Casebook)

## CRIMINAL LAW AND CRIMINAL PROCEDURE—Continued

Vorenberg's Cases on Criminal Law and Procedure, 2nd Ed., 1088 pages, 1981 (Casebook)

See also Corrections, Juvenile Justice

## DECEDENTS ESTATES

See Trusts and Estates

## DOMESTIC RELATIONS

Clark's Cases and Problems on Domestic Relations, 3rd Ed., 1153 pages, 1980 (Casebook)

Clark's Hornbook on Domestic Relations, 754 pages, 1968 (Text)

Krause's Cases and Materials on Family Law, 2nd Ed., 1221 pages, 1983 (Casebook)

Krause's Family Law in a Nutshell, 400 pages, 1977 (Text)

Krauskopf's Cases on Property Division at Marriage Dissolution, 250 pages, 1984 (Casebook)

## ECONOMICS, LAW AND

Goetz' Cases and Materials on Law and Economics, 547 pages, 1984 (Casebook)

Manne's The Economics of Legal Relationships—Readings in the Theory of Property Rights, 660 pages, 1975 (Text)

See also Antitrust, Regulated Industries

## EDUCATION LAW

Alexander and Alexander's The Law of Schools, Students and Teachers in a Nutshell, 409 pages, 1984 (Text)

Morris' The Constitution and American Education, 2nd Ed., 992 pages, 1980 (Casebook)

## EMPLOYMENT DISCRIMINATION

Player's Cases and Materials on Employment Discrimination Law, 2nd Ed., 782 pages, 1984 (Casebook)

Player's Federal Law of Employment Discrimination in a Nutshell, 2nd Ed., 402 pages, 1981 (Text)

See also Women and the Law

## ENERGY AND NATURAL RESOURCES LAW

Rodgers' Cases and Materials on Energy and Natural Resources Law, 2nd Ed., 877 pages, 1983 (Casebook)

Selected Environmental Law Statutes, 758 pages, 1984

Tomain's Energy Law in a Nutshell, 338 pages, 1981 (Text)

See also Environmental Law, Oil and Gas, Water Law

## ENVIRONMENTAL LAW

Bonine and McGarity's Cases and Materials on the Law of Environment and Pollution, 1076 pages, 1984 (Casebook)

Findley and Farber's Cases and Materials on Environmental Law, 738 pages, 1981, with 1983 Supplement (Casebook)

Findley and Farber's Environmental Law in a Nutshell, 343 pages, 1983 (Text)

Rodgers' Hornbook on Environmental Law, 956 pages, 1977 (Text)

Selected Environmental Law Statutes, 758 pages, 1984

See also Energy and Natural Resources Law, Water Law

## EQUITY

See Remedies

## ESTATES

See Trusts and Estates

## ESTATE PLANNING

Kurtz' Cases, Materials and Problems on Family Estate Planning, 853 pages, 1983 (Casebook)

Lynn's Introduction to Estate Planning, in a Nutshell, 3rd Ed., 370 pages, 1983 (Text)

See also Taxation

## EVIDENCE

Broun and Meisenholder's Problems in Evidence, 2nd Ed., 304 pages, 1981 (Problem book)

Cleary and Strong's Cases, Materials and Problems on Evidence, 3rd Ed., 1143 pages, 1981 (Casebook)

Federal Rules of Evidence for United States Courts and Magistrates, approximately 325 pages, 1984

Graham's Federal Rules of Evidence in a Nutshell, 429 pages, 1981 (Text)

Kimball's Programmed Materials on Problems in Evidence, 380 pages, 1978 (Problem book)

Lempert and Saltzburg's A Modern Approach to Evidence: Text, Problems, Transcripts and Cases, 2nd Ed., 1296 pages, 1983 (Casebook)

Lilly's Introduction to the Law of Evidence, 486 pages, 1978 (Text)

McCormick, Elliott and Sutton's Cases and Materials on Evidence, 5th Ed., 1212 pages, 1981 (Casebook)

McCormick's Hornbook on Evidence, 3rd Ed., Student Ed., 1155 pages, 1984 (Text)

Rothstein's Evidence, State and Federal Rules in a Nutshell, 2nd Ed., 514 pages, 1981 (Text)

# LAW SCHOOL PUBLICATIONS—Continued

## EVIDENCE—Continued

Saltzburg's Evidence Supplement: Rules, Statutes, Commentary, 245 pages, 1980 (Casebook Supplement)

## FEDERAL JURISDICTION AND PROCEDURE

Currie's Cases and Materials on Federal Courts, 3rd Ed., 1042 pages, 1982 (Casebook)

Currie's Federal Jurisdiction in a Nutshell, 2nd Ed., 258 pages, 1981 (Text)

Federal Rules of Civil-Appellate-Criminal Procedure—West Law School Edition, approximately 477 pages, 1984

Forrester and Moye's Cases and Materials on Federal Jurisdiction and Procedure, 3rd Ed., 917 pages, 1977 with 1981 Supplement (Casebook)

Redish's Cases, Comments and Questions on Federal Courts, 878 pages, 1983 (Casebook)

Vetri and Merrill's Federal Courts, Problems and Materials, 2nd Ed., 232 pages, 1984

Wright's Hornbook on Federal Courts, 4th Ed., Student Ed., 870 pages, 1983 (Text)

## FUTURE INTERESTS

See Trusts and Estates

## IMMIGRATION LAW

Weissbrodt's Immigration Law and Procedure in a Nutshell, 345 pages, 1984 (Text)

## INDIAN LAW

See American Indian Law

## INSURANCE

Dobbyn's Insurance Law in a Nutshell, 281 pages, 1981 (Text)

Keeton's Cases on Basic Insurance Law, 2nd Ed., 1086 pages, 1977

Keeton's Basic Text on Insurance Law, 712 pages, 1971 (Text)

Keeton's Case Supplement to Keeton's Basic Text on Insurance Law, 334 pages, 1978 (Casebook)

Keeton's Programmed Problems in Insurance Law, 243 pages, 1972 (Text Supplement)

York and Whelan's Cases, Materials and Problems on Insurance Law, 715 pages, 1982 (Casebook)

## INTERNATIONAL LAW

Henkin, Pugh, Schachter and Smit's Cases and Materials on International Law, 2nd Ed., 1152 pages, 1980, with Documents Supplement (Casebook)

## INTERNATIONAL LAW—Continued

Jackson's Legal Problems of International Economic Relations, 1097 pages, 1977, with Documents Supplement (Casebook)

Kirgis' International Organizations in Their Legal Setting, 1016 pages, 1977, with 1981 Supplement (Casebook)

Weston, Falk and D'Amato's International Law and World Order—A Problem Oriented Coursebook, 1195 pages, 1980, with Documents Supplement (Casebook)

Wilson's International Business Transactions in a Nutshell, 2nd Ed., 476 pages, 1984 (Text)

## INTERVIEWING AND COUNSELING

Binder and Price's Interviewing and Counseling, 232 pages, 1977 (Text)

Shaffer's Interviewing and Counseling in a Nutshell, 353 pages, 1976 (Text)

## INTRODUCTION TO LAW

Dobbyn's So You Want to go to Law School, Revised First Edition, 206 pages, 1976 (Text)

Hegland's Introduction to the Study and Practice of Law in a Nutshell, 418 pages, 1983 (Text)

Kinyon's Introduction to Law Study and Law Examinations in a Nutshell, 389 pages, 1971 (Text)

See also Legal Method and Legal System

## JUDICIAL ADMINISTRATION

Carrington, Meador and Rosenberg's Justice on Appeal, 263 pages, 1976 (Casebook)

Nelson's Cases and Materials on Judicial Administration and the Administration of Justice, 1032 pages, 1974 (Casebook)

## JURISPRUDENCE

Christie's Text and Readings on Jurisprudence—The Philosophy of Law, 1056 pages, 1973 (Casebook)

## JUVENILE JUSTICE

Fox's Cases and Materials on Modern Juvenile Justice, 2nd Ed., 960 pages, 1981 (Casebook)

Fox's Juvenile Courts in a Nutshell, 3rd Ed., 291 pages, 1984 (Text)

## LABOR LAW

Gorman's Basic Text on Labor Law—Unionization and Collective Bargaining, 914 pages, 1976 (Text)

Leslie's Labor Law in a Nutshell, 403 pages, 1979 (Text)

Nolan's Labor Arbitration Law and Practice in a Nutshell, 358 pages, 1979 (Text)

## LABOR LAW—Continued

Oberer, Hanslowe and Andersen's Cases and Materials on Labor Law—Collective Bargaining in a Free Society, 2nd Ed., 1168 pages, 1979, with 1979 Statutory Supplement and 1982 Case Supplement (Casebook)

See also Employment Discrimination, Social Legislation

## LAND FINANCE

See Real Estate Transactions

## LAND USE

Hagman's Cases on Public Planning and Control of Urban and Land Development, 2nd Ed., 1301 pages, 1980 (Casebook)

Hagman's Hornbook on Urban Planning and Land Development Control Law, 706 pages, 1971 (Text)

Wright and Gitelman's Cases and Materials on Land Use, 3rd Ed., 1300 pages, 1982 (Casebook)

Wright and Webber's Land Use in a Nutshell, 316 pages, 1978 (Text)

## LEGAL HISTORY

Presser and Zainaldin's Cases on Law and American History, 855 pages, 1980 (Casebook)

See also Legal Method and Legal System

## LEGAL METHOD AND LEGAL SYSTEM

Aldisert's Readings, Materials and Cases in the Judicial Process, 948 pages, 1976 (Casebook)

Bodenheimer, Oakley and Love's Readings and Cases on an Introduction to the Anglo-American Legal System, 161 pages, 1980 (Casebook)

Davies and Lawry's Institutions and Methods of the Law—Introductory Teaching Materials, 547 pages, 1982 (Casebook)

Dvorkin, Himmelstein and Lesnick's Becoming a Lawyer: A Humanistic Perspective on Legal Education and Professionalism, 211 pages, 1981 (Text)

Fryer and Orentlicher's Cases and Materials on Legal Method and Legal System, 1043 pages, 1967 (Casebook)

Greenberg's Judicial Process and Social Change, 666 pages, 1977 (Coursebook)

Kelso and Kelso's Studying Law: An Introduction, 587 pages, 1984 (Coursebook)

Kempin's Historical Introduction to Anglo-American Law in a Nutshell, 2nd Ed., 280 pages, 1973 (Text)

Kimball's Historical Introduction to the Legal System, 610 pages, 1966 (Casebook)

Mashaw and Merrill's Introduction to the American Public Law System, 1095 pages, 1975, with 1980 Supplement (Casebook)

## LEGAL METHOD AND LEGAL SYSTEM—Continued

Murphy's Cases and Materials on Introduction to Law—Legal Process and Procedure, 772 pages, 1977 (Casebook)

Reynolds' Judicial Process in a Nutshell, 292 pages, 1980 (Text)

See also Legal Research and Writing

## LEGAL PROFESSION

Aronson's Problems in Professional Responsibility, 280 pages, 1978 (Problem book)

Aronson and Weckstein's Professional Responsibility in a Nutshell, 399 pages, 1980 (Text)

Mellinkoff's The Conscience of a Lawyer, 304 pages, 1973 (Text)

Mellinkoff's Lawyers and the System of Justice, 983 pages, 1976 (Casebook)

Pirsig and Kirwin's Cases and Materials on Professional Responsibility, 4th Ed., approximately 650 pages, 1984 (Casebook)

Schwartz and Wydick's Problems in Legal Ethics, 285 pages, 1983 (Casebook)

Selected Statutes, Rules and Standards on the Legal Profession, approximately 260 pages, Revised 1984

Smith's Preventing Legal Malpractice, 142 pages, 1981 (Text)

## LEGAL RESEARCH AND WRITING

Cohen's Legal Research in a Nutshell, 4th Ed., approximately 425 pages, 1984 (Text)

Cohen and Berring's How to Find the Law, 8th Ed., 790 pages, 1983. Problem book by Foster and Kelly available (Casebook)

Cohen and Berring's Finding the Law, 8th Ed., Abridged Ed., 556 pages, 1984 (Casebook)

Dickerson's Materials on Legal Drafting, 425 pages, 1981 (Casebook)

Felsenfeld and Siegel's Writing Contracts in Plain English, 290 pages, 1981 (Text)

Gopen's Writing From a Legal Perspective, 225 pages, 1981 (Text)

Mellinkoff's Legal Writing—Sense and Nonsense, 242 pages, 1982 (Text)

Rombauer's Legal Problem Solving—Analysis, Research and Writing, 4th Ed., 424 pages, 1983 (Coursebook)

Squires and Rombauer's Legal Writing in a Nutshell, 294 pages, 1982 (Text)

Statsky's Legal Research, Writing and Analysis, 2nd Ed., 167 pages, 1982 (Coursebook)

Statsky's Legislative Analysis: How to Use Statutes and Regulations, 2nd Ed., 217 pages, 1984 (Text)

Statsky and Wernet's Case Analysis and Fundamentals of Legal Writing, 2nd Ed., 441 pages, 1984 (Text)

**LEGAL RESEARCH AND WRITING—Continued**

Teply's Programmed Materials on Legal Research and Citation, 334 pages, 1982. Student Library Exercises available (Coursebook)

Weihofen's Legal Writing Style, 2nd Ed., 332 pages, 1980 (Text)

**LEGISLATION**

Davies' Legislative Law and Process in a Nutshell, 279 pages, 1975 (Text)

Nutting and Dickerson's Cases and Materials on Legislation, 5th Ed., 744 pages, 1978 (Casebook)

Statsky's Legislative Analysis: How to Use Statutes and Regulations, 2nd Ed., 217 pages, 1984 (Text)

**LOCAL GOVERNMENT**

McCarthy's Local Government Law in a Nutshell, 2nd Ed., 404 pages, 1983 (Text)

Michelman and Sandalow's Cases-Comments-Questions on Government in Urban Areas, 1216 pages, 1970, with 1972 Supplement (Casebook)

Reynolds' Hornbook on Local Government Law, 860 pages, 1982 (Text)

Valente's Cases and Materials on Local Government Law, 2nd Ed., 980 pages, 1980 with 1982 Supplement (Casebook)

**MASS COMMUNICATION LAW**

Gillmor and Barron's Cases and Comment on Mass Communication Law, 4th Ed., 1076 pages, 1984 (Casebook)

Ginsburg's Regulation of Broadcasting: Law and Policy Towards Radio, Television and Cable Communications, 741 pages, 1979, with 1983 Supplement (Casebook)

Zuckman and Gayne's Mass Communications Law in a Nutshell, 2nd Ed., 473 pages, 1983 (Text)

**MEDICINE, LAW AND**

King's The Law of Medical Malpractice in a Nutshell, 340 pages, 1977 (Text)

Shapiro and Spece's Problems, Cases and Materials on Bioethics and Law, 892 pages, 1981 (Casebook)

Sharpe, Fiscina and Head's Cases on Law and Medicine, 882 pages, 1978 (Casebook)

**MILITARY LAW**

Shanor and Terrell's Military Law in a Nutshell, 378 pages, 1980 (Text)

**MORTGAGES**

See Real Estate Transactions

**NATURAL RESOURCES LAW**

See Energy and Natural Resources Law, Environmental Law, Oil and Gas, Water Law

**NEGOTIATION**

Edwards and White's Problems, Readings and Materials on the Lawyer as a Negotiator, 484 pages, 1977 (Casebook)

Williams' Legal Negotiation and Settlement, 207 pages, 1983 (Coursebook)

**OFFICE PRACTICE**

Hegland's Trial and Practice Skills in a Nutshell, 346 pages, 1978 (Text)

Strong and Clark's Law Office Management, 424 pages, 1974 (Casebook)

See also Computers and Law, Interviewing and Counseling, Negotiation

**OIL AND GAS**

Hemingway's Hornbook on Oil and Gas, 2nd Ed., Student Ed., 543 pages, 1983 (Text)

Huie, Woodward and Smith's Cases and Materials on Oil and Gas, 2nd Ed., 955 pages, 1972 (Casebook)

Lowe's Oil and Gas Law in a Nutshell, 443 pages, 1983 (Text)

See also Energy and Natural Resources Law

**PARTNERSHIP**

See Agency—Partnership

**PATENT AND COPYRIGHT LAW**

Choate and Francis' Cases and Materials on Patent Law, 2nd Ed., 1110 pages, 1981 (Casebook)

Miller and Davis' Intellectual Property—Patents, Trademarks and Copyright in a Nutshell, 428 pages, 1983 (Text)

Nimmer's Cases on Copyright and Other Aspects of Law Pertaining to Literary, Musical and Artistic Works, 2nd Ed., 1023 pages, 1979 (Casebook)

**POVERTY LAW**

Brudno's Poverty, Inequality, and the Law: Cases-Commentary-Analysis, 934 pages, 1976 (Casebook)

LaFrance, Schroeder, Bennett and Boyd's Hornbook on Law of the Poor, 558 pages, 1973 (Text)

See also Social Legislation

**PRODUCTS LIABILITY**

Noel and Phillips' Cases on Products Liability, 2nd Ed., 821 pages, 1982 (Casebook)

Noel and Phillips' Products Liability in a Nutshell, 2nd Ed., 341 pages, 1981 (Text)

**PROPERTY**

Aigler, Smith and Tefft's Cases on Property, 2 volumes, 1339 pages, 1960 (Casebook)

Bernhardt's Real Property in a Nutshell, 2nd Ed., 448 pages, 1981 (Text)

Boyer's Survey of the Law of Property, 766 pages, 1981 (Text)

**PROPERTY**—Continued

Browder, Cunningham and Smith's Cases on Basic Property Law, 4th Ed., 1431 pages, 1984 (Casebook)

Bruce, Ely and Bostick's Cases and Materials on Modern Property Law, 1004 pages, 1984 (Casebook)

Burby's Hornbook on Real Property, 3rd Ed., 490 pages, 1965 (Text)

Burke's Personal Property in a Nutshell, 322 pages, 1983 (Text)

Chused's A Modern Approach to Property: Cases-Notes-Materials, 1069 pages, 1978 with 1980 Supplement (Casebook)

Cohen's Materials for a Basic Course in Property, 526 pages, 1978 (Casebook)

Cunningham, Whitman and Stoebuck's Hornbook on the Law of Property, Student Ed., 916 pages, 1984 (Text)

Donahue, Kauper and Martin's Cases on Property, 2nd Ed., 1362 pages, 1983 (Casebook)

Hill's Landlord and Tenant Law in a Nutshell, 319 pages, 1979 (Text)

Moynihan's Introduction to Real Property, 254 pages, 1962 (Text)

Phipps' Titles in a Nutshell, 277 pages, 1968 (Text)

Uniform Land Transactions Act, Uniform Simplification of Land Transfers Act, Uniform Condominium Act, 1977 Official Text with Comments, 462 pages, 1978

See also Real Estate Transactions, Land Use

**REAL ESTATE TRANSACTIONS**

Bruce's Real Estate Finance in a Nutshell, 2nd Ed., approximately 300 pages, 1985 (Text)

Maxwell, Riesenfeld, Hetland and Warren's Cases on California Security Transactions in Land, 3rd Ed., 728 pages, 1984 (Casebook)

Nelson and Whitman's Cases on Real Estate Transfer, Finance and Development, 2nd Ed., 1114 pages, 1981, with 1983 Supplement (Casebook)

Osborne's Cases and Materials on Secured Transactions, 559 pages, 1967 (Casebook)

Osborne, Nelson and Whitman's Hornbook on Real Estate Finance Law, 3rd Ed., 885 pages, 1979 (Text)

**REGULATED INDUSTRIES**

Gellhorn and Pierce's Regulated Industries in a Nutshell, 394 pages, 1982 (Text)

Morgan's Cases and Materials on Economic Regulation of Business, 830 pages, 1976, with 1978 Supplement (Casebook)

**REGULATED INDUSTRIES**—Continued

Pozen's Financial Institutions: Cases, Materials and Problems on Investment Management, 844 pages, 1978 (Casebook)

See also Mass Communication Law, Banking Law

**REMEDIES**

Dobbs' Hornbook on Remedies, 1067 pages, 1973 (Text)

Dobbs' Problems in Remedies, 137 pages, 1974 (Problem book)

Dobbyn's Injunctions in a Nutshell, 264 pages, 1974 (Text)

Friedman's Contract Remedies in a Nutshell, 323 pages, 1981 (Text)

Leavell, Love and Nelson's Cases and Materials on Equitable Remedies and Restitution, 3rd Ed., 704 pages, 1980 (Casebook)

McCormick's Hornbook on Damages, 811 pages, 1935 (Text)

O'Connell's Remedies in a Nutshell, 2nd Ed., approximately 330 pages, 1984 (Text)

York and Bauman's Cases and Materials on Remedies, 4th Ed., approximately 1200 pages, 1985 (Casebook)

**REVIEW MATERIALS**

Ballantine's Problems
Black Letter Series
Smith's Review Series
West's Review Covering Multistate Subjects

**SECURITIES REGULATION**

Hazen's Hornbook on The Law of Securities Regulation, approximately 520 pages, 1984 (Text)

Ratner's Securities Regulation: Materials for a Basic Course, 2nd Ed., 1050 pages, 1980 with 1982 Supplement (Casebook)

Ratner's Securities Regulation in a Nutshell, 2nd Ed., 322 pages, 1982 (Text)

Selected Securities and Business Planning Statutes, Rules and Forms, 485 pages, 1982

**SOCIAL LEGISLATION**

Hood and Hardy's Workers' Compensation and Employee Protection Laws in a Nutshell, 274 pages, 1984 (Text)

LaFrance's Welfare Law: Structure and Entitlement in a Nutshell, 455 pages, 1979 (Text)

Malone, Plant and Little's Cases on Workers' Compensation and Employment Rights, 2nd Ed., 951 pages, 1980 (Casebook)

See also Poverty Law

**TAXATION**

Dodge's Federal Taxation of Estates, Trusts and Gifts: Principles and Planning, 771 pages, 1981 with 1982 Supplement (Casebook)

**TAXATION**—Continued

Garbis and Struntz' Cases and Materials on Tax Procedure and Tax Fraud, 829 pages, 1982 with 1984 Supplement (Casebook)

Gunn's Cases and Materials on Federal Income Taxation of Individuals, 785 pages, 1981 with 1983 Supplement (Casebook)

Hellerstein and Hellerstein's Cases on State and Local Taxation, 4th Ed., 1041 pages, 1978 with 1982 Supplement (Casebook)

Kahn's Handbook on Basic Corporate Taxation, 3rd Ed., Student Ed., 614 pages, 1981 with 1983 Supplement (Text)

Kahn and Gann's Corporate Taxation and Taxation of Partnerships and Partners, 2nd Ed., approximately 1300 pages, 1984 (Casebook)

Kragen and McNulty's Cases and Materials on Federal Income Taxation, Vol. I: Taxation of Individuals, 3rd Ed., 1283 pages, 1979 with 1983 Supplement (Casebook)

Kragen and McNulty's Cases and Materials on Federal Income Taxation, Vol. II: Taxation of Corporations, Shareholders, Partnerships and Partners, 3rd Ed., 989 pages, 1981 with 1983 Supplement (Casebook)

McNulty's Federal Estate and Gift Taxation in a Nutshell, 3rd Ed., 509 pages, 1983 (Text)

McNulty's Federal Income Taxation of Individuals in a Nutshell, 3rd Ed., 487 pages, 1983 (Text)

Posin's Hornbook on Federal Income Taxation of Individuals, Student Ed., 491 pages, 1983 (Text)

Rice and Solomon's Problems and Materials in Federal Income Taxation, 3rd Ed., 670 pages, 1979 (Casebook)

Rose and Raskind's Advanced Federal Income Taxation: Corporate Transactions—Cases, Materials and Problems, 955 pages, 1978 (Casebook)

Selected Federal Taxation Statutes and Regulations, 1255 pages, 1983

Sobeloff and Weidenbruch's Federal Income Taxation of Corporations and Stockholders in a Nutshell, 362 pages, 1981 (Text)

**TORTS**

Christie's Cases and Materials on the Law of Torts, 1264 pages, 1983 (Casebook)

Green, Pedrick, Rahl, Thode, Hawkins, Smith and Treece's Cases and Materials on Torts, 2nd Ed., 1360 pages, 1977 (Casebook)

Green, Pedrick, Rahl, Thode, Hawkins, Smith, and Treece's Advanced Torts: Injuries to Business, Political and Family Interests, 2nd Ed., 544 pages, 1977 (Casebook)—reprint from Green, et al. Cases and Materials on Torts, 2nd Ed., 1977

**TORTS**—Continued

Keeton, Keeton, Sargentich and Steiner's Cases and Materials on Torts, and Accident Law, 1360 pages, 1983 (Casebook)

Kionka's Torts in a Nutshell: Injuries to Persons and Property, 434 pages, 1977 (Text)

Malone's Torts in a Nutshell: Injuries to Family, Social and Trade Relations, 358 pages, 1979 (Text)

Prosser and Keeton's Hornbook on Torts, 5th Ed., Student Ed., 1286 pages, 1984 (Text)

Shapo's Cases on Tort and Compensation Law, 1244 pages, 1976 (Casebook)

See also Products Liability

**TRADE REGULATION**

McManis' Unfair Trade Practices in a Nutshell, 444 pages, 1982 (Text)

Oppenheim, Weston, Maggs and Schechter's Cases and Materials on Unfair Trade Practices and Consumer Protection, 4th Ed., 1038 pages, 1983 (Casebook)

See also Antitrust, Regulated Industries

**TRIAL AND APPELLATE ADVOCACY**

Appellate Advocacy, Handbook of, 249 pages, 1980 (Text)

Bergman's Trial Advocacy in a Nutshell, 402 pages, 1979 (Text)

Binder and Bergman's Fact Investigation: From Hypothesis to Proof, 354 pages, 1984 (Coursebook)

Goldberg's The First Trial (Where Do I Sit?, What Do I Say?) in a Nutshell, 396 pages, 1982 (Text)

Hegland's Trial and Practice Skills in a Nutshell, 346 pages, 1978 (Text)

Hornstein's Appellate Advocacy in a Nutshell, 325 pages, 1984 (Text)

Jeans' Handbook on Trial Advocacy, Student Ed., 473 pages, 1975 (Text)

McElhaney's Effective Litigation, 457 pages, 1974 (Casebook)

Nolan's Cases and Materials on Trial Practice, 518 pages, 1981 (Casebook)

Parnell and Shellhaas' Cases, Exercises and Problems for Trial Advocacy, 171 pages, 1982 (Coursebook)

Sonsteng, Haydock and Boyd's The Trialbook: A Total System for Preparation and Presentation of a Case, Student Ed., approximately 400 pages, 1984 (Coursebook)

**TRUSTS AND ESTATES**

Atkinson's Hornbook on Wills, 2nd Ed., 975 pages, 1953 (Text)

Averill's Uniform Probate Code in a Nutshell, 425 pages, 1978 (Text)

Bogert's Hornbook on Trusts, 5th Ed., 726 pages, 1973 (Text)

Clark, Lusky and Murphy's Cases and Materials on Gratuitous Transfers, 2nd Ed., 1102 pages, 1977 (Casebook)

**TRUSTS AND ESTATES**—Continued

Gulliver's Cases and Materials on Future Interests, 624 pages, 1959 (Casebook)

Gulliver's Introduction to the Law of Future Interests, 87 pages, 1959 (Casebook)—reprint from Gulliver's Cases and Materials on Future Interests, 1959

McGovern's Cases and Materials on Wills, Trusts and Future Interests: An Introduction to Estate Planning, 750 pages, 1983 (Casebook)

Mennell's Cases and Materials on California Decedent's Estates, 566 pages, 1973 (Casebook)

Mennell's Wills and Trusts in a Nutshell, 392 pages, 1979 (Text)

Powell's The Law of Future Interests in California, 91 pages, 1980 (Text)

Simes' Hornbook on Future Interests, 2nd Ed., 355 pages, 1966 (Text)

Turrentine's Cases and Text on Wills and Administration, 2nd Ed., 483 pages, 1962 (Casebook)

Uniform Probate Code, 5th Ed., Official Text With Comments, 384 pages, 1977

Waggoner's Future Interests in a Nutshell, 361 pages, 1981 (Text)

**WATER LAW**

Getches' Water Law in a Nutshell, 439 pages, 1984 (Text)

Trelease's Cases and Materials on Water Law, 3rd Ed., 833 pages, 1979, with 1984 Supplement (Casebook)

See also Energy and Natural Resources Law, Environmental Law

**WILLS**

See Trusts and Estates

**WOMEN AND THE LAW**

Kay's Text, Cases and Materials on Sex-Based Discrimination, 2nd Ed., 1045 pages, 1981, with 1983 Supplement (Casebook)

Thomas' Sex Discrimination in a Nutshell, 399 pages, 1982 (Text)

See also Employment Discrimination

**WORKERS' COMPENSATION**

See Social Legislation

# CASES AND MATERIALS ON PROFESSIONAL RESPONSIBILITY

**Fourth Edition**

By

**Maynard E. Pirsig**
*Professor of Law Emeritus, University of Minnesota*
*Professor of Law, William Mitchell College of Law*

**Kenneth F. Kirwin**
*Professor of Law, William Mitchell College of Law*

AMERICAN CASEBOOK SERIES

WEST PUBLISHING CO.
ST. PAUL, MINN., 1984

50 West Kellogg Boulevard
P.O. Box 43526
St. Paul, Minnesota 55164

Printed in the United States of America

**Library of Congress Cataloging in Publication Data**

Pirsig, Maynard E., 1902–
Cases and materials on professional responsibility.

(American casebook series)
Includes bibliographical references and indexes.
1. Legal ethics—United States—Cases. I. Kirwin, Kenneth F. II. Title. III. Title: Cases and materials on professional responsibility. IV. Series.
KF306.A4P5 1984 174.'.3'0973 84–7566

**ISBN** 0–314–83001–4

# Preface

Eight years have elapsed since we presented the third edition of our casebook. Much has since occurred in the field of professional responsibility that makes the present fourth edition a most necessary one. Some of these developments have been brought about by the legal profession itself. But others have been produced by outside forces imposed upon the legal profession largely against its will.

Public criticism of the bar has been widespread, going beyond the usual complaints perennially made.[1] Such leaders as Derek Bok, president of Harvard University and former dean of Harvard Law School, and former President Jimmy Carter have expressed their concern over, among other things, the bar's failure to provide needed services for large segments of society, the cost of legal services and the overemphasis and reliance on the adversary system in the resolution of disputes.[2]

But the legal profession has been met with more specific developments many of which have affected the profession profoundly.

Lawyer advertising is no longer a forbidden practice, the United States Supreme Court finding none of the reasons given for the former almost total prohibition to have substantial validity.[3]

The organized bar has made a general retreat from its former aggressive attack on those deemed to be engaged in the unauthorized practice of law. The retreat was stimulated in very considerable part by the fear that charges of violation of the antitrust laws would be leveled against the bar.[4] The Supreme Court of the State of Washington has initiated a new program whereby it prescribes the qualifications and conditions of practice by real estate brokers.[5] Does this foretell the development of new sub-bar groups not unlike the division in England between barristers and solicitors?

The SEC continues to insist that lawyers who give legal assistance to clients in the corporate security field, assume responsibility for and if need be disclose to the SEC questionable information received from clients in order to protect investors who might otherwise be misled in relying on the information.[6] Should this responsibility extend beyond the securities field?

The corporate lawyer's status and role are receiving increasing attention both as to his or her duties to the corporation and its constituents, but also to the general public.[7]

1. See infra pp. 10–14.
2. See infra p. 11 n. b.
3. See infra pp. 541–54.
4. See infra pp. 82, 435–36.
5. See infra pp. 90–91.
6. See infra pp. 267–71.
7. See infra pp. 256–71.

Large numbers of women are entering the legal profession, from which they have been too long excluded. The United States Supreme Court, in holding that law firms may not discriminate against women in promotions within the firm, has given added emphasis to the right of women lawyers to equal status and recognition.[8]

Programs for group legal services have continued to flourish since the United States Supreme Court held in a series of cases that efforts of the organized bar, supported by state appellate courts, to stifle these programs were unconstitutional.[9]

One could continue. If entering lawyers are to understand these criticisms and developments and what can be done about them, they must have some understanding of the lawyer's role and responsibilities and how that role and those responsibilities affect society. The end result should be a greater appreciation of the indispensible function that lawyers serve in our society, better understanding of how that function can best be performed, and pride in being a participant.

It is from that point of view that this casebook has been prepared. Prominence has been given to the Model Rules of Professional Conduct, supplemented by the earlier Code of Professional Responsibility. The Model Rules are the organized bar's latest expression of what it conceives to be the role and responsibilities of the individual lawyer. When, and to the extent, adopted by courts, the Model Rules will be obligatory on members of the legal profession. Like any subject of higher education, they should be examined critically by both student and teacher. The same holds for the other materials contained in the casebook, including judicial decisions, scholarly works, and bar association opinions.

The materials begin with an examination of the basic concepts of professionalism as applied to lawyers, including their relationship to clients, and proceed to concrete issues, problems and obligations with which the legal profession and lawyers in the practice of their profession must deal.

Once again we wish to express our appreciation for the permission given by the various organizations, law reviews, publishers, and authors to reproduce portions of their materials in this casebook. To keep this casebook within manageable proportions, most selections have been severely edited. Much important material will be found in the footnotes, which the teacher and students may utilize depending upon the amount of time available for the course. Citations and footnotes of the courts and commentators have been omitted without so specifying; omissions of other matters are indicated by asterisks or brackets. Numbered footnotes in the reprinted materials are from the original; lettered footnotes

**8.** See infra p. 56 n. b. See generally infra pp. 53–56.

**9.** See infra pp. 527–34.

are ours. It is hoped that users of this book will turn to the originals in pursuing the subject further.

MAYNARD E. PIRSIG
KENNETH F. KIRWIN

William Mitchell College of Law
June, 1984.

*

# Acknowledgments

The editors are very grateful to the many persons and organizations who have granted permission to reprint portions of copyrighted materials in this casebook.

First, the editors desire to express their appreciation to the American Bar Association regarding the following:

Numerous matters excerpted from the ABA Model Rules of Professional Conduct (1983), ABA Model Code of Professional Responsibility and Code of Judicial Conduct (1982), and ABA Formal Opinions, all copyrighted by the American Bar Association. All rights reserved. Reprinted with permission.

Numerous excerpts from ABA Standards for Criminal Justice (2d ed. 1980), copyrighted by American Bar Association and reprinted with permission of the ABA and Little, Brown & Co.

Excerpts from ABA Handbook on Specialization (1983); Special Committee on Clients' Security Fund Report, 91 A.B.A. Rep. 596, 599 (1966); Crouch, Divorce Mediation and Legal Ethics, 16 Fam.L.Q. 219 (1982); and Wasserstrom, Lawyers as Professionals: Some Moral Issues, 5 Human Rights 1 (1975), all copyrighted by the American Bar Association and reprinted with permission.

Excerpts from Hill, Ethics for the Unelected, 68 A.B.A.J. 950 (1982), and Swaine, Impact of Big Business on the Profession: An Answer to Critics of the Modern Bar, 35 A.B.A.J. 89 (1949). Copyrighted by American Bar Association and reprinted with permission of the ABA and the American Bar Association Journal.

Excerpts from Marden, The American Bar and Unauthorized Practice of Law, excerpted from 33 Unauthorized Practice News 1, copyright 1967 by American Bar Association. All rights reserved. Reprinted with permission.

Excerpts from Maupin, Environmental Law, The Corporate Lawyer and the Model Rules of Professional Conduct, 36 Bus.Law. 431 (1981). Copyright 1981 by the American Bar Association. All rights reserved. Reprinted with the permission of the American Bar Association and its Section of Corporation, Banking and Business Law.

Secondly, the authors wish to thank the American Bar Foundation for its permission to reprint portions of Landon, Lawyers and Localities: The Interaction of Community Content and Professionalism, 1982 Am.B. Found. Research J. 459, and Nelson, The Changing Structure of Opportunity: Recruitment and Careers in Large Law Firms, 1983 Am.B.Found. Research J. 109.

Finally, the authors wish to thank those who have granted permission to reprint portions of the following materials:

ABA Annual Meeting, 49 U.S.L.W. 2125 (1980), reprinted by special permission from The United States Law Week, copyright 1980, by the Bureau of National Affairs, Inc., Washington, D.C.

Administrative Law—Workmen's Compensation Proceedings—Use of Lay Representatives, 58 Mich.L.Rev. 456 (1960), with permission of the Michigan Law Review Association.

Michael D. Bayles, Professional Ethics, copyright 1981 by Wadsworth, Inc. Reprinted by permission of Wadsworth Publishing Company, Belmont, California 94002.

Burger, The Role of the Law School in the Teaching of Legal Ethics and Professional Responsibility, 29 Clev.St.L.Rev. 377 (1980), with permission of Cleveland State University and Chief Justice Warren E. Burger.

Burt, Conflict and Trust Between Attorney and Client, 69 Geo. L.J. 1015 (1981), with permission of the copyright holder Phi Delta Phi Legal Institute, Inc.

Comment, National Survey of Bar Admission Application Forms: Need for Reform, 22 St. Louis U.L.J. 638 (1978), with permission of St. Louis University School of Law and of Ms. Anne D. Crane, the student author.

Ferren, The Lawyer's Professional Responsibility to the Legal System, 55 Wis.B.Bull. 10 (Sept. 1982), with permission of State Bar of Wisconsin.

W. Fisher, What Every Lawyer Knows (1974), with permission of the copyright holder Mr. Walter T. Fisher.

Freedman, Personal Responsibility in a Professional System, 27 Cath.U.L.Rev. 191 (1978), with permission of Catholic University of America Press, Inc.

Fried, The Lawyer as Friend: The Moral Foundations of the Lawyer-Client Relation, 85 Yale L.J. 1060 (1976), with permission of the copyright holder Professor Charles Fried.

The Government Client and Confidentiality: Opinion 73–1, 32 Fed.B.J. 71 (1973), with permission of the Federal Bar Association.

Heinz & Laumann, The Legal Profession: Client Interests, Professional Roles and Social Hierarchies, 76 Mich.L.Rev. 1111 (1978), with permission of the Michigan Law Review, Professor John P. Heinz, and Professor Edward O. Laumann.

Heise, Chemical Tests for Intoxication—Scientific Background and Public Acceptance, 41 Marq.L.Rev. 296 (1958), with permission of Marquette Law Review.

Jayanne A. Hino, Unauthorized Practice of Law—Limited Practice of Law for Real Estate Closing Officers, 57 Wash.L.Rev. 781

(1982), reprinted by permission of the author and the Washington Law Review Association.

J. Lieberman, Crisis at the Bar (1978), with permission of W.W. Norton & Co., Inc.

Leubsdorf, Communicating with Another Lawyer's Client: The Lawyer's Veto and the Client's Interests, 127 U.Pa.L.Rev. 683 (1979), with permission of the copyright holder Professor John Leubsdorf.

MacIver, The Social Significance of Professional Ethics, 297 Annals 118 (1955), with permission of the American Academy of Political and Social Science.

Platt & Friedman, The Limits of Advocacy: Occupational Hazards in Juvenile Court, 116 U.Pa.L.Rev. 1156 (1968), copyright 1968 by University of Pennsylvania, with permission of University of Pennsylvania Law Review and Fred B. Rothman & Co.

C. Rembar, The End of Obscenity (1968), with permission of the copyright holder Mr. Charles Rembar.

Shaffer, Christian Theories of Professional Responsibility, 48 So.Cal.L.Rev. 721 (1975), with permission of University of Southern California.

Weil & Roy, Start-Up Costs of a One-Lawyer Office, 52 N.Y.St. B.J. 601 (1980), with permission of the copyright holder Altman & Weil, Inc.

Weinstein, Judicial Notice and the Duty to Disclose Adverse Information, 51 Iowa L.Rev. 807 (1966), copyright 1966 University of Iowa (Iowa Law Review), with permission of University of Iowa (Iowa Law Review) and Judge Jack B. Weinstein.

Welch, Delinquency Proceedings—Fundamental Fairness for the Accused in a Quasi-Criminal Forum, 50 Minn.L.Rev. 653 (1966), with permission of Minnesota Law Review Foundation and Professor Thomas A. Welch.

Wentworth, Attorneys' Liens—A Survey and a Proposal, 35 Conn.B.J. 191 (1961), with permission of Connecticut Bar Association, Incorporated.

8 H. Wigmore, Evidence § 2291 (McNaughton rev. 1961), with permission of Little, Brown & Co.

Youngwood, The Contingent Fee—Reasonable Alternative? 28 Mod.L.Rev. 330 (1965), with permission of Modern Law Review Limited.

*

# Summary of Contents

# Table of Contents

# Table of Cases

**The principal cases are in italic type. Cases discussed in notes and footnotes are in roman type. References are to Pages.**

---

*

# Table of Rules of Professional Conduct

# Code of Professional Responsibility

## Canons



## Ethical Considerations



## Disciplinary Rules

# A.B.A. Standards



*

# A.B.A. Formal Opinions

Opinions from which extracts have been taken are in italic type. Opinions cited or discussed are in roman type.



*

# Other Authorities

Authorities from which extracts have been taken are in italic type. Authorities cited or discussed are in roman type.

*

# CASES AND MATERIALS ON
# PROFESSIONAL RESPONSIBILITY

**Fourth Edition**

*

# Chapter 1

# THE MEANING OF PROFESSIONAL RESPONSIBILITY

## A. UNDERLYING CONCEPTS

### M. BAYLES, PROFESSIONAL ETHICS

pp. 7–11, 13 (1981).[a]

No generally accepted definition of the term *profession* exists, yet a working concept is needed for our study of professional ethics. Because the purpose of this study is to consider common ethical problems raised by and within professions, a good definition will delineate characteristics of occupations with similar ethical problems. (These characteristics may prove to be related to some of those problems in important ways.) One need not characterize professions by a set of necessary and sufficient features possessed by all professions and only by professions. The variety of professions is simply too great for that approach. Rather, some features can be taken as necessary for an occupation to be a profession, and others as simply common to many professions and as raising similar ethical concerns.

Three necessary features have been singled out by almost all authors who have characterized professions. First, a rather extensive training is required to practice a profession. Lawyers now generally attend law school for three years, and in the past they underwent years of clerkship with an established lawyer. Many, if not most, professionals have advanced academic degrees, and one author has plausibly contended that at least a college baccalaureate is necessary to be a professional.

Second, the training involves a significant intellectual component. The training of bricklayers, barbers, and craftspeople primarily involves physical skills. Accountants, engineers, lawyers, and physicians are trained in intellectual tasks and skills. Although physical

a. From PROFESSIONAL ETHICS by Michael D. Bayles. © 1981 by Wadsworth, Inc. Reprinted by permission of Wadsworth Publishing Company, Belmont, California 94002.

skill may be involved in, for example, surgery or dentistry, the intellectual aspect is still predominant. The intellectual component is characteristic of those professionals who primarily advise others about matters the average person does not know about or understand. Thus, providing advice rather than things is a characteristic feature of the professions.

Third, the trained ability provides an important service in society. Physicians, lawyers, teachers, accountants, engineers, and architects provide services important to the organized functioning of society—which chess experts do not. The rapid increase in the numbers of professions and professionals in the twentieth century is due to this feature. To function, technologically complex modern societies require a greater application of specialized knowledge than did the simpler societies of the past. The production and distribution of energy requires activity by many engineers. The operation of financial markets requires accountants, lawyers, and business and investment consultants. In short, professions provide important services that require extensive intellectual training.

Other features are common to most professions, although they are not necessary for professional status. Usually a process of certification or licensing exists. Lawyers are admitted to the bar and physicians receive a licence to practice medicine. However, licensing is not sufficient to constitute an occupation a profession. One must be licensed to drive a car, but a driver's license does not make one a professional driver. Many professionals need not be officially licensed. College teachers are not licensed or certified, although they must usually possess an advanced university degree. Similarly, many accountants are not certified public accountants, and computer scientists are not licensed or certified.

Another feature common to professions is an organization of members. All major professions have organizations that claim to represent them. These organizations are not always open to all members of a profession, and competing organizations sometimes exist. Some bar associations, at least in the past, did not admit all lawyers. The organizations work to advance the goals of the profession—health, justice, efficient and safe buildings, and so on—and to promote the economic well-being of their members. Indeed, one author has stated that "the ethical problem of the profession, then, is * * * to fulfill as completely as possible the primary service for which it stands while securing the legitimate economic interest of its members." If this claim is even approximately correct, one must expect professional organizations to be deeply involved in securing the economic interests of their members. Nevertheless, such organizations do generally differ from trade unions, which are almost exclusively devoted to members' economic interests. One does not expect to find carpenters' or automobile workers' unions striking for well-designed and constructed buildings or automobiles, yet public school teachers do strike for smaller classes and other benefits for students, and physicians and nurses for improved conditions for patients.

A third common feature of the professional is autonomy in his or her work. Given the present concern with reconciling professions and liberal values, how far such autonomy should extend is an open question. The minimum lies perhaps in the tasks of the work itself. For example, surgeons are free to use their own judgment about the details of operating procedure and lawyers to use their judgment about how to draft a contract, provided they remain within the bounds of acceptable professional practice. If professionals did not exercise their judgment in these aspects, people would have little reason to hire them. However, many professionals now work in large bureaucratic organizations in which their autonomy is limited by superiors who direct their activity and overrule their judgments. Nurses are often thought to have an equivocal status as professionals simply because their superiors can overrule their judgments about specific aspects of their work. In these cases, however, an element of autonomy remains since the professionals are expected to exercise a considerable degree of discretionary judgment within the work context. Thus, an element of autonomy is a common and partially defining feature of a profession, though it might not be a necessary feature and the extent of such autonomy is debatable.

One may bias an investigation of professional ethics by using normative features (those saying how matters *should* be) to define or characterize professions. One common bias is to characterize professionals as primarily devoted to providing service and only secondarily to making money. Such claims may be legitimate contentions about what should govern professions and motivate professionals, but they do not define the professions. If lawyers are, in the words of one of the earliest American writers on legal ethics, George Sharswood, "a hord of pettifogging, barratrous, custom-seeking, money-making" persons, they nonetheless constitute a profession. An extreme example of the use of normative features to define professions is the following "consideration" presented by Maynard Pirsig: "The responsibility for effectuating the rendition of these services to all that need them and in such a manner that the public interest will best be served is left to the profession itself." In this one condition, Pirsig manages to assume three different normative principles. First, services should be provided to all who need them. Second, the services should be provided so as best to promote the public interest. Third, the profession itself should be the sole judge of the method for achieving the first two principles. Even if these normative principles are correct, they should not be erected into the defining features of a profession.

Distinctions among kinds of professions are usually related to the kinds of activities pursued by most but not all members of the professions. An important distinction in professional ethics is between *consulting* and *scholarly* professions. The consulting professions, such as law, medicine, and architecture, have traditionally practiced on a fee-for-service basis with a personal, individual relationship between client and professional. A consulting professional (or a professional in a consulting role) acts primarily in behalf of an individual client. A scholarly professional, such as a college teacher or scientific researcher, usually has either many clients at the same time (students) or no personal client (jobs assigned by superiors in a corporation). A scholarly professional usually works for a salary rather than as an entrepreneur who depends on attracting individual clients. Of course, this distinction is blurred in many cases. For example, a junior lawyer in a large law firm is more like a scientific researcher, and nurses have individual clients even though they usually work for a large organization (hospital). Among the consulting professionals are physicians, lawyers, accountants, consulting engineers, architects, dentists, psychiatrists, and psychological counselors. Other persons with tasks similar to some of the consulting professions include nurses, pharmacists, stock brokers, the clergy, insurance brokers, social workers, and realtors. Among the scholarly professions are nonconsulting engineers, teachers, scientists, journalists, and technicians.

These differences between the roles of consulting and scholarly professionals are crucial in defining the kinds of ethical problems each confronts. The economic considerations of the consulting professional—fees, advertising, and so on—are not important problems for the professional employed by a large organization on a salary. Although consulting architects and accountants have many ethical problems in the professional-client relationship, research scientists or engineers in large organizations do not normally deal with clients. University teachers do have clients, but they typically confront them in a group and have fewer problems of confidentiality, and so forth.

This discussion focuses on the consulting professions. Special emphasis is placed upon the legal and medical professions because they are among the oldest and largest professions and have often been models for newer professions. Moreover, they have the most developed codes of professional ethics, and there is considerable documented material about problems that arise. Finally, most people will deal with a physician or lawyer sometime during their life, whereas fewer people will deal with an architect or consulting engineer.

Three salient features of the role of the consulting professions in the United States during the last half of the twentieth century lie at the heart of the problem of their positions in a liberal society. First, they all provide an important service. Consulting engineers and architects design the structures and facilities essential to modern life—buildings, houses, power stations, transportation systems, and so on. Most of us depend on the medical and dental professions to protect our health and well-being, even our lives. The legal profession provides services essential for justice and equality before the law. Accountants, as auditors, testify to the financial integrity of institutions and keep track of the wealth in society. The services of professionals are important for individuals to realize the values they seek in their personal lives—health, wealth, justice, comfort, and safety.

Second, not only do the professions serve basic values, they also have a monopoly over the provision of services. In many professions, one must be legally certified to practice. Laws often make it a criminal offense to practice a profession without a license. Attempting to do without professionals or to be one's own professional can realistically have only minimal success. If one decides to be one's own physician, one cannot obtain access to the most useful medicines and technology; most drugs can only be obtained legally with a prescription from a licensed physician and from another professional, a pharmacist. Although one may legally represent oneself, the legal profession has waged continuous war against allowing people access to information that would enable them to handle their own legal problems, such as divorce and probate of wills. * * *

The legal monopoly of professional services has an important implication for professional ethics. Professionals do not have a right to practice; it is a privilege conferred by the state. One must carefully distinguish between a right and a privilege in this context. A right is a sound claim that one be permitted (or assisted) to act in some manner without interference. A privilege is a permission to perform certain acts provided specified conditions are fulfilled. With a privilege, the burden is upon the person obtaining it to demonstrate that he or she has the necessary qualifications. For example, one must pass tests for the privilege of driving a car. In the case of a right, the burden is upon anyone who fails to respect it, for example, by prohibiting the publication of one's opinions. Individual professionals have only a privilege to practice; in addition, the profession as a whole is a privileged activity created by the state to further social values.

A third feature of the consulting professional's role is that although some professions have secured legally protected monopolies, none of them has been subject to much public control. Monopolies such as public utilities that provide essential services have usually been subject to strict public control as to the conditions and types of services provided. In contrast, the professions have claimed and been accorded a large degree of self-regulation. They have claimed that because of the intellectual training and judgment required for their practice, nonprofessionals are unable to properly evaluate their conduct. Thus, in addition to control over membership and the disciplining of members, the professions also control the conditions of practice (including until recently the setting of fees and the regulation of advertising).

The combined effects of these three features—serving basic social values, monopoly, and self-regulation—are central to the issue of the role of professions in a modern, liberal society. Monopoly and self-regulation, if exercised improperly, may be detrimental to society and the quality of human life. As the number of professions and professionals increases and their decisions become more essential for the operation of a technologically complex modern society, the conduct and ethical principles of the professions as well as the enforcement of standards become a matter of increasing importance to everyone. If the principles of professional conduct are designed to favor professionals more than their clients and others, then liberal values are threatened. Monopolies are created for the benefit of society, and if they do not serve society well, then they are not justified. * * *

Professional ethics seeks to determine what the role of professions and the conduct of professionals should be. As a discipline, it includes aspects of social, political, and legal philosophy as well as individual ethics. The study of professional ethics will not automatically make one more ethical, but it should develop sensitivity to ethical problems and clearer thinking, provide some general guiding principles, and help one better understand the role and importance of professions in contemporary society. Professional ethics has gained popularity due to recent dramatic cases of unethical conduct or difficult issues, but deeper reasons may underlie this new popularity. The contemporary concern with professional ethics reflects consumerism and the need for society to reconsider the role and conduct of professionals.[b]

### *Comment*

The term "profession" may be used in a sense different from that when applied to attorneys, doctors, ministers, etc. For example, "the professional athlete" or "the oldest profession."

Which of the following are properly deemed persons engaged in a profession: engineer, architect, accountant, journalist, social worker, banker, real estate broker? Some of these have codes of ethics adopted by their organizations. See pp. 116–18 below. Should that have a bearing on the question?

## MacIVER, THE SOCIAL SIGNIFICANCE OF PROFESSIONAL ETHICS

297 Annals 118, 120–21, 123 (1955).

### STANDARDS COMMON, CODES DISTINCTIVE

The demarcation and integration of the profession is a necessary preliminary to the establishment of the [professional] code. Each profession becomes a functional group in a society whose tendency is to organize itself less and less in terms of territory or race or hereditary status, and more and more in terms of function. Each profession thus acquires its distinctive code. It is important to observe that what is

**b.** See also R. Dingwall & P. Lewis, The Sociology of the Professions (1982); M. Larson, The Rise of Professionalism (1977); Wade, Public Responsibilities of the Learned Professions, 21 La.L.Rev. 130 (1960); Weckstein, Training for Professionalism, 4 Conn.L.Rev. 409 (1972).

distinctive is the code rather than the standard. [T]he different codes of professional groups represent * * * the deliberate application of a generally accepted social standard to particular spheres of conduct. Medical ethics do not necessarily differ in quality or level from engineering ethics, nor the ethics of law or of statesmenship from those of architecture. * * *

Ethics cannot be summed up in a series of inviolate rules or commandments which can be applied everywhere and always without regard to circumstances, thought of consequences or comprehension of the ends to be attained. What is universal is the good in view, and ethical rules are but the generally approved ways of preserving it. The rules may clash with one another, and then the only way out is to look for guidance to the ideal. The physician may have to deceive his patient in order to save his life. The lawyer, the priest, and the physician may have to observe secrecy and keep confidences under conditions where it might be the layman's duty to divulge them, for the conception of the social welfare which should induce the one to speak out may equally in the peculiar professional relationship compel the other to silence. Every profession has its own problems of conduct, in the interpretation within its own province of the common principles of ethical conduct. The [doctor] to whom is entrusted, under conditions which usually admit of no appeal save to his own conscience, the safeguarding of the health of his patient, with due consideration for the health of the whole community, has to depend upon a special code applicable to that situation. So with the legal profession which, for example, has to provide professional service for all litigants, irrespective of the popularity or unpopularity of the cause. So with the architect, who has to determine his responsibility alike to the client, to the contractor, to the workmen, to the "quantity surveyor," and to the community. So with the university professor, who has to uphold the necessity of academic freedom against the pressure of prejudice and the domination of controlling interests which care less for truth than for their own success. So with the journalist, in his peculiarly difficult situation as the servant of a propagandist press. So with the engineer, the surveyor, the accountant, or the technician generally, who has to maintain standards of service and of efficiency against the bias of profit making. So with the manager, the secretary, or the officer of a corporation—for here business assumes most nearly the aspect of a profession—who has to reconcile the trust imposed on him by his employers with the duty he owes to himself and to those whose services he in turn controls. Out of such situations develop the written and the unwritten codes of professional ethics. * * *

### Professional Interest and General Welfare

Every organized profession avows itself to be an association existing primarily to fulfill a definite service within the community. Some codes distinguish elaborately between the various types of obligation incumbent on the members of the profession. The lawyer, for example, is declared to have specific duties to his client, to the public, to the court or to the law, to his professional brethren, and to himself. It would occupy too much space to consider the interactions, harmonies, and potential conflicts of such various duties. * * *

In addition it must suffice to show that the conception of communal service is apt to be obscured alike by the general and by the specific bias of the profession. It is to the general bias that we should attribute such attempts to maintain a vested interest as may be found in the undue restriction of entrants to the profession—undue when determined by such professionally irrelevant considerations as high fees and expensive licenses; in the resistance to specialization, whether of tasks or of men * * *; in the insistence on a too narrow orthodoxy, which would debar from professional practice men trained in a different school; in the unnecessary multiplication of tasks, of which a flagrant example is the English severance of barrister and solicitor. Another aspect of the general bias is found in the shuffling of responsibility under the cloak of the code. This is most marked in the public services, particularly the civil service and the army and navy—and incidentally it may be noted that the problem of professional ethics is aggravated when the profession as a whole is in the employ of the state. "An official," says Emile Faguet in one of his ruthless criticisms of officialdom, "is a man whose first and almost only duty is to have no will of his own." [a]

**a.** Compare C. Rembar, The End of Obscenity 218–21 (1968):

"A lawyer usually lives on what his clients pay him, an arrangement that clashes with his social function. The inconsistency appears in the curious transformation of the word 'client.' It originally referred to one who was a dependent, in a status inferior to that of the person he depended upon. Part of the protection the Roman *patronus* gave his clients was legal advice and representation in court. Now, however, there is too often a mutual dependency between attorney and client, an unhealthy symbiosis, and the dominance may point the other way. Lawyers need the patronage of their clients, which in etymological terms is a contradiction. * * *

"The word 'client' has spread to other commercial activities, and its most recent meaning is its most debased. Even in the law, it denotes, to an unhappy extent, nothing more than customer. And nothing less: lawyers who accept that meaning also accept the postulate that the important client, like customers generally, is always right.

"This is a poor state of affairs. It is not merely training and experience that the lawyer offers his client; there is also his detachment. He has a cool and distant perspective, and can see things clearer—not because he is always a clear-headed man, but because the problem is not his own. * * * Partisanship and detachment are in no way inconsistent when the partisanship is professional, but financial dependence and detachment are not congenial. His objectivity is even more important in the lawyer's broader obligations * * * to the law, to the interests of society. He is part of the judicial system, an officer of the court.

"And so, like the judge, the lawyer ought to get his pay from the government. Such a proposal would at first provoke fiercer opposition than did tax-supported medical care in the American Medical Association; Medicare, after all, affects only part of a doctor's practice. But lawyers might be reminded, gently, that being officers of the court, they are by tradition in the service of the government. And in modern government—federal, state and local—a great number of lawyers are already public employees. As a practical matter, once the shock had worn off, the opposition would probably be less solid than that of the doctors; there are impecunious practitioners who would stand to gain.

"The idea would be attacked as radical and socialistic, but it would in fact be reactionary. The *patronus* did not charge fees for

DANGER OF SPECIFIC GROUP BIAS

This last case brings us near to what we have called the specific bias of the profession. Each profession has a limited field, a special environment, a group psychology. * * * The group environment creates a group bias. The [lawyer] develops his respect for property at the risk of his respect for personal rights. The teacher is apt to make his teaching an over-narrow discipline. The priest is apt to underestimate the costs of the maintenance of sanctity. The diplomat may overvalue good form and neglect the penalty of exclusiveness. The civil servant may make a fetish of the principle of seniority, and the soldier may interpret morality as mere *esprit de corps*.

All this, however, is merely to say that group ethics will not by themselves suffice for the guidance of the group unless they are always related to the ethical standards of the whole community. This fact has a bearing on the question of the limits of professional self-government, though we cannot discuss that here. Professional group codes are, as a matter of fact, never isolated, and thus they are saved from the narrowness and egotism characteristic of racial group ethics. Their dangers are far more easily controlled, and their services to society, the motive underlying all codes, vastly outweigh what risks they bring. They provide a support for ethical conduct less diffused than that inspired by nationality, less exclusive than that derived from the sense of class, and less instinctive than that begotten of the family. As they grow they witness to the differentiation of community. Their growth is part of the movement by which the fulfillment of function is substituted as a social force for the tradition of birth or race, by which the activity of service supersedes the passivity of station. For all their present imperfections these codes breathe the inspiration of service instead of the inspiration of mere myth or memory. As traditional and authoritative ethics weaken in the social process, the ethics formulated in the light of function bring to the general standard of the community a continuous and creative reinforcement.

his advice or his advocacy. And the legal profession has never been entirely at ease with the way it earns its living. England and the United States differ on whether a lawyer may sue for unpaid fees and on whether contingent fees are permissible. (England says no to both.) Barristers' tailcoats still have a discreet pocket reached from the back, a vestige of the time when payment was made in a way supposed to keep the lawyer unaware of it.

"The proposal would solve one of the acute problems of our legal system: how to provide counsel to the poor. Moreover, it is not only the very poor who suffer. Every lawyer has had the excruciating experience of telling a client he must relinquish a just claim or yield to an unjust one because the client cannot afford litigation against a rich opponent. Contingent fees, a device to make payment easy, sometimes have unwholesome side effects; in any event, they cannot help the poor person who is a defendant. And it is not merely cases that require the presence of a lawyer; it is often required when there is no case at all.

"The law provides the structure in which we work and live. Our property and our incomes, as well as our freedom, depend upon the law; they are in essence, no more than legal concepts. Rights have a strange meaning when they cannot be enforced; hence counsel must be available to everyone. The ability to pay fees is irrelevant to justice. That some people should be advised of their rights and represented in their enforcement while others are not—that some should have rights in fact and others have them only in theory—is a flat denial of law."

## B. CRITICISMS OF THE LEGAL PROFESSION

### BURGER, THE ROLE OF THE LAW SCHOOL IN THE TEACHING OF LEGAL ETHICS AND PROFESSIONAL RESPONSIBILITY

29 Clev.St.L.Rev. 377, 378–80 (1980).

Our profession carries public and ethical burdens with its privileges. Daniel Webster spoke of justice as "the greatest interest of man on earth." As a profession with a monopoly over the performance of certain services, we have special obligations to the consumers of justice to be energetic and imaginative in producing the best quality of justice at the lowest possible costs for those who use it, and with a minimum of delay. It was in these respects that my late colleague, Charles Fahy, hoped that we would think of a lawyer and the law as forces for moral good, "as a civilization of its own, enhancing the whole of our civilization."

Unfortunately, few members of the general public see us this way. In one poll lawyers ranked in ninth place among professions on a public credibility rating, just above law enforcement officers, television news reporters and plumbers. In 1974, a poll sponsored by the American Bar Association showed: sixty-eight percent (68%) of the public believed that lawyers charged more for their services than they were worth; sixty percent (60%) believed that lawyers work harder for wealthy, influential clients than for others; eighty-two percent (82%) believed that many matters could be handled as well and cheaper by accountants, bank officers, and insurance agents; and forty-two percent (42%) believed that "lawyers are not concerned about doing anything about the bad apples in the legal profession." A 1977 Gallup poll on the honesty and ethical standards of lawyers found that only twenty-six percent (26%) of the sample rated honesty and ethical standards of lawyers as being high or very high, while twenty-seven percent (27%) rated lawyers' honesty and ethical standards low or very low. These results were substantially lower than those for members of the clergy, medical doctors, engineers, college teachers, bankers, police, journalists, undertakers, business executives, building contractors and others. Lawyers did rank higher than members of Congress, realtors, labor union leaders, state office holders, advertising practitioners and car salesmen.

One can reasonably question the validity of such surveys, but the findings of these polls—accurate or not—suggest that the public's perception of lawyers is that they needlessly complicate the problems of life; that average citizens do not seek legal advice as often as they could or should; that lawyers are not prompt in getting things done; and that lawyers do not care whether their clients fully understand what needs to be done and why. For my part, I would seriously question that these public perceptions are accurate—or fair—but as "straws in the wind," they afford little basis for complacency. These results, to some degree, are due to age-old, popular suspicions of the jargon and technicality in the profession, and to a failure to understand that lawyers are specialists who become identified with the interests they represent in conflicts. It is inevitable that lawyers, to some extent, become scapegoats. Over the centuries artists like Daumier, Shakespeare, Samuel Johnson, Dickens and Shaw, have had harsh things to say about the law's delays, lawyers' avarice, and the role of lawyers in fomenting conflicts.

But, as Harlan Fiske Stone wrote almost a half-century ago:

> "We cannot brush aside this lay dissatisfaction with lawyers with the comforting assurance that it is nothing more than the chronic distrust of the lawyer class which the literature of every age has portrayed. It is, I fear, the expression of a belief too general and too firmly held for us to shut our eyes to it." [a]

Nor can we take comfort in the diagnosis that lawyers are not alone among American institutions and professions—public and private—to suffer declining respect. A significant part of our profession has been, and continues to be, guilty of grave ethical lapses over which public awareness and resentment have grown. More serious is the complacency of the organized bar with even the most grave lapses of professional propriety.[b]

**a.** The quotation is from Stone, The Public Influence of the Bar, 48 Harv.L.Rev. 1 (1934).

**b.** Other leading public figures have been ciritical of the legal profession and the administration of justice. See the address of then President Carter before the Los Angeles County Bar Association, 64 A.B.A. J. 840 (1978). A reply to President Carter was made by the then president of the American Bar Association, in which he stated in part:

> "Specifically, I am concerned over the charge that the organized bar has resisted innovation. I have been authorized by Chief Justice Warren Burger to say on his behalf that the ABA has co-operated fully in every innovation he has advocated since he became chief justice. There is much more to be done to improve our legal system—and heaven knows we have been late getting to some problems—but we are getting there. We are committed to getting there."

Response of President Spann, 64 A.B.A. J. 841 (1978)

Five years later, Derek Bok, president of Harvard University and former dean of the Harvard Law School, in an address before the Bar Association of the City of New York, leveled a broad criticism against the organized bar and the failures of the legal system. Bok, Law and its Discontents: A Critical Look at Our Legal System, 38 Rec.A.B.City N.Y. 12 (1983). (A version of President Bok's address appears in Bok, A Flawed System of Law Practice and Training, 33 J. Legal Educ. 570 (1983).) Compare McKay, Too Many Bright Law Students? 33 J.Legal Educ. 596 (1983). For some thoughtful comments by several authors on Mr. Bok's criticisms, see 35 Harv.L.Sch.Bull. 7–21 (Winter 1984).

One reason the American Bar Association may not have been "getting there" sooner, or at all if Mr. Bok is correct, may be that the Association President's term is but a year. At the end of his term, Mr. Spann remarked, "Unfortunately, however, there's almost nothing that one president can start and then finish in his term." He listed the Kutak Commission as the most important achievement of his term. It "was my own idea, I proposed it, and it is functioning." Wm. B. Spann, Jr., Reviews His Year as President, 64 A.B.A. J. 1707 (1978). The ABA adopted the Commission's proposed Model Rules of Professional Conduct in August 1983.

The British administration of justice also is not without its critics. See Report of Royal Commission on Legal Services, Cmnd. 7648 (1979); Zander, The Report of the Royal Commission on Legal Services, 33 Current Legal Probs. 33 (1980).

## WASSERSTROM, LAWYERS AS PROFESSIONALS: SOME MORAL ISSUES

5 Human Rights 1 (1975).

[The author addresses two criticisms that have been made of the legal profession:]

The first criticism centers around the lawyer's stance toward the world at large. The accusation is that the lawyer-client relationship renders the lawyer at best systematically amoral and at worst more than occasionally immoral in his or her dealings with the rest of mankind.

The second criticism focuses upon the relationship between the lawyer and the client. Here the charge is that it is the lawyer-client relationship which is morally objectionable because it is a relationship in which the lawyer dominates and in which the lawyer typically, and perhaps inevitably, treats the client in both an impersonal and a paternalistic fashion.

[Speaking to the first criticism:]

[T]here is a special, complicated relationship between the professional, and the client or patient. For each of the parties in this relationship, but especially for the professional, the behavior that is involved is to a very significant degree, what I call, role-differentiated behavior. And this is significant because it is the nature of role-differentiated behavior that it often makes it both appropriate and desirable for the person in a particular role to put to one side considerations of various sorts—and especially various moral considerations—that would otherwise be relevant if not decisive. * * *

* * * Most clients come to lawyers to get the lawyers to help them do things that they could not easily do without the assistance provided by the lawyer's special competence. They wish, for instance, to dispose of their property in a certain way at death. They wish to contract for the purchase or sale of a house or a business. They wish to set up a corporation which will manufacture and market a new product. They wish to minimize their income taxes. And so on. In each case, they need the assistance of the professional, the lawyer, for he or she alone has the special skill which will make it possible for the client to achieve the desired result.

And in each case, the role-differentiated character of the lawyer's way of being tends to render irrelevant what would otherwise be morally relevant considerations. Suppose that a client desires to make a will disinheriting her children because they opposed the war in Vietnam. Should the lawyer refuse to draft the will because the lawyer thinks this a bad reason to disinherit one's children? Suppose a client can avoid the payment of taxes through a loophole only available to a few wealthy taxpayers. Should the lawyer refuse to tell the client of a loophole because the lawyer thinks it an unfair advantage for the rich? Suppose a client wants to start a corporation that will manufacture, distribute and promote a harmful but not illegal substance, e.g., cigarettes. Should the lawyer refuse to prepare the articles of incorporation for the corporation? In each case, the accepted view within the profession is that these matters are just of no concern to the lawyer *qua* lawyer. The lawyer need not of course agree to represent the client (and that is equally true for the unpopular client accused of a heinous crime), but there is nothing wrong with representing a client whose aims and purposes are quite immoral. And having agreed to do so, the lawyer is required to provide the best possible assistance, without regard to his or her disapproval of the objective that is sought.

The lesson, on this view, is clear. The job of the lawyer, so the argument typically concludes, is not to approve or disapprove of the character of his or her client, the cause for which the client seeks the lawyer's assistance, or the avenues provided by the law to achieve that which the client wants to accomplish. The lawyer's task is, instead, to provide that competence which the client lacks and the lawyer, as professional, possesses. In this way, the lawyer as professional comes to inhabit a simplified universe which is strikingly amoral—which regards as morally irrelevant any number of factors which nonprofessional citizens might take to be important, if not decisive, in their everyday lives. And the difficulty I have with all of this is that the arguments for such a way of life seem to be not quite so convincing to me as they do to many lawyers. I am, that is, at best uncertain that it is a good thing for lawyers to be so professional—for them to embrace so completely this role-differentiated way of approaching matters.

* * * It is especially hard, if not impossible, because of the nature of the professions, for one's professional way of thinking not to dominate one's entire adult life. * * * The nature of the professions—the lengthy educational preparation, the prestige and economic rewards, and the concomitant enhanced sense of self—makes the role of professional a difficult one to shed even in those obvious situations in which that role is neither required nor appropriate. In important respects, one's professional role becomes and is one's dominant role, so that for many persons at least they become their professional being. This is at a minimum a heavy price to pay for the professions as we know them in our culture, and especially so for lawyers. Whether it is an inevitable price is, I think, an open question, largely because the problem has not begun to be fully perceived as such by the professionals in general, the legal profession in particular, or by the educational institutions that train professionals."

[As to the second criticism, the author observes:]

One way to begin to explore the problem is to see that one pervasive, and I think necessary, feature of the relationship between any professional and the client or patient is that it is in some sense a relationship of inequality. This relationship of inequality is intrinsic to the existence of professionalism. For the professional is, in some respects at least, always in a position of dominance vis-a-vis the client, and the client in a position of dependence vis-a-vis the professional. To be sure, the client can often decide whether or not to enter into a relationship with a professional. And often, too, the client has the power to decide whether to terminate the relationship. But the significant thing I want to focus upon is that while the relationship exists, there are important respects in which the relationship cannot be a relationship between equals and must be one in which it is the professional who is in control. As I have said, I believe this is a necessary and not merely a familiar characteristic of the relationship between professionals and those they serve. * * *

[As reasons for this inequality, the author discusses the "expert knowledge" of the attorney, the "technical language" employed by attorneys, the inability, for these and other reasons, of the client to evaluate the attorney's work, the client's own lack of objectivity, and the acculturation of the attorney. "It is hard, I think, if not impossible, for a person to emerge from professional training and participate in a profession without the belief that he or she is a special kind of person, both different from and somewhat better than those non-professional members of the social order. It is equally hard for the other members of society not to hold an analogous view of the professionals."]

Without developing the claim at all adequately in terms of scope or detail, I want finally to suggest the direction this might take. Desirable change could be brought about in part by a sustained effort to simplify legal language and to make the legal processes less mysterious and more directly available to lay persons. The way the law works now, it is very hard for lay persons either to understand or to evaluate or solve legal problems more on their own. But it is not at all clear that substantial revisions could not occur along these lines. Divorce, probate, and personal injury are only three fairly obvious areas where the lawyers' economic self-interest says a good deal more about resistance to change and simplification than does a consideration on the merits.

The more fundamental changes, though, would, I think, have to await an explicit effort to alter the ways in which lawyers are educated and acculturated to view themselves, their clients, and the relationships that ought to exist between them. It is, I believe, indicative of the state of legal education and of the profession that there has been to date extremely little self-conscious concern even with the possibility that these dimensions of the attorney-client relationship are worth examining—to say nothing of being capable of alteration. That awareness, is surely, the prerequisite to any serious assessment of the moral character of the attorney-client relationship as a relationship among adult human beings. * * * [a]

a. See also Shaffer, The Practice of Law as Moral Discourse, 55 Notre Dame Law. 231 (1979).

## FRIED, THE LAWYER AS FRIEND: THE MORAL FOUNDATIONS OF THE LAWYER-CLIENT RELATION

85 Yale L.J. 1060, 1066–67, 1071–73 (1976).

[In this article, Professor Fried's approach to the criticisms of the legal profession is that the lawyer is properly acting as a friend, "a limited friend" of the client. The lawyer's loyalties and duties are similar to those owed to a friend or close relative. He identifies two criticisms and discusses them from this approach:

(1) The profession's failure to provide its services to those in greater need and to those in need in greater numbers;

(2) In acting for the client, the lawyer's "loyalty appears to authorize tactics which procure advantages for the client at the direct expense of some identified opposing party. Examples are discrediting a nervous but probably truthful complaining witness or taking advantage of the need or ignorance of an adversary in a negotiation."]

I will argue in this essay that it is not only legally but also morally right that a lawyer adopt as his dominant purpose the furthering of his client's interests—that it is right that a professional put the interests of his client above some idea, however valid, of the collective interest. I maintain that the traditional conception of the professional role expresses a morally valid conception of human conduct and human relationships, that one who acts according to that conception is to that extent a good person. Indeed, it is my view that, far from being a mere creature of positive law, the traditional conception is so far mandated by moral right that any advanced legal system which did not sanction this conception would be unjust.

The general problem raised by the two criticisms is this: How can it be that it is not only permissible, but indeed morally right, to favor the interests of a particular person in a way which we can be fairly sure is either harmful to another particular individual or not maximally conducive to the welfare of society as a whole?

The resolution of this problem is aided, I think, if set in a larger perspective. Charles Curtis made the perspicacious remark that a lawyer may be privileged to lie for his client in a way that one might lie to save one's friends or close relatives.[17] I do not want to underwrite the notion that it is justifiable to lie even in those situations, but there is a great deal to the point that in those relations—friendship, kinship—we recognize an authorization to take the interests of particular concrete persons more seriously and to give them priority over the interests of the wider collectivity. One who provides an expensive education for his own children surely cannot be blamed because he

17. Curtis, [The Ethics of Advocacy, 4 Stan.L.Rev. 3 (1951)] at 8. Analogizing the lawyer to a friend raises a range of problems upon which I shall not touch. These have to do with the lawyer's benevolent and sometimes not so benevolent tyranny over and imposition on his client, seemingly authorized by the claim to be acting in the client's interests. Domineering paternalism is not a normal characteristic of friendship. This point is due to Jay Katz.

does not use these resources to alleviate famine or to save lives in some distant land. Nor does he blame himself. Indeed, our intuition that an individual is authorized to prefer identified persons standing close to him over the abstract interests of humanity finds its sharpest expression in our sense that an individual is entitled to act with something less than impartiality to that person who stands closest to him—the person that he is. There is such a thing as selfishness to be sure, yet no reasonable morality asks us to look upon ourselves as merely plausible candidates for the distribution of the attention and resources which we command, plausible candidates whose entitlement to our own concern is no greater in principle than that of any other human being. Such a doctrine may seem edifying, but on reflection it strikes us as merely fanatical.

This suggests an interesting way to look at the situation of the lawyer. As a professional person one has a special care for the interests of those accepted as clients, just as his friends, his family, and he himself have a very general claim to his special concern. But I concede this does no more than widen the problem. It merely shows that in claiming this authorization to have a special care for my clients I am doing something which I do in other contexts as well. * * *

In explicating the lawyer's relation to his client, my analogy shall be to friendship, where the freedom to choose and to be chosen expresses our freedom to hold something of ourselves in reserve, in reserve even from the universalizing claims of morality. These personal ties and the claims they engender may be all-consuming, as with a close friend or family member, or they may be limited, special-purpose claims, as in the case of the client or patient. The special-purpose claim is one in which the beneficiary, the client, is entitled to all the special consideration *within* the limits of the relationship which we accord to a friend or a loved one. It is not that the claims of the client are less intense or demanding; they are only more limited in their scope. After all, the ordinary concept of friendship provides only an analogy, and it is to the development of that analogy that I turn.

How does a professional fit into the concept of personal relations at all? He is, I have suggested, a limited-purpose friend. A lawyer is a friend in regard to the legal system. He is someone who enters into a personal relation with you—not an abstract relation as under the concept of justice. That means that like a friend he acts in your interests, not his own; or rather he adopts your interests as his own. I would call that the classic definition of friendship. To be sure, the lawyer's range of concern is sharply limited. But within that limited domain the intensity of identification with the client's interests is the same. It is not the specialized focus of the relationship which may make the metaphor inapposite, but the way in which the relation of legal friendship comes about and the one-sided nature of the ensuing "friendship." But I do insist upon the analogy, for in overcoming the arguments that the analogy is false, I think the true moral foundations of the lawyer's special role are illuminated and the utilitarian objections to the traditional conception of that role overthrown.

The claims that are made on the doctor or lawyer are made within a social context and are defined, at least in part, by social expectations. Most strikingly, in talking about friendship the focus of the inquiry is quite naturally upon the free gift of the donor; yet in professional relationships it is the recipient's need for medical or legal aid which defines the relationship. So the source of the relationship seems to be located at the other end, that of the recipient. To put this disquiet another way, we might ask how recognizing the special claims of friendship in any way compels society to allow the doctor or the lawyer to define his role on the analogy of those claims. Why are these people not like other social actors designated to purvey certain, perhaps necessary, goods? Would we say that one's grocer, tailor, or landlord should be viewed as a limited-purpose friend? Special considerations must be brought forward for doctors and lawyers.

A special argument is at hand in both cases. The doctor does not minister just to any need, but to health. He helps maintain the very physical integrity which is the concrete substrate of individuality. To be sure, so does a grocer or landlord. But illness wears a special guise: it appears as a critical assault on one's person. The needs to which the doctor ministers usually are implicated in crises going to one's concreteness and individuality, and therefore what one looks for is a kind of ministration which is particularly concrete, personal, individualized. Thus, it is not difficult to see why I claim that a doctor is a friend, though a special purpose friend, the purpose being defined by the special needs of illness and crisis to which he tends.

But what, then, of the lawyer? Friendship and kinship are natural relations existing within, but not defined by, complex social institutions. Illness too is more a natural than social phenomenon. The response here requires an additional step. True, the special situations—legal relations or disputes—in which the lawyer acts as a limited-purpose friend are themselves a product of social institutions. But it does not follow that the role of the lawyer, which is created to help us deal with those social institutions, is defined by and is wholly at the mercy of the social good. We need only concede that at the very least the law must leave us a measure of autonomy, whether or not it is in the social interest to do so. Individuals have rights over and against the collectivity. The moral capital arising out of individuals' concrete situations is one way of expressing that structure of rights, or at least part of it. It is because the law must respect the rights of individuals that the law must also create and support the specific role of legal friend. For the social nexus—the web of perhaps entirely just institutions—has become so complex that without the assistance of an expert adviser an ordinary layman cannot exercise that autonomy which the system must allow him. Without such an adviser, the law would impose constraints on the lay citizen (unequally at that) which it is not entitled to impose explicitly. Thus, the need which the lawyer serves in his special-purpose friendship may not be, as in the case of the doctor, natural, pre-social. Yet it is a need which has a moral grounding analogous to the need which the physician serves:

the need to maintain one's integrity as a person. When I say the lawyer is his client's legal friend, I mean the lawyer makes his client's interests his own insofar as this is necessary to preserve and foster the client's autonomy within the law. This argument does not require us to assume that the law is hostile to the client's rights. All we need to assume is that even a system of law which is perfectly sensitive to personal rights would not work fairly unless the client could claim a professional's assistance in realizing that autonomy which the law recognizes.

### FREEDMAN, PERSONAL RESPONSIBILITY IN A PROFESSIONAL SYSTEM

27 Cath.U.L.Rev. 191, 194–99 (1978).

[After referring to Professor Wasserstrom's discussion of John Dean's list of attorneys involved in the Watergate coverup, the author continues:]

Professor Wasserstrom holds that the core of the problem is professionalism and its concomitant, *role-differentiated behavior*. Role-differentiation refers, in this context, to situations in which one's moral response will vary depending upon whether one is acting in a personal capacity or in a professional, representative one. As Wasserstrom says, the "nature of role-differentiated behavior * * * often makes it both appropriate and desirable for the person in a particular role to put to one side considerations of various sorts—and especially various moral considerations—that would otherwise be relevant if not decisive."

An illustration of the "morally relevant considerations" that Wasserstrom has in mind is the case of a client who desires to make a will disinheriting her children because they opposed the war in Vietnam. Professor Wasserstrom suggests that the lawyer should refuse to draft the will because the client's reason is a "bad" one. But is the lawyer's paternalism toward the client preferable—morally or otherwise—to the client's paternalism toward her children?

"[W]e might all be better served," says Wasserstrom, "if lawyers were to see themselves less as subject to role-differentiated behavior and more as subject to the demands of the *moral* point of view." Is it really that simple? What, for example, of the lawyer whose moral judgment is that disobedient and unpatriotic children should be disinherited? Should that lawyer refuse to draft a will leaving bequests to children who opposed the war in Vietnam? If the response is that we would then have a desirable diversity, would it not be better to have that diversity as a reflection of the clients' viewpoints, rather than the lawyers'?

In another illustration, Wasserstrom suggests that a lawyer should refuse to advise a wealthy client of a tax loophole provided by the legislature for only a few wealthy taxpayers. If that case is to be generalized, it seems to mean that the legal profession can properly regard itself as an oligarchy whose duty is to nullify decisions made by the people's duly elected representatives. Therefore, if the lawyers believe that particular clients (wealthy or poor) should not have been given certain rights, the lawyers are morally bound to circumvent the legislative process and to forestall the judicial process by the simple device of keeping their clients in ignorance of tempting rights.

Nor is that a caricature of Wasserstrom's position. The role-differentiated amorality of the lawyer is valid, he says, "only if the enormous degree of trust and confidence in the institutions themselves (that is, the legislative and judicial processes) is itself justified." "[W]e are today", he asserts, "certainly entitled to be quite skeptical both of the fairness and of the capacity for self-correction of our larger institutional mechanisms, including the legal system." If that is so, it is not a nonsequitur to suggest that we are justified in placing that same trust and confidence in the morality of lawyers, individually or collectively?

There is "something quite seductive," adds Wasserstrom, about being able to turn aside so many ostensibly difficult moral dilemmas with the reply that my job is not to judge my client's cause, but to represent his or her interest. Surely, however, it is at least as seductive to be able to say, "My moral judgment—or my professional responsibility—requires that I be your master. Therefore, you will conduct yourself as I direct you to."

[I]n an interesting and thought-provoking article, Professor Charles Fried has compared the lawyer to a friend—a "special-purpose" or "limited purpose" friend "in regard to the legal system." The lawyer, thereby, is seen to be "someone who enters into a personal relation with you—not an abstract relation as under the concept of justice." This means, Fried says, that "like a friend [the lawyer] acts in your interests, not his own; or rather he adopts your interests as his own."

The moral foundation upon which Fried justifies that special-purpose friendship is the sense of self, the moral concepts of "personality, identity, and liberty." He notes that social institutions are so complex that without the assistance of an expert adviser, an ordinary lay person cannot exercise the personal autonomy to which he or she is morally and legally entitled within the system. "Without such an adviser, the law would impose constraints on the lay citizen (unequally at that) which it is not entitled to impose explicitly." The limited purpose of the lawyer's friendship, therefore, is "to preserve and foster the client's autonomy within the law." * * *

The essence of Professor Fried's argument does not require the metaphor of friendship, other than as an analogy in justifying the lawyer's role-differentiation. It was inevitable, however, that Fried's critics would give the metaphor of friendship the same emphasis that Fried himself does and, thereby, consciously or not, miss the essential point he makes, that human autonomy is a fundamental moral concept that must determine, in substantial part, the answers that we give to some of the more difficult issues regarding the lawyer's ethical code. * * *

The most serious flaw in Professor Fried's friendship metaphor is that it is misleading when the moral focus is on the point at which the lawyer-client relationship begins. Friendship, like love, seems simply to happen, or to grow, often in stages of which we may not be immediately conscious. Both in fact and in law, however, the relationship of lawyer and client is a contract, which is a significantly different relationship, formed in a significantly different way.

Unlike friendship, a contract involves a deliberate choice by both parties at a particular time. Thus, when Professor Fried says that friendship is "an aspect of the moral liberty of self to enter into personal relations freely," the issue of the morality of the decision to enter the relationship is blurred by the amorphous nature in which friendships are formed. Since entering a lawyer-client contract is a more deliberate, conscious decision, however, that decision can justifiably be subjected to a more searching moral scrutiny.

In short, a lawyer should indeed have the freedom to choose clients on any standard he or she deems appropriate. As Professor Fried points out, the choice of client is an aspect of the lawyer's free will, to be exercised within the realm of the lawyer's moral autonomy. That choice, therefore, cannot properly be coerced. Contrary to Fried's view, however, it can properly be subjected to the moral scrutiny and criticism of others, particularly those who feel morally compelled to persuade the lawyer to use his or her professional training and skills in ways that the critics consider to be more consistent with personal, social, or professional ethics.

As I have stressed elsewhere, however, once the lawyer has assumed responsibility to represent a client, the zealousness of that representation cannot be tempered by the lawyer's moral judgments of the client or of the client's cause. That point is of importance in itself, and is worth stressing also because it is one of the considerations that a lawyer should take into account in making the initial decision whether to enter into a particular lawyer-client relationship.

### *Comment*

Elsewhere in his article, Professor Fried recognizes that his concept of the lawyer acting as a "special friend" for a client whom the lawyer is free to accept or reject does not apply to a lawyer who is under an obligation to accept appointment as defense counsel for an indigent defendant in a criminal case. "This is not a large qualification to the general liberty I proclaim. The obligation is, and must remain, exceptional; it cannot become a kind of general conscription of the particular lawyer involved."

He believes the concept does apply to clients who are corporations or government agencies. These are "only formal arrangements of real persons pursuing their real interests. If the law allows real persons to pursue their interests in these complex forms, then why are they not entitled to loyal legal assistance, 'legal friendship,' in this exercise of their autonomy just as much as if they pursued their interests in simple arrangements and associations?" The government lawyer's client "might be thought to be the government of the United States, or the people of the United States mediated by an intricate political and institutional framework." Is this persuasive? See pages 272–76 below.

### BURT, CONFLICT AND TRUST BETWEEN ATTORNEY AND CLIENT

69 Geo.L.J. 1015, 1019–21 (1981).

Though an attorney and client may want a harmonious relationship, recurrent aspects of their dealings inevitably interfere with this goal. There has been little systematic empirical investigation of this question. The legal profession has not pressed for such investigation; and, as will be developed below, attorneys have many incentives to avoid acknowledging mutual mistrust in their dealings with specific clients and in their general ruminations concerning professional roles. The profession currently assumes the importance and attainability of attorney-client trust. Some speculation will, however, reveal enough possible, recurrent sources of attorney-client mistrust to justify a reexamination by the profession of its current assumptions that are unsupported by clear data.

Consider, for example, the effect of an attorney's advice that the client's position is contrary to law and therefore that the client's adversary will likely prevail. The client rarely welcomes this enunciation and its delivery can breed suspicion that the attorney is not committed wholeheartedly to the client's cause. The attorney may expect this suspicion when he realizes that he lacks sympathy for the client because, for example, he approves of the law opposing his client's interests. Even when the attorney disapproves of the law that adversely affects the client or regards the law as morally neutral, the client nonetheless might believe the attorney secretly harbors disapproval.

Many attorneys recognize this mistrust through the old adage that the messenger of bad news is always despised. Many clients, however, attempt to hide their suspicion because they fear the attorney's anger and abandonment or because they hope ultimately to persuade the attorney to their side. Moreover, many attorneys see, and only want to see, their own good intentions toward the client and fail to notice the suspicion engendered by their unwelcome prognosis and advice. Thus, mistrust that influences the entire course of the relation between attorney and client can arise though neither is prepared to acknowledge this fact to the other.

Well-disguised though palpably influential mistrust between attorney and client does not end here. Even when the attorney gives the most favorable prognosis—that the client's wishes will ultimately prevail over his adversaries'—some clients remain unassured. Some clients find conflict, or even the anticipation of conflict, psychologically intolerable. Like Vince Lombardi, these clients feel that winning is not the important thing, but the only thing. They find the prospect of any loss unacceptable; even a brief delay before total victory may be viewed as a defeat. Like Lombardi, some of these clients openly flaunt their aggressiveness. Thus, their insatiability and consequent irrational mistrust might be apparent even to an attorney unambivalently committed to their cause. Many such clients, however, do not reveal this attitude to their attorneys and might not admit even to themselves that any defeat is intolerable and that they resent anyone, including their attorney, who fails to satisfy their wishes at once. * * *

In disputes involving only money, clients and their attorneys often have directly conflicting financial interests because the attorneys' fees do not depend on the clients' success against their third-party adversaries. Indeed, the more difficult, less assuredly victorious battles frequently demand more lawyers' time; legal fees mount as prospects for success progressively appear more questionable. Although some clients might reap great financial rewards from the ultimate defeat of their adversaries, many clients cannot avoid suspecting that their attorney is the only assured beneficiary in these long, drawn-out battles. This suspicion may be perceived by attorneys and might lead them to propose compromises that feed greater client suspicion that the attorneys are "selling them down the river." Contingent fee arrangements in personal injury cases do not fully solve this problem because even the financially successful client might feel left with a long-term disability and only a portion of his "true financial due" while the lawyer pockets a large chunk of the recovery and enjoys it in good health.

No amount of self-righteous professional preaching about the basic harmony of interest between lawyer and client can obscure this particular intrinsic conflict: Lawyers grow rich on their clients' troubles and greater woe to the client typically means greater profit to the lawyer. Legal and medical practice are the same in this respect, and it is not surprising that intense suspicion of financial gouging pervades consumer attitudes toward both professions.

## MORRIS v. SLAPPY

— U.S. —, 103 S.Ct. 1610, 75 L.Ed.2d 610 (1983).

CHIEF JUSTICE BURGER delivered the opinion of the Court.

[When the defendant's assigned public defender became ill, another attorney from the same office was substituted. The defendant objected claiming the substitute was poorly prepared and that the original attorney was still his attorney. The trial court denied his request for continuance until "his attorney" had recovered. Following conviction, he petitioned for a writ of habeas corpus.]

In reversing the District Court's denial of the writ, the Court of Appeals acknowledged that "an indigent defendant does not have an unqualified right to the appointment of counsel of his own choosing," but argued that respondent was not seeking appointment of counsel of his own choosing; rather, he "was merely seeking a continuance of the trial date so that his attorney [Goldfine] would be able to represent him at trial."

The Court of Appeals went on to announce a new component of the Sixth Amendment right to counsel. The Sixth Amendment right, it held, would

> "be without substance *if it did not include the right to a meaningful attorney-client relationship.*" ( [E]mphasis added).

The court seems to have determined, solely on the basis of respondent's confusing and contradictory remarks on the subject, that respondent had developed such a "meaningful attorney-client relationship" with Goldfine but not with Hotchkiss. * * *

The Court of Appeals' conclusion that the Sixth Amendment right to counsel "would be without substance if it did not include the right to a *meaningful attorney-client relationship*" is without basis in the law. No authority was cited for this novel ingredient of the Sixth Amendment guarantee of counsel, and of course none could be. No court could possibly guarantee that a defendant will develop the kind of rapport with his attorney—privately retained or provided by the public—that the Court of Appeals thought part of the Sixth Amendment guarantee of counsel. Accordingly, we reject the claim that the Sixth Amendment guarantees a "meaningful relationship" between an accused and his counsel. * * *

In its haste to create a novel Sixth Amendment right, the court wholly failed to take into account the interest of the victim of these crimes in not undergoing the ordeal of yet a third trial in this case. Of course, inconvenience and embarrassment to witnesses cannot justify failing to enforce constitutional rights of an accused: when prejudicial error is made that clearly impairs a defendant's constitutional rights, the burden of a new trial must be borne by the prosecution, the courts, and the witnesses; the Constitution permits nothing less. But in the administration of criminal justice, courts may not ignore the concerns of victims. Apart from all other factors, such a course would hardly encourage victims to report violations to the proper authorities; this is especially so when the crime is one calling for public testimony about a humiliating and degrading experience such as was involved here. Precisely what weight should be given to the ordeal of reliving such an experience for the third time need not be decided now; but that factor is not to be ignored by the courts. The spectacle of repeated trials to establish the truth about a single criminal episode inevitably places burdens on the system in terms of witnesses, records, and fading memories, to say nothing of misusing judicial resources.

Over 75 years ago, Roscoe Pound condemned American courts for ignoring "substantive law and justice," and treating trials as sporting contests in which the "inquiry is, Have the rules of the game been carried out strictly?" Pound, The Causes of Popular Dissatisfaction With the Administration of Justice, 29 ABA Ann.Rep. 395, 406 (1906). A criminal trial is not a "game," and nothing in the record of respondent's two trials gives any support for the conclusion that he was constitutionally entitled to a new trial. The state courts provided respondent a fair trial and the United States District Judge properly denied relief. * * *

Justice BRENNAN, with whom Justice MARSHALL joins, concurring in the result. * * *

Given the importance of counsel to the presentation of an effective defense, it should be obvious that a defendant has an interest in his relationship with his attorney. As we noted in Faretta v. California, 422 U.S. 806, 834, 95 S.Ct. 2525, 2540, 45 L.Ed.2d 562 (1975), "[t]he right to defend is personal." It is the defendant's interests, and freedom, which are at stake. Counsel is provided to assist the defendant in presenting his defense, but in order to do so effectively the attorney must work closely with the defendant in formulating defense strategy. This may require the defendant to disclose embarrassing and intimate information to his attorney. In view of the importance of uninhibited communication between a defendant and his attorney, attorney-client communications generally are privileged. See Upjohn Co. v. United States, 449 U.S. 383, 389, 101 S.Ct. 677, 682, 66 L.Ed.2d 584 (1981). Moreover, counsel is likely to have to make a number of crucial decisions throughout the proceedings on a range of subjects that may require consultation with the defendant. These decisions can best be made, and counsel's duties most effectively discharged, if the attorney and the defendant have a relationship characterized by trust and confidence.[4]

## C. CODES OF PROFESSIONAL CONDUCT

### *Comment*

(1) *Canons of Professional Ethics.* The original American Bar Association Canons of Professional Ethics were adopted by the ABA in 1908. They were patterned after the Alabama State Bar Associ-

4. The American Bar Association Standards for Criminal Justice state that "[d]efense counsel should seek to establish a relationship of trust and confidence with the accused." ABA Standards for Criminal Justice 4–3.1(a) (2d ed. 1980). The Standards also suggest that "[n]othing is more fundamental to the lawyer-client relationship than the establishment of trust and confidence." Id., at 4·29 (commentary).

In Linton v. Perini, 656 F.2d 207 (CA6 1981), the court stated that "[b]asic trust between counsel and defendant is the cornerstone of the adversary system and effective assistance of counsel." Similarly, in Lee v. United States, 98 U.S.App.D.C. 272, 235 F.2d 219 (1956), the court stated that " '[t]he relationship between attorney and client is highly confidential, demanding personal faith and confidence in order that they may work together harmoniously.' "

ation Code of Ethics, adopted in 1887. These, in turn, were patterned on the lectures of Judge George Sharswood published in 1854. These lectures reflected the standards and idealism of the legal profession as he saw them or thought they should be.

Following the 1908 adoption, numerous amendments were made from time to time and from the late twenties to the late thirties some attempts were made toward complete revisions. Little action resulted however.

(2) *Code of Professional Responsibility.* In 1964, the president of the ABA, Lewis F. Powell, Jr., now a justice of the U.S. Supreme Court, appointed a committee whose recommendations led to the ABA's adoption in 1969 of the Code of Professional Responsibility (CPR). The CPR has been adopted by the courts of nearly all of the states, with modifications of varying degrees. The CPR's provisions are cited in these materials as DR (Disciplinary Rule) or EC (Ethical Consideration).

It was not long before questions were raised about the adequacy of the CPR's provisions. These were in considerable part precipitated by the Watergate episode, by decisions of the Supreme Court on such subjects as advertising and solicitation by lawyers,[1] by attacks on corporate attorneys by the Securities and Exchange Commission,[2] and by criticisms that the CPR was too oriented toward the adversary model and insufficiently concerned with the public interests that may be affected by the activities of attorneys on behalf of their clients.[3]

(3) *Model Rules of Professional Conduct.* In 1977, the ABA appointed a Commission on Evaluation of Professional Standards, "charged with undertaking a comprehensive rethinking of the ethical premises and problems of the profession of law." [4]

After several revisions and numerous amendments, the Commission's Model Rules of Professional Conduct were adopted by the ABA in August, 1983, and are referred to in these materials as the Model Rules, or RPC.

To what extent and with what modifications the Model Rules will be adopted by the courts of the several states remains to be seen at the present writing. While there was considerable criticism of the proposed Rules during the drafting stage, they received widespread distribution and consideration by the legal profession and the objections were fully examined before the final adoption by the ABA. Much will depend upon the degree of support given the Model Rules by the bar organizations of the several states.

1. See infra pp. 541–91.

2. See infra pp. 269–71.

3. See supra pp. 12–14.

4. Chairman's Introduction, ABA Model Rules of Professional Conduct (Proposed Final Draft May 30, 1981).

For an informative account of the events leading to the creation of the Commission on Evaluation of Professional Standards, known as the Kutak Commission after its original Chairman, see Armstrong, The Kutak Commission Report: Retrospect and Prospect, 11 Cap.U.L.Rev. 475 (1982).

(4) *Self-government.* The RPC's Preamble states in part:

"The legal profession is largely self-governing. Although other professions also have been granted powers of self-government, the legal profession is unique in this respect because of the close relationship between the profession and the processes of government and law enforcement. This connection is manifested in the fact that ultimate authority over the legal profession is vested largely in the courts.

"To the extent that lawyers meet the obligations of their professional calling, the occasion for government regulation is obviated. Self-regulation also helps maintain the legal profession's independence from government domination. An independent legal profession is an important force in preserving government under law, for abuse of legal authority is more readily challenged by a profession whose members are not dependent on government for the right to practice."

The reference to government regulation is undoubtedly intended to refer to regulation by the executive and legislative branches. The legal profession is subject to substantial control and supervision by the judiciary, exercised usually by the highest appellate court. The standards of admission to the bar are fixed, and applicants admitted, by the court. Minimum standards of conduct of attorneys are in the form of codes of professional conduct promulgated by the court, and it disciplines members of the bar for professional misconduct. Anyone not so admitted who undertakes to practice law does so under threat of contempt of the court.

State supreme courts, relying upon state constitutional separation of powers provisions and their concept of the judicial power, have generally asserted inherent authority over these matters. While statutes attempting to deal with them are entitled to respect due determinations of coordinate branches, courts do not deem themselves bound by them.[5]

In the exercise of these powers, courts tend to rely heavily on the assistance of members of the bar or on bar organizations and to seek their recommendations before undertaking any particular action. In this respect, it may be said that the legal profession is a self-governing

5. See Board of Commissioners v. Baxley, 295 Ala. 100, 324 So.2d 256 (1976); Wallace v. Wallace, 225 Ga. 102, 166 S.E.2d 718, cert. denied 396 U.S. 939, 90 S.Ct. 369, 24 L.Ed.2d 240 (1969); Sharood v. Hatfield, 296 Minn. 416, 210 N.W.2d 275 (1973). Cf. ABA Standards for Lawyer Discipline and Disability Proceedings 2.1 (Approved Draft 1979); Williams, State Constitutional Law Processes, 24 Wm. & Mary L.Rev. 169, 210 (1983).

Compare Beardsley, The Judicial Claim to Inherent Power over the Bar, 19 A.B.A. J. 509 (1933) (challenging inherent power rationale); Note, The Inherent Power of the Judiciary to Regulate the Practice of Law—A Proposed Delineation, 60 Minn.L.Rev. 783 (1976).

For a description of voters "overruling" a state supreme court's assertion of inherent authority to restrict unauthorized practice of law, see Hamner, Title Insurance Companies and the Practice of Law, 14 Baylor L.Rev. 384 n. 1 (1962), relating the 132,492 to 34,451 adoption of Ariz.Const. art. 26, § 1 permitting brokers to draft real estate instruments.

profession. Consider again the criticisms made of the legal profession discussed above at pages 10–24. To what extent should the profession be self-governing in the sense of not being accountable to the public?

## D. PROFESSIONAL ORGANIZATION

### *Comment*

(1) *England.*[1] The legal profession in England is divided into solicitors or attorneys and barristers or counsel. The division is due largely to historical reasons but also in part to a natural division of function.[2] Basically, solicitors perform the work of an office lawyer, while barristers, who cannot accept lay clients, are employed by solicitors to appear in court, draft pleadings and other legal documents, advise on matters relating to preparation for trial, and give opinions on difficult questions of law.

A client must take his or her legal problem to a solicitor. The client cannot employ a barrister directly except in exceptional cases. The solicitor makes the necessary preparations for trial if there is to be one, such as investigating the facts, and securing the witnesses and documentary evidence. It is the solicitor, not a barrister, who negotiates with the opponent or the opponent's solicitor if the opponent has one. The solicitor may or may not ask a barrister to prepare the necessary pleadings and may seek a barrister's advice on what is needed by way of preparation for trial. Having completed the preparation, the solicitor prepares a brief for the barrister who will try the case. This contains a statement of the facts contended for, a list of the witnesses to be called and their testimony. On the basis of this brief, the barrister will try the case, the solicitor participating only through the barrister. Reasons for the noted skills of English barristers may be gathered from the observations of a distinguished English jurist:

> "In England, no barrister can appear in court as counsel unless he has been instructed by a solicitor. The livelihood of a barrister is thus wholly dependent upon solicitors and what they think of him. Solicitors are the judges of the Bar; they brief the good, they

1. Of necessity, only the barest outline can be given here and interesting and important qualifications, such as those relating to Queen's Counsel, have not been noted. For more detailed accounts, see A. Cordery, Law Relating to Solicitors (1981); R. Jackson, The Machinery of Justice in England, ch. 6 (5th ed. 1977); Q. Johnstone & D. Hopson, Lawyers and Their Work 357–531 (1967); M. Zander, Lawyers and the Public Interest (1968); Gilbert, Lawyers in England, 52 Judicature 243 (1969); Wheatcroft, The Education and Training of the Practicing Lawyer in England, 30 B. Exam. 3 (1961). The ethical obligations of barristers, including their relation to solicitors, are set out in W. Boulton, Conduct and Etiquette at the Bar (4th ed. 1965).

See also Megarry, Barristers and Judges in England Today, 51 Ford.L.Rev. 387 (1982); Ablard, Observations on the English System of Legal Education: Does it Point the Way to Changes in the United States? 29 J.Legal Educ. 148 (1978).

2. See Niles, Ethical Prerequisites to Certification, 49 A.B.A. J. 83 (1963).

ignore the bad. The judgment of forensic ability is made not by laymen, who too often think that storm and fury make good advocacy, even when empty of content. It is made by solicitors, lawyers who are skilled in litigation and well accustomed to appreciating quiet and effective competence, and to discounting froth, however impressively uttered."[3]

Each of the two branches of the profession has its own organization. The Law Society represents the solicitors. It has been given extensive power.[4] Subject to some judicial approval, it fixes the requirements for admission and passes on the applicant's moral fitness to be a solicitor.[5] It keeps the roll of those admitted.[6] It issues the practicing certificate required of all practicing solicitors, for a fee which it retains.[7] It may "make rules for regulating in any respect of any matter the professional practice, conduct and discipline of solicitors."[8] It presents disciplinary proceedings, brought against offending solicitors, to a Discipline Committee made up of members of its Council selected by the Master of the Rolls.[9]

The Law Society is a voluntary organization. A solicitor need not become a member, but is still subject to the foregoing powers.

The organization of the barristers centers around the famous Inns of Court located in London; Lincoln's Inn, Gray's Inn, The Inner Temple, and the Middle Temple, which have existed from time immemorial. The chambers of the great majority of barristers are located in these Inns. A barrister cannot engage in the practice of law without being a member of one of these Inns, and membership begins as a student prior to his admission to the Bar. The Inns control the admission or "call to the Bar," the rules of conduct, and the discipline of barristers.

In 1974, a Senate of the Inns of Court and the Bar was created to supersede the earlier General Council of the Bar. Its function appears to be to centralize and coordinate matters common to the several Inns, including legal education and discipline. In discipline cases, the Senate, after appropriate proceedings, may recommend to the particular Inn to which the barrister belongs the disciplinary measures it believes should be taken.[10]

(2) *United States.*[11] The simple and pioneer conditions of life in early colonial times did not require much law and did not permit the

3. Megarry, supra note 1, at 397.

4. See Lund, The Professional Discipline of Solicitors, appearing in R. Pollard, Administrative Tribunals at Work (1950).

5. Solicitors Act, 1974 § 3.

6. Id. § 6.

7. Id. §§ 9, 10.

8. Id. § 28.

9. Id. § 46(1) et seq.

10. See May, Some Thoughts on the English Bar, 60 Cornell L.Rev. 699, 716 (1975). This article is an informative one on the then current educational requirements for admission to the bar and on the work and methods of the practicing barrister.

Major changes appear not to have since been made, see Megarry, supra note 1.

11. See Chroust, The Rise of the Legal Profession in America (1965); R. Pound, The Lawyer from Antiquity to Modern Times 129-349 (1953); Reed, Present-Day Law Schools in the United States and Canada (1928); Warren, History of the American Bar (1911); Winters, Bar Association Organization and Activities (1954).

existence of a legal profession. Even courts of justice were manned by laypersons. But as the population grew and economic conditions became more complex, the need for a legal system and hence for lawyers led to the development of a substantial profession before the Revolution. The first lawyers were generally trained in England, but as the profession grew, the apprenticeship system, characteristic of training of solicitors in England, became the prevailing method of training candidates for the bar. Substantial periods of apprenticeship and standards of admission appear to have been required. The division of the bar into solicitors and barristers as prevailed in England was quite unsuited to the conditions that existed. The single lawyer served the functions of both.

Following the Revolution and with the advent of Jacksonian democracy, bar admission standards declined. There were but a few law schools, located in the east. The great majority of lawyers received such training as they may have gotten, in a lawyer's office. The wide sparsely settled geographical areas contributed to the general absence of any professional consciousness. A bar organization under these circumstances would have had little meaning and none existed.

The movement for organization of the bar first began following the Civil War with the creation of the Association of the Bar of the City of New York in 1870 and the American Bar Association in 1878. This led to state and local associations in other areas, the greatest impetus occurring after the turn of the Century.

The history of the ABA reflects the growing organizational consciousness of the American bar. Professor Sunderland, in his History of the American Bar (1953), divided the ABA's growth into three periods. The first, 1878 to 1902, he called the Saratoga Era, the annual meetings being held at Saratoga Springs, New York. This was a period of relatively slow growth in membership and activity, the annual meetings being confined more to social activity than to professional problems. The second period, 1903 to 1935 was called the Era of National Expansion. Meetings of the Association were held in various parts of the country acquainting lawyers with the organization, its purposes and activities, and the need of organization. Membership and program expanded rapidly. The last period, 1936 to the present, has been under the present constitution of the Association, adopted in 1936. This constitution recognized that a new form of organization of the Association was required by the large membership, which made representative action at annual meetings of the assembly virtually impossible, and by the need to bring into the Association representatives of the state and local bar associations.

The House of Delegates, rather than the Assembly, is now the controlling body. It is made up of delegates from each state, elected by the Association membership, of delegates selected by state and larger local bar associations and of delegates from certain specified allied organizations.

ABA Membership is open to all lawyers on a voluntary basis. There are innumerable standing and special committees and numerous sections. To appreciate the scope of the ABA's activities, a recent volume of its Summary and Reports should be examined. The ABA is clearly the primary medium through which the bar can express itself on the national level.

The average practitioner, however, is more likely to identify his or her immediate professional concerns with the state and local bar associations, even though their activities are not and cannot be as extensive. He or she is more likely to attend their meetings, if for no other reason than proximity, more likely to participate in its committee activities and will turn to them for the assistance and guidance which a professional organization can give.

Bar associations perform an indispensible function for the members of the legal profession as well as for the public. It is through them that many of the professional responsibilities of the lawyer can most effectively be realized. It would appear to follow that all lawyers should contribute both financially and of their time and effort to the maintenance and functioning of their associations.[12] However, when bar associations were first organized, it would have been impossible to begin on any other basis than voluntary membership.

In the 1920s and after some earlier discussion, a movement began for the creation of what has been called the integrated or unified bar association. This is a statewide organization to which all practicing lawyers of the state are required to pay dues. The first such organization was established by statute in North Dakota in 1921. A rapid succession of other state integrated bar associations followed including such leading states as California, Michigan and Texas.[13]

At the present writing, all but nineteen states have integrated bar associations. They have been created either by statute, by court rule following statutory authorization, or by court rule pursuant to the inherent power of the court over the legal profession.[14]

Usually there has been substantial opposition within the bar of the state to the creation of such organizations and in some states, such as New York, New Jersey, Massachusetts and Pennsylvania, this opposition has prevailed. The opposition has been particularly strong in Wisconsin where opponents earlier received a sympathetic reception in the state supreme court.[15]

12. See EC 9–6 ["Every lawyer owes a solemn duty * * * to cooperate * * * in supporting the organized bar through the devoting of his time, efforts, and financial support as his profession standing and ability reasonably permit").

13. For a fuller account of these organizations, see McKean, The Integrated Bar (1963). See also American Judicature Soc'y, Citations and Bibliography on the Integrated Bar in the United States (1961).

The most recent and thorough discussion appears in Schneyer, The Incoherence of the Unified Bar Concept: Generalizing from the Wisconsin Case, 1983 Am.B.Found.Research J. 1.

14. See Schneyer, supra note 13.

15. In re Integration of the Bar, 249 Wis. 523, 25 N.W.2d 500 (1946) (integration denied) (discussed in Pirsig, Integration of the Bar and Judicial Responsibility, 32 Minn.L.Rev. 1 (1947)).

However in 1956, the Wisconsin court granted the request for integration for an experimental two year period and at the end of the period made the order of integration permanent. But the controversy did not end there. An attorney attacked the action of the court on constitutional grounds, lost in the Wisconsin courts, and appealed to the United States Supreme Court in Lathrop v. Donohue.[16] *Lathrop*, in a plurality opinion, upheld the order of integration against the principal objection that the attorney "cannot constitutionally be compelled to join and give support to an organization which has among its functions the expression of opinion on legislative matters and which utilizes its property, funds and employees for the purposes of influencing legislation and public opinion toward legislation."

The Court considered that the Wisconsin integrated bar served many professional functions which attorneys may properly be required to support and that "legislative activity is not the major activity." Moreover, the record in the case, according to the Court, did not show what legislative activities of the integrated bar were objectionable to the complaining attorney or what portion of the funds derived from dues were used for this purpose.

The debate within the Wisconsin bar, however, continued.[17] The opponents to integration found support for their position in other developments. The issue whether union members could be compelled to pay union dues which went to support political candidates and views was presented in Abood v. Detroit Board of Education.[18] The United States Supreme Court held that the members have a first amendment right to "prevent the Union's spending a part of their required service fees to contribute to political candidates and to express political views unrelated to its duties as exclusive bargaining representative." Opponents of integration succeeded in persuading some courts that the same constitutional right extended to lawyers who were required to become members of an integrated bar organization.[19]

In 1980, a rebellion against the District of Columbia's integrated bar erupted when its board sought an increase in dues from $50 to $150, the purpose of which was to enable purchase of a law library being offered for sale by another bar association. Opponents secured a referendum of the bar which voted to limit the dues to $75. The bar also voted in an accompanying referendum to limit the association's use of proceeds of mandatory bar dues to admission, registration, discipline and client security funds. The Court of Appeals of the District,

**16.** 367 U.S. 820, 81 S.Ct. 1826, 6 L.Ed.2d 1191 (1961).

**17.** For a detailed account of the numerous Wisconsin cases, see Schneyer, supra note 13, at 5 n. 27.

**18.** 431 U.S. 209, 97 S.Ct. 1782, 52 L.Ed.2d 261 (1977).

**19.** See Schneider v. Colegio de Abogados, 546 F.Supp. 1251 (D. Puerto Rico 1982); Arrow v. Dow, 544 F.Supp. 458 (D.N.M.1982); Falk v. State Bar, 411 Mich. 63, 305 N.W.2d 201 (1981) (members of court widely divided on what action should or should not be taken; additional evidentiary hearing ordered) (discussed in 1982 Det.C.L.Rev. 737), petition dismissed, 418 Mich. 270, 342 N.W.2d 504 (1983).

by a divided court, felt obligated to give effect to the results of the referenda and amended its Rules governing the bar accordingly.[20] As could be anticipated, the adverse impact on the organization was substantial.[21]

One possible explanation for the rebellion is the composition of the bar of the District resulting from the influx of large numbers of lawyers from outside the District. The clients of many probably do not come from the District. It would not be surprising if these lawyers did not have a sufficiently strong and conscious identity with the local community of the District or with its legal profession to feel the need for a District organization which advances common professional interests and responsibilities.[22]

It is against the foregoing background that the next case should be examined.

## REPORT OF COMMITTEE TO REVIEW THE STATE BAR

— Wis.2d —, 334 N.W.2d 544 (1983).

PER CURIAM. * * *

[At the end of 1981, the Wisconsin Supreme Court appointed a committee "to review the performance of the bar in carrying out its public functions."]

### THE UNIFIED BAR

The committee recommends that the state bar be retained as an organization in which membership is required of all persons licensed to practice law in Wisconsin. This recommendation, however, is not unqualified, for the committee noted that compulsory membership in the association raises "certain legitimate concerns about individual freedom of association and expression." Consequently, the committee's recommendation for continued bar unification is conditioned on the adoption of recommended changes in the manner in which the association engages in legislative activity and the establishment of a procedure whereby a member may obtain a refund of that portion of as-

20. On Petition to Amend Rule 1 of Rules, 431 A.2d 521 (D.C.App.1981).

21. Some indication of the immediate impact appears in the 1980–81 annual report of the organization: "The Public Service Activities Office, including the Lawyer Referral and Information Service; the Professional Services Activities Office; the Continuing Legal Education Office; and the Citizens' Advisory Committee no longer may be funded through mandatory D.C. Bar dues. On July, excluding the Disciplinary Board staff, dues-funded, fulltime positions will be reduced from thirty-six to fourteen." 5 Dist.Law. 39, 40 (July–Aug.1981).

On the other hand, interest in the Divisions of the organization (corresponding to Sections in most bar organizations) has substantially increased. Membership in these Divisions, consisting of those specially interested in the subject-matter of a Division, is voluntary with annual dues ranging from $5.00 to $7.50. See The Volunteer Effort: Lifeblood of the Organized Bar, President's Page, 8 Dist. Law. (Sept.–Oct.1983), pointing out that the Divisions, in whatever public representations they may make, must make clear that they are not acting for the Bar as a whole.

22. See infra pp. 38–40.

sociation dues which are used to support legislation which the member opposes.

The committee was unanimous in its conclusion that membership in the legal profession carries with it certain obligations to the public, as well as to the profession. The report lists the following activities, which it feels every lawyer can properly be required to support, whether by membership in and financial support of a unified bar association or otherwise:

" * the provision of continuing legal education to members of the bar;

" * the provision of a disciplinary system to insure the quality of legal services in the state;

" * the provision of a system for admission to practice which assures the qualification of lawyers admitted to practice;

" * the provision of a system to control the unauthorized practice of law;

" * the provision of a client security fund, and a system to make reparations for losses by clients;

" * the maintenance of a mailing list of all licensed attorneys;

" * the maintenance of a program to control trust funds held by attorneys;

" * the operation of a program of public information with respect to legal questions, the functions of the courts, and the administration of justice;

" * the collection of funds to support the obligatory programs just identified."

We agree that lawyers may properly be required to financially support these functions, and we also agree with the committee's conclusion that a unified bar association, which all licensed practitioners are required to join, is better suited than a voluntary association to accomplish them. The committee notes that a unified bar association is more likely to administer its programs in the public interest, that the performance of such functions is more efficient and economical if conducted by a single association financially supported by all lawyers and that voluntarism, on which the accomplishment of these goals by the existing association almost exclusively depends, is better promoted by a unified bar association. Whether or not these considerations are sufficient to justify the requirement that all lawyers be members of the association, it is our opinion, as it has been for more than 25 years, that a bar association in which membership is mandatory is the best means for the profession to fulfill its obligations to the public. We do not see as a practicable alternative a voluntary association of lawyers to which all practitioners, members or not, would be required to contribute for the performance of only those functions which we deem to be the obligation of every lawyer.

However, there is one area of the association's activity which the committee believes must be more particularly circumscribed if membership in the association is to continue being mandatory, and that is legislative activity. While all members of the committee believe that a bar association should maintain an active involvement in the legislative process, a majority of the committee urges that we, by rule, alleviate the concerns of those members who oppose all or any particular association involvement in the legislative process, since the dues they pay to maintain membership are used to finance such activity.

We have been sensitive to this issue since the association was unified in 1956 and have addressed it on numerous occasions. See, Lathrop v. Donohue, 10 Wis.2d 230, 102 N.W.2d 404 (1960), In re Regulation of the Bar of Wisconsin, 81 Wis.2d xxxv (1977), Matter of Discontinuation of the Wisconsin State Bar, 93 Wis.2d 385, 286 N.W.2d 601 (1980). In our 1977 opinion we limited the state bar association's authorization to engage in legislative activities to "only as to matters concerning the administration of justice and the practice of law, including matters of substantive law on which the views of lawyers have special relevance." We then enunciated the guiding principle of the association's legislative activities, indeed, of all its activities, namely, the public interest.

The committee suggests that the "administration of justice and the practice of law" standard is too broad and that it obscures the demarcation between technical information and advocacy on legislative matters. The committee considered but rejected the creation of a more restrictive definition of permissible legislative activity as a solution to this issue, believing that it would constitute "an unworkable and counterproductive approach" and would unduly hamper the association in its permissible legislative activity. Rather, the committee recommends that the extent possible, the legislative questions on which it is likely to take a position and to inform them as to the time and place of the board of governors' meetings at which action is likely to be taken. Further, the committee recommends that the state bar have the support of 60 percent of its board of governors on any position taken before the legislature. * * *

The committee apparently believes that no degree of "substantial unanimity" is sufficient to require that members opposed to the bar's position on legislation, whether legislation in general or specific legislative proposals, contribute to the advocacy of that position by the payment of dues, compulsorily exacted, which are used to finance the bar association's legislative activity. Consequently, the majority of the committee recommends that there be instituted a rebate procedure requiring the association to publish in its official publication, after each legislative session, the amount that has been expended from member dues on each legislative matter in which the association participated during that session, showing the total amount expended on all legislative activities, as well as the amount expended on each separate legislative issue. Further, the publication should show the cost to each member of all legislative activity and as to each separate legislative issue. Each member would then be entitled to request and receive a refund of his or her portion of dues expended either as to all legislative activity or only as to one or more specific legislative items. The committee also recommends that the request for a refund be treated in strict confidence and that the refund be granted as a matter of course.

This recommended rebate procedure is obviously in response to recent case law which addresses the issue of the use of mandatory membership dues to support political or ideological activity to which an individual member is opposed. See, Abood v. Detroit Board of Education, 431 U.S. 209, 97 S.Ct. 1782, 52 L.Ed.2d 261 (1977), Browne v. Milwaukee Board of School Directors, 83 Wis.2d 316, 265 N.W.2d 559 (1978), Falk v. State Bar of Michigan (plurality opinion), 411 Mich. 63, 305 N.W.2d 201 (1981), Arrow v. Dow, 544 F.Supp. 458 (D.N.M.1982), Schneider v. Colegio de Abogados de Puerto Rico, 546 F.Supp. 1251 (D.P.R.1982). Assuming, arguendo, that those cases are applicable here, we believe that the rebate procedure proposed by the committee is an acceptable and adequate response to any claimed infringement on the rights of those association members who oppose the association's position on specific legislation. Moreover, in order that a dissenting member not be required to specify those legislative issues on which the association has taken a position to which he or she is opposed, the rebate procedure should entitle a member to a rebate for that portion of his or her dues spent on all legislative activity, without specification, and if the objecting member wishes to contribute part of the rebated amount in proportion to the amount spent on legislative issues to which he or she was not opposed, he or she may do so voluntarily. In response to this recommendation of the committee, we will propose such a rebate procedure for inclusion in the rules governing the State Bar, and we will hold a public hearing on the proposal, with a view to implementing a rebate procedure prior to the conclusion of the coming legislative session. * * *

POLITICAL ACTIVITY

The committee states its belief that a bar association in which membership is compulsory ought not be involved in supporting political candidates, and it recommends that LAWPAC, the political action committee with which the state bar has been involved, directly or indirectly, in the past, be completely severed from the association. It notes that LAWPAC has made use of state bar facilities and services and that a state bar employee, the one most actively involved in communicating with the legislature as to the state bar's positions on legislation, is the person who operates LAWPAC. The committee recommends that no state bar personnel or facilities be used in connection with LAWPAC, whether or not arrangements for compensation from the latter to the former exist.

Again, we have addressed the issue of bar association political activity on prior occasions. * * * In the face of the committee's recommendations, we hold that, while lawyers may voluntarily form and participate in political action committees, it is impermissible for the state bar, funded as it is by compulsory member dues, to participate to *any* extent in LAWPAC or in its activities. * * * [a]

[a]. Justices Abrahamson and Steinmetz filed concurring opinions.

DAY, Justice (dissenting).

I dissent. * * *

In our review of the Kelly Committee report on the performance of the State Bar of Wisconsin in carrying out its public functions, we have had available to us a thorough, well-researched study of bar integration by Professor Theodore J. Schneyer of the University of Wisconsin Law School. Professor Schneyer's work serves to reinforce the position of those who believe that membership in a statewide association of lawyers ought not be required as a condition to practice law in Wisconsin. The study, entitled "Unified But Ungovernable: A Case Study of the Wisconsin State Bar,"[a] is the result of extensive research and investigation undertaken by Professor Schneyer, under a grant from the American Bar Foundation * * *. He concludes that a voluntary bar association can insure a respectable membership level by providing its members with quality programs and tangible benefits. * * *

Legislative activity by the bar association is of particular concern to many lawyers, as is compelled financial support of political or ideological activities. Acting on the Kelly Committee's recommendation, the majority would create a rebate system whereby that portion of a bar member's dues used to support legislation which the member opposes would be refunded at the end of each legislative session. This, however, is no more than a cosmetic remedy to a deeply rooted problem. It means the bar has the use of a dissenting member's money, without his consent for purposes of which he disapproves.

Lobbying can be a positive part of the legislative process, but the effectiveness of a statewide bar association's legislative efforts is diminished by the fact that membership in that association is made mandatory by court rule. The Wisconsin legislature is not fooled into believing that a position on a legislative matter taken by the State Bar of Wisconsin constitutes the composite judgment of its members. In my view, integration of the bar has hampered the bar's effectiveness in legislative matters.

Additionally, because of the nature of the bar association's legislative activity, the court, exercising its regulatory authority over the bar, has found it necessary to repeatedly demarcate the permissible limits of the association's participation in the legislative process. Thus, integration has consistently worked against the bar in this area: the association is not permitted to engage in lobbying, partisan politics or other legislative activity in which it might like to participate, it cannot speak with a "single voice" on behalf of its membership, and a significant portion of its membership has expressed resistance to being identified with policy positions taken by the association. These reasons in themselves warrant changing the association's status from mandatory to voluntary.

**a.** Published in 1983 Am.B. Found. Research J. 1.

On the practical side, Professor Schneyer discusses three distinct images of the unified bar, images which have proved to be conflicting and irreconcilable in terms of association governance: an autonomous association to be run as a private voluntary association, a public agency whose mission is to serve the public in all of its activities, and a compulsory membership organization, akin to a "closed shop." Tracing the history of bar integration in Wisconsin, Professor Schneyer illustrates the continuous struggle among these competing images of the state bar. For example, when the integrated bar is perceived as a public agency or a closed shop, the dominant theme in bar governance is regulation by the court to insure that the association's activities are in the public interest and that the rights of dissenting members are protected. He notes a trend in other jurisdictions for courts to view the unified bar as a closed shop, which serves as the basis for their closely scrutinizing its activities for potential infringement on the constitutional rights of its "captive" members. Such view of the unified bar runs directly contrary to the concept of associational autonomy, to which an organization of professionals, certainly should aspire. * * *

It is because of this "confused" status that the court has been required to closely supervise the association's activities, even in those areas in which it acts as a voluntary-type professional society. It is also for this reason that the court found it advisable to establish a periodic committee review of the state bar's activities to assess its performance in carrying out its public functions. However, such review has proven so costly, both in terms of time and money, that the majority now has abandoned the quadrennial review originally provided in favor of an "as needed" review.

* * * After all, there are nineteen states in which the statewide bar association is voluntary, and I have not yet heard it argued that the lawyers in those states are evading or avoiding their professional responsibility to render a public service.

### *Comment*

States which do not have integrated bar organizations usually require by court rule the payment of fees to support the expenses of the discipline of attorneys, and sometimes other activities relating to the profession.[1]

1. See Cuyahoga County Bar Association v. Ohio Supreme Court, 430 U.S. 901, 97 S.Ct. 1167, 51 L.Ed.2d 577 (1977), affirming mem. 45 U.S.L.W. 3583 (S.D. Ohio Oct. 1, 1976) (required fee did not deny due process, equal protection, or right of association); Ables v. Fones, 587 F.2d 850 (6th Cir. 1978) (fee for discipline upheld, citing *Cuyahoga County Bar Association*); Board of Overseers of Bar v. Lee, 422 A.2d 998 (Me.1980), appeal dismissed 450 U.S. 1036, 101 S.Ct. 1751, 68 L.Ed.2d 233 (1981) (fee upheld for attorney registration, discipline, expenses of fee arbitration and such other purposes as approved by the court, relying upon *Cuyahoga County Bar Ass'n*).

The cases cited were decided before *Abood* and were based on the inherent power of the courts over the practice of law.

### *Questions*

(1) Courts have assumed that *Abood* controls what states may do in compelling financial support from lawyers for activities which impinge on first amendment rights.[2]

May a distinction be drawn? The legal profession's intimate knowledge and understanding of the law and its purposes may warrant giving it, through its organization, wide latitude in expressing and advocating views relating to the improvement of the law and the administration of justice. If so, does *Abood* prevent imposing dues or fees on lawyers for these purposes?

(2) If compulsory dues-supported activities are to be limited by first amendment rights, what are the limits? Consider the following:

(a) Bar polls on candidates for judicial office;

(b) Seeking increases in judicial salaries;

(c) Compulsory attendance at continuing legal education programs;

(d) Adoption of the Model Rules of Professional Conduct to parts of which some lawyers have objected;

(e) Advocacy of arbitration and mediation as means of settling disputes;

(f) Expansion of legal services to the poor;

(g) Reforms by legislation or court rules in civil and criminal procedure;

(h) Advocacy of higher or lower standards for admission to the bar or discipline or unauthorized practice of law.

Which of these activities would be permissible under the Wisconsin court's analysis in *Report of Committee to Review the State Bar?*[3]

(3) The court in *Report of Committee to Review the State Bar* approved the refund to objecting lawyers of the portion of their dues used for objectionable activities. Is this feasible?

## E. COMPOSITION OF THE BAR

### 1. GENERALLY

#### LANDON, LAWYERS AND LOCALITIES: THE INTERACTION OF COMMUNITY CONTENT AND PROFESSIONALISM

1982 Am.B. Found. Research J. 459, 468–69.

The lawyer practicing in a small town experiences his local community differently than does the lawyer practicing in an urban or met-

2. See cases cited supra p. 31 n. 19. See also Note, First Amendment Proscriptions on the Integrated Bar: Lathrop v. Donohue Re-Examined, 22 Ariz.L.Rev. 939 (1980).

3. Compare Arrow v. Dow, 544 F.Supp. 458 (D.N.M.1982), stating, "I cannot conclude that advancing the administration of justice or improving the legal system are equivalent in the context of a Bar Association, to collec-

ropolitan setting. In the small town, relationships of every sort are presumed to be on a more personal level. The web of group associations and the likelihood of future encounters tend to narrow the range of motivations that apply to each situation. Friendship, intimacy, and altruism are the orienting principles of association, and even if the actual patterns of association contradict that image, the image remains intact in the mind of the small town actor. Obviously the lawyer experiences considerable cross-pressure as he functions in his legal role in such a setting. Clients are friends, adversaries are acquaintances, disputes often carry community-wide implications, and his independence may be constantly under the pressure of intimacy, familiarity, and community scrutiny.

The small town presumably involves greater group pressures to conform to community values and orientations. Small town lawyers are typically products of the settings in which they practice. Thus the "moral notions of the community" are likely to be internalized long before the small town citizen becomes a professional practitioner. The local ideological pattern includes a conception of the community, a set of preferences as to who (what principles) shall rule, a sense of social hierarchy both cultural and economic, and a sense of what constitutes an appropriate method of allocating values. It may also involve a uniquely local sense of what constitutes (and doesn't constitute) a legal problem. To practice law successfully within such realities requires a balancing of community roles and the professional role. Certainly, the small town practitioner does not have the protection a firm specialist enjoys in a metropolitan setting. Unlike the urban practitioner, the small town lawyer is not free from community-wide scrutiny and cannot insulate himself from a wide range of value-sensitive matters because he is a specialist. His is a broad-based practice. His economic survival is contingent upon working with a wide variety of cases and having good relations with all of the community. Thus, he is exposed to the full array of pressures.

Moreover, the selection of a small town setting in which to practice law implies something about the aspirations of the attorney. The rural lawyer is not likely to aspire to national prominence. His "aspiration group" is more likely to be local or regional in character. Thus from the viewpoint of opinion formation, the local context is likely very important for the small town attorney. As a member of the ongoing local system and with few, if any, aspirations beyond it, he will probably take those actions likely to lead to his personal enhancement locally. He is likely to reflect the "modal character" which any given social system tends to create as a product of its own operations. Thus he is likely to live in a universe of local groups, local opinions, and local expectations. All of this he must try to integrate into his profes-

tive bargaining activities [approved in *Abood*] in the context of a labor union." See the Appendix to the court's opinion listing the wide variety of legislative bills lobbied for or against by the association.

sional role. As Bell, speaking as a participant-observer of small town law practice, asserts:

> "The list of these local customs and traditions is endless. In the small group, they are understood and no formal statement is required. In the large group of lawyers at a city bar, there is no informal communication that includes the entire group, and the group therefore is bound only by the rules that are communicated (written)." [a]

Finally, the small town setting may affect the professional pattern of the practitioner because of his high visibility or identity. The small group setting tends to heighten the visibility and identity of all its members. This high visibility, of course, has positive value for the lawyer because it means clients—professional opportunity. But it also means that the lawyer is quickly caught up in the working and functioning of the community, which may involve some loss of professional independence.

### *Comment*

In addition to differences among attorneys based on geographical location, they differ also in the type of practice in which they are engaged. Thus it has been observed:

> "The fields of law differ in their substantive doctrines, in their characteristic tasks, in the settings in which the fields are practiced, and in the social origins of their practitioners. But we hypothesize that these differences are secondary to yet another variable: the type of client served. We suggest that differences between clients profoundly influence many of the other types of differentiation among the fields—that the legal profession is, to a great degree, externally oriented, and in consequence is shaped and structured by its clients.
>
> "Many of the recognized fields of law correspond to bodies of doctrine generally regarded as distinct legal subjects and taught as separate courses in law school—e.g., crimes, real estate, commercial transactions, personal injury, tax, labor, corporations, antitrust, and securities. But the practicing bar commonly distinguishes between two sides of many of these doctrinal areas, sides that serve adverse clients—e.g., criminal defense versus prosecution, personal-injury plaintiffs' work versus personal-injury defense, labor law on the union side versus the management side, and so on. Other fields divide into parts that, though not necessarily adverse, are nonetheless distinct. Corporate tax planning differs from personal income tax work, real estate development work from home-mortgage preparation and title searching, and corporate litigation from a "general trial" practice that may encompass bits of divorce, commercial, personal-injury or even criminal work. As

a. The reference is to an unpublished Ph.D. dissertation.

these examples make clear, lawyers are accustomed to think in terms of categories of work that distinguish, within broader doctrinal areas, fields or sub-fields defined by the types of clients served. One of the objectives of our research, therefore, was to ascertain the extent to which the operational definitions of the customary categories of legal work—which may, themselves, influence the structure of the profession—are determined by corresponding categories of client-types rather than by doctrinal categories or other systematic theory.

"The needs of a particular client or type of client often dictate the character and the diversity or homogeneity of the work of a lawyer or a law firm. The practitioner who serves a neighborhood's small businesses will often also handle the personal income tax returns of the owners of those businesses, will file their divorces, and will settle their automobile accident claims. The large firm that deals with a corporation's antitrust problems is also likely to handle its real estate acquisitions, its securities issues, and its corporate tax returns. But a lawyer who represents labor unions in one case is unlikely to represent management in another, and in this country a lawyer may not both prosecute and defend criminal cases simultaneously (though many young prosecutors later become defense lawyers). Broadly, the tendency of lawyers' work to address congeries of problems associated with particular types of clients organizes the profession into types of lawyers: those serving corporations, and those serving individuals and individuals' small businesses. Fields within each of these broad sectors of the legal profession have more in common—on a whole range of social variables—than do fields from different sectors." [1]

Can these differences affect the extent to which there can be a sense among lawyers of belonging to a common profession? The extent to which there can, or should, be a common code of ethics?

## SWAINE, IMPACT OF BIG BUSINESS ON THE PROFESSION: AN ANSWER TO CRITICS OF THE MODERN BAR

35 A.B.A.J. 89, 91 (1949).

Until the 1880's * * * the leaders of the American Bar [devoted] themselves almost exclusively to advocacy. While there were many law partnerships, they seldom had more than three or four partners and they had no legal assistants except uncompensated students preparing for examinations.

As trade and industry passed from individual into corporate ownership, lawyers, who in earlier days were seldom called into business transactions until litigation had broken out, were summoned to or-

1. Heinz & Lauman, The Legal Profession: Client Interests, Professional Roles and Social Hierarchies, 76 Mich.L.Rev. 1111, 1113–14 (1978).

ganize the new corporations and supervise their security issues. Naturally the important retainers went to those lawyers who had already achieved high professional position, and, during the 1880's and 1890's, many leading advocates of New York, Philadelphia, Boston and Chicago were devoting an increasing part of their practice to office work, drafting legal documents to create, consolidate and reorganize corporations and to effect public issues of securities and advising on mixed questions of law and business arising daily in the operations of their clients.

The new practice involved much larger sums than that of the earlier days. The problems were more intricate, requiring much more time and effort; and frequently the line between a legal question and a business question was hard to draw.

There was a new tempo. In the earlier days high pressure had been infrequent. A trial or an argument could go over to suit the convenience of counsel. But bankers who took large financial commitments in the purchase of securities were subject to the vagaries of the market; their counsel were under constant pressure to conclude the necessary proceedings with the greatest possible dispatch.

The new practice required a different approach. Litigation deals with events of the past. The advocate's duty to his client requires him to cull from existing facts those which support his client's position and so to arrange them as to paint the picture which best suits his client. He must urge that concept of the legal principles involved which will support the client. In handling a security issue, a consolidation or a reorganization, counsel must design a structure to withstand future attack. The exact truth of all present facts must be discovered and the principles of governing law determined, free in each case from color or bias. Whatever may be their personal views or those of the client as to the merits of the relevant decisions of the courts of last resort, or of changing legal concepts foreshadowed by changing personnel of such courts, counsel in a creative corporate matter are more rigidly controlled by those decisions and trends than is any judge sitting in a court of first instance.

The new practice was more lucrative than the old, for usually the clients were realizing large profits from the transactions on which their counsel were serving as legal engineers, and hence were ready to pay higher fees than for services in litigation.

By the 1890's many of the former great advocates were not only devoting most of their own time to the new corporate practice but had drawn around themselves other lawyers whose abilities lay rather in negotiation in the conference room and in drafting documents than in persuasiveness before the courts. The corporation lawyer had developed, with functions and working habits quite different from those of the advocate.[a]

a. For a discussion of ethical problems of corporate lawyers, see infra pp. 256–71.

## 2. FORM OF PRACTICE

### WEIL & ROY, START-UP COSTS OF A ONE-LAWYER OFFICE [a]

52 N.Y.St.B.J. 601 (1980).

The start-up and first year operating costs of a solo practitioner's general practice law office are estimated to be at least $33,000 today. In 1969, the cost of opening and operating a new one-lawyer office was about $14,500. This is a 228% increase. By comparison, the Consumer Price Index (1967 = 100) averaged 218 in 1979 and 110 in 1969, a 200% increase.

These figures are based on rental of a three-room office (lawyer and secretary work rooms and reception area), purchase of inexpensive new furniture, use of standard office machines such as dictation and transcription machines, a copier, a typewriter, a calculator and a clock radio, certain law books, publications, and miscellaneous office supplies. A significant factor in starting a law office is the cost of law books and publications. The approximate purchase price of a minimal law library will be over $5,000 (including shelving). A more complete law library could cost over $19,500 in most states. Library costs can be significantly reduced if the lawyer has convenient access to a public law library, or has a sharing arrangement with other lawyers.

One can, of course, start an office with less. The cost of supplies and equipment can be reduced through the acquisition of used furniture and office machines. Initially, many new law offices do not require the services of a full-time secretary. The lawyer may employ a secretary part-time or share a secretary with other lawyers. Many library materials can be bought, used, or financed over several years. This is not considered in our cost estimates.

The financing of capital equipment such as library materials and office machines such as typewriters and copiers can significantly reduce initial outlays. For example, the IBM Electronic Typewriter 75 can be leased for approximately $110 per month over four years, and purchase credits are accumulated with each lease payment. The major lawbook vendors, such as the West Publishing Company also offer extended purchasing plans.

Many of the items to be purchased can vary considerably in cost. The location, quality and vendors of the items to be bought are factors which will have a significant impact on the actual cost.

To begin a new office without clients or cash flow, the initial start-up funds available should include operating expenses for the first three months. These expenses would include the secretary's salary, office

a. Robert I. Weil is a Certified Management Consultant and a principal in the management consulting firm of Altman & Weil, Inc. Paul D. Roy is a staff consultant with Altman & Weil, Inc., and a member of the Pennsylvania Bar. The firm specializes in providing management and economic service to the legal profession.

rental, copy machine rental, liability insurance and telephone charges. Expenses for these items over three months would typically be approximately $4,800. Thus, the total start-up cost for a one lawyer office amounts to a minimum of just over $20,000.

### *Comment*

(1) *Buying a law practice.* One possible means of acquiring a law practice is by buying another lawyer's practice or that of a deceased lawyer. ABA Formal Opinion 266, rendered in 1945, found a number of reasons, then existing, why this could not be permitted, insofar as it involved payment for good will and future business from the clients. It would involve sharing legal fees with a lay person,[1] or if the payment went to a lawyer, the lawyer would not have rendered service or shared responsibility with the purchasing lawyer.[2]

The Committee also feared the prospect that confidential information in the selling lawyer files would be disclosed without the consent of the clients.[3] Permitting the sale was also deemed to entail the risk of solicitation and competitive bidding for the practice, which, at the time, was considered unethical.[4] Whether the last objection is any longer tenable, in the light of recent liberalization of the prohibition against advertising and solicitation, may be open to question.[5]

(2) *Taking clients along.* It is not an uncommon practice for a member or associate of a law firm to leave the firm, expecting clients the lawyer has served to follow him or her to the newly established office. There is no ethical impropriety in the lawyer's accepting these clients. It would appear that the lawyer may also announce to them his or her availability.[6] However, substantial personal solicitation of the clients may open the lawyer to the charge of interfering illegally with the contract between client and law firm.[7]

Attorneys have sought to prevent the loss of their clients through these means by insisting on an agreement from a prospective partner

1. See infra pp. 77–98, 538–39.

2. See infra pp. 452–53.

3. See infra Chapter 3.

4. The Opinion approved the sale of physical assets such as furniture and books and of claims for services already rendered.

Consistent with the Opinion is Detroit Bank & Trust Co. v. Coopes, 93 Mich.App. 459, 287 N.W.2d 266 (1979), citing DR 3-102(A)(2) (no sharing of fees with non-lawyer), DR 4-101 (confidences and secrets), DR 2-103 (prohibition against solicitation), and the previous edition of this casebook.

5. See infra pp. 541–91.

For a helpful discussion, see Minkus, The Sale of a Law Practice: Toward a Professionally Responsible Approach, 12 Golden Gate U.L.Rev. 353 (1982). See also Note, The Selling of a Law Practice, 2 J. Legal Educ. 147 (1977).

6. See Adler, Barish, Daniels, Levin & Creskoff v. Epstein, 482 Pa. 416, 393 A.2d 1175 (1978), appeal dismissed 442 U.S. 907, 99 S.Ct. 2817, 61 L.Ed.2d 272 (1979).

7. So held in the *Adler, Barish* case cited in the preceding footnote. The court relied upon the U.S. Supreme Court case of Ohralik v. Ohio State Bar Association, infra p. 570. The reliance may be open to question on the ground that whatever pressure was put on the clients to leave the firm was not of the magnitude contemplated in *Ohralik*. See the dissenting opinion in *Adler, Barish*.

or associate that on leaving the firm he or she will not practice law in the geographical area for a stated period of time.

RPC 5.6 proscribes these agreements:

"A lawyer shall not participate in offering or making:

"(a) a partnership or employment agreement that restricts the rights of a lawyer to practice after termination of the relationship, except an agreement concerning benefits upon retirement; or

"(b) an agreement in which a restriction on the lawyer's right to practice is part of the settlement of a controversy between private parties." [8]

RPC 5.6's Comment explains, "An agreement restricting the right of partners or associates to practice after leaving a firm not only limits their professional autonomy but also limits the freedom of clients to choose a lawyer." [9]

The prohibition may be particularly desirable for the young lawyer seeking association with a practicing lawyer or law firm. The lawyer may find after entering into the agreement that the work assigned is not to his or her liking, that advancement in the firm does not materialize, or that personal relationships are not good. RPC 5.6 protects the lawyer from being forced to either continue in the predicament or leave the area in order to remain in practice.

(3) *Dual practice.* In 1980, the ABA deleted DR 2–102(E) which prohibited a lawyer from indicating on a letterhead, office sign, or professional card that he or she was also engaged in another profession or business.[10] But other ethical limitations may remain. Because one is a lawyer, one may be subject to ethical obligations when acting, for example, as an accountant which would not apply to a nonlawyer accountant. Note the discussion in ABA Formal Opinion 328 (1972):

"There is little ethical difficulty with the operation of an unrelated occupation from the same location as a lawyer's law office * * *. In this situation there may be an increased risk, of course, that the lawyer will violate some other disciplinary rule. For example, a lawyer who also operates a retail store may be in violation of DR 2–104(A) if he accepts employment as a lawyer from a customer of his retail store after volunteering the suggestion to the customer that the customer needs to seek legal advice about some matter. Nevertheless, mere existence of this risk does not mean that the second occupation cannot be conducted from the premises where the lawyer has his law office.

8. DR 2-108(A) provides:

"A lawyer shall not be a party to or participate in a partnership or employment agreement with another lawyer that restricts the right of a lawyer to practice after the termination of a relationship created by the agreement, except as a condition to payment of retirement benefits."

9. See also ABA Formal Opinion 300 (1961).

10. See infra p. 566 n. 20.

"If the second profession or occupation is law-related, a greater ethical difficulty is encountered. It may be impossible to know whether the lawyer's work for another person is performed as part of the practice of law or as a part of his other occupation or profession. As stated in Opinion 57 (1932), 'It is difficult to conceive how a lawyer could conduct a claims adjustment bureau, a company for the organization of corporations, or a bureau for securing tax refunds, without practicing law.'

"In carrying on law-related occupations and professions the lawyer almost inevitably will engage to some extent in the practice of law, even though the activities are such that a layman can engage in them without being engaged in the unauthorized practice of law. * * *

"In Informal Opinion 709 (1964), it is said:

> 'A real estate brokerage business is so closely related to the practice of law that, when engaged in by a lawyer, it constitutes the practice of law.'

"If the second occupation is so law-related that the work of the lawyer in such occupation will involve, inseparably, the practice of law, the lawyer is considered to be engaged in the practice of law while conducting that occupation. Accordingly, he is held to the standards of the Bar while conducting that second occupation from his law offices. With this qualification, the lawyer may carry on a law-related occupation, such as that of a C.P.A., from the same office.

"The qualification just stated is a substantial one, however. Illustrations may indicate its scope. For example, fees set by a lawyer purporting to carry on, from his law office, a mortgage brokerage or loan brokerage business must conform with DR 2-106. Publicity given to the second occupation and methods of seeking business must be in accord with DR 2-101, DR 2-103 and DR 2-104. The lawyer may have a duty under DR 4-101 to preserve confidences and secrets, or information, acquired in carrying on the second occupation even though others engaged in that occupation do not have a similar duty. Similarly, the lawyer may, in connection with the second occupation, owe a duty as a fiduciary even though the relationship of others in that occupation to their clients and customers is not that of a fiduciary; see DR 5-101, DR 5-104 and DR 5-105.

"The answer to the * * * question is, therefore, that a lawyer may conduct * * * his law practice and a second occupation, not law-related from one office, and he may practice from the same office both as a lawyer and as a member of a law-related profession or occupation, such as a marriage counselor, accountant, labor relations consultant, real estate broker or mortgage broker, if he complies * * * with all provisions of the Code of Professional Responsibility while conducting his second, law-related occupation."[11]

(4) *Specialization.* It is a fact of modern professional life that many lawyers elect to confine their practice to one or a few areas of practice and to become specialists in those areas. This raises two problems, (a) how can the lawyer let prospective clients know of his or her special qualifications, and (b) how can prospective clients be assured that the lawyer does in fact have the asserted special skills? The first involves questions of advertising and solicitation discussed elsewhere.[12] The second involves control over the lawyer's asserted qualifications. One such control has been some form of certification that the lawyer has the necessary minimum special skills to qualify as a specialist in the given field. Since 1971, a number of states, including California, Florida, New Jersey, New Mexico, South Carolina and Texas, have adopted specialty certification programs. These vary in stringency from California's system with rigorous experience, education and examination requirements to New Mexico's which merely requires the lawyer to aver that he or she has spent at least 60% of his or her time in the specified field, and in number of available specialties from New Jersey's single specialty of trial practice, through California's four specialties and Texas' six, to New Mexico's 62 specialties.[13]

Supporters of this trend have urged that specialization certification will improve competency, help clients to select lawyers in a more informed manner and, by increasing efficiency, reduce the cost of legal services.[14]

Critics fear that specialization certification, by reducing competition, increasing education costs, and sometimes requiring a client to employ several lawyers instead of one, will increase rather than reduce the cost of legal services, and that it will fractionate the bar and spell the demise of the general practitioner.[15] They claim that certification is not necessary now that lawyers may advertise areas of practice.[16]

11. Problems concerning confidential communications occur when a lawyer-accountant acts for a client and accountants have no privilege not to disclose. See United States v. Schmidt, 360 F.Supp. 339, 345 (M.D.Pa.1973).

See generally Burke, Dueling Over the Dual Practice, 27 Md.L.Rev. 142 (1967); Mintz, Accountancy and Law: Should Dual Practice Be Proscribed? 53 A.B.A. J. 225 (1967).

12. See infra pp. 563–64.

13. Fromson, Let's Be Realistic About Specialization, 63 A.B.A. J. 74 (1977); Lumbard, Specialty Certification for Lawyers: The National Alternative to the Non-Existent State Programs, 67 Women Law. J. 23 (No. 1, 1981); Note, Regulation of Legal Specialization: Neglect by the Organized Bar, 56 Notre Dame Law. 293 (1980). See Florida Bar, In re Amendment to Integration Rule (Certification Plan), 414 So.2d 490 (Fla.1982).

Akin to certification in trial practice are certain federal court admission pilot programs the United States Judicial Conference is studying. See infra pp. 68–69.

14. See Fromson, supra note 13, at 76–77.

15. See M. Bayles, Professional Ethics 42–43 (1981); Mindes, Proliferation, Specialization and Certification: The Splitting of the Bar, 11 U. Toledo L.Rev. 273 (1980); Note,

In August 1979 the ABA adopted a "Model Plan of Specialization." [17] Under this Plan, the state supreme court sets up and appoints a Board of Legal Specialization including "lawyers who are in general practice as well as those who specialize." The Board exercises overall jurisdiction over the subject of lawyer specialization, subject to the following limitations:

"5.1 No standard shall be approved which shall in any way limit the right of a recognized specialist to practice in all fields of law. Any lawyer, alone or in association with any other lawyer, shall have the right to practice in all fields of law, even though he or she is recognized as a specialist in a particular field of law;

"5.2 No lawyer shall be required to be recognized as a specialist in order to practice in the field of law covered by that specialty. Any lawyer, alone or in association with any other lawyer, shall have the right to practice in any field of law, even though he or she is not recognized as a specialist in that field;

"5.3 All requirements for and all benefits to be derived from recognition as a specialist are individual and may not be fulfilled by nor attributed to the law firm of which the specialist may be a member;

"5.4 Participation in the program shall be on a completely voluntary basis;

"5.5 A lawyer may be recognized as a specialist in more than one field of law. The limitation on the number of specialties in which a lawyer may be recognized as a specialist shall be determined only by such practical limits as are imposed by the requirement of substantial involvement and such other standards as may be established by the Board as a prerequisite to recognition as a specialist;

"5.6 When a client is referred by another lawyer to a lawyer who is a recognized specialist under this Plan on a matter within the specialist's field of law, such specialist shall not take advantage of the referral to enlarge the scope of his or her representation and, consonant with any requirements of the Code of Professional Responsibility of this state, such specialist shall not enlarge the scope of representation of a referred client outside the area of the specialty field; and

"5.7 Any lawyer recognized as a specialist under this Plan shall be entitled to advertise that he or she is a 'Board Recognized Spe-

Legal Specialization and Certification, 61 Va.L.Rev. 434 (1975).

16. See In re Amendments to Code of Professional Responsibility, 267 Ark. 1181, 590 S.W.2d 2 (1979); M. Bayles, supra note 15, at 43; Mindes, supra note 15, at 284.

17. The Model Plan is set forth as an appendix to Mindes, supra note 15, at 296. See also the thorough discussion of specialization and the Model Plan in Handbook on Specialization (1983), prepared by the ABA Committee on Specialization.

> cialist' in his or her specialty to the extent permitted by the Code of Professional Responsibility of this state."

The Board in turn establishes and appoints "a separate Specialty Committee for each specialty in which specialists are to be recognized," comprising lawyers "who, in the judgment of the Board, are competent in the field of law to be covered by the specialty." The Specialty Committee, after public hearing on due notice, recommends standards to the Board for regulating the specialty, administers procedures established by the Board, and makes recommendations to the Board as to accreditation of continuing legal education and as to the granting, denying, suspending, or revoking of a lawyer's recognition as a specialist. The Board's standards must require *at least* the following for recognition of a lawyer in a specialty:

> (a) Substantial involvement in the specialty during the preceding three years (if measured on a time basis, at least 25% of a full-time practice),
>
> (b) An average of ten hours per year of continuing legal education in the specialty during the preceding three years, and
>
> (c) A satisfactory showing of competence through peer review by providing as references the names of five lawyers or judges familiar with the lawyer's competence in the specialty.[18]

Similar requirements are imposed for renewal of specialty recognition after five years, and the Board may require evidence of continued qualification during a five year recognition period.[19]

(5) *"Partners" and "associates."* ABA Formal Opinion 310 (1963) states:

> "An inquiry has been made as to the propriety of the use of the term 'associates' in connection with the name of a law firm or an individual practitioner of a law firm. There are three possible ways of using the term.
>
> "1. Smith and Jones are partners. They share in the responsibility and liability for the partnership, whatever their agreement may be pertaining to the division of fees.

18. The Board may establish "additional or more stringent standards, including, but not limited to, oral or written examinations."

19. Regarding the Model Plan's lack of success before state bar associations, see Lumbard, supra note 13, at 24–25. Lumbard opines that bar opposition and financial considerations will prevent most states from establishing specialty certification systems. He argues that an appropriate alternative is reliance upon certification by national organizations like the National Board of Trial Advocacy of which he is the Director. See In re Johnson, discussed infra p. 564.

Regarding the standard of care to which those holding themselves out as specialists are held in malpractice actions, see R. Mallen & V. Levit, Legal Malpractice § 253 (2d ed. 1981).

What should be the standard of care required of an attorney who is not certified as a specialist but who undertakes to act, as the Model Plan permits, in a field calling for special knowledge and a certified specialist is available? Should the answer be different if the available specialists are not certified or no certification program exists?

"2. Smith and Jones each are individual lawyers. Although they practice law together from the same suite of offices and share in some of the costs of the practice, each lawyer has his own clients and they do not share in the responsibility and liability of each other.

"3. An individual lawyer, or a partnership as in (1) above, employs or otherwise associates with him or it one or more additional lawyers to perform legal services for the individual lawyer's or the firm's clients and for the individual lawyer or the firm. Such a person does not share in both the responsibility and the liability for all of the activities of the individual lawyer or of the firm and is in essence an employee of the firm. * * *

"The Committee is of the opinion that:

"1. The word 'associates' would be misleading to describe the situation existing in paragraph (1) above, when there is a sharing of responsibility and liability.

"2. The word 'associates' would be misleading to describe the situation existing in paragraph (2) above, when there is no sharing of responsibility and liability. In the same way, the joining of two or more of the names of such persons practicing together into a title for the firm would be misleading * * *. For example: where there is no sharing of responsibility and liability, 'Law Offices of Jones & Smith,' or 'Jones & Smith Attorneys and Counselors at Law,' would be misleading. Each lawyer should use separate stationery, with his own name and not that of a firm on it. He should not join his name with others on cards, in law lists, or in telephone directories. The door of the firm, when otherwise appropriate, may contain the names of the persons practicing therein no more closely connected than the following example:

Law Offices
Charles W. Jones
Peter S. Smith

"3. Only in the situation described in (3) above is the term 'associates' used in a non-misleading manner. Those lawyers who are working for an individual lawyer or a law firm may be designated on the letterhead and in other appropriate places as 'associates.' Thus, a letterhead giving the name of the firm as Jones & Smith and listing as partners, Charles Jones and Peter Smith, could also list as 'associates' the names of other lawyers who are employed by the firm.

"Even without listing the 'associates,' the word may properly be used in connection with the name of the partnership or the individual in private practice to describe a situation in which the firm or the individual has other lawyers working for them or him who are not partners and who do not generally share in the responsibility and liability for the acts of the firm. Thus, the name 'Jones &

Smith and Associates' would be appropriate to describe a situation in which Jones and Smith were partners and were sharing the responsibility and liability for the partnership practice and who had associated with them other lawyers who were employees of the firm not generally sharing the responsibility and liability for the acts of the firm. In the same way, the name Charles H. Smith and Associates would imply that Mr. Smith was engaged in the individual practice of law without other partners but that he did have other lawyers employed by him to assist him in the practice of law.

"However, where there are other partners in addition to those indicated in the firm name, the Committee feels that it might be misleading to add, after the firm name the words 'and Associates,' unless on the letterhead the names of all the partners and, separately, the names of the associates, were shown."[20]

(6) *"Of counsel."* ABA Formal Opinion 330 (1972) states in part:

"The lawyer who is described as being 'Of Counsel' to another lawyer or law firm must have a continuing (or semipermanent) relationship with that lawyer or firm, and not a relationship better described as a forwarder-receiver of legal business. His relationship with that lawyer or firm must not be that of a partner (or fellow member of a professional legal corporation) nor that of an employee. His relationship with the lawyer or law firm must be a close, regular, personal relationship like, for example, the relationship of a retired or semiretired former partner, who remains available to the firm for consulting and advice, or a retired public official who regularly and locally is available to the firm for consultation and advice.

"While it would be misleading to refer to a lawyer who shares in the profits and losses and general responsibility of a firm as being 'Of Counsel,' the lawyer who is 'Of Counsel' may be compensated either on a basis of division of fees in particular cases or on a basis of consultation fees; see Informal Opinion 710. He is compensated as a *sui generis* member of that law office, however, and not as an outside consultant. Generally speaking, the close, personal relationship indicated by the term 'Of Counsel' contemplates either that the lawyer practice in the offices of the lawyer or law firm to which he is 'Of Counsel' or that his relationship, for example, by virtue

**20.** Accord: In re Sussman, 241 Ore. 246, 405 P.2d 355 (1965). See Equal Employment Opportunity Commission v. Rinella & Rinella, 401 F.Supp. 175 (N.D.Ill.1975) (associates held "employees" for purpose of anti-discrimination provisions of federal 1964 Civil Rights Act); Florida Bar v. Fetterman, 439 So.2d 835 (Fla.1983) (name may keep specifying "associates" when there is only one associate).

In ABA Formal Opinion 277 (1948), A and B held themselves out as a law partnership. A practiced in one locality; B, a specialist in trademark and copyright law, practiced in another. Under their agreement, A was to prepare and send to B all trademark and copyright applications originating in A's practice and was to receive a percentage of the fees charged. In other respects they did not share in each other's business. The arrangement was condemned as not a true partnership but a device for securing law practice for B.

of past partnership of a retired partner that has led to continuing close association, be so close that he is in regular and frequent, if not daily, contact with the office of the lawyer or firm; see Informal Opinion 1134. The term obviously does not apply to the relationship which is merely that of a forwarder and receiver of legal business.

"In short, the individual lawyer who properly may be shown to be 'Of Counsel' to a lawyer or law firm is a member or component part of that law office, but his status is not that of a partner or an employee (nor that of a controlling member of a professional legal corporation).

"Given this view of the relationship indicated by the term 'Of Counsel,' it follows that one lawyer possibly could have the requisite relationship with two firms simultaneously, for example, one with which he practiced for many years before his retirement and another at a location to which he has moved after his retirement. It has been recognized that a lawyer may be a member of two law firms (see New York State Opinion 231); and there is no per se prohibition against one's being 'Of Counsel' to two law firms, even though this would seem impossible if the lawyer were currently a partner in any other firm, and even though it may be difficult for the lawyers to avoid other ethical problems such as the problem of differing interests; see DR 5-105 (D) * * *." [21]

(7) *Nonlawyer partner.* RPC 5.4(b) prohibits a partnership with a nonlawyer "if any of the activities of the partnership consist of the practice of law." [22] The term "practice of law" as so used is subject to interpretation. Some activities, while law related, may be conducted by laypersons. However, if performed by a lawyer they are deemed to constitute the practice of law. The latter is probably the intended meaning.[23]

**21.** Formal Opinion 330 also states that the term "Of Counsel," while used in the Disciplinary Rules only with respect to letterheads, could also be used on announcement cards and shingles, and in directories and announcements which were otherwise appropriate.

See Mutual of Omaha Insurance Co. v. Chadwell, 426 F.Supp. 550 (N.D.Ill.1977), in which the court held that a retired partner whose name was kept in the firm's name and listed on its letterhead as "Of Counsel" was not an "employee" for purposes of an insurance policy where he had not done and was not required to do any work in return for the payments and other benefits the firm provided under its agreement with the retiree. The court concluded that the contract was not one for employment, but rather "could best be characterized as a licensing contract." In a footnote relying upon Formal Opinion 330 the court added:

"We believe it is appropriate to call attention to the questionable propriety of the contractual provision which allows the firm to retain the use of the [lawyer's] name on its letterhead when there was no expectation that the [lawyer] would render any services. DR 2-102(A)(4) provides that '[a] lawyer may be designated "Of Counsel" on a letterhead if he has a continuing relationship with a lawyer or law firm other than as a partner or associate.' Surely, the 'continuing relationship' referred to here means a relationship in the practice of law. The letterhead is a holding out to the public that such a working relationship exists."

**22.** DR 3-103 is identical.

**23.** ABA Formal Opinion 201 (1940) held improper a partnership by a lawyer (holding himself out as such) with a nonlawyer patent practitioner to represent applicants in the presentation and prosecution of applications for patent, saying:

"[W]hen the business is one which, handled by a lawyer, would be regarded as the

In State v. Willenson,[24] the lawyer's nonlawyer wife conducted, in the lawyer's office, without physical separation into two offices, an independent business of preparing income tax returns. This was held unprofessional conduct on the part of the lawyer:

> "We are aware that there are circumstances where it is economically advantageous for a lawyer to share office space, clerical help, and other items of expense with some other enterprise.
>
> "Where the lawyer chooses to make such an arrangement, the burden is on him to arrange it so that it will be obvious to the public that the law office and the other enterprise are totally independent, except for the sharing of space and the other expense. It must be clear that patrons of the other enterprise are not dealing with the lawyer, that he is not responsible for the services they receive, and if they require legal work as an incident of the business they do with the other enterprise, it must be clear that they are as free to consult or not to consult the lawyer as they are to consult or not to consult any other lawyer."[25]

## NELSON, THE CHANGING STRUCTURE OF OPPORTUNITY: RECRUITMENT AND CAREERS IN LARGE LAW FIRMS[a]

1983 Am.B. Found. Research J. 109, 116–25.

### PATTERNS OF RECRUITMENT

The general model of status attainment in the legal profession developed in prior research holds that certain ethnic and class groups are less likely to gain admission to prestigious law schools and there-

practice of law, it continues to be the practice of law so far as the lawyer who is engaged in business is concerned. The fact that a layman also is permitted to render the same services does not alter this conclusion."

ABA Formal Opinion 239 (1942) held improper a partnership by a lawyer (holding himself out as such) and a CPA "as consultants in all federal tax matters" and in representing taxpayers before the IRS, saying:

> "We do not pass upon the question as to whether a certified public accountant is guilty of unauthorized practice of the law when he performs [these services]. In any event, the services are clearly such as to constitute professional employment when performed by a practicing lawyer. Consequently, a member of the bar who is engaged in the practice and who holds himself out as a lawyer, cannot enter into a partnership with a layman for the rendition of such services * * *.
>
> "While a member of the bar may properly enter into a partnership with an accountant to carry on any activity which does not constitute the practice of law by a layman, if the services performed by the partnership are such as to constitute professional employment if performed by a lawyer, it is necessary that the lawyer withdraw from the active practice of the law and refrain from holding himself out as a lawyer in connection with the partnership activities."

See also ABA Formal Opinion 297 (1961), as narrowed by ABA Formal Opinion 305 (1962).

See also the discussion of dual practice in Comment (3) above. RPC 5.4(a) and DR 3-102 prohibit the sharing of "legal" fees with a nonlawyer. See also ABA Formal Opinions 297 (1961) and 201 (1940). Compare Blumenberg v. Neubecker, 12 N.Y.2d 456, 240 N.Y.S.2d 730, 191 N.E.2d 269 (1963), permitting a lawyer and an accountant to share a contingent fee for work each had done in their respective fields in an income tax case.

24. 20 Wis.2d 519, 123 N.W.2d 452 (1963).

25. Compare Crawford v. State Bar, 54 Cal.2d 659, 7 Cal.Rptr. 746, 355 P.2d 490 (1960).

a. The author made a study of four large Chicago law firms left unidentified.

fore are less likely to gain admission to large law firms. The major preceding study of large firms, Smigel's analysis of Wall Street firms, found such a similar pattern more than 20 years ago. Of the partners in the 20 largest firms in New York in 1962, 71.8% had graduated from Harvard, Yale, or Columbia law schools; 30% were listed in the Social Register. Although Smigel suggested that discrimination was on the wane in the fifties, a history of ethnic segmentation had produced "Irish," "Jewish," and "Anglo-Saxon" firms. Most large firms had begun to hire Jewish associates by the late fifties, but it was suggested that "the Jewish student must qualify twice," showing an exemplary law school record and a proper social background. Catholics were not directly discriminated against but tended to be barred on grounds of "lower class" origins, foreign born parentage, or lack of proper education. Very few blacks were "qualified" for large firms, lacking Ivy League credentials. Women were especially subject to discrimination by New York firms. Smigel found that only 18 of the 1,755 female attorneys listed in the New York City directory were listed with large firms. Women in large firms generally were concentrated in particular areas of the office practice—probate, estate planning, and tax. The general pattern in Chicago firms was apparently quite similar. Heinz and Laumann's study of Chicago lawyers makes clear that the profession is still segmented on ethnic grounds, with the odds of reaching a position in a large firm varying considerably depending on social background.

Although the social characteristics of my sample of Chicago firms reflects the continuing importance of ascriptive traits and law school background, growth and bureaucratization have had a substantial effect in recent years. The firms still manifest ethnoreligious segmentation; the ethnoreligious composition of the four firms in my sample is statistically significantly different. While I cannot report the findings in detail without tending to identify the four firms, the differences primarily result from the legacy of past ethnoreligious segmentation. If one examines the cohorts who entered the firms during different periods, hiring has become more heterogeneous across the board. For example, the proportion of Jews hired has risen substantially since 1970 at two of the firms. The one exception to the pattern of change is race. Minorities are still almost completely absent from large firms.

The large law firm predominantly has been the domain of graduates from prestigious law schools. Heinz and Laumann found that 39% of practicing lawyers in Chicago were graduates of elite or prestige law schools, while 15.5% graduated from various regional schools, and 45.6% graduated from local law schools. They found that the distribution of law schools was much different for lawyers in firms of 30 or more: 52.9% elite, 21.4% prestige, 17.1% regional, and 8.6% local. [T]he distribution of law schools in the four firms in my sample is very similar to their findings. * * *

More dramatic than differences in law school composition across firms are the differences over time. [A] total of only 17.3% of the lawyers entering the firms before 1970 graduated from local or regional schools. The proportion grew only slightly, to 18.4%, for the cohort hired 1970–74. But the burst of growth in firms during the late seventies doubled the proportion to 37.5% for the cohort hired since 1975. The graduating classes of elite and prestige schools have not grown nearly fast enough to meet the demands of firms. The 20 top-ranked law schools in the country experienced an average growth in total enrollment of only 7.1% from 1972 to 1981. Hence the greater heterogeneity of this most recent cohort was almost a demographic given. Another result of the scarcity in the graduating classes of prestigious schools has been a dramatic rise in starting salaries in firms.

This development has particular significance for some social groups. Women and Catholics are more likely than other groups to have graduated from local and regional schools. Almost half (42.9%) of the women in the sample graduated from regional or local law schools compared with only a quarter (25.2%) of the male respondents ($\chi^2 = 5.737$, $p = .1252$). The gap in the law school status between men and women is particularly interesting given the relatively higher status social origins of the women. A majority of women (52.8%) had fathers with professional or technical occupations; 36.1% had fathers who were managers or administrators; and only 11.1% had fathers from lower status occupations. The comparable proportions for men were 36.2% professional and technical, 34.1% managers and administrators, and 29.7% in lower status occupations. The statistically significant difference ($\chi^2 = 6.074, p = .048$) reflects the difficulties women have in converting social status into the single most important determinant of professional status, status of law school attended. Epstein found that 90% of the women lawyers she interviewed in 1965–66 chose law school based on nonprofessional criteria, primarily location near family. Because they are more often tied to a locality than are men, women have limited options for gaining admission to elite or prestige schools. Even though family relationships continue to work to the disadvantage of women's professional careers, increased demand for associates has improved their prospects.

Roman Catholics are twice as likely to have graduated from regional or local law schools as any other ethnic or religious group (48.1% versus 18% for Jews, 20.4% for Northern or Western Europeans, and 23% for others; $\chi^2 = 18.545$, $p = .0294$). Unlike for women, this may be due in part to lower status origins. More than a third (34.5%) of the Catholic respondents reported fathers with occupations in the lowest of my status categories, compared with a range of 20.7% to 22.4% for the other ethnoreligious groups ($\chi^2 = 9.226$, $p = .1612$). Hence in Chicago the two local law schools affiliated with Catholic universities only recently have provided a window of opportunity into large firms for lower class Catholics. In contrast, Jews have gained entry to Chicago firms by duplicating the high-status social origins and high-status law school credentials of the Protestant and nonidentifying groups.

The proportion of women in the legal profession has risen steadily over the past 15 years until today it represents 7.5% of the profession.

* * *

Despite these advances, however, women do not appear to be fully integrated into firms. The work roles of women in firms are still concentrated in the office fields that have been their traditional niche. If one drops Curran, the litigation firm, from the analysis, women are significantly less likely to practice in litigation than men (13.0% versus 40.1%, $\chi^2 = 7.718$, $p = .052$). * * * Women may fare better in a special representation practice because lawyer-client interactions are more specialized, making client sensibilities concerning gender a less salient consideration in recruitment and promotion. While such a suggestion is highly speculative, based on modest differences among four firms, it may warrant consideration in future research on the role of women in the profession. * * *

PATTERNS OF PROMOTION AND EXIT

With few exceptions large law firms are "up or out" hierarchies. Lawyers who fail to make partner in 6 to 9 years must leave. * * *

Firms are considering policy changes that may well change the general pattern of promotion and exit, however. During my interviews with elite members it was frequently suggested that partnership policies may become more restrictive for newer, larger cohorts, either by limiting the proportion of associates made partner or by increasing the number of years with the firm before admission to full partnership. * * * As one partner in a New York firm commented to me, any time an associate makes partner, the firm must hire four new associates—one to replace the lost associate and three to work for the new partner. Although Chicago firms have not made promotions based on such ratios alone, there is new concern about partnership policies. More so than the law firms of any other major city, Chicago firms have responded to the problem of larger cohorts by adopting a dual partnership structure, admitting lawyers to the partnership on a nonequity basis for 2 or 3 years before making them full partners. This effectively delays the division of partnership shares for 2 or 3 years and allows firms another opportunity to evaluate a lawyer before granting tenure in the organization.[b]

**b.** See also Auerbach, Unequal Justice, Ch. 1, 2 (1975).

In Hishon v. King & Spalding, — (U.S. —, 104 S.Ct. 2229, — L.Ed.2d — 1984), the Court held that Title VII's prohibition of sex discrimination applies to law firm partnership promotion decisions.

Professional corporations have been widely resorted to by lawyers in order to gain the tax advantages obtained by corporations but not received by individuals or partnerships. Recent federal legislation may have reduced these advantages, a subject beyond the scope of this work.

See Schnee & White, Sec. 269A: New Weapon in the IRS's Battle Against Professional Corporations, 1983 Tax Adviser 386; Bowman, The Professional Corporation, Has the Death Knell Been Sounded? 10 Pepperdine L.Rev. 515 (1983). Compare Phillips, McNider & Riley, Origins of Tax Law: The History of the Personal Service Corporation, 40 Wash. & Lee L.Rev. 433, 454 (1983). See also Chapman, The Future of Personal Service Corporations, 24 Ariz.L.Rev. 503 (1982).

For a discussion of the ethical aspects of lawyers organizing into professional corporations, see Note, Professional Corporations and Associations, 75 Harv.L.Rev. 776, 789–90 (1962).

# Chapter 2

# REGULATION OF THE PRACTICE OF LAW

## A. ADMISSION TO THE BAR

### MODEL RULES OF PROFESSIONAL CONDUCT

**RULE 8.1 Bar Admission and Disciplinary Matters**

An applicant for admission to the bar, or a lawyer in connection with a bar admission application or in connection with a disciplinary matter, shall not:

(a) knowingly make a false statement of material fact; or

(b) fail to disclose a fact necessary to correct a misapprehension known by the person to have arisen in the matter, or knowingly fail to respond to a lawful demand for information from an admissions or disciplinary authority, except that this Rule does not require disclosure of information otherwise protected by Rule 1.6.[a]

### *Comment*

The United States Supreme Court has left little doubt that a state may constitutionally require a showing of "good moral character" as a condition to admission to the bar, and to make the investigations to determine if it is present.[2] The phrase, however, is an indefinite one

**a.** Compare the following CPR provisions:

"**EC 1-2** The public should be protected from those who are not qualified to be lawyers by reason of a deficiency in education or moral standards or other relevant factors but who nevertheless seek to practice law. * * * "

"**DR 1-101 Maintaining Integrity and Competence of the Legal Profession**

"(A) A lawyer is subject to discipline if he has made a materially false statement in, or if he has deliberately failed to disclose a material fact requested in connection with, his application for admission to the bar.

"(B) A lawyer shall not further the application for admission to the bar of another person known by him to be unqualified in respect to character, education, or other relevant attribute."

**2.** Law Students Civil Rights Research Council v. Wadmond, 401 U.S. 154, 91 S.Ct. 720, 27 L.Ed.2d 749 (1971); Schware v. Board of Bar Examiners, 353 U.S. 232, 77 S.Ct. 752, 1 L.Ed.2d 796 (1957).

subject to wide interpretations,[3] and courts have varied in their application of it. Some courts are more inclined than others to give the benefit of the doubt to the applicant and to hold that past misconduct does not necessarily forever bar admission. Thus, admission has been granted notwithstanding the applicant's professed belief that disobedience of law is sometimes justified and his criminal convictions for past minor acts of civil disobedience.[4]

Other decisions have admitted applicants notwithstanding examining committees had rejected them for conduct such as speeches at demonstrations which appeared to have advocated violence,[5] giving false testimony before the House Committee on Un-American Activities and a labor union trial committee regarding communist organization membership,[6] misstatement of residence in bar admission application,[7] and excessive use of intoxicants leading to criminal behavior and other misconduct.[8]

Decisions upholding exclusion include conduct such as nondisclosure of desertion and nonsupport conviction in an application to register as a law student,[9] failure for several years to register for military service, nondisclosure of the failure in the application for admission, and evasiveness in answering inquiries relative thereto,[10] misstatements and nondisclosures of various activities in bar admission application,[11] unjustified defaulting on student loans,[12] securing another to take the LSAT to gain law school admission,[13] and failure to disclose bankruptcy

3. "[T]he term, by itself, is unusually ambiguous. It can be defined in an almost unlimited number of ways for any definition will necessarily reflect the attitudes, experiences, and prejudices of the definer. Such a vague qualification, which is easily adapted to fit personal views and predilections, can be a dangerous instrument for arbitrary and discriminatory denial of the right to practice law." Konigsberg v. State Bar, 353 U.S. 252, 262, 77 S.Ct. 722, 728, 1 L.Ed.2d 810, 819 (1957).

4. Hallinan v. Committee of Bar Examiners, 65 Cal.2d 447, 55 Cal.Rptr. 228, 421 P.2d 76 (1966) ("If we were to deny to every person who has engaged in a 'sit-in' or other form of nonviolent civil disobedience, and who has been convicted of it, the right to enter a licensed profession, we would deprive the community of the services of many highly qualified persons of the highest moral courage.").

5. Siegel v. Committee of Bar Examiners, 10 Cal.3d 156, 110 Cal.Rptr. 15, 514 P.2d 967 (1973) (applicant's explanation accepted). See also In re David H., 283 Md. 632, 392 A.2d 83 (1978) (past criminal conduct adds to applicant's burden of establishing present good moral character by requiring proof of full and complete rehabilitation).

6. March v. Committee of Bar Examiners, 67 Cal.2d 718, 63 Cal.Rptr. 399, 433 P.2d 191 (1967) (subsequently rehabilitated).

7. In re Farris, 87 Nev. 508, 489 P.2d 1156 (1971) (subsequently rehabilitated and strong evidence of good moral character); see also In re Moore, 301 N.C. 634, 272 S.E.2d 826 (1981) (failure to disclose prior arrests and convictions would warrant exclusion).

8. In re Monaghan, 126 Vt. 53, 222 A.2d 665 (1966) (rehabilitated for past several years); see also In re A.T., 286 Md. 507, 408 A.2d 1023 (1979) (subsequently rehabilitated drug addict admitted).

9. Ex parte Weinberg, 281 Ala. 200, 201 So.2d 38 (1967), cert. denied 389 U.S. 1042, 88 S.Ct. 785, 19 L.Ed.2d 833 (1968).

10. In re Walker, 112 Ariz. 134, 539 P.2d 891, 88 A.L.R.3d 1045 (1975), cert. denied 424 U.S. 956, 96 S.Ct. 1433, 47 L.Ed.2d 363 (1976).

11. In re Beasley, 243 Ga. 134, 252 S.E.2d 615 (1979).

12. In re Gahan, 279 N.W.2d 826 (Minn. 1979).

13. In re Capace, 110 R.I. 254, 291 A.2d 632 (1972).

in two different states in the application for admission and failure to justify the omissions.[14]

In In re Davis,[15] the Ohio Supreme Court held that a prior conviction of a felony was not an automatic bar to admission but did place an obligation on the applicant to show "full and complete rehabilitation" by disclosure of all relevant facts. Withholding information by invoking the attorney-client privilege was deemed inconsistent with this obligation.

There are, however, first amendment rights and constitutional limits under the due process and equal protection clauses to how far states may go in excluding applicants on the ground that they lack good character. This has been settled in a series of United States Supreme Court decisions. These cases have centered for the most part on the applicant's political, social and economic beliefs and associations, past and present, which the admitting authorities deemed undesirable and harmful to the profession and to the public. In Schware v. Board of Bar Examiners,[16] the Court held that the universally-used "good moral character" requirement is valid *insofar as it is narrowly construed to "have a rational connection with the applicant's fitness or capacity to practice law."* In *Schware*, the Court held that under the circumstances, an applicant's use of aliases, arrests, and past membership in the Communist Party, all occurring more than a dozen years before his application, did not rationally justify a finding that he was morally unfit to practice law. The Court noted that the use of aliases was not fraudulent but to enable him to secure employment from anti-Semitic employers and to more effectively organize non-Jewish employees, that "the mere fact that a man has been arrested has very little, if any, probative value in showing that he has engaged in misconduct," and that his Communist Party membership "when he was a young man during the midst of this country's greatest depression" did not appear to be "anything more than a political faith in a political party."

Later cases have refined or modified the position of the Court. Most of these are discussed in Carfagno v. Harris, which follows.

## CARFAGNO v. HARRIS

470 F.Supp. 219 (D.Ark.1979).

VAN SICKLE, District Judge.

This is a civil action arising under 42 U.S.C. § 1983 to protect rights given to the Plaintiffs by the first and fourteenth amendments to the Constitution of the United States. The Plaintiffs seek a declaratory judgment and injunctive relief. The facts involved in this case were

14. In re Fitzpatrick, 247 Ga. 55, 273 S.E.2d 618 (1981).

15. 38 Ohio St.2d 273, 313 N.E.2d 363 (1974).

16. 353 U.S. 232, 77 S.Ct. 752, 1 L.Ed.2d 796 (1957). See also the companion case, Konigsberg v. State Bar, 353 U.S. 252, 77 S.Ct. 722, 1 L.Ed.2d 810 (1957).

stipulated and the case was submitted to the Court on cross motions for summary judgment.

In January of 1976, Plaintiff James Carfagno graduated from the University of Arkansas Law School in Fayetteville. He applied for permission to take and he did pass the spring 1976 bar examination. * * *

[T]he Arkansas Supreme Court has established the requirements and standards for admission to the Bar of Arkansas * * *. One of the requirements established by the Arkansas Supreme Court is the completion of a "Certificate and Oath of Applicant for Admission to the Bar of Arkansas."

On March 31, 1976, Carfagno complied with the requirements of the Certificate and Oath, except that he declined to answer two of its questions. These two questions are as follows:

(1) "Are you now, or have you at any time been, a member of the Communist party?"

(2) "Are you now, or have you at any time been, a member or supporter of any party, organization, or group that believes in or teaches the overthrow of the United States Government by force or by any illegal or unconstitutional methods?"

Along with the Certificate and Oath, Carfagno submitted a "Memorandum Brief in Support of Petition for License", in which he set forth his legal position for refusing to answer the questions. * * *

The Arkansas Supreme Court denied Carfagno's application because of his "failure to answer all the questions propounded on the prescribed form of application." Carfagno was not allowed to participate in the formal admission ceremony held on April 5, 1976. On April 7, 1976, Carfagno complied in full with the requirements of the Certificate and Oath by answering the two questions and was subsequently admitted to the Arkansas Bar.

On November 15, 1976, Carfagno along with several individuals who in the future planned to seek admission to the Bar of the State of Arkansas filed the complaint against the Arkansas Supreme Court and each of its members. The action was brought as a class action seeking a declaration that the questions referred to above offend the first and fourteenth amendments to the Constitution of the United States. Since 1976, all of the named Plaintiffs have answered the questions and are now practicing law. However, a third year law student, Arnold Goodman, has intervened stating he will apply for and take the Arkansas Bar Examination and does not wish to respond to the two questions. Goodman asserts that he is willing to respond to all other questions on the character questionnaires, which set forth extensive personal history data.

The Arkansas Supreme Court continues to require an answer to all questions as a condition of admission to the Arkansas Bar. The court's avowed purpose and intent in propounding the questions in controversy is to enable the court to "investigate further" into past and present activities of persons applying for admission to the Bar of Arkansas.

The Plaintiffs contend that the two questions on the Certificate and Oath offend the constitution. They contend that the questions focus impermissibly on the political activities and viewpoints of bar applicants, that the questions thereby operate to inhibit the exercise of protected expressive and associational freedoms by law students and others that make up the class, and that this chilling effect is not justified as a necessary impact of the system designed to weed out bar applicants who are unfit to practice law.

The state may not subject a person to a civil disability for mere membership in a particular organization. Baird v. State Bar of Arizona, 401 U.S. 1, 6, 91 S.Ct. 702, 27 L.Ed.2d 639 (1971). A person's beliefs and associations are protected by the first amendment. However, the state may exclude a person from a profession for membership in a subversive organization if the individual has knowledge of its unlawful purposes and the specific intent to further those purposes. Law Students Research Council v. Wadmond, 401 U.S. 154, 165, 91 S.Ct. 720, 27 L.Ed.2d 749 (1971). Similarly, the first amendment limits the power of the state to make inquiries about an individual's beliefs and associations. Broad and sweeping inquiries into these protected areas discourage citizens from exercising rights protected by the Constitution. "When a State seeks to inquire about an individual's beliefs and associations a heavy burden lies upon it to show that the inquiry is necessary to protect a legitimate state interest." *Baird.*[a] However, "The Court has held that under some circumstances simple inquiry into present or past Communist Party membership of an applicant for admission to the Bar is not as such unconstitutional. Konigsberg v. State Bar, 366 U.S. 36, 81 S.Ct. 997, 6 L.Ed.2d 105; In re Anastaplo, 366 U.S. 82, 81 S.Ct. 978, 6 L.Ed.2d 135." *Baird.* Thus, though broad inquiries into a person's beliefs or associations are disfavored because they discourage the exercise of first amendment rights, inquiries concerning Communist affiliation may be justifiable on the grounds of a legitimate state interest.

The first question that the Plaintiffs feel is objectionable asks, "Are you now, or have you at any time been, a member of the Communist party?" In Konigsberg v. State Bar, 366 U.S. 36, 81 S.Ct. 997, 6 L.Ed.2d 105 (1961), the Supreme Court held that a state may inquire

**a.** In In re Stolar, companion case to *Baird* and *Wadmond*, the Court held that a bar applicant cannot be excluded for refusing to answer a question about simple (as opposed to "knowing") membership in any organization advocating forceful overthrow (at least where the question is not limited to inquiry about Communist Party membership).

In *Stolar* the Court (without dissent on this point) also held that an applicant could not be excluded for refusing to list all organizations of which he was or had been a member since registering as a law student.

For discussion of *Baird* and *Stolar* as well as *Wadmond*, see Comment, Bar Examinations: Good Moral Character and Political Inquiry, 1970 Wis.L.Rev. 471; 85 Harv.L.Rev. 212 (1971).

into a bar applicant's membership in the Communist Party under similar circumstances to those presented in this case. The Court stated:

> "As regards the questioning of public employees relative to Communist Party membership it has already been held that the interest in not subjecting speech and association to the deterrence of subsequent disclosure is outweighed by the State's interest in ascertaining the fitness of the employee for the post he holds, and hence that such questioning does not infringe constitutional protections. With respect to this same question of Communist Party membership, we regard the State's interest in having lawyers who are devoted to the law in its broadest sense, including not only its substantive provisions, but also its procedures for orderly change, as clearly sufficient to outweigh the minimal effect upon free association occasioned by compulsory disclosure in the circumstances here presented."

The Supreme Court also upheld, as appropriate, inquiries into Communist Party membership in In re Anastaplo, 366 U.S. 82, 81 S.Ct. 978, 6 L.Ed.2d 135 (1961) as follows:

> "We have also held in *Konigsberg* that the State's interest in enforcing such a rule as applied to refusals to answer questions about membership in the Communist Party outweighs any deterrent effect upon freedom of speech and association, and hence that such state action does not offend the Fourteenth Amendment."

Thus, to inquire into Communist Party membership, there must be a legitimate government purpose. In view of the lawyer's position of trust and confidence and in view of the lawyer's position of authority, the government has a legitimate purpose in asking the question "Are you now, or have you at any time been, a member of the Communist Party?"

The second question challenged by the Plaintiffs asks, "Are you now, or have you at any time been, a member or supporter of any party, organization, or group that believes in or teaches the overthrow of the United States Government by force or by any illegal or unconstitutional methods?" This question *does* offend the first amendment of the Constitution in that it is overbroad.

The first amendment protects political activities. Arkansas cannot constitutionally exclude a bar applicant for membership in an organization advocating forcible overthrow of the government unless he knew of these aims and he had a specific intent to help bring them about. Law Students Research Council v. Wadmond, 401 U.S. 154, 165–166, 91 S.Ct. 720, 27 L.Ed.2d 749 (1971). Because of this, any question asking about membership in an organization that advocates forcible overthrow of the government must be limited to those organizations whose aims he knew and had a specific intent to bring about. The question objected to asks only of membership and does not include the "knowledge" or "specific intent" requirements. Thus, the second question is overbroad and invalid because it violates the expressive and associational freedoms guaranteed by the first amendment.

* * * Defendants shall be enjoined from asking this question of persons seeking admission to practice law in Arkansas. * * * [b]

### *Comment*

(1) *Admission forms.* A comprehensive study of the admission forms used by state admitting authorities was made in 1978.[1] Some of the findings seem incredible.

> "Oregon requires a credit check; Florida asks for the names, addresses and occupations for 10 years of the applicant's parents and of all brothers and sisters and every place where the applicant has established credit in the last 15 years; New York requires the 'full name of all persons with whom you are presently living, and relationship to you.' Montana asks questions about federal and state income tax returns and Ohio asks 'When and where did you last vote in a public election?' Montana goes still further: 'Have you voted in the last seven years? If so, state the county and state in which you were registered in each year that you voted.'
>
> "Three states continue to ask about organizational memberships which are not specifically oriented to the violent overthrow of the United States or the various state governments."

The study notes that "most states compel the prospective lawyer to waive all rights relating to confidential communications with his spouse, doctor, clergy, and attorney (usually without a stated termination date) *before* the local Board of Bar Examiners will accept the application form for processing." [2]

A form reproduced in the study's appendix occupies over four pages of fine print.

> "If the applicant feels the inquiry is too expansive, he has few options. For if the question is left unanswered, the Examiners may, under *Konigsberg* find the refusal to reply an obstruction of the investigation and cause for rejection. The basis for refusal may involve privacy and preference not to have the information in a semi-public file, rather than one of self-incrimination or constitutional protection. The price of not answering is high: the risk of loss of the applicant's chosen profession."

(2) *Constitutional limits.* Bar admission, like other government action, must accord with constitutional limitations, e.g., the bill of

**b.** See Martineau, The Supreme Court and State Regulation of the Legal Profession, 8 Hast.Const.L.Q. 199 (1980).

**1.** Comment, National Survey of Bar Admission Application Forms: Need for Reform, 22 St. Louis U.L.J. 638 (1978).

**2.** See Ex parte Minor, 280 So.2d 217 (La.1973), upholding a requirement that the applicant execute a document authorizing the admissions committee to obtain information about him and releasing all claims resulting from disclosures made in reliance on the waiver.

attainder prohibition,[3] the religion clauses,[4] the speech, press and association protections,[5] and the due process[6] and equal protection clauses.[7]

(3) *Citizenship.* In In re Griffiths,[8] a 7-2 U.S. Supreme Court held that total exclusion of resident aliens from the practice of law violated equal protection in that use of this "suspect classification" was not shown necessary to accomplish a substantial permissible state interest:

> "Connecticut has wide freedom to gauge on a case-by-case basis the fitness of an applicant to practice law. Connecticut law can,

3. Ex parte Garland, 71 U.S. (4 Wall.) 333, 18 L.Ed. 366 (1867). The Court struck down as a bill of attainder the requirement, to practice in federal courts, of an oath that the applicant has never voluntarily borne arms against, aided persons engaged in armed hostility against, or held office in or given voluntary support to any authority or pretended government hostile to, the United States.

4. See Nicholson v. Board of Commissioners, 338 F.Supp. 48 (D.Ala.1972) (state may not, over applicant's religious objection, condition admission on taking of oath ending with "so help me God").

The Court's 5-4 action in In re Summers, 325 U.S. 561, 65 S.Ct. 1307, 89 L.Ed. 1795 (1945), upholding exclusion of an applicant because he was a conscientious objector, does not seem to square with the requirement that qualifications must have a rational connection with fitness to practice law. Nor does it seem consistent with current free exercise clause interpretation, see, e.g., Wisconsin v. Yoder, 406 U.S. 205, 92 S.Ct. 1526, 32 L.Ed.2d 15 (1972). The Court's current approach would sustain excluding COs from the bar only if this were shown necessary to serve a compelling government interest. The fact that compelling selective COs to serve in the armed forces has been held to meet this test, see Gillette v. United States, 401 U.S. 437, 91 S.Ct. 828, 28 L.Ed.2d 168 (1971), does not show that excluding selective or general COs from the bar meets it.

The Washington Supreme Court's 7-2 action in In re Brooks, 57 Wash.2d 66, 355 P.2d 840 (1960), cert. denied 365 U.S. 813, 81 S.Ct. 694, 5 L.Ed.2d 692 (1961), upholding exclusion of a CO because of his federal felony conviction for violating (on conscience grounds) an order requiring COs to report to an alternative service camp, is similarly questionable.

5. See Moity v. Louisiana State Bar Association, 414 F.Supp. 176 (D.La.1976) (constitutionally permissible scope of inquiry regarding applicant's character and professional competence must be limited by traditional high regard for first amendment freedoms of speech and association), affirmed mem. 537 F.2d 1141 (5th Cir. 1976); In re Levine, 97 Ariz. 88, 397 P.2d 205 (1964) (applicant cannot be excluded for criticism, even if erroneous, of FBI Director).

6. It is a denial of procedural due process to withhold admission to the bar on the basis of confidential information not disclosed to the applicant. Willner v. Committee of Character & Fitness, 373 U.S. 96, 83 S.Ct. 1175, 10 L.Ed.2d 224, 2 A.L.R.3d 1254 (1963); In re Burke, 87 Ariz. 336, 351 P.2d 169 (1960) (information from National Conference of Bar Examiners); In re Lobb, 157 So.2d 75 (Fla.1963). See Note, Procedural Due Process and Character Hearings for Bar Applicants, 15 Stan.L.Rev. 500 (1963).

In In re Kellar, 79 Nev. 28, 377 P.2d 927 (1963), the court denied the applicant's request for disclosure of the report of the National Conference of Bar Examiners on the ground that "Our study of the record reveals that every subject of significance contained in the confidential reports and touching upon Kellar's character and fitness to practice law in Nevada was referred to during the mentioned hearings and is, therefore, contained in the non-confidential or open record of this matter." Does this meet the constitutional objection? Compare In re Warren, 149 Conn. 266, 178 A.2d 528 (1962).

In In re Berkan, 648 F.2d 1386 (1st Cir. 1981), the court decided that having satisfied threshold requirements for admission to the bar, applicant fell within the class of those entitled to be admitted to practice, and so should not have been rejected upon charges of her unfitness without giving her an opportunity by notice for hearing and answer.

7. See Schware v. Board of Bar Examiners, 353 U.S. 232, 77 S.Ct. 752, 1 L.Ed.2d 796 (1957) (qualification must have rational connection with fitness to practice law).

Further, if a restriction infringes a "fundamental right" (e.g., privacy or travel) or uses a "suspect classification" (e.g., race, national origin, or alienage), it must be shown necessary to serve a compelling government interest. See Memorial Hospital v. Maricopa County, 415 U.S. 250, 94 S.Ct. 1076, 39 L.Ed.2d 306 (1974) (travel); In re Griffiths, infra Comment (3) (alienage).

8. 413 U.S. 717, 93 S.Ct. 2851, 37 L.Ed.2d 910 (1973).

and does, require appropriate training and familiarity with Connecticut law. [I]t requires a new lawyer to take [oaths] to perform his functions faithfully and honestly and * * * to 'support the constitution of the United States, and the constitution of the state of Connecticut.' * * * Connecticut may quite properly conduct a character investigation to insure in any given case that an applicant is not one who swears to an oath pro forma while declaring or manifesting his disagreement with or indifference to the oath. [Footnote: "We find no merit in the contention that only citizens can in good conscience take an oath to support the Constitution. We note that all persons inducted into the Armed Services, including resident aliens, are required to take [such an] oath."] Moreover, once admitted to the bar, lawyers are subject to continuing scrutiny by the organized bar and the court. * * * In sum, the Committee simply has not established that it must exclude all aliens from the practice of law in order to vindicate its undoubted interest in high professional standards."

(4) *Residence.* A good number of states have adopted requirements, usually by court rule, requiring that the applicant for admission be a resident of the state in which he or she is seeking admission, either before taking the bar examination or before beginning practice in the state. State and lower federal courts are in conflict over whether these requirements can withstand attacks on constitutional grounds, usually under the privileges and immunities clause of article IV.

Several kinds of practitioners are adversely affected if they must become residents of the state in which they want to engage in practice. It would confine their state practice to that of a single state. This strikes particularly at attorneys practicing near state borders with sizeable populations in both states, e.g., New York City and Newark, New Jersey; St. Louis and East St. Louis; Washington D.C. and the surrounding suburbs in Delaware and Virginia.

Other attorneys adversely affected include those who specialize in particular fields of practice and are retained throughout the country, and corporate attorneys representing corporations with extensive interstate activities.[9]

Courts which have upheld the validity of the residence requirement have assigned several reasons.

"The state interests most commonly identified as supportive of residency requirements for admission to the bar include: (1) convenience in administering the mechanics of the bar admission process—registration, testing, and interviewing; (2) the need to observe the prospective attorney's behavior and character; (3) the importance of general familiarity with local customs and court procedures; and (4) the facilitation of various interests served by the

9. For a discussion of admission of out-of-state attorneys pro hac vice, see infra pp. 98–108.

physical presence of the attorney within the state, such as ease of service of process and attorney-client communication, availability for malpractice investigation and bar discipline, rapid response to motion calls, and simplifying the task of court appointments of counsel for indigent defendants." [10]

The courts which hold the residence requirements violative of the privileges and immunity clause do not find these reasons persuasive.[11] They do not find it to have been shown that states would suffer the handicaps portrayed in investigating, supervising and disciplining out-of-state attorneys who practice in the state. The state may require the attorney to designate local counsel as the attorney's representative,[12] and a state official, such as a state clerk of court, as the attorney's agent for service of process.[13] It may require an attorney to have an office in the state.[14]

(5) *Education requirements.* The courts have upheld requirements as to pre-law school education[15] and graduation from a law school accredited by the ABA.[16] It has been held that an applicant can be excluded on the ground that his or her law school did not give final course exams "whenever such an examination is appropriate to test the student's understanding of the course." [17]

(6) *Bar exams.* The courts have likewise upheld requiring successful completion of a bar exam as a prerequisite to admission,[18] and

10. Note, A Constitutional Analysis of State Bar Residency Requirements Under the Interstate Privileges and Immunities Clause of Article IV, 92 Harv.L.Rev. 1461, 1480 (1979).

11. See Piper v. Supreme Court of New Hampshire, 723 F.2d 110 (1st Cir. 1983) (equally divided court), prob. juris. noted 52 U.S.L.W. 3776 (U.S. Apr. 23, 1984); Gordon v. Committee on Character & Fitness, 48 N.Y.2d 266, 422 N.Y.S.2d 641, 397 N.E.2d 1309 (1979); Noll v. Alaska Bar Association, 649 P.2d 241 (Alaska 1982); Sargus v. West Virginia Board of Law Examiners, 294 S.E.2d 440 (W.Va.1982); Note, supra note 10.

12. See Sargus v. West Virginia Board of Law Examiners, 294 S.E.2d 440 (W.Va.1982).

13. See Gordon v. Committee on Character & Fitness, 48 N.Y.2d 266, 422 N.Y.S.2d 641, 397 N.E.2d 1309 (1979).

14. See White River Paper Co. v. Ashmont Tissue, Inc., 110 Misc.2d 373, 441 N.Y.S.2d 960 (1981).

In In re Sackman, 90 N.J. 521, 448 A.2d 1014 (1982), the court, in order to avoid the constitutional question, amended its Rule requiring out-of-state attorneys to have their "principal offices" in the state, to require both in-state and out-of-state attorneys to have a "bona fide office" in the state.

15. Heiberger v. Clark, 148 Conn. 177, 169 A.2d 652 (1961).

16. Hackin v. Lockwood, 361 F.2d 499 (9th Cir. 1966), cert. denied 385 U.S. 960, 87 S.Ct. 396, 17 L.Ed.2d 305 (1966). See also Louis v. Supreme Court, 490 F.Supp. 1174 (D.Nev.1980); Ostroff v. New Jersey Supreme Court, 415 F.Supp. 326 (D.N.J.1976); In re Urie, 617 P.2d 505 (Alaska 1980); In re Hansen, 275 N.W.2d 790 (Minn.1978), appeal dismissed 441 U.S. 938, 99 S.Ct. 2154, 60 L.Ed.2d 1040 (1979).

17. In re Rules of Court, 29 N.Y.2d 653, 324 N.Y.S.2d 949, 274 N.E.2d 440 (1970).

18. Bailey v. Board of Law Examiners, 508 F.Supp. 106 (W.D.Tex.1980); Attwell v. Nichols, 608 F.2d 228 (5th Cir. 1979), cert. denied 446 U.S. 955, 100 S.Ct. 2924, 64 L.Ed.2d 813 (1980). See also Avery v. Board of Governors, 576 P.2d 488 (Alaska 1978), where the practice of offering attorney-applicant a choice of taking the multistate bar exam or the essay portion of the general exam was approved as fair and appropriate, modifying In re Stephenson, 516 P.2d 1387 (Alaska 1973), in which the court ordered that the applicant, who had practiced for 35 years in Oklahoma and passed the essay-type Alaska section of the general bar exam but failed the multistate portion, be certified for admission.

have held that the applicant is not entitled to insist on an evidentiary hearing or a court review of the exam results absent an indication of fraud or other misconduct by the bar examiners.[19]

(7) *Reciprocal admission of lawyers from other states.* It has been held that a state may limit admission without exam to lawyers from states which accord lawyers from it the same treatment.[20]

(8) *Admission to federal practice.* "On account of pragmatic difficulties, the separate United States District Courts do not recognize a comity in this regard with each other or with the appellate courts. Each is a separate tribunal and governed by its own rules. Some United States District Courts do not recognize admission to the courts of the state in which they are situated as the test for admission to their own bars. These courts themselves require independent examinations into character and fitness as well as oral examinations into the candidates' knowledge of the federal statutes and rules among the tests for admission. Some federal District Courts give general admission to lawyers who are admitted by the courts of other states and who are nonresidents of the state in which the District Court sits. But there is no requirement by any law or regulation, state or national, that this be done."[21]

### *Questions*

(1) Given the necessity that only those of reliability, honesty and integrity, that is, of good moral character, be admitted to the legal profession, how are these qualities to be ascertained?

(2) Are written form questionnaires an appropriate method of obtaining the information sought and for judging the character of the applicant?

(3) How much weight should be given to sworn statements obtained from relatives, friends, lawyer acquaintances, political figures, employers in non-law areas, or ministers of the applicant's church, attesting to the applicant's good character?

**19.** See In re Pacheco, 85 N.M. 600, 514 P.2d 1297 (1973) ("a number of jurisdictions have held that a review of one's bar examination answers will not be made by a court in the absence of an allegation that there was fraud, coercion, imposition or other misconduct on the part of the bar examiners"). See also Richardson v. McFadden, 563 F.2d 1130 (4th Cir. 1977) (applicants admitted to bar upon showing that law examiners acted arbitrarily and capriciously in scoring exams) cert. denied 435 U.S. 968, 98 S.Ct. 1606, 56 L.Ed.2d 59 (1978); Whitfield v. Illinois Board of Law Examiners, 504 F.2d 474 (7th Cir. 1974) (fact that bar exam has prevented one exceptionally qualified individual from practicing is not sufficient to declare it violative of fourteenth amendment); In re Reardon, 378 A.2d 614 (Del.1977) (Board of Examiners' actions must be clearly arbitrary and manifestly unfair to warrant change in examinee's scores).

**20.** Hawkins v. Moss, 503 F.2d 1171 (4th Cir. 1974), cert. denied 420 U.S. 928, 95 S.Ct. 1127, 43 L.Ed.2d 400 (1975).

Regarding pro hac vice admission of lawyers from other states, see infra p. 98–108.

**21.** In re Wasserman, 240 F.2d 213 (9th Cir. 1956).

"[E]xcept in the District of Columbia, there is no federal procedure for examining applicants either as to legal ability or moral character and so reliance is placed on prior admission to the bar of a state supreme court." In re Dreier, 258 F.2d 68 (3d Cir. 1958).

(4) Would it be an invasion of the applicant's privacy if these persons were interviewed by the admitting authority about all aspects of the applicant's private and public life? If so, does the state's interest in a qualified legal profession override this consideration?

(5) Should the applicant be examined under oath by the admitting authority? If so, should the applicant be able to invoke the privilege against self-incrimination? Compare Spevack v. Klein,[22] where the U.S. Supreme Court held that a lawyer may take the fifth in disciplinary proceedings if testifying would expose the lawyer to possible criminal prosecution.[23]

## SPEARS, FEDERAL COURT ADMISSION STANDARDS— A 45-YEAR SUCCESS STORY[a]

83 F.R.D. 235 (1979).

The Committee of the Judicial Conference of the United States to Consider Standards for Admission to Practice in the Federal Courts, better known as the Devitt Committee, has made its final report to the Judicial Conference of the United States.[b] Among the proposals for action by the individual districts were three recommendations which bear directly upon admission to practice in the federal court system. They were that:

1. As a condition of admission to practice, applicants pass a bar examination, covering the Federal Rules of Civil, Criminal and Appellate Procedure, the Federal Rules of Evidence, federal jurisdiction, and the Code of Professional Responsibility. (This examination requirement will not apply to present members of the Federal Bar.)

2. Attorneys who conduct a federal civil trial or any phase of a criminal proceeding satisfy an experience requirement of four supervised trial experiences, at least two of which involve actual trials in state or federal courts. (Present members of the Federal Bar may satisfy the requirement by experience in prior unsupervised trials and lawyers not satisfying this requirement may become or remain members of the Federal Bar, and may conduct, without assistance, pre-trial civil matters.)

3. District courts establish a peer or performance review procedure to advise and give guidance to Federal Bar members whose trial performances are substandard.

The Committee recommended that these three standards of examination, experience, and peer review be instituted in a number of pilot

22. 385 U.S. 511, 87 S.Ct. 625, 17 L.Ed.2d 574 (1967).

23. See infra p. 76.

a. Adrian A. Spears is Chief Judge, Western District of Texas, Member, Committee to Consider Standards for Admission to Practice in the Federal Courts.

b. Committee to Consider Standards for Admission to Practice in the Federal Courts, Final Report to the Judicial Conference of the United States, 83 F.R.D. 215 (1979).

districts; that district courts adopt a student practice rule; and that district courts support continuing legal education programs on trial advocacy and federal practice subjects and encourage Federal Bar members to attend. In addition, the Committee proposed that the Judicial Conference recommend to the American Bar Association that it re-examine its law school accreditation standards with a view toward requiring that each law school provide trial advocacy training, including student participation in actual or simulated trials under the supervision of instructors with trial experience, and encourage the Bench and Bar to support the law schools in attaining the goal of providing trial skills training to every student desiring it.

On September 20, 1979, the Judicial Conference unanimously approved the recommendations of the Devitt Committee * * *.

The proposals recommended by the Devitt Committee have been met with a variety of reactions ranging from outright disapproval and skepticism,[6] to acceptance with pride within the Western District of Texas, where similar proposals have been in effect for many years and are considered neither radical nor unreasonable. In fact, in many respects, the admission standards of the Western District of Texas, which have stood the test of forty-five years, strongly parallel those recommended by the Devitt Committee. * * *[c]

## B. DISCIPLINE

### 1. MISCONDUCT SUBJECT TO DISCIPLINE

#### MODEL RULES OF PROFESSIONAL CONDUCT

**RULE 8.4 Misconduct**

It is professional misconduct for a lawyer to:

(a) violate or attempt to violate the Rules of Professional Conduct, knowingly assist or induce another to do so, or do so through the acts of another;

(b) commit a criminal act that reflects adversely on the lawyer's honesty, trustworthiness or fitness as a lawyer in other respects;

(c) engage in conduct involving dishonesty, fraud, deceit or misrepresentation;

(d) engage in conduct that is prejudicial to the administration of justice;

6. "The overwhelming majority of all the respondents, about 85%, are opposed to the idea of a federal Bar examination and a trial experience requirement as prerequisites for admission to practice in the federal trial courts * * * The overall response of those who appeared at the public hearings, to put it kindly, was less than enthusiastic." Committee to Consider Standards for Admission to Practice in the Federal Courts to the Judicial Conference of the United States, Staff Report of Written Comments and Public Hearings (June 1979) at 2–3.

c. See Law Scope, 67 A.B.A. J. 550 (1981) (fourteen federal district courts have implemented one or more of the three recommendations).

(e) state or imply an ability to influence improperly a government agency or official; or

(f) knowingly assist a judge or judicial officer in conduct that is a violation of applicable rules of judicial conduct or other law.[a]

### *Question*

Under RPC 8.4(b), a criminal act must reflect the lawyer's unfitness *as a lawyer*, while under DR 1–102(A)(3), "illegal conduct" must involve *moral turpitude.* Which of the following examples of misconduct would be affected by this difference?

(1) Failure to file income tax returns.[1]

(2) Possession or distribution of marijuana or other controlled substance.[2]

(3) Sexual misconduct and exploitation.[3]

**a.** Compare the following CPR provision:

**"DR 1–102 Misconduct**

"(A) A lawyer shall not:

(1) Violate a Disciplinary Rule.

(2) Circumvent a Disciplinary Rule through actions of another.

(3) Engage in illegal conduct involving moral turpitude.

(4) Engage in conduct involving dishonesty, fraud, deceit, or misrepresentation.

(5) Engage in conduct that is prejudicial to the administration of justice.

(6) Engage in any other conduct that adversely reflects on his fitness to practice law."

**1.** Compare Attorney Grievance Commission v. Walman, 280 Md. 453, 374 A.2d 354 (1977) (misdemeanor not involving moral turpitude per se, distinguishable from more serious crime of willful tax evasion involved in Maryland State Bar Association v. Agnew, 271 Md.App. 543, 318 A.2d 811 (1974)) with In re Nicholson, 243 Ga. 803, 257 S.E.2d 195 (1979) (moral turpitude if "pattern of repetitious non-filing for multiple years and for which there were taxes due").

See also In re Bunker, 294 Minn. 47, 199 N.W.2d 628 (1972):

"There is no law of the state or nation which so uniformly affects every citizen as the income tax regulations. * * * Any violation of the income tax laws represents a threat to the ability of our government units to function, whether such action is done with corrupt intent or not. * * *

" * * * We will not * * * attempt to distinguish a failure-to-file-income tax-returns proceeding on the question of moral turpitude. Rather, we hold that the failure to file income tax returns represents a violation of a lawyer's oath of office and further represents a violation of the Code of Professional Responsibility. [The court quoted DR 1–102 without indicating which clause(s) controlled.]"

See Annot., 63 A.L.R.3d 476 (1975); Annot., 63 A.L.R.3d 512 (1975).

**2.** See State ex rel. Oklahoma Bar Association v. Denton, 598 P.2d 663 (Okl.1979) (suspension for possession of marijuana as involving moral turpitude); In re Rabideau, 102 Wis.2d 16, 306 N.W.2d 1 (1981) (suspension for possessing marijuana and giving it to a juvenile as evincing moral turpitude); In re Roberson, 429 A.2d 530 (D.C.App.1981) (conspiracy to sell and to receive and conceal narcotic drugs inherently involves moral turpitude).

In In re Preston, 616 P.2d 1 (Alaska 1980), the attorney, who disagreed with the laws relating to marijuana and cocaine, gave small amounts of both to a 13-year-old son of a friend with the friend's consent. He was suspended for two years:

"We reject Preston's contentions that because his conduct was unrelated to his professional skills and ability to practice law that he should receive no discipline. [T]he major concern here is the damage done to the reputation and integrity of the legal profession."

**3.** See ABA Commission on Evaluation of Professional Standards, Model Rules of Professional Conduct 8.4 Legal Background at 211 (Proposed Final Draft May 30, 1981), indicating that such behavior is intended to be covered since it shows the attorney to be unworthy of confidence in him or her as an

(4) Negligent or intentional defective notarial acts. The not uncommon loose practice in executing the functions of a notary public has been held to be grounds for disciplinary sanctions.[4]

## 2. PROCEDURE FOR DISCIPLINE

### MODEL RULES OF PROFESSIONAL CONDUCT

**RULE 8.3 Reporting Professional Misconduct**

(a) A lawyer having knowledge that another lawyer has committed a violation of the Rules of Professional Conduct that raises a substantial question as to that lawyer's honesty, trustworthiness or fitness as a lawyer in other respects, shall inform the appropriate professional authority.

(b) A lawyer having knowledge that a judge has committed a violation of applicable rules of judicial conduct that raises a substantial question as to the judge's fitness for office shall inform the appropriate authority.

(c) This Rule does not require disclosure of information otherwise protected by Rule 1.6 [dealing with confidential communications.][a]

#### *Comment*

(1) *Whistle blowing.* "This obligation of the profession appears to many to contain an element of informing on another person—an act that seems contrary to the nature of most of us. If personal relationships and reluctance to cause trouble for another lawyer are the hallmarks of the legal profession, then we should immediately cease claiming to be a profession and acknowledge that it is a fraternity. Standards of camaraderie that may be appropriate for a fraternal organization are not appropriate for a profession that plays an integral part in the proper functioning of our system of justice."[1]

attorney. A series of cases are cited showing predominantly sexual abuse of children. See, e.g., In re Kamin, 262 N.W.2d 162 (Minn.1978) (abuse of client's children).

Should fornication with a voluntarily consenting client be considered within the RPC 8.4(b)? Or adultery with a client seeking a divorce? Would these fall within RPC 8.4(b)'s terms "fitness as a lawyer in other respects"?

4. See In re Finley, 261 N.W.2d 841 (Minn.1978) (public censure for falsely notarizing documents not signed in lawyer's presence); In re Surgent, 79 N.J. 529, 401 A.2d 522 (1979); In re Kraus, 289 Or. 661, 616 P.2d 1173 (1980). See also In re Smith, 292 Or. 84, 636 P.2d 923 (1981) (persuading secretary to make false acknowledgement is "conduct prejudicial to the administration of justice"; emergency is no defense); In re McGuinn, 272 S.C. 366, 252 S.E.2d 122 (1979) (court "shocked" at attorney's "long standing practice" of signing secretary's name as notary with her consent).

a. Compare the following CPR provisions:

**"DR 1-103 Disclosure of Information to Authorities**

"(A) A lawyer possessing unprivileged knowledge of a violation of DR 1-102 shall report such knowledge to a tribunal or other authority empowered to investigate or act upon such violation.

"(B) A lawyer possessing unprivileged knowledge or evidence concerning another lawyer or a judge shall reveal fully such knowledge or evidence upon proper request of a tribunal or other authority empowered to investigate or act upon the conduct of lawyers or judges."

1. Thode, The Duty of Lawyers and Judges to Report Other Lawyers' Breaches of the Standards of the Legal Profession, 1976 Utah L.Rev. 95, 100.

(2) *Clark Report.* The 1970 Report of the ABA Special Committee on Evaluation of Disciplinary Enforcement, chaired by former U.S. Supreme Court Justice Tom C. Clark, found great laxity in enforcement of professional standards against lawyers:

> "The Committee has found that in some instances disbarred attorneys are able to continue to practice in another locale; that lawyers convicted of federal income tax violations are not disciplined; that lawyers convicted of serious crimes are not disciplined until after appeals from their convictions have been concluded, often a matter of three or four years, so that even lawyers convicted of serious crimes, such as bribery of a governmental agency employee, are able to continue to practice before the very agency whose representative they have corrupted; that even after disbarment lawyers are reinstated as a matter of course; that lawyers fail to report violations of the Code of Professional Responsibility committed by their brethren, much less conduct that violates the criminal law; that lawyers will not appear or cooperate in proceedings against other lawyers but instead will exert their influence to stymie the proceedings; that in communities with a limited attorney population disciplinary agencies will not proceed against prominent lawyers or law firms and that, even when they do, no disciplinary ac- is taken, because the members of the disciplinary agency simply will not make findings against those with whom they are professionally and socially well acquainted; and that, finally, state disciplinary agencies are undermanned and underfinanced, many having no staff whatever for the investigation or prosecution of complaints."[2]

The Clark Report's recommendations, and other actions by the ABA such as the 1975 ABA Standing Committee on Professional Discipline's Suggested Guidelines for Rules of Disciplinary Enforcement and the 1979 ABA Standards for Lawyer Discipline and Disability Proceedings, stimulated extensive changes in disciplinary procedure among the states.[3]

The case which follows contains a description of a typical state disciplinary proceeding. Most of the Court's discussion of the abstention doctrine has been omitted.

## MIDDLESEX COUNTY ETHICS COMMITTEE v. GARDEN STATE BAR ASSOCIATION

457 U.S. 423, 102 S.Ct. 2515, 73 L.Ed.2d 116 (1982).

Chief Justice BURGER delivered the opinion of the Court.

We granted certiorari to determine whether a federal court should abstain from considering a challenge to the constitutionality of disci-

2. ABA Special Committee on Evaluation of Disciplinary Enforcement, Problems and Recommendations in Disciplinary Enforcement (Final Draft 1970).

3. The ABA Standards for Lawyer Discipline and Disability Proceedings may be found in West Publishing Co., Selected Statutes, Rules and Standards on the Legal Profession 187 (1984).

plinary rules that are the subject of a pending state disciplinary proceeding within the jurisdiction of the New Jersey Supreme Court. The Court of Appeals held that it need not abstain under Younger v. Harris, 401 U.S. 37, 91 S.Ct. 746, 27 L.Ed.2d 669 (1971). We reverse.

The Constitution of New Jersey charges the State Supreme Court with the responsibility for licensing and disciplining attorneys admitted to practice in the State. Under the rules established by the New Jersey Supreme Court, enacted pursuant to its constitutional authority, a complaint moves through a three-tier procedure. First, local District Ethics Committees appointed by the State Supreme Court are authorized to receive complaints relating to claimed unethical conduct by an attorney. New Jersey Court Rule 1:20–2(d). At least two of the minimum of eight members of the District Ethics Committee must be nonattorneys. Complaints are assigned to an attorney member of the Committee to report and make a recommendation. Rule 1:20–2(h). The decision whether to proceed with the complaint is made by the person who chairs the Ethics Committee. If a complaint is issued by the Ethics Committee it must state the name of the complainant, describe the claimed improper conduct, cite the relevant rules, and state, if known, whether the same or a similar complaint has been considered by any other Ethics Committee. The attorney whose conduct is challenged is served with the complaint and has 10 days to answer.

Unless good cause appears for referring the complaint to another committee member, each complaint is referred to the member of the Committee who conducted the initial investigation for review and further investigation, if necessary. The committee member submits a written report stating whether a prima facie indication of unethical or unprofessional conduct has been demonstrated. The report is then evaluated by the chairman of the Ethics Committee to determine whether a prima facie case exists. Absent a prima facie showing, the complaint is summarily dismissed. If a prima facie case is found, a formal hearing on the complaint is held before three or more members of the Ethics Committee, a majority of whom must be attorneys. The lawyer who is charged with unethical conduct may have counsel, discovery is available, and all witnesses are sworn. The panel is required to prepare a written report with its findings of fact and conclusions. The full Committee, following the decision of the panel, has three alternatives. The Committee may dismiss the complaint, prepare a private letter of reprimand, or prepare a presentment to be forwarded to the Disciplinary Review Board. Rule 1:20–2(*o*).

The Disciplinary Review Board, a statewide board which is also appointed by the Supreme Court, consists of nine members, at least five of whom must be attorneys and at least three of whom must be nonattorneys. The Board makes a *de novo* review. Rule 1:20–3(d)(3). The Board is required to make formal findings and recommendations to the New Jersey Supreme Court.

All decisions of the Disciplinary Review Board beyond a private reprimand are reviewed by the New Jersey Supreme Court. Briefing and oral argument are available in the Supreme Court for cases involving disbarment or suspension for more than one year. Rule 1:20–4.

Respondent Lennox Hinds, a member of the New Jersey bar, served as executive director of the National Conference of Black Lawyers at the time of his challenged conduct. Hinds represented Joanne Chesimard in a civil proceeding challenging her conditions of confinement in jail. In 1977 Chesimard went to trial in state court for the murder of a policeman. Respondent Hinds was not a counsel of record for Chesimard in the murder case. However, at the outset of the criminal trial Hinds took part in a press conference, making statements critical of the trial and of the trial judge's judicial temperament and racial insensitivity. In particular, Hinds referred to the criminal trial as "a travesty," a "legalized lynching," and "a kangaroo court."

One member of the Middlesex County Ethics Committee read news accounts of Hinds' comments and brought the matter to the attention of the Committee. In February of 1977 the Committee directed one of its members to conduct an investigation. A letter was written to Hinds, who released the contents of the letter to the press. The Ethics Committee on its own motion then suspended the investigation until the conclusion of the Chesimard criminal trial.

After the trial was completed the Committee investigated the complaint and concluded that there was probable cause to believe that Hinds had violated DR 1–102(A)(5). That section provides that "A lawyer shall not * * * [e]ngage in conduct that is prejudicial to the administration of justice." Respondent Hinds also was charged with violating DR 7–107(D), which prohibits extrajudicial statements by lawyers associated with the prosecution or defense of a criminal matter. The Committee then served a formal statement of charges on Hinds.

Instead of filing an answer to the charges in accordance with the New Jersey bar disciplinary procedures, Hinds and the three respondent organizations filed suit in the United States District Court for the District of New Jersey contending that the disciplinary rules violated respondents' First Amendment rights. In addition, respondents charged that the disciplinary rules were facially vague and overbroad. The District Court granted petitioner's motion to dismiss based on Younger v. Harris, 401 U.S. 37, 91 S.Ct. 746, 27 L.Ed.2d 669 (1971), concluding that "[t]he principles of comity and federalism dictate that the federal court abstain so that the state is afforded the opportunity to interpret its rules in the face of a constitutional challenge." * * *

The question in this case is threefold: *first,* do state bar disciplinary hearings within the constitutionally prescribed jurisdiction of the State Supreme Court constitute an ongoing state judicial proceeding; *second,* do the proceedings implicate important state interests; and *third,* is there an adequate opportunity in the state proceedings to raise constitutional challenges.

The State of New Jersey, in common with most States,[11] recognizes the important state obligation to regulate persons who are authorized to practice law. New Jersey expresses this in a state constitutional provision vesting in the New Jersey Supreme Court the authority to fix standards, regulate admission to the bar, and enforce professional discipline among members of the bar. New Jersey Const. Art. 6, § 2, ¶ 3. The Supreme Court of New Jersey has recognized that the local District Ethics Committees act as the arm of the court in performing the function of receiving and investigating complaints and holding hearings. Rule 1:20–2; In re Logan, 70 N.J. 222, 358 A.2d 787 (1976). The New Jersey Court has made clear that filing a complaint with the local ethics and grievance committee "is in effect a filing with the Supreme Court. * * *" Toft v. Ketchum, 18 N.J. 280, 284, 113 A.2d 671, 674, cert. denied, 350 U.S. 887 (1955). "From the very beginning a disciplinary proceeding is judicial in nature, initiated by filing a complaint with an ethics and grievance committee."[12] Ibid. It is clear beyond doubt that the New Jersey Supreme Court considers its bar disciplinary proceedings as "judicial in nature."[13] As such, the proceedings are of a character to warrant federal court deference. The remaining inquiries are whether important state interests are implicated so as to warrant federal court abstention and whether the federal plaintiff has an adequate opportunity to present the federal challenge.

The State of New Jersey has an extremely important interest in maintaining and assuring the professional conduct of the attorneys it licenses. States traditionally have exercised extensive control over the professional conduct of attorneys. See *supra*, n. 11. The ulti-

**11.** See Shoaf, State Disciplinary Enforcement Systems Structural Survey (ABA National Center for Professional Responsibility 1980).

The New Jersey allocation of responsibility is consistent with § 2.1 of the ABA Standards for Lawyer Discipline and Disability Proceedings (Proposed Draft 1978), which states that the "[u]ltimate and exclusive responsibility within a state for the structure and administration of the lawyer discipline and disability system and the disposition of individual cases is within the inherent power of the highest court of the state."

The rationale for vesting responsibility with the judiciary is that the practice of law "is so directly connected and bound up with the exercise of judicial power and the administration of justice that the right to define and regulate it naturally and logically belongs to the judicial department." Id., commentary at § 2.1.

**12.** The New Jersey Supreme Court has concluded that bar disciplinary proceedings are neither criminal nor civil in nature, but rather are *sui generis*. In re Logan, 70 N.J. 222, 358 A.2d 787 (1976). See also, Standards for Lawyer Discipline and Disability Proceedings § 1.2 (Proposed Draft 1978). As recognized in Juidice v. Vail, supra, however, whether the proceeding "is labeled civil, quasi-criminal, or criminal in nature," the salient fact is whether federal court interference would unduly interfere with the legitimate activities of the state. Id., 430 U.S., at 335–336, 97 S.Ct. at 1217.

The instant case arose before the 1978 rule change. In 1978 the New Jersey Supreme Court established a Disciplinary Review Board charged with review of findings of District Ethics Committees. Nothing in this rule change, however, altered the nature of such proceedings. The responsibility under Art. 6, § 2, ¶ 3 remains with the New Jersey Supreme Court.

**13.** The role of local ethics or bar association committees may be analogized to the function of a special master. Anonymous v. Assn of the Bar of City of New York, 515 F.2d 427 (CA2), cert. denied, 423 U.S. 863, 96 S.Ct. 122, 46 L.Ed.2d 92 (1975). The essentially judicial nature of disciplinary actions in New Jersey has been recognized previously by the federal courts. * * *

mate objective of such control is "the protection of the public, the purification of the bar and the prevention of a reoccurrence." In re Baron, 25 N.J. 445, 449, 136 A.2d 873, 875 (1957). The judiciary as well as the public is dependent upon professionally ethical conduct of attorneys and thus has a significant interest in assuring and maintaining high standards of conduct of attorneys engaged in practice. The state's interest in the professional conduct of attorneys involved in the administration of criminal justice is of special importance. Finally, the state's interest in the present litigation is demonstrated by the fact that the Middlesex County Ethics Committee, an agency of the Supreme Court of New Jersey, is the named defendant in the present suit and was the body which initiated the state proceedings against respondent Hinds.

The importance of the state interest in the pending state judicial proceeding and in the federal case calls *Younger* abstention into play. So long as the constitutional claims of respondents can be determined in the state proceedings and so long as there is no showing of bad faith, harassment or some other extraordinary circumstance that would make abstention inappropriate, the federal courts should abstain. * * * [a]

### *Comment*

(1) *Self-incrimination.* In Spevack v. Klein,[1] the U.S. Supreme Court held that an attorney could not be compelled, by threat of disbarment, to give evidence in a disciplinary proceeding against him, if to do so would expose him to possible criminal prosecution. State courts have generally construed the case as not preventing such compulsion if only disbarment, as distinguished from criminal prosecution, is the prospect faced by the attorney. Disbarment, of itself, is not deemed within the protection of the fifth amendment.[2]

Consistent with this position, it is held that testimony compelled in a criminal prosecution under a grant of immunity may be used against the attorney in a disciplinary proceeding.[3]

**a.** Justice Brennan and Justice Marshall (joined by Justices Brennan, Blackmun, and Stevens) filed concurring opinions.

For the New Jersey Supreme Court's subsequent disposition of the disciplinary proceeding, see In re Hinds, p. 381.

**1.** 385 U.S. 511, 87 S.Ct. 625, 17 L.Ed.2d 574 (1967).

**2.** See, e.g., McInnis v. State, 618 S.W.2d 389 (Tex.Civ.App.1981), cert. denied 456 U.S. 976, 102 S.Ct. 2242, 72 L.Ed.2d 851 (1982). Earlier cases are reviewed in Comment, Self-Incrimination in Bar Disciplinary Proceedings: What ever Happened to *Spevack?* 23 Vill.L.Rev. 125 (1977).

**3.** See In re Mann, 270 Ind. 358, 385 N.E.2d 1139 (1979); Maryland State Bar Association v. Sugerman, 273 Md. 306, 329 A.2d 1 (1974), cert. denied 420 U.S. 974, 95 S.Ct. 1397, 43 L.Ed.2d 654 (1975); Anonymous Attorneys v. Bar Association, 41 N.Y.2d 506, 362 N.E.2d 592, 393 N.Y.S.2d 961 (1977) (disbarment not "penalty or forfeiture" within statute conferring immunity from prosecution, nor does use in disciplinary proceeding of resulting testimony violate fifth amendment); Annot., 62 A.L.R.3d 1145 (1975).

In In re Daley, 549 F.2d 469 (7th Cir. 1977), cert. denied 434 U.S. 829, 98 S.Ct. 110, 54 L.Ed.2d 89 (1977), the federal district court, in granting the attorney immunity, prohibited state disciplinary agencies from using the attorney's testimony. The prohibition was held invalid and the testimony could be used. The case is discussed in 17 Washburn L.J. 438, (1978).

(2) *Non-cooperation.* Failure of the attorney to heed the notices and requests of, and otherwise cooperate with the disciplinary agency may, in itself, be ground for some disciplinary sanction.[4]

## C. UNAUTHORIZED PRACTICE OF LAW

### 1. NONLAWYERS

#### MODEL RULES OF PROFESSIONAL CONDUCT

**RULE 5.5 Unauthorized Practice of Law**

A lawyer shall not:

* * *

(b) assist a person who is not a member of the bar in the performance of activity that constitutes the unauthorized practice of law.[a]

***Comment***

The underlying justification for restricting unauthorized practice is given in EC 3–1:

> "The prohibition against the practice of law by a layman is grounded in the need of the public for integrity and competence of those who undertake to render legal services. Because of the fiduciary and personal character of the lawyer-client relationship and the inherently complex nature of our legal system, the public can better be assured of the requisite responsibility and competence if the practice of law is confined to those who are subject to the requirements and regulations imposed upon members of the legal profession."[1]

#### PEOPLE EX REL. MacFARLANE v. BOYLS

197 Colo. 242, 591 P.2d 1315 (1979).

GROVES, Justice.

The Grievance Committee of this court, after a full disciplinary hearing, recommended that the respondent attorney, Pipp Marshall Boyls, be suspended from the practice of law for a period of two years and that he be assessed the cost of the disciplinary proceedings.

The recommendation of the Committee was based upon violations of DR3–101(A) * * *.

4. In re Cartwright, 282 N.W.2d 548 (Minn.1979).

a. DR 3–101(A) provides: "A lawyer shall not aid a non-lawyer in the unauthorized practice of law." Regarding sharing fees or forming partnership with nonlawyer, see RPC 5.4(a)(b); DR 3–102, 3–103.

1. The stated policy is developed further in EC 3–2 to 3–5.

The Comment to RPC 5.5, is much briefer on the reasons for the restriction: "[L]imiting the practice of law to members of the bar protects the public against rendition of legal services by unqualified persons."

DR3-101(A) reads: "A lawyer shall not aid a nonlawyer in the unauthorized practice of law."

We paraphrase the findings of the Committee. This court admitted the respondent to the practice of law in 1970. In 1973, he met James R. Walsh of Educational Scientific Publishers (ESP). ESP enrolled "students" who wanted to learn to set up "pure" trusts (also called "equity" trusts, "pure equity" trusts or "common law" trusts) which ESP claimed would reduce students' taxes materially.

ESP trusts allegedly would reduce or eliminate income, capital gains, estate and gift taxes provided they were operated or managed properly. ESP non-lawyer salesmen and the respondent were available to assist purchasers to formulate effective trusts.

Neither the Internal Revenue Service (IRS) nor any courts of record have found the trusts to be viable tax saving mechanisms. Since 1973, the IRS has publicized its opinion that "the entire ESP approach [is] little more than an ill-conceived scheme to improperly avoid taxes which would not accomplish any of its objectives." The publicity included letters sent from the IRS to all known holders of such trusts, a public news release and Revenue Rulings 75-257, through 75-260.

ESP "educators" marketed the trusts at presentations where they claimed: (1) that most bankers and lawyers were ignorant of their method; (2) that ESP retained attorneys with knowledge of, and experience with such trusts and that the "pure" trust forms were time-tested, copyrighted, patented by the federal government, court-declared and water tight.

One salesman testified that the respondent answered questions which the salesman relayed from clients regarding individual problems in setting up the trust, e.g. whether or not to include certain real property or business assets in the trust. The respondent himself testified that he attended several sales presentations and prepared promotional materials which challenged the IRS' analysis as legally incorrect. ESP distributed these challenges in connection with its promotions. * * *

Respondent's reliance upon Grievance Committee v. Dacey, 154 Conn. 129, 222 A.2d 339 (1966), appeal dismissed, 387 U.S. 938 (1967) is unavailing. The case is distinguishable since Dacey did not participate in tailoring his standardized forms to an individual's needs.[a] * * *

We have reviewed the length of suspension recommended by the Committee and have concluded to set the length of the suspension at one year. The respondent is suspended for one year commencing forthwith and assessed the costs of these proceedings in the amount of $952.64 to be paid within 90 days.

**a.** The *Dacey* case is discussed infra p. 93.

See also Kentucky Bar Association v. Tiller, 641 S.W.2d 421 (Ky.1982) in which an attorney was disciplined for allowing his client, a collection agency to, in effect, engage in the unauthorized practice of law by permitting the agency to conduct legal proceedings in his name.

### *Questions*

(1) If the attorney had been correct, and the IRS wrong, concerning the validity of the trust plan, should this have a bearing on whether the attorney should be disciplined?

(2) What is objectionable about ESP, after receiving competent legal advice, originating and promoting a tax-saving plan? Would the public be better served if the attorney himself were to develop and advance such a plan? Or if neither is permitted to do so?

(3) Every civilized society with a legal system of any degree of complexity has a legal profession to master the principles of the system and to apply them as needed for the effective functioning of that society. We have previously noted the educational and character requirements imposed to qualify for admission to the profession. It may appear as a corollary that those not meeting these requirements should not be permitted to engage in providing services which can be characterized as falling within the purview of the practice of law.[1] But is this necessarily so? It would be possible to permit laypersons to engage in at least some forms of practice but forbid them from holding themselves out as attorneys. By analogy, there are certified public accountants, but there are also practicing accountants not so certified. There are registered nurses, but there are also mid-wives and practical nurses. What harm would come to the public if clients were free to choose between an attorney and a layperson who the client believes to be qualified for the client's needs? Isn't this merely free competition?

This has indeed been urged by Justice Douglas. After referring to "the increasing complexities of our governmental apparatus" which makes it "difficult for a person to process a claim or even to make a complaint," Justice Douglas stated,

> "There are not enough lawyers to manage or supervise all of these affairs; and much of the basic work done requires no special legal talent. Yet there is a closed-shop philosophy in the legal profession that cuts down drastically active roles for laymen * * *.
>
> " * * * Laymen * * * should be allowed to act as 'next friend' to any person in the preparation of any paper or document or claim, so long as he does not hold himself out as practicing law or as being a member of the Bar."[2]

1. "Restricting the practice of law to persons licensed by the state is both a legitimate and necessary exercise of this power ["to establish standards for licensing practitioners and regulating the practice of professions"]. The underlying rationale behind this grant of a monopoly is twofold: (1) it insures that persons rendering legal services are qualified to do so; and (2) it subjects persons rendering such services to the Virginia Code of Professional Responsibility * * *." Surety Title Insurance Agency, Inc. v. Virginia State Bar Association, 431 F.Supp. 298 (E.D.Va.1977), vacated on other grounds 571 F.2d 205 (4th Cir.), cert. denied 436 U.S. 941, 98 S.Ct. 2838, 56 L.Ed.2d 781 (1978).

2. Johnson v. Avery, 393 U.S. 483, 491, 89 S.Ct. 747, 752, 21 L.Ed. 718, 725 (1969). (Douglas, J., concurring). The majority held that a state may not deny to prison inmates the assistance of other inmates in preparing

This position has not been adopted by the courts or the profession. With limited exceptions, if a given activity falls within the practice of law, only attorneys may engage in it. This raises a number of questions:

(a) What constitutes the practice of law? Some occupations require some knowledge of the law relevant to the occupation, such as the practice of accounting, architecture, the sale and rental of real estate, and insurance brokerage.

(b) Who should decide where the lines between the practice of law and the activities of these other occupations should be drawn? The bar? The courts? The legislature? The other occupations? Which one is most likely to protect the public interest in making the decision?

(c) Should simple transactions requiring a minimum of knowledge of the law be excluded from the definition of the practice of law? E.g., preparation of simple income tax returns, aiding a claimant or defendant in a small claims court; filing applications for welfare relief?

(d) Should answers to these questions take into account whether or not the legal profession is as qualified, ready, or able to provide the needed services as the laypersons whom it seeks to exclude, and at the same or lower cost? [3]

### *Comment*

Approximately 50 years ago, the organized bar began to move aggressively against those not lawyers whom it considered to be engaged illegally in the practice of law. The enactment of statutes making unauthorized practice a criminal offense was secured, litigation was resorted to to curb unauthorized practice, conferences were held and agreements sought and secured delineating the respective areas of practice between the legal profession and other organized groups, and in 1934, publication of the periodical Unauthorized Practice News was begun. The ABA committee on the subject sought and obtained the

habeas writs, absent provision of some other form of legal assistance. In a footnote, the Court stated:

> "[T]he Court of Appeals relied on the power of the State to restrict the practice of law to licensed attorneys as a source of authority for the prison regulation. The power of the States to control the practice of law cannot be exercised so as to abrogate federally protected rights. NAACP v. Button, 371 U.S. 415, 83 S.Ct. 328, 9 L.Ed.2d 405 (1963); Sperry v. Florida, 373 U.S. 379, 83 S.Ct. 1322, 10 L.Ed.2d 428 (1963)."

In *Sperry*, Florida attempted to restrict the activities within the state of a patent attorney registered with the U.S. Patent Office but not admitted to the Florida bar. The U.S. Supreme Court conceded that the patent attorney's activities could properly be classified as the practice of law, but held that the state's restriction was invalid as interfering with the federal government's proper exercise of authority in this field. After referring to the Patent Office's requirements for nonlawyers to be granted registration, the Court noted, "So successful have the efforts of the Patent Office been that the Office was able to inform the Hoover Commission that 'there is no significant difference between lawyers and nonlawyers either with respect to their ability to handle the work or with respect to their ethical conduct.' "

3. Compare Johnson v. Avery, discussed in the preceding footnote.

cooperation of state and local bar committees and assisted them in their efforts to prevent the unauthorized practice of law in their jurisdictions. Also, from time to time, the ABA committee issued opinions on what was or was not the unauthorized practice of law.[4]

In these efforts, the bar and the courts, at the urging of the bar, have given an expansive interpretation of what constitutes the practice of law. The justification has been that it is in the public interest to assure the public of competence and integrity in the legal services it receives. Note the 1967 statement of the then president of the ABA:

## MARDEN, THE AMERICAN BAR AND UNAUTHORIZED PRACTICE

33 Unauth. Prac. News 1–2 (Spring-Summer 1967).

There are numerous other groups whose activities touch on the practice of law. Accountants and auditors number about 490,000, and real estate agents and brokers another 200,000. There are architects, life insurance salesmen, chartered life underwriters, labor consultants, patent agents, tax specialists and so on, almost ad infinitum. The newest one to appear on the scene is the computer specialist.[a] * * *

We believe that the proper functioning of our society requires a system of courts and lawyers to resolve justifiable disputes between citizens and between the citizen and government. We believe that without judges and lawyers, specially educated, continuously trained, admitted to practice by specific license, and subject to stern standards of conduct, our liberties and our way of life would be in jeopardy.

Now, if it is in the interest of our entire society that lawyers and lawyers alone are to be licensed to practice law, it then follows that there must be a line drawn between lawyers and other groups whose work touches on the practice of law.

* * * Our concern in this subject matter is governed by broad considerations of social policy and the public interest. It must not be motivated by selfishness, by competition-for-competition's sake, or by avaricious materialism. The lawyer who thinks that unauthorized

4. These activities are recounted in detail in the volumes of Unauthorized Practice News.

a. "Basically, Electronic Data Retrieval is unobjectionable so long as it is merely a means of storing textual information for later retrieval. In that respect, it is similar to a library. So long as it is a library, there would appear to be no unauthorized practice of law problems present. When, however, the system becomes so sophisticated that facts are fed into it from which the system draws legal conclusions based on *specific legal analysis*, it would involve the practice of law. On well established principles these services may be *rendered only to lawyers* for as soon as the spectrum of services becomes broader, so that the services are rendered to *non-lawyers*, it impinges upon the unauthorized practice of law." ABA Standing Committee on Unauthorized Practice of Law Annual Report, 33 Unauth.Prac.News 62, 70 (Spring-Summer 1970).

For more recent analyses, see Sprowl, Automating the Legal Reasoning Process: A Computer That Uses Regulations and Statutes to Draft Legal Documents, 1979 Am.B. Found. Research J. 1; Thomas, Unauthorized Practice and Computer Aided Legal Analysis Systems, 20 Jurimetrics J. 41 (1979).

practice work is simply a means for increasing his own income has no place in this discussion.

We are here to protect the public from the hidden dangers of dealing with the unlicensed and unauthorized practitioner; not to protect the lawyer from competition. We are not a trade union, and we must beware of giving the appearance of acting for our selfish interests when we attack the illegal practitioner.

### *Comment*

This position of the bar has met more recently with growing criticism and has been undermined by developments on the federal level bringing into question whether the bar's activities violated the Sherman Antitrust Act.[1]

During the 1970s, the U. S. Department of Justice began an investigation into the bar's activities. One consequence was that the Board of Governors of the California State Bar Association terminated some 20 agreements previously entered into with other groups.[2] In 1979, the ABA Board of Governors authorized its committees to work with other professional organizations to rescind all statements of principles.[3] Other action taken to meet possible challenges included termination, in 1977, of the publication of Unauthorized Practice News.

States have adopted a variety of measures such as greater control and participation by the judiciary,[4] addition of laypersons to unauthorized practice committees, and, in at least seven states, the abolition of the committees.[5]

Efforts by the bar, and particularly by the medical profession, to secure the enactment of federal legislation excluding the professions from the terms of the Sherman Act have not, to the time of this writing, been successful.[6]

In considering the materials which follow, these developments should be kept in mind, recognizing that where and how the line should be drawn between what is and what is not the practice of law still remains unsettled to a considerable degree.

Bear in mind also the questions raised at pp. 79–80 above.

1. For a discussion of the cases dealing with the antitrust aspects of various activities of the bar, see infra pp. 426–37. See also Rhode, Policing the Professional Monopoly: A Constitutional and Empirical Analysis of Unauthorized Practice Prohibitions, 34 Stanford L. Rev. 1 (1981). See also Weckstein, Limitations on the Right to Counsel: The Unauthorized Practice of Law, 1978 Utah L. Rev. 649 (1978).

2. See Law Scope, 66 A.B.A. J. 129 (1980).

3. Id.

4. One effect of this might be to bring the activity within the "state action" exception to the Sherman Act. See infra pp. 430–35.

5. See Rhode, supra note 1, at 55–62.

6. See Kauper, Antitrust and the Professions: An Overview, 52 Antitrust L.J. 163 (1983).

## BENNION, VAN CAMP, HAGEN & RUHL v. KASSLER ESCROW, INC.

96 Wash.2d 443, 635 P.2d 730 (1981).

DIMMICK, Justice.

Is RCW 19.62 authorizing escrow agents and other lay persons to perform certain actions with regard to real estate or personal property transactions constitutional? We hold, affirming the trial court, that the legislative action violates Const. art. 4, § 1 inasmuch as therein, the Supreme Court is given the exclusive power to regulate the practice of law.

Defendant petitioner is a registered escrow agent under the Escrow Agent Registration Act, RCW 18.44, and employs licensed escrow officers for closing real estate transactions. Petitioner closed several real estate transactions and in the process prepared documents and performed other services. Two of these transactions involved earnest money agreements specifying that the place of closing was to be the office of the plaintiff/respondent, a law firm. Respondent brought suit alleging that the escrow company had engaged in the unauthorized practice of law in violation of RCW 2.48.170, .180 and .190. Respondent sought a permanent injunction enjoining petitioner from performing any acts constituting the practice of law.

Subsequent to the filing of the action, the legislature enacted RCW 19.62 authorizing certain lay persons to perform tasks relating to real estate transactions. Specifically, the act allows escrow agents and officers to

> "select, prepare, and complete documents and instruments relating to such loan, forbearance, or extension of credit, sale, or other transfer of real or personal property, limited to deeds, promissory notes, deeds of trusts, mortgages, security agreements, assignments, releases, satisfactions, reconveyances, contracts for sale or purchase of real or personal property, and bills of sale * * * "

RCW 19.62.010(2).[1]

Petitioner, in reliance upon the statute, moved to dismiss the action for injunctive relief, which motion was denied by the trial court. Re-

1. RCW 19.62.010 reads in full:

"The following individuals, firms, associations, partnerships, or corporations:

"(1) Any person or entity doing business under the laws of this state or the United States relating to banks, trust companies, bank holding companies and their affiliates, mutual savings banks, savings and loan associations, credit unions, insurance companies, title insurance companies and their duly authorized agents exclusively engaged in the title insurance business, federally approved agencies or lending institutions under the National Housing Act; or

"(2) Any escrow agent or escrow officer subject to the jurisdiction of the department of licensing; when acting in such capacity in connection with a loan, forbearance, or other extension of credit, or closing, or insuring title with respect to any loan, forbearance, or extension of credit or sale or other transfer of real or personal property, may select, prepare, and complete docu-

spondent moved for, and the trial court granted, a partial summary judgment declaring RCW 19.62 unconstitutional.

The line between those activities included within the definition of the practice of law and those that are not is oftentimes difficult to define. Recently, in Washington State Bar Ass'n v. Great W. Union Fed. Sav. & Loan Ass'n, 91 Wash.2d 48, 586 P.2d 870 (1978), we concluded that preparation of legal instruments and contracts that create legal rights is the practice of law.

> "The 'practice of law' does not lend itself easily to precise definition. However, it is generally acknowledged to include not only the doing or performing of services in the courts of justice, throughout the various stages thereof, but in a larger sense includes legal advice and counsel and the preparation of legal instruments by which legal rights and obligations are established. Further, selection and completion of preprinted form legal documents has been found to be the 'practice of law.'
>
> "The services at issue here are ordinarily performed by licensed attorneys, involve legal rights and obligations, and by their very nature involve the practice of law. We thus must agree with the trial court's conclusion that the selection and completion of form legal documents, or the drafting of such documents, including deeds, mortgages, deeds of trust, promissory notes and agreements modifying these documents constitutes the practice of law."

*Great Western.*

The statute in question is a direct response to our holding. We reaffirm that definition. RCW 19.62 authorizes a lay person involved with real estate transactions to "select, prepare, and complete documents and instruments" that affect legal rights. As such the statute allows the practice of law by lay persons. Petitioner requests this court to redefine the practice of law so that the conduct allowed by the statute does not constitute the practice of law. Petitioner asserts that there is a trend allowing lay persons to perform certain services such as those authorized by RCW 19.62 and our holding RCW 19.62

ments and instruments relating to such loan, forbearance, or extension of credit, sale, or other transfer of real or personal property, limited to deeds, promissory notes, deeds of trusts, mortgages, security agreements, assignments, releases, satisfactions, reconveyances, contracts for sale or purchase of real or personal property, and bills of sale, provided:

"(a) No such person or entity makes an additional charge for the selection, preparation, or completion of any such document or instrument;

"(b) All parties to the transaction are given written notice substantially as follows: IN CONNECTION WITH THE * * * (describe the transaction) * * * (name of person or entity) * * * SELECTS, PREPARES, AND COMPLETES CERTAIN INSTRUMENTS OR DOCUMENTS WHICH MAY SUBSTANTIALLY AFFECT YOUR LEGAL RIGHTS, BUT IS DOING SO FOR ITS OWN BENEFIT AND TO PROTECT ITS OWN INTEREST IN THIS TRANSACTION. IF YOU HAVE ANY QUESTION REGARDING SUCH DOCUMENTS OR INSTRUMENTS OR YOUR RIGHTS, YOU SHOULD CONSULT AN ATTORNEY OF YOUR CHOICE; and

"(c) No attorney or other agent had previously been designated in writing by a party to such documents or instruments to select and prepare the same."

competence required of an attorney * * * even though the statute attempts to require a similar standard.[5] The statute fails to consider who is to determine whether such agents and employees of banks, etc., are possessed of the requisite skill, competence and ethics. Only the Supreme Court has the power to make that determination through a bar examination, yearly Continuing Legal Education requirements, and the Code of Professional Responsibility. The public is also protected against unethical attorneys by a client's security fund maintained by the Washington State Bar Association.

Petitioner further contends that even if the court finds that the activities authorized by RCW 19.62 are the practice of law, the services rendered are within an exception to the general prohibition against lay persons practicing law. We have recognized this exception when a party to a legal document selects, prepares or drafts the document or represents himself in court proceedings. Both of these exceptions are based upon a

> "belief that a layperson may desire to act *on his own behalf* with respect to *his* legal rights and obligations without the benefit of counsel.
>
> "The 'pro se' exceptions are quite limited and apply only if the layperson is acting solely *on his own behalf*."

*Great Western. See also* EC 3–5. The instant statute also attempts to establish this exception by specific language. RCW 19.62.010(2)(a), (b).

Petitioner asserts that it falls within this "pro se" exception because as escrow agent it was a party to the documents and it charged no additional fees for the service. The interest of an escrow agent in the real estate transaction is not substantial enough to allow the services performed by it to fall within the exception. See State Bar of Arizona v. Arizona Land Title and Trust Co., 90 Ariz. 76, 366 P.2d 1 (1961); Oregon State Bar v. Security Escrows, Inc., 233 Or. 80, 377 P.2d 334 (1962). The petitioner in performing the services authorized by the statute was not acting solely on its own behalf. Simply stating the proposition does not make it accurate. Petitioner may have had a substantial interest in insuring the documents were correct but it

at law or qualified to do work of a legal nature, unless he is a citizen of the United States and a bona fide resident of this state and has been admitted to practice law in this state: *Provided,* That any person may appear and conduct his own case in any action or proceeding brought by or against him, or may appear in his own behalf in the small claims department of the justice's court: *And provided further,* That an attorney of another state may appear as counselor in a court of this state without admission, upon satisfying the court that his state grants the same right to attorneys of this state."

5. RCW 19.62.020 reads in full:

"Notwithstanding any provision of RCW 19.62.010, in the event any individual, firm, association, partnership, or corporation described in RCW 19.62.010 selects, prepares, or completes any document or instrument in connection with a transaction described in RCW 19.62.010, such individual, firm, association, partnership, or corporation shall be held to a standard of care equivalent to that of an attorney had such attorney selected, prepared, or completed any such instrument or document."

unconstitutional would not protect the public in any way. We dis gree.

It is the duty of the court "to protect the public from the activi of those who, because of lack of professional skills, may cause inju whether they are members of the bar or persons never qualified f or admitted to the bar." *Great Western.* Even the simplest of co veyances may involve issues of taxation, estate planning, future i terests, water rights, equitable conversion, covenants, equitable se vitudes, easements, statute of frauds and contract law. As stated Washington State Bar Ass'n v. Washington Ass'n of Realtors, 41 Wash.2 697, 712, 251 P.2d 619 (1952) (Donworth, J., concurring), "there is r such thing as a simple legal instrument in the hands of a layman Even escrow agents who may be well trained in certain aspects conveyancing could face complexities that are beyond the scope of tha escrow agent's knowledge. Additionally, the agent could fail to ider tify and address obscure issues.

A dangerous flaw of RCW 19.62 lies in the fact that it virtuall gives free rein to almost anyone of any degree of intelligence to perforr any task related to real property or personal property transactions Arguably, any employee of banks, trust companies, bank holding com panies, savings and loans, credit unions, insurance companies, or an federally approved agencies or lending institutions under the Nationa Housing Act, as well as escrow agents and officers, may select, com plete and prepare a host of documents in connection with any loan closing, sale or transfer of any real or personal property. * * *

Alternately, petitioner contends that the definition of the practice of law, as it now exists, should not be applied by this court to escrow agents. This assertion is based upon the fact that escrow agents must comply with state licensing requirements (RCW 18.44.010 et seq.) and with warning provisions notifying parties to seek legal advice if desired. RCW 19.62.010(2)(b). This argument focuses on who is performing the services rather than the nature and character of the services. This is clearly counter to prior case law. *Great Western; Washington Ass'n of Realtors.* In addition, if the agent is practicing law, a license and warning does not satisfy RCW 2.48.170, .180, and .190.[3] Such agent is not held to the high standards of conduct and

3. RCW 2.48.170 provides:

"No person shall practice law in this state subsequent to the first meeting of the state bar unless he shall be an active member thereof as hereinbefore defined: *Provided,* That a member of the bar in good standing in any other state or jurisdiction shall be entitled to appear in the courts of this state under such rules as the board of governors may prescribe."

RCW 2.48.180 provides:

"Any person who, not being an active member of the state bar, or who after he has been disbarred or while suspended from membership in the state bar, as by this chapter provided, shall practice law, or hold himself out as entitled to practice law, shall be guilty of a misdemeanor: *Provided, however,* Nothing herein contained shall be held to in any way affect the power of the courts to grant injunctive relief or to punish as for contempt."

RCW 2.48.190 provides:

"No person shall be permitted to practice as an attorney or counselor at law or to do work of a legal nature for compensation, or to represent himself as an attorney or counselor

did not have a substantial interest in the transaction itself. Petitioner relies heavily upon the fact that no additional charges were made for the services. Petitioner relies on the holding in *Great Western* to support this aspect of its argument. Such reliance is misplaced. Great Western did charge a fee so the court expressly limited its holding in the case to a situation where a fee is charged. The fact of compensation is irrelevant, however, except as to provide evidence of the fact that a lay person is acting for another. We have clearly held that it is the nature and character of the service rendered rather than the fact of compensation for it that governs. *Washington Ass'n of Realtors.* Realistically, since these businesses are profit-making ventures, compensation is inherent.

Petitioner's activities and those activities authorized by RCW 19.62 constitute the practice of law and do not come within any exception. Inasmuch as RCW 19.62 authorizes lay persons to perform services we have defined as the practice of law, it must fall. The statutory attempt to authorize the practice of law by lay persons is an unconstitutional exercise of legislative power in violation of the separation of powers doctrine.

Const. art. 4, § 1 provides in pertinent part: "judicial power of the state shall be vested in a supreme court * * * " An essential concomitant to express grants of power is the inherent powers of each branch. See generally In re Juvenile Director, 87 Wash.2d 232, 552 P.2d 163 (1976). Inherent power is that

> "authority not expressly provided for in the constitution but which is derived from the creation of a separate branch of government and which may be exercised by the branch to protect itself in the performance of its constitutional duties."

*In re Juvenile Director.*

It is a well established principle that one of the inherent powers of the judiciary is the power to regulate the practice of law. * * * Thus, the power to regulate the practice of law is solely within the province of the judiciary and this court will protect against any improper encroachment on such power by the legislative or executive branches. In passing RCW 19.62, allowing lay persons to practice law, the legislature impermissibly usurped the court's power. Accordingly, RCW 19.62 is unconstitutional as a violation of the separation of powers doctrine.

We affirm the trial court's summary judgment on the constitutional issue as well as that court's refusal to dismiss the request for injunctive relief. The cause is hereby remanded for trial.[a]

**a.** See also Chicago Bar Association v. Quinlan & Tyson, Inc., 34 Ill.2d 116, 214 N.E.2d 771 (1966) (injunction against real estate broker sustained except as to use of "preliminary or earnest money contract form"—but note the dissent that the form in fact determines the legal rights of the parties). The case is discussed in 69 W.Va.L.Rev. 59.

Recent cases tend to permit real estate brokers to fill in simple forms to complete the negotiated sale. See State Bar v. Guardian

## RECENT DEVELOPMENT, UNAUTHORIZED PRACTICE OF LAW—LIMITED PRACTICE OF LAW FOR REAL ESTATE CLOSING OFFICERS?

57 Wash.L.Rev. 781, 792–97 (1982).

The prohibition against the unauthorized practice of law theoretically protects the public from unnecessary litigation, excessive fees, incompetent work, lack of professional ethics and disciplinary procedures, and the conflicts of interests. The [*Bennion-*] *Hagan* court's policy discussion centered around two of these problems: competence and discipline.

First, the court stated that RCW chapter 19.62 was dangerously flawed because it authorized "almost anyone of any degree of intelligence to perform * * * property transactions." Many lawyers, however, have only limited training in the procedures for transferring title and preparing closing documents. Escrow agents at least have the benefit of performing these procedures every day and are also probably policed by lending institutions and title companies.

Requiring lawyers to perform incidental closing services will add to the already high cost of land transfers. Even if lawyers take over the escrow function, they may assess additional charges for more extensive client counseling. Most people are not willing to pay for extensive legal advice. As one commentator notes, "[r]ightly or wrongly, ill advised or well, the public has in fact been choosing Brand X over the real thing to do its legal work in these closings."

Ironically, the forced introduction of lawyers after the closing raises costs without helping the consumer to plan the transaction. What clients really need is legal advice before they sign the earnest money contract that determines the rights of the parties. Even the Washington court has not required lawyer participation at this stage, probably because of the inconvenience and the certainty of resistance from consumers and real estate brokers. Yet the forced introduction of

Abstract & Title Co., 91 N.M. 434, 575 P.2d 943 (1978) (the "filling in blanks in the legal instruments here involved, where the forms have been drafted by attorneys and where filling in the blanks requires only the use of common knowledge regarding the information to be inserted" not objectionable); Pope County Bar Association v. Suggs, 274 Ark. 250, 624 S.W.2d 828 (1981) (is in public interest to allow real estate brokers to fill in simple real estate forms where party has declined to employ lawyer, no charge is made, and forms have been prepared by attorney).

A contrary position had been taken in State Bar v. Arizona Land Title & Trust Co., 90 Ariz. 76, 366 P.2d 1 (1961). A public reaction ensued, led by real estate brokers, which resulted in an overwhelming electoral vote adopting a constitutional amendment permitting real estate brokers to use and execute the disputed documents. For a description of these events, see Hamner, Title Insurance Companies and the Practice of Law, 14 Baylor L.Rev. 384 n.1 (1962).

See generally, Note, Document Preparation by the Real Estate Broker: How Far is Far Enough? 14 Willamette L.J. 475 (1975).

Title insurers have also been under attack on the ground that they are engaged in the unauthorized practice of law. See State Bar v. Arizona Land Title & Trust Co., 90 Ariz. 76, 366 P.2d 1 (1961); Ballbach Title Assurance: A New Approach to Unauthorized Practice, 41 Notre Dame Law. 192 (1965); Brossman & Rosenberg, Title Companies and the Unauthorized Practice Rules: The Exclusive Domain Reexamined, 83 Dick.L.Rev. 437 (1979); Payne, Title Insurance and the Unauthorized Practice of Law Controversy, 53 Minn.L.Rev. 423 (1969).

lawyers as mere scriveners after the closing misplaces the emphasis. Lawyers should be involved in the planning as well as routine drafting if the public policy concerns of the court and the legislature are to be adequately met.

Secondly, the *Hagan* court was concerned that escrow agents were not subject to attorneys' rules of ethics and discipline. The court found that the statute's licensing and warning provisions were inadequate to ensure that escrow agents possessed the requisite discipline and ethical standards to draw up real estate documents. Yet, it is questionable whether the absence of bar or court supervision significantly increases the risk to the public in routine land transfers. The court's assertion that escrow agents are not held to the standards of attorneys is unsupported either by case law or by RCW chapter 19.62, which had established a standard of care equivalent to that of attorneys. Further, escrow agents must be licensed and must prove the financial ability to provide a security fund for their clients.

The *Hagan* court was also concerned with ethical problems such as conflicts of interest. The interests of brokers or sales officers in making a deal and earning a commission may not always coincide with the interests of their customers. Yet, similar risks of conflicts of interest may arise when lawyers provide real estate services. Lawyers might have to negotiate with lenders and real estate companies. These companies may be actual or potential clients, capable of giving lawyers much more profitable business than real estate consumers. An equally unhealthy relationship may arise when real estate companies and lawyers provide free services or reduced fees in exchange for directing business to each other.

The twin rationales advanced by the *Hagan* court—ensuring professional competence and discipline—seem unpersuasive in the context of real estate transactions. The court's underlying goal of protecting the public interest, of course, remains commendable. The court should retain this goal as its paramount concern while redefining the limits that it places on the practice of law.

The public already views unauthorized practice prohibitions as "self-protective, monopolistic, or greedy." Exclusive judicial regulation of the practice of law and concurrent absolute denial of legislative power may result not only in strained relations between the government branches, but also in reduced public confidence in the judiciary. More specifically, the judiciary's refusal to allow lay participation in the preparation of real estate documents may lead to the public perception that the judiciary and lawyers are acting in concert to increase lawyers' workloads and fees.

By asserting an inherent power to protect against the danger of legislative encroachment on an exclusive judicial function, the Washington Supreme Court instead may have cast a shadow upon the integrity of the judiciary and the legal system without advancing the public welfare.

### Recommended Alternatives

#### A. Public Policy Test

Courts in other jurisdictions have adopted a public policy test that balances the costs and benefits of lay assistance. Because the small risk of injury from lay consultation is outweighed by the inconvenience, delay, and expense of forced legal consultation, some courts have authorized real estate brokers to complete forms or to perform services incidental to their primary employment. These courts have found a noticeable absence of injury to the public from the change. The New Mexico Supreme Court, for example, found that the changeover from attorneys to title services completing real estate forms did not result in any detriment or inconvenience to the public. Instead, uncontroverted evidence demonstrated that using lawyers considerably slowed loan closings and increased costs. Similarly, in Colorado, where realtors have completed forms and given advice for the majority of real estate transactions, the court found no instance of injury to the public, laypersons, or lawyers. Many commentators agree that the use of lawyers to perform routine tasks such as real estate closings and title searches constitutes an enormous waste of skill and causes increased costs to parties.

In RCW chapter 19.62, the Washington legislature imposed reasonable conditions on lay preparation of documents. The disclosure statement required by the statute informs the consumer of the limited nature of the services provided and recommends legal counseling if necessary. While disclosure has never been suggested as a defense to unauthorized practice, the disclosure statement does emphasize that the agents are not holding themselves out as lawyers and gives the public notice of the limited nature of the services provided. Because the statute does not appear to impair the court unreasonably in its adjudicatory process and functions, it was improper for the court to assert its inherent judicial power in this case. A more thorough consideration of public policy issues would have required the court to defer to the legislature.

#### B. Limited Practice Rule

The Washington Supreme Court has recently published a draft of a proposed "Limited Practice Rule for Closing Officers." The proposed rule provides for a new group of practitioners known as closing officers, who will have their own licensure, admission, examination, control, and discipline. These officers would be subject to the ultimate control of the state supreme court. The rule classifies closing officers conceptually as members of a profession practicing law in a limited area.

A "Limited Practice Board," composed of no less than four bar representatives and four business representatives nominated by the bar association and appointed by the supreme court, would supervise the examination, investigation, and recommendation of each applicant.

The board would also handle complaints and could impose or recommend disciplinary action. The supreme court, however, would retain the ultimate power to admit or suspend laypersons from limited practice.

Under this proposed rule, laypersons would be allowed to prepare documents if they pass an examination, pay an annual fee, take an oath, and enroll as certified closing officers. The rule would also require proof of financial responsibility to respond in damages for malpractice. The officer would have to advise the parties that the documents affect the parties' legal rights, that their interests may differ, and that they may wish to consult a lawyer. Both parties to the transaction would have to agree in writing to the terms of the transaction and to the officer's legal limitations.

The scope of the limited practice rule would extend to the selection, preparation, and completion of certain documents in a form previously approved by the board. The documents would be limited to deeds, promissory notes, guarantees, deeds of trust, reconveyances, mortgages, satisfactions, security agreements, releases, Uniform Commercial Code documents, assignments, contracts, real estate excise tax affidavits, bills of sale, and such other documents as may be approved by the board.

Adoption of a limited practice rule would best serve both the judiciary and the public. Because the court would retain the power to admit, discipline, and suspend closing officers, it could wield this power to protect the public and to ensure its own dignity and proper functioning. While recognizing the court's primacy in regulating legal practice, the Limited Practice Rule harmonizes the legislative declaration of public policy implicit in RCW chapter 19.62 with the judicial concern for competence and ethical standards.

The public will also best be served by adoption of this rule. Enforcement of the competence and ethical standards will reduce the possibility of injury to the public arising from real estate transactions. Further, members of the public will avoid the added costs of forced legal counselling. Finally, the public's view of the judiciary may improve with the realization that the judiciary has acted, not to increase business for attorneys, but to better serve and protect the public interest.[a]

### *Questions*

(1) Are the Rules described a desirable solution to the issues presented by the *Bennion-Hagan* case?

(2) Should similar Rules be adopted to cover accountants, banks and trust companies, laypersons practicing before administrative agen-

a. The Washington Supreme Court adopted the proposed Rules in substantially the form proposed on December 22, 1982 to become effective January 21, 1983.

cies, collection agencies, estate planners, insurance claims adjusters[1] and others whose activities impinge on the practice of law?

### *Comment*

(1) *Accountants.* The dispute between the legal profession and accountants over their respective fields of practice in the area of taxation has asserted itself in two directions. One has been by resort to the courts to secure a determination that the accountant was or was not engaged in the unauthorized practice of law. In In re Bercu,[2] a New York court laid down the test that if the legal advice and activity of the accountant was incidental to proper accounting activities, the accountant was not engaged illegally in the practice of law. This approach was rejected in the Minnesota case of Gardner v. Conway,[3] in favor of a "difficult or doubtful question of law" test.

The other course of action has been the "conference approach." In 1951, a statement of principles was agreed upon and adopted by both the ABA and the Council of the American Institute of Accountants. The conference approach as a method of settling disputes over the unauthorized practice of law is no longer pursued.[4]

(2) *Estate planning.* In Oregon State Bar v. John H. Miller & Co.,[5] the court said:

> "The defendant company solicits business through salesmen who are paid a percentage of the fee charged for an analysis of the client's estate. A variety of factors reflecting upon tax liability are considered in preparing the analysis. For example, a report to the client might contain suggestions relating to the transfer of assets, the making of gifts, the use of the marital deduction, the use of inter vivos and testamentary trusts, and other devices designed to minimize taxes. The client's will is examined for the purpose of determining the need for change with regard to reducing taxes. These and other suggestions are a standard part of the service performed by defendants.
>
> "Much of the advice contained in the report to the client could not be given without an understanding of various aspects of the law, principally the law of taxation. Most of the advice is in terms

1. In Professional Adjusters, Inc. v. Tandon, 433 N.E.2d 779, 29 A.L.R.4th 1144 (Ind. 1982), the court held invalid as permitting unauthorized practice of law a statute which permitted licensed "Certified Public Insurance Adjusters" to represent claimants in adjusting claims against insurers. The court distinguished adjusters representing insurers, a distinction to which there was a dissent. See Dauphin County Bar Association v. Mazzacaro, 465 Pa. 545, 351 A.2d 229 (1976).

Compare Comment to RPC 5.5 (Rule "does not prohibit lawyers from providing professional advice and instruction to nonlawyers whose employment requires knowledge of law; for example, claims adjusters").

2. 273 App.Div. 524, 78 N.Y.S.2d 209 (1948), affirmed 299 N.Y. 728, 87 N.E.2d 451 (1949) (discussed in 47 Mich.L.Rev. 787 (1949); 56 Yale L.J. 1438 (1947)).

3. 234 Minn. 468, 48 N.W.2d 788 (1951) (discussed in 32 B.U.L.Rev. 95 (1952); 100 U.Pa.L.Rev. 290 (1951)).

4. See supra p. 82. But see 1981 joint statement by ABA and AICPA, 36 Tax Law. 26 (1982).

5. 235 Or. 341, 385 P.2d 181 (1963) (discussed in 13 DePaul L.Rev. 330 (1964); 39 N.Y.U.L.Rev. 364 (1964)).

of 'suggestions.' In each instance the client is urged to consult his own attorney. But whether the report takes the form of suggestions for further study or as a recommendation that the suggestions be subjected to further scrutiny by a lawyer, the fact remains that the client receives advice from defendants and the advice involves the application of legal principles. This constitutes the practice of law."

(3) *Kits, books, and forms.* A layperson may represent him or herself in and out of court in attempting to resolve any legal problem he or she may face,[6] however unwise it may be to do so. The person may consult textbooks, acquire and use legal forms, and read statutes and judicial decisions.

Lay efforts to provide the necessary information to those who seek to follow the do-it-yourself course have been met with charges that the prohibition against the unauthorized practice of law was being violated.

One of the first cases to deal with this issue was New York County Lawyers' Association v. Dacey.[7] A best-selling book written for laypersons, entitled "How to Avoid Probate," was held not to violate the prohibition. "There is no personal contact or relationship with a particular individual. Nor does there exist that relationship of confidence and trust so necessary to the status of attorney and client."

So-called "divorce kits" have also appeared in considerable numbers. The nation-wide shift from a fault to a no-fault basis for divorce, accompanied, usually, with simplified procedures has led to their considerable use, and ensuing charges that they violated the prohibition against the unauthorized practice of law. The line drawn in *Dacey* usually has been followed. If the kit is accompanied with personal contacts or advice on how to proceed or how to fill in the prescribed forms, the practice of law is held to exist and, hence, not permitted.[8]

Writers have been critical of the restrictions as unnecessary for the protection of the public and as not based on empirical evidence as to their need.[9]

6. Faretta v. California, 422 U.S. 806, 95 S.Ct. 2525, 45 L.Ed. 562 (1975) (a criminal case); EC 3–7. See State v. Peterson, 266 N.W.2d 103, (S.D. 1978), holding that *Faretta* does not entitled a defendant to be represented by a layperson in a criminal case.

7. 21 N.Y.2d 694, 287 N.Y.S.2d 422, 234 N.E.2d 459 (1967), reversing on the dissenting opinion in 28 A.D.2d 161, 283 N.Y.S.2d 984 (1967).

8. See, e.g., State Bar v. Cramer, 399 Mich. 116, 249 N.W.2d 1 (1976); Oregon State Bar v. Gilchrist, 272 Or. 552, 538 P.2d 913 (1975).

Compare Florida Bar v. Brumbaugh, 355 So.2d 1186 (Fla.1978) (earlier Florida decisions modified to permit personal contact and the rendering of secretarial services, but not the giving of advice or assistance in the filling of the necessary forms).

9. Note, Divorce Kit Dilemma: Finding the Public Interest, 19 J.Fam.L. 729 (1981); Project, The Unauthorized Practice of Law and Pro Se Divorce: An Empirical Analysis, 86 Yale L.J. 104 (1976) (a study of uncontested divorce cases in New Haven and Bridgeport, Conn.) The latter authority concludes:

> "The conclusion is inescapable that the formalities requisite to divorce need not be the exclusive domain of lawyers. From this flow two corollaries. The first is that the public should not be denied access to lay divorce assistance * * *. A second, more elemental proposition is that there are major social costs involved in imposing the Procrustean frame of an adversarial system

(4) *Law school clinics.* Court rules have been widely adopted permitting upper class law school students to represent clients in both civil and criminal cases but under the supervision of a practicing attorney. In People v. Perez,[10] a student represented a defendant in a felony prosecution under the supervision of an attorney who also took an active part in the trial.[11] The student examined the witnesses and presented the argument to the jury. The client had consented to this arrangement. The California Supreme Court held that the right to counsel had not been violated and that it was unnecessary to decide whether the student was engaged in the unauthorized practice of law since even if conceded it would not affect the validity of the conviction, the defendant having received competent representation.

The case has been criticized on the ground that the defense of felony cases should not be entrusted to inexperienced students, even under the supervision of an attorney, the risk of irreparable errors and missteps being made by the student being too great.[12] The use of paralegals has also raised ethical questions as to the extent of their proper use.[13]

(5) *Collection agencies.* The collection agency is a medium, long in existence, for the collection for creditors of money claims, usually of small amounts, which it would be uneconomical for an attorney to undertake. Following a history of efforts to define the proper role of the agency without its engaging in the unauthorized practice of law,[14] a Declaration of Fair Practices of Collection Agencies was adopted by the 1968 National Conference of Lawyers and Collections Agencies,[15] which appears, at the present writing, to remain in effect.

upon nondisputants. It generates needless expense for the parties and a less than optimal allocation of the expertise of lawyers and judges."

10. 24 Cal.3d 133, 155 Cal.Rptr. 176, 594 P.2d. 1 (1979).

11. The Rule permitting this had been adopted by the State Bar, an integrated bar association.

12. Galperin, Law Students as Defense Counsel in Felony Trials: The "Guiding Hand" Out of Hand, 46 Alb.L.Rev. 400 (1982); Comment, People v. Perez, Constitutional Implications of Law Student Representation of Indigent Criminal Defendants, 13 Marshall L.Rev. 461 (1980).

For other uses of law students, see infra footnote 27.

13. See Lehan, Ethical Considerations of Employing Paralegals in Florida, 53 Fla.B.J. 14 (1979) (full discussion under CPR); Note, Increase in Paralegals Stirs Ethical Concerns, 67 A.B.A. J. 1445 (1981). Compare Comment to RPC 5.5:

"Paragraph (b) does not prohibit a lawyer from employing the services of paraprofessionals and delegating functions to them, so long as the lawyer supervises the delegated work and retains responsibility for their work. See Rule 5.3."

Is this helpful to a lawyer who wants to know what kind of legal work may be delegated to a paraprofessional, as distinguished, for example, from a competent secretary or a law student?

14. For a summary of this history, see Milbourne, Principles for Commercial Collection Agencies to Follow to Avoid Involvement in the Unauthorized Practice of Law, 86 Com. L.J. 126 (1981).

15. Reproduced in Milbourne, supra note 14. Selected portions follow:

"1. A collection agency may engage in the business of collecting past-due accounts for customer-creditors (hereinafter 'creditors'), *provided, however,* that the agency may not:

"(a) Furnish legal advice or perform legal services or represent that it is competent to do so, or institute judicial proceedings on behalf of creditors or other persons;

"(b) Communicate with debtors in the name of an attorney or upon the stationery

Judicial decisions have generally been in accord with the principles stated in the Declaration. A collection agency may solicit and accept claims for collection from the debtor and contact the debtor for this purpose. It may not, however, give legal advice to the creditor, prepare and file pleadings, or appear in court.[16]

Attempts by collection agencies to circumvent these limitations by taking an assignment of the claim from the creditor and bringing suit as the real party in interest have not always been successful. Some courts have deemed them a "sham and a fraud upon the court" to avoid the prohibition against the unauthorized practice of law.[17] Other courts have taken a contrary view.[18]

(6) *Administrative agency practice.* Statutes creating administrative agencies and rules made by agencies pursuant to the statutes commonly provide that attorneys or agents or representatives may appear on behalf of a party.[19] State courts have usually taken the position that appearance before these agencies constitutes the practice of law and therefore only members of the bar are permitted to appear before the agencies.[20] More recent cases show some tendency to relax the restrictions.[21]

of an attorney, or prepare any forms of instrument which only attorneys are authorized to prepare;

"(c) Solicit and receive assignment of accounts for the purpose of suit thereon;

* * *

"(g) Intervene between creditor and attorney in any manner which would control or exploit the services of the attorney or which would direct those services in the interest of the agency * * *."

The declaration further states that the agency is not to control or otherwise interfere with the relation between the creditor and the attorney or with the decisions as to the manner in which the claim is to be handled by the attorney.

A note appended to the declaration states it is subject to applicable statutes and decisions.

**16.** State ex rel. Porter v. Alabama Association of Credit Executives, 338 So.2d 812 (Ala.1976); State ex rel. Frieson v. Isner, 285 S.E.2d 641 (W.Va.1981); Annot., 27 A.L.R.3d 1152 (1969).

**17.** See, e.g., State ex rel. Frieson v. Isner, 285 S.E.2d 641 (W.Va.1981). Cf. State ex rel. Norvell v. Credit Bureau, 85 N.M. 521, 514 P.2d 40 (1973).

**18.** See, e.g., Cruz v. Lusk Collection Agency, 119 Ariz. 356, 580 P.2d 1210. (App.1978), quoting from Note, The Real Party in Interest Rule Revitalized: Recognizing Defendant's Interest in the Determination of Proper Parties Plaintiff, 55 Calif.L.Rev. 1452, 1476–77 (1967):

"Commercial necessity is the primary justification for allowing suits by assignees for collection only. Refusal to permit such parties to sue results in unnecessary economic waste. If assignees for collection only were not permitted to sue, merchants might be forced to decide between abandoning their enterprises while suing on delinquent accounts, or abandoning their delinquent accounts."

**19.** 5 U.S.C. § 500 permits an attorney qualified before the highest court of his state to represent clients before federal administrative agencies without further qualification. The regulations of these agencies usually provide that nonlawyers must take certain prescribed tests of competence. See, e.g., 26 CFR § 601.502 and 31 CFR §§ 10.3–10.4 (IRS), 49 CFR §§ 1100.8–1100.13 (ICC). But see 31 CFR §§ 10.2(a) ("preparation of a tax return * * * is [not] considered practice before the Service"), 10.31 ("Nothing in the regulations in this part shall be construed as authorizing persons not members of the bar to practice law"). See Clark, Accountants in Treasury Practice: The Department Regulations Should Adopt the Bercu Rule, 24 Geo.Wash.L.Rev. 377 (1956).

**20.** See discussion and citation of cases and authorities in Note, Representation of Clients Before Administrative Agencies: Authorized or Unauthorized Practice of Law, 15 Val.U.L.Rev. 567 (1981).

**21.** See Hunt v. Maricopa County Employees Merit System Commission, 127 Ariz.

A state may not prohibit the practice of law by a layperson before a federal administrative agency if it is permitted by the agency acting under federal law enacted within the scope of federal power.[22]

(7) *Corporate officers.* In Merco Construction Engineers v. Municipal Court,[23] a California statute provided that a corporation "may appear through a director, an officer, or an employee, whether or not such person is an attorney at law." The authorization extended only to municipal and justice courts. Exercising its inherent power over the practice of law, the California court held the provision invalid. The majority of the court thought that the Act would authorize almost anyone to appear for the corporation regardless of his or her qualification. This might include disbarred lawyers and paraprofessionals who had failed the bar examinations. Such persons could hire themselves out on a part time basis to a number of corporations, creating

259, 619 P.2d 1036 (1980) (nonlawyer union agent permitted to represent employee in an appeal to a Commission in a discharge dispute). The court allowed "lay representatives in administrative hearings dealing with personnel matters under the following conditions: 1) the lay representative must be provided without a fee; 2) the subject matter of the hearing must have a value or represent an amount insufficient to warrant the employment of an attorney" and not exceed $1000.

The court noted that communications to the layperson would not be privileged.

See also Florida Bar v. Moses, 380 So.2d 412 (Fla.1980), in which the state administrative procedure act authorized appearances by "counsel or other qualified representative." The court held (1) representing a litigant before an administrative agency is the practice of law; (2) the state may validly authorize non-lawyers to practice before administrative agencies and the Act under consideration has done so; (3) but it had not been shown that the layperson in the instant case was "qualified."

It has been held not to be the practice of law to assist a claimant to workers' compensation in filing the claim which requires little skill and little more than the filling in of forms and submission of statements and affidavits. Goodman v. Beale, 130 Ohio St. 427, 200 N.E. 470 (1936). Compare In re Unauthorized Practice of Law, 175 Ohio St. 149, 192 N.E.2d 54, 2 A.L.R.3d 712 (1963), cert. denied 376 U.S. 970, 84 S.Ct. 1136, 12 L.Ed.2d 85 (1964). See Denver Bar Association v. Public Utilities Commission, 154 Colo. 273, 391 P.2d 467 (1964).

Note the comment in 58 Mich.L.Rev. 456, 457–58 (1960) critical of West Virginia State Bar v. Earley, 144 W.Va. 504, 109 S.E.2d 420 (1959):

"Under the majority view, if the claimant does not want to plead his case himself, a lawyer is required in proceedings before the workmen's compensation commissions. This often imposes a hardship. Numerous claimants for compensation are indigent and in many cases the compensation allowed by the commission is so small as not to justify the engagement of a lawyer. The great majority of claims for compensation are for temporary disabilities, for which the maximum award in West Virginia is $30 a week. From this, the attorney's fees, which are unrestricted in amount, must be paid. Other states, recognizing that the laborer cannot afford unrestricted attorney's fees, but not wanting to allow laymen to practice law, have solved the problem in different ways. In some, the insurer must pay the claimant's attorney fee, provided the claimant wins the case; in others, the commission itself will represent the claimant; and in still other states a reasonable limit is set on the amount that a lawyer may receive for his services, and any contracts between the client and the attorney calling for greater compensation are void. If West Virginia does not want to adopt one of these remedies, then perhaps it should be more lenient concerning lay representation. If tests are given and only competent and morally acceptable persons admitted, such representation seems unobjectionable. Furthermore, practice before the workmen's compensation commission is a specialty. Proceedings are traditionally informal and free from technical rules of evidence."

**22.** Sperry v. Florida ex rel. Florida Bar, 373 U.S. 379, 83 S.Ct. 1322, 10 L.Ed.2d 428 (1963).

**23.** 21 Cal.3d 724, 147 Cal.Rptr. 631, 581 P.2d 636 (1978).

a "cadre of unprofessional practitioners." Three justices dissented on the ground that the likelihood of the horribles appearing had not been shown and if they appeared they could be remedied.

That a lay officer of a bank may not draw mortgages securing loans made by the bank was held in Kentucky State Bar Association v. Tussey.[24] The court considered a corporation not a person within a provision that "No rule * * * shall * * * prevent a person from drawing any instrument to which he is a party." "That this has the effect of denying to a corporation what natural men can do occurs by virtue of the inherent nature of a corporation as an artificial entity."[25]

(8) *Nonlawyer assistants.* RPC 5.3 provides:

"**Responsibilities Regarding Nonlawyer Assistants**

"With respect to a nonlawyer employed or retained by or associated with a lawyer:

"(a) a partner in a law firm shall make reasonable efforts to ensure that the firm has in effect measures giving reasonable assurance that the person's conduct is compatible with the professional obligations of the lawyer;

"(b) a lawyer having direct supervisory authority over the nonlawyer shall make reasonable efforts to ensure that the person's conduct is compatible with the professional obligations of the lawyer; and

"(c) a lawyer shall be responsible for conduct of such a person that would be a violation of the Rules of Professional Conduct if engaged in by a lawyer if:

(1) the lawyer orders or, with the knowledge of the specific conduct, ratifies the conduct involved; or

(2) the lawyer is a partner in the law firm in which the person is employed, or has direct supervisory authority over the person, and knows of the conduct at a time when its consequences can be avoided or mitigated but fails to take reasonable remedial action."[26]

RPC 5.3's Comment states:

"Lawyers generally employ assistants in their practice, including secretaries, investigators, law student interns, and paraprofessionals. Such assistants, whether employees or independent contractors, act for the lawyer in rendition of the lawyer's professional services. A lawyer should give such assistants appropriate instruction and supervision concerning the ethical aspects of their employment, particularly regarding the obligation not to disclose information relating to representation of the client, and should be

24. 476 S.W.2d 177 (Ky.1972).

25. See also Strong Delivery Ministry Association v. Board of Appeals of Cook County, 543 F.2d 32 (7th Cir. 1976); Note, Representation of a Corporation by Its Lay Employees, 5 J. Legal Prof. 217 (1980).

26. There is no similar disciplinary Rule.

responsible for their work product. The measures employed in supervising nonlawyers should take account of the fact that they do not have legal training and are not subject to professional discipline."[27]

## 2. THE OUT-OF-STATE LAWYER

### MODEL RULES OF PROFESSIONAL CONDUCT

**RULE 5.5 Unauthorized Practice of Law**

A lawyer shall not:

(a) practice law in a jurisdiction where doing so violates the regulation of the legal profession in that jurisdiction * * *[a]

### *Comment*

"[L]icenses to practice law, granted by the courts of one state, have no extraterritorial effect or value and can vest no right in the holder to practice law in another state."[1]

As a matter of comity, courts usually recognize lawyers, admitted elsewhere, for appearance *pro hac vice*, that is, in the particular case. Frequently, association with a resident attorney is required by court rule, a requirement that has been upheld by the United States Supreme Court.[2]

### LEIS v. FLYNT

439 U.S. 438, 99 S.Ct. 698, 58 L.Ed.2d 717 (1979).

PER CURIAM * * *

Petitioners contend that the asserted right of an out-of-state lawyer to appear *pro hac vice* in an Ohio court does not fall among those interests protected by the Due Process Clause of the Fourteenth Amendment. Because we agree with this contention, we grant the petition for certiorari and reverse the judgment of the Sixth Circuit.

27. See also ABA Formal Opinions 316 (1967) and 85 (1932), the latter stating:

"A lawyer cannot delegate his professional responsibility to a law student employed in his office. He may avail himself of the assistance of the student in many of the fields of the lawyer's work, such as examination of case law, finding and interviewing witnesses, making collections of claims, examining court records, delivering papers, conveying important messages, and other similar matters. But the student is not permitted, until he is admitted to the Bar, to perform the professional functions of a lawyer, such as conducting court trials, giving professional advice to clients or drawing legal documents for them. The student in all his work must act as agent for the lawyer employing him, who must supervise his work and be responsible for his good conduct."

See generally, Ulrich & Clarke, Working with Legal Assistants: Professional Responsibility, 67 A.B.A. J. 992 (1981).

a. Accord, DR 3–101(B).

1. Hawkins v. Moss, 503 F.2d 1171 (4th Cir. 1974), (citing numerous cases), cert. denied 420 U.S. 928, 95 S.Ct. 1127, 43 L.Ed.2d 400 (1975).

2. Martin v. Walton, 368 U.S. 25, 82 S.Ct. 1, 7 L.Ed.2d 5 (1961).

[After referring to several prior procedural steps, the Court continued:]

Respondents next filed this suit in the United States District Court for the Southern District of Ohio to enjoin further prosecution of the criminal case until the state trial court held a hearing on the contested *pro hac vice* applications. The court ruled that the lawyers' interest in representing Flynt and Hustler Magazine was a constitutionally protected property right which petitioners had infringed without according the lawyers procedural due process. Further prosecution of Flynt and Hustler Magazine therefore was enjoined until petitioners tendered Fahringer and Cambria the requested hearing. The Sixth Circuit affirmed * * *.

As this Court has observed on numerous occasions, the Constitution does not create property interests. Rather it extends various procedural safeguards to certain interests "that stem from an independent source such as state law." The Court of Appeals evidently believed that an out-of-state lawyer's interest in appearing *pro hac vice* in an Ohio court stems from some such independent source. It cited no state law authority for this proposition, however, and indeed noted that "Ohio has no specific standards regarding *pro hac vice* admissions * * *." Rather the court referred to the prevalence of *pro hac vice* practice in American courts and instances in our history where counsel appearing *pro hac vice* have rendered distinguished service. We do not question that the practice of courts in most States is to allow an out-of-state lawyer the privilege of appearing upon motion, especially when he is associated with a member of the local bar. In view of the high mobility of the bar, and also the trend toward specialization, perhaps this is a practice to be encouraged. But it is not a right granted either by statute or the Constitution. Since the founding of the Republic, the licensing and regulation of lawyers has been left exclusively to the States and the District of Columbia within their respective jurisdictions. The States prescribe the qualifications for admission to practice and the standards of professional conduct. They also are responsible for the discipline of lawyers.[4]

4. The dissenting opinion relies heavily on dictum in Spanos v. Skouras Theatres, Corp., 364 F.2d 161 (CA2 1966). The facts of that case were different from those here, and the precise holding of the court was quite narrow. The court ruled that where a client sought to defend on the ground of illegality against an out-of-state attorney's action for his fee, and where the illegality stemmed entirely from the failure of the client's in-state attorneys to obtain leave for the out-of-state attorney to appear in federal district court, the client would not be allowed to escape from the contract through his own default. The balance of the opinion, which declared that "under the privileges and immunities clause of the Constitution no state can prohibit a citizen with a federal claim or defense from engaging an out-of-state lawyer to collaborate with an in-state lawyer and give legal advice concerning it within the state," must be considered to have been limited, if not rejected entirely, by Norfolk & Western R. Co. v. Beatty, 423 U.S. 1009, 96 S.Ct. 439, 46 L.Ed.2d 381 (1975).

The dissenting opinion also suggests that a client's interest in having out-of-state counsel is implicated by this decision. The court below, however, "did not reach the issue of whether the constitutional rights of Flynt and Hustler Magazine had also been violated," recognizing as it did that a federal court injunction enjoining a state criminal prosecution on a ground that could be asserted by the defendant in the state proceeding would conflict with this Court's holding in Younger v. Harris, 401 U.S. 37, 91 S.Ct. 746, 27 L.Ed.2d 669 (1971).

A claim of entitlement under state law, to be enforceable, must be derived from statute or legal rule or through a mutually explicit understanding. The record here is devoid of any indication that an out-of-state lawyer may claim such an entitlement in Ohio, where the rules of the Ohio Supreme Court expressly consign the authority to approve a *pro hac vice* appearance to the discretion of the trial court. Even if, as the Court of Appeals believed, respondents had "reasonable expectations of professional service," they have not shown the requisite *mutual* understanding that they would be permitted to represent their clients in any particular case in the Ohio courts.

Nor is there a basis for the argument that the interest in appearing *pro hac vice* has its source in federal law. The speculative claim that Fahringer's and Cambria's reputation might suffer as the result of the denial of their asserted right cannot by itself make out an injury to a constitutionally protected interest. * * * Further, there is no right of federal origin that permits such lawyers to appear in state courts without meeting that State's bar admission requirements. This Court, on several occasions, has sustained state bar rules that excluded out-of-state counsel from practice altogether or on a case-by-case basis. See Norfolk & Western R. Co. v. Beatty, 423 U.S. 1009, 96 S.Ct. 439, 46 L.Ed.2d 381 (1975), summarily aff'g 400 F.Supp. 234 (SD Ill.1975); Brown v. Supreme Court of Virginia, 414 U.S. 1034, 94 S.Ct. 533, 38 L.Ed.2d 327 (1973), summarily aff'g 359 F.Supp. 549 (ED Va.1973). These decisions recognize that the Constitution does not require that because a lawyer has been admitted to the bar of one State, he or she must be allowed to practice in another. See Ginsburg v. Kovrak, 392 Pa. 143, 139 A.2d 889, dismissed for want of a substantial federal question, 358 U.S. 52, 79 S.Ct. 95, 3 L.Ed.2d 46 (1958). Accordingly, because Fahringer and Cambria did not possess a cognizable property interest within the terms of the Fourteenth Amendment, the Constitution does not obligate the Ohio courts to accord them procedural due process in passing on their application for permission to appear *pro hac vice* before the Court of Common Pleas of Hamilton County.[5] * * *

5. The dissenting opinion of Mr. Justice Stevens argues that a lawyer's right to "pursu[e] his calling is protected by the Due Process Clause * * * when he crosses the border" of the State that licensed him. Mr. Justice Stevens identifies two "protected" interests that "reinforce" each other. These are said to be "the 'nature' of the interest in *pro hac vice* admissions or the 'implicit promise' inhering in Ohio custom."

The first of these lawyer's "interests" is described as that of "discharging [his] responsibility for the fair administration of justice in our adversary system." As important as this interest is, the suggestion that the Constitution assures the right of a lawyer to practice in the court of every State is a novel one, not supported by any authority brought to our attention. Such an asserted right flies in the face of the traditional authority of state courts to control who may be admitted to practice before them. If accepted, the constitutional rule advanced by the dissenting opinion would prevent those States that have chosen to bar all *pro hac vice* appearances from continuing to do so, see, e.g., Cal.Bus. & Prof.Code Ann. §§ 6062, 6068; Fla. Rules of the Sup. Ct. Relating to Admissions to the Bar, Art. I, § 1, and would undermine the policy of those States which do not extend reciprocity to out-of-state lawyers, see, e.g., Ariz.Sup.Ct.Rule 28(c) I; Fla. Rules of the Sup. Ct. Relating to Admissions to the Bar, Art. I, § 1.

The second ground for due process protection identified in the dissenting opinion is the "implicit promise" inherent in Ohio's past practice in "assur[ing] out-of-state practitioners that they are welcome in Ohio courts

Mr. Justice WHITE would grant certiorari and set the case for oral argument.

Mr. Justice STEVENS, with whom Mr. Justice BRENNAN and Mr. Justice MARSHALL join, dissenting.

A lawyer's interest in pursuing his calling is protected by the Due Process Clause of the Fourteenth Amendment.[1] The question presented by this case is whether a lawyer abandons that protection when he crosses the border of the State which issued his license to practice.

The Court holds that a lawyer has no constitutionally protected interest in his out-of-state practice. In its view, the interest of the lawyer is so trivial that a judge has no obligation to give any consideration whatsoever to the merits of a *pro hac vice* request, or to give the lawyer any opportunity to advance reasons in support of his application. The Court's square holding is that the Due Process Clause of the Fourteenth Amendment simply does not apply to this kind of ruling by a state trial judge.[2]

The premises for this holding can be briefly stated. A nonresident lawyer has no right, as a matter of either state or federal law, to appear in an Ohio court. Absent any such enforcible entitlement, based on an explicit rule or mutual understanding, the lawyer's interest in making a *pro hac vice* appearance is a mere "privilege" that Ohio may grant

* * *." We recall no other claim that a constitutional right can be created—as if by estoppel—merely because a wholly and *expressly* discretionary state privilege has been granted generously in the past. That some courts, in setting the standards for admission *within their jurisdiction,* have required a showing of cause before denying leave to appear *pro hac vice* provides no support for the proposition that the Constitution imposes this "cause" requirement on state courts that have chosen to reject it.

1. Konigsberg v. State Bar, 353 U.S. 252, 77 S.Ct. 722, 1 L.Ed.2d 810; Schware v. Board of Bar Examiners, 353 U.S. 232, 238–239, and n. 5, 77 S.Ct. 752, 756 and n. 5, 1 L.Ed.2d 796.

2. Although the Court does not address it, this case also presents the question whether a defendant's interest in representation by nonresident counsel is entitled to any constitutional protection. The clients, as well as the lawyers, are parties to this litigation. Moreover, the Ohio trial judge made it perfectly clear that his ruling was directed at the defendants, and not merely their counsel. After striking the appearances of Fahringer and Cambria, the trial judge stated:

> "I will tell you this then, Mr. Flynt. [T]he case is set for the second of May, 1977. * * * *The only thing is that you will be restricted to having an attorney that's admitted to practice in the State of Ohio.*"

A defendant's interest in adequate representation is "perhaps his most important privilege" protected by the Constitution. Powell v. Alabama, 287 U.S. 45, 70, 53 S.Ct. 55, 64, 77 L.Ed. 158. Whatever the scope of a lawyer's interest in practicing in other States may be, Judge Friendly is surely correct in stating that the client's interest in representation by out-of-state counsel is entitled to some measure of constitutional protection:

> "We are persuaded, however, that where a right has been conferred on citizens by federal law, the constitutional guarantee against its abridgment must be read to include what is necessary and appropriate for its assertion. In an age of increased specialization and high mobility of the bar, this must comprehend the right to bring to the assistance of an attorney admitted in the resident state a lawyer licensed by 'public act' of any other state who is thought best fitted for the task, and to allow him to serve in whatever manner is most effective, subject only to valid rules of courts as to practice before them. Cf. Lefton v. City of Hattiesburg, 333 F.2d 280, 285 (5 Cir. 1964). Indeed, in instances where the federal claim or defense is unpopular, advice and assistance by an out-of-state lawyer may be the only means available for vindication."

Spanos v. Skrouras Theatres Corporation, 364 F.2d 161, 170 (en banc) (CA2 1966) (Friendly, J.).

or withhold in the unrestrained discretion of individual judges. The conclusion that a lawyer has no constitutional protection against a capricious exclusion[3] seems so obvious to the majority that argument of the question is unnecessary. Summary reversal is the order of the day. * * *

I

The notion that a state trial judge has arbitrary and unlimited power to refuse a nonresident lawyer permission to appear in his courtroom is nothing but a remnant of a bygone era. Like the body of rules that once governed parole, the nature of law practice has undergone a metamorphosis during the past century. Work that was once the exclusive province of the lawyer is now performed by title companies, real estate brokers, corporate trust departments and accountants. Rules of ethics that once insulated the local lawyer from competition are now forbidden by the Sherman Law[6] and by the First Amendment to the Constitution of the United States.[7] Interstate law practice and multistate law firms are now commonplace.[8] Federal questions regularly

3. In this case there is no dispute about the capricious character of the Ohio court's action. Notwithstanding respondents' unblemished professional careers—in Ohio and elsewhere—their adherence to the same application procedures that they had followed successfully in the past, and their demonstrated familiarity with the issues involved in the litigation, Judge Morrissey refused to allow them to appear *pro hac vice*.

In full, Judge Morrissey ruled that: "Mr. Fahringer and Mr. Cambria are not attorneys of record in this case and will not be permitted to try this case." So far as the record shows, this was the second official action taken with respect to the *pro hac vice* applications of Fahringer and Cambria. In the first, Judge Rupert A. Doan, who presided at Flynt's arraignment, issued two orders designating both lawyers counsel "of record" in case No. B77031, the case eventually assigned to Judge Morrissey for trial. According to Rule 10(E) of the Rules of Practice of the Court of Common Pleas, Hamilton County, Ohio, under which Judges Doan and Morrissey were operating, once a designation order is filed, "such attorney shall become attorney of record * * * and shall not be permitted to withdraw except upon written motion and for good cause shown." Despite Rule 10(E), no objection to respondents' appearance, nor any argument either for or against their request, was heard in advance of the final ruling. In point of fact, nothing in the record identifies a legitimate reason for the Judge's action.

The record does suggest, and in any case the Court's broad holding would certainly encompass, one explanation for Judge Morrissey's unusual ruling, but it can hardly be characterized as legitimate. This is an obscenity case. Conceivably Judge Morrissey has strong views about the distribution of pornographic materials to minors and about lawyers who specialize in defending such activity. Perhaps these are not the kind of lawyers that he wants practicing in his courtroom. That Judge Morrissey reportedly referred to Fahringer as a "fellow traveler" of pornographers is at least consistent with these speculations. Cincinnati Post, Feb. 9, 1977. Indeed, after denying respondents' request to have Judge Morrissey removed from the case for bias, the Supreme Court of Ohio without explanation ordered that another judge of the Hamilton County Court of Common Pleas try the case.

6. Because the "transactions which create the need for the particular legal services in question frequently are interstate transactions," the practice of law is now regarded as a commercial activity subject to the strictures of the Sherman Act. Goldfarb v. Virginia State Bar [infra p. 426].

7. Lawyers now have a constitutional right to advertise because "significant societal interests are served by such speech." Bates v. State Bar [infra p. 541].

8. "Multistate or interstate practice by attorneys in this country is an expanding phenomenon. While no published quantitative data specifically support that assertion, a variety of established or verifiable facts exist that make the inference virtually indisputable. First is the increased mobility * * * of legal problem-solvers, problem-bringers and hence the legal problems themselves. Sec-

arise in state criminal trials and permeate the typical lawyer's practice. Because the assertion of federal claims or defenses is often unpopular, "advice and assistance by an out-of-state lawyer may be the only means available for vindication."[9] The "increased specialization and high mobility"[10] of today's Bar is a consequence of the dramatic change in the demand for legal services that has occurred during the past century.

History attests to the importance of *pro hac vice* appearances. As Judge Merritt, writing for the Court of Appeals, explained:

> "Nonresident lawyers have appeared in many of our most celebrated cases. For example, Andrew Hamilton, a leader of the Philadelphia bar, defended John Peter Zenger in New York in 1735 in colonial America's most famous freedom-of-speech case. Clarence Darrow appeared in many states to plead the cause of an unpopular client, including the famous *Scopes* trial in Tennessee where he opposed another well-known, out-of-state lawyer, William Jennings Bryan. Great lawyers from Alexander Hamilton and Daniel Webster to Chalres Evans Hughes and John W. Davis were specially admitted for the trial of important cases in other states. A small group of lawyers appearing *pro hac vice* inspired and initiated the civil rights movement in early stages. In a series of cases brought in courts throughout the South, out-of-state lawyers Thurgood Marshall, Constance Motley and Spotswood Robinson, before their appointments to the federal bench, developed the legal principles which gave rise to the civil rights movement.
>
> "There are a number of reasons for this tradition. 'The demands of business and the mobility of our society' are the reasons given by the American Bar Association in Canon 3 of the Code of Professional Responsibility. That Canon discourages 'territorial limitations' on the practice of law, including trial practice. There are other reasons in addition to business reasons. A client may want a particular lawyer for a particular kind of case, and a lawyer may want to take the case because of the skill required. Often, as in the case of Andrew Hamilton, Darrow, Bryan and Thurgood Marshall, a lawyer participates in a case out of a sense of justice. He may feel a sense of duty to defend an unpopular defendant and in this way to give expression to his own moral sense. These are

ond, an outgrowth of the first set of facts is the increased degree of uniformity of our laws, to a point where we are now commonly confronted with model codes, uniform state acts, federal practice rules (often copied by state) and similar substantive and procedural developments. Third, partly a response to the first two sets of facts and partly a reflection of the growing general complexity of our society, is a gradual change in the character of law practice from a generalist skill to an increasingly specialized one; hence the emergence of lawyers regarded and operating as * * * specialists * * * equipped to cope with problems that transcend jurisdictional boundaries and the legal competence of local generalists." Brakel & Loh, Regulating the Multistate Practice of Law, 50 U.Wash.L.Rev. 699, 699–700 (1975). See also 19 Stan.L.Rev. 856, 869 (1967).

**9.** Spanos v. Skouras Theatres Corporation, supra, 364 F.2d, at 170.

**10.** Ibid.

important values, both for lawyers and clients, and should not be denied arbitrarily." [11]

The modern examples identified by Judge Merritt, though more illustrious than the typical *pro hac vice* appearance, are not rare exceptions to a general custom of excluding nonresident lawyers from local practice. On the contrary, appearances by out-of-state counsel have been routine throughout the country for at least a quarter of a century.[12] The custom is so well recognized that, as Judge Friendly observed in 1966, there "is not the slightest reason to suppose" that a qualified lawyer's *pro hac vice* request will be denied.[13]

This case involves a *pro hac vice* application by qualified legal specialists; [14] no legitimate reason for denying their request is suggested by the record.[15] They had been retained to defend an unpopular litigant in a trial that might be affected by local prejudicies and attitudes.[16] It is the classic situation in which the interests of justice would be served by allowing the defendant to be represented by counsel of his choice.

The interest these lawyers seek to vindicate is not merely the pecuniary goal that motivates every individual's attempt to pursue his calling. It is the profession's interest in discharging its responsibility for the fair administration of justice in our adversary system. The nature of that interest is surely worthy of the protection afforded by the Due Process Clause of the Fourteenth Amendment.

II

In the past, Ohio has implicitly assured out-of-state practitioners that they are welcome in Ohio's courts unless there is a valid, articulable reason for excluding them. Although the Ohio Supreme Court dismissed respondents' petition for an extraordinary writ of mandamus in this case, it has not dispelled that assurance because it did not pur-

11. See also Judge Soper's discussion in In re Ades, 6 F.Supp. 467, 475–476 (Md.1934).

12. Brakel & Loh, supra, n. 8, at 702, and n. 8; Note, Attorneys and Federal Practice, 80 Harv.L.Rev. 1711, 1716 (1967).

13. Spanos v. Skouras Theatres Corporation, supra, 364 F.2d, at 168.

14. Both Fahringer and Cambria are members of the Bar of New York, who specialize in criminal defense and obscenity law. In 1975, the former received the Outstanding Practitioner of the Year award from the New York State Bar Association. The latter received his legal education in Ohio at the University of Toledo Law School where he graduated first in his class. While in law school, he was admitted by the State of Ohio as a legal intern and practiced as such in the Municipal Prosecutor's office in Toledo.

15. "No evidence of any disciplinary action against [plaintiffs] by any bar association has been presented to the Court, nor is there reason to believe that any such action is presently contemplated. Both are competent, experienced and qualified in the representation of persons charged with crimes." 434 F.Supp., at 483.

16. Ohio charged that Respondent Flynt's publication entitled "War, The Real Obscenity," is harmful to youth contrary to Ohio Rev.Code § 2907.31. Among his defenses are several based on the Federal Constitution. Respondent claims that § 2907.31 is "void for vagueness and overbreadth, impos[es] an impermissible prior restraint on the publication and circulation of materials protected by the First and Fourteenth Amendments to the Constitution," and "bears no rational or reasonable relationship to a legitimate state interest."

port to pass on the merits of their claim. In my opinion the State's assurance is adequate to create an interest that qualifies as "property" within the meaning of the Due Process Clause.

* * * This surely is not a case that should be decided before respondents have been given an opportunity to address the merits. Summary reversal "should be reserved for palpably clear cases of * * * error." Eaton v. City of Tulsa, 415 U.S. 697, 707, 94 S.Ct. 1228, 1234, 39 L.Ed.2d 693 (Rehnquist, J., dissenting). Such reversals are egregiously improvident when the Court is facing a "novel constitutional question." Pennsylvania v. Mimms, 434 U.S. 106, 124, 98 S.Ct. 330, 340, 54 L.Ed. 331 (Stevens, J., dissenting). Accordingly, I respectfully dissent from the Court's summary disposition of a question of great importance to the administration of justice.[a]

### *Comment*

(1) *Litigant's rights*. The *Leis* Court, in footnote 4, distinguished Spanos v. Skouras Theatres, Corp. and indicated that the constitutional basis relied upon in *Spanos* was open to question. To what extent does *Leis* permit a state to prevent a *party* in a civil or criminal case from retaining an out-of-state attorney? [1]

(2) *Policy considerations*. Compare the holding in *Leis* with the following statements in EC 3–9:

> "[T]he demands of business and the mobility of our society pose distinct problems in the regulation of the practice of law by the states. In furtherance of the public interest, the legal profession should discourage regulation that unreasonably imposes territorial limitations upon the right of a lawyer to handle the legal affairs of his client or upon the opportunity of a client to obtain the services

**a.** For critical comment, see Kalish, Pro Hac Vice Admission: A Proposal, 1979 S.Ill.U.L.J. 367; Comment, Leis v. Flynt: Retaining a Nonresident Attorney for Litigation, 79 Colum.L.Rev. 572 (1979).

In August 1980, the ABA House of Delegates refused to approve a proposal for a national rule standardizing requirements for *pro hac vice* appearances which specified:

> "An applicant for admission pro hac vice who has been admitted to the Bar of another state, the District of Columbia, or the Commonwealth of Puerto Rico, and who is presently in good standing at that Bar shall be permitted, pro hac vice, to participate in any pending matter before this Court in the same manner as an attorney authorized to practice law in this state. The filing of applicant's appearance on behalf of a party to an action, except where the appearance is solely to test the jurisdiction of the Court, shall be deemed to be applicant's agreement to submit to the jurisdiction of the disciplinary system of the state where applicant seeks admission pro hac vice. The Court may, however, condition its grant of admission pro hac vice by requiring, when circumstances so dictate, that the applicant associate with local counsel. In criminal cases the Court may impose reasonable conditions designed to assure the defendant's right to effective assistance of counsel.
>
> "The application for admission pro hac vice may be denied only if, after a hearing in which the applicant has been given due notice, the Court finds that the applicant has in any matter, whether in the forum or any other jurisdiction, engaged in unethical conduct warranting discipline in the forum jurisdiction."

See ABA Annual Meeting, 49 U.S.L.W. 2125 (1980). (Reprinted by special permission from The United States Law Week, Copyright 1980 by The Bureau of National Affairs, Inc., Washington, D.C.)

**1.** See Comment, 79 Colum.L.Rev. 572 (1979).

of a lawyer of his choice in all matters including the presentation of a contested matter in a tribunal before which the lawyer is not permanently admitted to practice." [2]

Among the more specific reasons assigned for permitting an attorney to render legal services in states other than the state of admission are:

(a) The need for the assistance of a specialist not available in the local state.[3]

(b) The inability to obtain counsel in the local state because of local prejudice or bias.[4]

(c) The need of large organizations engaged in multistate activities to have their own counsel assist and represent their interests in the several states. Local counsel are unlikely to have the same competence with respect to the special problems of the organization.[5]

(d) A single legal problem may have multistate ramifications best dealt with by a single counsel.

Among the reasons given for not permitting an attorney to render such services are:

(a) Ignorance of the substantive and procedural law and professional traditions peculiar to the local state.

(b) Protection of local professional standards evidenced by high bar admission requirements not obtaining in the state from which the out-of-state attorney comes.

(c) The difficulty of controlling unethical behavior of an out-of-state attorney, in view of his or her temporary presence. Withdrawal of admission *pro hac vice*[6] may not be an adequate deterrent or remedy.

2. See also the observations about the need for liberal admission of attorney *pro hac vice* in Spanos v. Skouras Theatres Corp., 364 F.2d 161 (2d Cir.), cert. denied 385 U.S. 987, 87 S.Ct. 597, 17 L.Ed.2d 448 (1966).

3. See e.g., Burlington County Internal Medicine Associates v. American Medicorp, Inc., 168 N.J.Super. 382, 403 A.2d 43 (Ch.1979) (anti-trust expert); Hahn v. Boeing Co., 95 Wn.2d 28, 621 P.2d 1263, 20 A.L.R.4th 846 (1980) (specialist in aviation law).

In Silverman v. Browning, 414 F.Supp. 80, 85 (D.Conn.1976), the majority held that a state trial court's denying a (specialist in admiralty and railroad law) *pro hac vice* admission was within the court's discretion. But note the dissent:

> "[The state trial judge's reasons] bear no rational relationship to any legitimate interests of the state in regulating the practice of law. * * * He said he was denying the application because there had been no showing plaintiff had a long-standing relationship with the out-of-state counsel he had selected, nor that Connecticut counsel were not available * * *."

4. See Sanders v. Russell, 401 F.2d 241 (5th Cir. 1968); Sherman, The Right to Representation by Out-of-State Attorneys in Civil Rights Cases, 4 Harv.C.R.-C.L.L.Rev. 65 (1968).

It has been pointed out that poverty lawyers frequently need to go from one state to another in order to carry out their chosen missions. The residence requirements have posed serious obstacles for them and have sometimes been used to frustrate the attacks on the legal problems of the poor. Lytton, Crossing State Lines to Practice Law: The Poverty Lawyer and Interstate Practice, 20 Am.U.L.Rev. 7 (1970).

5. See Spencer, The House Counsel and the Unauthorized Practice of Law, 33 Unauth.Prac.News 20 (Fall 1967); Note, The Practice of Law by Out-of-State Attorneys, 20 Vand.L.Rev. 1276 (1967).

6. See State v. Kavanaugh, 52 N.J. 7, 243 A.2d 225 (1968). See also Johnson v. Trueblood, 629 F.2d 302 (3d Cir. 1980) (district court has power to revoke *pro hac vice* appearance at close of trial where conduct of

(d) Availability for service of process.

(e) The need to protect the local bar against competition from out-of-state attorneys who have little concern for or identification with the interests of the local state.[7]

(f) Misconduct in the attorney's local state.[8]

(g) Competent counsel is locally available.[9]

(h) Permitting admission would create a conflict of interest on the part of the attorney.[10]

Which of the above reasons for denying admission are consistent with EC 3–9?

(3) *Decisions recognizing right.* Some judicial decisions are more liberal than others in recognizing the client's right to have an attorney, or the attorney's right to be, admitted *pro hac vice.*

In In re Waring's Estate,[11] New York attorneys had been legal advisors to the decedent, a New Jersey resident, prior to his death and were intimately acquainted with his affairs. His executors employed these attorneys for the administration of the estate and they in turn employed a New Jersey attorney. The will was admitted to probate in New Jersey. The New York attorneys handled such matters as the termination of a Massachusetts lease, preparation of federal income tax returns, etc. Their activities in New Jersey were limited to consultations with the New Jersey attorney who handled the administration of the estate in New Jersey. The New York attorneys were allowed recovery of their fee: "[T]he subject must be viewed practically and realistically and must be dealt with in common-sensible fashion and with due regard for the customary freedom of choice in the selection of counsel." [12]

counsel has exceeded bounds of proper conduct), cert. denied 450 U.S. 999, 101 S.Ct. 1704, 68 L.Ed.2d 200 (1981); In re Rappaport, 558 F.2d 87 (2d Cir. 1977) (admission *pro hac vice* is at most admission for a single proceeding so attorney who seeks to represent defendant on retrial must secure second admission).

7. In Brown v. Wood, 516 S.W.2d 98 (Ark.1974), cert. denied 421 U.S. 963, 95 S.Ct. 1951, 44 L.Ed.2d 449 (1975), the court found no arbitrary and capricious abuse of discretion in the trial court's withdrawing permission to appear *pro hac vice,* in light of the trial court's "concern about the extent of [the lawyer's] practice in Arkansas, and elsewhere, and the potential effect of this extensive practice on the ability of the judge to control and expedite his docket as well as the progress of cases in which [the lawyer] participated without sacrificing the interest of litigants, witnesses, and other participants in his court."

8. See also Hicks v. Committee for Admissions, 439 F.Supp. 302 (D.Tenn.1977) (federal district court could properly require that to be admitted *pro hac vice* attorney must appear before Tennessee Supreme Court and take an oath and be officially admitted).

9. In re Rappaport, 558 F.2d 87 (2d Cir. 1977).

10. Ross v. Reda, 510 F.2d 1172 (6th Cir.), cert. denied 423 U.S. 892, 96 S.Ct. 190, 46 L.Ed.2d 124 (1975) (in addition, attorney refused to limit out-of-court statements about case); State v. Reed, 174 Conn. 287, 386 A.2d 243 (1978) (attorney, in another independent trial, represented client who was to testify for present prosecution); State v. Hunter, 290 N.C. 556, 227 S.E.2d 535 (1976).

11. 47 N.J. 367, 221 A.2d 193 (1966).

12. See also Appell v. Reiner, 43 N.J. 313, 204 A.2d 146 (1964), in which a New York attorney negotiated the settlement of numerous obligations of a New Jersey client whose creditors were located in both New York and New Jersey. Recovery of the attorney's fee was permitted.

In In re Evans,[13] the Fifth Circuit held that a motion for admission *pro hac vice* may not be denied absent "a complaint rising to a level justifying disbarment."

The Washington Supreme Court adopted a somewhat similar test in Hahn v. Boeing Co.[14]:

> "The purpose of [the governing court Rule] can be achieved and the legitimate interests of the court and opposing counsel, as well as those of the client, can be protected if inquiries into the ethical conduct of an applicant are limited to matters which would warrant disqualification, were the attorney a member of the local bar, or which would justify discipline under the court's contempt powers."

The court held that solicitation of cases was not a sufficient ground for denying the application.[15]

(4) *Revocation of pro hac vice admission.* It has been held that the admission may not be revoked without notice and an opportunity to be heard.[16]

(5) *Scope of pro hac vice admission*. The admission is only for a particular pending proceeding. It would appear inapplicable to legal advice, the preparation of documents or settlement negotiations absent such litigation.[17]

(6) *Federal practice.* In Ginsburg v. Kovrak,[18] the attorney, admitted to the bar of the District of Columbia and before a federal

13. 524 F.2d 1004 (5th Cir. 1975).

14. 95 Wn.2d 28, 621 P.2d 1263 (1980) (citing EC 3–9, supra, p. 105, and Brakel & Loh, Regulating the Multistate Practice of Law, 50 Wash.L.Rev. 699 (1975)).

15. For examples of less liberal decisions, see In re Belli, 371 F.Supp. 111 (D.D.C.1974) (Melvin Belli denied admission *pro hac vice* because he criticized impartiality of district court judge who had decided against him, the criticism being made on a national television broadcast and without foundation in fact); State v. Ross, 36 Ohio App.2d 185, 304 N.E.2d 396 (1973), cert. denied 415 U.S. 904, 94 S.Ct. 1397, 39 L.Ed.2d 461 (1974) (denial of William Kunstler's appearance as co-counsel for criminal defendant upheld on ground that Kunstler showed a disregard for Disciplinary Rules on publicity and that local counsel could adequately represent defendant). (In Ross v. Reda, 510 F.2d 1172 (6th Cir.), cert. denied 423 U.S. 892, 96 S.Ct. 190, 46 L.Ed.2d 124 (1975), the court found that the action just described did not deny the defendant's sixth amendment right to counsel).

16. Johnson v. Trueblood, 629 F.2d 302 (3d Cir. 1980), cert. denied 450 U.S. 999, 101 S.Ct. 1704, 68 L.Ed.2d 200 (1981); Hallmann v. Sturm Ruger & Co., Inc., 31 Wn.App. 50, 639 P.2d 805 (1982), holding also that the standards stated in *Hahn* supra, apply.

17. See Lozoff v. Shore Heights, Limited, 66 Ill.2d 398, 6 Ill.Dec. 225, 362 N.E.2d 1047 (1977), holding that a Wisconsin attorney aiding the execution of a sale of real estate in Illinois was engaged in the unauthorized practice of law and hence not entitled to a fee. The court noted that since there was no litigation, the Rule on admission *pro hac vice* could not apply.

Compare the following: "A Massachusetts domiciliary is free to consult a licensed New York attorney on the merits of her estate plan. [The New York attorney's] overseeing the execution of the will in Boston is not unauthorized practice." Lindsey v. Ogden, 10 Mass.App.Ct. 142, 406 N.E.2d 701 (1980). See Dietrich Corp. v. King Resources Co., 596 F.2d 422 (10th Cir. 1979) (consultation with and advice to local attorney treated as equivalent to assistance of law clerks).

18. 392 Pa. 143, 139 A.2d 889 (1958), appeal dismissed for want of a substantial federal question 358 U.S. 52, 79 S.Ct. 95, 3 L.Ed.2d 46 (1958).

district court in Pennsylvania but not to the bar of Pennsylvania, maintained he was practicing only federal law in Pennsylvania and not state law. In the lower court's opinion, adopted by the Pennsylvania Supreme Court, this was rejected since "what with only such Federal questions as taxation and due process, defendant would have a large field in which to practice. The real point concerns practicing law of any kind and being subject to regulation as to mental and character fitness in the public interest." The Pennsylvania Supreme Court stated:

> "It is readily apparent that the injunction is intended to, and does, prohibit only the maintenance of an office and the practice of law in Philadelphia County (and, of course, anywhere else in the Commonwealth of Pennsylvania). It in no way affects the appellant's right to engage in the practice of law in Washington, D.C., or to try cases in the United States District Court for the Eastern District of Pennsylvania or in any other federal court or jurisdiction where he may be entitled to practice." [19]

### *Questions*

(1) Does the foregoing discussion suggest the desirability of a national bar examination, passing of which would entitle the candidate to be admitted in all states? [20] In all federal courts? [21] What impact would this have on law school education and on state bar examinations?

(2) A Mexican lawyer, located in New York but not a member of its bar, (a) advises New York clients on Mexican law, (b) advises New York lawyers on Mexican law for use with their clients and (c) testifies in New York litigation as an expert on Mexican law. Which, if any, of these activities are permissible? [22]

(3) A New Jersey resident goes to a New York lawyer for advice on a problem which calls for the application of New York law. May the lawyer give the advice? Is the answer the same if New Jersey law or the law of other states or federal or foreign law must be applied?

Is the answer the same if the New York lawyer, in response to the New Jersey resident's inquiry, gives the advice by phone from New

19. See In re Perrello, 270 Ind. 390, 386 N.E.2d 174 (1979).

20. See Note, Attorneys: Interstate and Federal Practice, 80 Harv.L.Rev. 1711, 1727 (1967).

21. See Note, Certification of Out-of-State Attorneys Before the Federal District Courts: A Plea for National Standards, 36 Geo.Wash.L.Rev. 204 (1967).

See also Wilkey, A Bar Examination for Federal Courts, 61 A.B.A. J. 1091 (1975).

22. See In re Roel, 3 N.Y.2d 224, 165 N.Y.S.2d 31, 144 N.E.2d 24 (1957), appeal dismissed 355 U.S. 604, 78 S.Ct. 535, 2 L.Ed.2d 524 (1958). Cf. Bluestein v. State Bar, 13 Cal.3d 162, 118 Cal.Rptr. 175, 529 P.2d 599 (1975).

In Bracken, Restrictions on Lawyers Qualified in One Country and Practicing in Another Country, 32 Unauth.Prac.News 18 (Fall 1966), it was urged that a system be inaugurated whereby a lawyer from a foreign country may be admitted to practice, in the state, the law for which the lawyer is licensed, provided he or she agrees to subject himself to the state's ethical requirements. New York has adopted such a system. See Slomanson, Foreign Legal Consultant: Multistate Model for Business and the Bar, 39 Alb.L.Rev. 199 (1975).

York? Mails the advice from New York?[23] Goes to New Jersey and gives the advice?[24]

Are the answers to these questions, under the present state of law, a bit absurd?

23. See In re Waters, 84 Nev. 712, 447 P.2d 661 (1968) ("The rules of professional conduct do not preclude a Texas attorney from corresponding with a California prisoner about his California case"); Martindale, Attorney's Liability in Non-Client and Foreign Law Situations, 14 Clev.-Mar.L.Rev. 44, 51 (1965).

Compare Mayes v. Leipziger, 674 F.2d 178 (2d Cir. 1982). A California attorney represented a New York resident in litigation in California, in the course of which he made telephone calls and sent letters to New York. In a malpractice suit against him by his client, it was held that New York's long arm jurisdiction statute did not permit the acquiring of personal jurisdiction over him.

24. See supra note 17.

# Chapter 3

# CONFIDENTIALITY OF INFORMATION

---

## MODEL RULES OF PROFESSIONAL CONDUCT

### RULE 1.6 Confidentiality of Information

(a) A lawyer shall not reveal information relating to representation of a client unless the client consents after consultation, except for disclosures that are impliedly authorized in order to carry out the representation, and except as stated in paragraph (b).

(b) A lawyer may reveal such information to the extent the lawyer reasonably believes necessary:

(1) to prevent the client from committing a criminal act that the lawyer believes is likely to result in imminent death or substantial bodily harm; or

(2) to establish a claim or defense on behalf of the lawyer in a controversy between the lawyer and the client, to establish a defense to a criminal charge or civil claim against the lawyer based upon conduct in which the client was involved, or to respond to allegations in any proceeding concerning the lawyer's representation of the client.[a]

**a.** Compare the following CPR provisions:

**"DR 4–101 Preservation of Confidences and Secrets of a Client**

"(A) 'Confidence' refers to information protected by the attorney-client privilege under applicable law, and 'secret' refers to other information gained in the professional relationship that the client has requested be held inviolate or the disclosure of which would be embarrassing or would be likely to be detrimental to the client.

"(B) Except when permitted under DR 4–101 (C), a lawyer shall not knowingly:

(1) Reveal a confidence or secret of his client.

(2) Use a confidence or secret of his client to the disadvantage of the client.

(3) Use a confidence or secret of his client for the advantage of himself or of a third person, unless the client consents after full disclosure.

"(C) A lawyer may reveal:

(1) Confidences or secrets with the consent of the client or clients affected, but only after a full disclosure to them.

(2) Confidences or secrets when permitted under Disciplinary Rules or required by law or court order.

(3) The intention of his client to commit a crime and the information necessary to prevent the crime.

(4) Confidences or secrets necessary to establish or collect his fee or to defend himself or his employees or

### *Comment*

RPC 1.6 states the ethical obligation of a lawyer and is broader in scope than the evidentiary attorney-client privilege.[1]

The Comment to the rule states:

"The principle of confidentiality is given effect in two related bodies of law, the attorney-client privilege (which includes the work product doctrine) in the law of evidence and the rule of confidentiality established in professional ethics. The attorney-client privilege applies in judicial and other proceedings in which a lawyer may be called as a witness or otherwise required to produce evi-

associates against an accusation of wrongful conduct.

"(D) A lawyer shall exercise reasonable care to prevent his employees, associates, and others whose services are utilized by him from disclosing or using confidences or secrets of a client, except that a lawyer may reveal the information allowed by DR 4–101 (C) through an employee."

1. See, e.g., Uniform Rules of Evidence (1974), Rule 502:

"(b) **General rule of privilege.** A client has a privilege to refuse to disclose and to prevent any other person from disclosing confidential communications made for the purpose of facilitating the rendition of professional legal services to the client (1) between himself or his representative and his lawyer or his lawyer's representative, (2) between his lawyer and the lawyer's representative, (3) by him or his representative or his lawyer or a representative of the lawyer to a lawyer or a representative of a lawyer representing another party in a pending action and concerning a matter of common interest therein, (4) between representatives of the client or between the client and a representative of the client, or (5) among lawyers and their representatives representing the same client.

"(c) **Who may claim the privilege.** The privilege may be claimed by the client, his guardian or conservator, the personal representative of a deceased client, or the successor, trustee, or similar representative of a corporation, association, or other organization, whether or not in existence. The person who was the lawyer or the lawyer's representative at the time of the communication is presumed to have authority to claim the privilege but only on behalf of the client.

"(d) **Exceptions.** There is no privilege under this rule:

"(1) **Furtherance of crime or fraud.** If the services of the lawyer were sought or obtained to enable or aid anyone to commit or plan to commit what the client knew or reasonably should have known to be a crime or fraud;

"(2) **Claimants through same deceased client.** As to a communication relevant to an issue between parties who claim through the same deceased client, regardless of whether the claims are by testate or intestate succession or by inter vivos transaction;

"(3) **Breach of duty by a lawyer or client.** As to a communication relevant to an issue of breach of duty by the lawyer to his client or by the client to his lawyer;

"(4) **Document attested by a lawyer.** As to a communication relevant to an issue concerning an attested document to which the lawyer is an attesting witness;

"(5) **Joint clients.** As to a communication relevant to a matter of common interest between or among two or more clients if the communication was made by any of them to a lawyer retained or consulted in common, when offered in an action between or among any of the clients or

"(6) **Public officer or agency.** As to a communication between a public officer or agency and its lawyers unless the communication concerns a pending investigation, claim, or action and the court determines that disclosure will seriously impair the ability of the public officer or agency to process the claim or conduct a pending investigation, litigation, or proceeding in the public interest."

The evidentiary aspect of the attorney-client privilege is left to other courses.

See the thorough discussion of the subject in Sagor, The Attorney-Client and Work-Product Privileges: Protection and Assertion, in J. Glekel, Business Crimes 127 (Practising Law Institute 1982).

dence concerning a client. The rule of client-lawyer confidentiality applies in situations other than those where evidence is sought from the lawyer through compulsion of law. The confidentiality rule applies not merely to matters communicated in confidence by the client but also to all information relating to the representation whatever its source." [2]

The materials which follow include cases dealing with the attorney-client privilege. They provide concrete examples to which the ethical obligation may apply. When the privilege is held not to apply, the lawyer may still be under an ethical obligation under the Model Rules and under the CPR's Disciplinary Rules.

## A. UNDERLYING POLICIES

### J. BENTHAM, RATIONALE OF JUDICIAL EVIDENCE

Vol. VII, p. 474 (Banring ed. 1827).

When, in consulting with a law adviser, attorney or advocate, a man has confessed his delinquency, or disclosed some fact which, if stated in court, might tend to operate in proof of it, such law adviser is not to be suffered to be examined as to any such point. The law adviser is neither to be compelled, nor so much as suffered, to betray the trust thus reposed in him. Not suffered? Why not? Oh, because to betray a trust is treachery; and an act of treachery is an immoral act. * * *

But if such confidence, when reposed, is permitted to be violated, and if this be known (which, if such be the law, it will be,) the consequence will be, that no such confidence will be reposed. Not reposed?—Well: and if it be not, wherein will consist the mischief? The man by the supposition is guilty; if not, by the supposition there is nothing to betray: let the law adviser say everything he has heard, everything he can have heard from his client, the client cannot have anything to fear from it. That it will often happen that in the case supposed no such confidence will be reposed, is natural enough: the first thing the advocate or attorney will say to his client, will be—Remember that, whatever you say to me, I shall be obliged to tell, if asked about it. What, then, will be the consequence? That a guilty person will not in general be able to derive quite so much assistance

2. See also DR 4–101(A), supra note a.

The court applied the distinction in Brennan's, Inc. v. Brennan's Restaurants, Inc., 590 F.2d 168 (5th Cir. 1979). The attorney had represented both plaintiff and defendant in a mutually agreed upon division of the business in which they had been engaged. He now appeared for the defendant in a dispute over who was entitled to the trade name of the prior business. In resisting disqualification, the attorney contended that since his prior representation had been a joint one of both parties, the attorney privilege did not apply and disqualification was not warranted. The court held that granted the privilege was not applicable, the attorney's broader ethical duties under the CPR did apply and made him disqualified.

from his law adviser, in the way of concerting a false defence, as he may do at present.[a]

### *Comment*

The leading defense of the privilege is in Wigmore on Evidence.[1] After stating Bentham's central argument that the guilty deserve no privilege and the innocent have nothing to hide, Dean Wigmore gives four reasons for not accepting the argument.

First, in civil cases there is no hard and fast line between the guilty and the innocent. He gives as an example contesting claimants to title to land, each claiming from a different source.

Second, not all the guilt or innocence in civil cases is on one or the other side. In criminal cases, to abolish the privilege would expose the client to the same risks as if the right against self incrimination were absent. The client would simply not state incriminating matters to his lawyer.

Third, even assuming in civil cases that "one party's case is wholly right and the other's wholly wrong—still, so far as the wrongdoer is consequently deterred from seeking legal advice, that result is not, as Bentham would have it, an unmixed good; for *it does not follow* that '*a guilty person would not* in general *derive quite so much assistance* from his law adviser, in the way of concerting a false defence, as he may do at present.' This does not follow except on the assumption that every legal adviser invariably proceeds, on request, to assist, by litigation or otherwise, the unjust causes that may be laid before him by his clients. How far this assumption is true varies no doubt with the individual and the locality. But there are at least many fraternities of the bar among whom are many practitioners who do not pursue such a course. Either they decline the cause utterly, in heinous cases (and even the privilege as it exists would not protect them if they consented to concert with the client a fraud or a crime), or they persuade the client that the cause is hopeless to support, or they secure a settlement with the opponent in which the client's interests are satisfied to the extent that there is any moral justice in them. To guarantee for clients of unjust causes a freedom of consultation with legal advisers cannot be deemed an evil except to the extent that the Bar is unprincipled; and in that condition more radical remedies are needed than the denial of the privilege."

Fourth, "the *sense of treachery* in disclosing such confidences in impalpable and somewhat speculative, but it is there nevertheless.

**a.** See in accord, Morgan, Suggested Remedy for Obstructions to Expert Testimony by Rules of Evidence, 10 U.Chi.L.Rev. 285, 288 (1943). See also Note, The Attorney-Client Privilege: Fixed Rules, Balancing and Constitutional Entitlement, 91 Harv.L.Rev. 464 (1977), urging greater flexibility in the application of the privilege.

See generally, Hazard, An Historical Perspective on the Attorney-Client Privilege, 66 Calif.L.Rev. 1061 (1978); Popkin, Client-Lawyer Confidentiality, 59 Tex.L.Rev. 755 (1981) (focuses primarily on pre-adoption drafts of the Model Rules).

**1.** 8 J. Wigmore, Evidence § 2291 (J. McNaughton rev. 1961).

* * * Certainly the position of the legal adviser would be a difficult and disagreeable one, for it must be repugnant to any honorable man to feel that the confidences which his relation naturally invites are liable at the opponent's behest to be laid open through his own testimony. He cannot but feel the disagreeable inconsistency of being at the same time the solicitor and the revealer of the secrets of the cause."

Wigmore contends further that the loss to truth is limited since today the opponent can be compelled to take the stand in civil cases and subjected to interrogation, but he concedes there is still a loss and that the privilege should be "strictly confined within the narrowest possible limits consistent with the logic of its principle."

### SHAFFER, CHRISTIAN THEORIES OF PROFESSIONAL RESPONSIBILITY

48 S.Cal.L.Rev. 721, 724–25 (1975).

Suppose a man comes to me seeking divorce, and I discover that he has not lived in the state long enough to meet statutory residence requirements. I explain that he may not have a divorce—at least not yet—and he leaves in a huff. Consider the following situations;

(1) I learn later that he has seen another lawyer and suspect that, having learned a recondite bit of law from me, he has lied about residence to the other lawyer.

(2) I learn that the other lawyer has filed a petition for divorce on his client's behalf, and I *know* that the client has lied to the lawyer or that they have both lied to the court.

(3) I learn that the client has been brought to trial for perjury and that my testimony would be useful to the prosecution.

In none of these three cases may I say what I know—not to prevent the abuse of my brother or sister lawyer; not to prevent a fraud on the court; not to assist in the administration of criminal justice. None of these reasons is as important to the State—to the law—as is my silence.

Every secular theory I can think of to explain this social preference seems somehow inadequate. The theories I have in mind can be summed up in three brief paragraphs.

*First*, the State may recognize that people need people. There is something about human beings, in their emotional need of one another, that the State cannot supplant or for which it can find no substitute. The best thing for the State to do is to respect the need, and to respect what people do in response to the need. My divorce client might have needed me, and I was obliged to be available to his need. A relationship between two people becomes a third personality. And that third personality, so this first theory suggests, is beyond the power of the State, immune to the blunt instruments of government.

*Second,* the State has found a usefulness it decides to respect in the narrower relationship between a person who is suffering and a person who proposes to be helpful in easing the pain. There is social utility in the "helping person" relationship. Just as a religiously-neutral government accords respect to religious schools because of their value to the secular good, respect is accorded "helping person" relationships because of their social utility.

*Third,* it is socially useful that human difficulties be resolved in the arena which involves the fewest people and the least social machinery. Aspirations aside, this is a principle of secular economy. A Christian who specially adheres to St. Paul's injunction against repairing to the courts saves the State time and money, as does a Jew who takes his quarrel to the rabbi. For example, the State has respected the dispute-settlement apparatus within a family by affording intra-family immunity in tort. There is social value in mediation and conciliation, and therefore in whatever machinery for reconciliation men invent. The professional interaction between lawyer and client is one such mediating relationship.

Any of these three theories could provide justification for a paraphrasing of Canon Four: *our duty not to speak of what our clients tell us is as broad as the need which brings people to us.* This duty has social value; our function as professionals depends on it, because our function as professionals requires that we learn the truth as often as we can. Because our social function is valuable, the means we must have to perform it well are also valuable. I reflect, for example, on cases in which I have represented indigent criminal defendants and prisoners in the Indiana State Prison. My recurrent problem has been to convince the client in that situation that I am on his side. He sees me as part of the machinery which put him behind bars. He tells me what he thinks the judge wants to hear. Canon Four seeks to provide lawyers with the means to encourage free and truthful communication, whenever possible.

### *Comment*

Viewed as a duty of professional ethics, the obligation not to disclose confidential communications is not one peculiar to the legal profession. Many other groups, rendering service to others which involves the receipt of confidential information, have asserted the same ethical obligation and have succeeded in some instances in securing legal recognition and protection of this duty.[1]

*Physicians,* for centuries, have deemed it their professional obligation not to disclose to others what they have learned from their

1. See Note, Functional Overlap Between the Lawyer and Other Professionals: Its Implications for the Privileged Communications Doctrine, 71 Yale L.J. 1226 (1962), for a general survey of the legal status of various groups' claims of privilege not to disclose.

patients.[2] The Oath of Hippocrates, formulated 2000 years ago, provided:

> "Whatsoever in the course of practice I see or hear (or even outside my practice in social intercourse) that ought never to be published abroad, I will not divulge, but consider such things to be holy secrets." [3]

In the majority of states, statutes have elevated this professional duty to a legal privilege.[4]

The *clergy* has likewise maintained that it is its members' professional duty not to disclose what they learn from those who come to them for spiritual guidance, advice and comfort and for confessionals. This has also received widespread statutory recognition.[5]

*Public accountants* have observed a similar professional obligation which has attained statutory recognition in some states.[6]

2. See American Medical Association, Principles of Medical Ethics, ch. 1, § 2; Marshall, The Ethics of Medical Pratice 37 (1960).

3. As translated by W. H. S. Jones and appearing in Percival, Medical Ethics 213 (Leake ed. 1927).

4. It is included in Uniform Rules of Evidence (1974), Rule 503.

See Slovenko, Psychotherapy, Confidentiality and Privileged Communications (1966).

5. See Tiemann, The Right to Silence (1964); Kuhlmann, Communications to Clergymen—When Are They Privileged? 2 Val.U.L.Rev. 265 (1965) (collecting statutes). See also Uniform Rules of Evidence (1974), Rule 505.

6. See Carey, Professional Ethics of Certified Public Accountants 164 (1956); Note, Privileged Communications—Accountants and Accounting—A Critical Analysis of Accountant-Client Privilege Statutes, 66 Mich.L.Rev. 1264 (1968).

In United States v. Arthur Young & Co., — U.S. —, 104 S.Ct. 1495, 79 L.Ed.2d 826 (1984), the Court held that the tax accrual workpapers of an independent certified public accountant, prepared in auditing a corporation's financial statement, were not exempt from compulsory disclosure to the IRS. Disclosure was deemed essential to protecting the investing public which relies upon these audits. Concepts of privileged communications and work product exemptions were held inapplicable. "[T]he independent auditor assumes a *public* responsibility transcending any employment relationship with the client." (Emphasis by the Court.)

Should this reasoning apply to attorneys who issue legal opinions knowing they will be relied upon by members of the public? Consider the following:

(1) An "independent" accountant, who is auditing the corporate client's financial statement, asks the corporation's attorney whether there are any claims outstanding against the corporation not paid and not included in the financial statement. The attorney replies there are none, knowing there are some claims being made and not included, but which the lawyer regards as unfounded. The SEC demands disclosure of what the attorney knew. The attorney insists disclosure would breach the confidences of the client and harm the client's competitive position.

For the problems raised for attorneys when responding to such accountants' inquiries, see Hinsey, Auditors' Inquiries and Lawyers' Responses, 62 A.B.A. J. 1572, (1976). The author summarizes the ABA Policy Statement on the subject adopted in 1975. The Statement is referred to, without amplification, in the Comment to RPC 2.3 as a permissible standard to follow.

For criticism of the answers received from attorneys by accountants, see Hall & Butler, Assuring Adequate Attorneys' Replies to Audit Inquiries, 152 J. of Accounting 83 (1981).

(2) A corporation lawyer, at the client's request, issues an opinion that the income from securities about to be issued by the client will be exempt from state and federal taxes. The lawyer knows the client will accompany the public offering with a statement of the opinion. The IRS contends the opinion is wrong and demands disclosure of the information upon which the attorney based the opinion.

*Psychologists* recognize a like duty to those they serve and it has been urged that this be erected into a statutory privilege.[7]

The *social workers'* position has been stated as follows:

> "Confidentiality in social work is an ethical obligation, based on the rights of the individuals and of the community to the protection of intimate personal disclosures made in a professional relationship * * * Specifically, the social work obligation arises from the ethics of one type of entrusted secrets—those given in a relationship of trust, the very nature of which implies that information given in it will not be disclosed against the will of the individual."[8]

## B. SCOPE

### PEOPLE v. MEREDITH

29 Cal.3d 682, 175 Cal.Rptr. 612, 631 P.2d 46 (1981).

TOBRINER, Justice.

Defendants Frank Earl Scott and Michael Meredith appeal from convictions for the first degree murder and first degree robbery of David Wade. Meredith's conviction rests on eyewitness testimony that he shot and killed Wade. Scott's conviction, however, depends on the theory that Scott conspired with Meredith and a third defendant, Jacqueline Otis, to bring about the killing and robbery. To support the theory of conspiracy the prosecution sought to show the place where the victim's wallet was found, and, in the course of the case this piece of evidence became crucial. The admissibility of that evidence comprises the principal issue on this appeal.

At trial the prosecution called Stephen Frick, who testified that he observed the victim's partially burnt wallet in a trash can behind Scott's

Compare Ernst & Ernst v. Hochfelder, 425 U.S. 185, 96 S.Ct. 1375, 47 L.Ed.2d 668 (1976), holding an accountant immune from liability for not discovering the client's fraud. Knowledge of the fraud is required, negligence alone not being sufficient.

Note the dissent of Blackmun, J. (joined by Brennan, J.) and its relevance to the above illustrative cases: "The critical importance of the auditing accountant's role in insuring full disclosure cannot be overestimated. The SEC has emphasized that in certifying statements the accountant's duty 'is to safeguard the public interest, not that of his client.' In re Touche, Niven, Bailey & Smart, 37 S.E.C. 629, 670–671 (1957). 'In our complex society the accountant's certificate and the lawyer's opinion can be instruments for inflicting pecuniary loss more potent than the chisel or the crowbar.' United States v. Benjamin, 328 F.2d 854, 863 (CA2), cert. denied sub nom. Howard v. United States, 377 U.S. 953, 84 S.Ct. 1631, 12 L.Ed.2d 497 (1964)."

See Bradford Securities Processing Services, Inc. v. Plaza Bank & Trust, described infra 512 n.a.

For a discussion of the ethical duties of corporate attorneys see infra pp. 256–71.

7. See Louisell, The Psychologist in Today's Legal World, 41 Minn.L.Rev. 731 (1957); Note, The Psychologist in Criminal Proceedings, 40 N.D.L.Rev. 173 (1964). See also In re Queen, 233 N.Y.S.2d 798 (Sup.Ct.1962) (applying N.Y. Education Code § 7611, creating a privilege of nondisclosure "on the same basis as those provided by law between attorney and client").

8. American Association of Social Workers, Dist. of Col. Chap., p. 3 (1946). See also Alves, Confidentiality in Social Work (1959).

The work of marriage counsellors would appear particularly to demand adherence to this obligation. See Note, A Suggested Privilege for Confidential Communications for Marriage Counsellors, 106 U.Pa.L.Rev. 266 (1957).

residence. Scott's trial counsel then adduced that Frick served as a defense investigator. Scott himself had told his former counsel that he had taken the victim's wallet, divided the money with Meredith, attempted to burn the wallet, and finally put it in the trash can. At counsel's request, Frick then retrieved the wallet from the trash can. Counsel examined the wallet and then turned it over to the police.

The defense acknowledges that the wallet itself was properly admitted into evidence. The prosecution in turn acknowledges that the attorney-client privilege protected the conversations between Scott, his former counsel, and counsel's investigator. Indeed the prosecution did not attempt to introduce those conversations at trial. The issue before us, consequently, focuses upon a narrow point: whether under the circumstances of this case Frick's observation of the *location* of the wallet, the product of a privileged communication, finds protection under the attorney-client privilege.

This issue, one of first impression in California, presents the court with competing policy considerations. On the one hand, to deny protection to observations arising from confidential communications might chill free and open communication between attorney and client and might also inhibit counsel's investigation of his client's case. On the other hand, we cannot extend the attorney-client privilege so far that it renders evidence immune from discovery and admission merely because the defense seizes it first.

Balancing these considerations, we conclude that an observation by defense counsel or his investigator, which is the product of a privileged communication, may not be admitted unless the defense by altering or removing physical evidence has precluded the prosecution from making that same observation. In the present case the defense investigator, by removing the wallet, frustrated any possibility that the police might later discover it in the trash can. The conduct of the defense thus precluded the prosecution from ascertaining the crucial fact of the location of the wallet. Under these circumstances, the prosecution was entitled to present evidence to show the location of the wallet in the trash can; the trial court did not err in admitting the investigator's testimony. * * *

We now recount the evidence relating to Wade's wallet, basing our account primarily on the testimony of James Schenk, Scott's first appointed attorney. Schenk visited Scott in jail more than a month after the crime occurred and solicited information about the murder, stressing that he had to be fully acquainted with the facts to avoid being "sandbagged" by the prosecution during the trial. In response, Scott gave Schenk the same information that he had related earlier to the police. In addition, however, Scott told Schenk something Scott had not revealed to the police: that he had seen a wallet, as well as the paper bag, on the ground near Wade. Scott said that he picked up the wallet, put it in the paper bag, and placed both behind a parking lot fence. He also said that he later retrieved the bag, took it home, found $100 in the wallet and divided it with Meredith, and then tried to burn the wallet in his kitchen sink. He took the partially burned wallet, Scott told Schenk, placed it in a plastic bag, and threw it in a burn barrel behind his house.

Schenk, without further consulting Scott, retained Investigator Stephen Frick and sent Frick to find the wallet. Frick found it in the location described by Scott and brought it to Schenk. After examining the wallet and determining that it contained credit cards with Wade's name, Schenk turned the wallet and its contents over to Detective Payne, investigating officer in the case. Schenk told Payne only that, to the best of his knowledge, the wallet had belonged to Wade.

The prosecution subpoenaed Attorney Schenk and Investigator Frick to testify at the preliminary hearing. When questioned at that hearing, Schenk said that he received the wallet from Frick but refused to answer further questions on the ground that he learned about the wallet through a privileged communication. Eventually, however, the magistrate threatened Schenk with contempt if he did not respond "yes" or "no" when asked whether his contact with his client led to disclosure of the wallet's location. Schenk then replied "yes," and revealed on further questioning that this contact was the sole source of his information as to the wallet's location.

At the preliminary hearing Frick, the investigator who found the wallet, was then questioned by the district attorney. Over objections by counsel, Frick testified that he found the wallet in a garbage can behind Scott's residence.

Prior to a trial, a third attorney, Hamilton Hintz, was appointed for Scott. Hintz unsuccessfully sought an *in limine* ruling that the wallet of the murder victim was inadmissible and that the attorney-client privilege precluded the admission of testimony concerning the wallet by Schenk or Frick.

At trial Frick, called by the prosecution, identified the wallet and testifed that he found it in a garbage can behind Scott's residence. On cross-examination by Hintz, Scott's counsel, Frick further testified that he was an investigator hired by Scott's first attorney, Schenk, and that he had searched the garbage can at Schenk's request. Hintz later called Schenk as a witness: Schenk testified that he told Frick to search for the wallet immediately after Schenk finished talking to Scott. Schenk also stated that Frick brought him the wallet on the following day; after examining its contents Schenk delivered the wallet to the police. Scott then took the stand and testified to the information about the wallet that he had disclosed to Schenk.

The jury found both Scott and Meredith guilty of first degree murder and first degree robbery. It further found that Meredith, but not Scott, was armed with a deadly weapon. Both defendants appeal from their convictions.

Defendant Scott concedes, and we agree, that the wallet itself was admissible in evidence. Scott maintains, however, that Evidence Code section 954 bars the testimony of the investigator concerning the location of the wallet. We consider, first, whether the California attorney-client privilege codified in that section extends to observations which are the product of privileged communications. We then discuss whether that privileged status is lost when defense conduct may have frustrated prosecution discovery.

Section 954 provides, "[T]he client * * * has a privilege to refuse to disclose, and to prevent another from disclosing, a confidential communication between client and lawyer * * *." Under that section one who seeks to assert the privilege must establish that a confidential communication occurred during the course of the attorney-client relationship. (8 Wigmore, Evidence (McNaughton rev. ed. 1961) § 2292; Witkin, Cal. Evidence (2d ed. 1966) § 794.)

Scott's statements to Schenk regarding the location of the wallet clearly fulfilled the statutory requirements. Moreover, the privilege did not dissolve when Schenk disclosed the substance of that communication to his investigator, Frick. Under Evidence Code section 912, subdivision (d), a disclosure which is "reasonably necessary" to accomplish the purpose for which the attorney has been consulted does not constitute a waiver of the privilege. If Frick was to perform the investigative services for which Schenk had retained him, it was "reasonably necessary," that Schenk transmit to Frick the information regarding the wallet.[3] thus, Schenk's disclosure to Frick did not waive the statutory privilege.

The statutes codifying the attorney-client privilege do not, however, indicate whether that privilege protects facts viewed and observed as a direct result of confidential communication. To resolve that issue, we turn first to the policies which underlie the attorney-client privilege, and then to the cases which apply those policies to observations arising from a protected communication.

The fundamental purpose of the attorney-client privilege is, of course, to encourage full and open communication between client and attorney. "Adequate legal representation in the ascertainment and enforcement of rights or the prosecution or defense of litigation compels a full disclosure of the facts by the client to his attorney. * * * Given the

3. Although prior cases do not consider whether section 912, subdivision (d) applies to an attorney's investigator, the language of that subdivision covers the circumstances of the instant case. An investigator is as "reasonably necessary" as a physician or psychiatrist (People v. Lines (1975) 13 Cal.3d 500, 119 Cal.Rptr. 225, 531 P.2d 793), or a legal secretary, paralegal or receptionist. (See Anderson v. State (Fla.App.1974) 297 So.2d 871; City & County of S. F. v. Superior Court (1951) 37 Cal.2d 227, 231 P.2d 26). Because the investigator, then, is a person encompassed by the privilege, he stands in the same position as the attorney for purposes of the analysis and operation of the privilege; the investigator cannot then disclose that which the attorney could not have disclosed. Thus, the discussion in this opinion of the conduct of defense counsel, and of counsel's right to invoke the attorney-client privilege to avoid testifying, applies also to a defense investigator.

privilege, a client may make such a disclosure without fear that his attorney may be forced to reveal the information confided to him." (City & County of S. F. v. Superior Court, supra, 37 Cal.2d at p. 235, 231 P.2d 26.)

In the criminal context, as we have recently observed, these policies assume particular significance: " 'As a practical matter, if the client knows that damaging information could more readily be obtained from the attorney following disclosure than from himself in the absence of disclosure, the client would be reluctant to confide in his lawyer and it would be difficult to obtain fully informed legal advice.' * * * Thus, if an accused is to derive the full benefits of his right to counsel, he must have the assurance of confidentiality and privacy of communication with his attorney." (Barber v. Municipal Court (1979) 24 Cal.3d 742, 751, 157 Cal.Rptr. 658, 598 P.2d 878, citing Fisher v. United States (1976) 425 U.S. 391, 403, 96 S.Ct. 1569, 1577, 48 L.Ed.2d 39.)

Judicial decisions have recognized that the implementation of these important policies may require that the privilege extend not only to the initial communication between client and attorney but also to any information which the attorney or his investigator may subsequently acquire as a direct result of that communication. In a venerable decision involving facts analogous to those in the instant case, the Supreme Court of West Virginia held that the trial court erred in admitting an attorney's testimony as to the location of a pistol which he had discovered as the result of a privileged communication from his client. That the attorney had observed the pistol, the court pointed out, did not nullify the privilege: "All that the said attorney knew about this pistol, or where it was to be found, he knew only from the communications which had been made to him by his client confidentially and professionally, as counsel in this case. And it ought therefore, to have been entirely excluded from the jury. It may be, that in this particular case this evidence tended to the promotion of right and justice, but as was well said in Pearce v. Pearce, 11 Jar. 52, in page 55, and 2 De Gex & Smale 25–27: 'Truth like all other good things may be loved unwisely, may be pursued too keenly, may cost too much.' " (State of West Virginia v. Douglass (1882) 20 W.Va. 770, 783.)

This unbearable cost, the *Douglass* court concluded, could not be entirely avoided by attempting to admit testimony regarding observations or discoveries made as the result of a privileged communication, while excluding the communication itself. Such a procedure, *Douglass* held, "was practically as mischievous in all its tendencies and consequences, as if it has required [the attorney] to state everything, which his client had confidentially told him about this pistol. It would be a slight safeguard indeed, to confidential communications made to counsel, if he was thus compelled substantially, to give them to a jury, although he was required not to state them in the words of his client."

More recent decisions reach similar conclusions. In State v. Olwell (1964) 64 Wash.2d 828, 394 P.2d 681, the court reviewed contempt charges against an attorney who refused to produce a knife he obtained from his client. The court first observed that "[t]o be protected as a privileged communication * * * the securing of the knife * * * must have been *the direct result of information* given to Mr. Olwell by his client." (Emphasis added.) The court concluded that defense counsel, after examining the physical evidence, should deliver it to the prosecution, but should not reveal the source of the evidence; "[b]y thus allowing the prosecution to recover such evidence, the public interest is served, and by refusing the prosecution an opportunity to disclose the source of the evidence, the client's privilege is preserved and a balance reached between these conflicting interests." [4] (See also Anderson v. State (D.C.App.Fla.1974) 297 So.2d 871).

Finally, we note the decisions of the New York courts in People v. Belge (Sup.Ct.1975) 83 Misc.2d 186, 372 N.Y.S.2d 798, affirmed in People v. Belge (App.Div.1975) 50 A.D.2d 1088, 376 N.Y.S.2d 771. Defendant, charged with one murder, revealed to counsel that he had committed three others. Counsel, following defendant's directions, located one of the bodies. Counsel did not reveal the location of the body until trial, 10 months later, when he exposed the other murders to support an insanity defense. Counsel was then indicted for violating two sections of the New York Public Health Law for failing to report the existence of the body to proper authorities in order that they could give it a decent burial. The trial court dismissed the indictment; the appellate division affirmed, holding that the attorney-client privilege shielded counsel from prosecution for actions which would otherwise violate the Public Health Law.[5]

The foregoing decisions demonstrate that the attorney-client privilege is not strictly limited to communications, but extends to protect observations made as a consequence of protected communications.[6]

4. The parties discuss an earlier Washington case, State v. Sullivan (1962) 60 Wash.2d 214, 373 P.2d 474. Defendant in that case revealed the location of the victim's body to his counsel, who informed the sheriff. At trial the prosecution called defense counsel to testify to the location. The appellate court reversed the conviction, apparently on the ground that it was unnecessarily prejudicial to call defense counsel as a prosecution witness when sheriff's deputies and other witnesses who had seen the body were available.

The *Sullivan* court stated a general rule which supports the result we reach here—that attorney-client communications remain privileged "regardless of the manner in which it is sought to put the communications in evidence, whether by direct examination, cross-examination, or *indirectly as by bringing of facts brought to knowledge solely by reason of a confidential communication.*" (P. 476, quoting 58 Am.Jur., Witnesses, § 466.) (Emphasis by the *Sullivan* court.) The decision expressly left open, however, whether defense counsel could be called to prove the location of the body if other witnesses were unavailable.

5. In each of the cases discussed in text, a crucial element in the court's analysis is that the attorney's observations were the direct product of information communicated to him by his client. Two decisions, People v. Lee (1970) 3 Cal.App.3d 514, 83 Cal.Rptr. 715 and Morrell v. State (Alaska 1978) 575 P.2d 1200, held that an attorney must not only turn over evidence given him by *third parties*, but also testify as to the source of that evidence. Both decisions emphasized that the attorney-client privilege was inapplicable because the third party was not acting as an agent of the attorney or the client.

6. In advancing the observable fact doctrine, the Attorney General relied largely on civil cases involving pretrial discovery of expert's observations, opinions, and reports. (See, e.g., San Diego Professional Assn. v. Superior Court (1962) 58 Cal.2d 194, 23

We turn therefore to the question whether that privilege encompasses a case in which the defense, by removing or altering evidence, interferes with the prosecution's opportunity to discover that evidence.[7]

In some of the cases extending the privilege to observations arising from protected communications the defense counsel had obtained the evidence from his client or in some other fashion removed it from its original location (State v. Olwell, supra, 394 P.2d 681; Anderson v. State, supra, 297 So.2d 871); in others the attorney did not remove or alter the evidence (People v. Belge, supra, 372 N.Y.S.2d 798; State v. Sullivan, supra, 373 P.2d 474). None of the decisions, however, confronts directly the question whether such removal or alteration should affect the defendant's right to assert the attorney-client privilege as a bar to testimony concerning the original location or condition of the evidence.

When defense counsel alters or removes physical evidence, he necessarily deprives the prosecution of the opportunity to observe that evidence in its original condition or location. As the Amicus Appellate Committee of the California District Attorneys Association points out, to bar admission of testimony concerning the original condition and location of the evidence in such a case permits the defense in effect to "destroy" critical information; it is as if, he explains, the wallet in this case bore a tag bearing the words "located in the trash can by Scott's residence," and the defense, by taking the wallet, destroyed this tag. To extend the attorney-client privilege to a case in which the defense removed evidence might encourage defense counsel to race the police to seize critical evidence. (See In re Ryder (E.D.Va.1967) 263 F.Supp. 360, 369; Comment, The Right of a Criminal Defense Attorney to Withhold Physical Evidence Received From His Client (1970) 38 U.Chi.L.Rev. 211, 227–228.)

We therefore conclude that courts must craft an exception to the protection extended by the attorney-client privilege in cases in which counsel has removed or altered evidence. Indeed, at oral argument defense counsel acknowledged that such an exception might be nec-

Cal.Rptr. 384, 373 P.2d 448; Oceanside Union School Dist. v. Superior Court (1962) 58 Cal.2d 180, 23 Cal.Rptr. 375, 373 P.2d 439.) Such cases arise in a context which differs from the present case; in civil cases, pretrial discovery is extensive and seldom restricted by a party's privilege against self-incrimination. Even in the cited cases, however, the court in allowing discovery carefully notes that the expert's observations do not derive from information submitted in confidence by the client.

7. We agree with the parties' suggestion that an attorney in Schenk's position often may best fulfill conflicting obligations to preserve the confidentiality of client confidences, investigate his case, and act as an officer of the court if he does not remove evidence located as the result of a privileged communication. We must recognize, however, that in some cases an examination of evidence may reveal information critical to the defense of a client accused of crime. If the usefulness of the evidence cannot be gauged without taking possession of it, as, for example, when a ballistics or fingerprint test is required, the attorney may properly take it for a reasonable time before turning it over to the prosecution. (*Olwell*, supra, 394 P.2d, pp. 684–685.) Similarly, in the present case the defense counsel could not be certain the burnt wallet belonged in fact to the victim; in taking the wallet to examine it for identification, he violated no ethical duty to his client or to the prosecution. (See generally Legal Ethics and the Destruction of Evidence (1979) 88 Yale L.J. 1665).

essary in a case in which the police would have inevitably discovered the evidence in its original location if counsel had not removed it. Counsel argued, however, that the attorney-client privilege should protect observations of evidence, despite subsequent defense removal, unless the prosecution could prove that the police probably would have eventually discovered the evidence in the original site.

We have seriously considered counsel's proposal, but have concluded that a test based upon the probability of eventual discovery is unworkably speculative. Evidence turns up not only because the police deliberately search for it, but also because it comes to the attention of policemen or bystanders engaged in other business. In the present case, for example, the wallet might have been found by the trash collector. Moreover, once physical evidence (the wallet) is turned over to the police, they will obviously stop looking for it; to ask where, how long, and how carefully they would have looked is obviously to compel speculation as to theoretical future conduct of the police.

We therefore conclude that whenever defense counsel removes or alters evidence, the statutory privilege does not bar revelation of the original location or condition of the evidence in question.[8] We thus view the defense decision to remove evidence as a tactical choice. If defense counsel leaves the evidence where he discovers it, his observations derived from privileged communications are insulated from revelation. If, however, counsel chooses to remove evidence to examine or test it, the original location and condition of that evidence loses the protection of the privilege. Applying this analysis to the present case, we hold that the trial court did not err in admitting the investigator's testimony concerning the location of the wallet. * * *[a]

### *Questions*

(1) In *Meredith* the defense attorney turned over the evidence to the police. He had obtained it while the criminal prosecution was pending. Assume that he had received it prior to the defendant's arrest and had destroyed it to prevent its use in the event of a later

8. In offering the evidence, the prosecution should present the information in a manner which avoids revealing the content of attorney-client communications or the original source of the information. In the present case, for example, the prosecutor simply asked Frick where he found the wallet; he did not identify Frick as a defense investigator or trace the discovery of the wallet to an attorney-client communication.

In other circumstances, when it is not possible to elicit such testimony without identifying the witness as the defendant's attorney or investigator, the defendant may be willing to enter a stipulation which will simply inform the jury as to the relevant location or condition of the evidence in question. When such a stipulation is proffered, the prosecution should not be permitted to reject the stipulation in the hope that by requiring defense counsel personally to testify to such facts, the jury might infer that counsel learned those facts from defendant. (Cf. People v. Hall (1980) 28 Cal.3d 143, 152, 167 Cal.Rptr. 844, 616 P.2d 826.)

a. The case is criticized in 70 Calif.L.Rev. 1048 (1982). See Comment, Ethics, Law, and Loyalty: The Attorney's Duty to Turn Over Incriminating Physical Evidence, 32 Stan.L.Rev. 977 (1980) (extended review of cases); see also People v. Nash, 110 Mich.App. 428, 313 N.W.2d 307 (1981).

prosecution. Most states and federal laws do not make it a criminal offense to destroy evidence in the absence of a pending or impending criminal prosecution or investigation.[1] Under these circumstances should the destruction of the evidence be deemed unethical?

> "What if Richard Nixon had burned the tapes? During the period before the recordings were subpoenaed when the President could have destroyed the tapes without direct legal consequences, it is not clear what ethical considerations would have guided presidential counsel in suggesting such action."[2]

RPC 3.3(a)(2) provides that a lawyer shall not knowingly "fail to disclose a material fact to a tribunal when disclosure is necessary to avoid assisting a criminal or fraudulent act by the client." Does this provide the answer?

(2) In People v. Belge,[3] the attorney's client, charged with murder, told the attorney of his unrelated murders of two young women who were being sought as missing persons. From information given him by the client, the attorney found the bodies in an abandoned mine shaft and photographed them. He did not disclose his discovery to anyone including the father of one of the victims who sought information from the attorney that might enable him to find his daughter. The attorney's reason was that he was bound by his ethical duty not to reveal

1. See Fedders & Guttenplan, Document Retention and Destruction; Practical, Legal and Ethical Considerations, 56 Notre Dame Law. 5 (1980) (a thorough discussion of the subject); Comment, Legal Ethics and the Destruction of Evidence, 88 YaleL.J. 1665, 1669, (1979).

2. Comment, supra note 1, at 1665. The author asserts that, as interpreted by ABA Opinions, DR 7–102(A) (3) (concealing or knowingly failing to disclose when required by law), DR 7–102(A) (7) (counseling or assisting client in illegal or fraudulent conduct), and DR 7–102 (B) (1) (revealing client's fraud perpetrated in course of representation), do not provide an answer. The author also refers to a statement reportedly made by former attorney general Richard Kleindienst that Nixon was "stupid" in not burning the tapes.

See also Fedders & Guttenplan, supra note 1 (dealing with the subject in terms of the need of business organizations to destroy outdated and unneeded records); Note, Disclosure of Incriminating Physical Evidence Received From a Client: The Defense Attorney's Dilemma, 52 Colo.L.Rev. 419 (1981) (reviewing major cases); Note, The Attorney's Duty to Turn Over Incriminating Physical Evidence, 32 Stan.L.Rev. 977 (1980).

The fourth amendment does not prevent seizure of incriminating evidence received and retained by the attorney if it were subject to seizure in the hands of the client. See Andresen v. Maryland, 427 U.S. 463, 96 S.Ct. 2737, 49 L.Ed.2d 627 (1976) (search warrant to search attorney's office); Fisher v. United States, 425 U.S. 391, 96 S.Ct. 1569, 48 L.Ed.2d 39 (1976) (summons directing attorney to produce documents delivered to him by his client).

In United States v. Authement, 607 F.2d 1129 (5th Cir. 1980), admission of incriminating evidence compelled from an attorney was upheld where it was authenticated by independent testimony and the jury was not told that the evidence had been secured from the attorney or that it had been produced in response to a subpoena.

Compare O'Connor v. Johnson, 287 N.W.2d 400 (Minn. 1979), holding that a warrant authorizing search of an attorney's office was invalid under the state constitution. The court deemed its holding "necessary to protect the overriding interest of our society in preserving the attorney-client privilege, client confidentiality, the work product doctrine, and the constitutional right to counsel."

Development of the constitutional aspects of the subject is left to other courses.

3. 83 Misc.2d 186, 372 N.Y.S.2d 798 (1975), affirmed 50 A.D.2d 1088, 376 N.Y.S.2d 771, affirmed on other grounds, 41 N.Y.2d 60, 390 N.Y.S.2d 867, 359 N.E.2d 377 (1976).

information harmful to his client and obtained through a confidential communication.

There was a public uproar when the news media reported these facts.[4] The attorney was indicted for violating a criminal statute requiring notice to the coroner of the death. The indictment was dismissed since the constitutional privilege against self-incrimination exempted the client from the statutory requirement and the attorney-client privilege made the lawyer "not only equally exempt but under a positive stricture precluding such disclosure."

In Opinion 479,[5] the Committee on Professional Ethics of the New York State Bar Association upheld the attorney's withholding of the information he had obtained as being required by the attorney-client privilege under DR 4–101 (B).[6] It also considered it proper, absent a statute to the contrary, for the attorney to destroy the records of his conversation with his client, the photographs taken of the bodies of the victims and the diagram showing the bodies' physical location. But any moving of the bodies would be improper as giving an "appearance of impropriety in violation of Canon 9."[7]

In considering the ethical propriety of the attorney's conduct, should any consideration be given to the adverse public reaction to what the attorney had done?[8]

(3) The client, charged with theft, tells his attorney he committed the offense and where the stolen property is located. Opinion 405, issued by the New York State Bar Association's Ethics Committee,[9] concluded that the attorney is under a duty not to disclose the property's location since it would risk linking the client with possession of the property and hence, by implication, with the past offense of theft.

Does this permit the attorney to advise entering a plea of not guilty and putting the prosecution to proof of the offense? See pp. 290–97 below. If so, and the client is acquitted, what disposition of the property may the attorney advise?

(4) The general rule developed by the courts is that the identity of the attorney's client is not a matter of confidence and hence is not covered by the attorney-client privilege. But if its disclosure would also expose the purpose of the attorney's employment or disclose communications between lawyer and client the privilege applies. In a

4. See New York Times, June 20, 1974, p. 1.

5. 50 N.Y.St.B. A. J. 259 (1978).

6. Reproduced supra p. 11 n.a.

See also M. Freedman, Lawyer's Ethics in an Adversary System, ch. 1 (1975) (attorney acted properly).

7. Canon 9 provides, "A Lawyer Should Avoid Even the Appearance of Professional Impropriety." The Model Rules do not include a similar provision.

8. The attorney's affidavit stated that the events had been "disastrous to his law practice." See In re Armani, 83 Misc.2d 252, 371 N.Y.S.2d 563 (1975). Mr. Armani was one of the two attorneys representing the defendant.

9. 47 N.Y.St.B.J. 527 (1975).

leading case, Baird v. Koerner,[10] the attorney sent a letter to the IRS on behalf of an unnamed client, stating the client owed additional taxes for which a cashier's check was enclosed. It was held that the attorney could not be compelled to disclose the identity of the client, for the volunteer payment might "well be the link that could form the chain of testimony necessary to convict an individual of a federal crime."

In In re Grand Jury Proceedings,[11] the attorney refused to disclose to a grand jury, investigating narcotics and income tax violations, whether a third party had employed him to represent his client, or posted bond or paid his fee. His refusal was upheld as within the privilege because on the facts in the case the client, if his identity were disclosed, "might very well be indicted."

But in In re Grand Jury Proceedings (Pavlick),[12] the attorney and probably the client, whose identity was sought, did not fare so well. One of three defendants in a narcotics prosecution had been granted immunity and testified before the grand jury that he had been promised "he would be taken care of" if arrested. The attorney for the defendants was then asked who the third person was who had employed him. His refusal was held by a divided court not to be within the privilege. The identity sought was not the last link in the evidence that might lead to indictment and, further, in view of the quoted testimony, his employment was in furtherance of criminal activity and hence within the crime/fraud exception to the attorney-client privilege.

The case has been criticized by a commentator, who notes that the "last link" concept is difficult to define or apply and "the prosecutor could force the attorneys to reveal their clients' identities before the identities provide the last link."[13] With respect to the crime/fraud exception, the commentator maintains that *Pavlick* is inconsistent with *Baird*, and that the exception is inapplicable since the attorney was not a party to the alleged agreement that one defendant "would be taken care of" and was not employed until later.[14]

Are these criticisms convincing?[15]

10. 279 F.2d 623 (9th Cir. 1960) (discussed in 49 Calif.L.Rev. 382 (1961); 47 Va.L.Rev. 126 (1961) ).

11. 517 F.2d 666 (5th Cir. 1975).

12. 680 F.2d 1026 (5th Cir. 1982).

13. 21 Am.Crim.L.Rev. 81 (1983).

14. "According to the *Pavlick* majority, an attorney is used in furtherance of a crime when legal services are *promised* to the co-conspirators as an inducement to enter the conspiracy. The actual date of the attorney's hiring is irrelevant." Id. at 94.

15. Compare United States v. Pape, 144 F.2d 778 (2d Cir. 1944), cert. denied 323 U.S. 752, 65 S.Ct. 86, 89 L.Ed. 602, in which the attorney, retained by the defendant in a prosecution for transporting a woman for prostitution, was compelled to disclose that he had also been retained by the defendant to defend the woman being prosecuted for the prostitution. Judge L. Hand dissented:

"Pape retained Buckley as his own lawyer at the same time that he retained him for the woman. I agree that his retainer of an attorney for himself involved no privileged communication * * *. Moreover, it goes without saying that Pape's retainer of Buckley for the woman would not have been privileged, had he not retained him as his own attorney. On the other hand I attach no importance to the fact that he retained him in both capacities at the same time; the case stands as it would if he had retained

## ABA FORMAL OPINION 287 (1953)

[The ABA Committee considered two inquiries submitted to it. Its answer to the first follows:]

An attorney represents a client in a suit for divorce and a decree for divorce from bonds of matrimony is duly entered by the court on November 6, 1952, in favor of the client on the grounds of willful desertion and abandonment by his wife as of March 15, 1950. The wife was represented by counsel in the divorce action and she was fully apprised of the evidence presented on behalf of her husband. Three months after entry of the decree, the client again comes to the attorney seeking advice by reason of the following situation: The client tells the attorney that he, the client, gave false testimony at the taking of the depositions upon which his decree for divorce was based; that the date of desertion was not March 15, 1950, as he had testified, but was actually the early part of November 1951 (which, under the local law, would have made the action premature); that his former wife threatens to disclose the true facts to the court unless support money is forthcoming. The client has not remarried, nor has his former wife.

What is the duty of the attorney to the court, as an officer of the court, after learning that the testimony of his client in the suit for divorce was false?

What is the duty of the attorney to his client, who, when seeking advice, disclosed the fact that he had testified falsely in the suit for divorce? * * *

[Opinion of the Committee stated by Mr. Drinker:] * * *

Canon 37 recognizes and specifies conditions under which the privilege is not applicable, the second paragraph providing that the announced intention of a client to commit a crime is not included within the confidences which he is bound to respect, and states that he may properly make such disclosure as may be necessary to prevent the criminal act or to protect those against whom it is threatened.[a]

The case put is clearly not one coming within the exception. The crime of perjury has already been committed; the question is not one of preventing the commission of the crime, and the wife, being at least a tacit party to the fraud on the court, requires no protection. * * *

him for himself first. Yet if he had done that when he told him to appear for her, I think it was a communication between attorney and client, a step in his own defense; it may have been also a step in hers but that, I submit, is irrelevant * * *. That it was an important step in connecting him with the woman's prostitution, admits of no debate."

In child custody cases, the interests and welfare of the child may cause courts to require disclosure of, e.g., the location of the client charged with holding the child illegally. See, e.g., In re Jacqueline F., 47 N.Y.2d 215, 391 N.E.2d 967, 417 N.Y.S.2d 884 (1979); Brennan v. Brennan, 281 Pa.Super. 362, 422 A.2d 510 (1980) (disclosure denied because client expressly so requested and not shown child's interest required disclosure) (but note the dissent).

a. Cf. RPC 1.6 and DR 4–101, reproduced supra p. 111 n.a.

In the case submitted to us, the communication by the client to the lawyer that he had committed perjury was made to the lawyer in his professional capacity, when seeking advice as to what to do, and is within the letter and the spirit of Canon 37, which would apply unless controlled by some other Canon or consideration.

Canon 41 provides as follows:

> "When a lawyer discovers that some fraud or deception has been practiced, which has unjustly imposed upon the court or a party, he should endeavor to rectify it; at first by advising his client, and if his client refuses to forego the advantage thus unjustly gained, he should promptly inform the injured person or his counsel, so that they may take appropriate steps." [b]

We do not believe that Canon 41 was directed at a case such as that here presented but rather at one in which, in a civil suit, the lawyer's client has secured an improper advantage over the other through fraud or deception.

Nor do we not think that because the state is considered an interested party to proceedings to sever the matrimonial relation of its citizens the state or the court may therefore be treated as an "injured person" within the meaning of Canon 41.

More forcible argument for an exception to Canon 37 is found in Canon 29, which provides:

> "The counsel upon the trial of a cause in which perjury has been committed owe it to the profession and to the public to bring the matter to the knowledge of the prosecuting authorities." [c]

On its face this provision would apparently make it the duty of the lawyer to disclose his client's prior perjury to the prosecuting au-

**b.** See RPC 3.3:

"(a) A lawyer shall not knowingly:

* * *

(2) fail to disclose a material fact to a tribunal when disclosure is necessary to avoid assisting a criminal or fraudulent act by the client.

"(b) The duties stated in paragraph (a) continue to the conclusion of the proceeding, and apply even if compliance requires disclosure of information otherwise protected by Rule 1.6."

RPC 4.1 deals with disclosures to third persons in representing a client and is identical to RPC 3.3(a) (2), but adds "unless disclosure is prohibited by Rule 1.6."

See also DR 7–102(B):

"A lawyer who receives information clearly establishing that:

"(1) His client has, in the course of the representation, perpetrated a fraud upon a person or tribunal shall promptly call upon his client to rectify the same, and if his client refuses or is unable to do so, he shall reveal the fraud to the affected person or tribunal, except when the information is protected as a privileged communication.

"(2) A person other than his client has perpetrated a fraud upon a tribunal shall promptly reveal the fraud to the tribunal."

**c.** See RPC 3.3(a) (4), which specifies, "A lawyer shall not knowingly * * * offer evidence that the lawyer knows to be false. If a lawyer has offered material evidence and comes to know of its falsity, the lawyer shall take reasonable remedial measures."

See also DR 7–102(A) (4), which specifies, "In his representation of a client, a lawyer shall not * * * Knowingly use perjured testimony or false evidence."

thorities. However, to do so in this case would involve the direct violation of Canon 37.

Accordingly, it is essential to determine which of the Canons controls.

Neither Canon 41 nor Canon 29 specifically requires the lawyer to advise the *court* of his client's perjury, even where this was committed in a case in which the lawyer was acting as counsel and an officer of the court. We do not consider that either the duty of candor and fairness to the court as stated in Canon 22, or the provisions of Canons 29 and 41 above quoted are sufficient to override the purpose, policy and express obligation under Canon 37.

In the case stated the lawyer should urge his client to make the disclosure, advising him that this is essential to secure for him any leniency in the event of the court's finding out the truth. He should also advise him to tell his wife that he proposes to do so, and thus avoid further blackmail. If the client will not take this advice, the lawyer should have nothing further to do with him, but despite Canons 29 and 41, should not disclose the facts to the court or to the authorities.

[The second inquiry was as follows:]

(1) A convicted client stands before the judge for the sentence. The custodian of criminal records indicates to the court that the defendant has no record. The court thereupon says to the defendant, "You have no criminal record, so I will put you on probation."

Defense counsel knows by independent investigation or from his client that his client in fact has a criminal record and that the record clerk's information is incorrect. Is it the duty of defense counsel to disclose to the court the true facts as to his client's criminal record?

(2) Suppose, under the above circumstances, that the judge before disposing of the case asks the defendant himself whether he has a criminal record and the defendant answers that he has none. Is it the duty of defense counsel to disclose to the court the true facts as to his client's criminal record?

(3) Assume further a situation in which the judge following the conviction asks the defendant's lawyer whether his client has a criminal record.

* * *

Turning to the second inquiry, relative to the convicted client up for sentence, whose lawyer sees the court put him on probation by reason of the court's misinformation as to his criminal record, known to the lawyer: If the client's criminal record was communicated by him to his counsel when seeking professional advice from him, Canon 37 would prevent its disclosure to the court unless the provisions of Canons 22,[d] 29 and 41 require this. If the court asks the defendant

d. Canon 22 dealt with "candor and fairness" "before the court and with other lawyers." Cf. RPC 3.3 and DR 7–102, discussed infra pp. 305–29.

whether he has a criminal record and he answers that he has none, this, although perhaps not technical perjury, for the purposes of the present question amounts to the same thing. Despite this, we do not believe the lawyer justified in violating his obligation under Canon 37. He should, in due course, endeavor to persuade the client to tell the court the truth and if he refuses to do so should sever his relations with the client, but should not violate the client's confidence. We yield to none in our insistence on the lawyer's loyalty to the court of which he is an officer. Such loyalty does not, however, consist merely in respect for the judicial office and candor and frankness to the judge. It involves also the steadfast maintenance of the principles which the courts themselves have evolved for the effective administration of justice, one of the most firmly established of which is the preservation undisclosed of the confidences communicated by his clients to the lawyer in his professional capacity.

If the fact of the client's criminal record was learned by the lawyer without communication, confidential or otherwise, from his client, or on his behalf, Canon 37 would not be applicable, and the only problem would be as to the conflicting loyalties of the lawyer on the one hand to represent his client with undivided fidelity and not to divulge his secrets (Canon 6),[e] and on the other to treat the court in every case in which he appears as counsel, with the candor and fairness (Canon 22) which the court has the right to expect of him as its officer. In this case we deem the following considerations applicable.

If the court asks the lawyer whether the clerk's statement is correct, the lawyer is not bound by fidelity to the client to tell the court what he knows to be an untruth, and should ask the court to excuse him from answering the question, and retire from the case, though this would doubtless put the court on further inquiry as to the truth.

Even, however, if the court does not directly ask the lawyer this question, such an inquiry may well be implied from the circumstances, including the lawyer's previous relations with the court. * * * If, under all the circumstances, the lawyer believes that the court relies on him as corroborating the correctness of the statement by the clerk or by the client that the client has no criminal record, the lawyer's duty of candor and fairness to the court requires him, in our opinion, to advise the court not to rely on counsel's personal knowledge as to the facts of the client's record. While doubtless a client who would permit the court, because of misinformation, to be unduly lenient to him would be indignant when his lawyer volunteered to ruin his chance of escaping a jail sentence, such indignation would be unjustified since the client's bad faith had made the lawyer's action necessary. The indignation of the court, however, on learning that the lawyer had

e. Cf. RPC 1.6 and DR 4-101, reproduced supra p. 111.

deliberately permitted him, where no privileged communication is involved, to rely on what the lawyer knew to be a misapprehension of the true facts, would be something that the lawyer could not appease on the basis of loyalty to the client. No client may demand or expect of his lawyer, in the furtherance of his cause, disloyalty to the law whose minister he is (Canon 32),[f] or "any manner of fraud or chicane." (Canon 15).[g]

If the lawyer is quite clear that the court does not rely on him as corroborating, by his silence, the statement of the clerk or of his client, the lawyer is not, in our opinion, bound to speak out.[h]

### *Questions*

(1) The Committee states that if the attorney obtains information "without communication, confidential or otherwise from his client, or on his behalf" the Canon prohibiting disclosure would not apply. Can the same conclusion be drawn under RPC 1.6 and DR 4-101, page 111 above? A dissenting member of the Committee maintained that even under the Canon then in force, this distinction should not be drawn.

(2) To what extent, if any, should you as a lawyer refuse to comply with a court order requiring you to testify, where you feel that the order may be erroneous because the information sought is protected by the attorney-client privilege? RPC 3.4(c) specifies that a lawyer shall not "knowingly disobey an obligation under the rules of a tribunal except for an open refusal based on as assertion that no valid obligation exists."[1] Compare the following—

(a) Shinn, Presiding Justice, concurring in the California case of People v. Kor[2] (wherein the court reversed a conviction because defendant's lawyer was erroneously required to testify to information protected by the attorney-client privilege):

"Defendant's attorney should have chosen to go to jail and take his chances of release by a higher court. This is not intended as a criticism of the action of the attorney. It is, however, a

f. Cf. RPC Preamble, ("A lawyer should demonstrate respect for the legal profession and for those who serve it, including judges, other lawyers and public officials."); EC 1–5 ("To lawyers especially, respect for the law should be more than a platitude.").

g. Cf. RPC 1.2(d) ("A lawyer shall not counsel or assist a client in conduct that the lawyer knows is criminal or fraudulent"); DR 7–102(A) (7) (identical except "illegal" instead of "criminal").

h. Two members of the Committee dissented on the ground that former Canons 29, 41, 15 and 22 should control.

1. See also DR 4–101(C)(2) (lawyer "may reveal * * * confidences or secrets when * * * required by * * * court order"); DR 7–101(A)(1) (lawyer shall not intentionally "fail to seek the lawful objectives of his client through reasonably available means permitted by law and the Disciplinary Rules"); DR 7–106(A) (lawyer "shall not disregard * * * a ruling of a tribunal made in the course of a proceeding, but he may take appropriate steps in good faith to test the validity of such * * * ruling").

2. 129 Cal.App.2d 436, 441, 277 P.2d 94, 101 (1954).

suggestion to any and all attorneys who may have the misfortune to be confronted by the same or a similar problem."[3]

(b) Wigmore on Evidence:

"[T]he privilege not being the attorney's but the client's, the *attorney* is not justified (when the client is a party to the cause) in refusing to obey a ruling (though erroneous) against the privilege. The client is the one to protect himself by appellate proceedings * * *."[4]

Should the answer be affected by the extent to which appeal is likely to be a completely adequate remedy for the erroneously-required disclosure? Note that the Wigmore quotation recognizes that appeal will not provide a remedy where the client is not a party to the cause. Must it be presumed that appeal is a complete remedy for any harm that erroneously-required disclosure does to the client's case? Or is it proper to note that the placement of the burden upon the appellant and the harmless error rule may prevent appeal from being a completely adequate remedy? What about harm apart from the client's case, such as disclosure of trade secrets or injury to reputation? It has been suggested that considerations like these, together with consideration of the degree of likelihood that the privilege claim will ultimately prevail, should be carefully explored *in consultation with the client* before deciding to comply with a trial court order to disclose information that may be protected by the attorney-client privilege.[5]

(3) Should a lawyer suing to recover a fee be able to attach the client's property about which the lawyer learned through a confidential communication?[6]

(4) If the client telephones the attorney and states he is about to commit suicide, should the attorney report it to the appropriate authorities to prevent it?

"To exalt the oath of silence, in the face of imminent death, would, under these circumstances, be not only morally reprehensible, but ethically unsound. As Professor Monroe Freedman reminds us, 'At one extreme, it seems clear that the lawyer should

3. It may be noted that although not cited in the opinion, Cal.Bus. & Prof. Code § 6068(e) specifies, "It is the duty of an attorney * * * to maintain inviolate the confidence and at every peril to himself to preserve the secrets, of his client."

4. 8 J. Wigmore, Evidence § 2321 (J. McNaughton rev. 1961).

5. Comment, The Attorney-Client Privilege: The Remedy of Contempt, 1968 Wis.L.Rev. 1192. See Levine, Self-Interest or Self-Defense: Lawyer Disregard of the Attorney-Client Privilege for Profit and Protection, 5 Hofstra L.Rev. 783, 813–14 (1977).

6. ABA Formal Opinion 250 (1943) says yes, reasoning, "The general rule should not be carried to the extent of depriving the lawyer of the means of obtaining or defending his own rights."

Compare Opinion 278, Association of the Bar of the City of New York: "It would certainly offend the sense of propriety if an attorney who was retained in a matter which from its nature was highly confidential should, in an action for the recovery of his fees, give publicity to the very facts which he was employed to suppress."

See RPC 1.6(b) (2); DR 4–101(C)(4); G. Hazard, Ethics in the Practice of Law 32–33 (1978).

reveal information necessary to save a life,' 10 Crim.L.Bull., No. 10, p. 987. If the ethical duty exists primarily to protect the client's interests, what interest can there be superior to the client's life itself?

"The issue was addressed in N.Y. State Bar Op. 486 [1978] [New York State Bar Journal, August 1978]. Posing the question 'May a lawyer disclose his client's expressed intention to commit suicide?' the New York State Bar Association, in interpreting EC 4–2 and DR 4–101[C] [3] answered in the affirmative, despite the repeal of suicide as a crime." [7]

(5) Assume a client tells his attorney that a third person is being charged with murder which he, the client, committed. What is the duty of the attorney? What factors are relevant? That the third person faces a death sentence if convicted? Verification and belief by the attorney of his client's version? The express admonition by the client before disclosure that it be kept in confidence? Deferring decision until the third person has in fact been convicted and sentenced to death? [8] Should the answer be different if capital punishment is not involved?

(6) A client tells his attorney that, he, and not the defendant in a hit and run prosecution, was the driver of the car involved. May the attorney, without the consent of his client, inform the prosecutor that the client was the violator? May the attorney give the information without identifying the client? [9]

7. People v. Fentress, 103 Misc.2d 179, 425 N.Y.S.2d 485 (1980) (dicta). Accord, ABA Informal Opinion 83–1500 (1983).

8. That preventing the execution of the third person, if innocent, by disclosing the client's statement, is ethically justified, see J. Lieberman, Crisis at the Bar 1141–43 (1978); A. Kaufman, Problems in Professional Responsibility 181–82 (1976); Gardner, A Reevaluation of the Attorney-Client Privilege, 8 Vill. L. Rev. 447, 477–79 (1963).

9. Compare Colman v. Heidenreich, 269 Ind. 419, 381 N.E.2d 866 (1978). The client had told the attorney that the client's friend, who was not the attorney's client directly or indirectly, had told the client that he, the friend, had been the driver. The attorney was required to inform the prosecution of the name of the friend but not of the client. How long do you suppose the friendship lasted? Or the client remained a client?

# Chapter 4

# CONFLICT OF INTEREST AND DISQUALIFICATION

---

### *Comment*

In addition to disciplining lawyers,[1] courts have granted motions to disqualify counsel,[2] enjoined or stayed proceedings,[3] reversed judgments,[4] denied lawyers their fees,[5] imposed constructive trusts,[6] and subjected lawyers to civil liability,[7] upon finding lawyer conflict of interest situations.[8]

Disqualification may be based upon grounds other than conflict of interest, including the risk of possible (as opposed to proof of actual) use of confidential information to the client's disadvantage.[9]

## A. LAWYER'S OWN INTEREST

### 1. GENERALLY

#### MODEL RULES OF PROFESSIONAL CONDUCT

**Terminology**

* * *

"Consult" or "Consultation" denotes communication of information rea-

1. See Annot., 17 A.L.R.3d 835 (1968).

2. See Annot., 31 A.L.R.3d 715 (1970); Annot., 31 A.L.R.3d 953 (1970).

3. See Watson v. Watson, 171 Misc. 175, 11 N.Y.S.2d 537, 539 (1939).

4. See People v. Cross, 30 Ill.App.3d 199, 331 N.E.2d 643 (1975); Commonwealth v. Geraway, 364 Mass. 168, 301 N.E.2d 814 (1973).

5. See Weil v. Neary, 278 U.S. 160, 49 S.Ct. 144, 73 L.Ed. 243 (1929); City of Little Rock v. Cash, 277 Ark. 494, 644 S.W.2d 229 (1982), cert. denied — U.S. — 103 S.Ct. 2464, 77 L.Ed.2d 1341 (1983); Anderson v. Eaton, 211 Cal. 113, 293 P. 788 (1930); Hill v. Douglass, 271 So.2d 1 (Fla. 1973); Rice v. Perl, 320 N.W.2d 407 (Minn. 1982); In re Clarke's Estate, 12 N.Y.2d 183, 237 N.Y.S.2d 694, 188 N.E.2d 128 (1962).

6. See City of Hastings v. Jerry Spady Pontiac-Cadillac, Inc., 212 Neb. 137, 322 N.W.2d 369 (1982).

7. See Annot., 28 A.L.R.3d 389 (1969).

8. See generally Developments in the Law—Conflicts of Interest in the Legal Profession, 94 Harv.L.Rev. 1244, 1470–1503 (1981) (discussing relative merits of disqualification, malpractice liability, denial of fee, and discipline as sanctions).

9. See RPC 1.10(b), 1.11; DR 9-101(B). Compare RPC 1.8(b); DR 4–101(B) (2), (3).

sonably sufficient to permit the client to appreciate the significance of the matter in question.

**RULE 1.7 Conflict of Interest: General Rule**

* * *

(b) A lawyer shall not represent a client if the representation of that client may be materially limited * * * by the lawyer's own interests, unless:

(1) the lawyer reasonably believes the representation will not be adversely affected; and

(2) the client consents after consultation. * * *

**RULE 1.8 Conflict of Interest: Prohibited Transactions**

* * *

(i) A lawyer related to another lawyer as parent, child, sibling or spouse shall not represent a client in a representation directly adverse to a person who the lawyer knows is represented by the other lawyer except upon consent by the client after consultation regarding the relationship.

COMMENT:

* * * The disqualification stated in Rule 1.8(i) is personal and is not imputed to members of firms with whom the lawyers are associated.[a]

## BLUMENFELD v. BORENSTEIN

247 Ga. 406, 276 S.E.2d 607 (1981).

H: not enough to disqual.

CLARKE, Justice.

This appeal is from an order * * * disqualifying an attorney and his law firm from representation of the executrix of the estate of Simon Silbermintz * * *.

Simon Silbermintz died in May, 1977. His will, naming his sister Regina Borenstein as executrix, was submitted for probate in solemn form. The will was challenged by another sister, Fela Blumenfeld, who was represented by the firm of Gershon, Ruden, Pindar & Olim. The executrix was represented by the firm of [Meals & McLaughlin].

---

a. Compare the following CPR provisions:

"DEFINITIONS

"(1) 'Differing interests' include every interest that will adversely affect either the judgment or the loyalty of a lawyer to a client, whether it be a conflicting, inconsistent, diverse, or other interest."

**"DR 5-101 Refusing Employment When the Interests of the Lawyer May Impair His Independent Professional Judgment**

"(A) Except with the consent of his client after full disclosure, a lawyer shall not accept employment if the exercise of his professional judgment on behalf of his client will be or reasonably may be affected by his own financial, business, property, or personal interests."

**"DR 5-105 Refusing to Accept or Continue Employment if the Interests of Another Client May Impair the Independent Professional Judgment of the Lawyer**

* * *

"(D) If a lawyer is required to decline employment or to withdraw from employment under a Disciplinary Rule, no partner or associate, or any other lawyer affiliated with him or his firm may accept or continue such employment."

During an eight-day trial held in the Probate Court * * * a new associate in the law firm of Meals & McLaughlin, Kathie G. McClure, assisted Mr. Meals, lead counsel for the propounder. Following the trial in the probate court, the propounder appealed to the Superior Court * * * for a trial de novo. The caveator, Blumenfeld, associated the firm of Howard & Gilliland as local counsel to assist in the trial in the superior court. Kathie McClure is and was at the time of the probate trial married to Jay Y. McClure, a partner in the firm of Howard & Gilliland. Following the probate trial, and prior to the caveator's association of Howard & Gilliland, Ms. McClure left the firm of Meals & McLaughlin to become an Assistant United States Attorney for the Northern District of Georgia.

Following the association of Howard & Gilliland by the caveator, the propounder moved to disqualify Jay Y. McClure and the firm of Howard & Gilliland on the ground of conflict of interest and "the appearance of impropriety, in violation of Canons 4 and 9 of the Code of Professional Responsibility." A hearing was held * * * . [T]he [Superior Court] specifically found that the integrity of the law firm of Howard & Gilliland had not been questioned and that Ms. McClure at all times kept the confidences and secrets of her former client inviolate. The court found that Mr. McClure's practice was limited to real estate and corporate matters and that he had not participated in the handling of the will case, nor had other members of the firm discussed the case with him. Finally, the court found that there had been no impropriety committed by any of the parties in the matter. However, the court found that the marital relationship between the propounder's former counsel and the caveator's present co-counsel might tend to raise a question of impropriety in the minds of some laymen. Therefore, the court granted the motion to disqualify Jay Y. McClure and the firm of Howard & Gilliland on the basis of Canon 9 of the Code of Professional Responsibility: "A lawyer should avoid even the appearance of professional impropriety." We find that the court disqualified the law firm solely on the basis of Mr. McClure's marital status. We further find that per se disqualification based on marital status is neither mandated nor justified by the Code of Professional Responsibility. Having decided that disqualification of Mr. McClure would not have been justified under the circumstances of this case, we need not reach the question whether if disqualified he could have been so isolated as to obviate the necessity for disqualification of his law firm. * * *

Basic fairness will not permit the disqualification of an attorney because of wrongdoing imputed to the attorney by reason of his status when as a matter of fact no wrongdoing exists. More important, the right to counsel is an important interest which requires that any curtailment of the client's right to counsel of choice be approached with great caution. The mere fact that the public may perceive some conduct as improper is, without some actual impropriety, insufficient justification for interference with a client's right to counsel of choice.

This becomes even more apparent when the perceived impropriety is not conduct at all but is, instead, status. Absent a showing that special circumstances exist which prevent the adequate representation of the client, disqualification based solely on marital status is not justified.

A per se rule of disqualification on the sole ground that an attorney's spouse is a member of a firm representing an opposing party would be not only unfair to the lawyers so disqualified and to their clients but would also have a significant detrimental effect upon the legal profession.[4] Such a rule could be expected to affect the hiring practices of law firms and the professional opportunities of lawyers. A per se rule would effectively create a category of legal "Typhoid Marys," chilling both professional opportunities and personal choices.

[A]ppellee argues that the marital relationship is substantially different from any other type relationship and that because of its confidential nature the parties are liable to share even professional secrets. While we cannot disagree with the proposition that the marital relationship may be the most intimate relationship of a person's life, it does not follow that professional people allow this intimacy to interfere with professional obligations. If this court endorsed a rule imputing professional wrongdoing to an attorney on the basis of marital status alone, it would be difficult to avoid the extension of that rule to other relationships as well.

Appellees have not shown us a case where a per se rule was applied to disqualify an attorney on the basis of an appearance of impropriety alone. * * * In the instant case, the trial court specifically found that Ms. McClure kept the secrets of her client inviolate. Consequently, there was no violation of Canon 4. Canon 5 requires the preservation of independent judgment and deals primarily with the representation of multiple clients by a single attorney. This circumstance is not in question here.

It is perhaps helpful to view the issue of attorney disqualification as a continuum. At one end of the scale where disqualification is always justified and indeed mandated, even when balanced against a client's right to an attorney of choice, is the appearance of impropriety coupled with a conflict of interest or jeopardy to a client's confidences. In these instances, it is clear that the disqualification is necessary for the protection of the client. Somewhere in the middle of the continuum is the appearance of impropriety based on conduct on the part of the attorney. [T]his generally has been found insufficient to outweigh the client's interest in counsel of choice. This is probably so because absent danger to the client, the nebulous interest of the public at large in the propriety of the Bar is not weighty enough to justify disqualification. Finally, at the opposite end of the continuum is the ap-

4. According to the amicus curiae brief filed by the Atlanta Bar Association, Inc., at least 45 law firms and over 1,000 attorneys in the Atlanta area would be affected by a per se disqualification rule based on marital status.

pearance of impropriety based not on conduct but on status alone. This is an insufficient ground for disqualification. This is particularly clear in this case in light of the trial court's specific finding that there was no actual impropriety on the part of any of the parties.

It has been suggested that the trial court's order of disqualification should not be disturbed on appeal absent an abuse of discretion. The trial court's finding of fact was that there was no actual impropriety. We do not disturb this finding. The disqualification is in the nature of a conclusion of law rather than a finding of fact. United States v. Miller, 624 F.2d 1198 (3rd Cir. 1980). This conclusion, based as it is solely on an appearance of impropriety due to status, cannot stand.

Having decided that disqualification based on marital status alone was improper in this case, Mr. McClure should not have been disqualified. This being so, we need not reach the question whether his law firm's disqualification on the basis of some vicarious taint was error. * * *

Judgment reversed.

HILL, Presiding Justice, concurring.

I join the majority opinion. I write separately only to point out that there is nothing said by the majority to indicate that the burden of proving that a client's confidential communication has been transmitted from one attorney spouse to the other is upon the party moving for disqualification. The record before us shows that the spouses here discussed the case but that no confidences or secrets were discussed. In my view, it would be an intolerable burden, a burden possibly requiring disclosure of the confidential communication itself, to require the movant to prove not only that one attorney spouse discussed the case with the other but also transmitted the client's confidential communications to the other. Because the majority opinion does not place such burden on the movant, I concur in it.[a]

## 2. TRANSACTION WITH CLIENT

### MODEL RULES OF PROFESSIONAL CONDUCT

**RULE 1.8 Conflict of Interest: Prohibited Transactions**

(a) A lawyer shall not enter into a business transaction with a client or knowingly acquire an ownership, possessory, security or other pecuniary interest adverse to a client unless:

(1) the transaction and terms on which the lawyer acquires the interest are fair and reasonable to the client and are fully disclosed and

a. See ABA Formal Opinion 340 (1975); Recent Development, Ethical Issues Facing Lawyer-Spouses and Their Employers, 34 Vand.L.Rev.1435 (1981); Note, Legal Ethics—Representation of Differing Interests by Husband and Wife: Appearances of Impropriety and Unavoidable Conflicts of Interest? 52 Denver L.J. 735 (1975); Comment, Ethical Concerns of Lawyers Who Are Related by Kinship or Marriage, 60 Or.L.Rev. 399 (1981).

transmitted in writing to the client in a manner which can be reasonably understood by the client;

(2) the client is given a reasonable opportunity to seek the advice of independent counsel in the transaction; and

(3) the client consents in writing thereto.

(b) A lawyer shall not use information relating to representation of a client to the disadvantage of the client unless the client consents after consultation.

(c) A lawyer shall not prepare an instrument giving the lawyer or a person related to the lawyer as parent, child, sibling, or spouse any substantial gift from a client, including a testamentary gift, except where the client is related to the donee.

(d) Prior to the conclusion of representation of a client, a lawyer shall not make or negotiate an agreement giving the lawyer literary or media rights to a portrayal or account based in substantial part on information relating to the representation.[a]

## IN RE MONTGOMERY

292 Or. 796, 643 P.2d 338 (1982).

PER CURIAM.

This is an attorney discipline case involving a loan from the client to the lawyer. We find that the accused lawyer, Kenneth M. Montgomery, violated DR 5–104(A), and we impose a public reprimand.

a. Compare the following CPR provisions:

**"DR 4–101 Preservation of Confidences and Secrets of a Client**

* * *

"(B) Except when permitted under DR 4–101(C), a lawyer shall not knowingly:

* * *

(2) Use a confidence or secret of his client to the disadvantage of the client.

(3) Use a confidence or secret of his client for the advantage of himself or of a third person, unless the client consents after full disclosure."

**"EC 5–5** A lawyer should not suggest to his client that a gift be made to himself or for his benefit. If a lawyer accepts a gift from his client, he is peculiarly susceptible to the charge that he unduly influenced or over-reached the client. If a client voluntarily offers to make a gift to his lawyer, the lawyer may accept the gift, but before doing so, he should urge that his client secure disinterested advice from an independent, competent person who is cognizant of all the circumstances. Other than in exceptional circumstances, a lawyer should insist that an instrument in which his client desires to name him beneficially be prepared by another lawyer selected by the client."

**"DR 5–101 Refusing Employment When the Interests of the Lawyer May Impair His Independent Professional Judgment**

"(A) Except with the consent of his client after full disclosure, a lawyer shall not accept employment if the exercise of his professional judgment on behalf of his client will be or reasonably may be affected by his own financial, business, property, or personal interests."

**"DR 5–104 Limiting Business Relations With a Client**

"(A) A lawyer shall not enter into a business transaction with a client if they have differing interests therein and if the client expects the lawyer to exercise his professional judgment therein for the protection of the client, unless the client has consented after full disclosure.

"(B) Prior to conclusion of all aspects of the matter giving rise to his employment,

Montgomery practices law in Portland. MacLellan and Farnham were two of the three principal owners of a corporation, BLT Enterprises, Inc. Montgomery represented BLT on an ongoing basis. He also represented MacLellan and Farnham on some personal matters and was personally involved in other business ventures with MacLellan. The third principal in BLT was a man named Thompson, who was inactive in the management of BLT. Both MacLellan and Farnham were highly competent in their fields. MacLellan handled the business and financial end of the corporation, and Farnman was largely responsible for the other operations of the company.

Prior to 1979, Montgomery made an unsuccessful investment and he needed cash. From previous discussions MacLellan was aware that Montgomery needed cash. Montgomery testified that after he was turned down by a bank he asked MacLellan whether BLT would be interested in lending him $20,000 for 45 days at a 20 percent annual interest rate, a then usurious rate of interest. Montgomery knew that the rate was usurious. MacLellan did not.

Montgomery testified that he knew that if usury were asserted as a defense the interest would be uncollectible and the principal forfeited to the common school fund. He also understood the risks of making an unsecured loan. None of these facts were disclosed to MacLellan or to BLT prior to the time that the loan was made.

MacLellan was highly sophisticated in business and financial matters and routinely handled large financial transactions without consulting Farnham or Thompson. However, in view of the unique nature of this loan, he consulted with Farnham and obtained Farnham's approval before lending the money to Montgomery.

Montgomery prepared and delivered a handwritten note. * * * The note was not paid within the 45 days. Thereafter, the principals in BLT had a falling out, separate counsel were obtained, and the matter was reported to the Oregon State Bar.[2] A complaint was filed charging that Montgomery violated DR 5–104(A), which provides (the Arabic numbers are ours, and do not appear in the disciplinary rule itself):

> "A lawyer shall not [1] enter into a business transaction with a client if [2] they have differing interests therein and if [3] the client expects the lawyer to exercise his professional judgment therein

a lawyer shall not enter into any arrangement or understanding with a client or a prospective client by which he acquires an interest in publication rights with respect to the subject matter of his employment or proposed employment."

See also ABA Standards for Criminal Justice 4–3.4 (2d ed. 1980) (substantially identical to DR 5–104(B) ).

2. As required by DR 1–103(A), the matter was reported to the Bar by the lawyers who subsequently represented the principals in BLT. DR 1–103(A) provides:

> "A lawyer possessing unprivileged knowledge of a violation of DR 1–102 shall report such knowledge to a tribunal or other authority empowered to investigate or act upon such violation."

[Eds.] Compare RPC 8.3.

for the protection of the client, unless [4] the client has consented after full disclosure."

* * * Montgomery concedes that the requirements of clauses (1) and (2) of DR 5–104 have been met. The determinative question is whether a violation of the third clause has been made out, that is, whether there is clear and convincing evidence that the client expected the lawyer " * * * to exercise his professional judgment therein for the protection of the client * * *."

Prior to this transaction, BLT had loaned money to its employees at low rates of interest. There is no question that BLT, MacLellan and Farnham viewed this loan simply as a business loan and that BLT was aware of Montgomery's somewhat precarious financial situation. In that sense, we agree * * * that BLT was not relying upon Montgomery for any advice regarding the creditworthiness of the borrower. Even so, we are convinced that the lender was relying upon Montgomery's exercise of professional judgment, at least to the extent that (a) the loan was valid and legally enforceable, and (b) that the documents prepared by him were in proper form and evidenced a legally enforceable obligation.

MacLellan was a sophisticated businessman with " * * * far greater business experience and knowledge than [Montgomery]." And true, MacLellan testified that he " * * * would not have gotten another attorney involved in a minor transaction like that." But that analysis is incomplete.

MacLellan testified:

"Q BY MR. CROW: If Ken had said to you at the time he requested the loan or at any time prior to making the loan, that you should seek the advice of another attorney, what would your reaction have been? What would you have done?

"A If the same thing were repeated tomorrow or today, *I would have probably asked him why. Why would I need an attorney for this transaction? And based on what the response would be,* based on the track record before and after that particular transaction, I wouldn't have gotten another attorney for a $20,000 note." (Emphasis added.)

When a lawyer regularly represents a financial institution such as a bank, savings and loan association or finance company, and applies for a loan of a type which the client makes in the normal course of business, it may be that the lawyer need not advise the client to seek independent legal counsel or otherwise advise the client in the transaction. * * * It is clear that there is no expectation that the lawyer will "exercise his professional judgment for the protection of the client" because the client is already fully informed.

But that is not the situation here. * * * The key is found in the response quoted above, " * * * *I would have asked him why* [I should consult another lawyer]," which confirms the unspoken but existing belief on the client's part that the transaction was what the client believed it to be—a loan at a favorable rate of interest which was legally enforceable.

When a lawyer borrows money from a non-lawyer client who is not in the business of lending money, the lawyer should assume that the client is relying on the lawyer for the legal aspects of the transaction to the same extent that the client would rely on the lawyer for advice were the client making the loan to a third person, unless the opposite is expressly stated.

It would not occur to a trusting client that the lawyer would advise the client to enter into an unlawful contract. Thus, had BLT consulted Montgomery about a loan to a third person, although advice as to the creditworthiness of the third person would likely not be expected, advice as to the legal effect of the usurious rate of interest would likely have been given. In addition, a competent lawyer might have recommended that security be given by the borrower.

In many situations the client would not be dealing with the lawyer but for the client's trust and confidence in the lawyer born of past associations. This trust is indispensable in some lawyer-client relationships. Requiring the lawyer-borrower to assume that the client is relying on the lawyer as to the legal aspects of the transaction is consistent with the realities of the situation, and perhaps more importantly, will tend to maintain a healthy, aboveboard relationship between the lawyer and the client with maximum protection to the client.

* * * We are convinced that had Montgomery advised [MacLellan] of the consequences of usury, or had MacLellan sought outside legal advice, the loan in this form would not have been made. We find that the requirements of the third clause have been met.

Although we are convinced that Montgomery would not have asserted a usury defense, that is beside the point, for as we observed in In re Drake, 292 Or. 704, 642 P.2d 296 (1982), which also involved a loan at a usurious interest rate:

> "Although Drake testified that he felt morally bound, had he died or become incompetent his personal representative or conservator might successfully have avoided the payment of any interest by asserting that the interest rate was usurious, and Gallagher would have been unable to recover either the principal or a legal rate of interest. * * * "

If the situation described in clauses (1), (2) and (3) of DR 5–104(A) is shown to exist, then the business transaction cannot be concluded " * * * unless the client has consented after full disclosure." One way for consent to be obtained is by having the client obtain outside counsel * * * . If the advice to seek outside counsel has not been given, or though given has not been taken, then the lawyer must make "full disclosure." In this case, full disclosure would require the type of advice which a prudent lawyer would be expected to give the client if the client consulted the lawyer regarding such a loan to a third person. * * *

Montgomery has violated DR 5-104(A) and [is] publicly reprimanded. * * *

### *Comment*

(1) *Discipline—transaction with client.* In other cases, lawyers have been held subject to discipline for borrowing a substantial sum from a client without insisting upon the client getting independent counsel,[1] for improperly purchasing property from a client,[2] for improperly accepting large gifts of money from an elderly client,[3] for exercising control over property bought by the lawyer's spouse at an execution sale regarding which the lawyer represented the judgment creditor,[4] or for obtaining an interest adverse to the client even with the client's consent.[5] It has been asserted that "The twin desires to protect the legal profession from undesirable publicity and to ensure fair representation of client interests have resulted in strict regulation of a lawyer's business dealings with clients."[6]

(2) *Discipline—drawing will naming lawyer.* A number of courts have disciplined lawyers for drawing a will leaving the lawyer a gift.[7] One court explained:

> "Among the reasons for including such action, absent exempting circumstances, within the definitions of unprofessional conduct sub-

1. See In re Darrow, 39 A.D.2d 62, 331 N.Y.S.2d 533 (1972).

2. See In re Temrowski, 409 Mich. 262, 293 N.W.2d 346 (1980); Annot., 35 A.L.R.3d 674 (1971). See also State v. Hartman, 54 Wis.2d 47, 194 N.W.2d 653 (1972) (lawyer acting as executor and attorney for estate selling estate property to lawyer's spouse).

3. See In re Schuyler, 91 Ill.2d 6, 61 Ill.Dec. 540, 434 N.E.2d 1137 (1982) (lawyer did not carry burden of rebutting presumption of undue influence arising from receipt of client's gifts of almost $10,000).

4. See Marlowe v. State Bar, 63 Cal.2d 304, 46 Cal.Rptr. 326, 405 P.2d 150 (1965).

5. See Ames v. State Bar, 8 Cal.3d 910, 106 Cal.Rptr. 489, 506 P.2d 625 (1973), construing the California Business and Professions Code to prohibit this. The client had a second mortgage on real estate securing the purchase price of a sale which the client asked the lawyer to get rescinded. The first mortgage holder proceeded to foreclose his mortgage. The client, being unable to pay off the first mortgage, entered into an agreement with his lawyer whereby the lawyer would purchase the first mortgage interest and then permit the client later to repay the lawyer. This was held to create an impermissible adverse interest in the lawyer.

6. Developments in the Law—Conflicts of Interest in the Legal Profession, 94 Harv.L.Rev. 1244, 1287 (1981).

7. See In re Vogel, 92 Ill.2d 55, 65 Ill.Dec. 30, 440 N.E.2d 885 (1982) (censure for violating DR 5-101(A) ); Committee on Professional Ethics & Conduct v. Behnke, 276 N.W.2d 838 (Iowa) (suspension for violating EC 5-5), appeal dismissed 444 U.S. 805, 100 S.Ct. 27, 62 L.Ed.2d 19 (1979); In re Jones, 254 Or. 617, 462 P.2d 680 (1969); State v. Collentine, 39 Wis.2d 325, 159 N.W.2d 50 (1968); Annot., 98 A.L.R.2d 1234 (1964). See also In re Gallop, 85 N.J. 317, 426 A.2d 509 (1981) (drawing trust in which lawyer received share to compensate for past legal services and loans); State v. Gulbankian, 54 Wis.2d 599, 196 N.W.2d 730 (1972) (bequest to lawyer's sister).

Courts have held that this impropriety is not cured by having the will drawn by a lawyer with whom one shares office space, see People v. Berge, 620 P.2d 23 (Colo. 1980), or by a lawyer who functioned merely as a scrivener rather than an independent attorney, State v. Beaudry, 53 Wis.2d 148, 191 N.W.2d 842 (1971), cert. denied 407 U.S. 912, 92 S.Ct. 2441, 32 L.Ed.2d 686 (1972).

However, in other cases, arising under the CPR, courts have refused to discipline lawyers for drawing a will under which the lawyer received a gift. See In re Barrick, 87 Ill.2d 233, 57 Ill.Dec. 725, 429 N.E.2d 842 (1981) (conduct complied with DR 5-101(A)); In re Tonkon, 292 Or. 660, 642 P.2d 660 (1982) (EC violation not basis for discipline). Compare In re Amundson, 297 N.W.2d 433 (N.D. 1980) (conduct committed before CPR adopted).

jecting the doer to disciplinary action are that it may well involve a disservice to the client for it involves the attorney in a conflict of interests, may affect his competency to testify, jeopardizes the will if a contest ensues, thus harming other beneficiaries and possibly nullifying the testator's intended distribution of his estate, and diminishes confidence in the integrity of the legal profession." [8]

### GOLDMAN v. KANE

3 Mass.App.Ct. 336, 329 N.E.2d 770 (1975).

HALE, Chief Justice. The defendants, Barry Kane and Higley Hill, Inc., appeal from a judgment of a Probate Court ordering them to pay $50,806, plus interest, to the plaintiff Goldman, as the executor of the estate of Lawrence E. Hill.[1] * * *

Lawrence Hill, a fifty-three year old law school graduate, and his wife moved to Cape Cod in October, 1967. At that time Hill was the income beneficiary of two trusts. He received weekly income from one trust of about $200, and from the other he received approximately $30,000 a year, which was divided into two semi-annual payments. In 1968 Hill was introduced to Barry Kane, a practicing attorney with offices in Chatham and Yarmouth, after Hill had decided to purchase a parcel of real estate in Chatham (Kent Road property). As Hill's attorney, Kane set up a corporation, Lawrence Properties, Inc. (the other plaintiff in this suit and of which Hill owned all the outstanding shares), drew up a purchase and sale agreement for the Kent Road property whereby title to the parcel was to be taken by Lawrence Properties, Inc., and arranged for and obtained a mortgage loan on Hill's behalf. Between 1968 and 1970 Kane acted as Hill's attorney on a number of matters, including matters arising from the death of Hill's wife. During that period he received fees for legal services performed by him. It also appears that at various times throughout their relationship Hill paid money to Kane, who in turn paid Hill's bills.

In October, 1970, Hill decided to "change his lifestyle and live aboard a boat," whereupon he left for Florida in the "Alas II," a twenty-two foot sloop which he owned. At about this time, Hill decided that he needed a larger vessel. While he was in the process of looking for an appropriate vessel to buy, Hill continuously sought advice from Kane both by telephone and letter. On April 17, 1971, Hill signed an agreement to purchase a forty-three foot ketch called the "Sea Chase" for $31,500, towards which he paid a deposit of $3,150, agreeing to pay the balance on or before May 17, 1971. Prior to Hill's signing the agreement Kane advised him on matters such as negotiations for the transfer of the "Sea Chase," the registration thereof, and technical nautical requirements of the vessel. Hill also asked Kane to arrange for the

8. In re Vogel, 92 Ill.2d 55, 65 Ill.Dec. 30, 440 N.E.2d 885 (1982).

1. Hill (who initiated this suit) died on January 14, 1974, and the executor of his estate was substituted.

financing of the balance of $28,350 which would have to be paid by May 17.

In early May, 1971, Kane informed Hill that he was unable to arrange a loan with a bank, whereupon Hill instructed Kane to sell the Kent Road property. That property was put on the market at an offering price of $85,000, but Kane was unable to effect a sale. On May 30, Hill telephoned Kane on two or three occasions and told him he was in dire need of the money because he stood to lose the $3,150 deposit if he should be unable to raise the balance of the purchase price of the "Sea Chase" by the next day. In one of those conversations Kane told Hill that "it was virtually impossible" to get a loan in view of Hill's financial predicament and in view of the time limitation. In a subsequent conversation Kane told Hill that Kane's corporation[2] would loan him $30,000 but that, in consideration of making the loan, Hill would have to convey to the corporation absolute title to (1) the Kent Road property, (2) all of the personal property located therein, and (3) the "Alas II." In addition, Hill and Lawrence Properties, Inc. would have to execute a note to Kane's corporation for the repayment of the $30,000, and to secure the performance of the note, Hill would have to convey to Kane's corporation title to the "Sea Chase," which would be reconveyed upon full repayment of the note. After Hill agreed to the terms of the loan, Kane obtained the $30,000, prepared some of the necessary documents, and left for Florida, arriving there shortly after midnight on June 2. During that day he advised Hill not to enter into the agreement and to "walk away" from his deposit (see n. 3). However, Hill insisted on going forward, and the transaction was consummated on June 2, when Hill signed the following documents prepared by Kane: (1) a quit-claim deed transferring the title of the Kent Road property from Lawrence Properties, Inc. to Kane's corporation, subject to two outstanding mortgages; (2) a bill of sale transferring the "Alas II" from Hill to Kane's corporation; (3) a bill of sale transferring all of the personal property located in the Kent Road property from Lawrence Properties, Inc. to Kane's corporation; and (4) a non-interest bearing note for $30,000 requiring payment in two installments of $15,000 each on September 15, 1971, and March 1, 1972. Hill also signed an agreement, prepared by Kane, which recited the terms of the loan and which indicated that Hill was aware of the drawbacks of the agreement and that Kane had advised him against entering into it.[3] Shortly thereafter, by arrangement of the parties, title to the "Sea Chase" was taken in the name of Kane's corporation.

2. Kane's corporation is the defendant, Higley Hill, Inc., of which Kane owned ninety-five per cent of the outstanding stock.

3. The agreement stated in part: "I fully understand that Barry Kane, Esq., my attorney, is a major stockholder of Higley Hill, Inc., the transferee named herein. As my attorney, he has strongly advised me that this transfer is adverse to my financial welfare and has recommended that I not make said transfer. My only expectations from this said transfer are that I shall receive legal title to the aforesaid Bluenose ketch upon having completed repayment of the $30,000 loan to Higley Hill, Inc., in accordance with the terms of the note."

In July, 1971, Kane's corporation sold the Kent Road property with furnishings for $86,000. In September, 1971, Hill defaulted on the first payment of the $30,000 note, whereupon Kane, without notice to Hill, took possession of the "Sea Chase."

The judge concluded that at the time of the transaction the relationship of attorney and client existed between Kane and Hill and that Kane breached his fiduciary obligations to Hill by taking unfair advantage of that relationship. As a result the judge ordered that the defendants pay to Hill's executor $50,806, plus interest.[4]

The defendants contend that the judge erred in concluding that an attorney-client relationship existed between Kane and Hill at the time of the transaction. This contention is without merit * * *.

The defendants argue that even if an attorney-client relationship existed the record does not support the conclusion that there was a breach of that relationship. We disagree. The relationship of attorney and client is highly fiduciary in nature. * * *

The law looks with great disfavor upon an attorney who has business dealings with his client which result in gains to the attorney at the expense of the client. "The attorney is not permitted by the law to take any advantage of his client. The principles holding the attorney to a conspicuous degree of faithfulness and forbidding him to take personal advantage of his client are thoroughly established." Berman v. Coakley, [243 Mass. 348,] 355, 137 N.E. [667,] 671 [1923]. When an attorney bargains with his client in a business transaction in a manner which is advantageous to himself, and if that transaction is later called into question, the court will subject it to close scrutiny. In such a case, the attorney has the burden of showing that the transaction "was in all respects fairly and equitably conducted; that he fully and faithfully discharged all his duties to his client, not only by refraining from any misrepresentation or concealment of any material fact, but by active diligence to see that his client was fully informed of the nature and effect of the transaction proposed and of his own rights and interests in the subject matter involved, and by seeing to it that his client either has independent advice in the matter or else receives from the attorney such advice as the latter would have been expected to give had the transaction been one between his client and a stranger." Hill v. Hall, 191 Mass. 253, 262, 77 N.E. 831, 835 (1906).

Applying these principles to the case at bar, it is clear that the judge was correct in concluding that Kane, by entering into the transaction, breached his fiduciary duty to Hill. While the defendants con-

4. This figure was apparently reached as a result of the judge's findings that the values of the assets transferred from Hill to Kane or his corporation in consideration for the making of the loan were as follows: 1. Hill's equity in the Kent Road property—$42,000; 2. The "Alas II"—$7,000; 3. Furniture from the Kent Road property which was retained by Kane—$1,000. The $806 concerned a different matter which is not argued by the parties. The judge found that the fair market value of "Sea Chase" was $30,000 (which amount was offset by the loan) and that any additional money paid by Hill was offset by reason of his use and enjoyment of the vessel.

tend that Kane's conduct did not constitute a breach of his fiduciary duty because Hill fully understood the nature and effect of the transaction and because Kane advised Hill against it,[5] in the circumstances of this case, Kane's full disclosure and his advice were not sufficient to immunize him from liability. The fundamental unfairness of the transaction and the egregious overreaching by Kane in his dealings with Hill are self-evident. In light of the nature of the transaction, Kane, at a bare minimum, was under a duty not to proceed with the loan until he was satisfied that Hill had obtained independent advice on the matter. The purpose of such requirement is to be certain that in a situation where an attorney deals with a client in a business relationship to the attorney's advantage, the "presumed influence resulting from the relationship has been neutralized." Israel v. Sommer, 292 Mass. [113,] 123, 197 N.E. [442,] 447 [1935]. * * *

Judgment affirmed.

### *Comment*

(1) *Civil consequences—lawyer-client transaction.* In civil suits regarding lawyer-client transactions, most courts put the burden on the lawyer to prove the transaction was fair, conscionable, and free of overreaching. This approach has been applied to sales,[1] loans,[2] gifts,[3] bequests or devises to lawyers who drew the wills,[4] and fee agreements made after commencement of representation.[5] But several courts have held that this approach does not apply if the lawyer's employment was not related to the subject matter of the lawyer-client transaction.[6]

(2) *Civil consequences—purchase at judicial sale.* If a lawyer purchases property at a judicial sale with respect to which the lawyer represents a client, it has been held that the client may recover the property purchased and that the lawyer is liable for any profits resulting from the purchase, the lawyer being deemed a "constructive trustee."[7]

5. It is important to note that after Hill agreed to the loan arrangement on the telephone and prior to any negative advice given by Kane, Kane prepared some of the documents necessary to consummate the agreement. Two days later Kane went to Florida where he advised Hill not to go through with the loan. However, this advice was given only a short time before the transaction was consummated.

1. See Toner v. Hubbard, 105 So.2d 180 (Fla.1958); McFail v. Braden, 19 Ill.2d 108, 166 N.E.2d 46 (1960); Anderson v. Wolfe, 368 P.2d 655 (Okl.1962).

2. See Gerlach v. Donnelly, 98 So.2d 493 (Fla.1957).

3. See Annot., 24 A.L.R.2d 1288 (1952).



4. See Annot., 19 A.L.R.3d 575, 589–90 (1968).

5. See infra p. 447.

6. See Palmer v. Arnett, 352 Mich. 22, 88 N.W.2d 445 (1958); Smoot v. Lund, 13 Utah 2d 168, 369 P.2d 933 (1962).

But see Flanagan v. DeLapp, 533 S.W.2d 592 (Mo.1976) (deed of property owned by person lawyer represented only in person's capacity as guardian for another).

7. See In re Bond & Mortgage Guarantee Co., 303 N.Y. 423, 103 N.E.2d 721 (1952); Western Flour Co. v. Alosi, 216 Pa.Super. 341, 264 A.2d 413 (1970); Annot., 20 A.L.R.2d 1280 (1951).

(3) *Civil consequences—purchase from third person.* A lawyer may be held similarly liable to the client for acquiring from a third person an interest in property which it was the lawyer's duty to acquire or protect for the client.[8] But it has been held that the fact that a lawyer was previously consulted about certain property does not preclude the lawyer from purchasing it later if the client has indicated no further interest in the property and the purchase is not inconsistent with any obligation owed to the client during or arising out of the consultation.[9]

(4) *Effect of literary rights agreement.* In Ray v. Rose,[10] the Sixth Circuit held that defendant, convicted of murdering Dr. Martin Luther King, was entitled to an evidentiary hearing on his habeas corpus allegation that because of his lawyer's interest in defendant's publication rights, the lawyer did not represent him effectively and intimidated and coerced him into pleading guilty.[11] Similarly, in United States v. Hearst,[12] the Ninth Circuit held that defendant was entitled to a hearing on her allegations that her counsel, F. Lee Bailey, preferred his interest in publication to her interest in acquittal by (a) failing to seek a continuance so public interest would not flag and competing authors would not get the jump on him, (b) failing to seek a change of venue so publicity would be maximized by a trial in San Francisco, and (c) putting defendant on the stand so that her story would go on the public record, freeing him from attorney-client privilege problems.

In People v. Corona,[13] a California court reversed defendant's conviction upon a showing that counsel's literary rights had caused him to avoid defenses based on defendant's mental condition where those defenses clearly would have been in defendant's best interests.[14]

However, in Maxwell v. Superior Court,[15] the Supreme Court of California, (where no flat prohibition like that in RPC 1.8(d) and DR 5–104(B) was adopted) held that it violated due process to disqualify a criminal defendant's chosen counsel merely because counsel had obtained literary rights where defendant wanted that counsel after being advised in detail of the potential conflicts.[16] Justice Richardson dis-

8. Gaffney v. Harmon, 405 Ill. 273, 90 N.E.2d 785, 20 A.L.R.2d 1273 (1950). Compare Nadler v. Treptow, 166 N.W.2d 103 (Iowa 1969).

9. Tuab Mineral Corp. v. Anderson, 3 Ariz.App. 512, 415 P.2d 910 (1966); Day v. Cowart, 212 Miss. 280, 54, So.2d 385 (1951); Kauder v. Lautman, 114 N.J.Eq. 197, 168 A. 660 (1933), affirmed, 116 N.J.Eq. 145, 172 A. 565 (1934).

10. 491 F.2d 285 (6th Cir.), cert. denied 417 U.S. 936, 94 S.Ct. 2650, 41 L.Ed.2d 240 (1974).

11. After the evidentiary hearing, the allegations in *Ray* were found to be unsubstantiated. See Ray v. Rose, 535 F.2d 966 (6th Cir.), cert. denied 429 U.S. 1026, 97 S.Ct. 648, 50 L.Ed.2d 629 (1976).

12. 638 F.2d 1190 (9th Cir. 1980), cert. denied 451 U.S. 938, 101 S.Ct. 2018, 68 L.Ed.2d 325 (1981).

13. 80 Cal.App.3d 684, 145 Cal.Rptr. 894 (1978).

14. Regarding the approach that Corona's defense counsel *did* adopt, see infra pp. 410–12.

15. 30 Cal.3d 606, 180 Cal.Rptr. 177, 639 P.2d 248, 18 A.L.R.4th 333 (1982).

16. Chief Justice Bird, concurring and dissenting, agreed that the lawyer's acquisition of literary rights did not inevitably require disqualification, but did not think the record showed adequate informing of the defendant regarding the potential conflicts.

sented, feeling that the literary rights agreement created unconsentable conflicts.

**IN RE RYAN**

66 N.J. 147, 329 A.2d 553 (1974).

PER CURIAM. This is a disciplinary case. Respondent, a member of the bar of this State, was retained by Edward C. Clarke, a New York attorney representing a decedent's estate, to handle the details of the sale of a five-acre tract of vacant land in Atlantic County, New Jersey, owned by the estate. A $2500 offer for the land had been submitted by J. Fred Ellis, Jr., an adjoining property owner, which offer was acceptable to Clarke and the executrix of the estate. Accordingly, on June 29, 1970, Clarke wrote to respondent asking him to prepare a contract of sale to Ellis for $2500, forward it to Ellis for his signature and obtain a downpayment from him. The same day that respondent received the letter he got a telephone call from Ellis, who had obtained respondent's name from the Clarke office, saying he was ready to sign a contract "right now." Respondent told Ellis that his secretary was going on vacation for the next few weeks and that respondent would "get to this after she returns." About a week later, respondent telephoned Clarke and "indicated that it was a sort of a low price on the property and that he'd like to take a look at it and see what it was like." Clarke assented, and a few days later respondent drove to Atlantic County and inspected the property. He liked the property, "thought it was beautiful," and got in touch with Clarke who said he had no objection to respondent making a personal offer for the property, whereupon respondent submitted a bid of $3000. Clarke took the matter up with the executrix who was told that the new offer had been made by the New Jersey attorney who had been engaged to represent the estate. According to Clarke, she had no objection to respondent purchasing the property himself and was satisfied with the higher offer. Respondent immediately prepared and caused to be executed a contract of sale naming his wife as the purchaser. In February 1971, after certain title matters had been cleared, the property was conveyed to Mrs. Ryan for a purchase price of $3000.

In the meantime, in early August 1970, Ellis, having heard nothing from respondent, wrote to him about the contract. Respondent did not answer Ellis' letter. Ellis next telephoned respondent, also in early August 1970, and was told by respondent that the property had been sold for a higher price. Ellis then called Clarke who verified the information and told Ellis that "he understood the sale was final."

Neither respondent nor Clarke told Ellis that respondent was the purchaser, nor was Ellis afforded the opportunity to submit a higher offer. Ellis did not find out until a year later that respondent had purchased the property in his wife's name for $3000. Respondent sold the property on April 17, 1973 for $10,000.

Ellis filed a complaint with the Union County Ethics Committee which, after a full hearing, concluded that, since there was no attorney-client relationship between respondent and Ellis, and since full disclosure had been made to the executrix of the estate, respondent had not violated any of the canons of ethics. * * *

Ellis wrote to the Administrative Director of the Courts expressing his dissatisfaction with the foregoing decision. The matter was referred to the Central Ethics Unit of the Administrative Office of the Courts which, after investigation, filed a petition with this Court charging respondent with unethical conduct. * * *

We conclude that respondent's conduct in this matter fell far short of the high standards expected of him. While there was no attorney-client relationship between respondent and Ellis, Ellis was dealing with respondent as an attorney who, he understood, was going to prepare a contract of sale. He was not informed that respondent had stepped out of his attorney status and had become personally interested in purchasing the property for himself. Under basic concepts of fair dealing, respondent should have informed Ellis of his changed status and higher bid so that Ellis would at least have had the opportunity to make an informed decision as to what he might do in the circumstances. Granted the executrix ordinarily would be free to sell to whomever she chose respondent still should have made a full disclosure to Ellis instead of letting Ellis assume that respondent was only the attorney representing the estate. In these circumstances the concealment from Ellis amounted to misrepresentation. As was stated in In re Boyle, 18 N.J. 415, 416, 113 A.2d 818 (1955):

> "Because of the education and training of members of the legal profession and the opportunities inherent in their practice, they very clearly have a duty and a challenge to exert a wholesome influence by fostering high ideals."

An attorney does not discard his professional standing and obligation to maintain a high standard of conduct when he engages in a business transaction. In In re Carlsen, 17 N.J. 338, 346, 111 A.2d 393, 397 (1955) we said:

> " * * * In In re Genser, 15 N.J. 600, 606, 105 A.2d 829, 832 (1954), this court expressly recognized that an attorney who wishes to be a business man must act in his business transactions with high standards and that his professional obligation reaches all persons who have reason to rely on him even though 'not strictly clients.' And in In re Howell, 10 N.J. 139, 140, 141, 89 A.2d 652 (1952), we approved the doctrine that conduct by an attorney which engenders disrespect for the law calls for disciplinary action even in the total absence of the attorney-client relationship."

* * * This principle is essentially embodied in our DR 1–102(A) (4) (5) (6).[a]

**a.** DR 1–102(A) provides that a lawyer shall not:

"(4) Engage in conduct involving dishonesty, fraud, deceit, or misrepresentation.

"(5) Engage in conduct that is prejudicial

In Marco v. Dulles, 169 F.Supp. 622, 631 (S.D.N.Y.1959) it is stated that a lawyer is:

> "* * * held to the same 'highest standards of ethical and moral uprightness and fair dealing' when acting as a businessman or when acting as a lawyer and is subject to disciplinary action if he fails to maintain those standards in either capacity."

It cannot be doubted that Ellis' experience with respondent, whom he dealt with as an attorney, has resulted in a feeling on his part of frustration, and disillusionment with the trustworthiness of lawyers.

Respondent's conduct was ethically remiss in the particulars heretofore indicated and merits censure. He is hereby reprimanded for such conduct with the admonition that any future transgression of a similar nature on his part will be dealt with more severely.

## 3. INTEREST IN LITIGATION

### MODEL RULES OF PROFESSIONAL CONDUCT

**RULE 1.8 Conflict of Interest: Prohibited Transactions**

* * *

(e) A lawyer shall not provide financial assistance to a client in connection with pending or contemplated litigation, except that:

(1) a lawyer may advance court costs and expenses of litigation, the repayment of which may be contingent on the outcome of the matter; and

(2) a lawyer representing an indigent client may pay court costs and expenses of litigation on behalf of the client.

* * *

(j) A lawyer shall not acquire a proprietary interest in the cause of action or subject matter of litigation the lawyer is conducting for a client, except that the lawyer may:

(1) acquire a lien granted by law to secure the lawyer's fee or expenses; and

(2) contract with a client for a reasonable contingent fee in a civil case.[a]

to the administration of justice.

"(6) Engage in any other conduct that adversely reflects on his fitness to practice law."

Compare RPC 8.4.

a. Compare the following CPR provisions:

**"DR 5–103 Avoiding Acquisition of Interest in Litigation**

"(A) A lawyer shall not acquire a proprietary interest in the cause of action or subject matter of litigation he is conducting for a client, except that he may:

(1) Acquire a lien granted by law to secure his fee or expenses.

(2) Contract with a client for a reasonable contingent fee in a civil case.

"(B) While representing a client in connection with contemplated or pending litigation, a lawyer shall not advance or guarantee financial assistance to his client, except that a lawyer may ad-

### MAHONING COUNTY BAR ASSOCIATION v. RUFFALO

176 Ohio St. 263, 199 N.E.2d 396, 8 A.L.R.3d 1142, cert. denied 379 U.S. 931, 85 S.Ct. 328, 13 L.Ed.2d 342 (1964).

PER CURIAM. * * * As to charge No. 8, it is stated in respondent's brief:

> "The facts * * * which are alleged in this charge are that respondent 'did advance monies to certain clients * * * while their claims were pending, which advances were deducted from any settlements * * * later received in settlement of said claims.' * * *
>
> "The record shows that respondent did advance monies to certain clients, but with the understanding that such monies were to be repaid irrespective of the outcome of the pending litigation. * * * "

It is obvious that, where the advancement of living expenses is made, as in the instant case, to enable a disabled client and his family to survive, any agreement by the disabled client to repay them would not have the effect of providing the attorney with any reasonable source of repayment other than the proceeds received on trial or settlement of his client's claim. In effect, the attorney has purchased an interest in the subject matter of the litigation that he is conducting. [This is] proper only where the advance is for "expenses of litigation." * * *

[Respondent was disciplined for this and other conduct.]

HERBERT, Judge (dissenting). * * * The importance of financial aid from his lawyer to an injured workman may spell the difference between injustice and justice.

For example, a member of a railroad train crew or yard crew is injured or killed by reason of the negligence of the railroad. * * *

The railroad offers a meager totally inadequate settlement—a small percentage of what a lawful judgment could reasonably be expected. In making this inadequate settlement offer, the claims department of the railroad advises that the railroad can delay final decision for years. In short, the powerful can close the doors of the courts to the weak by reason of the lack of finances of the claimant.

Under the pronouncement in the case at bar, lawyers in Ohio are not permitted to give or loan financial assistance to a client even though the injured employee or the dependents in case of death are in want and hungry.

#### *Questions*

(1) Is lawyer advancement of living expenses an appropriate way to deal with problems like those the dissent cites?

vance or guarantee the expenses of litigation, including court costs, expenses of investigation, expenses of medical examination, and costs of obtaining and presenting evidence, provided the client remains ultimately liable for such expenses."

Regarding attorneys' liens, see infra pp. 465–73. Regarding contingent fees, see infra pp. 437–52.

(2) What reasons support the general rule against advancements?

(3) What considerations support the exception to that rule for litigation expenses?

### *Comment*

Lawyers have been disciplined for advancing living expenses in a number of cases.[1] But in Louisiana State Bar Association v. Edwins,[2] the Louisiana Supreme Court was "unwilling to hold that the spirit or the intent of DR 5–103(B) is violated by the advance or guarantee by a lawyer to a client (who has already retained him) of minimal living expenses, of minor sums necessary to prevent foreclosures, or of necessary medical treatment." The court reasoned:

> "In the first place, the disciplinary rule was adopted to implement Canon 5: 'A lawyer should exercise independent professional judgment on behalf of a client.' In interpreting the disciplinary rule, we should do so in the light of the canon and the ethical considerations on which it is based. At least two of the ethical considerations point out policies which permit lawyer-client fee arrangements or advances when they represent the only practicable method by which a client can enforce his cause of action. [Footnote quoting EC 5–7 and 5–8 referring to contingent fees and advancement of expenses of litigation].
>
> "If an impoverished person is unable to secure subsistence from some source during disability, he may be deprived of the only effective means by which he can wait out the necessary delays that result from litigation to enforce his cause of action. He may, for reasons of economic necessity and physical need, be forced to settle his claim for an inadequate amount.
>
> "We do not believe any bar disciplinary rule can or should contemplate depriving poor people from access to the court so as effectively to assert their claim. Cf. Canon 2: 'A lawyer should assist the legal profession in fulfilling its duty to make legal counsel available.' Nor do we see how a lawyer's guarantee of necessary

1. See In re Stewart, 121 Ariz. 243, 589 P.2d 886 (1979) (censure for advancing $265 for living expenses); Committee on Professional Ethics Conduct v. Bitter, 279 N.W.2d 521 (Iowa 1979) (discipline for advancing $986 for living expenses); In re Berlant, 458 Pa. 439, 328 A.2d 471, 476 (1974) (fact of "client's indigency, since the money was generally used for rent, food, and other necessities * * * may be a mitigating factor [but] is irrelevant to the commission of the offense itself under DR 5–103(B)"), cert. denied 421 U.S. 964, 95 S.Ct. 1953, 44 L.Ed.2d 451 (1975); Annot., 8 A.L.R.3d 1155, 1177–80 (1966).

Regarding DR 5–103(B)'s requirement that the client be ultimately liable for litigation expenses (which was not included in RPC 1.8(e) ), see Golub v. Mid-Atlantic Toyota Distributors, Inc., 93 F.R.D. 485 (D.Md.1982); Gould v. Lumonics Research Limited, 495 F.Supp. 294, 298 (N.D.Ill.1980); In re Carroll, 124 Ariz. 80, 602 P.2d 461 (1979). See also United Transportation Union v. State Bar, infra p. 533 n.9, where the United States Supreme Court (without noting DR 5–103(B) ) found constitutional protection for a union's "securing an agreement from the counsel it recommends that the fee will not exceed 25% of the recovery, and that the percentage will include all expenses incident to investigation and litigation" and held that this practice could not validly be subjected to an injunction against the union's "stating or suggesting that a recommended lawyer will defray expenses of any kind or make advances for any purpose to such injured persons or their families pending settlement of their claim."

2. 329 So.2d 437 (La.1976).

medical treatment for his client, even for a non-litigation related illness, can be regarded as unethical, if the lawyer for reasons of humanity can afford to do so.

"The advances and guarantees here made are, in our opinion, more akin to the authorized advance of 'expenses of litigation' than to the prohibited advances made with improper motive to buy representation of the client or by way of advertising to attract other clients. We note that the disciplinary rule permitting the advance of 'expenses of litigation' includes certain instances as illustrative, but that it does not clearly exclude other expenses similarly necessary to permit the client his day in court, such as arguably are the present.

"Additionally, however, if the intent of the disciplinary rule were indeed to prohibit the type of advances and guarantees here made, we have some doubt as to its constitutionality. In Brotherhood of Railroad Trainmen v. Virginia [infra p. 527], the United States Supreme Court struck down a state regulation of the practice of law, holding that such regulation could not unreasonably handicap a claimant's right to petition the courts nor unreasonably inhibit the enforcement of a federal statutory right. For similar reasons, a court-adopted bar disciplinary rule which places an unreasonable burden upon an individual's right to enforce claims allowed him by law might be deemed violative of the access to courts guaranteed to all our people by our state constitution.

"In our opinion, the better view of those decisions which applied the former canons of ethics * * * was that the advancement of living expenses did not constitute a violation of professional responsibility, so long as: (a) the advances were not promised as an inducement to obtain professional employment, nor made until after the employment relationship was commenced; (b) the advances were reasonably necessary under the facts; (c) the client remained liable for repayment of all funds, whatever the outcome of the litigation; and (d) the attorney did not encourage public knowledge of this practice as an inducement to secure representation of others. See: Annotation, Attorneys—Clients' Expenses, 8 A.L.R.3d 1155 (1966); Strelow, Loans to Clients for Living Expenses, 55 Calif. L.Rev. 1419 (1967).

"A similar interpretation of the present Code of Professional Responsibility may be more difficult in view of the different wording of the present-day disciplinary rule at issue. Nevertheless, for the reasons earlier stated, we believe that it is justified."

Compare Roscoe Pound—American Trial Lawyers Foundation, American Lawyer's Code of Conduct 5.6 (Public Discussion Draft June 1980),[3] which provides:

"5.6 A lawyer shall not give money or anything of substantial value to any person in order to induce that person to become or

3. 16 Trial 44, 55 (Aug.1980).

remain a client, or to induce that person to retain or to continue the lawyer as counsel on behalf of someone else. However, a lawyer may (a) advance money to a client on any terms that are fair; (b) give money to a client as an act of charity; (c) give money to a client to enable the client to withstand delays in litigation that would otherwise induce the client to settle a case because of financial hardship, rather than on the merits of the client's claim; or (d) charge a fee that is contingent in whole or in part on the outcome of the case."[4]

## 4. LAWYER AS WITNESS

### MODEL RULES OF PROFESSIONAL CONDUCT

**RULE 3.7 Lawyer as Witness**

(a) A lawyer shall not act as advocate at a trial in which the lawyer is likely to be a necessary witness except where:

(1) the testimony relates to an uncontested issue;

(2) the testimony relates to the nature and value of legal services rendered in the case; or

(3) disqualification of the lawyer would work substantial hardship on the client.

(b) A lawyer may act as advocate in a trial in which another lawyer in the lawyer's firm is likely to be called as a witness unless precluded from doing so by Rule 1.7 or Rule 1.9.

COMMENT:

Combining the roles of advocate and witness can prejudice the opposing party and can involve a conflict of interest between the lawyer and client.

The opposing party has proper objection where the combination of roles may prejudice that party's rights in the litigation. A witness is required to testify on the basis of personal knowledge, while an advocate is expected to explain and comment on evidence given by others. It may not be clear whether a statement by an advocate-witness should be taken as proof or as an analysis of the proof.

Paragraph (a)(1) recognizes that if the testimony will be uncontested, the ambiguities in the dual role are purely theoretical. Paragraph (a)(2) recognizes that where the testimony concerns the extent and value of legal services rendered in the action in which the testimony is offered, permitting the lawyers to testify avoids the need for a second trial with new counsel to resolve that issue. Moreover, in such a situation the judge has first hand knowledge of the matter in issue; hence, there is less dependence on the adversary process to test the credibility of the testimony.

4. The American Lawyers' Code of Conduct was drafted under the auspices of the Roscoe Pound—American Trial Lawyers Foundation, is copyrighted by the Foundation and is reproduced here by permission.

See also Lynch, Ethical Rules in Flux: Advancing Costs of Litigation, 7 Litigation 19 (Winter 1981); Note, Guaranteeing Loans to Clients under Minnesota's Code of Professional Responsibility, 66 Minn.L.Rev. 1091 (1982); Comment, Advancing Money to Clients for Living Expenses, 2 J.Legal Prof. 107 (1977).

Apart from these two exceptions, paragraph (a)(3) recognizes that a balancing is required between the interests of the client and those of the opposing party. Whether the opposing party is likely to suffer prejudice depends on the nature of the case, the importance and probable tenor of the lawyer's testimony, and the probability that the lawyer's testimony will conflict with that of other witnesses. Even if there is risk of such prejudice, in determining whether the lawyer should be disqualified due regard must be given to the effect of disqualification on the lawyer's client. It is relevant that one or both parties could reasonably foresee that the lawyer would probably be a witness. * * * [a]

## MacARTHUR v. BANK OF NEW YORK

524 F.Supp. 1205 (S.D.N.Y. 1981).

SOFAER, District Judge:

During the jury trial of this action, it became apparent that a partner in the firm representing the defendant ought to testify on behalf of his client. The court *sua sponte* disqualified defendant's counsel and declared a mistrial. Several of the issues raised by the disqualification deserve comment.

This is an action sounding in contract. Plaintiff alleges that the defendant Bank entered into a joint venture with him to manage and reorganize four failing companies that were indebted to defendant. The companies' indebtedness to the Bank allegedly was to be reduced by repayment or sale of the companies to a third party. The plaintiff claims that the defendant breached the joint venture agreement by failing to compensate him in accordance with its terms. Specifically,

a. Compare the following CPR provisions:

**"DR 5–101 Refusing Employment When the Interests of the Lawyer May Impair His Independent Professional Judgment**

* * *

"(B) A lawyer shall not accept employment in contemplated or pending litigation if he knows or it is obvious that he or a lawyer in his firm ought to be called as a witness, except that he may undertake the employment and he or a lawyer in his firm may testify:

(1) If the testimony will relate solely to an uncontested matter.

(2) If the testimony will relate solely to a matter of formality and there is no reason to believe that substantial evidence will be offered in opposition to the testimony.

(3) If the testimony will relate solely to the nature and value of legal services rendered in the case by the lawyer or his firm to the client.

(4) As to any matter, if refusal would work a substantial hardship on the client because of the distinctive value of the lawyer or his firm as counsel in the particular case.

**"DR 5–102 Withdrawal as Counsel When the Lawyer Becomes a Witness**

"(A) If, after undertaking employment in contemplated or pending litigation, a lawyer learns or it is obvious that he or a lawyer in his firm ought to be called as a witness on behalf of his client, he shall withdraw from the conduct of the trial and his firm, if any, shall not continue representation in the trial, except that he may continue the representation and he or a lawyer in his firm may testify in the circumstances enumerated in DR 5–101(B) (1) through (4).

"(B) If, after undertaking employment in contemplated or pending litigation, a lawyer learns or it is obvious that he or a lawyer in his firm may be called as a witness other than on behalf of his client, he may continue the representation until it is apparent that his testimony is or may be prejudicial to his client."

he alleges that the defendant refused to execute a sale of the companies to a third party and that the defendant refused to transfer the companies' common stock to him as agreed. The plaintiff contends that these acts deprived him of compensation. Alternatively, plaintiff seeks recovery in quantum meruit.

The defendant denies that a joint venture existed and alleges that plaintiff received full compensation for services rendered. Alternatively, he claims that, even if a joint venture agreement did exist, it was conditioned upon reduction of the companies' debt. Defendant contends that the escalation of the debt during plaintiff's management precludes any recovery. Defendant has also interposed a counterclaim for money due under a promissory note.

On the second day of plaintiff's direct testimony, it became evident to the court that Donald McNicol, a senior partner in the firm representing defendant (Hall, McNicol, Hamilton, Clark & Murray), was intimately involved in the events at the heart of this litigation, and that other members of the firm (particularly William Collins) were involved to a lesser extent.[1] Absent testimony of McNicol and others in the firm it appeared impossible for the bank effectively to explain or rebut plaintiff's testimony. For this reason, the court suggested to the litigants, outside the presence of the jury, that defendant would need to call McNicol as its witness and that this might require his firm to withdraw from further representation of defendant in this suit.

In the discussions that followed, the parties repeatedly revised their positions on the disqualification issue. Plaintiff's attorney declined to move either for disqualification or for a mistrial, but nevertheless repeatedly raised questions as to the propriety of defendant's counsel's continued participation. Initially, defendant's attorney took the po-

1. The record at trial, along with plaintiff's supplemental answers to interrogatories, indicate that McNicol and Collins in particular, and the Hall, McNicol firm in general, participated actively in many of the contested events. Plaintiff's allegations as to particular incidents illustrate why the testimony of defendant's attorneys is imperative. First, plaintiff alleged that McNicol stated in a meeting with him on July 6, 1978, that McNicol would investigate the transfer of common stock. Second, plaintiff testified that he discussed with Collins the law firm's failure to transfer shares of common stock in a telephone conversation on July 21, 1978. Third, a meeting took place on January 17, 1979, between plaintiff, his attorney (Paul Mishkin), and McNicol regarding defendant's compensation of plaintiff. No other representative of the Bank was present. Fourth, on December 20, 1978, negotiations took place between McNicol, the plaintiff, a bank officer, and a prospective purchaser of the business (Salinas), regarding the sale of the business. Fifth, on January 2, 1979, at the office of Hall, McNicol, the plaintiff and McNicol allegedly altered the terms of the sale. The negotiations that took place are in sharp dispute. Finally, on May 4, 1979, McNicol acted as agent of defendant when he called plaintiff to fire him. The testimony of defendant's witnesses on that conversation would be based on McNicol's report to them.

Aside from these particular incidents, the firm's conduct permeates this case. McNicol appears to have acted as the lead negotiator and agent for defendant in many of the contested matters. Moreover, plaintiff asserts that members of the firm repeatedly interfered with his performance of his duties with respect to the companies and joined in defendant's misrepresentations. In essence, plaintiff claims that the law firm either was following the Bank's secret orders, in which case defendant is liable for breach of the alleged contract, or the firm disobeyed the Bank's orders, in which case the firm itself might be culpable, making defendant liable in turn for adopting the firm's actions as its agent.

sition that McNicol's testimony was unnecessary. Later, counsel for defendant said they would not call McNicol, but asked the court to instruct the jury that the reason McNicol did not testify was that this firm could not act as counsel if he had done so. Ultimately, defense counsel agreed that McNicol and other members of the firm ought to testify on behalf of defendant, but argued that disqualification was inappropriate as it would cause substantial hardship to the client. The defendant Bank of New York, through its officers, remained adamant in its position that it wanted Hall, McNicol to continue as its counsel, even if that would preclude defendant from offering testimony of firm members.

The court followed the mandate of Disciplinary Rule 5–102(A) and ordered defendant's counsel to withdraw. That Rule provides:

> If, after undertaking employment in contemplated or pending litigation, a lawyer learns or it is obvious that he or a lawyer in his firm ought to be called as a witness on behalf of his client, he shall withdraw from the conduct of the trial and his firm, if any, shall not continue representation in the trial, except that he may continue the representation and he or a lawyer in his firm may testify in the circumstances enumerated in DR 5–101(B)(1) through (4).[a]

The court declared a mistrial because of the disqualification. The defendant needed several weeks to retain and properly inform new trial counsel, making it impracticable to retain the jury that had already been impanelled. The fact that the jury would conceivably speculate to the prejudice of either party as to the reason counsel had been changed after two days of testimony was sufficient reason to warrant a new trial.

Strong policies underlie DR 5–102(A). Calling a party's attorney as a witness undermines the integrity of the judicial process. The rule operates to protect the interests of the plaintiff, the interests of the adverse party, and the reputation of the legal profession as a whole. See generally 6 J. Wigmore, Evidence § 1911 (Chadbourn rev. ed. 1976); Note, The Advocate Witness Rule: If Z, then X. But Why? 52 N.Y.U.L.Rev. 1365 (1977); American Bar Association Committee on Ethics and Professional Responsibility, Formal Opinion 339 (January 31, 1975). These interests are well expressed in Ethical Consideration 5–9:

> "Occasionally a lawyer is called upon to decide in a particular case whether he will be a witness or an advocate. If a lawyer is both

**a.** Compare RPC 3.7.

Regarding disqualification under DR 5–101(B) and 5–102 because a firm member ought to be a witness, see generally Annot., 5 A.L.R.4th 574 (1981).

For decisions finding it permissible for one *prosecutor* to serve as advocate while another prosecutor from the same office testifies, see People ex rel. Younger v. Superior Court, 86 Cal.App.3d 180, 150 Cal.Rptr. 156 (1978); People v. Hauschel, 37 Colo.App. 114, 550 P.2d 876 (1976); People v. Thomas, 38 Ill.App.3d 685, 348 N.E.2d 282 (1976); State v. Martinez, 89 N.M. 729, 557 P.2d 578 (1976), cert. denied 430 U.S. 973, 97 S.Ct. 1663, 52 L.Ed.2d 367 (1977).

counsel and witness, he becomes more easily impeachable for interest and thus may be a less effective witness.[b] Conversely, the opposing counsel may be handicapped in challenging the credibility of the lawyer when the lawyer also appears as an advocate in the case.[c] An advocate who becomes a witness is in the unseemly and ineffective position of arguing his own credibility.[d] The roles of an advocate and of a witness are inconsistent; the function of an advocate is to advance or argue the cause of another, while that of a witness is to state facts objectively.[e] "

DR 5–102(A) implicitly recognizes the potential conflict of interest with which an attorney may be faced in this situation: attorneys anxious to participate in the litigation might fail to step aside as counsel and testify even if their testimony could help the client; other attorneys might fail to step aside and testify because the client insists upon their continued representation. The Code of Professional Responsibility seeks to prevent such conflicts by keeping separate the roles of attorney and witness.

DR 5–102(A) also operates to protect the interests of the adverse party. A jury may view an attorney as possessing special knowledge of a case and therefore accord a testifying attorney's arguments undue weight. Also, as EC 5–9 suggests, the adverse party's attorney may, for reasons of professional courtesy and court etiquette, be handicapped in challenging the testimony of another lawyer. General Mill Supply Co. v. SCA Services, Inc., 505 F.Supp. 1093 (D.Mich.1981). Finally, the bar is ill-served when an attorney's veracity becomes an issue in a case; lay observers especially might speculate whether counsel has compromised his integrity on the stand in order to prevail in the litigation. International Electronic Corp. v. Flanzer, 527 F.2d 1288, 1294 (2d Cir. 1975); United States ex rel. Sheldon Electronic Co. v. Blackwood Heating & Plumbing Co., 423 F.Supp. 486, 489 (S.D.N.Y.1976); 6 J. Wigmore, supra, § 1911. Cf. EC 7–24 (attorney may not claim innocence of client or justness of position to the jury). Having seen the attorney take an oath on the witness stand, the jury

**b.** See Wasserman v. Buckeye Union Cas. Co., 32 Ohio St.2d 69, 290 N.E.2d 837 (1972) (proper for defense to argue that plaintiff's lawyer who testified was the sole person interested in plaintiff's action or who would benefit from a verdict for plaintiff—as witness, lawyer was subject to "same tests for credibility as any other witness").

**c.** See People v. Smith, 13 Cal.App.3d 897, 91 Cal.Rptr. 786 (1971):

"The attorney would attempt to shift between the sworn objectivity of the witness and the duty-bound partisanship of the advocate. Because of his professional and official role, his sworn testimony would lay silent claim to a heightened degree of credibility. He would thrust upon his opponent a sticky choice between vigorous cross-examination of his professional colleague and abdication of his own professional responsibility."

**d.** See State v. McCuistion, 88 N.M. 94, 537 P.2d 702 (1975) ("I wouldn't come up here, I can assure you, ladies and gentlemen, and take that stand and fabricate a story like that because that would be perjury"); Siefring v. Marion, 22 A.D.2d 765, 253 N.Y.S.2d 619 (1964) ("If I did * * * what he said I did, I should be disbarred * * *. Are you going to convict me on that kind of testimony?").

**e.** See Enker, The Rationale of the Rule that Forbids a Lawyer to Be Advocate and Witness in the Same Case, 1977 Am.B.Found.Research J. 455.

might accord testimonial weight to his closing arguments, or might simply place undue weight on the testimony of a court officer. See Developments in the Law, Conflicts of Interest in the Legal Profession, 94 Harv.L.Rev. 1244, 1290 (1981).

DR 5–102(A) applies when a lawyer "ought to be called as a witness on behalf of his client." That the lawyer may not actually testify is not controlling. What matters is that he ought to testify. J.P. Foley & Co., Inc. v. Vanderbilt, 523 F.2d 1357 (2d Cir.1975). Defendant's argument that McNicol's testimony would merely corroborate other testimony, even if accurate, is unavailing. The test is whether the attorney's testimony could be significantly useful to his client; if so, he ought to be called.

This rule, of course, requires a careful evaluation of the relevant issues in the case and of other available testimony. An additional corroborative witness would almost always be of some use to a party, but might nevertheless be essentially cumulative. At some point, the utility of additional corroboration is de minimus and does not require the attorney's disqualification. EC 5–10 ("It is not objectionable for a lawyer who is a potential witness to be an advocate if it is unlikely that he will be called as a witness because his testimony would be merely cumulative or if his testimony will relate only to an uncontested issue.") Here, independent counsel would seem likely to call McNicol, both to supply his own account of the events in question (even if corroborative) and to prevent the jury from speculating about his absence. His testimony would be far from cumulative, since his role was pivotal, and his conduct was brought into question. See note 1 supra.

A second feature of DR 5–102(A) is that the stricture is mandatory: the party cannot choose between the attorney's testimony and his representation. The rule embodies a conclusive preference for testimony: "Where the question [of testimony versus representation] arises doubts should be resolved in favor of the lawyer testifying and against his becoming or continuing as an advocate." EC 5–10. A party can be represented by other attorneys, but cannot obtain substitute testimony for a counsel's relevant, personal knowledge.

In deciding whether an attorney should be disqualified, courts have balanced the interests underlying the rule against the potential damage to the client. General Mill Supply Co. v. SCA Services, Inc., supra, 505 F.Supp. at 1096. Yet, absent extreme hardship to the client, the mandate of 5–102(A) has been strictly invoked.

> "Aside from the likelihood of actual prejudice * * *, the court must be mindful of the possibility that testimony by an attorney in the case may lead the public to think 'that lawyers may as witnesses distort the truth,' thereby diminishing the public's respect for and confidence in the profession. * * * Where doubt may becloud the public's view of the ethics of the legal profession and thus impugn the integrity of the judicial process, *it is the responsibility of the court to insure that the standards of ethics remain high.*"

United States ex rel. Sheldon Electric Co. v. Blackhawk Heating & Plumbing Inc., 423 F.Supp. 486, 489 (S.D.N.Y.1976) (emphasis supplied).

Nor may the client waive the rule's protection by promising not to call the attorney as a witness.[f] The ostensible paternalism of disregarding such waivers is justified by the circumstances in which the problem arises. The client will generally be reluctant to forego the assistance of familiar counsel or to incur the expense and inconvenience of retaining another lawyer. The most serious breaches of the rule, in which an attorney has become intimately involved in the subject matter of the dispute, will often be the very situations in which withdrawal is most burdensome. Moreover, the party will generally be guided in its decision by the very attorney whose continued representation is at issue. At the same time, the attorney will be reluctant to jeopardize good relations with the client and may—against his better judgment—defer to the client's desire for representation.

The mandatory nature of DR 5–102(A) also requires that the court be able to disqualify counsel *sua sponte* when the need arises. Normally, a party will seek to have opposing counsel disqualified, and that moving party will have the burden of showing that continued participation in the case would violate the Code of Professional Responsibility. See, e.g., Zions First National Bank, N.A. v. United Health Clubs, Inc., 505 F.Supp. 138 (E.D.Pa.1981); Freeman v. Kulicke & Soffa Industries, Inc., 449 F.Supp. 974 (E.D.Pa.1978), aff'd, 591 F.2d 1334 (3d Cir. 1979). While all members of the bar share responsibility for avoiding breaches of ethical rules, an attorney may avoid pressing for disqualification out of a desire to avoid clashing with opposing counsel or to obtain tactical advantages from the prospect that the opposing firm's attorneys might be prevented from testifying. Thus, where neither party moves for disqualification, the court must intervene to ensure that the mandate of DR 5–102(A) is followed. Furthermore, although the problem of disqualification should be anticipated as early as possible to minimize expense, inconvenience, and needless expenditure of judicial resources, the rule controls irrespective of when the need for the attorney's testimony becomes evident. "Regardless of when the problem arises, [the lawyer's] decision is to be governed by the same basic considerations." EC 5–10. The mandatory ethical obligations imposed by DR 5–102(A) cannot be overcome by the equitable defenses of laches, waiver, or estoppel, although the burden on the party seeking disqualification may be greater as a result of his undue delay and may, in some cases, justify invocation of the substantial-hardship exception to DR 5–102(A) discussed below.[g]

**f.** Compare J.D. Pflaumer, Inc. v. United States Department of Justice, 465 F.Supp. 746 (E.D.Pa.1979) (court should give some deference to determination of party and counsel on whether counsel "ought" to testify because they should be permitted to present the case according to their own best judgment).

**g.** Compare White v. Superior Court, 98 Cal.App.3d 51, 159 Cal.Rptr. 278 (1979) (abuse of discretion for trial court to grant disqualification motion not made at first reasonable opportunity) (motion should have been made six months earlier).

The remedy for abuse of DR 5–102(A) by opposing counsel is not to disregard the rule, but rather to impose other sanctions. Parties might well attempt to use this ethical rule, like others, as a litigation tactic. The Court must therefore be careful to determine whether the testimony of the implicated attorney is genuinely necessary or merely a fabrication of his adversary. DR 5–102(B), which governs situations in which the opposing party seeks to call its adversary's attorney as a witness, makes clear that the court must prevent a litigant from using the witness disqualification rule to rob a party of its chosen representative. Even if disqualification is appropriate, the court can impose costs upon the adverse party for culpable failure to raise the ethical issue at an earlier stage.[2] Use of the Code of Professional Responsibility as a strategic tool can itself constitute unethical conduct that must be referred to disciplinary authorities. But any such abuse by opposing counsel does not cure the original violation and cannot vitiate the disciplinary rule.

Finally, the substantial-hardship exception invoked by defendant must be narrowly construed.[h] Despite the strictures of DR 5–102(A),

2. The court denied defendant's motion for costs in this case. Plaintiff did not hide the pertinent issues from defendant and did not fabricate the need for McNicol to appear. Plaintiff's second set of interrogatories, in particular, put defendant on ample notice of the substantial involvement of McNicol and others.

h. See Draganescu v. First National Bank, 502 F.2d 550, (5th Cir. 1974), cert. denied 421 U.S. 929, 95 S.Ct. 1655, 44 L.Ed.2d 86 (1975), upholding disqualification of a lawyer who, on a percentage contingency basis, represented certain Romanian nationals on their claim that defendant had negligently failed to prepare a will for a certain decedent, where the lawyer was the only one who had spoken with defendant regarding the exact terms and time requirements of the proposed will. The court said:

> "Plaintiffs' claim that removal of their lawyer will work a substantial hardship and that, under exception (4) to 5–101(B), he should therefore be reinstated. They argue that [he] is uniquely qualified to represent them because he can speak the Romanian language, knew decedent for many years, and has great familiarity with the task of representing Romanians. Moreover, they insist, other lawyers are reluctant to take cases involving Romanians on a contingent fee basis.
>
> "We are not convinced of these claims and do not believe that [the lawyer's] removal will work a substantial hardship. His knowledge of the Romanian language will be of limited utility since he admits, '[T]he plaintiffs do not have any information to impart which will be of any value * * *. All of the operative facts of our cause of action took place in Florida and the witnesses who shall establish them are in the United States.' In any case, the trial court's order does not bar [him] from acting as translator, should the need for a Romanian presence be established. The fact that [he] had known decedent for many years may make him a more credible witness on the nature of the will she is alleged to have commissioned, but it is not relevant to actions he would take in his lawyerly capacity. Plaintiffs fail to specify how [his] familiarity with Romanians bears on the quality of the representation he can give. Finally, they do not demonstrate that the lack of such familiarity makes disinterested counsel unwilling to work on a contingent fee basis."

Compare Schwartz v. Wenger, 267 Minn. 40, 124 N.W.2d 489 (1963), wherein defendant testified near the end of trial to a conversation she overheard the preceding day between plaintiff and plaintiff's lawyer. The court upheld the propriety of the lawyer's taking the stand to refute the testimony, saying:

> "In those rare cases where the testimony of an attorney is needed to protect his client's interests, it is not only proper but mandatory that it be forthcoming. This is such a case. Certainly plaintiff's attorney could not have predicted before trial this unusual turn of events. His failure to take the stand might well have been construed by the jury as a tacit admission, and it was to avoid this inference that he was obliged to act."

See Cartin v. Continental Homes, 134 Vt. 362, 360 A.2d 96 (1976) (where need for testimony only became apparent during trial, lawyer could take stand without withdrawing as counsel).

a lawyer who ought to testify may continue to represent the client if his withdrawal "would work a substantial hardship on the client because of the distinctive value of the lawyer or his firm as counsel in the particular case." DR 5–102(A) (incorporating DR 5–101(B)(4)). Defendant claims that, because of counsel's familiarity with the underlying facts and extensive preparations for trial, withdrawal would cause substantial hardship.

Hardship alone, however substantial, is insufficient to permit continued representation. The deprivation to the client will often be greatest precisely when the attorney was most intimately involved in, and familiar with, the events giving rise to the suit. See e.g., United States ex. rel Sheldon Electric Co. v. Blackhawk Heating & Plumbing Co., supra, 423 F.Supp. at 490. The familiarity of the Hall, McNicol law firm with the client's case is not sufficient to permit an exception to the rule. General Mill Supply Co. v. SCA Services, supra, 505 F.Supp. at 1099. Withdrawal will be costly whenever it occurs (though the expense can be minimized by invocation of the rule at the earliest possible time). But if the expense and delay routinely incident to disqualification satisfied the substantial-hardship exception, that exception would soon swallow the rule.

The exception expressly qualifies the hardship that must be shown to permit continued representation as one that arises "because of the distinctive value of the lawyer or his firm as counsel in the particular case." [i] For example, in a highly technical case, an attorney might have acquired unique expertise with respect to the matters in dispute, and no substitute counsel could supply the client with comparably adequate representation; in such a case, the serious prejudice to the client, when weighed against the significance of the testimony, might justify invocation of the exception. Similarly, a long-standing professional relationship could conceivably create a situation where an attorney has an extraordinary and irreplaceable familiarity with the affairs of his client. ABA [Formal Opinion 339], supra, at 3; Miller Electric Construction, Inc. v. Devine Lighting Co., Inc., 421 F.Supp. 1020, 1023 (W.D.Pa.1976). This latter exception could work to alleviate, in at least some cases, the use of DR 5–102(A) as a tactical weapon because an attempt to have opposing counsel disqualified is most likely to occur when that counsel is for some reason irreplaceable. But such instances will be rare, ABA [Formal Opinion 339], supra, at 4, and the burden of establishing their existence must fall upon the party opposing disqualification. Supreme Beef Processors v. American Consumer Industries, 441 F.Supp. 1064 (N.D.Tex.1977). Here, defendant failed to demonstrate that his attorney has distinctive value as trial counsel.

Finally, defendant objects that the effect of the court's ruling, if consistently applied, would be to prevent a law firm from maintaining a continuing relationship with a client. That fear is groundless. A

i. Compare RPC 3.7(a) (3).

lawyer can choose, as McNicol did here, to participate actively in a client's business affairs—not just as an adviser, but also as a negotiator and agent. (McNicol was also a director and a member of the executive committee of the company that plaintiff claims to have rehabilitated.) Such conduct is entirely proper. But if an attorney chooses to become intimately involved in the client's business, then he or she must be prepared to step aside if the matters involved result in litigation. This may be displeasing to firms that wish to have some members act as businessmen and others as litigators. But when these firms place themselves in the position of having an attorney acquire information that makes his testimony necessary, they must accept the consequences.

The circumstances of this case do not suggest culpability on the part of defendant's counsel. They acted in good faith, and appear to believe—however unjustifiably—that their continued representation of defendant is proper. But DR 5–102(A) must be applied despite the purest intentions. The parties concede that McNicol ought to appear as a witness for defendant, so his firm must withdraw as trial counsel.[3]

SO ORDERED.

### *Comment*

(1) *Withdrawal.* The required withdrawal of testifying counsel must be total. Withdrawal only while testifying under questioning by another lawyer and then returning to the trial of the case is not sufficient.[1]

(2) *Civil consequences.* Although courts sometimes grant a party's motion to disqualify opposing counsel because his or her testimony may be needed,[2] compel a party to choose between retaining the lawyer

3. The disqualified firm may consult with defendant's substitute counsel and assist in preparing for trial. Norman Norrell, Inc. v. Federated Department Stores, Inc., 450 F.Supp. 127 (S.D.N.Y.1978). The firm's request that it be permitted to continue to represent defendant in renewing a motion for summary judgment was also granted, since no witness will be called and since counsel have previously made such a motion and could renew it with far less cost than would be entailed in requiring new attorneys to perform this task. * * *

[Eds.] See generally, Lewis, The Ethical Dilemma of the Testifying Advocate: Fact or Fancy, 19 Hous.L.Rev. 75 (1981) (urging abrogation of advocate-witness restrictions); Wydick, Trial Counsel as Witness: The Code and the Model Rules, 15 U.Cal. Davis L.Rev. 651 (1982) (comparing operation of CPR and Proposed Final Draft of RPC provisions); Comment, Application of the Advocate-Witness Rule, 1982 So.Ill.U.L.J. 291 (discussing operation of CPR provisions).

1. People v. Spencer, 182 Colo. 189, 512 P.2d 260 (1973); Bauman v. Ballard Fish Co., 185 A.2d 506 (D.C.Mun.App. 1962). See Gutierrez v. Travelers Insurance Co., 358 So.2d 349 (La.App.1978). Compare State v. Newman, 179 Neb. 746, 140 N.W.2d 406 (1966) (not objectionable for county attorney who withdrew to sit at counsel table and give some aid to special prosecutor).

2. See Draganescu v. First National Bank, 502 F.2d 550 (5th Cir. 1974), cert. denied 421 U.S. 929, 95 S.Ct. 1655, 44 L.Ed.2d 86 (1975); Cottonwood Estates v. Paradise Builders, 128 Ariz. 99, 624 P.2d 296 (1981); Comden v. Superior Court, 20 Cal.3d 906, 145 Cal.Rptr. 9, 576 P.2d 971, cert. denied 439 U.S. 981, 99 S.Ct. 568, 58 L.Ed.2d 652 (1978); Auseon v. Reading Brass Co., 22 Mich.App. 505, 177 N.W.2d 662 (1970); Perazzelli v. Perazzelli, 147 N.J.Super. 53, 370 A.2d 535 (1977).

Compare Kroungold v. Triester, 521 F.2d 763 (3d Cir. 1975) (defendant moving to disqualify plaintiff's lawyer because defendant intends to call that lawyer as witness must show specifically how lawyer's testimony would prejudice plaintiff).

the party wants and the lawyer's testimony,[3] or deny a lawyer's fee for legal services rendered after the lawyer should have withdrawn because the lawyer knew it would be necessary to testify for the client,[4] courts generally will not reverse a judgment because the prevailing party's lawyer violated ethical standards in not withdrawing before testifying.[5]

(3) *Prosecutor testimony as denying fair trial.* But courts generally reverse a criminal conviction if a prosecutor who could have withdrawn takes the stand to testify on material facts, on the ground this denies the defendant a fair trial.[6]

(4) *Calling opposing counsel generally.* Trial courts generally are held to have discretion on whether to allow a party to call opposing counsel as a witness, on the view that "attempting to call opposing counsel * * * to establish some fact that can be readily proved in a different manner should be discouraged." [7]

3. See People v. Smith, 13 Cal.App.3d 897, 91 Cal.Rptr. 786 (1971) (criminal case); Town of Mebane v. Iowa Mutual Insurance Co., 28 N.C.App. 27, 220 S.E.2d 623 (1975) (civil case).

Compare Carlile v. State, 451 S.W.2d 511 (Tex.Crim.App.1970) (applying court rule permitting exclusion of witnesses while others testify to criminal defense counsel who intends to testify would violate constitutional right to counsel).

Regarding criminal defense counsel as witness generally, see Annot., 52 A.L.R.3d 887 (1973).

4. See Hill v. Douglass, 271 So.2d 1 (Fla.1973).

5. See Erwin M. Jennings Co. v. Di Genova, 107 Conn. 491, 141 A. 866 (1928); Pittman v. Currie, 414 So.2d 423 (Miss.1982); In re Estate of Elvers, 48 Wis.2d 17, 179 N.W.2d 881 (1970).

But see Gutierrez v. Travelers Ins. Co., 358 So.2d 349 (La.App.1978). Compare Commonwealth v. Rondeau, 392 N.E.2d 1001 (Mass.1979) (conviction reversed because defense counsel failed to withdraw when it became apparent counsel's alibi testimony would be necessary to client's proper defense). Regarding discipline, compare State v. Ledvina, 71 Wis.2d 195, 237 N.W.2d 683 (1976) (discipline for violation of DR 5–101(B) with In re Lathen, 294 Or. 157, 654 P.2d 1110 (1982) (no discipline because not shown by clear and convincing evidence that it was "obvious" before trial that lawyer ought to be witness).

6. See People v. Spencer, 182 Colo. 189, 512 P.2d 260 (1973); State v. McCuistion, 88 N.M. 94, 537 P.2d 702 (1975); Annot., 54 A.L.R.3d 100 (1973).

See also United States v. Gold, 470 F.Supp. 1336 (N.D.Ill.1979) (reversal because government lawyer testified before *grand jury* and participated as prosecutor before grand jury); Jenkins v. State ex rel. Sweat, 242 Miss. 646, 136 So.2d 580 (1962) (prosecutor's *injunction* dissolved because prosecutor testified); People v. Bonilla, 101 Misc.2d 146, 420 N.Y.S.2d 665 (1979) (prosecutor who participated in videotaped interrogation of defendant disqualified from presenting summation at trial). But see People v. Langdon, 91 Ill.App.3d 1050, 47 Ill.Dec. 573, 415 N.E.2d 578 (1980) (defendant did not demonstrate prejudice from failure of prosecutor who testified to withdraw).

For situations where the prosecutor's taking the stand was found justifiable, see People v. Stokley, 266 Cal.App. 2d 930, 72 Cal.Rptr. 513 (1968) (prosecutor testified to refute unexpected denial by defendant of conversation with prosecutor—prosecutor "was in the position of either doing nothing and thereby letting the jury think that he could not be trusted in matters he was bringing before the jury or else testifying in order to rehabilitate his position before the jury"), cert. denied 395 U.S. 914, 89 S.Ct. 1761, 23 L.Ed.2d 227 (1969); Tomlin v. State, 81 Nev. 620, 407 P.2d 1020 (1965) (prosecutor surprised by accomplice's trial testimony contradicting pretrial statement, unable to locate another prosecutor to take over, and in summation to jury did not comment on own testimony), cert. denied, 384 U.S. 990, 86 S.Ct. 1894, 16 L.Ed.2d 1006 (1966).

7. Rude v. Algiers, 11 Wis.2d 471, 482, 105 N.W.2d 825, 831 (1960). See Jones v. Kansas City Embalming & Casket Co., 192 Kan. 136, 386 P.2d 217 (1963). Compare Romeo v. Jumbo Market, 247 Cal.App.2d 817, 56 Cal.Rptr. 26 (1967) (counsel properly compelled to testify as to facts to which counsel refused to stipulate). See also Galarowicz v. Ward, 119 Utah 611, 230 P.2d 576 (1951) (lawyer criticized for putting opposing counsel on stand and then objecting to his continuing as opposing counsel).

(5) *Prosecution calling criminal defense counsel.* It has been held reversible error for the prosecution unnecessarily to call defendant's lawyer as a witness, on the ground this infringes defendant's constitutional right to effective counsel.[8] But the prosecutor's calling defense counsel has been held proper where defense counsel's testimony is necessary and not obtainable elsewhere.[9]

(6) *Defense calling prosecutor.* It has been held that the defendant's constitutional right to be fully heard requires allowing the defense to call the prosecutor as a witness, on the view that "litigants, and especially defendants in criminal cases, should not be hampered in their choice of those by whom they choose to prove their cases."[10] But refusal to allow the prosecutor to be called has been upheld where it appeared other witnesses were available to establish the point sought to be made,[11] and where the defense failed to show the relevance and materiality of the desired testimony.[12]

### *Question*

ABA Standards for Criminal Justice 4-4.3(d) (2d ed. 1980) states: "Unless the lawyer for the accused is prepared to forego impeachment of a witness by the lawyer's own testimony as to what the witness stated in an interview or to seek leave to withdraw from the case in order to present such impeaching testimony, the lawyer should avoid interviewing a prospective witness except in the presence of a third person."[13] Is this the best approach to this problem? What other means might be used?

8. See People v. Lathrom, 192 Cal.App.2d 216, 13 Cal.Rptr. 325, 88 A.L.R.2d 785 (1961); Annot., 9 A.L.R.Fed. 500, 523-24 (1971); Annot., 88 A.L.R.2d 796 (1963). Compare State v. Jenkens, 203 Kan. 354, 454 P.2d 496 (1969) (error "deplorable" but no reversal where defendant not prejudiced).

9. United States v. Crockett, 506 F.2d 759 (5th Cir.), cert. denied 423 U.S. 824, 96 S.Ct. 37, 46 L.Ed.2d 40 (1975). See United States v. Freeman, 519 F.2d 67 (9th Cir. 1975):

> "Merely requiring a defendant's lawyer to testify does not alone constitute a material interference with his function as an advocate or operate to deprive the accused of a fair trial. Here the matter was treated with considerable circumspection. The government first proposed that the fact sought to be proven be stipulated; when defense counsel rejected that method, the court appointed an associate counsel *pro tempore* who stated objections to the several questions put the witness and enabled the latter to devote his attention to his temporary testimonial role."

10. State v. Lee, 203 S.C. 536, 28 S.E.2d 402, 149 A.L.R. 1300 (1943).

11. See People v. Gendron, 41 Ill.2d 351, 243 N.E.2d 208 (1968), cert. denied 396 U.S. 889, 90 S.Ct. 179, 24 L.Ed.2d 164 (1969). More questionable is Chatman v. State, 263 Ind. 531, 334 N.E.2d 673 (1975), upholding a similar refusal even though the defendant had testified that the prosecutor had extracted a statement by duress and was questioning him about it.

12. Johnson v. State, 23 Md.App. 131, 326 A.2d 38 (1974), affirmed mem. 275 Md. 291, 339 A.2d 289 (1975); See United States v. Nanz, 471 F.Supp. 968 (E.D.Wis.1979).

13. Accord id. 3-3.1(f) (prosecutor).

# B. MULTIPLE CLIENTS' INTERESTS

## MODEL RULES OF PROFESSIONAL CONDUCT

**RULE 1.7 Conflict of Interest: General Rule**

(a) A lawyer shall not represent a client if the representation of that client will be directly adverse to another client, unless:

(1) the lawyer reasonably believes the representation will not adversely affect the relationship with the other client; and

(2) each client consents after consultation.

(b) A lawyer shall not represent a client if the representation of that client may be materially limited by the lawyer's responsibilities to another client or to a third person, or by the lawyer's own interests, unless:

(1) the lawyer reasonably believes the representation will not be adversely affected; and

(2) the client consents after consultation. When representation of multiple clients in a single matter is undertaken, the consultation shall include explanation of the implications of the common representation and the advantages and risks involved.

**RULE 1.8 Conflict of Interest: Prohibited Transactions**

* * *

(g) A lawyer who represents two or more clients shall not participate in making an aggregate settlement of the claims of or against the clients, or in a criminal case an aggregated agreement as to guilty or nolo contendere pleas, unless each client consents after consultation, including disclosure of the existence and nature of all the claims or pleas involved and of the participation of each person in the settlement.

**RULE 1.10 Imputed Disqualification: General Rule**

(a) While lawyers are associated in a firm, none of them shall knowingly represent a client when any one of them practicing alone would be prohibited from doing so by Rules 1.7, 1.8(c), 1.9 or 2.2

* * *

(d) A disqualification prescribed by this Rule may be waived by the affected client under the conditions stated in Rule 1.7.[a]

**a.** Compare the following CPR provisions:

"**EC 5–15** If a lawyer is requested to undertake or to continue representation of multiple clients having potentially differing interests, he must weigh carefully the possibility that his judgment may be impaired or his loyalty divided if he accepts or continues the employment. He should resolve all doubts against the propriety of the representation. A lawyer should never represent in litigation multiple clients with differing interests; and there are few situations in which he would be justified in representing in litigation multiple clients with potentially differing interests. If a lawyer accepted such employment and the interests did become actually differing, he would have to withdraw from employment with likelihood of resulting hardship on the clients; and for this reason it is preferable that he refuse the employment initially. On the other hand, there are many instances in which a lawyer may properly serve

## 1. CRIMINAL CASES

### HOLLOWAY v. ARKANSAS

435 U.S. 475, 98 S.Ct. 1173, 55 L.Ed.2d 426 (1978).

Mr. Chief Justice BURGER delivered the opinion of the Court.

Petitioners, codefendants at trial, made timely motions for appointment of separate counsel, based on the representations of their appointed counsel that, because of confidential information received from the codefendants, he was confronted with the risk of representing conflicting interests and could not, therefore, provide effective assistance for each client. We granted certiorari to decide whether petitioners were deprived of the effective assistance of counsel by the denial of those motions.

I

Early in the morning of June 1, 1975, three men entered a Little Rock, Ark., restaurant and robbed and terrorized the five employees of the restaurant. During the course of the robbery, one of the two female employees was raped once; the other, twice. The ensuing police investigation led to the arrests of the petitioners.

multiple clients having potentially differing interests in matters not involving litigation. If the interests vary only slightly, it is generally likely that the lawyer will not be subjected to an adverse influence and that he can retain his independent judgment on behalf of each client; and if the interests become differing, withdrawal is less likely to have a disruptive effect upon the causes of his clients.

**"DR 5–105 Refusing to Accept or Continue Employment if the Interests of Another Client May Impair the Independent Professional Judgment of the Lawyer**

"(A) A lawyer shall decline proffered employment if the exercise of his independent professional judgment in behalf of a client will be or is likely to be adversely affected by the acceptance of the proffered employment, or if it would be likely to involve him in representing differing interests, except to the extent permitted under DR 5–105(C).

"(B) A lawyer shall not continue multiple employment if the exercise of his independent professional judgment in behalf of a client will be or is likely to be adversely affected by his representation of another client, or if it would be likely to involve him in representing differing interests, except to the extent permitted under DR 5–105(C).

"(C) In the situations covered by DR 5–105(A) and (B), a lawyer may represent multiple clients if it is obvious that he can adequately represent the interest of each and if each consents to the representation after full disclosure of the possible effect of such representation on the exercise of his independent professional judgment on behalf of each.

"(D) If a lawyer is required to decline employment or to withdraw from employment under a Disciplinary Rule, no partner, or associate, or any other lawyer affiliated with him, or his firm, may accept or continue such employment.

**"DR 5–106 Settling Similar Claims of Clients**

"(A) A lawyer who represents two or more clients shall not make or participate in the making of an aggregate settlement of the claims of or against his clients, unless each client has consented to the settlement after being advised of the existence and nature of all the claims involved in the proposed settlement, of the total amount of the settlement, and of the participation of each person in the settlement."

See also EC 5–14, 5–16, 5–17, 5–19.

On July 29, 1975, the three defendants were each charged with one count of robbery and two counts of rape. On August 5, the trial court appointed Harold Hall, a public defender, to represent all three defendants. Petitioners were then arraigned and pleaded not guilty. Two days later, their cases were set for a consolidated trial to commence September 4.

On August 13 Hall moved the court to appoint separate counsel for each petitioner because "the defendants ha[d] stated to him that there is a possibility of a conflict of interest in each of their cases * * *." After conducting a hearing on this motion, and on petitioners' motions for a severance, the court declined to appoint separate counsel.

Before trial, the same judge who later presided at petitioners' trial conducted a Jackson v. Denno hearing to determine the admissibility of a confession purportedly made by petitioner Campbell to two police officers at the time of his arrest. The essence of the confession was that Campbell had entered the restaurant with his codefendants and had remained, armed with a rifle, one flight of stairs above the site of the robbery and rapes (apparently serving as a lookout), but had not taken part in the rapes. The trial judge ruled the confession admissible, but ordered deletion of the references to Campbell's codefendants. At trial one of the arresting officers testified to Campbell's confession.

On September 4, before the jury was empaneled, Hall renewed the motion for appointment of separate counsel "on the grounds that one or two of the defendants may testify and if they do, then I will not be able to cross-examine them because I have received confidential information from them." The court responded, "I don't know why you wouldn't," and again denied the motion.

The prosecution then proceeded to present its case. The manager of the restaurant identified petitioners Holloway and Campbell as two of the robbers. Another male employee identified Holloway and petitioner Welch. A third identified only Holloway. The victim of the single rape identified Holloway and Welch as two of the robbers but was unable to identify the man who raped her. The victim of the double rape identified Holloway as the first rapist. She was unable to identify the second rapist but identified Campbell as one of the robbers.

On the second day of trial, after the prosecution had rested its case, Hall advised the court that, against his recommendation, all three defendants had decided to testify. He then stated:

"Now, since I have been appointed, I had previously filed a motion asking the Court to appoint a separate attorney for each defendant because of a possible conflict of interest. This conflict will probably be now coming up since each one of them wants to testify.

"THE COURT: That's all right; let them testify. There is no conflict of interest. Every time I try more than one person in this court each one blames it on the other one.

"MR. HALL: I have talked to each one of these defendants, and I have talked to them individually, not collectively.

"THE COURT: Now talk to them collectively."

The court then indicated satisfaction that each petitioner understood the nature and consequences of his right to testify on his own behalf, whereupon Hall observed:

"I am in a position now where I am more or less muzzled as to any cross-examination.

"THE COURT: You have no right to cross-examine your own witness.

"MR. HALL: Or to examine them.

"THE COURT: You have a right to examine them, but have no right to cross-examine them. The prosecuting attorney does that.

"MR. HALL: If one [defendant] takes the stand, somebody needs to protect the other two's interest while that one is testifying, and I can't do that since I have talked to each one individually.

"THE COURT: Well, you have talked to them, I assume, individually and collectively, too. They all say they want to testify. I think it's perfectly alright for them to testify if they want to, or not. It's their business.

* * *

"Each defendant said he wants to testify, and there will be no cross-examination of these witnesses, just a direct examination by you.

"MR. HALL: Your Honor, I can't even put them on direct examination because if I ask them—

"THE COURT: (interposing) You can just put them on the stand and tell the Court that you have advised them of their rights and they want to testify; then you tell the man to go ahead and relate what he wants to. That's all you need to do." [4]

Holloway then took the stand on his own behalf, testifying that during the time described as the time of the robbery he was at his brother's home. His brother had previously given similar testimony. When Welch took the witness stand, the record shows Hall advised him, as he had Holloway, that "I cannot ask you any questions that might tend to incriminate any one of the three of you * * *. Now, the only thing I can say is tell these ladies and gentlemen of the jury what you know about this case * * *." Welch responded that he did not "have any kind of speech ready for the jury or anything. I

4. The record reveals that both the trial court and defense counsel were alert to defense counsel's obligation to avoid assisting in the presentation of what counsel had reason to believe was false testimony, or, at least, testimony contrary to the version of facts given to him earlier and in confidence. Cf. ABA, Standards Relating to the Administration of Criminal Justice—The Defense Function § 7.7(c), at 133 (1974). [Eds.: see infra pp. 305–29]

thought I was going to be questioned." When Welch denied, from the witness stand, that he was at the restaurant the night of the robbery, Holloway interrupted, asking:

> "Your Honor, are we allowed to make an objection?
>
> "THE COURT: No, sir. Your counsel will take care of any objections.
>
> "MR. HALL: Your Honor, that is what I am trying to say. I can't cross-examine them.
>
> "THE COURT: You proceed like I tell you to, Mr. Hall. You have no right to cross-examine your own witnesses anyhow."

Welch proceeded with his unguided direct testimony, denying any involvement in the crime and stating that he was at his home at the time it occurred. Campbell gave similar testimony when he took the stand. He also denied making any confession to the arresting officers.

The jury rejected the versions of events presented by the three defendants and the alibi witness, and returned guilty verdicts on all counts. On appeal to the Arkansas Supreme Court, petitioners raised the claim that their representation by a single appointed attorney, over their objection, violated federal constitutional guarantees of effective assistance of counsel. [T]he court concluded that the record demonstrated no actual conflict of interests or prejudice to the petitioners and therefore affirmed.

II

More than 35 years ago, in Glasser v. United States, 315 U.S. 60, 62 S.Ct. 457, 86 L.Ed. 680 (1942), this Court held that by requiring an attorney to represent two codefendants whose interests were in conflict the District Court had denied one of the defendants his Sixth Amendment right to the effective assistance of counsel. In that case, [t]wo of the defendants, Glasser and Kretske, were represented initially by separate counsel. On the second day of trial, however, Kretske became dissatisfied with his attorney and dismissed him. The District Judge thereupon asked Glasser's attorney, Stewart, if he would also represent Kretske. Stewart responded by noting a possible conflict of interests; his representation of both Glasser and Kretske might lead the jury to link the two men together. Glasser also made known that he objected to the proposal. The District Court nevertheless appointed Stewart, who continued as Glasser's retained counsel, to represent Kretske. Both men were convicted.

Glasser contended in this Court that Stewart's representation at trial was ineffective because of conflicts between the interests of his two clients. This Court held "the 'Assistance of Counsel' guaranteed by the Sixth Amendment contemplates that such assistance be untrammeled and unimpaired by a court order requiring that one lawyer should simultaneously represent conflicting interests." The record disclosed that Stewart failed to cross-examine a Government witness whose testimony linked Glasser with the conspiracy and failed to object to the admission of arguably inadmissible evidence. This failure was viewed by the Court as a result of Stewart's desire to protect Kretske's interests, and was thus "indicative of Stewart's struggle to serve two masters * * *." After identifying this conflict of interests, the Court declined to inquire whether the prejudice flowing from it was harmless and instead ordered Glasser's conviction reversed. Kretske's conviction, however, was affirmed.

One principle applicable here emerges from *Glasser* without ambiguity. Requiring or permitting a single attorney to represent co-defendants, often referred to as joint representation, is not *per se* violative of constitutional guarantees of effective assistance of counsel. This principle recognizes that in some cases multiple defendants can appropriately be represented by one attorney; indeed, in some cases, certain advantages might accrue from joint representation. In Mr. Justice Frankfurter's view: "Joint representation is a means of insuring against reciprocal recrimination. A common defense often gives strength against a common attack." Glasser v. United States, supra, at 92, 62 S.Ct., at 475 (dissenting).[5]

* * * Here trial counsel, by the pretrial motions of August 13 and September 4 and by his accompanying representations, made as an officer of the court, focused explicitly on the probable risk of a conflict of interests. The judge then failed either to appoint separate counsel or to take adequate steps to ascertain whether the risk was too remote to warrant separate counsel. We hold that the failure, in the face of the representations made by counsel weeks before trial and again before the jury was empanelled, deprived petitioners of the guarantee of "assistance of counsel."

* * * It is arguable, perhaps, that defense counsel might have presented the requests for appointment of separate counsel more vigorously and in greater detail. As to the former, however, the trial court's responses hardly encouraged pursuit of the separate counsel claim; and as to presenting the basis for that claim in more detail, defense counsel was confronted with a risk of violating, by more disclosure, his duty of confidentiality to his clients.

Additionally, since the decision in *Glasser*, most courts have held that an attorney's request for the appointment of separate counsel, based on his representations as an officer of the court regarding a conflict of interests, should be granted. In so holding, the courts have acknowledged and given effect to several interrelated considerations. An "attorney representing two defendants in a criminal matter is in the best position professionally and ethically to determine when a conflict of interest exists or will probably develop in the course of a trial."

5. By inquiring in *Glasser* whether there had been a waiver, the Court also confirmed that a defendant may waive his right to the assistance of an attorney unhindered by a conflict of interests. In this case, however, Arkansas does not contend that petitioners waived that right.

State v. Davis, 110 Ariz.[29,] 31, 514 P.2d [1025,] 1027 [1973]. Second, defense attorneys have the obligation, upon discovering a conflict of interests, to advise the court at once of the problem. Ibid.[a] Finally, attorneys are officers of the court, and " 'when they address the judge solemnly upon a matter before the court, their declarations are virtually made under oath.' " State v. Brazile, 226 La. [254,] 266, 75 So.2d [856,] 860–61.[9] We find these considerations persuasive.

The State argues, however, that to credit Hall's representations to the trial court would be tantamount to transferring to defense counsel the authority of the trial judge to rule on the existence or risk of a conflict and to appoint separate counsel. In the State's view, the ultimate decision on those matters must remain with the trial judge; otherwise unscrupulous defense attorneys might abuse their "authority," presumably for purposes of delay or obstruction of the orderly conduct of the trial.[10]

The State has an obvious interest in avoiding such abuses. But our holding does not undermine that interest. When an untimely motion for separate counsel is made for dilatory purposes, our holding does not impair the trial court's ability to deal with counsel who resort to such tactics. Nor does our holding preclude a trial court from exploring the adequacy of the basis of defense counsel's representations regarding a conflict of interests without improperly requiring disclosure of the confidential communications of the client.[11] See State v. Davis, supra. In this case the trial court simply failed to take adequate steps in response to the repeated motions, objections and

a. At this point, the Court in footnote quoted the predecessor of ABA Standards for Criminal Justice 4–3.5(b) (2d ed. 1980), which currently specifies:

> "Except for preliminary matters such as initial hearings or applications for bail, a lawyer or lawyers who are associated in practice should not undertake to defend more than one defendant in the same criminal case if the duty to one of the defendants may conflict with the duty to another. The potential for conflict of interest in representing multiple defendants is so grave that ordinarily a lawyer should decline to act for more than one of several codefendants except in unusual situations when, after careful investigation, it is clear that:
>
> (i) no conflict is likely to develop;
>
> (ii) the several defendants give an informed consent to such multiple representation; and
>
> (iii) the consent of the defendants is made a matter of judicial record. In determining the presence of consent by the defendants, the trial judge should make appropriate inquiries respecting actual or potential conflicts of interest of counsel and whether the defendants fully comprehend the difficulties that an attorney sometimes encounters in defending multiple clients.
>
> In some instances, accepting or continuing employment by more than one defendant in the same criminal case is unprofessional conduct."

9. When a considered representation regarding a conflict in clients' interests comes from an officer of the court, it should be given the weight commensurate with the grave penalties risked for misrepresentation.

10. Such risks are undoubtedly present; they are inherent in the adversary system. But courts have abundant power to deal with attorneys who misrepresent facts.

11. This case does not require an inquiry into the extent of a court's power to compel an attorney to disclose confidential communications that he concludes would be damaging to his client. Cf. DR 4–101(C)(2). Such compelled disclosure creates significant risks of unfair prejudice, especially when the disclosure is to a judge who may be called upon later to select sentences for the attorney's clients.

representations made to it, and no prospect of dilatory practices was present to justify that failure.

III

The issue remains whether the error committed at petitioners' trial requires reversal of their convictions. * * *

We read the Court's opinion in *Glasser* * * * as holding that whenever a trial court improperly requires joint representation over timely objection reversal is automatic. The *Glasser* Court stated:

> "To determine the precise degree of prejudice sustained by Glasser as a result of the [District] Court's appointment of Stewart as counsel for Kretske is at once difficult and unnecessary. The right to have the assistance of counsel is too fundamental and absolute to allow courts to indulge in nice calculations as to the amount of prejudice arising from its denial."

This language presupposes that the joint representation, over his express objections, prejudiced the accused in some degree. But from the cases * * * it is clear that the prejudice is presumed regardless of whether it was independently shown. * * *

Moreover, this Court has concluded that the assistance of counsel is among those "constitutional rights so basic to a fair trial that their infraction can never be treated as harmless error." Chapman v. California, 386 U.S., [18,] 23, 87 S.Ct. [824,] 827 [1967]. Accordingly, when a defendant is deprived of the presence and assistance of his attorney, either throughout the prosecution or during a critical stage in, at least, the prosecution of a capital offense, reversal is automatic.

That an attorney representing multiple defendants with conflicting interests is physically present at pretrial proceedings, during trial, and at sentencing does not warrant departure from this general rule. Joint representation of conflicting interests is suspect because of what it tends to prevent the attorney from doing. For example, in this case it may well have precluded defense counsel for Campbell from exploring possible plea negotiations and the possibility of an agreement to testify for the prosecution, provided a lesser charge or a favorable sentencing recommendation would be acceptable. Generally speaking, a conflict may also prevent an attorney from challenging the admission of evidence prejudicial to one client but perhaps favorable to another, or from arguing at the sentencing hearing the relative involvement and culpability of his clients in order to minimize the culpability of one by emphasizing that of another. Examples can be readily multiplied. The mere physical presence of an attorney does not fulfill the Sixth Amendment guarantee when the advocate's conflicting obligations has effectively sealed his lips on crucial matters.

Finally, a rule requiring a defendant to show that a conflict of interests—which he and his counsel tried to avoid by timely objections to the joint representation—prejudiced him in some specific fashion would not be susceptible to intelligent, evenhanded application. In the normal case where a harmless error rule is applied, the error occurs at trial and its scope is readily identifiable. Accordingly, the reviewing court can undertake with some confidence its relatively narrow task of assessing the likelihood that the error materially affected the deliberations of the jury. But in a case of joint representation of conflicting interests the evil—it bears repeating—is in what the advocate finds himself compelled to *refrain* from doing, not only at trial but also as to possible pretrial plea negotiations and in the sentencing process. It may be possible in some cases to identify from the record the prejudice resulting from an attorney's failure to undertake certain trial tasks, but even with a record of the sentencing hearing available it would be difficult to judge intelligently the impact of a conflict on the attorney's representation of a client. And to assess the impact of a conflict of interests on the attorney's options, tactics and decisions in plea negotiations would be virtually impossible. Thus, an inquiry into a claim of harmless error here would require, unlike most cases, unguided speculation.

Accordingly, we reverse and remand for further proceedings not inconsistent with this opinion.

Mr. Justice POWELL with whom Mr. Justice BLACKMUN and Mr. Justice REHNQUIST join, dissenting.

* * * I agree that the representations made by defense counsel in this case, while not as informative as the affidavit of counsel Stewart in *Glasser,* were sufficient to bring into play the trial court's duty to inquire further into the possibility of "conflicting interests." I question, however, whether the Constitution is violated simply by the failure to conduct that inquiry, without any additional determination that the record reveals a case of joint representation in the face of "conflicting interests." * * *

***Comment***

(1) *Setting aside conviction.* Following the Supreme Court's lead in *Glasser,* courts often have set aside criminal convictions (including guilty plea convictions[1]) on the ground that a lawyer's representing codefendants with conflicting interests violates the constitutional right

1. See Bishop v. Parratt, 509 F.Supp. 1140 (D.Neb.1981) (granting habeas to all three defendants where two defendants and lawyer persuaded reluctant third defendant to plead guilty as required by aggregate plea arrangement); LaFrance v. State, 585 S.W.2d 317 (Mo.1979) (reversing conviction where plea bargain was that if one of four jointly represented defendants pleaded guilty charges against others would be dismissed).

But see United States ex rel. Robinson v. Housewright, 525 F.2d 988 (7th Cir. 1975) (no habeas where defendant did not prove lawyer persuaded him to plead guilty in order to benefit other defendants who went to trial).

Regarding continued representation of codefendants through trial after rejection of an aggregate plea arrangement, compare Walker v. Garrington, 521 F.Supp. 1313 (M.D.Tenn.1981) (habeas where one defendant had wanted to accept arrangement and other had not) with Smith v. Regan, 583 F.2d 72 (2d Cir. 1978) (no habeas where both defendants had wanted to reject arrangement and there was no indication separate counsel could have obtained individual plea agreement).

to effective counsel.[2] Thus, courts have reversed convictions or granted habeas where:

(a) one defendant's testimony accused the other of the crime (whether the accusing codefendant denied the crime[3] or admitted it[4]),

(b) a *witness* for one defendant implicated the other defendant (whether counsel called[5] or did not call[6] the witness),

(c) one defendant admitted being at the scene of the crime and the other did not,[7]

(d) pressing one defendant's defense would have shifted responsibility to the other,[8]

(e) one defendant's testimony accepted the blame (because counsel's advice on this may have been intended to help the other defendant),[9]

(f) one defendant could not take the stand to exonerate the other without risking prejudice to his own case,[10]

(g) one defendant could not take the stand to exonerate *himself* without prejudicing the other defendant's case,[11]

(h) one defendant's *failure* to take the stand eroded the other defendant's consent defense,[12]

(i) one defendant claimed not only that he did not participate with the other defendant but that he did not *know* the other defendant,[13] and

2. See Hyman, Joint Representation of Multiple Defendants in a Criminal Trial: The Court's Headache, 5 Hofstra L.Rev. 315 (1977); Lowenthal, Joint Representation in Criminal Cases: A Critical Appraisal, 64 Va.L.Rev. 939 (1978); Annot., 18 A.L.R.4th 360 (1982); Annot., 53 A.L.R.Fed. 140 (1981); Annot., 34 A.L.R.3d 470 (1970).

Regarding *discipline* for representing multiple criminal defendants, see State v. Hilton, 217 Kan. 694, 538 P.2d 977 (1975).

3. See United States ex rel. Williams v. Franzen, 687 F.2d 944 (7th Cir. 1982); Baty v. Balkcom, 661 F.2d 391 (5th Cir. 1981); cert. denied 456 U.S. 1011, 102 S.Ct. 2307, 73 L.Ed.2d 1308 (1982); State v. Coleman, 9 Ariz.App. 526, 454 P.2d 196 (1969); Commonwealth v. Booker, 219 Pa.Super. 91, 280 A.2d 561 (1971).

4. See People v. Ware, 39 Ill.2d 66, 233 N.E.2d 421 (1968); Kent v. State, 11 Md.App. 293, 273 A.2d 819 (1971); People v. Lamere, 39 A.D.2d 15, 331 N.Y.S.2d 178 (1972); Commonwealth v. Breaker, 456 Pa. 341, 318 A.2d 354 (1974); Moran v. State, 4 Tenn.Crim.App. 399, 472 S.W.2d 238 (1971); Gonzales v. State, 605 S.W.2d 278 (Tex.Crim.App.1980).

5. See People v. Hilton, 26 Mich.App. 274, 182 N.W.2d 29 (1971).

6. See Turnquest v. Wainwright, 651 F.2d 331 (5th Cir. 1981); State v. Nielsen, 29 Wn.App. 451, 629 P.2d 1333 (1981).

7. See State v. Bush, 108 Ariz. 148, 493 P.2d 1205 (1972); People v. Gardner, 385 Mich. 392, 189 N.W.2d 229 (1971).

8. United States ex rel. Vriñer v. Hedrick, 500 F.Supp. 977 (C.D.Ill.1980); People v. Thompson, 13 Cal.App.3d 47, 91 Cal.Rptr. 341 (1970); McIver v. United States, 280 A.2d 527 (D.C.App.1971).

9. See Commonwealth v. Smith, 228 Pa.Super. 256, 323 A.2d 838 (1974).

10. See Horowitz v. Henderson, 514 F.2d 740 (5th Cir. 1975); State v. Weese, 424 A.2d 705 (Me.1981); State v. Martiñeau, 257 Minn. 334, 101 N.W.2d 410 (1960).

11. See Alvarez v. Wainwright, 552 F.2d 100 (5th Cir. 1975); Holland v. Henderson, 460 F.2d 978 (5th Cir. 1972).

12. See Commonwealth v. Knight, 245 Pa.Super. 337, 369 A.2d 431 (1976).

13. See Smith v. Anderson, 689 F.2d 59 (6th Cir. 1982).

But see Washington v. State, 419 So.2d 1100 (Fla.App.1982).

(j) the case against one defendant was stronger than that against the other.[14]

Similarly, cases have been remanded for resentencing with separate representation where one defendant's past record was better than the other's (whether the joint lawyer at sentencing emphasized this[15] or did not[16]).

(2) *Cuyler v. Sullivan.* In Cuyler v. Sullivan,[17] a 7–2 United States Supreme Court, while recognizing that the sixth amendment right to counsel free from conflicting interests applies to retained as well as appointed counsel and to cases where each defendant has a separate trial as well as where the defendants are tried jointly, held that a trial court is not constitutionally required to make inquiry about multiple representation on its own initiative absent any objection and absent any particular indication of a conflict of interest. Although this kind of inquiry is a desirable practice and is required of federal courts by F.R.Crim.P. 44(c), it is not constitutionally mandated. The Court said:

> "*Holloway* requires state trial courts to investigate timely objections to multiple representation. But nothing in our precedents suggests that the Sixth Amendment requires state courts themselves to initiate inquiries into the propriety of multiple representation in every case. Defense counsel have an ethical obligation to avoid conflicting representations and to advise the court promptly when a conflict of interest arises during the course of trial. Absent special circumstances, therefore, trial courts may assume either that multiple representation entails no conflict or that the lawyer and his clients knowingly accept such risk of conflict as may exist. * * * Unless the trial court knows or reasonably should know that a particular conflict exits, the court need not initiate an inquiry."

14. See United States v. Olsen, 453 F.2d 612 (2d Cir.) (counsel argued case for one "even stronger" than for other), cert. denied, 406 U.S. 927, 92 S.Ct. 1801, 32 L.Ed.2d 128 (1972). See also United States ex rel. Hart v. Davenport, 478 F.2d 203 (3d Cir. 1973); Campbell v. United States, 122 U.S.App.D.C. 143, 352 F.2d 359 (1965); Cavallaro v. United States, 359 F.Supp. 1276 (D.Conn.1973); People v. Chacon, 69 Cal.2d 765, 73 Cal.Rptr. 10, 447 P.2d 106, 34 A.L.R.3d 454 (1968); People v. Gallardo, 269 Cal.App.2d 86, 74 Cal.Rptr. 572 (1969); People v. Keesee, 250 Cal.App.2d 794, 58 Cal.Rptr. 780 (1967).

But see United States v. Benavidez, 664 F.2d 1255 (5th Cir.), cert. denied 457 U.S. 1121, 102 S.Ct. 2936, 73 L.Ed.2d 1334 (1982); United States v. Gallagher, 437 F.2d 1191 (7th Cir.), cert. denied 402 U.S. 1009, 91 S.Ct. 2190, 29 L.Ed.2d 430 (1971); Washington v. State, 419 So.2d 1100 (Fla.App.1982); People v. Tillman, 59 Mich.App.768, 229 N.W.2d 922 (1975); Holloway v. State, 32 Wis.2d 559, 146 N.W.2d 441 (1966).

15. See Commonwealth v. Bolduc, 375 Mass. 530, 378 N.E.2d 661 (1978) (remanding case of defendant with worse record).

16. See Commonwealth v. Cox, 441 Pa. 64, 270 A.2d 207 (1970) (remanding case of defendant with better record).

Compare State v. Kruchten, 101 Ariz. 186, 417 P.2d 510 (1966) (affirming where slight differences would not have justified different sentences), cert. denied 385 U.S. 1043, 87 S.Ct. 784, 17 L.Ed.2d 687 (1967); In re Watson, 6 Cal.3d 831, 100 Cal.Rptr. 720, 494 P.2d 1264 (1972) (similar).

17. 446 U.S. 335, 100 S.Ct. 1708, 64 L.Ed.2d 333 (1980).

The Court also held that "to establish a violation of the Sixth Amendment, a defendant who raised no objection at trial must demonstrate that an actual conflict of interest adversely affected his lawyer's performance"—showing a "possibility of conflict" is insufficient.[18]

### *Questions*

(1) Should a court be able to disqualify counsel from representing multiple criminal defendants if the defendants voluntarily and intelligently waive the right to conflict-free counsel?[1]

(2) May a lawyer simultaneously represent a criminal defendant and (in a completely unrelated civil matter not involving the criminal defendant) the victim of the crime with which the criminal defendant is charged?[2]

(3) May two lawyers from the same public defender office represent criminal defendants with conflicting interests? The RPC's Terminology defines "Firm" as including "lawyers employed in the legal department of a corporation or other organization and lawyers em-

18. Compare Developments in the Law, Conflicts of Interest in the Legal Profession, 94 Harv.L.Rev. 1244, 1390–97 (1981), discussing *Cuyler* and concluding that the "most needed change is a categorical rule forbidding * * * joint representation of codefendants" and "[a]t the very least, the requirement of proving prejudice on appeal should be eliminated when conflicts arise" therefrom. See Geer, Representation of Multiple Criminal Defendants: Conflicts of Interest and the Professional Responsibilities of the Defense Attorney, 62 Minn.L.Rev. 119 (1978) (urging flat prohibition on representing multiple criminal defendants).

1. Compare Flanagan v. United States, 679 F.2d 1072 (3d Cir. 1982) (trial court did not abuse discretion in disqualifying counsel although codefendants voluntarily and intelligently waived any conflict of interest claim), rev'd on other grounds, — U.S. —, 104 S.Ct. 1051, 79 L.Ed.2d 288 (1984) and Fleming v. State, 246 Ga. 90, 270 S.E.2d 185 (waiver not permitted in capital case), cert. denied 449 U.S. 904, 101 S.Ct. 278, 66 L.Ed.2d 136 (1980) with United States v. Curcio, 694 F.2d 14 (2d Cir. 1982) (defendant has right to counsel of choice if defendant makes voluntary and intelligent waiver of potential conflicts and if according right will not unduly delay trial, harm other defendants, or create actual conflict) and Margolin & Coliver, Pretrial Disqualification of Criminal Defense Counsel, 20 Am.Crim.L.Rev. 227 (1982) (prosecutors often use disqualification motions merely to disqualify the most competent lawyers). See also infra pp. 253–55.

Compare United States v. Bendetti, 498 F.Supp. 450 (D.N.J.1980) (lawyer desired by three defendants not permitted to *replace* defendants' three separate lawyers, but allowed to advise defendants' individual lawyers and, if they agree, handle some of the cross examination and legal arguments), affirmed mem. 642 F.2d 444 (3d Cir.), cert. denied 452 U.S. 938, 101 S.Ct. 3080, 69 L.Ed.2d 952 (1981).

2. See Castillo v. Estelle, 504 F.2d 1243 (5th Cir. 1974); People v. Stoval, 40 Ill.2d 109, 239 N.E.2d 441 (1968).

See also Commonwealth v. Hodge, 386 Mass. 165, 434 N.E.2d 1246 (1982) (lawyer's *partner* was representing prosecution *witness* in unrelated civil matter).

Compare Zuck v. Alabama, 588 F.2d 436 (5th Cir.), cert. denied 444 U.S. 883, 100 S.Ct. 63, 62 L.Ed.2d 42 (1979) (lawyer was representing *prosecutor* in unrelated civil matter).

Regarding *previous* representation of prosecution witness, see United States v. Jeffers, 520 F.2d 1256 (7th Cir. 1975), cert. denied 423 U.S. 1066, 96 S.Ct. 805, 46 L.Ed.2d 656 (1976); Shelton v. State, 254 Ark. 815, 496 S.W.2d 419 (1973); Olds v. State, 302 So.2d 787 (Fla.App.1974), cert. denied 312 So.2d 743 (1975); People v. Drysdale, 51 Ill.App.3d 667, 9 Ill.Dec. 137, 366 N.E.2d 394 (1977); Commonwealth v. Smith, 362 Mass. 782, 291 N.E.2d 607 (1973); Annot., 27 A.L.R.3d 1431 (1969).

Regarding counsel's personal acquaintance with murder victim, see People v. Lewis, 88 Ill.2d 429, 58 Ill.Dec. 743, 430 N.E.2d 994 (1981), cert. denied — U.S. —, 103 S.Ct. 1501, 75 L.Ed.2d 932 (1983).

Regarding simultaneous representation of a judgment creditor and, in an unrelated criminal prosecution, the debtor, see infra p. 200, Comment (6).

ployed in a legal services organization,"[3] and the Comment to RPC 1.10 states:

> "Lawyers employed in the same unit of a legal service organization constitute a firm, but not necessarily those employed in separate units. As in the case of independent practitioners, whether the lawyers should be treated as associated with each other can depend on the particular rule that is involved, and on the specific facts of the situation."

Courts generally apply traditional imputed disqualification rules to lawyers in the same public defender office,[4] in line with the view that "[l]awyers who practice their profession side-by-side, literally and figuratively, are subject to subtle influences that may well affect their professional judgment and loyalty to their clients, even though they are not faced with the more easily recognized economic conflict of interest."[5] But it has been held that imputed disqualification does not extend to public defenders who although employed by the same authority work out of separate offices, principally on the ground that they do not share files.[6]

OL

## 2. CIVIL MATTERS GENERALLY

### a. *Representing Multiple Parties in Same Matter*

#### WOODRUFF v. TOMLIN

616 F.2d 924 (6th Cir.), cert. denied 449 U.S. 888, 101 S.Ct. 246, 66 L.Ed.2d 114 (1980).

LIVELY, Circuit Judge.

This case involves a claim of legal malpractice arising from the manner in which the defendants handled litigation on behalf of the plaintiffs

3. Compare CPR Definition (2) (" 'Law firm' includes a professional legal corporation.").

4. See Allen v. District Court, 184 Colo. 202, 519 P.2d 351 (1974); Turner v. State, 340 So.2d 132 (Fla.Dist.Ct.App.1976); Commonwealth v. Westbrook, 484 Pa. 534, 400 A.2d 160 (1979); State v. Smith, 621 P.2d 697 (Utah 1980); Breger, Disqualification for Conflicts of Interest and the Legal Aid Attorney, 62 B.U.L.Rev. 1115 (1982); Webster, The Public Defender, the Sixth Amendment, and the Code of Professional Responsibility: The Resolution of a Conflict of Interest, 12 Am.Crim.L.Rev. 739 (1975).

Compare People v. Miller, 79 Ill.2d 454, 38 Ill.Dec. 775, 404 N.E.2d 199 (1980) (no per se rule; "in determining whether separate [assistant public defenders] can properly represent competing interests, we are to apply the general guidelines enunciated in our prior cases and those of the United States Supreme Court on the subject of conflicts of interest").

5. Borden v. Borden, 277 A.2d 89 (D.C.App.1971) (legal services program lawyers may not represent both parties in divorce suit).

6. See People v. Puckett, 70 Ill.App.3d 743, 27 Ill.Dec. 244, 388 N.E.2d 1293 (1979) (part-time public defenders appointed by court and paid by county "do not share offices, files, expenses, cases, or even communicate with one another except in a fashion common to all attorneys").

But see In re Bruce W., 114 Misc.2d 91, 450 N.Y.S.2d 734 (1982) (lawyer from juvenile division and lawyer from criminal defense division of legal aid society may represent alleged co-perpetrators with conflicting interests only with clients' informed consent); ABA Informal Opinion 1418 (1978) (lawyers in different cities within public defender department are "affiliated" for purposes of DR 5–105(D)).

in the Tennessee state courts. Jurisdiction of the district court was based on diversity of citizenship. The district court severed the plaintiffs' claims based on alleged conflict of interests in the defendants' representation of multiple parties. * * * The case was tried to a jury on the plaintiffs' claims that the defendants negligently conducted "the investigation, preparation for trial and presentation at trial" of the plaintiffs' claims for personal injuries arising from an auto-truck collision. The jury in the district court was unable to agree on a verdict. * * * The defendants then filed a motion for judgment n. o. v. * * * This motion was granted.

[A] panel of [this] court reversed the judgment of the district court. Thereafter this court granted rehearing *en banc* * * *. [W]e adopt the following statement from the panel opinion:

"The plaintiffs, Joan Woodruff and her sister Patricia, then 15 and 16 years of age respectively, were severely injured on May 22, 1968, when an automobile driven by Patricia and owned by her father, in which automobile Joan was riding as a passenger, was struck by a large truck loaded with gravel weighing about 73,000 pounds, on Highway 100 in Chester County, Tennessee. Joan was thrown out of the car and [a second] truck ran over her legs, crushing the bones and tearing the skin off her legs, crippling her for life. Patricia sustained a skull and brain injury resulting in traumatic amnesia, so that she had no memory of the accident.

"The girls' hospital bills alone exceeded $20,000.

"The girls' father, Charles Woodruff, carried liability insurance on his car with Tennessee Farmers Mutual Insurance Company, with limits of $10,000 for one person, and $20,000 for more than one person. While the girls were in the hospital Theo. Leathers, the Claims Adjuster for the insurer, contacted Mr. Woodruff and gave him a check for medical reimbursement. Leathers advised Mr. Woodruff that he should retain a lawyer. Leathers told Mr. Woodruff that the statements of witnesses to the collision were inconsistent and were changing.

"Leathers recommended to Woodruff that he retain Hewitt P. Tomlin, stating that Tomlin was a good lawyer. Tomlin was also the attorney for Tennessee Farmers Mutual Insurance Company. Woodruff then engaged Tomlin to represent his two daughters, and also to represent himself in his claim for damages to his car.

"Tomlin filed two suits for personal injuries sustained by the girls and one for damages to the car, against Pomeroy, the driver of the large truck, Teague, the owner of the truck, and Nobles, the owner of the second truck. The suits were filed in the Circuit Court of Chester County, Tennessee.

"Pomeroy, the truck driver, and Teague, the owner of the truck, filed suits in said Circuit Court against Patricia Woodruff and her sister Joan, to recover damages for personal injury sustained by Pomeroy, and for damages to the truck. They alleged negligence on the part of Patricia, and that Joan, the passenger, aided and abetted. Tomlin, as attorney for Tennessee Farmers Mutual Insurance Company, defended the suits against the two girls. The suits were all consolidated for trial.

"The cases in the state court were tried before a jury, which disagreed 9–3, and a mistrial was declared. At the second trial in the state court the jury returned a verdict in favor of the defendants in the personal injury actions of Patricia and Joan against Pomeroy, Teague and Nobles. In the suit of Pomeroy and Teague against Patricia and Joan the jury returned verdicts in favor of Pomeroy for $600, and Teague in the amount of $3,000.

"Upon appeal to the state court of appeals the judgments for the defendants in the personal injury cases of Patricia and Joan against Pomeroy, Teague and Nobles, were affirmed. The judgments in favor of Pomeroy and Teague against Patricia, totaling $3,600, were affirmed, but were reversed as to Joan, the Court holding that there was no evidence to prove that Joan, the passenger, aided and abetted in the negligence of Patricia. Therefore Joan was not contributorily negligent, and Patricia's negligence could not be imputed to her."

In the district court the plaintiffs contended that the loss of their personal injury actions in the state trial and appellate courts was proximately caused by negligence of the defendants and by their breach of fiduciary duties arising from the attorney-client relationship. * * *

[Discussion of negligence claim omitted.]

* * * We conclude that it was error to grant judgment n. o. v. in favor of the defendants on [the negligence] claim.

The jury heard no evidence on the charge of malpractice based on alleged conflict of interests. Nevertheless, the district court included this claim in its judgment n. o. v. We believe the true effect of the court's action with respect to this claim was that it granted summary judgment for the defendants. * * *

The alleged conflict of interests arose from the fact that Tomlin undertook to represent Tennessee Farmers Mutual Insurance Company, Charles Woodruff, Patricia Woodruff and Joan Woodruff. The interests of the insurance company, the insured father and Patricia, who was driving with her father's permission, appear to have been identical. The legal rights and obligations of all three, insofar as the consolidated actions were concerned, were the same. Thus this claim is centered on the continued representation of the passenger, Joan Woodruff. As a passenger, Joan had a potential claim against her sister Patricia, which it would have been the duty of the insurance company to defend. Though there is a dispute as to whether the policy contained a family exclusion which would have prevented Joan from recovering damages, the policy was never filed in the record. The district court assumed there would have been coverage. The question is what duty was imposed upon the attorney in this situation.

The plaintiffs argue that it was malpractice for Tomlin to continue to represent Joan and that he had an absolute duty to withdraw as her counsel if he continued to represent her sister, her father and his insurer. The plaintiffs' expert, an Arizona attorney, testified to this effect and gave several examples of how the multiple representation would be damaging. So far as this record reveals, Tennessee has no rule which absolutely forbids multiple representation. However, the attorney-client relationship requires an attorney to be alert to potential conflicts and to decline multiple representation when actual conflicts develop. [DR] 5–105(C) * * * provides in cases where multiple representation is likely to involve him in representing differing interests, "a lawyer may represent multiple clients if it is obvious that he can adequately represent the interest of each and if each consents to the representation *after full disclosure of the possible effect of such representation on the exercise of his independent professional judgment on behalf of each.*" [Emphasis supplied.]

We recognize that the Code of Professional Responsibility "does not undertake to define standards for civil liability of lawyers for professional conduct." [CPR Preliminary Statement.] Nevertheless, it certainly constitutes some evidence of the standards required of attorneys. See Annot., Malpractice: Liability of Attorney Representing Conflicting Interests, 28 A.L.R.3d 389 (1969); Crest Investment Trust, Inc. v. Comstock, 23 Md.App. 280, 327 A.2d 891, 904 (1974); Lysick v. Walcom, 258 Cal.App.2d 136, 65 Cal.Rptr. 406, 414 (1968).

It is clear that the defendant Tomlin never advised Charles Woodruff that Joan had a potential claim against Patricia. It appears that Tomlin had no knowledge of a family exclusion which would have prevented Joan from recovering damages under her father's policy, if such exclusion existed. Tomlin testified that both Mr. and Mrs. Woodruff were firm that Patricia was free of any negligence and wanted to protect her from any inference of responsibility. Further, Patricia had no memory of the events surrounding the collision and Joan consistently stated that it was not Patricia's fault. On the other hand, Charles Woodruff testified that he would have permitted Joan to sue Patricia and that he did not know of this possibility until after the trials were over.

Though it appears unlikely that Charles Woodruff would have sought other counsel for Joan if he had known of her potential claim against Patricia, this did not relieve the attorney of his obligation to disclose the differing interests and potential conflict. Woodruff's testimony, which must be taken as true for purpose of this appeal, at least created an issue of fact on the question of conflict of interests. The district court does not appear to have held that there was no conflict in the multiple representation. Rather, it dismissed this claim on a finding that it would be speculation for a jury to find that Tomlin's multiple representation affected the outcome of the trial. We think the harm to Joan may be more than a different outcome of the trial of the action against Pomeroy, Teague and Nobles. She may have lost the opportunity for a recovery based on the negligence of Patricia, remote as that possibility may appear.

The speculative nature of the damages disturbed the district court throughout the proceedings in this malpractice action. This is understandable, given the Tennessee rule that a client may only recover from an attorney for malpractice if he shows that "but for" the malpractice he would have been successful in the case in question. * * * Nevertheless, causation is a jury question. The jury could determine, on the basis of expert testimony, whether Joan suffered any injury in fact as the result of Tomlin's failure to advise her father of the potential conflict of interests inherent in his representation of all three plaintiffs and the insurance carrier. A trial of this issue would produce evidence of the actual coverage of the policy (whether there was an exclusion as to Joan) and expert opinion as to whether Joan's case against Pomeroy and Nobles would have been strengthened if she had been independently represented. Such evidence will involve "second guessing." Nevertheless, if the concept of legal malpractice, recognized by the Tennessee courts, is to be more than a mirage, plaintiffs who can produce evidence of negligence or breach of fiduciary responsibility by their attorneys must be given the opportunity to show that they have been damaged. See Story Parchment Co. v. Paterson Parchment Paper Co., 282 U.S. 555, 563, 51 S.Ct. 248, 250, 75 L.Ed. 544 (1931). * * *

Some comment is required on Judge Merritt's dissent. His broadside attack on the court's opinion misstates our holding * * *.

The court does not hold that Joan should have been persuaded to change her story to make out a claim against Patricia. The evidence of breach of duty consisted of Tomlin's failure to advise Joan and her father of the possible existence of a cause of action by Joan against Patricia. All this court holds on the conflict of interests issue is that the plaintiffs were entitled to have a jury determine whether Tomlin's failure to advise his clients fully, in the light of his multiple representation, was legal malpractice.

The dissent implies that the majority is encouraging unethical conduct by suggesting that another lawyer might persuade Joan to change her "consistent claim that her sister was not at fault." Of course, the majority makes no such suggestion. Another attorney, without attachments to Patricia's insurance carrier, might have concluded from Joan's testimony that Patricia was, in fact, at fault. What was important was not whether Joan thought Patricia was at fault, but whether the facts testified to by Joan would indicate legal liability on the part of Patricia. Interestingly, in its restatement of the facts, the dissent says that Joan's testimony demonstrated that "Patsy Woodruff panicked, slammed on the brakes and lost control of her car." A completely neutral lawyer hearing such testimony might conclude that Joan, as a passenger, had a claim against the driver.

Finally, the dissent completely ignores the fact that we are reviewing a judgment notwithstanding verdict. The decision of this court is not that Tomlin was guilty of malpractice or breach of duty, but that the Woodruffs produced sufficient evidence to have their claims submitted to a jury.

The judgment of the district court is * * * reversed in part. The cause is remanded for a new trial * * *.

WEICK, Circuit Judge, concurring * * * in part. * * *

The fact that Tomlin was honest and was acting in good faith, as he claims, did not give him a license to violate the ABA Canons of Professional Ethics as adopted by the Supreme Court of Tennessee or authorize him to represent clients when he had conflicts of interest which he never disclosed to his clients. * * *

In New Jersey, the Supreme Court issued a directive:

> "The Supreme Court is of the view, because of the conflict of interest inherent in the situation, that an attorney should not represent both the driver of a car and his passenger in an action against the driver of another car, unless there is a legal bar to the passenger suing his own driver, as, for example, where they are husband and wife, unemancipated child and parent, or employees of the same employer and the accident occurred in the course of their employment. Where an attorney does represent both a driver and his passenger and no such legal bar exists, if a cross-claim or counterclaim is made by the other driver, a conflict of interest arises and the Supreme Court has advised the Assignment Judges that the attorney should not be permitted to continue to represent either the driver or his passenger." 91 N.J.L.J. 68 (Feb. 1, 1968). And see Weinberg v. Underwood, 101 N.J.Super. 448, 244 A.2d 538 at 540 (1968). * * *

If Joan had been represented by separate counsel, without any conflict of interest and had included her sister Patricia as a party defendant in her suit in the state court against Teague, Pomeroy and Nobles, the jury could not very well have returned a verdict against Patricia in favor of Teague and Pomeroy based on Patricia's negligence without also returning a verdict in favor of Joan against Patricia. As a matter of fact, it would have changed the complexion of the entire case and could have resulted in a verdict against both truck drivers who were blocking both lanes of the highway. * * *

MERRITT, Circuit Judge, dissenting. * * *

On the so-called "conflict of interest" issue, there is a short answer. Had Joan, the passenger, decided to sue her sister, Patsy, the driver, she would have recovered nothing. The family's automobile liability insurance policy apparently contained an exclusion disallowing recovery by family members. Even if Joan had obtained a verdict against

Patsy, there would have been no insurance funds to pay the judgment. How can the lawyer be liable for failing to advise Joan Woodruff to sue her sister when such a suit would have profited her nothing?

Moreover, the majority opinion is remarkably silent on the subject of Joan's consistent claim that her sister was not at fault. Should another lawyer have been called in to try to persuade Joan to change her story to make out a claim aginst Patsy? Before my brothers condemn the lawyer, they should at least consider the ethical implications of such a course of conduct.

Lastly, and most important, the girls' legal guardian, the father, as a moral man, would not have consented for these injured girls to sue and testify against one another and thereby run the risk of lasting damage to the emotional stability of his children and the harmony of his family. As admitted by the Court, the record shows that Mrs. Woodruff did not want Patricia to feel that she was responsible for Joan's injuries. Charles Woodruff stated that he never thought Patricia caused the injury to Joan and both testified that they were a close family. There was testimony by Charles Woodruff, Lila Woodruff and Louis Hamilton, Patricia's husband, that, after the accident, Patricia had a drastic personality change. She became depressed, defensive and had a short breaking point. She asked her father if she was at fault and had caused the accident. Patricia also began doing poorly in school. She eventually had to drop out because of her inability to concentrate. If Joan had, in fact, brought suit against her sister Patricia, what would that have done to Patricia's state of mind?

Thus, there was no real conflict of interest between Joan and Patsy Woodruff. The issue is purely imaginary. Joan did not want to sue Patsy. She would have recovered nothing if she had. It would have been a stupid thing to do.

In closing, it should also be pointed out that the whole Woodruff family testified that they felt Hewitt Tomlin had done a commendable job and, in fact, thanked him for a "job well done." It was not until Charles Woodruff talked to the Arizona lawyer, Norman Herring, that he concluded Tomlin had not done a satisfactory job. For our Court to permit this lawyer to continue to be harassed in this way is unjust.

For these reasons, I would affirm * * *.[a]

**a.** See Jedwabny v. Philadelphia Transportation Co., 390 Pa. 231, 135 A.2d 252 (1957) (upholding new trial for defendant because trial court did not make sure that driver appreciated the conflict of interest in having same lawyer as passengers in suing defendant where defendant named driver as additional defendant and defendant and driver were held jointly liable to passengers), cert. denied 355 U.S. 966, 78 S.Ct. 557, 2 L.Ed.2d 541 (1958); Developments in the Law—Conflicts of Interest in the Legal Profession, 94 Harv.L.Rev. 1244, 1295–96 (1981). See also DuPont v. Southern Pacific Co., 366 F.2d 193, 1 A.L.R.Fed. 216 (5th Cir. 1966) (trial court should not have required lawyers representing driver and passenger plaintiffs to designate single lead counsel).

Regarding the practice of a litigant having one lawyer as plaintiff and another as defendant, see Berkey v. Puliafico, 485 Pa. 187, 401 A.2d 356 (1979); Burish v. Digon, 416 Pa. 486, 206 A.2d 497 (1965).

Regarding conflicts in representing multiple creditors against a debtor who may be unable to pay everyone in full, see Meyers, Ethical Considerations in the Representation of Multiple Creditors Against a Single Debtor, 51 Am.Bankr.L.J. 19 (1977).

### *Comment*

(1) *Informed consent.* Compare the Southern District of New York case of Altschul v. Paine Webber, Inc.,[1] where plaintiffs sued a company for mismanaging their securities account. The company brought a third party complaint against plaintiff's son, who was the company's employee who serviced plaintiffs' account, and the same lawyer represented both plaintiffs and their son. The court held that although the company had standing to seek the lawyer's disqualification (on the ground that ethical misconduct is a matter of public concern implicating the bar's integrity that should be brought to the proper forum's attention by anyone aware of it), the motion should be denied where plaintiffs filed an affidavit stating that they had no wish to sue their son and where plaintiffs' and the son's interests were parallel—to prove that the company mismanaged the account and that the son did not.

(2) *Adequacy of multiple representation.* But in another case from the same jurisdiction, Sapienza v. New York News,[2] the court disqualified a lawyer from simultaneously representing the plaintiffs and one of the defendants in an antitrust suit notwithstanding consent because it was not "obvious that [the lawyer could] adequately represent the interests of each" as required by DR 5–105(C). Compare RPC 1.7(b)(1)'s requirement that "the lawyer reasonably believes that the representation will not be adversely affected."

(3) *Aggregate settlements.* In In re Lauderdale,[3] a Washington court held that where a wrongful death settlement is to be apportioned among a widower, two adult children, and two minor children and court approval is needed for the settlement to become binding upon the minors:

(a) *each* minor must have a separate lawyer or guardian ad litem, and

(b) the adult claimants must either:

(i) all consent to the apportionment as specified in DR 5–106 (the predecessor of RPC 1.8(g)),

(ii) have separate lawyers at the apportionment hearing, or

(iii) "if all agree after full disclosure of the conflict that the financial costs are such that separate counsel are not warranted, then each adult client should be given the opportunity to testify as to his or her circumstances, needs, and recommended apportionment with [their joint lawyer] conducting the examination [but] not advocat[ing] for one client to the detriment of the other without informed consent of each claimant."

In Hayes v. Eagle-Picher Industries, Inc.,[4] the Tenth Circuit held jointly-represented plaintiffs not bound by their agreement to abide by a majority vote on whether to settle. The court said:

"We hold that the arrangement presented allowing the majority to govern the rights of the minority is violative of the basic tenets of

1. 488 F.Supp. 858 (S.D.N.Y.1980).

2. 481 F.Supp. 676 (S.D.N.Y.1979).

3. 15 Wn.App. 321, 549 P.2d 42 (1976).

4. 513 F.2d 892 (10th Cir. 1975).

the attorney-client relationship in that it delegates to the attorney powers which allow him to act not only contrary to the wishes of his client, but to act in a manner disloyal to his client and to his client's interests. Because of this, it is essential that the final settlement be subject to the client's ratification particularly in a non-class action case such as the present one."

(4) *Class actions.* Compare Parker v. Anderson,[5] wherein the Fifth Circuit upheld a class action settlement which counsel presented to the court over the objection of ten of the eleven *named* plaintiffs, saying:

"This inquiry must be placed in proper perspective. Objectors' personal claims were not before the district court and are not before us; they were severed and are still pending. Rather, the objectors stand before us as representatives of the absentee class members. The question presented by this appeal is whether class counsel provided fair and adequate legal representation to the class as a whole. Necessarily, much of what counsel does for the class is by and through the class representatives, but that is neither the ultimate nor the key determinant. The compelling obligation of class counsel in class action litigation is to the group which makes up the class. Counsel must be aware of and motivated by that which is in the maximum best interests of the class considered as a unit.

"The duty owed to the client sharply distinguishes litigation on behalf of one or more individuals and litigation on behalf of a class. * * *

"The courts have recognized that the duty owed by class counsel is to the entire class and is not dependent on the special desires of the named plaintiffs. It has been held that agreement of the named plaintiffs is not essential to approval of a settlement which the trial court finds to be fair and reasonable. 'Because of the unique nature of the attorney-client relationship in a class action, the cases cited by appellants holding that an attorney cannot settle his individual client's case without the authorization of the client are simply inapplicable.' Kincade [v. General Tire & Rubber Co.,] 635 F.2d [501,] 508 [5th Cir. 1981]. The rationale implicit in [the] decisions is sound: the named plaintiffs should not be permitted to hold the absentee class hostage by refusing to assent to an otherwise fair and adequate settlement in order to secure their individual demands. The trial court was not impressed favorably by the motivation of the objectors, finding as a fact that: 'Plaintiff-objectors opposed the settlement in bad faith, primarily to gain leverage in settling their individual claims * * * at exorbitant figures.'

"We measure class counsel's performance of the duty to represent the class fairly and adequately as we gauge the fairness and adequacy of the settlement. It will follow generally that an at-

5. 667 F.2d 1204 (5th Cir. 1982), cert. denied 459 U.S. 828, 103 S.Ct. 63, 74 L.Ed.2d 65 (1982).

torney who secures and submits a fair and adequate settlement has represented the client class fairly and adequately."[6]

### *b. Opposing Current Client in Different Matter*

## INTERNATIONAL BUSINESS MACHINES CORP. v. LEVIN

579 F.2d 271 (3d Cir. 1978).

MARIS, Circuit Judge.

[T]hese appeals and cross-appeals seek our review of an interlocutory order of the United States District Court for the District of New Jersey entered in this private antitrust suit directing Carpenter, Bennett & Morrissey (herein "CBM"), counsel for the plaintiffs, Howard S. Levin (herein "Levin") and Levin Computer Corporation (herein "LCC"), to withdraw from the case and allowing CBM to turn over its past work on the case to substitute counsel for the plaintiffs with consultation with such counsel to effect the turnover permitted for a period of sixty days.

The plaintiffs' lawsuit against the International Business Machines Corporation (herein "IBM"), alleging [antitrust] violations * * * was filed [on June 23, 1972,] after Levin caused LCC to be incorporated * * * for the purpose * * * of engaging in the business of purchasing for lease certain data processing equipment manufactured by IBM [and] IBM refused to extend installment credit to Levin and LCC on other than terms which the latter considered to be unfair and unreasonable * * *.

In June 1977 IBM moved for an order disqualifying CBM from further participation in the case on the ground that the law firm had represented both the plaintiffs and IBM during the pendency of the action in the district court in violation of the disciplinary rules of the Code of Professional Responsibility * * *.

The district court * * * disqualified CBM from further representation of the plaintiffs in the case but permitted CBM to turn over its past work product on the case to the plaintiffs' new counsel and allowed consultation between CBM and the plaintiffs' substitute counsel with respect thereto for a period of sixty days. * * *

* * * IBM * * * appealed from the portions of the district court's order which permit [the] turnover of work product and consultation. * * *

CBM and the plaintiffs cross-appealed from the district court's order disqualifying CBM. * * *

We turn then to outline the facts out of which this controversy arose. It appears that CBM had represented * * * Levin [since 1965].

6. See generally Rhode, Class Conflicts in Class Actions, 34 Stan.L.Rev. 1183 (1982).

* * * In the latter part of 1971 * * * CBM arranged for the incorporation of LCC on behalf of Levin. One of the firm's partners, Stanley Weiss, became a director of LCC and another, David M. McCann, assumed the office of secretary of the corporation.

LCC's effort in late 1971 and 1972 to secure installment credit on terms acceptable to it for the purchase of IBM equipment was handled by McCann dealing with Joseph W. S. Davis, Jr., counsel for IBM's Data Processing Division located in White Plains, New York. As LCC's prospects for a satisfactory credit arrangement with IBM diminished with IBM's successive rejections of LCC's applications for installment credit, Levin's determination to take legal action against IBM grew. In February 1972 McCann advised Davis of the plaintiffs' intention to file suit to enjoin IBM from imposing more stringent credit requirements on LCC than were applied to prospective lessees of the equipment LCC desired to purchase.

Davis reported this information to Nicholas Katzenbach, IBM vice-president and general counsel, and Chester B. McLaughlin, assistant general counsel, both working out of the general counsel's office located at IBM's corporate headquarters in Armonk, New York.

In March 1972 a meeting, attended by McCann and Weiss of CBM, Davis and R. G. O'Neill of IBM, and Levin and the treasurer of LCC, was held at LCC's New York City office in an unsuccessful attempt to resolve the dispute. IBM, thereafter, engaged the law firm of Riker, Danzig, Scherer & Debevoise to represent it in any ensuing suit. On June 23, 1972, CBM filed the present suit on behalf of the plaintiffs and has prosecuted it until the present time.

In April 1970 a member of IBM's legal staff in the general counsel's office at Armonk, Robert Troup, contacted Edward F. Ryan, a CBM partner and one of five members of the firm specializing in labor matters, for the purpose of retaining CBM's services in the preparation of an opinion letter for IBM regarding a jurisdictional dispute with an electrical workers' union. The CBM partners considered and rejected the possibility that acceptance of the IBM assignment in the labor matter might create a conflict of interest in the light of CBM's former representation of [Levin]. Ryan prepared an opinion on the jurisdictional dispute question and accepted a second assignment from Troup in July 1970 dealing with a union's right to picket IBM in the event IBM cancelled a subcontracting arrangement and a third assignment in May 1971 relating to the availability of injunctive relief against certain union picketing.

In April 1972 Ryan accepted Troup's telephoned request for another opinion letter in a labor matter concerning the right of temporary employees to form a separate bargaining unit. At this point Ryan's account of the facts diverges from that of Troup. Ryan's sworn statement is that his acceptance of IBM's fourth assignment caused him some concern since he was aware of CBM's current representation of LCC and LCC's difficulty in procuring credit from IBM. Consequently, a few days after Troup's call, Ryan consulted with McCann and Weiss about a possible conflict of interest in CBM's representation of both IBM and LCC simultaneously. Weiss informed Ryan of the contemplated antitrust suit against IBM and advised him to obtain IBM's consent to the firm's representation of both IBM and the plaintiffs. Ryan stated that shortly thereafter he called Troup at his Armonk office and in a conversation lasting about three minutes brought to Troup's attention the contemplated antitrust suit against IBM by CBM's client, Levin. Troup's response, according to Ryan's testimony, was that the matter was not significant from IBM's point of view and he directed Ryan to proceed with the assignment given him. Various members of the CBM firm testified to their understanding at the time that Ryan had obtained IBM's consent to the dual representation. Troup, however, by affidavit and deposition, denied ever having been informed by Ryan of the proposed Levin lawsuit or that CBM might represent another client in a suit against IBM. CBM obtained Levin's consent to CBM's representation of IBM in labor matters and the antitrust suit was filed by Weiss acting for the firm June 23, 1972, one week after the completion of CBM's fourth opinion letter for IBM.

Weiss testified, also, in connection with IBM's knowledge of CBM's possible conflict of interest involving IBM, that in July 1973 while he and Charles Danzig, a partner of Riker, Danzig, Scherer & Debevoise, IBM's counsel in the antitrust suit, rode together in a train from Philadelphia to Newark, Weiss mentioned that CBM performed occasional work for IBM in labor matters. Danzig denied that such a statement was made to him by Weiss.

It is undisputed that during CBM's prosecution of the antitrust suit, Ryan accepted four additional labor relations assignments from Troup without further discussing with Troup CBM's concurrent representation of Levin and LCC [in February and June of 1974 and June and July of 1976].

Subsequently, at a law school alumni luncheon in New York City on January 28, 1977, John Lynch, a partner of CBM, met Richard McDonough, then a member of IBM's legal staff, and Lynch mentioned to McDonough his role in prosecuting the plaintiffs' antitrust suit against IBM. McDonough indicated surprise in that CBM was, to his knowledge, representing IBM in labor matters. In April 1977, at a dinner attended by McDonough and counsel for IBM in the antitrust suit, McDonough expressed to the latter an interest in knowing how CBM's conflict of interest had been reconciled to permit CBM's representation of Levin and LCC in the suit against IBM. McDonough's remarks caused IBM to investigate the matter further and led to the filing in June 1977 of the motion to disqualify CBM.

These being the facts we turn to the consideration of the questions raised by the parties. * * *

* * * If the facts found by the district court establish that practitioners before it have acted in a way which disqualifies them under

its rules and established standards of professional conduct, it would ordinarily be error for the court to fail to declare the disqualification. But in its order of disqualification the court has a wide discretion in framing its sanctions so as to be just and fair to all parties involved. Except where purely legal issues are involved, the district court's action in these matters may be reversed only for a clear abuse of this discretion.

CBM's principal contention does raise a legal question, however. It is that under a proper interpretation of the disciplinary rules * * * an attorney who has asserted a claim against a client pursuant to his representation of a second client may continue to represent the first client with respect to matters unrelated to the lawsuit without disclosing fully the facts of the dual representation to the client being sued and without obtaining his consent. * * *

CBM argues that clauses (A) and (B) of DR 5–105 are not applicable since no effect adverse to IBM resulted from CBM's concurrent representation of both IBM and the plaintiffs and no adverse effect on CBM's exercise of its independent professional judgment on behalf of IBM was likely to result from CBM's representation of these clients in two entirely unrelated areas. Since clauses (A) and (B) do not apply, CBM argues, the consent requirement of clause (C) of DR 5–105 also is not applicable.

We think that CBM takes too narrow a view of the meaning of the phrase "adversely affected" in clauses (A) and (B), and that a somewhat more generous interpretation is called for. The rule does not define the nature or extent of the adverse effect contemplated on the attorney's exercise of independent judgment. However, DR 5–105(C) makes clear that situations entailing the likelihood of an adverse effect include circumstances in which such an effect may be minor permitting the performance of adequate services in spite of it. In those cases the multiple representation may take place if the attorney believes in good faith that he can adequately represent both clients and if the consent of the clients is obtained.

We think, however, that it is likely that some "adverse effect" on an attorney's exercise of his independent judgment on behalf of a client may result from the attorney's adversary posture toward that client in another legal matter. See Cinema 5, Ltd. v. Cinerama, Inc., 528 F.2d 1384, 1386–1387 (2d Cir. 1976); Grievance Committee of the Bar of Hartford County v. Rottner, 152 Conn. 59, 65, 203 A.2d 82, 84 (1964); Advisory Committee on Professional Ethics of the Supreme Court of New Jersey, Opinion No. 282, 97 N.J.L.J. 362 (1974), and Opinion No. 301, 98 N.J.L.J. 209 (1975). For example, a possible effect on the quality of the attorney's services on behalf of the client being sued may be a diminution in the vigor of his representation of the client in the other matter. See *Cinema 5*. A serious effect on the attorney-client relationship may follow if the client discovers from a source other than the attorney that he is being sued in a different matter by the attorney. The fact that a deleterious result cannot be identified subsequently as having actually occurred does not refute the existence of a likelihood of its occurrence, depending upon the facts and circumstances, at the time the decision was made to represent the client without having obtained his consent.

[A]s the Court of Appeals for the Second Circuit stated in *Cinema 5*, in connection with the prosecution of a lawsuit by an attorney or his partner against an actively represented client as opposed to a former one,

> "The propriety of this conduct must be measured not so much against the similarities in litigation as against the duty of undivided loyalty which an attorney owes to each of his clients. * * *
>
> "Putting it as mildly as we can, we think it would be questionable conduct for an attorney to participate in any lawsuit against his own client without the knowledge and consent of all concerned."

[W]e turn to the question of whether the district court erred in disqualifying CBM and, if not, whether the court abused its discretion in permitting CBM to turn over its work product to plaintiffs' new counsel during a period of sixty days.

The district court concluded that its rule applying the Code required that CBM obtain IBM's consent to the firm's representation of it after full disclosure of the facts of CBM's representation of the plaintiffs. In support of this conclusion the court made several findings. The court found as a fact that at all relevant times CBM had an on-going attorney-client relationship with both IBM and the plaintiffs. This assessment of the relationship seems entirely reasonable to us. Although CBM had no specific assignment from IBM on hand on the day the antitrust complaint was filed and even though CBM performed services for IBM on a fee for service basis rather than pursuant to a retainer arrangement, the pattern of repeated retainers, both before and after the filing of the complaint, supports the finding of a continuous relationship.

The court also found that although the services required of CBM by IBM dealt consistently exclusively with labor matters, this was not the result of any special arrangement between them and that at any time IBM, unaware of CBM's participation in the plaintiffs' action, might have sought CBM's assistance in legal matters more closely related to the lawsuit. Thus, it was perhaps fortuitous that CBM, as the court found, never acquired any confidential information from IBM useful in the prosecution of the antitrust suit.

These findings, with which we agree, support the district court's conclusion, which seems to us reasonable and just, that CBM was obligated in these circumstances at the very least to disclose fully to IBM the facts of its representation of the plaintiffs and obtain its consent.

The district court determined that CBM did not meet its burden of proving that such a full disclosure was made and that consent by IBM to CBM's dual representation was obtained thereafter. CBM asserts that disclosure and consent were not necessary in that IBM had constructive knowledge of the pertinent facts since its labor lawyers knew of CBM's representation of IBM in that area and its lawyers handling the defense of IBM in the antitrust action knew of CBM's participation in that matter. This assertion is without merit. Clause (C) of DR 5–105 specifically imposes upon an attorney the burden of affirmatively providing disclosure and obtaining consent. Clearly, full and effective disclosure of all the relevant facts must be made and brought home to the prospective client.[3] The facts required to be disclosed are peculiarly within the knowledge of the attorney bearing the burden of making the disclosure. To accept CBM's position would be to engraft an unwarranted exception on the requirement of DR 5–105 that disclosure must be sufficient to enable the prospective client himself to make an informed decision as to whether in the circumstances counsel will be retained. See E. F. Hutton & Co. v. Brown, 305 F.Supp. 371, 398 (S.D.Tex.1969); In re Kushinsky, 53 N.J. 1, 4, 247 A.2d 665 (1968).

CBM alternatively argues that IBM's consent was in fact obtained. As we have stated earlier, Ryan testified that he called Troup at the IBM Armonk headquarters in April or May 1972 for the express purpose of informing Troup of the facts of CBM's representation of the plaintiffs and that Troup, after hearing the disclosure, directed Ryan to proceed with the preparation of the requested opinion in the labor matter. It appears that a telephone call lasting no more than three minutes was placed from Ryan's Newark office on May 3, 1972, to Troup's office in Armonk. Troup denied that he ever received the information which Ryan alleged had been conveyed and denied having given the consent Ryan alleged he sought to elicit or having had the authority to do so. Weiss testified that in July 1973 he had in a casual conversation with Danzig, IBM's counsel in the antitrust suit, mentioned that IBM employed CBM to perform occasional legal services in labor matters. Danzig denied that the statement was made to him by Weiss.

The district court did not deem it necessary to resolve these issues of credibility between Ryan and Troup and between Weiss and Danzig since it determined that even accepting CBM's version of this disputed testimony a full and adequate disclosure as required by DR 5–105 had not been made to IBM and that the IBM antitrust attorneys did not in fact know during the relevant period that CBM was representing

3. In the words of Justice Story, "An attorney is bound to disclose to his client every adverse retainer, and even every prior retainer, which may affect the discretion of the latter. No man can be supposed to be indifferent to the knowledge of facts, which work directly on his interests, or bear on the freedom of his choice of counsel. When a client employs an attorney, he has a right to presume, if the latter be silent on the point, that he has no engagements, which interfere, in any degree, with his exclusive devotion to the cause confided to him; that he has no interest, which may betray his judgment, or endanger his fidelity." Williams v. Reed, 3 Mason 405, 418, Fed.Case No. 17,733 (C.C.Maine 1824).

IBM in labor matters. We conclude that the district court did not err in so determining and in concluding that since IBM's informed consent to the concurrent representation by CBM of it and the plaintiffs had not been obtained, CBM had violated DR 5–105. While we accept the district court's finding that the antitrust lawyers in IBM's legal department did not know that its labor lawyer in the same department was repeatedly retaining the services of CBM in labor matters, we cannot refrain from expressing our belief that such a situation could not have existed for over five years if the activities of the IBM legal department had been properly coordinated and controlled. Apparently in IBM's case the practice was to "let not thy left hand know what thy right hand doeth", a Biblical[4] injunction directed to almsgiving which is hardly applicable to the internal operation of a corporate legal department.

CBM and the plaintiffs urge that even if CBM is held to have violated DR 5–105, the district court's disqualification of CBM from the case is too harsh a sanction and penalizes the plaintiffs unnecessarily in view of the termination of CBM's relationship with IBM and the district court's finding that, in the course of its representation of IBM, CBM did not obtain any information which would aid it in the prosecution of the antitrust suit against IBM.

In considering this contention, we bear in mind the proposition that the plaintiffs do not have an absolute right to retain particular counsel. Kramer v. Scientific Control Corp., 534 F.2d 1085, 1093 (3d Cir. 1976). The plaintiffs' interest in retaining counsel of its choice and the lack of prejudice to IBM resulting from CBM's violation of professional ethics are not the only factors to be considered in this disqualification proceeding. An attorney who fails to observe his obligation of undivided loyalty to his client injures his profession and demeans it in the eyes of the public. The maintenance of the integrity of the legal profession and its high standing in the community are important additional factors to be considered in determining the appropriate sanction for a Code violation. See Hull v. Celanese Corp., 513 F.2d 568, 572 (2d Cir. 1975). The maintenance of public confidence in the propriety of the conduct of those associated with the administration of justice is so important a consideration that we have held that a court may disqualify an attorney for failing to avoid even the appearance of impropriety. *Kramer*; Richardson v. Hamilton International Corp., 469 F.2d 1382, 1385–1386 & n. 12 (3d Cir. 1972), cert. denied 411 U.S. 986, 93 S.Ct. 2271, 36 L.Ed.2d 964 (1973). Indeed, the courts have gone so far as to suggest that doubts as to the existence of an asserted conflict of interest should be resolved in favor of disqualification. Hull v. Celanese Corp.; Chugach Elec. Ass'n v. United States D.C. for Dist. of Alaska, 370 F.2d 441, 444 (9th Cir.), cert. denied 389 U.S. 820, 88 S.Ct. 40, 19 L.Ed.2d 71 (1967). Mindful of these considerations, we cannot say that the district court erred in ordering the disqualification of CBM.

4. Matthew 6:3.

It is true that the plaintiffs will be injured by the disqualification of CBM, their counsel for a number of years. Here the district court ameliorated the harsh effect upon the plaintiffs of its sanction against CBM by permitting the turnover to substitute counsel for the plaintiffs within sixty days of the past work product of CBM on the case. IBM contends that the allowance of a turnover of work product with consultation, particularly work product prepared after the filing of IBM's motion, was an abuse of discretion.

In support of its contention IBM cites First Wisconsin Mortgage Trust v. First Wisconsin Corp., 571 F.2d 390 (7th Cir. 1978), and Fund of Funds, Ltd. v. Arthur Andersen & Co., 567 F.2d 225 (2d Cir. 1977). To the extent that the Seventh Circuit Court of Appeals lays down a legal tenet in *First Wisconsin Mortgage Trust* against permitting the turnover of a disqualified attorney's work product, we disagree, but we note that the court in that case expressly limited its holding to the facts of the case. *Fund of Funds*, also cited by IBM, involves a complex situation not comparable to the facts present here. It deals with the question of the disqualification of counsel because of his relationship with disqualified co-counsel and in it the court does not address the question of the turnover of a disqualified attorney's work product.

As we have already indicated, disqualification in circumstances such as these where specific injury to the moving party has not been shown is primarily justified as a vindication of the integrity of the bar. We think the turnover provisions of the district court's order of disqualification are sufficient for that purpose and a proper exercise of the court's discretion. * * *

### *Comment*

(1) *RPC 1.7(a).* RPC 1.7(a) is much more straightforward than the CPR in prohibiting unconsented opposing of a current client (on the same, related, *or unrelated* matter), by barring unconsented representation of a client "if the representation of that client will be directly adverse to another client."[1]

1. CPR provisions, on the other hand, reach the problem only by prohibiting:

(a) unconsented representation where—

(i) representation of one client (likely) will adversely affect the exercise of the lawyer's independent professional judgment in behalf of another client (DR 5–105(A), (B)),

(ii) the representation likely would involve the lawyer in representing differing interests (including interests that will adversely affect the lawyer's judgment *or loyalty* to a client) (DR 5–105(B)), or

(iii) the lawyer's *own* "financial * * * or personal interests" will or reasonably may affect the exercise of the lawyer's professional judgment on behalf of a client (DR 5–101(A)), and

(b) use of a confidence or secret to a client's disadvantage or, absent consent, another's advantage (DR 4–101(B)).

(Note that (a)(iii) and (b) will sometimes bar opposing a *former* client.)

The *IBM v. Levin* court based its decision upon point (a)(i). See also Unified Sewerage Agency v. Jelco, 646 F.2d 1339, 1345 (9th Cir. 1981) (opposing current client *presumed* to affect adversely the representation of each affected client).

But other courts have based their decisions on point (a)(ii). See McCourt Co. v. FPC Properties, Inc., 386 Mass. 145, 434 N.E.2d 1234 (1982) (acting for client in one action and against same client in another action constitutes "representing differing interests" within meaning of DR 5–105(B)). See also Cinema

(2) *"Two masters."* In one sense, the frequently cited [2] maxim that "no man can serve two masters" [3] is too broad, in that "[m]any fiduciaries—including lawyers—simultaneously serve the interests of scores of 'masters' without [ever] betraying any of them." [4] In another sense, to the extent that the maxim means that "the attorney should avoid inner conflicts of loyalty," it arguably "errs by overrating the lawyer's discomposure and underrating the client's" whereas—

> "Professional responsibility rules seek the objective of public confidence as well as internal integrity. [The basis for condemning] acceptance of employment adverse to a client even though the employment is unrelated to the existing representation * * * is the client's loss of confidence, not the attorney's inner conflicts." [5]

(3) *"Adversity" client v. "nonadversity" client.* An excellent Harvard Law Review developments piece[6] makes a significant observation not squarely recognized in the cases—that where a lawyer represents C1 in the "adversity matter" (C1 v. C2) and represents C2 in the "nonadversity matter" (e.g., C2 v. X), the risks to C1 and C2 are quite different:

(a) C1's risk is diminished vigor in the lawyer's performance.

(b) C2's risk is not diminished vigor in the lawyer's performance, but rather—

(i) C2's own loss of confidence in the lawyer (whom C2 probably expected to favor C2's interests *generally*, not just in the nonadversity (C2 v. X) matter), and

(ii) the lawyer-client relationship being undermined by the lawyer using antagonizing tactics (like burdensome discovery or cross-examination) in the adversity (C1 v. C2) matter.

(4) *Clients covered.* Courts have applied the prohibition against unconsented opposing of a current client to cases where the "nonad-

5, Limited v. Cinerama, Inc., 528 F.2d 1384 (2d Cir. 1976) ("The propriety of this conduct must be measured * * * against the duty of undivided loyalty which an attorney owes to each of his clients"); Jeffry v. Pounds, 67 Cal.App.3d 6, 136 Cal.Rptr. 373 (1977) (client is likely to doubt loyalty of lawyer who accepts unrelated but antagonistic employment); Grievance Committee v. Rottner, 152 Conn. 59, 203 A.2d 82 (1964) (when client is sued by own lawyer "all feeling of loyalty is necessarily destroyed").

Decision may be based upon point (b) to bar opposing a current client on a (substantially) related matter. See Westinghouse Electric Corp. v. Kerr-McGee Corp., 580 F.2d 1311 (7th Cir.), cert. denied 439 U.S. 955, 99 S.Ct. 353, 58 L.Ed.2d 346 (1978); Fund of Funds, Limited v. Arthur Andersen & Co., 567 F.2d 225 (2d Cir. 1977).

2. See, e.g., Fund of Funds, Limited v. Arthur Andersen & Co., 567 F.2d 225, 233 (2d Cir. 1977); Cinema 5, Limited v. Cinerama, Inc., 528 F.2d 1384, 1386 (2d Cir. 1976).

3. Matthew 6:24.

4. Developments in the Law—Conflicts of Interest in the Legal Profession, 94 Harv.L.Rev. 1244, 1295 (1981). This authority goes on to recognize, however, that "the maxim expresses an obvious truth: If a fiduciary attempts to serve two beneficiaries in a matter in which their interests are adverse, in a matter in which one's loss translates directly into another's gain, the fiduciary will almost certainly be unable to avoid a breach of his duty to promote the interest of each with loyal vigor." Id. at 1295–96.

5. Jeffry v. Pounds, 67 Cal.App.3d 6, 10–11, 136 Cal.Rptr. 373, 376–77 (1977).

6. Developments in the Law–Conflicts of Interest in the Legal Profession, 94 Harv.L.Rev. 1244, 1297–1303 (1981).

versity" (C2) client was a governmental entity[7] or a large corporation,[8] as well as where that client was an individual.[9]

In McCourt Co. v. FPC Properties, Inc.,[10] the Massachusetts Supreme Judicial Court disqualified a firm from representing plaintiff C1 where an amended complaint added C2 as a defendant because C2, as parent corporation of the primary defendant, had guaranteed some of the latter's obligations and where the firm was defending C2 in several unrelated personal injury suits only because a liability insurer had retained it to do so. The court reasoned:

> "A law firm that represents [C2] in the defense of an action may not, at the same time, be counsel for [C1] in an action brought against [C2], at least without the consent of both clients. It does not matter that the law firm represents [C2] as a defendant because it was selected as [C2's] counsel by [C2's] liability insurer. The law firm is attorney for the insured as well as the insurer. Nor does it matter that [C2] is a corporation or that [C2] consists, collectively, of a parent corporation and various wholly owned subsidiaries. It is also irrelevant that the lawsuits are unrelated in subject matter and that it appears probable that [C2] will not in fact be prejudiced by the concurrent participation of the law firm in both actions. The undivided loyalty that a lawyer owes to his clients forbids him, without the clients' consent, from acting for [C2] in one action and at the same time against [C2] in another. If there are any special circumstances in which an exception to this general rule should be recognized, no such circumstances have been demonstrated here, and we are aware of no case in which such an exception has been recognized and applied."

The court referred to a Massachusetts Bar Association ethics opinion questioning whether the bar on opposing a client in an unrelated matter should apply if "a large bank, insurance company, or industrial company which has a considerable volume of legal work * * * spread that work among a number of local lawyers or law firms in the

7. See City of Little Rock v. Cash, 277 Ark. 494, 644 S.W.2d 229 (1982), cert. denied — U.S. —, 103 S.Ct. 2464, 77 L.Ed.2d 1341 (1983), where the court denied attorney fees to a lawyer representing taxpayers suing the city because the lawyer still represented the city in unrelated litigation (although the latter had been submitted for decision and required no further action by the lawyer). The court held that the city's consent made no difference, on the basis of older authorities stating that "[w]here the public interest is involved, [a lawyer] may not represent conflicting interests even with consent of all concerned." But see RPC 1.11(a)'s provision for government agency consent in the former-government employee area.

Compare City Council v. Sakai, 58 Hawaii 390, 570 P.2d 565 (1977) (upholding fees for firm's acting as city *council's* special investigative counsel while representing claimants against city in unrelated matters).

8. See, e.g., IBM v. Levin and the *Cinema 5* case discussed therein.

9. See, e.g., Jeffry v. Pounds, 67 Cal. App.3d 6, 136 Cal.Rptr. 373 (1977) (no fee for firm's representing husband in personal injury suit while representing wife in marriage dissolution proceedings); Grievance Committee v. Rottner, 152 Conn. 59, 203 A.2d 82 (1964) (discipline for firm representing person suing client for assault and battery while representing client in unrelated collection case); In re Kushinsky, 53 N.J. 1, 247 A.2d 665 (1968) (discipline for simultaneously representing creditor and, in unrelated criminal case, debtor).

10. 386 Mass. 145, 434 N.E.2d 1234 (1982).

expectation that none of them then will be left free to handle cases against the company," but concluded that it "need not pass on the question because [law firm] has not shown any such anticipatory defensive behavior by [C2]."

(5) *Law firms covered.* It has been held that a law firm's size and geographical scope cannot exempt it from ordinary disqualification rules.[11] Similarly, courts have rejected claims that lawyers should be permitted to sue C2 if a "Chinese wall" is constructed to "screen" the lawyers suing C2 from the lawyers representing C2 in the nonadversity matter.[12]

(6) *Alignment of interests.* In In re Kushinsky,[13] the New Jersey Supreme Court disciplined a lawyer representing a judgment creditor (C1) for defending the debtor (C2) in an unrelated criminal prosecution, notwithstanding the argument that a successful defense would improve C1's prospect of collection. The court said:

> "[W]ithout the consent of [C1] the [lawyer] could not fulfill his obligations as an adversary to do all in his power to press [C2] for payment of the judgment, and at the same time defend [C2] against the criminal charge. What would [the lawyer's] duties be to [C1] if in representing [C2] he were to discover a previously undisclosed asset? "[14]

(7) *Consent and "consentability."* In Unified Sewerage Agency v. Jelco, Inc.,[15] C2, general contractor on a project, asked a law firm to defend it against the claim of X, an electrical subcontractor, for additional compensation on the ground that a change in suppliers by C2 constituted a change in the subcontract's terms. The law firm informed C2 of a claim that C1, the concrete subcontractor and a long-time client of the law firm, had against C2 based upon C2's alleged delay and interference in scheduling the concrete work. With full knowledge of C1's claim and the law firm's long-standing relationship with C1, C2 retained the law firm.

Later, after a proposed settlement of the C1–C2 dispute collapsed, the law firm told C2 that the C1–C2 dispute could ripen into a lawsuit, and asked C2 to re-evaluate whether it wished the law firm to keep

11. See Westinghouse Electric Corp. v. Kerr-McGee Corp., 580 F.2d 1311 (7th Cir. 1978) (eight to 14 of the 130 lawyers in the firm's Chicago office represented plaintiff while six of the 40 lawyers in the firm's Washington office were representing some of the defendants in a different but related matter), cert. denied 439 U.S. 955, 99 S.Ct. 353, 58 L.Ed.2d 346 (1978). See Cinema 5, Limited v. Cinerama, Inc., 528 F.2d 1384 (2d Cir. 1976) (New York City firm disqualified from representing plaintiff because one of the firm's partners was also partner in Buffalo firm representing defendant in unrelated case).

12. See Westinghouse Electric Corp. v. Kerr-McGee Corp., 580 F.2d 1311 (7th Cir.), cert. denied 439 U.S. 955, 99 S.Ct. 353, 58 L.Ed.2d 346 (1978); Fund of Funds, Limited v. Arthur Andersen & Co., 567 F.2d 225 (2d Cir. 1977). See generally Annot., 51 A.L.R.Fed. 678 (1981).

Regarding screening of former government employee-lawyers, see infra pp. 279–80, 287–89.

13. 53 N.J. 1, 247 A.2d 665 (1968).

14. Compare In re Hansen, 586 P.2d 413 (Utah 1978) (lawyer must refund fee for representing client in civil suit while defending client's opponent in unrelated criminal case).

15. 646 F.2d 1339 (9th Cir. 1981).

representing it in X v. C2. C2 replied unequivocally that it wanted the law firm to continue as counsel in that case regardless of what happened in the C1–C2 dispute.

Still later, after the law firm filed suit for C1 against C2, the law firm again asked C2 if it wanted the law firm to keep representing it, and C2 again decided that it did. But several months later C2 discharged the law firm from representing it in X v. C2, and then moved to disqualify the law firm from representing C1 in C1 v. C2.

Affirming the district court's refusal to disqualify the law firm, the Ninth Circuit upheld findings that, within the meaning of DR 5–105(C):

(a) C2 had consented to the representation after full disclosure, and

(b) it was obvious that the law firm could adequately represent the interests of each client.

(Compare RPC 1.7(a)'s requirements for representation directly adverse to another client, of "consent after consultation" and that "the lawyer reasonably believes the representation will not adversely affect the relationship with the * * * client.")

Regarding consent after full disclosure, the court recognized that "it is not sufficient that both parties be informed of the fact that the lawyer is undertaking to represent both of them." Rather, the lawyer "must explain to them the nature of the conflict of interest in such detail so that they can understand the reasons why it may be desirable for each to have independent counsel, with undivided loyalty to the interests of each of them." But the court found the record showed that "there was an informed and knowing waiver by [C2] of any conflict or apparent conflict" and that C2 knew that the law firm would accept C2 as a client only if doing so would not inhibit its continuing to act as C1's counsel.

Noting that C2 obviously *no longer* consented to the law firm's representating C1, the court said, "Our analysis nonetheless turns on the effectiveness of [C2's] consent, however, because [C2] would be estopped from revoking its consent by everyone's reliance on its long-standing position."

Regarding the obviousness that the law firm could adequately represent each client's interests, the court first relied upon an "analysis of the history of DR 5–105(C),[a] the structure of the Code, and the

**a.** In this connection, the court noted:

"DR 5–105(C) underwent one significant change during the drafting process. In the Tentative Draft, the rule read 'a lawyer may represent multiple clients if a lawyer of ordinary prudence would believe that he could adequately represent the interest of each. * * *' In the Preliminary Draft, the words 'a lawyer of ordinary prudence would believe he could' were replaced by the current wording, 'it is obvious that he can.' See American Bar Foundation, Annotated Code of Professional Responsibility, Textual & Historical Notes p. 242 (1979). The Annotation notes that some confusion over the meaning of 'obvious' has occurred. Id. at 243. Without belaboring the point, we think 'obvious' must refer to an objective standard under which the ability of the attorney adequately to represent each client is free from substantial doubt."

relevant policy considerations" [b] to reject the approach "that if an adverse [effect] is shown, it is never *obvious* that an attorney can adequately represent both" clients. The court went on to say:

> "In determining whether it is obvious that an attorney can [adequately] represent adverse parties, the court should look at factors such as: the nature of the litigation; the type of information to which the lawyer may have had access; whether the client is in a position to protect his interests or know whether he will be vulnerable to disadvantage as a result of the multiple representation; the questions in dispute (e.g., statutory construction versus disputes over facts) and whether a government body is involved.
>
> "[Here i]t is sufficiently obvious * * * that [the law firm] could adequately represent both [C2] and [C1] in the several actions. The litigation in the two cases was quite different; one involved a question of contract interpretation and the other was a highly disputed factual claim concerning each party's performance. [The law firm] did not have access to any specific information that would help [C1] prevail against [C2] (other than general information concerning the personality of a client, which is always helpful in later suits against that client). [C2] was in a position to know all the risks it was taking in employing [the law firm].
>
> "We find no facts that suggest that [the law firm] would be tempted to 'soft pedal' the rights of one client in these cases so as not to jeopardize the position of another client. Nothing suggests that [the law firm] had an incentive *not* to represent zealously the interests of each client in their respective cases. Accordingly, we find that it was as 'obvious' as necessary that [the law firm] could adequately represent [C2] and [C1]." [16]

**b.** In this connection, the court said:

"[F]rom its representation of [C2] in the [X v. C2] matter, [the law firm] was likely to gain information and insights from [C2] about such things as [C2's] institutional attitudes towards negotiation and settlement and [C2's] method of doing business. Such information undoubtedly could prove useful to an opponent. Nevertheless, while the practice of suing a client can be neither condoned nor encouraged, we are not prepared to enunciate a *per se* rule that a client must forego in all circumstances his choice of a particular attorney merely because there is the foreseeability of a future conflict with one of the attorney's existing clients.

"It is true that the court has an obligation to safeguard the integrity of the judicial process in the eyes of the public. But the impact upon the public's respect for lawyers may be too speculative to justify overriding the client's right to take a calculated risk and, with full knowledge, engage the attorney of his choice. We do not find it necessary to create a paternalistic rule that would prevent the client in every circumstance from hiring a particular attorney if the client knows that some detriment may result from that choice in a later suit. Clients who are fully advised should be able to make choices of this kind if they wish to do so. Our responsibility is to preserve a balance, delicate though it may be, between an individual's right to his own freely chosen counsel and the avoidance of representations where undivided loyalty is impossible."

**16.** See Note, Unified Sewerage Agency v. Jelco, Inc.: The Client's Right to Consent to Potential Conflicts of Interest, 11 Cap.U.L.Rev. 625 (1982). See generally Note, Prospective Waiver of the Right to Disqualify Counsel for Conflicts of Interest, 79 Mich.L.Rev. 1074 (1981).

Compare In re Holmes, 290 Or. 173, 619 P.2d 1284 (1980), wherein the court disciplined a collection agency's lawyer for endeavoring to collect debts for it from another

### c. *Opposing Former Client in Related Matter*

#### MODEL RULES OF PROFESSIONAL CONDUCT

**RULE 1.9 Conflict of Interest: Former Client**

A lawyer who has formerly represented a client in a matter shall not thereafter:

(a) represent another person in the same or a substantially related matter in which that person's interests are materially adverse to the interests of the former client unless the former client consents after consultation; or

(b) use information relating to the representation to the disadvantage of the former client except as Rule 1.6 would permit with respect to a client or when the information has become generally known.[a]

**RULE 1.10 Imputed Disqualification: General Rule**

(a) While lawyers are associated in a firm, none of them shall knowingly represent a client when any one of them practicing alone would be prohibited from doing so by Rules 1.7, 1.8(c), 1.9 or 2.2.

(b) When a lawyer becomes associated with a firm, the firm may not knowingly represent a person in the same or a substantially related matter in which that lawyer, or a firm with which the lawyer was associated, had previously represented a client whose interests are materially adverse to that person and about whom the lawyer had acquired information protected by Rules 1.6 and 1.9(b) that is material to the matter.

(c) When a lawyer has terminated an association with a firm, the firm is not prohibited from thereafter representing a person with interests materially adverse to those of a client represented by the formerly associated lawyer unless:

(1) the matter is the same or substantially related to that in which the formerly associated lawyer represented the client; and

(2) any lawyer remaining in the firm has information protected by Rules 1.6 and 1.9(b) that is material to the matter.

(actual knowledge)

of the lawyer's clients. The lawyer told the client that if the debt could not be resolved the lawyer would have to sign a complaint, erroneously adding, "I suppose it's better to have a friendly adversary than an enemy." The court held that even if both clients consented after full disclosure, the lawyer could not adequately represent each client's interests.

a. Compare the following CPR provisions:

"**EC 4–6** The obligation of a lawyer to preserve the confidences and secrets of his client continues after the termination of his employment. * * * "

"**DR 4–101 Preservation of Confidences and Secrets of a Client**

* * *

"(B) Except when permitted under DR 4–101(C), a lawyer shall not knowingly:

* * *

(2) Use a confidence or secret of his client to the disadvantage of the client.

(3) Use a confidence or secret of his client for the advantage of himself or of a third person, unless the client consents after full disclosure."

(d) A disqualification prescribed by this Rule may be waived by the affected client under the conditions stated in Rule 1.7.[b]

### *Comment*

While RPC 1.9's heading contains the term "Conflict of Interest," and the Rule covers representations which may conflict with duties owed to former clients, e.g., seeking to set aside a contract prepared for a prior client, the Rule also encompasses the obligation not to disclose the former client's confidential information. In that respect, RPC 1.9 is essentially a codification of the principles developed by judicial decisions under the CPR. See, e.g., Cheng v. GAF Corp., which follows.

## CHENG v. GAF CORP.

631 F.2d 1052 (2d Cir. 1980), vacated 450 U.S. 903, 101 S.Ct. 1338, 67 L.Ed.2d 327 (1981).[a]

MESKILL, Circuit Judge:

James K. J. Cheng appeals from an order entered in the United States District Court for the Southern District of New York (Owen, J.) denying his motion to disqualify the law firm representing his opponent, GAF Corporation. Cheng argued below that because one of the attorneys employed by the law firm representing GAF previously had been employed by the legal services office representing Cheng, disqualification was necessary to avoid violations of various Canons of the American Bar Association Code of Professional Responsibility. The district court, concluding that disqualification was not warranted, denied Cheng's motion. For the reasons set forth below, we reverse the district court's decision and remand for entry of an order of disqualification.

### Background

In 1977, Cheng, represented by Legal Services for the Elderly Poor ("LSEP"), instituted an employment discrimination action against GAF. From the start, GAF has been represented in this litigation by the law firm of Epstein, Becker, Borsody & Green ("Epstein firm"). In October, 1979, while the *Cheng* case was still in the discovery phase, the Epstein firm hired Philip Gassel as an associate in its health law department. From 1974 until his association with the Epstein firm,

b. Compare the following CPR provision:

**"DR 5–105 Refusing to Accept or Continue Employment if the Interests of Another Client May Impair the Independent Professional Judgment of the Lawyer**

* * *

"(D) If a lawyer is required to decline employment or to withdraw from employment under a Disciplinary Rule, no partner or associate, or any other lawyer affiliated with him or his firm may accept or continue such employment."

a. The Supreme Court vacated on grounds of its ruling in Firestone Tire & Rubber Co. v. Risjord, 449 U.S. 368, 101 S.Ct. 669, 66 L.Ed.2d 571 (1981), that orders denying disqualification are not appealable prior to final judgment in the underlying civil case.

Gassel had been employed as a senior attorney at LSEP. Although Cheng concedes that while Gassel was employed at LSEP he did not represent Cheng in any litigation, Cheng claims that Gassel did participate in discussions with other members of the staff about the GAF case.

After learning of Gassel's new association, Cheng filed a motion to disqualify the Epstein firm from representing GAF in the instant case. Cheng alleged that the "continued participation of the Epstein firm * * * seriously jeopardizes the integrity of confidences and secrets of [Cheng] which were imparted to Mr. Gassel under the cloak of attorney-client relationship." Citing the small size of the LSEP legal staff, which consisted of four to six attorneys working with several part-time students, and noting the frequency of cooperation and consultation among the LSEP attorneys, Cheng claimed that Gassel had actual knowledge of Cheng's confidences and secrets when he joined the Epstein firm. Cheng argued, therefore, that under Canons Four, Five and Nine of the [CPR],[1] the Epstein firm should be disqualified.

Opposing the disqualification motion, the Epstein firm averred in its affidavits that Gassel had been hired as a health law attorney and had functioned only in that capacity, aside from handling some commercial litigation and miscellaneous matters. The Epstein firm emphasized that Gassel had not worked on the *Cheng* case, had not divulged any confidential information and would not be required to do so in the future. Gassel submitted an affidavit disclaiming any present involvement in the *Cheng* case and urging acceptance of the technique of insulation practiced by the Epstein firm.

In his opinion denying the disqualification motion, Judge Owen discussed Gassel's involvement in the *Cheng* case, and expressed the belief that Gassel possessed minimal confidential information, that he had not disclosed the information yet and that the Epstein firm had effectively screened him from the attorneys handling GAF's defense. Stating that the prejudice that would result from requiring GAF to change law firms after extensive discovery and trial preparation would be substantial, Judge Owen concluded that "to order disqualification under these circumstances would not serve any interest which the law recognizes." Because we disagree with Judge Owen's view of the effectiveness of the screening procedures employed by the Epstein firm, we reverse.

1. The [CPR] consists of Canons which are "axiomatic norms, expressing in general terms the standards of professional conduct expected of lawyers." While the Ethical Considerations accompanying each Canon are "aspirational in character," the Disciplinary Rules keyed to each Canon "state the minimum level of conduct below which no lawyer can fall without being subject to disciplinary action." [CPR] Preliminary Statement.

Canon 4 states: "A Lawyer Should Preserve the Confidences and Secrets of a Client." Canon 5 provides: "A lawyer should Exercise Independent Professional Judgment on Behalf of a Client" and Canon 9 warns that: "A Lawyer Should Avoid Even the Appearance of Professional Impropriety."

DISCUSSION

It is well settled in this Circuit that a motion to disqualify an attorney is addressed to the discretion of the district court, and a ruling thereon will not be overturned absent a determination of abuse of discretion. Hull v. Celanese Corp., 513 F.2d 568, 571 (2d Cir. 1975). See also Fund of Funds, Ltd. v. Arthur Andersen & Co., 567 F.2d 225 (2d Cir. 1977). The question raised in this appeal is whether Judge Owen's refusal to disqualify the Epstein firm was such an abuse.

I. DISQUALIFICATION UNDER CANON 4

The American Bar Association Code of Professional Responsibility has been recognized in this Circuit as providing appropriate guidelines for proper professional behavior. *Fund of Funds*; NCK Organization Ltd. v. Bregman, 542 F.2d 128, 129 n.2 (2d Cir. 1976); Cinema 5, Ltd. v. Cinerama, Inc., 528 F.2d 1384, 1386 (2d Cir. 1976); Hull v. Celanese Corp., supra, 513 F.2d at 571 n.12. Cf. Armstrong v. McAlpin, 625 F.2d 433, 446 n.26 (2d Cir. 1980) (although ABA committee that drafted Code has indicated rules were intended for use in disciplinary proceedings rather than in disqualification proceedings, Court refers to Code for guidance).[b]

Canon 4 and its Ethical Considerations and Disciplinary Rules provide standards to guide an attorney in preserving the confidences and secrets of a client. Cheng argues vigorously that under these standards Gassel should be disqualified from representing GAF in the present action. Although Gassel is not actively involved in GAF's defense, his disqualification under Canon 4 would implicate the sweeping prohibition of representation by a tainted attorney's co-workers contained in Canon 5. Disciplinary Rule 5–105(D) provides: "If a lawyer is required to decline employment or to withdraw from employment under a Disciplinary Rule, no partner, or associate, or any other lawyer affiliated with him or his firm, may accept or continue such employment." Although the district court below did not decide whether Gassel himself had to be disqualified under Canon 4, we must address this question briefly as it bears upon our analysis of Disciplinary Rule 5–105(D).

Determination of a violation of Canon 4 sufficient to disqualify an attorney traditionally has been based on a finding of concurrent or successive representation in the same or substantially related matters.

> "[T]he former client need show no more than that the matters embraced within the pending suit wherein his former attorney appears on behalf of his adversary are substantially related to the matters or cause of action wherein the attorney previously represented him, the former client. The Court will assume that during the course of the former representation confidences were disclosed to the attorney bearing on the subject matter of the representation."

b. Vacated 449 U.S. 1106, 101 S.Ct. 911, 66 L.Ed.2d 835 (1981), (on ground that order denying disqualification is not appealable prior tc final judgment in underlying civil case).

T. C. Theatre Corp. v. Warner Bros. Pictures, 113 F.Supp. 265, 268 (S.D.N.Y.1953). It is well established that a court may not inquire into the nature of the confidences alleged to have been revealed to the tainted attorney. To require proof of access to privileged information would "put the former client to the Hobson's choice of either having to disclose his privileged information in order to disqualify his former attorney or having to refrain from the disqualification motion altogether." Government of India v. Cook Industries, Inc., 569 F.2d 737, 740 (2d Cir. 1978). See also *Fund of Funds;* United States v. Standard Oil Co., 136 F.Supp. 345, 354 (S.D.N.Y.1955) (Kaufman, *J.*) ("complainant need only show *access* to such *substantially related* material and the inference that defendant received these confidences will follow.") (emphasis in original). In the instant case, there is no dispute that the matters involved in Gassel's former association with Cheng are substantially related to his present association; the suit and the parties have remained the same throughout the proceedings. The only changing factor has been Gassel, who has moved from the plaintiff's firm to the defendant's firm, thus becoming subject to a disqualification challenge.[4]

In Silver Chrysler Plymouth Inc. v. Chrysler Motors Corp., 518 F.2d 751 (2d Cir. 1975) (overruled on other grounds in Armstrong v. McAlpin, supra), we recognized that although there may be an inference that an attorney has knowledge of the confidences and secrets of his firm's clients, that inference is rebuttable. We also noted an earlier caution that the standard of proof to rebut this presumption should not become "unattainably high." Id., at 754, quoting Laskey Bros. of W. Va., Inc. v. Warner Bros. Pictures, 224 F.2d 824, 827 (2d Cir. 1955), cert. denied, 350 U.S. 932, 76 S.Ct. 300, 100 L.Ed. 814 (1956). After considering the affidavits submitted by all parties in the instant case, including Gassel, Judge Owen assumed for the purposes of the motion that Gassel had been privy to some confidential disclosures, but he admitted that the extent of Gassel's exposure to the *Cheng* case through informal discussions or general strategy conferences had not been conclusively determined. Thus, the district court refrained from deciding whether Gassel had rebutted the presumption that he had obtained impermissible knowledge of Cheng's confidences and secrets. If we accept Judge Owen's assumption that Gassel was privy to those confidences, however, it is clear that Gassel would have to be dis-

4. In our recent decision in *Armstrong, supra,* we noted that

> "with rare exceptions disqualification has been ordered only in essentially two kinds of cases: (1) where an attorney's conflict of interests in violation of Canons 5 and 9 of the Code of Professional Responsibility undermines the court's confidence in the vigor of the attorney's representation of his client, * * * or more commonly (2) *where the attorney is at least potentially in a position* to *use privileged information concerning the other side through prior representation,* for example, in violation of Canons 4 and 9, thus giving his present client an unfair advantage * * *." 625 F.2d at 444, quoting Board of Education v. Nyquist, 590 F.2d 1241, 1246 (2d Cir. 1979) (emphasis added).

In the instant case, because the Epstein firm is defending the still pending suit brought on Cheng's behalf by LSEP, Gassel is potentially in a position to use Cheng's confidential information to Cheng's disadvantage.

qualified under Canon 4 from representing Cheng's adversary in the identical proceedings.[5] *Government of India; Fund of Funds;* Emle Industries, Inc. v. Patentex, Inc., 478 F.2d 562 (2d Cir. 1973).

Applying Disciplinary Rule 5–105(D), it appears that the Epstein firm should be disqualified as well. Judge Owen did not reach this conclusion, choosing instead to find that regardless of the extent of Gassel's knowledge, Cheng was adequately protected because Gassel had not yet divulged any confidences and was not inclined to do so in the future. We have considered the affidavits submitted to the district court and we conclude that there is ample support for Judge Owen's assumption that Gassel had been privy to Cheng's confidences, thus we find that under Canon 4 he would be disqualified from representing the defendant in the *Cheng* case. We next address Canon 5 and the screening procedures instituted to avoid disqualification of the Epstein firm.

## II. The "Chinese Wall" Defense

Anticipating difficulties caused by a strict application of Disciplinary Rule 5–105(D), law firms have employed various methods of screening a possibly tainted attorney from the rest of the firm's involvement in a particular case. The Epstein firm in the instant case cites the division of duties within its firm to demonstrate the height and thickness of the "Chinese Wall" they have constructed between Gassel and the *Cheng* case. They note in their affidavits that Gassel has been assigned to the health law division of their firm while GAF's defense is being handled by its labor division. The affidavits also aver that Gassel has not worked on the *Cheng* case, disclosed Cheng's confidences nor discussed the merits of the case while at the Epstein firm, and that the firm will not permit him to have any substantive involvement in the *Cheng* defense. Judge Owen accepted the Epstein firm's position, finding that the "risk of disclosure of confidential information is negligible." We take a different view of the potential for disclosure, keeping in mind that, as Judge Owen noted, one of the purposes of disqualification is "to guard against the danger of inadvertent use of confidential information."

Although Gassel may not be personally involved in the *Cheng* defense, he is a member of a relatively small firm.[6] The matter involved

5. The following allegations appeared in the affidavits submitted on Cheng's behalf: Gassel was personally introduced to Cheng; he "was present at and participated in several discussions with other LSEP attorneys and law students regarding the conduct, strategy, and facts of Mr. Cheng's case;" he discussed Cheng's communications with the representing attorney. These allegations were not challenged or refuted in any of the Epstein firm's affidavits; indeed, they appear also in the Epstein firm's brief on appeal. * * * Because we find that the affidavits demonstrate that Gassel did have knowledge of Cheng's confidences and secrets, we accept Judge Owen's assumption for purposes of this appeal.

6. The Epstein firm's affidavit states that a total of 35 attorneys are employed in their New York and Washington, D.C. offices, with approximately 60 percent of the total located in the New York office where Gassel is an associate.

in his prior exposure to Cheng while at LSEP is still being actively pursued by attorneys for GAF at the Epstein firm. Despite the Epstein firm's protestations, it is unclear to us how disclosures, admittedly inadvertent, can be prevented throughout the course of this representation. Unlike many disqualification motions that appear before this Court, here there exists a continuing danger that Gassel may unintentionally transmit information he gained through his prior association with Cheng during his day-to-day contact with defense counsel. Compare *NCK Organization* and *Hull v. Celanese Corp.* See also *Government of India.* If after considering all of the precautions taken by the Epstein firm this Court still harbors doubts as to the sufficiency of these preventive measures, then we can hardly expect Cheng or members of the public to consider the attempted quarantine to be impenetrable. Although we do not question Mr. Gassel's integrity or his sincere efforts to disassociate himself from the *Cheng* case, we are not satisfied that under the facts of this case the screening will be effective, thus we look to Disciplinary Rule 5–105(D) and order the district court to disqualify the Epstein firm.[7] See *Cinema 5* and cases cited therein. See also *Fund of Funds.*

### III. Appearance of Impropriety

Although we rest our holding on the clear direction in Disciplinary Rule 5–105(D), the result is compelled also by Canon 9's warning that "A Lawyer Should Avoid Even the Appearance of Professional Impropriety."[b] In Armstrong v. McAlpin, we cited the restrained approach to disqualification that had been adopted in Board of Education

7. Although the Epstein firm urges that the result in this case should be controlled by our recent decision in *Armstrong*, supra, we find many factors distinguishing the two situations. In *Armstrong*, a former government attorney was concedely disqualified from private employment in a matter in which he had had substantial responsibility while employed by the Securities and Exchange Commission. This Court held that the attorney's law firm could continue representation where the tainted attorney was screened effectively.

In the instant case the tainted attorney is disqualified under Canon 4's commendable intent to protect a client's confidences and secrets, while in *Armstrong*, the attorney was disqualified under Disciplinary Rule 9–101(B) which forbids a lawyer to accept private employment in a matter in which he had substantial responsibility while a public employee. In *Armstrong* we noted the absence of a threat of taint of the underlying trial, and cited several policy reasons for approving the screening employed there. Primary among these reasons was a recognition that to disallow screening in all cases involving government attorneys might hamper the "government's efforts to hire qualified attorneys." 625 F.2d at 443. In the instant case, by contrast, there *does* exist a threat of taint of the underlying trial, but there are no public policy reasons against disqualification as compelling as those involved in *Armstrong*. In addition, the tainted attorney's former employer in *Armstrong* agreed to the representation as long as proper screening techniques were used; here, Cheng and LSEP, Gassel's former employer, have objected to the representation since the Epstein firm hired Gassel. Finally, although the prejudice to the client separated from his attorney is also a factor, we must note that the prejudice to GAF caused by changing firms at this point is much less than the hardship that would have resulted from disqualification in *Armstrong*. "[S]eparating the receiver from his counsel at this late date will seriously delay and impede, and perhaps altogether thwart his attempt to obtain redress for defendants' alleged frauds." Id. at 445.

**b.** A similar provision does not appear in the RPC.

v. Nyquist, [discussed infra p. 252], noting that where there is no danger that the underlying trial will be tainted, appearances of impropriety alone are insufficient to justify disqualification. Judge Owen, in his opinion below, also cited *Nyquist's* recommendation of restraint and concluded that it was "virtually assured" that the underlying trial in *Cheng* would not be tained. We disagree. Such assurances would not seem to be possible in a situation such as this where Gassel is "potentially in a position to use privileged information," *Nyquist*, which he gained through his prior contact with the *Cheng* case. It is possible that, despite attempts by the Epstein firm to screen Gassel, the underlying trial could be tainted through GAF's inadvertent use of the unfair advantage it has over Cheng. This case presents, therefore, both the danger of tainting the underlying trial and the unacceptable appearance of impropriety condemned in Canon 9. Cf. Emle Industries, 478 F.2d at 565 (where public confidence in Bar would be undermined, "even an appearance of impropriety requires prompt remedial action by the court.").

Thus, it is clear that under Canon 9 as well as Canons 4 and 5, Gassel and the Epstein firm must be disqualified. Judge Owen's decision to the contrary was an abuse of discretion. Moreover, if there were any doubt as to the propriety of our action, we would resolve it in favor of disqualification. Hull v. Celanese Corp.; accord, *Silver Chrysler Plymouth*.

The order of the district court is reversed and the case is remanded for entry of an order of disqualification.

## FREEMAN v. CHICAGO MUSICAL INSTRUMENT CO.

689 F.2d 715 (7th Cir. 1982).

COFFEY, Circuit Judge.

The Chicago Musical Instrument Company (CMI) appeals an order of the United States District Court for the Northern District of Illinois, Eastern Division, the Honorable Stanely J. Roszkowski presiding, disqualifying CMI's co-counsel, the law firm of Fitch, Even, Tabin, Flannery & Welsh (Fitch or the Fitch firm), in this patent infringement action. * * * [W]e reverse the order of the district court and remand for proceedings consistent with this opinion.

Alfred B. Freeman brought this action in July of 1973 against the Chicago Musical Instrument Company, alleging that CMI had infringed upon several patents owned by Freeman. The patents involve chord organs having an electronic system for sounding bass notes. CMI denied both infringement of the patents and actual ownership of them by Freeman.

On October 16, 1978, Freeman retained the law firm of Dressler, Goldsmith, Shore, Sutker & Milnamow, Ltd. (Dressler) to represent him in this action. Prior to this, since 1975, the Dressler law firm had represented Freeman in other electronic organ matters but did not directly represent Freeman in this case. Throughout the entire course of this action, CMI has been represented by the Chicago law firm of Hill, Van Santen, Steadman, Chiara & Simpson, P.C. (Hill).

The ownership aspect of the lawsuit was tried before the district court in November of 1978 and was resolved in Freeman's favor. Shortly thereafter, CMI engaged the services of the Chicago law firm of attorneys of Fitch, Even, Tabin, Flannery & Welsh to act as co-counsel with the Hill law firm. Appearances were entered in district court by John Flannery and Roger Greer on behalf of the Fitch law firm. Apparently when the new litigation was made known to the members of the Fitch firm, Eric C. Cohen, an associate in Fitch since May 1979, notified Flannery that he had previously been employed as an associate lawyer in the Dressler law firm from July 1976 until April 1979. Cohen told Flannery that he had neither worked on nor had he any knowledge of the subject matter of the present litigation. Flannery then notified opposing counsel at Dressler of these facts and was informed that Dressler objected to the further representation of CMI by the Fitch law firm. Dressler claimed that Cohen had access to the confidences and secrets of their client, Freeman, in that it was a Dressler firm policy to distribute various legal opinions and memoranda to all lawyers of the firm. The Dressler law firm also claimed that cases were often discussed by members of the firm among each other, implying that Cohen was privy to Freeman's secrets and confidences.

CMI then filed a motion with the district court requesting a declaration that the Fitch law firm be allowed to continue to represent CMI in this action. In support of their motion, an affidavit by Cohen was submitted. In it Cohen averred that while he was an associate at Dressler he never performed work on behalf of Freeman and that he, Cohen, had no knowledge of the subject matter of the present lawsuit. He also averred that although various legal memoranda and opinions circulated at Dressler, he typically had been too busy to read them.

The Dressler firm in response filed an affidavit executed by Talivaldis Cepuritis, a member of Dressler and counsel for Freeman, in which Cepuritis averred that the Freeman litigation files were stored in cabinets immediately outside of Cohen's former office and also that it was the practice of the firm to circulate and discuss among the members of the law firm correspondence, opinions, memoranda, etc. generated from the firm's cases. In a supplemental affidavit, Cohen responded that he had never met Mr. Freeman and that he recalled neither reading nor discussing any memoranda or files related to the Freeman case.

The district court, without making any findings of fact, concluded that "there can be little doubt that permitting the Fitch firm to represent defendant in the instant case would result in an appearance of impropriety." Relying upon Westinghouse Electric Corp. v. Gulf Oil Corp., 588 F.2d 221 (7th Cir. 1978), the district court went on to state that "it is not appropriate for the court to inquire into whether actual confidences were disclosed." Concluding that Cohen was tainted by his prior association with the Dressler law firm, the district court imputed the taint to the Fitch law firm and accordingly disqualified it. It is from this order that CMI appeals. * * *

The question of propriety that has arisen in this case concerns a law firm attempting to represent a party where an associate of the law firm was at one time an associate member for the law firm representing the adverse party. The resolution of the ethical question presented in this case must be guided by prior caselaw and the precepts of the Code of Professional Responsibility itself. Before we begin our analysis, however, it is necessary to briefly note the ethical considerations which are implicated by the issue presented here. A fundamental principle in the lawyer-client relationship is that a lawyer shall maintain the confidentiality of the information relating to the representation. This principle is expressly recognized by Canon 4[7] of the ABA Code of Professional Responsibility and is also encompassed within the parameters of Canon 9.[8] It is part of a court's duty to safeguard the sacrosanct privacy of the attorney-client relationship. See American Can Company v. Citrus Feed Co., 436 F.2d 1125, 1128 (5th Cir. 1971). In doing so, a court helps to maintain public confidence in the legal profession and assists in protecting the integrity of the judicial proceeding. United States v. Agosto, 675 F.2d 965, 969 (8th Cir. 1982). Disqualification of counsel is but one of several avenues available to a court in its attempt to insure that Canons 4 and 9 are not violated.[9] On the other hand, we also note that disqualification, as a prophylactic device for protecting the attorney-client relationship, is a drastic measure which courts should hesitate to impose except when absolutely necessary. A disqualification of counsel, while protecting the attorney-client relationship, also serves to destroy a relationship by depriving a party of representation of their own choosing. See Comden v. Superior Court, 20 Cal.3d 906, 145 Cal.Rptr. 9, 16, 576 P.2d 971, 978, cert. denied 439 U.S. 981, 99 S.Ct. 568, 58 L.Ed.2d 652 (1978). We do not mean to infer that motions to disqualify

7. Canon 4 states: "A Lawyer Should Preserve the Confidences and Secrets of a Client."

8. Canon 9 states: "A Lawyer Should Avoid Even the Appearance of Professional Impropriety."

9. The Eighth Circuit has proffered one justification for the merger of Canon 9's concern for the appearance of impropriety with Canon 4's injunction against disclosure of secrets:

"Clients who retain, are billed by, and pay a law firm, can reasonably expect, and often their problems require, that confidences disclosed in one lawyer in the firm will be shared with others in the firm. Indeed, the ability to bring various fields of expertise to bear on the client's problem often serves as a justification for practice as a firm and the very reason for the client's decision to retain the firm. If the reputation and status of the legal profession, and more importantly the freedom and opportunity of the public to obtain adequate legal counseling, are to be preserved, a client must have every reason to expect that disclosures to 'his' law firm will not be used against him by any member or associate lawyer in that firm."

State of Arkansas v. Dean Foods Products Company, Inc., 605 F.2d 380, 385–86 (8th Cir. 1979).

counsel may not be legitimate, for there obviously are situations where they are both legitimate and necessary; nonetheless, such motions should be viewed with extreme caution for they can be misused as techniques of harassment.

The analysis which we will employ to resolve the issue presented has been developed through the prior caselaw of the Seventh Circuit. We must * * * first ascertain whether the representation of Freeman by the Dressler firm, at the time Cohen was an associate there, is substantially related to the present litigation. If we conclude that it is, we must then determine whether the presumption that Cohen shared in the confidences and secrets of Freeman while he was an associate for the Dressler firm has been rebutted. Only if we find that it has not been rebutted may we reach the dispositive issue of whether the Fitch firm was properly disqualified.

The first step in our analysis requires that we ascertain whether the subject matter of the representation of Freeman by the Dressler firm, at the time Cohen was an associate there, is "substantially related" to the present litigation.[10] If the subject matter of the former representation is not substantially related to the subject matter of the present representation, obviously no ethical problem exists. See Unimweld Products, Inc. v. Union Carbide Corp., 385 F.2d 992, 994–95 (5th Cir. 1967), cert. denied 390 U.S. 921, 88 S.Ct. 853, 19 L.Ed.2d 980 (1968). Our determination need not detain us here long. There is no dispute that the matters involved are substantially related. They involve, in fact, the same case. The suit and the parties have remained the same throughout the proceedings. The only factor to have changed has been Cohen, who, by moving from Freeman's firm to CMI's law firm, exposed the Fitch firm to the disqualification challenge. It is without doubt that the matters are substantially related.

Implicit in a finding of substantial relationship is a presumption that particular individuals in a law firm freely share their client's confidences with one another. See Novo Terapeutisk, Etc. v. Baxter Travenol Lab., 607 F.2d [186,] 196 [7th Cir. 1979]. It was upon this presumption that the district court relied when it disqualified the Fitch firm. Our decision in *Novo*, however, indicates that further analysis was and is necessary.

10. The "substantial relationship" test was first espoused in the seminal case T. C. Theatre Corp. v. Warner Bros. Pictures, 113 F.Supp. 265 (S.D.N.Y. 1953). Essentially, the test has been held to require three levels of inquiry:

> "Initially, the trial judge must make a factual reconstruction of the scope of the prior legal representation. Second, it must be determined whether it is reasonable to infer that the confidential information allegedly given would have been given to a lawyer representing a client in those matters. Finally, it must be determined whether the information is relevant to the issues raised in the litigation pending against the former client."

Westinghouse Electric Corp. v. Gulf Oil Corp., 588 F.2d 221, 225 (7th Cir. 1978). In *Westinghouse*, we also noted that the determination of whether there is a substantial relationship turns on the possibility, or appearance thereof, that confidential information might have been given to the attorney in relation to the subsequent matter in which disqualification is sought.

In *Novo,* we recognized that the presumption that an attorney has knowledge of the confidences and secrets of his firm's clients is rebuttable. CMI argues that Cohen's affidavits, which state that he neither read the memoranda which circulated within the firm nor had he any knowledge of the Freeman case, satisfactorily rebuts the above described presumption. The district court failed to make any determination as to this issue.

O.L.

The question as to what quality or quantity of proof is actually necessary to rebut the presumption of imputed knowledge was expressly left open in *Novo.* The purposes behind the disqualification remedy, namely, the need to enforce the lawyer's duty of absolute fidelity and to guard against the danger of inadvertent use of confidential information, Ceramco, Inc. v. Lee Pharmaceuticals, 510 F.2d 268, 271 (2d Cir. 1975), as well as to continue to achieve a high regard for the legal profession in the public mind, General Motors Corp. v. City of New York, 501 F.2d 639, 649 (2d Cir. 1974), seem to indicate that a rather strict standard of proof is required. The Second Circuit, however, has cautioned that:

> "It will not do to make the presumption of confidential information rebuttable and then to make the standard of proof for rebuttal unattainably high. This is particularly true where, as here, the attorney must prove a negative, which is always a difficult burden to meet."

Laskey Bros. of W. Va., Inc. v. Warner Bros. Pictures, 224 F.2d 824, 827 (2d Cir. 1955), cert. denied 350 U.S. 932, 76 S.Ct. 300, 100 L.Ed. 814 (1956).[11]

In *Novo,* this Court held that the uncontroverted affidavits "clearly and effectively" rebutted the presumption existing in the case. A requirement for such a finding in order to rebut the presumption is not an unreasonable one. It creates no conflict with the purposes behind the disqualification order nor is it by any means impossible to meet or "unattainably high." Accordingly, if an attorney can clearly and effectively show that he had no knowledge of the confidences and secrets of the client, disqualification is unnecessary and a court order of such might reasonably be regarded as an abuse of discretion. A district court, in resolving this issue, may of course rely on any of a number of factors, among them being the size of the law firm, the area of specialization of the attorney, the attorney's position in the firm, and the demeanor and credibility of witnesses at the evidentiary hearing.

11. In support of its holding, the *Laskey* court expressed concern that an irrebuttable presumption "might seriously jeopardize [young lawyers'] careers by temporary affiliation with large law firms." The court also projected an adverse effect on clients, noting that strictly applied disqualification rules might result in "difficulty in discovering technically trained attorneys in specialized areas who were not disqualified, due to their peripheral or temporally remote connections with attorneys for the other side."

In this case, the district court failed to address the question of whether CMI had clearly and effectively shown that Cohen, while he was an associate for the Dressler law firm, had no knowledge of the confidences and secrets of the client Freeman. The possible appearance of impropriety, found to be determinative by the district court, is simply too weak and too slender a reed on which to rest a disqualification order in this case, particularly where the mere appearance of impropriety is far from clear. Accord, Armstrong v. McAlpin, supra, 625 F.2d at 445. If CMI is able to show that Cohen was not privy to the above information, there obviously is no need for the disqualification of the Fitch law firm. An evidentiary hearing is thus necessary to make these factual determinations. In so holding, in view of the limited record and scarcity of facts recited, we express no opinion as to how this issue should be resolved. What Cohen knew is a question of fact for the district court to decide in the first instance.[12]

Accordingly, the order of the District Court is reversed and remanded for proceedings consistent with this opinion.

### *Question*

Is *Freeman* consistent with *Cheng?* Are the issues in the two cases the same?

### *Comment*

(1) *General principles.* The principles first developed in T. C. Theatre Corp. v. Warner Brothers Pictures, and quoted in *Cheng,* have since been generally followed, and many courts do not permit the attorney sought to be disqualified to show that he or she in fact did not receive confidential information from the former client.[1]

As in *Cheng* and *Freeman,* principal reliance has been placed on CPR Canon 4. The "appearance of impropriety" language of Canon 9 has also frequently been invoked.[2]

One commentator has criticized the reliance on ethical rules to determine questions of disqualification, stating, "Disqualification occurs at a different time, in a different situation, and with different stakes from the original decision whether to take the case or continue representation."[3]

12. It will be necessary for the Fitch law firm to be disqualified should CMI be unable to show that Cohen was not privy to Freeman's confidences and secrets. See *Novo.*

1. See Riger, Disqualifying Counsel in Corporate Representation—Eroding Standards in Changing Times, 34 U. Miami L. Rev. 995, 1007 (1980); Developments in the Law—Conflicts of Interest in the Legal Profession, 94 Harv.L.Rev. 1244, 1328–33 (1981); Note, Motions to Disqualify Counsel Representing an Interest Adverse to a Former Client, 57 Tex.L.Rev. 726 (1979); Comment, The Chinese Wall Defense to Law-Firm Disqualification, 128 U.Pa.L.Rev. 677 (1980).

2. See, e.g., In re of Cipriano, 68 N.J. 398, 346 A.2d 393 (1975) (Canon 4 not mentioned).

3. Lindgren, Toward a New Standard of Attorney Disqualification, 1982 Am.B.Found. Research J. 419, 457.

For a criticism of courts using "appearance of impropriety" as a basis of disqualification, see Kramer, The Appearance of Impropriety

(2) *Ambiguities*. Several ambiguities inhere in the principles stated, among them:

(a) There must have been a prior attorney-client relationship. This may not always be clear.[4]

(b) There must be a "substantial relationship" between the present "matter" and the prior one. Whether that relationship exists depends on the facts of the particular case and upon views held as to the required closeness of the relationship. Courts are in disagreement. Some insist upon some degree of identity of issues between the present controversy and the earlier one in which the attorney had appeared.[5]

Others have held there is a substantial relationship if the attorney acquired confidential information about the practices, policies and techniques of conducting business, and tactics of litigation, of the former client which may be useful in representing the present client against his former one, even though none of the issues may be the same.[6]

Intermediate between these two situations are cases in which information obtained from the former client relevant to the issues in the former representation is relevant also to quite different issues in the later representation against the former client. Should the attorney be disqualified?[7]

Under Canon 9: A Study of the Federal Judicial Process Applied to Lawyers, 65 Minn.L.Rev. 243 (1981).

4. See, e.g., Westinghouse Electric Corp. v. Kerr-McGee Corp., 580 F.2d 1311 (7th Cir.), cert. denied 439 U.S. 955, 99 S.Ct. 353, 58 L.Ed.2d 346 (1978). The American Petroleum Institute (API) requested its members to provide information to the attorney which the API had employed preparatory to a report by the attorney for submission to Congress. The members were assured that the specific information they supplied would not be disclosed, even to API. The court held, after extended analysis, that, for purposes of disqualification, the members were clients of the attorney.

5. See, e.g., City of Cleveland v. Cleveland Electric Illuminating, 440 F.Supp. 193 (D.Ohio 1977) (no "patently clear" relationship existed; no "commonality of issues"), affirmed mem. 573 F.2d 1310 (6th Cir. 1977); Fleischer v. A. A. P., Inc., 163 F.Supp. 548 (S.D.N.Y.1958) (must be "clearly discernible that the issues involved in a current case do not relate to matters in which the attorney formerly represented the adverse party"), appeal dismissed 264 F.2d 515 (2d Cir.), cert. denied 359 U.S. 1002, 79 S.Ct. 1139, 3 L.Ed.2d 1030 (1959).

6. Chugach Electric Association v. United States District Court, 370 F.2d 441 (9th Cir. 1966).

Does this suggest that an attorney who has worked for a private corporation or government agency may not take any cases against it after leaving for private practice? Knowledge of the corporation or agency's inner operations would give the attorney an advantage over the prior client even in cases arising sub sequent to his or her leaving. Regarding former government agency lawyers, see infra pp. 279–89.

7. So held in Trone v. Smith, 621 F.2d 994 (9th Cir. 1980). The attorney made an investigation preparatory to issuing a legal opinion letter regarding the client's sale of shares of stock. The attorney was held barred from later representing a trustee in bankruptcy who brought suit against the former client for violation of various federal and state statutes. The court stated that even if no confidential information had been communicated, "the subject matters of the professional representation undertaken in each case were so interlinked by reason of common factual background that the requisite substantially of relation for disqualifying the attorneys existed here."

(3) *Consequences.* The consequences of disqualification may be substantial. The attorney has lost a client. The client is put to the necessity of finding and paying another lawyer, who may find it necessary to duplicate much of the work already done by the disqualified lawyer. This in turn may cause delay of the trial of the case. Motions to disqualify may be brought not to protect the movant but to harass the opponent into settling or getting rid of a good lawyer. Litigating the issue itself adds to cost and delay. The prospect of disqualification may make lawyers and law firms reluctant to bring in lawyers from other firms having a substantial clientele. Specialists may be particularly affected.[8]

The consequences become aggravated, especially for large law firms, when not only the disqualified lawyer is barred from a representation, but, as indicated in *Freeman*, all members of the lawyer's new firm are also barred.[9]

(4) *Relaxation of restrictions.* Because of these frequently harsh results, some courts have relaxed the principles governing disqualification. As noted in Comment (2), the principles may be given a narrow construction. In other instances, courts have allowed rebuttal of the presumption that the challenged attorney received confidential information from the former client or, if received, conveyed it to the attorney's later colleagues.

In Silver Chrysler Plymouth, Inc. v. Chrysler Motors Corp.,[10] the attorney was permitted to show that he had not received substantially related information from his former client. His relationship to the

The case is criticized in Dolmarch, Professional Responsibility, 1981 Ann.Surv.Am.L. 57, 60, as representing "an unduly harsh rule whereby substantial factual similarity creates an irrebuttable presumption that damaging confidences were disclosed." Is the criticism sound?

See also Analytica, Inc. v. NPD Research, Inc., 708 F.2d 1263 (7th Cir. 1983), in which the attorney was retained to effect a transfer of stock to a new member of a closely held corporation. To fix the value of the stock, the attorney obtained information about the corporation's financial condition, sales trends, and management. Later, the attorney represented a competitor in a suit against the corporation charging antitrust violations. He was held disqualified since the information he had obtained was "potentially germane to both the liability and damages phases of an antitrust suit."

The court distinguished *Freeman* in that there the attorney had "change[d] jobs" from one firm to the later one and so came within the exception to the disqualification requirement recognized in previous decisions. In *Analytica* "the firm itself changed sides." Is this a valid distinction? Compare the dissenting opinion.

8. The early cases of *T. C. Theatre* and *Laskey Brothers* cited in *Cheng* involved the disqualification of specialists. See also City of Cleveland v. Cleveland Electric Illuminating, 440 F.Supp. 193 (N.D. Ohio 1977) (municipal bond expert), affirmed mem. 573 F.2d 1310 (6th Cir.), cert. denied 435 U.S. 996, 98 S.Ct. 1648, 56 L.Ed.2d 85 (1978); Consolidated Theatres Corp. v. Warner Brothers Circuit Management Corp., 216 F.2d 920, 926 (2d Cir. 1954). ("[W]e are not unmindful of the drastic effect of the Canon on a lawyer of Mr. Nickerson's background. It comes close to preclude him as serving as a plaintiff's attorney in the lucrative anti-trust motion-picture field in which he has specialized during most of his professional life.").

9. See Liebman, The Changing Law of Disqualification: The Role of Presumption and Policy, 73 Nw.U.L.Rev. 996 (1979); Annot., 46 A.L.R.Fed. 189 (1982).

10. 518 F.2d 751 (2d Cir. 1975) (reviewing prior cases).

client was considered only a brief and subordinate one. "[T]here is reason to differentiate for disqualification purposes between lawyers who become heavily involved in the facts of a particular matter and those who enter briefly on the periphery for a limited and specific purpose relating solely to legal questions." The court also observed:

> "Several of New York's firms have well over 100 associates and over 50 partners. Many firms hire a dozen or more law graduates each year and it has now become the practice to hire for summer work (usually between their second and third years at law school) a substantial number of law students. These 'summer associates' most frequently perform tasks assigned to them by supervising associates or partners. Many of the summer students do not return to the same firms with which they have been associated or even remain in New York City. Even after an initial association with a firm upon graduation, it is not uncommon for young lawyers to change their affiliation once or even several times. It is equally well known that the larger firms in the metropolitan areas have hundreds (collectively thousands) of clients. It is unquestionably true that in the course of their work at large law firms, associates are entrusted with the confidences of some of their clients. But it would be absurd to conclude that immediately upon their entry on duty they become the recipients of knowledge as to the names of all the firm's clients, the contents of all files relating to such clients, and all confidential disclosures by client officers or employees to any lawyer in the firm."

(5) *Rebutting presumptions.* When all members of a law firm are deemed disqualified because one of them has previously represented the present adverse party, two presumptions are made. One is that the former client gave the attorney confidential information. The other, that the attorney conveyed the information to his or her present colleagues. Some courts have drawn a distinction between the two presumptions and permitted the latter to be rebutted by proof that the other members of the firm had not in fact received, or had access to, the information.[11]

Is this consistent with the purposes of disqualification, and of the presumption—to assure the client that his or her confidences will be kept? Should the client be expected to accept the word of the former attorney, whom the client is now challenging, that the confidences have been kept?

There are other variations. If all members of the ABC law firm are disqualified because C is tainted, and C leaves the firm for practice elsewhere, should A and B still be irrebuttably disqualified?[12]

11. Novo Terapeutisk Laboratorium v. Baxter Travenol Laboratories, 807 F.2d 186, 196–97 (7th Cir. 1979); Jenson v. Touche Ross & Co., 335 N.W.2d 720, 729 (Minn. 1983). Contra Arkansas v. Dean Foods Products Co., 605 F.2d 380 (8th Cir. 1979).

12. Yes, says Schloetter v. Railoc of Indiana, Inc. 546 F.2d 706, 711 (7th Cir. 1976), stating, "it would be unreasonable to expect the public or clients * * * who have reposed confidences in a member of a law firm, to accept the proposition that the danger of

If, B, instead of C, leaves the firm for practice elsewhere, should B still be irrebuttably disqualified? [13]

(6) *Screening.* When the tainted member of the firm is a former government attorney, law firms have been permitted to rebut the presumption that he or she has conveyed government confidences to other members of the firm. This is done by erecting a so-called "Chinese wall" within the firm. With respect to the representation in question, the tainted member is isolated from any contact with other firm members or relevant files or any portion of the fee.[14]

Whether this is permitted when a lawyer in private practice joins a law firm is unclear.[15] *Cheng* appears to assume that it is, but found holes in the "wall." A showing in the individual case that no confidences were revealed or available to other members of the firm has been rejected as not a sufficient "wall." There must be an "institutional mechanism" for screening within the firm.[16] "Chinese walls" evidently are not built just for the day.

Is the following Comment persuasive?

> "Once it is admitted that a Chinese wall can rebut the presumption of imputed knowledge in former government attorney cases, it becomes difficult to insist that the presumption is irrebuttable when the disqualified attorney's previous employment was private and not public. To hold fast to such a proposition would logically require a belief that privately employed attorneys are inherently incapable of being effectively screened, as though they were less trustworthy or more voluble than their ex-government counterparts." [17]

(7) *The Model Rules.* RPC 1.11 permits screening of former government attorneys.[18]

RPC 1.9 and 1.10, set forth above, which apply generally, do not provide for screening. The Model Rules do not retain a provision against creating an "appearance of impropriety" that is present in CPR Canon 9 and commonly used to bolster disqualification decisions. Of course, courts, independent of the Model Rules, may still adopt and apply "appearance of impropriety" concepts.

those confidences being used against the client in a closely related matter has entirely dissipated upon the departure of the individual member of the firm."

13. No, says Laskey Brothers v. Warner Brothers Pictures, 224 F.2d 824 (2d Cir. 1955). See also American Can Co. v. Citrus Feed Co., 436 F.2d 1125 (5th Cir. 1971).

Yes, says Arkansas v. Dean Foods Products Co., 605 F.2d 380 (8th Cir. 1979). B had joined the state attorney general's office and became D's supervisor. The court thought it made no sense to impute to D receipt of confidential information which B himself had only by imputation. But the court held that the "appearance of impropriety" required D's, as well as B's, disqualification. Is this sound?

14. For discussion of the former government lawyer, see infra pp. 279–89.

15. Comment, supra note 1, at 701, found no recent cases on the subject.

16. Analytica, Inc. v. NPD Research, Inc., 708 F.2d 1263 (7th Cir. 1983).

17. Comment, supra note 1, at 701.

18. See infra p. 279.

What effect will adoption of the Model Rules have on the principles we have examined?

### 3. NON-LITIGATION MATTERS

#### IN RE DOLAN

76 N.J. 1, 384 A.2d 1076 (1978).

PER CURIAM.

A complaint was filed with the Middlesex County Ethics Committee charging respondent with conflicts of interest in connection with certain real estate transactions. * * *

[O]n April 5, 1971, Gulya Bros. Redevelopment Corp. (Gulya) was established for the purpose of purchasing [and] developing [land] and marketing the townhouses which it erected thereon. * * *

Thereafter Gulya's attorney sought financing for the project on behalf of the developer but was unsuccessful. To aid in this endeavor the developer's attorney sought out the respondent, who had "handled matters for him in the past", was "familiar with mortgage financing", and had done "some extensive real estate work." In May or June of 1972 respondent, at the instance of Gulya's attorney, discussed the project with the principals of Gulya and at that point took over the representation of the developer * * *.

Respondent's efforts on Gulya's behalf produced the required financing through a New Jersey mortgage company. The financing consisted of both the construction mortgage and permanent mortgages available to the buyers of the townhouses. * * *

Respondent also represented the mortgage company in sales involving permanent mortgages used in the purchase of townhouses from Gulya. In those same transactions he came to act as well on behalf of purchasers-mortgagors of the housing units at their closings of mortgage loan and title, under the following circumstances. In order to market the townhouses the developer engaged a real estate agent, whose function it was to attract buyers and assist those buyers in obtaining FHA approvals. It was the agent who led the buyers through whatever preliminary steps were required leading to execution of the contracts, and it was the agent who secured execution of those contracts. Respondent did not enter the picture until after the contracts had been signed by the buyer. The contract forms utilized by the agent, pursuant to these procedures, contained the following clauses:

> "Purchaser shall be responsible for paying the closing attorneys for the mortgage (sic) their legal fee for examination of title and recording of deed and mortgage and shall also be responsible for and shall pay for survey, mortgage title insurance, hazard insurance premium, escrow funds for taxes and insurance, appraisal and inspection fees and a one percent processing fee except as may be otherwise provided herein. * * *

If purchaser uses seller's attorney, the seller will pay the legal fee for title examination, recording of deed and mortgage, survey, mortgage title insurance appraisal and inspection fees."

By virtue of the arrangement last referred to either respondent or an associate in his office attended closings not only for the seller in sixteen instances, but also for the purchasers-mortgagors in at least fourteen of those closings.[2] At these closings purchasers were notified for the first time of the potential conflicts of interest arising out of respondent's multiple representations. They were presented with and executed two separate waiver and consent forms, one acknowledging and approving respondent's representation of purchaser and seller and the other acknowledging and approving his representation of mortgagor, mortgagee and seller.

* * * At the outset we recognize the emphasis that our disciplinary rules place on the desirability of completely independent counsel. Specifically, DR 5–105 prohibits multiple representation except under certain severely circumscribed circumstances. The sense of our rules is that an attorney owes complete and individed loyalty to the client who has retained him. The attorney should be able to advise the client in such a way as to protect the client's interests, utilizing his professional training, ability and judgment to the utmost. Consequently, if any conflicting interest could arise which would stand in the way of that kind of unstinting zeal, then the client must be so informed and the attorney may continue his limited representation only with the client's informed consent.

In a real estate transaction, the positions of vendor and purchaser are inherently susceptible to conflict. In re Kamp, 40 N.J. 588, 595, 194 A.2d 236 (1963). This is likewise the case with a borrower-lender relationship. Id. at 596, 194 A.2d 236. The requirements of an attorney involved in such multiple representations of purchaser, vendor and mortgagee are set out in Justice Proctor's opinion in In re Kamp, supra, where he said:

"Full disclosure requires the attorney not only to inform the prospective client of the attorney's relationship to the seller, but also to explain in detail the pitfalls that may arise in the course of the transaction which would make it desirable that the buyer have independent counsel. The full significance of the representation of conflicting interests should be disclosed to the client so that he may make an intelligent decision before giving his consent. If the attorney cannot properly represent the buyer in all aspects of the transaction because of his relationship to the seller, full disclosure requires that he inform the buyer of the limited scope of his intended representation of the buyer's interest and point out the advantages of the buyer's retaining independent counsel. A similar situation

2. In a letter answer to the complaint, marked in evidence at the Committee's hearing, respondent indicated that "one or two of the people did bring their own attorney to the closing."

may occur, for example, when the buyer of real estate utilizes the services of the attorney who represents a party financing the transaction. To the extent that both parties seek a marketable title, there would appear to be no conflict between their interest. Nevertheless, a possible conflict may arise concerning the terms of the financing, and therefore at the time of the retainer the attorney should make clear to the buyer the potential area of conflict. In addition, if the buyer's interests are protected only to the extent that they coincide with those of the party financing the transaction, the attorney should explain the limited scope of this protection so that the buyer may act intelligently with full knowledge of the facts."

In the application of these principles to the matter before us we are mindful of the circumstances surrounding this type of transaction, namely, the purchase of low and moderate income dwellings with federally guaranteed financing, which serve to distinguish it from the conventional transfer of real estate. There is less flexibility in the terms. Federal auspices in this context brings with it a certain rigidity which leaves little room for negotiation of price and such other commonly negotiable features as limits and rates on borrowed money. The prescribed forms for bond and mortgage contain fixed terms from which variance is rarely, if ever, permitted. Nevertheless, the severely strictured nature of the relationship between mortgagor and mortgagee in no wise serves to diminish the essential obligation of full and timely disclosure. The opportunity for conflict to arise—for instance, in terms of a condition of title acceptable to one party but not the other—while perhaps remote is by no means non-existent. More apparent is the possibility that as between buyer and developer-seller there may ripen some disagreement respecting the physical condition of the premises. Without presuming to suggest an exhaustive list of potential areas of conflict, we draw attention to these as the kinds of matters of which consenting purchasers-mortgagors should be made aware before they consent to the attorney representing another party to the transaction.

Here the consent forms executed by purchasers at the eleventh hour amounted to little more than a perfunctory effort formally to comply with *Kamp's* admonition. After the respondent was retained, he had an "immediate" duty to explain to the client the nature of his relationship with the seller and inform the client of the significance of any consent that the client may have given to dual representation. In re Kamp, supra, 40 N.J. at 596, 194 A.2d 236; see In re Lanza, 65 N.J. 347, 350–51, 322 A.2d 445 (1974).[a]

**a.** The *Lanza* court said:

"It is utterly insufficient simply to advise a client that he, the attorney, foresees no conflict of interest and then to ask the client whether the latter will consent to the multiple representation. This is no more than an empty form of words. A client cannot foresee and cannot be expected to foresee the great variety of potential areas of disagreement that may arise in a real estate transaction of this sort. The attorney is or should be familiar with at least the more common of these and they should be stated and laid before the client at some length and with considerable specificity. Of course all eventualities cannot be foreseen, but a great many can."

The problems that can arise from the failure to heed that instructive warning are graphically demonstrated in the matter before us. The record reveals that a purchaser objected to signing one of the consent forms after the conflict of interest situation had been explained to him (because he believed it might place him in the position of approving a conflict which was "illegal"), but ultimately he executed the form as the result of persuasion from his wife and a desire to avoid the serious disruption of his moving plans resulting from any adjourned or cancelled closing. Although we agree with the Committee's conclusion that the consent form was signed voluntarily in the literal sense that neither respondent nor the seller exerted any overt pressure on the client, nevertheless we are left with the impression, as was the Committee, that execution of the form was due more to the exigencies of the situation than to an unfettered will. And this need not and should not have been. The circumstances surrounding the execution of the consent form in this instance and in every other instance where the forms were executed in like fashion should not have been permitted to arise. The record before us reveals that respondent's office dealt with the purchasers "for several weeks before * * * the closing." Somewhere in that interval the time should have been taken and the opportunity created to explain to the purchasers the potential conflicts—the "pitfalls"—so as to allow for execution of the consent forms after due deliberation.

While the practicalities of this type of purchase may generate joint representation of low or middle income purchasers-mortgagors and their sellers and mortgagees by a single attorney, those practicalities in no sense justify any relaxation of the requirement of full, complete and timely explanation of the pitfalls and implications of such representation and the potential for conflict. Indeed, given the increased likelihood that this class of clients may be without the resources to obtain separate representation, the need for meticulous observance of the requirement of full disclosure and informed consent is underscored.

While tenable arguments have been made in favor of a complete bar to any dual representation of buyer and seller in a real estate transaction, see e.g., In re Lanza, supra, 65 N.J. at 353, 322 A.2d 445 (Pashman, J., concurring); In re Rockoff, 66 N.J. 394, 397, 331 A.2d 609 (1975) (Pashman, J., concurring), on balance we decline to adopt an inflexible *per se* rule. Confining ourselves to the type of situation before us (assuredly there are others, entirely unrelated to financial pressures), the stark economic realities are such that were an unyielding requirement of individual representation to be declared, many prospective purchasers in marginal financial circumstances would be left without representation. That being so, the legal profession must be frank to recognize any element of economic compulsion attendant upon a client's consent to dual representation in a real estate purchase and to be circumspect in avoiding any penalization or victimization of those who, by force of these economic facts of life, give such consent.

This opinion should serve as notice that henceforth where dual representation is sought to be justified on the basis of the parties' consents, this Court will not tolerate consents which are less than knowing, intelligent and voluntary. Consents must be obtained in such a way as to insure that the client has had adequate time—manifestly not provided in the matter under consideration—to reflect upon the choice, and must not be forced upon the client by the exigencies of the closing. This applies with equal force to the dual representation of mortgagor and mortgagee.

In view of respondent's impeccable record, including a history of significant public service and contributions to the legal profession, we conclude that appropriate discipline is exercised by the imposition of this public reprimand.

PASHMAN, J., concurring and dissenting.

While I applaud the Court's tightening of the rules governing multiple representation in real estate transactions by further narrowing its permissible circumstantial basis. I am afraid that its effort to provide an additional safeguard for consumers of legal services simply does not go far enough. The prophylactic rule announced herein will do little to enhance the likelihood that the quality of representation provided in such circumstances will duplicate that which would be provided by counsel with undivided loyalty. Similarly, the Court's admonition that attorneys must avoid "any penalization or victimization" of clients who, as a result of economic constraints, consent to dual representation will be far from effective to prevent the various abuses endemic in such situations.

* * * The result herein continues the Court's acceptance of dual representation in circumstances where, notwithstanding full disclosure and knowing consent by the derivative client, the intrinsic degree of divided allegiance is so intolerable that the proscribed adverse effect on the exercise of the attorney's independent professional judgment on behalf of that client must *ipso facto* be conclusively presumed. See D.R. 5–105(B). In so doing, the Court relies on the fiction that a lay client can effectively consent to dual representation and perpetuates the cruel myth that adequate representation can be provided in such cases by an attorney who supposedly can simultaneously protect the inevitably adverse interests of his two masters. The reality, of course, is that it is well-nigh impossible for the derivative client to be so well attuned to the numerous legal nuances of the transaction that his consent can be said to have been truly informed.[3] The propriety

3. The most frequent topics of controversy at closing are:

(A) Difficulties with the quality of title deliverable by the seller.

(B) Disputes over alleged structural defects.

(C) Warranties.

(D) Unfinished work.

(E) Leaks.

(F) Cellar problems.

(G) Construction of roads and sidewalks in the development on schedule.

(H) Drainage problems.

(I) Problems as to utilities.

(J) Defective masonry foundations.

(K) Mortgage and tax escrows—amount and interest.

of according dispositive effect to consent so obtained is further undermined when it is frankly acknowledged that the consent is induced by the derivative client's reliance on a promise by the attorney which cannot be fulfilled—the promise of adequate representation of each of his two clients.

Surely the Court is not so naive as to the economic realities of such transactions as its utopian stance would indicate. Any conflicting interests which are potentially disruptive of the ultimate goal—the expeditious consummation of the sales transaction—must inevitably be resolved in favor of the primary client and for that same reason will probably not even be brought to the attention of the derivative client. This problem is even more aggravated in circumstances such as those of the instant case where the primary client of the attorney is a developer with whom the attorney has a potentially long-term and profitable relationship. Consequently, the attorney has a substantial economic stake in maintaining the continued goodwill of this primary client. * * *

Even assuming that dual representation in an "ordinary isolated" real estate transaction should not be *per se* impermissible, the practice is wholly unsupportable where the attorney involved is the representative of a developer. * * * I cannot countenance the Court's continued tolerance of such farcical and often duplicitous behavior by some members of the legal profession. The injustice of this is heightened by the fact that it occurs in what for most consumers is the transaction of greatest personal and financial moment in their lifetime in which their need for adequate representation is acute.

I am similarly distressed by this Court's continuing condonation of the concept of "limited" dual representation, first sanctioned in In re Kamp, 40 N.J. 588, 595–596, 194 A.2d 236 (1963). By securing the derivative client's consent to such a limitation on his duty, the attorney, in addition to his plenary representation of the primary client, "represents" the derivative client also as to some matters involved in the closing of title but not as to others. In practical terms what this arrangement means is that at the settlement table, moments after having purportedly acted on behalf of the derivative client's interest, the attorney will turn on his "former" client and act solely as the advocate for the primary client as to the matters reserved from dual representation. One can readily imagine the bewilderment of the derivative client as he sees the attorney transformed from ally to enemy in a matter of seconds. He didn't bargain for that result when he gave his "consent" to the limits of the dual representation he would receive.

(L) Escrows of a part of seller's money to assure complaince with above problems, including schedule for release of funds.

(M) Appropriate remedies for compliance with any agreements concerning the above.

There are, of course, innumerable variations of such problems within the above general areas. These are in addition to the many subjects as to which intolerable conflicts of interest result if the attorney provides dual representation at the contract negotiation stage as well as at the closing of title.

Agreeing to allow an attorney not to press certain matters on your behalf is not equatable with agreeing to have him press those very matters against you. This incongruous situation would be ludicrous were it not so tragic. Yet the Court sees fit to perpetuate such an arrangement, which in reality is nothing less than a travesty of the attorney-client relationship and mocks the very concept of the professionalism of lawyers. The impropriety of permitting an attorney to act as both the advocate and adversary of a client in a single transaction is too obvious even for statement. * * *

Moreover, the Court's assumption that adoption of a *per se* prohibition of dual representation in a real estate transaction would somehow prevent persons of modest means from being represented at all is unwarranted. The more likely result of a *per se* rule will be to alert such persons to the gravity of the contemplated transaction and consequently impel them to secure their own counsel. * * *

It is virtually impossible for an attorney to contend for that which duty to another client requires him to oppose. This impossible fact pattern prevents the fulfillment of that undivided loyalty owed by a lawyer to his client. We must decisionally or by Canons of Ethics discourage an attorney from taking any chances where such a highly charged potential for conflict exists. * * * [b]

### *Comment*

(1) *"Lawyer for the situation."* While in private practice, Justice Louis D. Brandeis believed that in some counseling situations involving potentially conflicting interests and informed consent, a single scrupulous lawyer handling all the legal details could best assure fairness to everyone.[1]

(2) *Pre-agreed plans.* "When amiable parties to a proposed event of legal import come to the attorney's office with what they believe to be a complete agreement embodying their compromises and desires [and] the lawyer concludes not to undertake the representation of multiple interests, his recommendation of separate, independent counsel * * * may be received with incredulity. From the clients' perspective, the lawyer's refusal is unfathomable: his excessive cautiousness will mean inefficiency, added legal expense, and the possibility of an undesired adversary atmosphere to their pre-agreed plan."[2]

**b.** See In re Robertson, 290 Or. 639, 624 P.2d 603 (1981) (thirty day suspension for simultaneously representing buyer and seller without consent after full disclosure or obviousness lawyer could adequately represent each client's interests).

**1.** Note, Simultaneous Representation: Transaction Resolution in the Adversary System, 28 Case W.Res.L.Rev. 86, 90 (1977). See G. Hazard, Ethics in the Practice of Law 58–68 (1978) (counsel for situation is "very important and socially estimable function that lawyers can perform and do perform); Frank, The Legal Ethics of Louis D. Brandeis, 17 Stan.L.Rev. 683, 702, 708 (1965) (counsel for situation unfortunate phrase; "the greatest caution to be gained from study of the Brandeis record is never be 'counsel for the situation.' * * * I have never attempted [to work out conflicts] without wishing I had not, and I have given up attempting it").

**2.** Note, supra note 1, at 86–88.

See Blevin v. Mayfield, 189 Cal.App.2d 649, 11 Cal.Rptr. 882 (1961) (lawyer drawing deed

(3) *Buyer and seller.* "[T]here are situations where it may be appropriate for the lawyer to accept a consent * * * to represent two clients with different interests. Of course the lawyer will not venture into this thicket unless he feels certain that under the particular circumstances he can represent each client fully and fairly. That may well be true of some standardized situations whose scope is widely understood, e.g., where the one client is buying the other's house, and says to him: 'I am well acquainted with your regular lawyer and know his high reputation. I want to save money and time and avoid delay by having him represent both of us in this sale.' Title questions may arise that are not understood, but they are within a definite range. The parties expect to give and receive a good title, upon customary terms. If special questions arise, either of title or terms, they can be discussed with both parties. The question will be of a well-defined class. It may turn out that one party or both will be disappointed if the lawyer raises issues that burden one or the other with unexpected expenses or that cause the deal to fall through; but there will be no feeling of disappointment with the lawyer's role. He was expected to raise such issues. Once raised, there were no practical alternatives to what had to be done about them: they had to be dealt with on lines established by real estate law or custom. Both clients understood this when they consented to be represented by the same lawyer. So the disappointed client does not blame the lawyer, for he knows that he had consented to have the lawyer do just what was done." [3]

Regarding difficulties that may arise in representing both buyer and seller, see Hill v. Okay Construction Co.,[4] wherein the Minnesota Supreme Court upheld malpractice judgments, saying:

> "An attorney who undertakes to represent at the same time adverse parties in any type of legal relationship, whether contractual or otherwise, does not obligate himself to adhere to any higher duty or standard of care than if he endeavored to represent only one of those parties. On the other hand, he clearly owes no lesser duty to each of his clients, and he must protect the interests of each as

acted only as "scrivener"); Beal v. Mars Larsen Ranch Corp., 99 Idaho 662, 586 P.2d 1378 (1978) (lawyer was requested only to draft land sale contract according to terms agreed upon after parties negotiated with aid of real estate broker).

3. W. Fisher, What Every Lawyer Knows 41–42 (1974). Other discussion in his book shows that Fisher is, in general, chary of consent to common representation given by persons with potentially adverse interests.

See Craft Builders, Inc. v. Ellis D. Taylor, Inc., 254 A.2d 233 (Del.1969) (lawyer "represented both buyer and seller so long as their interests coincided, but withdrew completely when they reached the parting of the ways"); Richards v. Wright, 45 N.M. 538, 119 P.2d 102 (1941) ("It is not unusual for the purchaser of real estate to require that his attorney be employed [by the seller] to quiet title to the property he is buying. There is no impropriety in such employment if it is clearly understood by all the parties"); Dillard v. Broyles, 633 S.W.2d 636 (Tex.App.1982) (representing both buyer and seller proper upon parties' agreement after full disclosure), cert. denied U.S., 103 S.Ct. 3539, 77 L.Ed.2d 1389 (1983).

See generally Annot., 68 A.L.R.3d 967 (1976).

4. 312 Minn. 324, 252 N.W.2d 107 (1977).

zealously as if their interests were his sole responsibility. In undertaking to represent both [seller] and [buyer], [lawyer] placed himself in a position which, by its very nature, made it more difficult for him to conform to the required standard of practice in protecting his clients' interests. In the opinion of the jury, [lawyer] failed both clients. We must accept that judgment."[5]

(4) *Borrower and lender.* In the 1897 case of Lawall v. Groman,[6] Pennsylvania Supreme Court stated that "it is not uncommon, in many places, including some, at least, of the counties of this state, for the same counsel to represent both borrower and lender, upon mortgage or similar security, although the former only is expected to pay the fees."[7]

An English commentator distinguished the mortgagor-mortgagee situation from the buyer-seller situation as follows:

> "There is rarely a contract between mortgagor and mortgagee (the point at which in cases of vendor and purchaser the conflict is most likely to arise), and in the investigation of title there is normally no conflict of interest between mortgagor and mortgagee. Indeed, where, as is usual, the mortgage is to be granted in connection with a purchase, the identity of interest of the potential purchaser and mortgagor with that of the mortgagee would appear to be complete. The interest of vendor and purchaser can never be identical."[8]

(5) *Principal and agent.* In the Wisconsin case of State v. Rogers,[9] Issuer Company engaged Seller Company to sell Issuer's securities. With consent of both companies, Seller's lawyer represented both companies as to the qualification and sale of the securities. Lawyer knew Seller was converting funds received from the sale. The court disciplined Lawyer for failing to disclose Seller's conversion to Issuer.

(6) *Adoption.* Representing both the consenting mother and the adopting parents in an adoption proceeding, after full disclosure, was

5. See Cultra v. Douglas, 60 Tenn.App. 116, 444 S.W.2d 575 (1969) (no specific enforcement of agreement to sell where lawyer did not adequately explain extent of conflicting interests and nature of transaction). See also Farr v. Newman, 14 N.Y.2d 183, 250 N.Y.S.2d 272, 199 N.E.2d 369, 4 A.L.R.3d 215 (1964) (lawyer's knowledge that seller had prior agreement to sell to someone else imputed to buyer: "A conflict of interest does not avoid the imputation of knowledge"). Contra, C.B. & T. Co. v. Hefner, 98 N.M. 594, 651 P.2d 1029 (App.1982) (knowledge not imputed where lawyer violated duty of disclosure owed by lawyer representing both buyer and seller).

6. 180 Pa. 532, 37 A. 98 (1897).

7. See Pyeatt v. Estus, 72 Okl. 160, 179 P. 42, 4 A.L.R. 1570 (1916) ("nothing inconsistent" in lender's lawyer representing borrower regarding title examination).

Compare In re Smith, 292 Or. 84, 636 P.2d 923 (1981) (discipline for representing both borrower and lender without consent after full disclosure). On problems that can arise, see Crest Inv. Trust, Inc. v. Comstock, 23 Md.App. 280, 327 A.2d 891 (1974) (mortgage set aside because lawyer did not adequately explain how unfair it was); Lawall v. Groman, 180 Pa. 532, 37 A. 98 (1897) (lawyer liable to lender for negligence in overlooking prior lien).

8. 79 L.Q.Rev. 25, 27 (1963).

9. 226 Wis. 39, 275 N.W. 910 (1937).

held not improper in the California case of Arden v. State Bar.[10] In the New York case of Tierney v. Flower,[11] a lawyer representing adopting parents, in fact also assumed to act for the mother, who was not to know who the adopting parents were. The lawyer was compelled to disclose to the mother their identity, partly on the ground that the lawyer was acting for the mother as well. The privilege of nondisclosure of confidential communications did not apply.[12]

## 4. LAWYER AS INTERMEDIARY

### MODEL RULES OF PROFESSIONAL CONDUCT

**RULE 2.2 Intermediary**

(a) A lawyer may act as intermediary between clients if:

(1) the lawyer consults with each client concerning the implications of the common representation, including the advantages and risks involved, and the effect on the attorney-client privileges, and obtains each client's consent to the common representation;

(2) the lawyer reasonably believes that the matter can be resolved on terms compatible with the clients' best interests, that each client will be able to make adequately informed decisions in the matter and that there is little risk of material prejudice to the interests of any of the clients if the contemplated resolution is unsuccessful; and

(3) the lawyer reasonably believes that the common representation can be undertaken impartially and without improper effect on other responsibilities the lawyer has to any of the clients.

(b) While acting as intermediary, the lawyer shall consult with each client concerning the decisions to be made and the considerations relevant in making them, so that each client can make adequately informed decisions.

(c) A lawyer shall withdraw as intermediary if any of the clients so requests, or if any of the conditions stated in paragraph (a) is no longer satisfied. Upon withdrawal, the lawyer shall not continue to represent any of the clients in the matter that was the subject of the intermediation.

COMMENT:

A lawyer acts as intermediary under this Rule when the lawyer represents two or more parties with potentially conflicting interests. A key factor in defining the relationship is whether the parties share responsibility for the lawyer's fee, but the common representation may be inferred from other circumstances. Because confusion can arise as to the lawyer's role where each party is not separately represented, it is important that the lawyer make clear the relationship. * * *

A lawyer acts as intermediary in seeking to establish or adjust a relationship between clients on an amicable and mutally advantageous basis; for example,

10. 52 Cal.2d 310, 341 P.2d 6 (1959).

11. 32 A.D.2d 392, 302 N.Y.S.2d 640 (1969).

12. See generally Comment, Surrogate Motherhood: The Attorney's Legal and Ethical Dilemma, 11 Cap.U.L.Rev. 593 (1982).

in helping to organize a business in which two or more clients are entrepreneurs, working out the financial reorganization of an enterprise in which two or more clients have an interest, arranging a property distribution in settlement of an estate or mediating a dispute between clients. * * *

In considering whether to act as intermediary between clients, a lawyer should be mindful that if the intermediation fails the result can be additional cost, embarrassment and recrimination. In some situations the risk of failure is so great that intermediation is plainly impossible. For example, a lawyer cannot undertake common representation of clients between whom contentious litigation is imminent or who contemplate contentious negotiations. * * *

In acting as intermediary between clients, the lawyer is required to consult with the clients on the implications of doing so, and proceed only upon consent based on such a consultation. The consultation should make clear that the lawyer's role is not that of partisanship normally expected in other circumstances.[a]

## CROUCH, DIVORCE MEDIATION AND LEGAL ETHICS[b]

16 Fam.L.Q. 219 (1982).

There is no denying that divorce mediation just now has enormous fad appeal. The public is being continually assaulted by articles at varying levels of sophistication extolling mediation as a remedy for the undeniable ills of divorce practice. The number of attorneys entering this lucrative field, and those waiting to enter it, is large. * * *

### SUBSTANTIVE BENEFITS OF MEDIATION

Obviously, there really are reasons for a desperate search for alternatives to the old system. There are right as well as wrong reasons for mediation's immense popularity, and some of the right ones are:

1. Avoidance of unnecessary hostility and artificial antagonism that can destroy all chances of cooperation in constructing a settlement.

2. A measure of client autonomy in constructing the solutions—which is generally agreed to increase the chances of voluntary adherence to the agreement in future years.

a. Compare the following CPR provision:

"**EC 5-20** A lawyer is often asked to serve as an impartial arbitrator or mediator in matters which involve present or former clients. He may serve in either capacity if he first discloses such present or former relationships. After a lawyer has undertaken to act as an impartial arbitrator or mediator, he should not thereafter represent in the dispute any of the parties involved."

b. Richard E. Crouch is a member of the Bar of Virginia; Consulting Editor, the Family Law Reporter, Bureau of National Affairs, Inc., Washington, DC; and Chairman, Ethical Practices and Procedures Committee, Family Law Section, American Bar Association. The views expressed herein do not reflect those of the Bureau of National Affairs, which as a reporter of legal news does not take or express positions. Nor do they necessarily represent the views of the ABA, except that the final section on recommendations for an ethical rule substantially represents a position taken by the Family Law Section's Council before the Kutak Commission and the ABA House of Delegates in June of 1982.

3. Avoiding the traditional two-attorney fight in the settlement process (to say nothing of litigation)—which holds out much promise of reducing costs.

Underlying all this, and more difficult to classify, is the advantage that usually results when one has to state demands and their rationalizations in the actual presence of the other party and that of a presumptively neutral and reasonable third person. Obviously if one has to face only one's own committed advocate, it is easier to state an extreme or unreasonable position.

### Specific Factors Making Mediation Attractive

To clients the appealing features include: (a) some consciousness of the above-listed substantive benefits, (b) the prospect of saving money, (c) the appeal of preserving client dignity by self-determination ("private ordering"), (d) attorney-avoidance and (e) conflict-avoidance (most clients understand, at varying levels of articulability, the appeal of laying the pertinent matters before a supposedly neutral third party immediately present with the two opponent parties, rather than filtering one's desires through a lawyer who must wrangle with another lawyer over the probabilities of decision by a distant judge who can ultimately, in theory, be appealed to), and (f) avoiding the terrors of the courtroom (few people enjoy going on the witness stand).

If we look at mediation's particular attractiveness to attorneys, it seems to lie primarily in the following considerations:

First there is money in it. Mediation, particularly in a city where there is already a raised mediation consciousness, or high susceptibility to fad appeal generally, is a potential gold mine for lawyers, and especially appealing as the salvation of a flagging, or young and struggling, law practice. If mediation is what the public wants, there are many lawyers who would rather give it to them than send the potential clients on to nonlawyers or—worse yet—the rival lawyer next door. Also, mediation practice feeds on itself geometrically. A mediation is likely to produce a measure of free advertising spread by two satisfied clients, whereas the lawyer who "successfully" litigates a divorce or negotiates a separation agreement is very lucky if his one client goes away satisfied.

And lawyers, too, are susceptible to fad appeal, and those of a reforming temperament can flatter themselves that they are participating in a pro-client and anti-lawyer movement. If this selfless nobility can be pursued while making good money, the lawyer can flatter himself for being shrewd as well. * * *

And despite professions to the contrary, mediation is easy money. For the family lawyer it spells an end to the rigors of trial practice. There is no uncertainty, no trial preparation, and no chance of losing fights. The tense atmosphere of the courtroom and the unpleasantness of facing an equally skilled professional across the negotiating table are both avoided.

There is also the promise of court-relief, which indirectly but substantially benefits the attorney. The severe overcrowding of dockets and courtrooms makes any alternative to litigation look inviting. * * *

CONTEXT OF THE MEDIATION/ETHICS DEBATE

There is no question as to the *need for a new rule*, because the rationalizations of dual representation of divorcing parties that now exist are quite ineffective. * * *

Also important in the context of the debate is the concept of the bar as soft target. Since its historical preoccupation with precise analysis of moral questions has given the bar a facility for self-criticism, the bar must take especially seriously any challenges to its integrity from outside. The idea persists that it cannot, ethically and in good conscience, oppose any idea that it is said to reduce lawyers' income, since opposing it would be economically self-serving. In this sense, the bar is the only group that cannot defend itself. * * *

Yet we all know that major reasons for the debate over mediation are the several real dangers it poses to the client population. Dual representation by either lay or legally trained mediators is an invitation to one party's overreaching, and it is judges and lawyers who will have to straighten out the results of mediated agreements that one party discovers cannot be lived with. Unlikely as the consumer/client population is to appreciate it, bar caution in approval of mediation also goes to the possible economic wastefulness of the process. * * *

DIFFICULT ETHICAL ISSUES RAISED BY MEDIATION SCHEMES

Obviously first among the ethical issues all this raises is the conflict of interest in single-lawyer "service" to a divorcing couple. I break this question down into several components.

1. WHETHER ANY "REPRESENTATION" IS INVOLVED

Obviously the rules concerning representation of opponents are not applicable in this context *if* there is no representation, *and no one thinks* there is any. * * *

a. *Dual Representation and Mediation.* Confusion of terminology has complicated the issue recently. Obviously there is much difference between mediation as traditionally conceived, service as an intermediary, common representation of coparty litigants, and "dual representation" of opponents in divorce. With amazing naivete, [RPC 2.2] confounded all these. Its ideas as to service "as an intermediary" are plainly inapplicable to divorce practice, as is the previous law and learning on the subject of intermediary service and co-plaintiff or co-defendant representation. *Dual representation* contemplates, in its most innocent form, representation by one lawyer to the court of the one desire that warring parties can unite in: their desire for a divorce that incorporates the written agreement they have reached. *Mediation,* as in labor-management conflicts, contemplates each side's presenting its arguments to the other in the presence of a neutral third party who aims at a resolution of the issues that will represent the least detriment to each party. * * *

b. *Representing Both or Neither.* Thus the New York City opinion[b] (which does not address the issue of the nature of common representation to the court for uncontested divorce purposes after agreement) held that no representation is involved in mediation and the lawyer must so declare. So did the Boston opinion.[8] * * *

The Boston Bar and the Oregon State Bar[10] concluded that mediation activities were proper because neither is represented. The New York City Bar opinion agrees. Silberman's article[c] says that the differences between these and the [RPC 2.2] conception is "only a semantic one." In that evaluation either the "semantic" or the "only" must be questioned. The difference is a loaded and dangerous one.

* * * It should be noted that the Coogler system,[14] and the Ohio[15] and Virginia[16] bar rulings, contemplate only one party's being represented in the divorce proceedings that follow mediation, with the other party consenting to being unrepresented.

c. *What Exactly Would "Representation" Be?* Does the representation that is disavowed (or shared, depending on how you look at it) include advice that benefits one party to the detriment of the other? Presumably so. The question that naturally arises is what happens when the attorney-mediator sees one party being "disadvantaged" in negotiations. If the mediator cannot advise one party to break off mediation without hurting the interests of the one who is gaining by mediation, then a real conflict of interests problem seems to arise. * * *

### 2. Abstract Representation Rationalization

For as long as dual representation has been around, long antedating the mediation fad, some lawyers have rationalized the compromising of adversary loyalty by saying that they "represent the whole family" when doing this. That rationalization has been rejected as untenable since the family is an abstraction incapable of being a client. * * *

**b.** Opinion 80–23, Association of the Bar of the City of New York, 7 Fam.L.Rep. 3097 (1981).

**8.** Opinion 78–1. Boston Bar Association Committee on Ethics, summarized 5 Fam.L.Rep. 2606.

**10.** Opinion 70–46. Oregon Bar Association Committee on Legal Ethics (1980).

**c.** Silberman, Professional Responsibility Problems of Divorce Mediation, 7 Fam.L.Rep. 4001 (1981). [Silberman finds it "dismaying * * * that mediation efforts may be stymied before they have even begun [by a] variety of restrictive professional responsibility rulings [from state and local] bar associations."]

**14.** See Coogler, Structured Mediation in Divorce Settlements, 1978.

**15.** Ohio S.B.A. Opinion 30, 1 Fam.L.Rep. 3109 (1975).

**16.** Informal Ethics Opinion No. 296. Virginia State Bar, Committee on Legal Ethics (1977); see 7 Fam.L.Rep. 2188.

### 3. The "Mere Scrivener" Theory

A comfortable way to view dual representation of the opposing parties in a divorce is to say that the lawyer only serves as an amanuensis, or notary in the European sense, who is educated enough to "put into legal language" the parties' common intentions once their thoughts have been straightened out and agreement reached in mutual discussion. There are difficulties with this rationalization, however, as the Maryland opinion,[d] pointed out. It said that "if the preparation of a property settlement agreement in mediation can be equated to filling in blanks on forms, then the services of an attorney are probably not necessary," but that if it requires "a professional choice of what language best expresses intent and any expression of opinion on what promotes the best interests of the clients and is not unjust to one or the other," then the preparation is likely to create conflict of interest.

Obviously there are more difficulties if the mere scrivener is also the mediator. * * *

### 4. Awkwardness of Post-Agreement Advice, Representation

* * * The authorities are radically divided on whether post-agreement common representation should be permissible. * * * The Boston Bar opinion contemplates an attorney-mediator * * * not being allowed to represent either party in court, and the Oregon and New York opinions forbid the involved lawyer's representing either party. As conceived by the Virginia and Ohio opinions the common attorney represents one party in presenting the agreement and divorce pleadings to the court while the other goes unrepresented. The California case of Klemm v. Superior Court,[32] hints at a permissible dual representation in divorce court for those who have worked out an agreement with the common attorney's help.[e] * * *

**d.** Opinion 80–55A, Maryland State Bar Association Committee on Ethics, 14 Md. B.J. 8 (Jan. 1981).

**32.** 75 Cal.App.3d 893, 142 Cal.Rptr. 509, 4 Fam.L.Rep. 2185, 2245 (1977).

**e.** In *Klemm*, lawyer consulted with husband and wife, her friends of very modest means, and worked out an agreement with joint custody and wife waiving child support. She represented only wife at the dissolution hearing. The court reversed her disqualification to represent both spouses, with their consent, at a subsequent hearing on the county's request for child support. The court found the conflict "strictly potential and not present" because the spouses had settled their differences by agreement and there was no point of difference to be litigated—the issue was only between the county, which wanted support ordered, and the spouses, who both maintained that husband should not be ordered to pay support. The court said:

> "While on the face of the matter it may appear foolhardy for the wife to waive child support [footnote: "It is to be noted that the parties' agreement that the children should not receive support would not prevent the court from awarding child support either at the hearing or at some time subsequent thereto. Therefore, the children's rights are not in issue nor are they jeopardized"], other values could very well have been more important to her than such support—such as maintaining a good relationship between the husband and the children and between the husband and herself despite the marital problems * * *. It could well have been if the wife was forced to choose between A.F.D.C. payments to be reimbursed to the county by the husband and no A.F.D.C. payments she would have made the latter choice.

The difficulties of post-agreement common representation are one more reason why there should be a warning to clients that this, like mediation and like common advice, is not what you traditionally pay an attorney for: it is a new kind of service designed to save the client money. In my opinion, exactly these words should be required. * * *

There is little question that lawyer scruples appear hypocritical to the public since the mystique of the profession has been demolished in recent decades. A public encouraged by many lawyer-reformers to think of themselves as "consumers" of "services," rather than clients of an advisor-advocate in a unique relationship, tends to look at all lawyer rationalizations of professional caution with a suspicious eye. When a lawyer elects to forgo any kind of employment to provide representation (and its financial rewards) for conflict-of-interest reasons, clients seldom appreciate a lawyer's scruples—especially if the whole fee from Day One is not to be refunded. It sounds like bad faith, a glaring example of economic determinism, and an indefensible featherbedding rule upheld by the chummy bonds of the bar's old-boy network, when a couple are told that they must get two or three lawyers to do what appears to be a single job. * * *

### 5. Whether There Is Always, Necessarily, an Unacceptably High Level of Conflict in the Divorce Situation

According to many authorities, the traditional view has been that representing both spouses is entirely prohibited because of the inextricable adversariness inherent in the situation. * * *

Legal scholars tend to make a distinction between "actual and potential" conflict of interest. Is this an irrelevant distinction here, or, indeed, is it a very apt one, requiring us to face the fact that divorcing spouses are opponents, with the advancement of one's interests necessarily diminishing those of the other? Though their desires may coincide on the sole issue of divorce itself, mediation necessarily involves many more issues.

* * * The problem, as described in the Maryland opinion, is that the lawyer who sees one party being disadvantaged cannot speak up and terminate the mediation without damaging the interests of the one who is prevailing.

### 6. Attorney as Judge of His Own Cause

The New York opinion's solution to all this is to say that the attorney must keep especially alert and be especially sensitive to evidence that one party is being disadvantaged—particularly by unfair exploitation on the other's part. This not only assumes a great deal about the lawyer's sensitivity to these concerns, and places great moral

"Of course, if the wife at some future date should change her mind and seek child support and if the husband should desire to avoid the payment of such support, [lawyer] would be disqualified from representing either in a contested hearing on the issue."

responsibility on his or her conscience, but also assumes scrupulous and rigorous honesty on the part of all mediating lawyers. However, assuming even a bit less of this last quality, one must worry about the desire of the lawyer and the mediation shop which referred the couple to him to see the mediation go through at all costs. In this sense, making the lawyer a judge of his own cause—although arguably lawyers' ethics codes do so, and have to do so, in many instances—is like appointing a vulpine poultry-conservator. * * *

Also, the assumption that the lawyer can always solve problems by bowing out is perhaps a naive one. The parties who invest their time and money, emotions and energies in a mediation lose something when forced to begin over again with another lawyer even if (as we assume they will understand) they avoid something worse. * * *

### Waiver and Its Difficulties

Consent of the parties has always been assumed to be the answer to the ethical difficulties posed by attempting to serve both sides of a marital dispute. However, it has long been held by a number of authorities that because there is severe "actual conflict" of interests, rather than just "potential conflict," consents in the divorce area are not valid, or are perpetually retractable after the fact. * * *

As for the adequacy of explanation, it is hard to see how the client can fully, or even adequately, understand the subtle forces involved in this conflict of interest without at least having had three years of law school, if not several years of law practice.

Especially in a climate of defensive practice, it would seem that a prudent attorney has to adopt an attitude requiring so full an explanation and so severe a warning that reconsideration and withdrawal of the request really is likely to follow (in other words, a warning so honestly and conscientiously given that it will be effective, and achieve its ostensible purpose, overcoming any subtextual promediation message). * * * Assuming such waivers can be effective, they would seem to have to take the form of agreements at the very outset between the lawyer and each party that if the lawyer sees something unfair, the lawyer is *not* going to blow the whistle. However, the theory with which most clients go into this would seem to be a very different one: that one of the mediator's main purposes is to referee or police the negotiations to see that fair play is observed.

Expressing these fears is somewhat akin to admitting the suspicion that there will be no such thing as "simple uncontested divorce" if a party's attorney does a thorough and conscientious job. Of course, that brings one immediately back to the often-expressed view that amicable divorces can "go along smoothly enough until the lawyers get involved." It cannot be denied that when the profession is at its most scrupulously ethical it sacrifices some public confidence in seeming to require a procedure that exacerbates adversary bitterness while lining lawyers' pockets. * * *

At least one question we should answer is whether, in order for there to have been a valid waiver, the lawyer must have informed each client individually what is the best financial result he or she could expect from a court fight and the best result to be expected from a pre-litigation settlement with full discovery, certain pressure tactics, and at least some wrangling.

### Militant Consumerism as a Factor in the Debate

The desire to use mediation as a means of saving divorce litigants from unnecessary expense as well as unnecessary acrimony has long been a factor in mediationist rhetoric. Suddenly, mediation is hotly desired by the prudent consumer of legal "services" approaching divorce—notwithstanding that much mediation as now practiced appears to be every bit as expensive as legal services in the same case, in a competent divorce lawyer's hands, would be. * * *

It is certain that consumerist rhetoric depends on the existence of entirely "simple, uncontested" divorces, and that there is a danger (noted above) of such simplicity falling apart when either lawyer does a scrupulous, honest, and professional job. Most "consumers" are surprised to find that the simple uncontested divorce does not include one involving property or children, and they regard this revelation as part of a bait-and-switch advertising scheme.

The lawyer's actions in mediation, dual representation, and other cost-saving schemes stand a good chance of later being labeled a sellout by dissatisfied "customers." This is because the "customer" hardly ever fully appreciates how much he or she is being asked to waive. The supposed "consumer" of "services" really wants the traditional loyalty and adversary advocacy that lawyering has always imported in the public's mind. He wants to get a good deal on "services" as a consumer, but also wants the almost-mystical formation of a patron-client relationship.

The important questions are whether the adversary system can ever be abolished, or even diminished, and lawyers still stay involved—and then whether that can be done in a climate of "defensive practice." * * *

### Possible Misuse of the Process

#### 1. Unwarranted Prolongation—Adding Unnecessary Layer

There is certainly some question whether mediation in many cases is indeed swifter or cheaper than either litigation, or traditional separation-agreement negotiation in the shadow of litigation. * * * Sometimes * * * it [means] sending battered parties back into the ring for another dull, grim round of stressful combat * * *. There may be cases where the traditional mechanism would be not only quicker and cheaper, but less stressful. * * *

2. FACILITATING EXPLOITATION OF ONE PARTY

The fear is sometimes expressed that imperfect human mediators, stepping into a godlike role in the process, are deceived into allowing, and even contributing to, the unconscionable exploitation of the weaker by the dominant party. (In the unfathomable subtleties of longstanding marital relationships, this dominant party can even be the one who appears the weaker party, and even trained observers can be fooled for at least an appreciable length of time.) * * *

From a lawyer's viewpoint it seems likely that ignorance of what a court would do nearly always operates to one party's benefit and the other's detriment. This is still true, even if it is both who are ignorant.

What the attorney does in the face of overreaching, too-aggressive bargaining, deceit or coercion is not as simple a question as it might appear. Supposedly, he or she sounds the alarm and alerts the victim and curbs the transgressor. However, what is overreaching may be such a subjective question that the lawyer has, or should have, real doubts about curbing that which in fairness should not be curbed. This might be tactics which are only the full and free expression of deep feelings that mediation supposedly allows * * *.

The mediator also has to ask just what is client self-determination and autonomy in the spirit of what has been called "private ordering." [62] If one person wishes to be a doormat (perhaps for the sake of a quick exit from the marriage, or for less obvious reasons), is it proper for the mediator to let that person do it? Such a person's reasons might include a very real and deep distaste for even mediation-flavored divorce negotiation, which the other party and the mediator, by reason of their temperament, do not share—or even understand.

It must take the wisdom of Solomon to know what to do in most situations if the fairness one strives for is imperfectly defined. The mediator who knows exactly when to bow out and call a halt to the cooperative effort is still disadvantaging in that way the one party who was profiting the most by letting mediation go on. It is sometimes a very subtle judgment on the mediator's part to say whether, and when, mediation has "broken down."

As noted above, there is also the tainted objectivity of the mediator-umpire whose stake in "successful" mediations would make him very reluctant to cut off the process too early. One of the great advantages to lawyers is the doubled "living advertisement" factor. Someone may be influenced to produce a compromise against justice and against reason because he is reluctant to jeopardize mediation by telling one party "you are just selfish and there is nothing more to this case." Nor is panel membership likely to last long for a lawyer who finds mediation unsuitable in over half of his or her cases.

62. *See* Mnookin and Kornhauser, Bargaining in the Shadow of the Law: The Case of Divorce, 88 Yale L.J. 950 (1979).

Obviously if the attorney, either as mediator or as post-mediation advisor, will be advising the couple what would happen in court or in non-face-to-face negotiations without mediation, there is a real danger of misrepresenting these potentials to one side unless the attorney is very exhaustively thorough. It is also arguable that an adequate explanation is not possible unless the attorney[63] sees each person separately for this purpose. * * *

Another great difficulty, briefly alluded to earlier, is posed by the possibly flawed philosophical basis of the whole mediation movement. As it is taught today, mediation theory is characterized by the underlying assumption that all issues can and must be compromised. However, there can be cases imagined wherein this is simply irrational. It could be that the compromiser role requires that one make peace with oppression, suffer fools gladly, redefine black as white, and meet utter nonsense halfway. The lawyer involved in the mediation process as mediator or legal advisor could find it very difficult to reconcile loyalty to the "situation" or process (or the mediation center) with loyalty or honesty to the individual from whom compromise is being unreasonably sought. It seems to come back to the homely truth that you really cannot serve two masters. * * *

RECOMMENDATIONS FOR A RULE

[RPC 2.2] aims at other kinds of law practice than domestic relations and for the most part misses divorce mediation and related phenomena. As a guide for any kind of legal practice in the family law field, including mediation by a lawyer, it [is] woefully inadequate. If a special rule to cover family law situations were acceptable, I would suggest a fairly detailed one. * * * Some essentials of honest and ethically safe mediation are suggested below:

1. Coverage. Divorce-related mediation requires a special rule. The rule should explicitly apply itself to any lawyer participating in divorce-related mediation, whether it be as mediator, as post-mediation legal advisor, as draftsman, or any combination of these.

63. This would mean the attorney in whatever one of a bewildering variety of roles and role combinations he or she might assume. The lawyer role in the various mediation schemes can be mediator, post-mediation advisor, post-mediation draftsman, post-mediation and post-drafting advisor, post-mediation and post-drafting representative to the court of the parties' joint desires, and various combinations. A very deep, and just-possibly insoluble, ethical problem is stirred up by the contemplation of this scene. If the lawyer does not see each party separately, to ascertain vital facts that one party is unable to speak of in the presence of the other, the mediation may proceed on the basis of ignorance or misapprehension as to a major factor—such as the amount of undeclared income, or the sexual exploitation or legal vulnerability of one party. The theory must be that, absent a full and frank discussion of this very matter of ignorance or distorted facts, the parties at least impliedly consent to a mediation that may proceed on a factually cockeyed basis. However, as soon as the mediator sees either party alone, suspicion as to what secrets the mediator may be holding can render absurd the assumptions on which the mediation proceeds. The mediator who is keeping secrets for one person or both can hardly rationalize his declarations of neutrality.

2. A preliminary written contract. The undertaking of mediation itself should be set forth in a written contract which both parties sign before entering into mediation. All the warnings, waivers, and informed consents contemplated by this unique form of divorce negotiation should be embodied in the contract, but that does not relieve the attorney who participates in mediation from his or her obligation to explain the understandings effectively. The attorney should be honestly satisfied that the parties fully understand and genuinely consent to the conditions of mediation as required below. After signing, nothing happens for three days.

3. The parties should be warned that their interests are presumed to be conflict on most points, and that they are waiving any objections to the conflict of interest a lawyer necessarily has when serving in any way the opposing parties in a conflict. It should be explained that this compromise of loyalties is being allowed only because they consent to it. The parties must also declare their informed satisfaction with mediation's proceeding on the basis of only that information that was brought out in joint sessions.

4. The parties should be expressly told that neither one is receiving legal representation. The lawyer should go on to warn them that the service to be provided is not what lawyers traditionally are paid to do, and that no attorney-client relationship will exist.

5. The parties must understand from the outset that the lawyer will not represent either spouse, or both spouses, before the court in the securing of a divorce if a written separation agreement is not produced or if any such agreement is contested or disavowed by either party.

6. If the lawyer is serving as a mediator (rather than post-mediation advisor or draftsman), he or she will not represent either party, or both, before the court in connection with this matter.

7. The lawyer, in whatever mediation-connected role he or she serves, will interview each party separately to ascertain the divorce-pertinent facts and listen to each party's individual concerns. However, the lawyer will give no legal advice while seeing either client alone. A party who objects to the lack of private legal advice will be informed of its availability from independent legal counsel unconnected with the mediation. If the lawyer decides that the interests are so opposed that this case is not an appropriate one for mediation, the parties should be told as soon as possible. Legal advice will be given to the parties only in the presence of each other.

8. The lawyer will interview the parties together before mediation, and will advise them *together* as to his best professional opinion, however imprecise, of what a court of competent jurisdiction would do with their case if required to review it. This opinion should be revised if warranted by facts that come out only in the course of the mediation. The lawyer must explain to the parties

at this time what he or she will do in the event that the lawyer perceives unfairness or overreaching.

9. The parties will be informed at the outset that any agreement which mediation should produce will be reduced to writing and, when signed by the parties, will be binding on both and enforceable by the court to whatever extent local law makes it so. That local law will itself be explained. It will also be explained that either party can retract the verbal agreement at any time before the written agreement is signed.

When reduced to writing, the agreement will include a line saying "first seen," followed by a blank which each party will fill in with initials and date. After the agreement is reduced to writing and the parties have initialed and dated the "first seen" line, the lawyer must fully explain to them the advantages of having the agreement reviewed before signature by independent legal counsel for each party. It will also be explained that independent legal counsel means a separate lawyer who does not serve and is not employed by the other spouse or by the mediator or the mediation organization. The agreement will be valid only if signed by the parties at least three days after the "first seen" date. The agreement will include a clause so explaining, and explaining that neither party has any legal obligation to return and sign the written agreement.

In addition, the lawyer should not undertake any of the above-described mediation roles at all unless the lawyer has satisfied himself or herself that in the lawyer's professional judgment the parties can prudently agree to a full settlement on all the legal issues without the advice of separate, independent legal counsel, and that the parties can intelligently and prudently consent to all the waivers involved in the particular process of mediation and dual representation being contemplated.

It may be objected that this rule is too long and detailed, and that [RPC] 2.2 and the [CPR's] DR 5–106 and EC 5–20 cover the matter. However, [RPC 2.2] is clearly designed for other kinds of co-representation and intermediary service, and the old rule leaves so many questions unanswered that perils for the lawyer without more specific guidance loom on all sides. * * * A rule elegant in its simplicity would have much to recommend it, but the issues and the dangers simply demand the express guidance offered by a detailed rule.[f]

f. For less restrictive views, see Moore, Conflicts of Interest in the Simultaneous Representation of Multiple Clients: A Proposed Solution to the Current Confusion and Controversy, 61 Tex.L.Rev. 211, 245–58 (1982); Morgan, The Evolving Concept of Professional Responsibility, 90 Harv.L.Rev. 702, 727–28 (1977); Note, Family Law—Attorney Mediation of Marital Disputes and Conflict of Interest Considerations, 60 N.C.L.Rev. 171 (1981); Note, Simultaneous Representation: Transaction Resolution in the Adversary System, 28 Case W. Res.L.Rev. 86, 105–09 (1977). See also Special Section on Mediation, 17 Fam.L.Q. 449 (1984).

### *Questions*

(1) Are Crouch's concerns and proposals sound?

(2) To what extent do they apply to other intermediary situations specified in RPC 2.2's Comment?

(3) What would you do as a lawyer if two clients asked you to organize a business which they would share 50-50, and you knew it was sounder to specify a 51-49 or 55-45 split to protect the business from crippling deadlocks?

### *Comment*

(1) *Validity of settlements.* Several courts have refused to set aside divorce property settlements on grounds of dual representation. In Levine v. Levine,[1] New York's highest court held that "the fact that the same attorney represented both parties in the preparation of the separation agreement does not, without more, establish overreaching on the part of the husband." It also ruled that the trial court properly rejected any inference of overreaching by the husband arising from joint representation in the following circumstances:

> "The husband initially contacted the attorney [who was related to the husband by marriage, had previously represented the husband in connection with his business, and had known both parties for a number of years] and informed him that he had discussed the possibility of a separation agreement with his wife and that the couple had agreed on the essential terms. The attorney then arranged to meet with the wife at his office.
>
> "At this meeting, the attorney told the wife that he was involved in the matter only because the basic terms of the agreement had already been settled by the parties and that the wife was free to seek the advice of another attorney. Based on conversations with both parties, the attorney prepared a draft agreement. Further negotiations and consultations followed, after which a final agreement was drawn up, thoroughly reviewed by plaintiff, and then signed by her.
>
> " * * * The [trial] court [found] that the agreement was fair, and * * * that the attorney had 'managed to preserve neutrality' throughout his joint representation of the couple."

In the Washington case of Halvorsen v. Halvorsen,[2] the court rejected a wife's action to set aside a divorce property settlement entered into with the family lawyer representing both the husband. The lawyer had previously represented the husband with reference to both personal affairs and the husband's million dollar tug boat enterprise. Nine doctors said the wife was able to cope despite fits of depression although a tenth doctor thought she was unable to understand complex matters or assert her own will in negotiation. The wife had written letters to the lawyer requesting the joint representation and saying

1. 56 N.Y.2d 42, 451 N.Y.S.2d 26, 436 N.E.2d 476 (1982).

2. 3 Wn.App. 827, 479 P.2d 161 (1970).

that she would be content if she received $500 per month and assurance that the business would go to one of the parties' two children. The court reasoned:

"The practice of one attorney's representing both parties to a divorce can, of course, lead to difficulties * * *. Here, however, [lawyer's] conduct appears to us to be proper under the circumstances. The record shows that plaintiff, after it was explained to her that she could obtain independent counsel and ought to do so if she felt any conflict of interest existed, chose to have [lawyer] represent her in what she appears to have regarded as an amicable division of the marital estate. She knew that the estate contained substantial assets. She spelled out her desires and got what she wanted * * *.

"Here [lawyer] told plaintiff she should get independent counsel if the matter were to be contested. He said he would have represented neither of the parties in a contested divorce. He inquired of plaintiff's psychiatrist and was told she could successfully cope with a divorce. Only then, and at plaintiff's request and to her apparent satisfaction, did he function in the case. We cannot find any unreasonable behavior on [lawyer's] part." [3]

(2) *Malpractice liability.* Compare the older California case of Ishmael v. Millington,[4] where lawyer, who represented husband in unrelated matters, with wife's consent prepared a settlement agreement and a divorce complaint in which wife was plaintiff. A default divorce and court approval of the settlement followed. Wife sued lawyer for malpractice in not discovering for her that the property involved in the settlement had been undervalued. The court found summary judgment for lawyer unwarranted, saying:

"Divorces are frequently uncontested; the parties may make their financial arrangements peaceably and honestly; vestigial chivalry may impel them to display the wife as the injured plaintiff; the husband may then seek out and pay an attorney to escort the wife through the formalities of adjudication. We describe these facts of life without necessarily approving them. Even in that situation the attorney's professional obligations do not permit his

3. For instances of improper dual representation in divorce suits, see Holmes v. Holmes, 145 Ind.App. 52, 248 N.E.2d 564 (1969) (new trial because husband's lawyer, acting for wife in obtaining default divorce, failed to protect her against unfair advantage husband had taken of her in settlement); In re Rubin, 7 N.J. 507, 81 A.2d 776 (1951); Staedler v. Staedler, 6 N.J. 380, 78 A.2d 896, 28 A.L.R.2d 1291 (1951).

For situations of *consecutive* representation without the former client's consent, where the lawyer was reprimanded for causing the danger that a former client's confidences would be used to the former client's disadvantage, see In re Braun, 49 N.J. 16, 227 A.2d 506 (1967) (lawyer represented wife in divorce suit after counseling both husband and wife with a view to reconciliation and conferring with husband on possibility of representing him); In re Blatt, 42 N.J. 522, 201 A.2d 715 (1964) (lawyer represented husband in divorce suit after ceasing to represent wife for whom he had commenced the suit).

Cf. In re Maltby, 68 Ariz. 153, 202 P.2d 902 (1949); Florida Bar v. Ethier, 261 So.2d 817 (Fla.1972); In re Themelis, 117 Vt. 19, 83 A.2d 507 (1951).

4. 241 Cal.App.2d 520, 50 Cal.Rptr. 592 (1966).

descent to the level of a scrivener. The edge of danger gleams if the attorney has previously represented the husband. A husband and wife at the brink of division of their marital assets have an obvious divergence of interests. Representing the wife in an arm's length divorce, an attorney of ordinary professional skill would demand some verification of the husband's financial statement; or, at the minimum, inform the wife that the husband's statement was unconfirmed, that wives may be cheated, that prudence called for investigation and verification. Deprived of such disclosure, the wife cannot make a free and intelligent choice. Representing both spouses in an uncontested divorce situation (whatever the ethical implications), the attorney's professional obligations demand no less. He may not set a shallow limit on the depth to which he will represent the wife."

Compare the Missouri malpractice case of Lange v. Marshall[5]:

"[Plaintiff wife's] charges of negligence were that defendant [lawyer] failed to (1) inquire as to the financial state of [husband] and advise plaintiff; (2) negotiate for a better settlement for plaintiff; (3) advise plaintiff she would get a better settlement if she litigated the matter; and (4) fully and fairly disclose to plaintiff her rights as to marital property, custody and maintenance. Defendant admitted that he did none of these things and contended that he had no duty to do them. He asserted that because he undertook to represent the parties as a mediator, a status disclosed fully to both parties, that he felt it would be improper for him to do any of the four things claimed to be negligence as it would place him in the position of an advocate for one party or the other. [Footnote: "The parties disagree as to the nature of the obligation defendant undertook. It is clear that he advised both parties that he would not represent either as an advocate. Although the terms 'arbitrator' and 'negotiator' were also used in the parties' conversations, 'mediator' would appear to be the proper term to apply to defendant's role."] We need not resolve the exact nature of defendant's status nor the duties which that status imposed upon him [because] we are unable to find that plaintiff sustained any damage as a proximate result of [the alleged] negligence."

## C. THIRD PERSON'S INTERESTS

### MODEL RULES OF PROFESSIONAL CONDUCT

**RULE 1.8 Conflict of Interest: Prohibited Transactions**

* * *

(f) A lawyer shall not accept compensation for representing a client from one other than the client unless:

(1) the client consents after consultation;

5. 622 S.W.2d 237 (Mo.App.1981).

(2) there is no interference with the lawyer's independence of professional judgment or with the client-lawyer relationship; and

(3) information relating to representation of a client is protected as required by Rule 1.6.[a]

## PARSONS v. CONTINENTAL NATIONAL AMERICAN GROUP

113 Ariz. 223, 550 P.2d 94 (1976).

GORDON, Justice:

* * * We are asked to determine whether an insurance carrier in a garnishment action is estopped from denying coverage under its policy when its defense in that action is based upon confidential information obtained by the carrier's attorney from an insured as a result of representing him in the original tort action.

* * * Michael Smithey, age 14, brutally assaulted his neighbors, appellants Ruth, Dawn and Gail Parsons, on the night of March 26, 1967.

During April, 1967 Frank Candelaria, CNA claims representative, began an investigation of the incident. On June 6, 1967 he wrote to Howard Watt the private counsel retained by the Smitheys advising him that CNA was "now in the final stages of our investigation," and to contact the Parsons' attorney to ascertain what type of settlement they would accept. Watt did contact the Parsons' attorney and requested that a formal demand settlement be tendered and the medical bills be forwarded to Candelaria. On August 11, 1967 Candelaria wrote a detailed letter to his company on his investigation of Michael's background in regards to his school experiences. He concluded the letter with the following:

> "In view of this information gathered and in discussion with the boy's father's attorney, Mr. Howard Watts, and with the boy's parents, I am reasonably convinced that the boy was not in control of his senses at the time of this incident.
>
> "It is, therefore, my suggestion that, and unless instructed otherwise, I will proceed to commence settlement negotiations with the claimant's attorney so that this matter may be disposed of as soon as possible."

[On three occasions,] Candelaria tried to settle with the Parsons for the medical expenses and was unsuccessful.

a. Compare the following CPR provisions:

**"DR 5-107 Avoiding Influence by Others Than the Client**

"(A) Except with the consent of his client after full disclosure, a lawyer shall not:

(1) Accept compensation for his legal services from one other than his client.

(2) Accept from one other than his client any thing of value related to his representation of or his employment by his client.

"(B) A lawyer shall not permit a person who recommends, employs, or pays him to render legal services for another to direct or regulate his professional judgment in rendering such legal services."

On October 13, 1967 the Parsons filed a complaint alleging that Michael Smithey assaulted the Parsons and that Michael's parents were negligent in their failure to restrain Michael and obtain the necessary medical and psychological attention for him. At the time that the Parsons filed suit they tendered a demand settlement offer of $22,500 which was refused by CNA as "completely unrealistic."

CNA's retained counsel undertook the Smithey's defense and also continued to communicate with CNA and advised him on November 10, 1967:

> "I have secured a rather complete and confidential file on the minor insured who is now in the Paso Robles School for Boys, a maximum-security institution with facilities for psychiatric treatment, and he will be kept there indefinitely and certainly for at least six months * * *.
>
> "The above referred-to confidential file shows that the boy is fully aware of his acts and that he knew what he was doing was wrong. It follows, therefore, that the assault he committed on claimants can only be a deliberate act on his part."

After CNA had been so advised they sent a reservation of rights letter to the Smitheys stating that the insurance company, as a courtesy to the insureds, would investigate and defend the Parsons' claim, but would do so without waiving any of the rights under the policy. The letter further stated that it was possible the act involved might be found to be an intentional act, and that the policy specifically excludes liability for bodily injury caused by an intentional act. This letter was addressed only to the parents and not to Michael.

In preparing for trial the CNA attorney retained to undertake the defense of the Smitheys interviewed Michael and received a narrative statement from him in regards to the events of March 26, 1967, and then wrote to CNA: "His own story makes it obvious that his acts were willful and criminal."

CNA also requested an evaluation of the tort case and the same attorney advised CNA: "Assuming liability and coverage, the injury is worth the full amount of the policy or $25,000.00."

On the issue of liability the trial court directed a verdict for Michael's parents on the grounds that there was no evidence of the parents being negligent. This Court affirmed. On the question of Michael's liability the trial court granted plaintiff's motion to a directed verdict after the defense presented no evidence and there was no opposition to the motion. Judgment was entered against Michael in the amount of $50,000.

The Parsons then garnished CNA, and moved for a guardian ad litem to be appointed for Michael which was granted by the trial court. On November 23, 1970 [the] Parsons offered to settle with CNA in the amount of its policy limits, $25,000. This offer was not accepted.

CNA successfully defended the garnishment action by claiming that the intentional act exclusion applied. The same law firm and attorney that had previously represented Michael represented the carrier in the garnishment action.

Appellants contend that CNA should be estopped to deny coverage and have waived the intentional act exclusion because the company took advantage of the fiduciary relationship between its agent (the attorney) and Michael Smithey. We agree.

The attorneys, retained by CNA, represented Michael Smithey at the personal liability trial, and, as a result, obtained privileged and confidential information from Michael's confidential file at the Paso Robles School for Boys, during the discovery process and, more importantly, from the attorney-client relationship. Both the A.B.A. Committee on Ethics and Professional Responsibility and the State Bar of Arizona, Committee on Rules of Professional Conduct have held that an attorney that represented the insured at the request of the insurer owes undivided fidelity to the insured, and, therefore, may not reveal any information or conclusions derived therefrom to the insurer that may be detrimental to the insured in any subsequent action. The A.B.A. Committee on Ethics and Professional Responsibility in Informal Opinion Number 949 [1966] stated:

> "If the firm does represent the insured in the personal injury action, to subsequently reveal to the insurer any information received from the insured for possible use by the insurer in defense of a garnishment proceeding by the injured person, would be a clear violation of both Canon 6 [adverse influences and conflicting interests] and Canon 37 regarding confidences of a client. * * * "

The Arizona Ethics Opinion No. 261 adopted November 15, 1968 stated:

> "A.B.A. Informal Opinion C728 makes it very clear that the inquiring attorney is the attorney for the insured, B, even though the attorney would be paid by G Insurance Company. The undivided fidelity owed by the attorney, then, is to B and not to G Insurance Company.
>
> " * * * it was unethical for the inquiring attorney to represent the insurance company in an action against the insured, after judgment against the insured, to declare that the policy did not provide coverage. * * * "

The State Bar Committee in its Arizona Ethics Opinion No. 282 adopted May 21, 1969 stated:

> "No better statement of the basis for our position on this question occurs to us than the following quotation from the Blakslee article cited above (55 A.B.A. Jour. at p. 263):
>
> 'Although the opinions of the Committe state that the lawyer represents both the insurer and insured, *it is clear that his highest duty is to the insured and that the lawyer cannot be used as an agent of the company to supply information detrimental to the insured.* The lawyer is a professional retained pursuant to the terms of a contract between the insurer and insured. The company has

a right to expect that the issue of liability for injury and damages will be effectively and forcefully presented by the lawyer it has chosen. It has agreed, by its contract, to pay damages once they are determined.

'The client, on the other hand, in order to obtain an insurance policy, has given up the right to direct the incidents of the trial by agreeing that the company shall have the right to choose the attorney. This also is fair since it is the company that will ultimately pay the judgment. *But counsel should not be expected to communicate information received in confidence or to betray confidences lodged in them by trusting clients.* To do so would not only destroy public confidence in the legal profession, but also would make defense attorneys investigators for carriers. That the company has not satisfied itself concerning coverage by its other, independent methods, is no compelling reason why defense counsel should be asked to betray the trust reposed in him by the insured. The fact that the company may be required to pay a monetary judgment does not alter the situation, since the company voluntarily has assumed this contractual obligation by virtue of its existence as an insurer. Its contractual obligation, voluntarily assumed, should not be permitted to be used as the basis for converting the defense counsel into something beyond a lawyer defending a client' (Emphasis supplied.)"

The attorney who represents an insured owes him "undeviating and single allegiance" whether the attorney is compensated by the insurer or the insured. Newcomb v. Meiss, 263 Minn. 315, 116 N.W.2d 593 (1962).

The attorney in the instant case should have notified CNA that he could no longer represent them when he obtained any information (as a result of his attorney-client relationship with Michael) that could possibly be detrimental to Michael's interests under the coverage of the policy.

The attorney representing Michael Smithey in the personal injury suit instituted by the Parsons had to be sure at all times that the fact he was compensated by the insurance company did not "adversely affect his judgment on behalf of or dilute his loyalty to [his] client, [Michael Smithey]". Ethical Consideration 5–14. Where an attorney is representing the insured in a personal injury suit, and, at the same time advising the insurer on the question of liability under the policy it is difficult to see how that attorney could give individual loyalty to the insured-client. "The standards of the legal profession require undeviating fidelity of the lawyer to his client. No exceptions can be tolerated." Van Dyke v. White, 55 Wash.2d 601, 349 P.2d 430 (1960).

* * *

The attorney in the present case continued to act as Michael's attorney while he was actively working against Michael's interests. When an attorney who is an insurance company's agent uses the confidential relationship between an attorney and a client to gather information so as to deny the insured coverage under the policy in the garnishment proceeding we hold that such conduct constitutes a waiver of any policy defense, and is so contrary to public policy that the insurance company is estopped as a matter of law from disclaiming liability under an exclusionary clause in the policy. Employers Casualty Company v. Tilley, 496 S.W.2d 552 (Tex.1973). In the *Tilley* case the Texas Supreme Court also noted that such conduct on the part of an attorney and insurance carrier has been the subject of litigation in other jurisdictions especially in regards to the situation where an attorney representing the carrier does not fully and completely disclose to the insured the specific conflict of interest involved.

> "Conduct in violation of the above principles by the insurer through the attorney selected by it to represent the insured has been condemned by the highest courts of several other jurisdictions. In Perkoski v. Wilson, 371 Pa. 553, 92 A.2d 189 (1952); Tiedtke v. Fidelity & Casualty Company of New York, 222 So.2d 206 (Fla.1969); Bogle v. Conway, 199 Kan. 707, 433 P.2d 407 (1967); Crum v. Anchor Casualty Company, 264 Minn. 378, 119 N.W.2d 703 (1963); Merchants Indemnity Corp. v. Eggleston, 37 N.J. 114, 179 A.2d 505 (1962); and Van Dyke v. White, 55 Wash.2d 601, 349 P.2d 430 (1960), analogous conduct in violation of such principles was held to preclude or estop the insurer from denying coverage or liability. See also general criticisms and consequences of such conduct discussed in Meirthew v. Last, 376 Mich. 33, 135 N.W.2d 353 (1965); and Newcomb v. Meiss, 263 Minn. 315, 116 N.W.2d 593 (1962)." Employers Casualty Company v. Tilley, 496 S.W.2d at 559.

Appellee urges that the personal liability matter was defended under a reservation of rights agreement and this agreement had the effect of allowing the insurance company to investigate and defend the claim and still not waive any defenses. We hold that the reservation of rights agreement is not material to this case because the same attorney was representing conflicting clients. Appellee further urges that the procedure followed in the instant case is provided for by statute in Arizona. A.R.S. § 20–1130 states inter alia:

> "Without limitation of any right or defense of an insurer otherwise, none of the following acts by or on behalf of an insurer shall be deemed to constitute a waiver of any provision of a policy or of any defense of the insurer thereunder:
>
> * * *
>
> "3. Investigating any loss or claim under any policy or engaging in negotiations looking toward a possible settlement of any such loss or claim."

Appellee misconstrues the protection offered to the carrier under A.R.S. § 20–1130. This statute does not grant to a carrier the right to engage an attorney to act on behalf of the insured to defend a claim against the insured while at the same time build a defense against the insured on behalf of the insurer. This conflict of interest constitutes a source of prejudice upon which the insured may invoke the doctrine of estoppel.

Appellee further urges that if the appellants are entitled to a judgment against the appellee insurance company the only judgment they are entitled to is in the amount of coverage $25,000.00. We do not agree. The evidence shows that the insurance company was advised by their legal counsel that if they were liable the injury was "worth the full amount of the policy." The evidence further shows that CNA could have settled the Parsons' claim against Michael Smithey well within the policy limits and refused to do so on the basis that the settlement was "completely unrealistic." It is clear from the record that the carrier failed to enter into good faith settlement negotiations. In the instant case the further fact that the carrier believed there was no coverage under the policy and so refused to give any consideration to the proposed settlements did not absolve them from liability for the entire judgment entered against the insured. [J]udgment of the trial court reversed and judgment entered in favor of appellants Parsons in the sum of $50,000.

### Comment

(1) *Client identification.* Although authorities have viewed the insurer-provided lawyer as engaged in a dual representation of insurer and insured,[1] the better (and emerging) position is that the lawyer owes allegiance "to one party and one party only: the insured."[2]

(2) *Disclosing or using information against insured.* In addition to preventing the lawyer from informing the insurer of noncoverage information,[3] the lawyer-client relationship bars the lawyer from such conduct as implying to the jury that insured is in collusion with plaintiff[4] or subsequently representing insurer on its noncoverage claim.[5]

(3) *Failure to settle—malpractice liability for excess judgment.* Although "insurer may feel it has nothing to lose by refusing a policy

1. Morris, Conflicts of Interest in Defending Under Liability Insurance Policies: A Proposed Solution, 1981 Utah L.Rev. 457, 461.

A few authorities have considered insured to be only a nominal client and the insurer to be the true client. Id. at 462.

2. Id. at 465; see authorities cited throughout Professor Morris' article, including ABA Formal Opinion 282 (1950).

3. See id. at 478–84; ABA National Conference of Lawyers and Liability Insurers, 20 Fed'n of Ins. Couns. Q. 95, 98 (1970) (Guiding Principle VI).

4. See Albinder v. Chrysler Corp., 79 A.D.2d 594, 433 N.Y.S.2d 511 (1980). Cf. Gass v. Carducci, 37 Ill.App.2d 181, 185 N.E.2d 285 (1962) (lawyer may not impeach insured for insurer's benefit).

5. See Hartford Fire Insurance Co. v. Masternak, 55 A.D.2d 472, 390 N.Y.S.2d 949 (1977).

Compare Lima v. Chambers, 657 P.2d 279 (Utah 1982) (if, after intervening in opposition to insured's action against uninsured motorist, insurer has duty to defend insured, e.g., against uninsured motorist's counterclaim, insured may choose independent counsel who insurer must compensate).

limit demand,"[6] it has been held that the lawyer's duty is to proceed "as if the insurance policy has no limits."[7]

In the California case of Lysick v. Walcom,[8] plaintiffs sued insured for $450,000. Lawyer, appointed by insurer to defend under the $10,000 liability policy, followed insurer's instruction to offer $9500, but did not so notify insured. When plaintiffs offered to settle for $12,500 and insured offered to pay the $2500 difference over the policy limits, lawyer did not advise insurer to pay $10,000. The matter went to trial, producing a $225,000 judgment. With an assignment of insured's rights, plaintiffs sued insurer and lawyer. Insurer settled for $89,000, and lawyer prevailed at trial.

The appellate court reversed lawyer's judgment, holding lawyer's conduct to be malpractice as a matter of law. Only the question of the damages' causation was remanded for retrial. If causation was found, the lawyer would have to pay $225,000 less $12,500 and $89,000. The court stated:

> "[Lawyer] acted solely upon practical considerations in the interests of [insurer] and considered his duties to the insurance company paramount to his duties to [insured]. By continuing to act as counsel for [insured] while entertaining the belief that his primary obligation in the matter of settlement was to the insurer, defendant violated the legal and ethical concepts which delineated his duties to [insured]."

(4) *Settling over objection—malpractice liability for premium hike.* In Lieberman v. Employers Insurance of Wausau,[9] the New Jersey Supreme Court held that an insured whose medical malpractice insurance premiums increased drastically because of a claim settlement could recover from the insurer-provided lawyer for settling the claim over insured's objection. Insured had signed an authorization for the claim to be settled within policy limits, but upon hearing that plaintiff (who claimed $3,000,000 for loss of use of his hands) had been using his hands normally, insured wrote insurer that no settlement was to be made without insured's consent. Insurer concluded that proving plaintiff's fraud or malingering would depend upon plaintiff's credibility and therefore be almost impossible, and so wrote back that unfortunately insured's request could not be honored. Knowing all of this, lawyer settled with plaintiff for $50,000. Upholding insured's right to recover from lawyer for malpractice, the court said:

> "We conclude * * * that [lawyer] breached a duty owed to [insured] inherent in their attorney-client relationship. The attorney's professional dereliction here was two-fold. It first consisted of his failure to inform [insured] of the clear conflict of interests and his subsequent failure either to withdraw from the case

6. Morris, supra note 1, at 467.

7. Hamilton v. State Farm Insurance Co., 83 Wn.2d 787, 523 P.2d 193 (1974).

8. 258 Cal.App.2d 136, 65 Cal.Rptr. 406, 28 A.L.R.3d 368 (1968).

9. 84 N.J. 325, 419 A.2d 417 (1980).

completely or to terminate his representation of either the insured or the insurer. It also consisted of [lawyer's] active participation thereafter in the actual settlement of the claim against the wishes of his client, the insured. This serious breach of duty constitutes actionable professional negligence or malpractice by the attorney."

The court remanded the case for trial on whether absent the settlement the medical malpractice claim would have been defeated at trial or settled for not more than $3500 (so it would not have caused the insurance premium increase).[10]

(5) *Group legal services lawyer opposing group members*. In Board of Education v. Nyquist[11], the Second Circuit held that a lawyer employed by a teacher's union's legal service program should not have been disqualified from representing certain male teachers on a seniority claim opposed by certain female teachers. Under the legal service program, union members could apply for free representation for matters the union's general counsel deemed both job related and meritorious. Reversing the disqualification, the court said:

> "The district court disqualified [lawyer] because a 'layman's faith would be severely troubled' by the fact that 'the female teachers are paying, in part, for their opponents' legal expenses.' There is no claim, however, that [lawyer] feels any sense of loyalty to the women that would undermine his representation of the men. Nor is there evidence that his representation of the men is anything less than vigorous. There is also no claim that the men have gained an unfair advantage through any access to privileged information about the women. Were there any such problem, the women would not be asking, and the district judge would not have ordered, as an alternative to disqualification of [lawyer], that [union] pay their attorney's fees. Thus, in no real sense can [lawyer's] representation of the men be said to taint the trial.
>
> "We agree that there is at least some possibility that [lawyer's] representation of the men has the appearance of impropriety, because of the large number of union members involved and the public importance of the civil rights issue at the heart of the dispute. But in any event, we think that disqualification was inappropriate. We believe that when there is no claim that the trial will be tainted, appearance of impropriety is simply too slender a reed on which to rest a disqualification order except in the rarest cases. This is particularly true where, as in this case, the appearance of impropriety is not very clear."[12]

10. See Rogers v. Robson, Masters, Ryan, Brumund & Belom, 81 Ill.2d 201, 40 Ill.Dec. 816, 407 N.E.2d 47 (1980), affirming 74 Ill.App.3d 467, 30 Ill.Dec. 320, 392 N.E.2d 1365 (1979).

11. 590 F.2d 1241 (2d Cir. 1979).

12. A concurring judge pointed out that generally "an organization financed with dues received from all members may properly take a position that benefits some members at the expense of others, provided it acts reasonably, in good faith and without hostility or arbitrary discrimination."

[Eds.: Teachers were not compelled to provide financial support for the union as in the *Abood* case discussed supra p. 31.]

(6) *Defendants' employer paying for attorney.* In the U.S. Supreme Court case of Wood v. Georgia,[13] theater employees facing obscenity charges were represented by a lawyer paid by the theater owner. They were convicted and given probation on condition that they pay monthly installments on their fines. When they failed to do so, their probation was revoked notwithstanding their showing that they were unable to make the payments and that they had expected the theater owner to pay their fines. Their lawyer sought Supreme Court review on the issue of whether it violates equal protection to imprison probationers solely because of their inability to make installment payments on fines. Instead of reaching that issue, the Court vacated and remanded for determination of whether the employees' lawyer had a conflict of interest which violated their due process rights. The Court said:

> "The fact that the employer chose to refuse payment of these fines * * * suggests the possibility that it was seeking—in its own interest—a resolution of the equal protection claim raised here. If offenders cannot be jailed for failure to pay fines that are beyond their own means, then this operator of 'adult' establishments may escape the burden of paying the fines imposed on its employees when they are arrested for conducting its business. To obtain such a ruling, however, it was necessary for petitioners to receive fines that were beyond their own means and then risk jail by failing to pay.
>
> "Although we cannot be sure that the employer and petitioners' attorney were seeking to create a test case, there is a clear possibility of conflict of interest on these facts. [I]f petitioners' counsel was serving his employer's interest in setting a precedent, this conflict in goals may well have influenced the decision of the trial court to impose such large fines, as well as the decision to revoke petitioners' probations rather than modifying the conditions.[14]
>
> "Courts and commentators have recognized the inherent dangers that arise when a criminal defendant is represented by a lawyer hired and paid by a third party, particularly when the third party is the operator of the alleged criminal enterprise. One risk is that the lawyer will prevent his client from obtaining leniency by preventing the client from offering testimony against his former employer or from taking other actions contrary to the employer's interest. Another kind of risk is present where, as here, the party

13. 450 U.S. 261, 101 S.Ct. 1097, 67 L.Ed.2d 220 (1981).

14. There is also a danger that petitioner's lawyer was influenced in his strategic decisions by other improper considerations. Rather than relying solely on the equal protection claims, he could have sought leniency at the probation hearing by arguing that the stiff sentences imposed on petitioners should be modified in light of the employer's unanticipated refusal to pay the fines. But this would have required him to dwell on the apparent bad faith of his own employer, and to emphasize the possibly improper arrangement by which he came to represent petitioners. Thus [e]ven if the employer's motives were unrelated to its interest in establishing a precedent, its refusal to pay the fines put the attorney in a position of conflicting obligations.

paying the fees may have had a long-range interest in establishing a legal precedent and could do so only if the interests of the defendants themselves were sacrificed. * * *

"Where a constitutional right to counsel exists, our Sixth Amendment cases hold that there is a correlative right to representation that is free from conflicts of interest. Here, petitioners were represented by their employer's lawyer, who may not have pursued their interests single-mindedly. It was his duty originally at sentencing and later at the revocation hearing, to seek to convince the court to be lenient. On the record before us, we cannot be sure whether counsel was influenced in his basic strategic decisions by the interests of the employer who hired him. If this was the case, the due process rights of petitioners were not respected * * *.

"[T]he record [demonstrates] that the *possibility* of a conflict of interest was sufficiently apparent at the time of the revocation hearing to impose upon the court a duty to inquire further. * * *

"[On remand, the trial] court should hold a hearing to determine whether the conflict of interest that this record strongly suggests actually existed at the time of the probation revocation or earlier. If the court finds that an actual conflict of interest existed at that time, and that there was no valid waiver of the right to independent counsel, it must hold a new revocation hearing that is untainted by a legal representative serving conflicting interests."

(7) *Grand jury witnesses represented by same attorney.* There has been increased judicial consideration of the ethical propriety of a single attorney representing several witnesses appearing before a grand jury in its investigation of a crime. The cases frequently involve so-called white collar crimes by officers and employees of corporations, associations and similar entities.

Conflicts of interest inhere in these situations depending on such factors as the degree of alleged participation of each witness, the possible advantage to one or more of them of testifying against the others, and the offer of immunity to one or more of them in exchange for such testimony.

The advantages of retaining a common attorney lie in the presentation of a common front, permitting a united and consistent defense strategy, the prosecution's inability to obtain sufficient evidence to support a criminal charge (which might not be the case if each witness had separate counsel), and the sharing of information about the prosecution's case learned as each witness appears and is questioned before the grand jury.

Several ethical issues are presented:

(a) Is the "stonewall" strategy an unethical obstruction to the grand jury's performance of its duty to investigate criminal activity?

(b) Should the witness be permitted to waive objection to any possible conflict, and should it make a difference if the witness is an employee, or otherwise under the control, of another witness represented by the common attorney?

The prevailing view is that the witness' right to choice of counsel should prevail if the choice is made after full explanation of the possible or actual conflicts and intelligent waiver of the objection.[15]

### *Question*

A asks A's lawyer to prepare a will to be executed by B leaving some or all of B's property to A. Should the lawyer accede to the request? [1]

15. The cases and the ethical issues involved are discussed in Mickenberg, Grand Jury Investigations: Multiple Representation and Conflicts of Interest in Corporate Criminality Cases, 17 Crim.L.Bull. 1 (1981); Moore, Disqualification of an Attorney Representing Multiple Witnesses before a Grand Jury: Legal Ethics and the Stonewall Defense, 27 U.C.L.A.L.Rev. 1 (1979); Tague, Representation of Targets and Witnesses During a Grand Jury Investigation, 17 Am.Crim.L.Rev. 301 (1980).

Regarding corporation lawyers, see infra pp. 260–62.

1. See In re Farrell's Estate, 219 Or. 164, 346 P.2d 634 (1959). Compare Ward v. Arnold, 52 Wn.2d 581, 328 P.2d 164 (1958). See also T. Atkinson, Handbook of the Law of Wills 261–62 (1953).

# Chapter 5

# THE ORGANIZATION LAWYER

## A. THE CORPORATE LAWYER

### MODEL RULES OF PROFESSIONAL CONDUCT

**RULE 1.13 Organization as Client**

(a) A lawyer employed or retained by an organization represents the organization acting through its duly authorized constituents.

(b) If a lawyer for an organization knows that an officer, employee or other person associated with the organization is engaged in action, intends to act or refuses to act in a matter related to the representation that is a violation of a legal obligation to the organization, or a violation of law which reasonably might be imputed to the organization, and is likely to result in substantial injury to the organization, the lawyer shall proceed as is reasonably necessary in the best interest of the organization. In determining how to proceed, the lawyer shall give due consideration to the seriousness of the violation and its consequences, the scope and nature of the lawyer's representation, the responsibility in the organization and the apparent motivation of the person involved, the policies of the organization concerning such matters and any other relevant considerations. Any measures taken shall be designed to minimize disruption of the organization and the risk of revealing information relating to the representation to persons outside the organization. Such measures may include among others:

(1) asking reconsideration of the matter;

(2) advising that a separate legal opinion on the matter be sought for presentation to appropriate authority in the organization; and

(3) referring the matter to higher authority in the organization, including, if warranted by the seriousness of the matter, referral to the highest authority that can act in behalf of the organization as determined by applicable law.

(c) If, despite the lawyer's efforts in accordance with paragraph (b), the highest authority that can act on behalf of the organization insists upon action, or a refusal to act, that is clearly a violation of law and is likely to result in substantial injury to the organization, the lawyer may resign in accordance with Rule 1.16.

(d) In dealing with an organization's directors, officers, employees, members, shareholders or other constituents, a lawyer shall explain the identity of the client when it is apparent that the organization's interests are adverse to those of the constituents with whom the lawyer is dealing.

(e) A lawyer representing an organization may also represent any of its directors, officers, employees, members, shareholders or other constituents, subject to the provisions of Rule 1.7. If the organization's consent to the dual representation is required by Rule 1.7, the consent shall be given by an appropriate official of the organization other than the individual who is to be represented, or by the shareholders.[a]

### Comment

(1) *Client identification.* A corporation's lawyer faces a number of ethical problems which a lawyer employed by an individual does not.[1] This because the corporation is treated as an entity separate and apart from its stockholders, director, officers and employees. It is the officers appointed by the directors who manage the affairs of the corporation and with whom the lawyer ordinarily deals.[2] Yet it

a. Compare the following CPR provision:

"**EC 5–18** A lawyer employed or retained by a corporation or similar entity owes his allegiance to the entity and not to a stockholder, director, officer, employee, representative, or other person connected with the entity. In advising the entity, a lawyer should keep paramount its interests and his professional judgment should not be influenced by the personal desires of any person or organization. Occasionally a lawyer for an entity is requested by a stockholder, director, officer, employee, representative, or other person connected with the entity to represent him in an individual capacity; in such case the lawyer may serve the individual only if the lawyer is convinced that differing interests are not present."

1. Some of these issues also arise with unincorporated associations. Labor unions are a prime example. See Yablonski v. United Mine Workers, 448 F.2d 1175 (D.C. Cir. 1971), cert. denied 406 U.S. 906, 92 S.Ct. 1609, 31 L.Ed.2d 816 (1972). There are differences, however. The members of a labor union do not have a property interest in the union, in the sense that stockholders own stock. The typical business corporation exists primarily to earn income to be distributed in the form of dividends to its stockholders. A labor union, on the other hand, serves primarily the welfare of its members by securing adequate wages, safe working conditions, job security, etc. See Bartosic & Minda, Union Fiduciaries, Attorneys, and Conflicts of Interest, 15 U.C.D. L.Rev. 229 (1981).

RPC 1.13's Comment states, "The duties defined in this Comment apply equally to unincorporated associations."

2. Thus RPC 1.13's Comment states:

"An organizational client is a legal entity, but it cannot act except through its officers, directors, employees, shareholders and other constituents.

"Officers, directors, employees and shareholders are the constituents of the corporate organizational client."

EC 5–18 provides:

"A lawyer employed or retained by a corporation or similar entity owes his allegiance to the entity and not to a stockholder, director, officer, employee, representative, or other person connected with the entity. In advising the entity [how does one do that?], a lawyer should keep paramount its interests and his professional judgment should not be influenced by the personal desires of any person or organization. * * *."

EC 5–24 points to some of the problems a corporate lawyer may face:

"* * * Although a lawyer may be employed by a business corporation with non-lawyers serving as directors or officers, and they necessarily have the right to make decisions of business policy, a lawyer must decline to accept direction of his professional judgment from any layman. Various types of legal aid offices are administered by boards of directors composed of

is only the corporation, the entity, which the lawyer is said to represent.[3]

In representing the corporation in dealings with third persons, no ethical issues substantially different from those in representing private individuals are involved. It is when the lawyer is brought into an internal controversy or the personal interests of the lawyer get enmeshed with those of the corporation or its representatives,[4] that problems arise.

(2) *Stock ownership*. It is not an uncommon practice for lawyers to purchase stock in corporations they represent or to receive payment of their fee in stock of the company they have incorporated. This gives the lawyer a personal interest in the success of the corporation which may affect or color the advice and assistance he or she gives the corporation. Is this good or bad?[5]

lawyers and laymen. A lawyer should not accept employment from such an organization unless the board sets only broad policies and there is no interference in the relationship of the lawyer and the individual client he serves. Where a lawyer is employed by an organization, a written agreement that defines the relationship between him and the organization and provides for his independence is desirable since it may serve to prevent misunderstanding as to their respective roles."

3. There are exceptions. When stock of a corporation is closely held, e.g., a family owned corporation, the lawyer is likely to deal directly with the stockholders dominating the affairs of the corporation, as officers or otherwise. In that situation, courts have disregarded the separate entity and held that the lawyer's duties run also to the stockholders with whom he has dealt. He may not, for example, oppose the stockholders on a matter in which he had previously dealt with the stockholders in the name of the corporation. See In re Brownstein, 288 Or. 83, 602 P.2d 655 (1979), stating:

"Where a small, closely held corporation is involved, and in the absence of a clear understanding with the corporate owners that the attorney represents solely the corporation and not their individual interests, it is improper for the attorney thereafter to represent a third party whose interests are adverse to those of the stockholders and which arise out of a transaction which the attorney handled for the corporation."

See also In re Banks, 283 Or. 459, 584 P.2d 284, 284 Or. 691, 588 P.2d 34 (1978).

4. See EC 5-3:

"The self-interest of a lawyer resulting from his ownership of property in which the client also has an interest or which may affect property of his client may interfere with the exercise of free judgment on behalf of his client. * * * After accepting employment, a lawyer should not acquire property rights that would adversely affect his professional judgment in the representation of his client. * * * "

Compare DR 5-103(A): "A lawyer shall not acquire a proprietary interest in the *cause of action or subject matter of litigation he is conducting for a client* * * *." (Emphasis added.)

The question receives even less consideration in the Model Rules. See the general conflict of interest provisions in RPC 1.7 and 1.8, discussed supra pp. 137-57.

5. See H. Drinker, Legal Ethics 101 (1953); H. Henn & J. Alexander, Laws of Corporations § 377 (3d ed. 1983); Developments in the Law—Conflicts of Interest in the Legal Profession, 94 Harv.L.Rev. 1244, 1350-52 (1981).

In Financial General Bankshares, Inc. v. Metzger, 523 F.Supp. 744, 767 (D.D.C.1981), vacated on other grounds 680 F.2d 768 (D.C. Cir. 1982), the court stated:

"Because 'what is in the best interests of the corporation' generally furthers an individual's interests as a stockholder, the lawyer-shareholder combination is not prohibited. ABA Informal Opinion 1057 (1968). But the combination is subject to the limits set forth in DR 5-101: the professional employment may not be affected by the lawyer's own personal interests. When an attorney's privileges as a shareholder collide with his obligations as a lawyer for the company in which he has invested, the lawyer's professional obligations predominate. Formal Opinion 86 (1932). At that point, the attorney should advise the corporate client to seek outside counsel. ABA Informal Opinion 1057 (1968). If that is not appropriate, the attorney should

Should it make a difference whether the amount of stock the lawyer has is large or small relative to the total outstanding or to be issued? Is this ownership consistent with the ethical principle that an attorney should not have a personal financial interest in the client's case?

If the company president tells the attorney in confidence that the company is insolvent and asks for advice, what should the attorney do? Advise the president and promptly sell the stock? Defer advice until the attorney has sold his or her stock? Tell the president to get another lawyer? [6]

(3) *Corporate directorship*. It is also a frequent practice for lawyers who represent a corporation to accept membership on the board of directors. This has been both defended and questioned. Arguments for accepting a directorship include:

(a) Sitting in with the meetings of the board will give the lawyer a better understanding of the legal issues with which he or she may have to deal.

(b) Having a responsibility as director will make the lawyer more careful and responsible in the legal services rendered.

(c) As a result of the personal contacts with members of the board, they will have greater confidence in the advice and assistance received from their attorney.

(d) The corporate management, i.e., the officers, will have more confidence in the lawyer's competence and reliability.

(e) Being on the board enables the lawyer to have greater influence in directing the activities of the corporation toward sound business, economic and social, as well as legal, policies.

(f) The fears of those opposed to corporate attorneys acting as directors have, in practice, not been realized.[7]

Arguments made against accepting a directorship include:

(a) The lawyer may not be able to exercise independent professional judgment as attorney for the corporation. Participation in, and suggestions made during, board meetings, may consciously or unconsciously, color the advice and recommendations the lawyer will make when acting as attorney for the corporation in the same matter.

(b) A retained outside attorney's judgment and vote as a member of the board may be affected, consciously or unconsciously, by the fact that the resulting action of the board will or will not result

relinquish his privileges as a shareholder, ABA Opinion 86 (1932), or resign. See DR 2–110(B)(2), 2–110(C)(2)."

6. See Walsh, The Advocate 34 (2d ed. 1926).

7. Hawes, Should Counsel to a Corporation be Barred From Serving as a Director?—A Personal View, 1 Corp.L.Rev. 14 (1978); Riger, The Lawyer-Director—"A Vexing Problem," 33 Bus.Law 2381, 2383 (1978); Thurston, Corporate Counsel on the Board of Directors: An Overview, 10 Cum.L.Rev. 791 (1980).

in legal business for the attorney or his or her firm. It may have the opposite effect on house counsel.

(c) The attorney's judgment, professional advice and action as attorney for the corporation may be colored by the duties and liabilities as director, which, with the attendent personal risks, have increased in recent years.[8]

(d) The application of the attorney-client privilege becomes confused. If facts concerning a legal controversy are discussed during a board meeting at which you are present, and you use this information later when the matter is turned over to you, have you received the information as director or as attorney? If the former, the privilege would appear not to apply.[9]

In terms of the public interest, or of the corporation, which position do you think has the more persuasive arguments?

(4) *Confidential communications*. It is generally accepted that a corporation falls within those entitled to assert the attorney-client privilege of confidentiality. The question is, to whom of those that make up the corporation does the privilege extend? The attorney may discuss a legal matter with any number of persons in varying degrees of authority within the corporation.

On the federal level this was resolved in Upjohn Co. v. United States.[10] The lower court had held that only those communications between the attorney and members of the "control group" of the corporation, who play a substantial part in deciding and directing the corporation's response to the legal advice sought, fell within the privilege. The chief officer of Upjohn had directed the lower echelon of the company to give to the corporate counsel any information they might have about payments to foreign government agents and to keep the information in strictest confidence. The lower court held that the information so obtained was not from the "control group" and hence not within the privilege and hence discoverable by the IRS.

The Supreme Court reversed because the purpose of the corporation's privilege could only be realized if it applied not only to the "con-

8. See the particularly helpful discussion in Knepper, Liability of Lawyers-Directors, 49 Ohio St.L.J. 341 (1979). See also W. Knepper & D. Bailey, Liability of Corporate Officers and Directors § 14.06 (3d ed.Supp.1982).

Compare American Law Institute, Principles of Corporate Governance and Structure: Restatement and Recommendations (Tent. Draft No. 1 1982), criticized in Scott, Corporate Governance, 35 Stan.L.Rev. 927 (1983), as, among other objections, imposing an unwarranted degree of responsibility and liability on corporate directors.

9. See Ruder, The Case Against the Lawyer-Director, 30 Bus. Law. 51 (1975); Thurston, Corporate Counsel on the Board of Directors? An Overview, 10 Cum.L.Rev. 791, 175 (1980); Note, Should Lawyers Serve as Directors of Corporations of Which They Act as Counsel? 1978 Utah L.Rev. 711, 712.

The Model Rules are ambivalent on the point. RPC 1.7's Comment states the lawyer "should determine whether the responsibilities of the two roles may conflict" and should not serve if "there is material risk that the dual role will compromise the lawyer's independence of professional judgment."

10. 449 U.S. 383, 101 S.Ct. 677, 66 L.Ed.2d 584 (1981). On confidentiality generally, see supra Chapter 3.

trol group" but to others of the corporation who had the information needed by the attorney.

The case has been the subject of wide comment [11] which has focused primarily on the effect of the decision on the right of corporations to the attorney-client privilege and, if the right exists, the scope and effect of that privilege.[12]

We are concerned here more with the significance of the decision in affecting the ethical duties of attorneys.

(a) The Court states that its decision does not prevent the government from still getting the desired information by questioning the members of the corporation directly. How far up the scale of corporate personnel may this go without violating the ethical rule against communicating with the adverse party represented by counsel without the counsel's consent? [13]

(b) If the corporation waives its privilege, the employee who gave the information to the attorney may not be protected against the use of the information in proceedings against him or her. Is the attorney under a duty to so inform the employee before questioning him or her? Is the attorney in a position to advise the employee on what the employee's best interests require? [14]

**11.** See, e.g., Gergacz, Attorney-Corporate Client Privilege: Cases Applying *Upjohn*, Waiver, Crime-Fraud Exceptions, and Related Issues, 38 Bus.Law. 1653 (1983); Sexton, A Post-*Upjohn* Consideration of the Corporate Attorney-Client Privilege, 57 N.Y.U.L.Rev. 443 (1982); Note, The Attorney-Client Privilege and the Corporate Client: Where Do We Go After *Upjohn*? 81 Mich.L.Rev. 665 (1983); 95 Harv.L.Rev. 270 (1981).

**12.** The difficulties encountered in interpreting the case are illustrated by Leer v. Chicago, Milwaukee, St. Paul & Pacific Railway, 308 N.W.2d 305 (Minn.1981), cert. denied 455 U.S. 939, 102 S.Ct. 1430, 71 L.Ed.2d 650 (1982). An employee of the defendant had witnessed an accident occurring on the defendant's right of the way. The plaintiff was held entitled to discovery of the product of an interview of the employee by defendant's investigator. The court said:

> "*Upjohn* is critically different from the instant case in that the communications in *Upjohn* regarded a matter within the scope of the employee's duties. In the instant case the witnessing of an accident was not within the scope of the employee's duties."

But note the dissent.

In Consolidated Coal Co. v. Bucyrus-Erie Co., 89 Ill.App.2d 103, 59 Ill.Dec. 666, 432 N.E.2d 250 (1982), the court declined to follow *Upjohn* since it did not "articulate an alternative standard to guide future cases in the Federal courts." Adopted, instead, after full review of authorities and competing considerations, was the "control group" test, but with the group extending beyond top management:

> "We believe that an employee whose advisory role to top management in a particular area is such that a decision would not normally be made without his advice or opinion, and whose opinion in fact forms the basis of any final decision by those with actual authority, is properly within the control group."

**13.** RPC 4.2 states: "In representing a client, a lawyer shall not communicate about the subject of the representation with a party the lawyer knows to be represented by another lawyer in the matter, unless the lawyer has the consent of the other lawyer or is authorized by law to do so."

Accord, DR 7-104(A)(1). See infra pp. 353–54.

**14.** See Gallagher, Legal and Professional Responsibility of Corporate Counsel to Employees During an Internal Investigation for Corporate Misconduct, 6 Corp. Law. 3 (1983). See also infra pp. 354–57.

Compare RPC 1.13's Comment, which states that when the corporation asks the lawyer to investigate and in the course of doing so, the lawyer interviews the employees of the corporation, the interviews are covered by RPC

(c) If the claim or charge is against both the corporation and the employee, based on conduct of the employee, and the employee asks the corporation attorney to represent him or her also, may the attorney accept? May the attorney ask the employee to become the attorney's client in the case? [15]

Absent a conflict of interests, an attorney may represent each of joint parties in both criminal and civil cases.[16] But a conflict of interest may inhere if an attorney represents both the corporation and its employee and the claim or charge is based on the conduct of the employee. The employee may feel compelled to defer to the wishes of the employer in order to retain his or her employment and the attorney may be inclined to look to the corporation as the principal client.[17]

Assume in a criminal prosecution against both the corporation and the employee, the employee asks the corporation attorney who represents also the employee whether to accept a generous recommendation made to the employee by the prosecution. What should the attorney do? [18]

(5) *Derivative suits against officers and directors*. Derivative suits place the corporate attorney in a quandary. Who is the lawyer to represent, the corporation, the officers and directors, all of them, or none of them? RPC 1.13(e) provides:

> "A lawyer representing an organization may also represent any of its directors, officers, employees, members, shareholders or other constituents, subject to the provisions of Rule 1.7.[a] If the organization's consent to the dual representation is required by Rule 1.7, the consent shall be given by an appropriate official of the organization other than the individual who is to be represented, or by the shareholders."

Does RPC 1.13(e) meet the problems involved in the following case?

## MESSING v. FDI, INC.

439 F.Supp. 776 (D.N.J.1977).

STERN, District Judge.

In this derivative action, shareholders of FDI, Inc., charge violations of the Securities Act of 1934, 15 U.S.C. §§ 78a et seq. * * *

1.6. The Comment continues, "This does not mean, however, that constituents [i.e., employees] of the organizational client are the clients of the lawyer."

15. See infra pp. 566–91 (solicitation).

16. See supra pp. 170–81 (criminal cases), 181–90 (civil cases).

17. See supra pp. 253–55.

This appears not to have influenced the court in In re Coordinated Pretrial Proceedings, 658 F.2d 1355 (9th Cir. 1981), cert. denied 455 U.S. 990, 102 S.Ct. 1615, 71 L.Ed.2d 850 (1982), when it held that, in an antitrust suit against the corporation, the corporation attorney was not disqualified from appearing for an employee whose discovery deposition was being taken. The decision of the trial court to the contrary was reversed.

18. See Miller, The Problems of Multiple Representation in the Investigation and Prosecution of Corporate Crime, 29 Fed.B. News & J. 217 (1982).

a. RPC 1.7 deals with conflict of interests. See supra Chapter 4.

At issue now is the question whether the defendant directors may share counsel with the corporation, which appears as a nominal defendant. * * *

The relevant allegations of the amended complaint are as follows. FDI, Inc. ("FDI") was formed in October, 1974 as a result of the merger of Rayco International, Inc. ("Rayco") and Filter Dynamics International, Inc. ("Filter"). One of the primary purposes of the merger—according to the joint proxy statement distributed to shareholders of Filter and Rayco—was to confer a tax benefit on the successor corporation by enabling it to offset Rayco's huge losses against Filter's projected high earnings. This purported tax benefit was treated as an actual asset of Rayco for purposes of determining the exchange ratio at which FDI shares would issue to the shareholders of Filter and Rayco. However, as a result of a change in Filter's inventory valuation, along with rising costs of raw materials and uncertainties in the tax laws—none of which were disclosed in the proxy statement—this tax benefit was not and could not be realized. Hence, or so plaintiffs allege, the joint proxy statement was false and misleading, FDI shares were issued at an excessively low price, and Rayco shares were purchased by FDI at an excessively high price.

Some of the numerous defendants in this action are charged with negligence in connection with this merger; others with outright fraud. The allegations of fraud are leveled against defendants Braun, Gregg, Peltz and Pearl. Prior to the merger, defendants Braun, Gregg, Peltz (the "insiders") served as directors of Filter; defendant Pearl was a member of the defendant law firm Katten, Muchin, Gittles, Zavis & Galler (the "Katten firm"), general counsel to both Filter and Rayco. It is alleged that defendant Pearl and the insiders controlled 42% of the stock of Rayco and that, as a result of various transactions not relevant here, they had personally assumed in excess of two million dollars of Rayco's liabilities. Thus, it is alleged, these defendants helped bring about the merger for the purpose of simultaneously ridding themselves of their control of Rayco and their consequent personal indebtedness.

The other defendants are charged with negligence in failing to detect that fraud. Specifically, it is alleged that the remaining directors of Filter, defendants Carr, Palmer, Cole and Stillman (the "outsiders") failed to act with due diligence when they approved the merger of Filter and Rayco. Also charged with negligence for their participation in the merger is the Katten firm, and defendants Prescott, Ball & Turben ("PBT"), and Joseph Miller and Russell, two investment firms engaged by Filter and Rayco, respectively, to opine on the fairness of the proposed exchange ratio. * * *

### PBT's Motion for Disqualification

PBT has brought to this Court's attention the fact that the same counsel represents FDI, two of the outsiders (defendants Carr and

Stillman) and all of the insiders (defendants Braun, Gregg and Peltz).[4]
* * *

PBT points out two possible conflicts inherent in the joint representation of these defendants: (1) the conflicting interests of the corporation and all of the directors; and (2) the conflicting interests of the insiders, who have been accused of fraud, and the outsiders, who have been charged with negligence in failing to detect that fraud. Accordingly, PBT moves this Court to disqualify the Weston-Sills firms from any further participation in this litigation and to appoint new counsel for FDI.

* * * DR 5–105 * * * provides that a lawyer may not represent multiple clients with adverse interests unless each client consents after full disclosure of the conflicts which might arise in their joint representation. Because a corporation acts only through its board of directors, and, here, all but two of FDI's directors are parties to this litigation, very different issues are presented with respect to each of the two conflicts asserted by PBT.

JOINT REPRESENTATION OF THE CORPORATION AND THE DIRECTORS

The propriety of the joint representation of a corporation and the directors in a derivative action is a question on which there in some division of authority. * * *

More recent decisions appear to have adopted the position that directors accused of *fraud* may not share counsel with the corporation in a derivative shareholder's action. Thus, in Lewis v. Shaffer Stores Co., 218 F.Supp. 238 (S.D.N.Y.1963), the court held that the corporation could not share counsel with individual directors accused of defrauding the corporation. The court noted that "[u]nder all the circumstances, including the nature of the charges * * * it would be wise for the corporation to retain independent counsel, who have had no previous connection with the corporation, to advise it as to the position it should take in this controversy." In Cannon v. U. S. Acoustics Co., 398 F.Supp. 209 (D.Ill.1975), aff'd in relevant part, 532 F.2d 1118, 1119 (7th Cir. 1976) (per curiam) the district court disqualified counsel from simultaneously representing the corporation and the individual directors accused of fraud, noting not only the conflicting interests of these defendants, but also the possibility that confidences obtained from one client might be used to the detriment of the other.[6]

The nature of the allegations against the directors is but one factor that has been considered in determining the propriety of the joint rep-

4. These defendants are represented by Weston, Hurd, Fallon, Paisley & Howley and locally through Sills, Beck, Cummis, Radin & Tischman. These firms will hereinafter be jointly referred to as the "Weston-Sills firms".

6. Other courts have likewise focused upon the diverse interests of the corporation and directors accused of fraud and prohibited their joint representation. See, e.g., Niedermeyer v. Niedermeyer, CCH Fed.Sec.L.Rep. [1973 Transfer Binder] ¶ 94.123 (D.Or.1973); Rowen v. LeMars Mutual Insurance Co. of Iowa, 230 N.W.2d 905 (Iowa 1975).

[Eds: See also In re Kinsey, 294 Or. 544, 660 P.2d 660 (1983).]

resentation of the corporation and the directors in a derivative action. The Association of the Bar of New York Committee on Ethics, while recognizing that a conflict of interests is always inherent in such arrangements, has indicated that the corporation should obtain independent counsel whenever the corporation elects to take an *active role* in the litigation. *Op.* 842, 15 Record N.Y.C.B.A. (1960). By contrast, commentators appear to have taken the broader view that the corporation should *always* be separately represented in a derivative action. See, e.g., Henn, Corporations § 370 (2d Ed. 1970); 13 Fletcher Corporations § 6025 (rev. ed. 1970). Note, Independent Representation for Corporate Defendants in Derivative Suits, 74 Yale L.J. 524 (1965).[7]

This Court perceives no basis for relying upon the nature of the charges against the directors for purposes of determining whether they may share counsel with the corporation. Irrespective of the nature of the charges against the directors—whether it be fraud or negligence—the interests of the two groups will almost always be diverse. Nor can we readily perceive the need for independent counsel turning upon the question whether the corporation has already elected to pursue an active or passive stance in the litigation, for that very election may have already been tainted by conflict. Moreover, just as it should be recognized that the corporate entity has a legitimate interest in recovering the fruits of past mismanagement or fraud on the part of its own directors, so too, it has a legitimate interest, and perhaps a role to play, in the defense of actions which have been frivolously or even wrongfully brought against its directors. The initial decision then as to what role if any the corporation should take must in the first instance be made completely free from any actual or apparent conflict.

However, because in the instant case the directors have been accused of fraud and the corporation has elected to take an active stance in the litigation, it is enough for now to decide that, under these combined circumstances, the corporation must retain independent counsel.[8]

Independent counsel for the corporation, unshackled by any ties to the directors, would be in the unique position of having only the

7. Similarly, the Court of Appeals for the District of Columbia Circuit, addressing the analogous problem of dual representation of the union and union officials in actions brought on behalf of the union, apparently has indicated that it would always require separate counsel for a corporation in a shareholder's derivative action. See Yablonski v. United Mine Workers of America, 145 U.S.App.D.C. 252, 258, 448 F.2d 1175, 1181 (1971), cert. denied 406 U.S. 906, 92 S.Ct. 1609, 31 L.Ed.2d 816 (1972).

8. The need for independent counsel is underscored by the duty of counsel for the corporation in a derivative action to safeguard the corporation's interest. While, historically, it has been the role of the plaintiff-shareholders to represent the corporation's interests, as a practical matter, the adequacy of such representation—particularly when the litigation reaches settlement stages—is open to serious doubt. See, Note, Independent Representation for Corporate Defendants in Derivative Suits, 74 Yale L.J. 524, 532 (1965). Thus, independent counsel for the corporation would be particularly useful in assisting the Court to approve any settlements reached between the plaintiffs and defendants.

corporation's interest at stake. For example, in this case, serious questions have been raised as to whether the corporation has expended funds on behalf of the directors in violation of law. Under Delaware law, a corporation may advance monies to the directors for their litigation expenses upon a resolution of the Board of Directors and receipt of an undertaking. § 145(e) Del.Corp.Law. A director is required to repay such expenses in the event that he is ultimately "adjudged to have been liable for negligence or misconduct in the performance of his duty to the corporation." Id., at § 145(b). On oral argument of this motion, Mr. Blackford, present counsel for FDI, conceded that the directors had not posted the undertaking required by Delaware law to ensure repayment of their litigation expenses in the event that it is later determined that they were guilty of misconduct in office. Counsel was also unclear whether FDI had passed the required resolution permitting the corporation to advance the directors' litigation expenses. He did indicate that he believed there had been no impropriety, although it was unclear whether he had made that judgment on behalf of his director clients, for whom the funds had been paid to him, or his corporate client, who had paid those fees.

PBT further contends that present counsel for FDI disregarded the corporation's interest by bringing frivolous cross-claims against PBT on FDI's behalf.[11] However, resolution of this issue, along with the issue of the directors' litigation expenses, will have to await the appointment of new counsel for FDI.

Accordingly, this Court will require FDI to retain independent counsel. This Court is next faced with the question of the manner in which such counsel is to be selected.

PBT urges that this Court itself appoint new counsel for FDI, a procedure with some, but scant, support in the case law.[12] Present counsel for FDI has indicated to the Court that the corporation has in the interim appointed an ad hoc committee consisting of the two di-

11. PBT alleges that, under the terms of its agreement with FDI, the corporation is required to reimburse it for litigation expenses incurred in connection with the merger in the event that PBT is found not to have been negligent. Accordingly, PBT questions on whose behalf—the directors' or the corporation's—the cross-claims were asserted, arguing that truly independent counsel for FDI will not be tempted to jeopardize corporate funds by bringing frivolous cross-claims against a party whom it may be required to reimburse. In any event, this Court agrees that the views of independent counsel for FDI would be beneficial.

12. See Rowen v. LeMars Mutual Insurance Co., 230 N.W.2d 905 (Iowa 1975); Niedermeyer v. Niedermeyer, CCH Fed.Sec.L.Rep. [1973 Transfer Binder] ¶ 94.123 (D.Ore.1973).

Most courts faced with this problem have refused to appoint counsel. See, e.g., Yablonski v. United Mine Workers of America, 145 U.S.App.D.C. 252, 448 F.2d 1175 (1971), cert. denied, 406 U.S. 906, 92 S.Ct. 1609, 31 L.Ed.2d 816 (1972); Cannon v. U. S. Acoustics Corp., 398 F.Supp. 209 (D.Ill.1975), aff'd, 532 F.2d 1118 (7th Cir. 1976) (per curiam); Lewis v. Shaffer Stores Co., 218 F.Supp. 238 (S.D.N.Y.1963).

The *Yablonski* court noted the anomaly of permitting union officials to choose new counsel for the union, but nevertheless declined court intervention:

> "We are cognizant that any counsel to represent U.M.W.A. selected by President Boyle will to some degree be under his control. But such counsel will still have only one client—the U.M.W.A.—to represent in matters growing out of the union's affairs."

rectors who are not parties to this litigation. If so ordered by the Court, he reports, this committee will retain new counsel for the corporation and supervise the corporation's role in the litigation.[13]

This Court, while not necessarily approving the procedure suggested by present counsel for FDI, will at this time direct only that the corporation resolve this problem as it would any other issue as to which the existence of interested directors renders the usual corporate decision-making process unavailable. Of course, the directors may request this or any other court with jurisdiction over the matter to relieve them of this duty. It may well be that there are other ways to fashion a solution to this problem. However, at this time, this Court declines to itself appoint counsel or to prospectively pass on the method proposed by present counsel for FDI. It is the duty of the directors, in this as in other matters, to act in the corporation's best interest. If they are disqualified from acting on this or on any other matter, then it is for them, in the first instance, to devise a method to accommodate the need to continue the corporate enterprise while refraining from participating in any corporate decision in which they might have a personal interest. They act, or fail to act, at their peril.
* * *

### *Comment*

(1) *Counsel involvement.* Note that Pearl was "general counsel to both Filter and Rayco"; that he and others "controlled 42% of the stock of Rayco and that * * * they had personally assumed in excess of two million dollars of Rayco's liabilities." What ethical questions does this raise, aside from the questions discussed in *Messing*?

(2) *"Blowing the whistle."* Under what obligation is a corporation's lawyer who knows, believes, or suspects that officers of the corporation are engaged in activities that are dishonest or unethical and, in the lawyer's opinion, are or may be harmful to the corporation or the public? The information the lawyer has received may have come from discussions with the officers in his or her capacity as attorney for the corporation. What action may or must the lawyer undertake to protect the corporate client or the public? Consider the following hypothetical situation:

> "You represent a corporate client—an electric utility—in connection with all its environmental affairs. The company has recently converted one of its generating units to coal pursuant to a DCO [Delayed Compliance Order] that you helped to secure. The Vice President Operations calls and advises you as follows: the conversion has been completed; the unit is not now operating, but based on tests at less than full capacity he knows that the old elec-

13. Present counsel for FDI apparently seeks Court approval of the arrangements it has made for choosing new counsel. PBT opposes this arrangement, arguing that the two "disinterested" directors may still have emotional or pecuniary ties to the defendant-directors. As indicated below, this Court declines at this time to pass on the parties' contentions with respect to the manner in which counsel for FDI is to be chosen.

trostatic precipitator on the unit is not working as well as expected; the unit cannot satisfy the interim particulate emission limitations prescribed in the DCO while operating at full capacity; a heat wave is in progress and expected to continue; and the client desperately needs to use the unit at full capacity. He asks you whether it is a violation of law to violate the order. You tell him it is.

"* * * Suppose the Vice President begins to ask you about EPA inspection practices; how many inspectors are assigned to the region; what is the likelihood that an inspection will occur in the near future; how should the EPA Staff be expected to react if the Company's continuous opacity monitors malfunction; how long would it take the Staff to consider the malfunctioning monitors and require the Company to correct them; how would EPA react if the Company was late filing the required reports; can EPA verify that the company's filed reports are correct?

"The case raises the question, to be sure, about your duty to your client and to the public * * *. But what duty, if any, do you have to the Vice President? His questions seem calculated, not to determine what the law requires, but to assess the risk of getting caught. He may be on the verge of causing your client to commit a crime and, to the same extent, about to commit one himself. The longer he talks the more evidence he is producing that if he violates the DCO, he will do so 'knowingly.'

"What he tells you may be subject to the attorney-client privilege that involves you and your corporate client. But you are not his lawyer. Presumably, whatever he tells you would not be protected in a proceeding against him if the corporation were to waive the privilege. Is he entitled to a warning from you?"[1]

The underlying issues presented by this hypothetical case are not new. In 1934, Justice William O. Douglas, then a professor at the Yale Law School, noted the failure of corporate directors to meet their responsibilities and the remedies that had been proposed, and observed:

"All of these measures, of course, merely check or control rather than cure a fundamental condition which underlies the whole problem. That condition has been reflected by the amazing absence of social consciousness on the part of directors and business executives and by their lack of any awareness of the implications and results of many practices which flourished in recent years. It has not been so much a matter of depravity and of evil intent as the consequence of cutting as close to the mythical legal line as possible. This lack of social mindedness has not been wholly or largely that of business.

1. Maupin, Environmental Law, The Corporate Lawyer and the Model Rules of Professional Conduct, 36 Bus.Law. 431, 434–35 (1981).

It has been equally shared by lawyers.[65] It has been evidenced by the almost perverted singleness of purpose with which they have championed the cause of their clients, whether it be in the drafting of a deposit agreement, the handling of a merger, the conduct of a reorganization, or the marketing of securities. It resulted in getting accomplished what clients wanted but without regard for the long-term consequences of those accomplishments. The singleness of purpose has been wholly incompatible with the use of these aggregations of capital for either the welfare of the investors or the good of the public." [2]

More recently, the issue has focused on the activities of the Securities and Exchange Commission in insisting that attorneys participating in such matters as the issuance of corporate securities, mergers, liquidations, and take-overs, assume substantial responsibility for preventing dishonesty or other violations of relevant laws and regulations.

In SEC v. National Student Marketing Corp.,[3] the SEC sought an injunction against attorneys for failing to disclose information having a substantial bearing on the merger of two companies which they were effecting. The SEC charged that the attorneys had received, at the point of closing, reliable information that the income of one of the companies was not as had been previously reported.[4]

The SEC position was widely criticized.[5] It was said that it would likely require disclosure of confidential information received from corporate clients and, if clients knew this, they would withhold the information and make the efforts of the attorney to prevent the misconduct less possible. Also, the attorney would be placed in the

65. A columnist has stated it more popularly as follows:

"But just as a fine, natural football player needs coaching in the fundamentals and schooling in the wiles of the sport, so, too, it takes a corporation lawyer with a heart for the game to organize a great stock swindle or income tax dodge and drill the financiers in all the precise details of their play.

"Otherwise in their natural enthusiasm to rush in and grab everything that happens not to be nailed down and guarded with shotguns, they would soon be caught offside and penalized, and some of the noted financiers who are now immortalized as all-time all-American larcenists never would have risen beyond the level of the petty thief or short-change man."

Westbrook Pegler, N.Y. World Telegram, Jan. 24, 1923, at 19.

2. Douglas, Directors Who Do Not Direct, 47 Harv.L.Rev. 1305, 1328–29 (1934). See also Stone, The Public Influence of the Bar, 48 Harv.L.Rev. 1 (1934).

3. 360 F.Supp. 284 (D.D.C.1973).

4. The injunction was denied because it was not shown that the misconduct was likely to continue.

5. See Bialkin, The Securities Laws and the Code of Professional Responsibility, 30 Bus.Law. 21 (Sp. Issue Mar. 1975); Burke, Duty of Confidentiality and Disclosing Corporate Misconduct, 36 Bus.Law. 240 (1981); Cheek, Professional Responsibility and Self-Regulation of the Securities Lawyer, 32 Wash. & Lee L.Rev. 597 (1975); Mathews, Litigation and Settlement of SEC Administrative Enforcement Proceedings, 29 Cath.U.L.Rev. 215 (1980); Panel Discussion, Lawyers Responsibilities and Liabilities Under the Securities Laws, 11 Colum.J.L. & Soc.Prob. 99 (1974).

precarious position of having to pass judgment on whether the client was in fact engaged in the prohibited conduct and suffer the consequences if he or she erred.[6]

In In re Carter,[7] the SEC brought disciplinary proceedings against two attorneys pursuant to Rule 2(e) of its Rules of Practice. The charge was that the attorneys, while advising their client to make certain required disclosures, failed to take any measures to cause the client to do so when they learned that their client was not following their advice.

While not taking any action against the attorneys before it, the SEC did state its views for prospective application:

> "When a lawyer with significant responsibilities in the effectuation of a company's compliance with the disclosure requirements of the federal securities laws becomes aware that his client is engaged in substantial and continuing failure to satisfy those disclosure requirements, his continuing participation violates professional standards unless he takes prompt steps to end the client's noncompliance."

The SEC observed that the attorney is not expected to correct every violation which he may think exists, but "he is not privileged to unthinkingly permit himself to be co-opted into an ongoing fraud and cast as a dupe or shield for a wrongdoing client."[8]

It was against this background that the ABA prepared and adopted RPC 1.13(b) which specifies:

> "If a lawyer for an organization knows that an officer, employee or other person associated with the organization is engaged in ac-

6. For the reaction of the American Bar Association, see Formal Opinion 341 and a statement of policy adopted by the House of Delegates, reproduced in 61 A.B.A. J. 1085, (1975). DR 7–102(B)(1), requiring disclosure of client fraud under certain conditions, was amended in 1974 by adding, "except when the information is protected as a privileged communication."

See Meyerhofer v. Empire Fire & Marine Insurance Co., 497 F.2d 1190 (2d Cir.), cert. denied 419 U.S. 998, 95 S.Ct. 314, 42 L.Ed.2d 272 (1974), where a young attorney resigned from his law firm because the firm declined to disclose in a registration of securities statement the substantial fee the firm was getting and reported the failure to the SEC. When he was included as a defendant in a law suit against the firm based on the nondisclosure, the young attorney informed the plaintiff of what he had done and was dismissed from the suit. The trial court upheld the propriety of his behavior. A commentator has observed the attorney "was only obeying the recent demands made by the SEC." Comment, The Duties and Obligations of the Securities Lawyer: The Beginning of a New Standard for the Legal Profession, 1975 Duke L.J. 121.

See also SEC v. Gulf & Western Industries, Inc., 518 F.Supp. 675 (D.D.C.1981), in which the defendant charged that the SEC had intentionally obtained confidential information from the defendant's former outside counsel which it was using against the defendant. Breach of the privilege was held not to have been established. See Comment, The Need for Attorney-Client Confidentiality in Securities Regulation: S. E. C. v. Gulf & Western Industries, Inc., 46 Alb.L.Rev. 1354 (1982).

7. [1981 Transfer Binder] Fed.Sec.L.Rep. (CCH) ¶ 82,847 (Sec Feb. 28, 1981).

8. For a helpful discussion of the Carter case and its implications, see Barber, Lawyer's Duties in Securities Transactions Under Rule 2(e): The Carter Opinions, 1982 B.Y.U.L.Rev. 513. See also Note, Attorney Discipline by the SEC: 2(e) or not 2(e)? 17 New Eng.L.Rev. 1267 (1982).

tion, intends to act or refuses to act in a manner related to the representation that is a violation of a legal obligation to the organization, or a violation of law which reasonably might be imputed to the organization, and is likely to result in substantial injury to the organization, the lawyer shall proceed as is reasonably necessary in the best interest of the organization. In determining how to proceed, the lawyer shall give due consideration to the seriousness of the violation and its consequences, the scope and nature of the lawyer's representation, the responsibility in the organization and the apparent motivation of the person involved, the policies of the organization concerning such matters and any other relevent considerations. Any measures taken shall be designed to minimize disruption of the organization and the risk of revealing information relating to the representation to persons outside the organization. * * * "

RPC 1.13(b) goes on to provide that the measures taken may include (1) asking reconsideration, (2) suggesting a separate legal opinion, and (3) referring the matter to a higher authority in the organization. If these fail and the organization's highest authority insists upon a clear violation of law likely to substantially injure the organization, the lawyer may resign.[9]

Note RPC 1.13(b)'s words "knows," "likely to result in substantial injury to the organization," "shall give due consideration," "minimize disruption of the organization," "risk of revealing information relating to the representation." How much information must the attorney have before he or she "knows" that a corporate officer "intends" to violate a law? Compare the hypothetical at the beginning of this Comment regarding the electric utility vice president.

Do RPC 1.13(b)'s provisions meet the criticism by Justice Douglas?

Are they consistent with the standards of conduct insisted upon by the SEC as outlined above? Both Justice Douglas and the SEC were concerned with protecting the public interest. Do you find sufficient recognition of this interest in RPC 1.13(b)?[10]

Is observation of RPC 1.13(b) likely to turn on whether the attorney is a house counsel, an outside counsel dependent heavily on the corporate client, or a general practitioner whose representation of the corporation is only sporadic?[11]

9. RPC 1.13(b) was much discussed and criticized during the drafting stage and revised considerably before adoption in its final form. See, e.g., Slovak, The Ethics of Corporate Lawyers: A Sociological Approach, 1981 Am.B. Found. Research J. 753 (1981), discussing the May 30, 1981 Proposed Final Draft.

10. Under RPC 2.1, an attorney, in representing a client, "may" refer "to other considerations such as moral, economic, social and political factors."

11. See Malin, Protecting the Whistleblower From Retaliatory Discharge, 16 U.Mich.J.L.Ref. 277 (1983), pointing to the limited protection against discharge usually afforded by common law decisions to whistle blowing employees. Discharge of corporate attorneys is not discussed.

# B. THE GOVERNMENT LAWYER

## 1. THE CURRENT GOVERNMENT LAWYER

### MODEL RULES OF PROFESSIONAL CONDUCT

**RULE 1.11 Successive Government and Private Employment**

* * *

(c) Except as law may otherwise expressly permit, a lawyer serving as a public officer or employee shall not:

(1) participate in a matter in which the lawyer participated personally and substantially while in private practice or nongovernmental employment, unless under applicable law no one is, or by lawful delegation may be, authorized to act in the lawyer's stead in the matter; or

(2) negotiate for private employment with any person who is involved as a party or as attorney for a party in a matter in which the lawyer is participating personally and substantially.

* * *

**RULE 1.13 Organization as Client**

(a) A lawyer employed or retained by an organization represents the organization acting through its duly authorized constituents.

* * *

COMMENT:

The duty defined in this Rule applies to governmental organizations. However, when the client is a governmental organization, a different balance may be appropriate between maintaining confidentiality and assuring that the wrongful official act is prevented or rectified, for public business is involved. In addition, duties of lawyers employed by the government or lawyers in military service may be defined by statutes and regulation. Therefore, defining precisely the identity of the client and prescribing the resulting obligations of such lawyers may be more difficult in the government context. Although in some circumstances the client may be a specific agency, it is generally the government as a whole. For example, if the action or failure to act involves the head of a bureau, either the department of which the bureau is a part or the government as a whole may be the client for purpose of this Rule. Moreover, in a matter involving the conduct of government officials, a government lawyer may have authority to question such conduct more extensively than that of a lawyer for a private organization in similar circumstances. This Rule does not limit that authority. * * *[a]

a. Compare the following CPR provisions:

"**DR 8–101 Action as a Public Official**

(A) A lawyer who holds public office shall not:

(1) Use his public position to obtain, or attempt to obtain, a special advantage in legislative matters for himself or for a client under circumstances where he knows or it is obvious that such action is not in the public interest.

(2) Use his public position to influence, or attempt to influence, a tribunal to act in favor of himself or of a client.

(3) Accept any thing of value from any person when the lawyer knows or it is obvious that the offer is for the purpose of influencing his action as a public official."

### *Comment*

(1) *Scope.* Attorneys serve in many governmental activities, executive, legislative, and of course, as judges. They become presidents, members of congress, legislators, cabinet members or heads of agencies. More often, their service is in the lower levels of government and they are subject to the supervision of superiors. Limitations of space permit consideration of only some of the several ethical issues which these attorneys sometimes face.[1]

(2) *Client identification.* To whom should the government attorney look as the "client" in the performance of his or her duties? The attorney's immediate superior, the head of the agency or department, the government itself, the public? Note that this question is similar to that faced by the corporate attorney.[2] Who is the client?

It has been said that this is the wrong question and does not aid in determining such ethical issues as "Whose confidences shall I respect? With whom may I further discuss 'confidences'? What role does my own judgment play in determining what I ought to do?"[3]

Bear these questions in mind in considering the following materials.

## HILL, ETHICS FOR THE UNELECTED

68 A.B.A. J. 950 (1982).

> "To a degree that would shock 99 per cent of the American people, many decisions that affect every aspect of their lives are not made by congressmen or senators but by those members' personal or committee staff, the Unelected Representatives of Capitol Hill."
>
> Gerald R. Ford, *A Time to Heal*

For young lawyers who choose Capitol Hill as the first test of their legal education, the most serious challenge they may face is associated more with the accountability issue that former president Gerald Ford raises than the lawyer's legal competence. More specifically, the lack of electoral or political accountability of congressional staff attorneys presents a peculiar dilemma: to whom are these unelected staff accountable and by what legal and ethical standards are they to be judged or guided?

This question is particularly important to address prior to a lawyer's entering the ranks of this amorphous group we call congressional staff, of which attorneys represent the largest professional occupation.

1. For a thorough study of the subject, see Developments in the Law—Conflicts of Interest in the Legal Profession, 94 Harv.L.Rev. 1244, 1413–46 (1981).

2. See supra pp. 250.

According to its Comment, RPC 1.13 applies to government lawyers as well as other organization's lawyers. Is the position of a government lawyer sufficiently different from that of a corporate lawyer to warrant separate provisions on the former's ethical obligations?

3. Lawry, Who is the Client of the Federal Government Lawyer? An Analysis of the Wrong Question, 37 Fed.B.J. 61 (1978).

Whether the attorney enters Congress as a committee or personal staff member, he or she has become part of the largest staff of any parliamentary body in the world and will become involved in national policy-making issues in a very short period of time.

The ability of the congressional staff to quietly but effectively influence the nature and substance of national legislation by virtue of their unique position in Congress magnifies the staff attorney's importance far beyond the visibility or the actual number of such staffers. Indeed, many congressional staff attorneys are fresh out of law school and thrust into an arena that is a potential minefield of ethical misconduct, ill-prepared for the political pressures that will soon confront them. The dangers of misconduct, both in a legal and ethical sense, by the politically uninitiated attorney can be severely damaging not only to the legal profession but also to our democratic institutions.

How the congressional staff attorney balances his or her ethical and professional obligations with the public responsibilities associated with this job and how the attorney is able to distinguish between the staff role of legal technician and the congressional role of policy makers are issues that go to the heart of the ethical considerations inherent in this job. Yet, little has been written about these conflicts and the issue has largely been ignored or lumped together with the issues facing elected public officials. * * *

The major ethical issue facing the staff attorney is: to whom is he or she accountable? To the senator or representative for whom the attorney works as a personal aide, or if a committee attorney, [to] the chairman of the committee? To the House or Senate? Or to the public? Obviously, the taxpayer pays the attorney's salary, but it is the representative or senator who hires and fires. When a staff attorney perceives a conflict between the political well-being of the Congressman and the well-being of the public as a whole, is there an ethical obligation beyond the loyalty owed to the congressional employer to represent the public's interest, in light of the public trust bestowed upon Congress and its staff?

On the other hand, can an individual staff attorney presume to pass ethical judgement over the decision of a Congressman elected by the people? Or should he or she accept a more passive role and bow to the political judgement of the Congressman? If the staff attorney disagrees, is resignation the only option available or is whistle blowing or leaking information to the press ever an acceptable alternative? Outside of personal conscience or vague notions of democratic theory, on what ethical or professional basis should his or her ultimate decision depend? * * *

### *Questions*

(1) Does RPC 1.13 permit the attorney to obtain the answers to the questions raised by Professor Hill?

(2) The attorney employed by a legislator may have less immunity from liability for action taken at the direction of his or her employer

than does the legislator.[1] Should this have a bearing on the ethical duties of the attorney?

(3) The ethical questions discussed by Professor Hill occur also for attorneys working for agencies or departments in the executive branch of government. What are their duties when they know or believe that their superiors are engaged in corrupt or other questionable conduct? Or the attorneys believe that the policies being pursued are not in the public interest?[2] Consider the following opinion of the Professional Ethics Committee of the Federal Bar Association:

## THE GOVERNMENT CLIENT AND CONFIDENTIALITY: OPINION 73–1

32 Fed.B.J. 71, 72–74 (1973).

The more usual situation of the federally employed lawyer * * * is that of the lawyer who is a principal legal officer of a department, agency or other legal entity of the Government, or a member of the legal staff of the department, agency, or entity. This lawyer assumes a public trust, for the government, over-all and in each of its parts, is responsible to the people in our democracy with its representative form of government. Each part of the government has the obligation of carrying out, in the public interest, its assigned responsibility in a manner consistent with the Constitution, and the applicable regulations. In contrast, the private practitioner represents the client's personal or private interest. In pointing out that the federally employed lawyer thus is engaged professionally in the furtherance of a particular governmental responsibility we do not suggest, however, that the public is the client as the client concept is usually understood. It is to say that the lawyer's employment requires him to observe in the performance of his professional responsibility the public interest sought to be served by the governmental organization of which he is a part.

[The "client" was stated to be "the agency where [the attorney] is employed" and that the attorney-client privilege applied. As to disclosure, the Opinion continued:]

The Committee does not believe there are any circumstances in which corrupt conduct may not be disclosed by the federally employed lawyer, apart from those situations * * * in which the lawyer has been designated to defend an individual in a proceeding against him with respect to a personal problem.

[After referring to 28 U.S.C. § 535, to a House Concurrent Resolution and to regulations of the Civil Service Commission, the Committee stated the attorney may report "corrupt conduct and any other illegal conduct of a criminal character, that is, the willful or knowing

1. See Dombrowski v. Eastland, 387 U.S. 82, 87 S.Ct. 1425, 18 L.Ed.2d 577 (1967).

2. See Schnapper, Legal Ethics and the Government Lawyer, 32 Rec. 649 (1977); Developments in the Law—Conflicts of Interest in the Legal Profession, 94 Harv.L.Rev. 1244, 1414–16 (1981).

disregard of or breach of the law" to the department or agency head who must report it to the Attorney General. The Committee continued:]

With respect to the second category of illegal conduct, conduct about which there may be reasonable differences of opinion as to its legality, and grossly negligent conduct, the Committee considers the problem to be different. Ordinarily there is no need of disclosure of such conduct beyond the personnel of the agency where it arises. Differences of opinion as to the legality of action are often unavoidable in the process of arriving at a course of action to be recommended or adopted. The lawyer may not deem the decision reached or the action taken to be legally sound, but in the situations in which the question arises it may not be misconduct at all. Moreover, when we turn particularly to the grossly negligent category, one must consider that the particular conduct may be accidental by a person ordinarily careful. There should usually be an adequate remedy in the public interest calling for no disclosure beyond the immediate persons involved, including if need be other members of the agency * * *.

## MONDALE, THE LAWYER IN PUBLIC LIFE [a]

The Minnesota legislature has many fine legislators. Its members, by and large, are dedicated, honest, intelligent, public servants. It works long hours for very little pay, and is generally a credit to the community.

Many of the most effective legislators are lawyers—far more than the proportion of lawyers to the general population might indicate—which again proves my point about the value of lawyers as public servants. Nevertheless, the position of the lawyer-legislator creates peculiarly difficult conflict-of-interest situations which I am personally convinced must be solved—and solved soon—if we are to continue Minnesota's tradition of good government.

These conflicts arise in three basic situations:

(1) Where a bill is introduced by another legislator which would injure the interests of a legislator's client;

(2) Where a bill is introduced by the legislator or by another which would help a client's interests;

(3) Where the legislator's client needs representation before a state administrative agency.

Every legislature sees the introduction of numerous bills which vitally affect the financial welfare of major interest groups. Lending institutions, railroads, insurance companies, retail businesses, professions, and every other kind of business enterprise, especially those

a. This is a portion of an address given to the 1964 graduating class of the University of Minnesota Law School by the Hon. Walter F. Mondale, while he was attorney general of the state of Minnesota before becoming U.S. Senator and Vice President of the United States.

which fall under state regulation, have important legislative interests at stake.

Business enterprises usually generate great amounts of legal business, encompassing all types of practice. Through intention, coincidence, or long-standing attorney-client relations having no tie-in with the fact that the lawyer is also a legislator, a legislator's practice may be significantly composed of business from one or another of these groups.

Depending upon the kind of practice in which the lawyer engages, bills in which a client is deeply interested may come up for consideration many times every session.

This can be very pernicious. When a lawyer who may be getting substantial fees from a given client notes that his vote on a piece of legislation can cost him that client, he would be a good deal less than human to disregard this in making up his mind on the bill. It is likely, if not certain, that the public interest will suffer a severe beating in his reasoning.

This situation becomes even more pernicious where the legal fees being paid to the legislator are out of proportion—sometimes significantly out of proportion—to the amount of work he actually does for the client.

The second kind of ethical problem which confronts the lawyer-legislator is not so much a question of conflict of interest, although that element is present, as of a possible abuse of his station for the private gain of one person or group of persons.

This can occur when the lawyer-legislator appears before state administrative agencies, as many legislators make a practice of doing. I wish to draw a distinction between the kind of work any legislator does for a constituent—interceding for him with agencies of government—and doing the same thing for a private client, for pay.

As an example of what happens, or may happen, by way of obtaining an unfair advantage for a client, I might recount an experience I had myself while in private practice.

I had occasion to present a matter before one of our Minnesota regulatory commissions. Among my opponents was a legislator—a member of the committee which handled that agency's legislative affairs.

A question arose concerning an interpretation of a recently passed law.

My opponent noted that he was a member of the committee which passed out the law, and that he certainly knew what the legislature had intended by the law, and proceeded to give an interpretation favorable to his own client.

The lawyer-legislator who practices before state agencies is in a peculiarly powerful position if he sits on the Appropriations Subcommittee or committee which handles the agency budget, or other committees which fundamentally affect the affairs of the agency. It is asking a truly Solomonic turn of mind to expect a man to decide without hesitation, cases which involve on one side—or even both—persons who have power to set his salary, determine his term of office, or slice his office budget.

Now I do not wish to be misunderstood. There are few pieces of legislation or matters before administrative agencies where the public interest is crystal-clear and where the private interest is obviously contrary to it. Reasonable men differ regarding the wisdom of proposed legislation. Reasonable men also differ on the merits of matters before administrative agencies—that is, in effect, why the agencies were created in the first place.

My concern is this—in a situation where the public interest is involved, and there is also involved in the mind of the same man who is voting on it or presenting the case a very strong private interest, involving possibly substantial fees or a long-standing attorney-client relationship, it is expecting a great deal of human nature to suppose that the public interest always wins. It would be suggested as insanity to allow judges to sit on cases wherein they had a personal financial interest—no one would even question the right, in fact the obligation, of the judge to disqualify himself, or for a lawyer to file an affidavit of prejudice if he did not. We should hardly expect less of those who make our laws than we do of those who interpret and apply them.

Legislatures are created to make major decisions of first importance to clashing and competing interests in the community. The conflicts before the average legislature are much more raw, much more basic, and much more fraught with substantial public importance than a year's cases before the average court.

It is the lawyer-legislator's professional obligation, it seems to me, to avoid these conflicts. Many of our legislators conscientiously do so, often at great personal cost to themselves. The answer, after all, cannot be to divorce all legislators from their law practices, or all lawyers from their legislative offices. In such case society would be deprived of the services of most of those best qualified to serve it.

It has been suggested that measures beyond self-regulation are needed, but self-regulation is of first importance.

It has also been suggested that legislators be required to disclose those private interests which conflict with public interests, either at the beginning or the end of the session.

Some say a commission on legislative ethics should be established to render opinions on the presence or absence of conflicts—just as the Ethics Committee of the Bar Association.

It has also been proposed, and very nearly enacted in New York, that lawyers be forbidden to represent clients before state agencies except for ministerial matters, and matters where the adversary system is certain to exist or the agency's discretion is not involved.

It has also been suggested that records be kept and published of committee hearings and floor debates.

The problem is also not confined to lawyers, nor is it confined to Minnesota. The problem exists, perhaps even on a grander scale, in the United States Congress, where, for an example, the late Senator Robert Kerr of Oklahoma, the owner of a vast oil empire, thought nothing of voting and lobbying on such matters as oil import quotas or the depletion allowance.

I suggest that the time has come in this state and in this nation to take a close, hard, look at problems of this sort. I say again that many lawyer-legislators are, as are many farmer-legislators or businessmen-legislators, conscientious about avoiding any situation which would involve a conflict of interest. But the problem nevertheless exists, and I think it must soon be solved.[b]

## 2. THE FORMER GOVERNMENT OFFICER OR EMPLOYEE

### MODEL RULES OF PROFESSIONAL CONDUCT

**RULE 1.11 Successive Government and Private Employment**

(a) Except as law may otherwise expressly permit, a lawyer shall not represent a private client in connection with a matter in which the lawyer participated personally and substantially as a public officer or employee, unless the appropriate government agency consents after consultation. No lawyer in a firm with which that lawyer is associated may knowingly undertake or continue representation in such a matter unless:

(1) the disqualified lawyer is screened from any participation in the matter and is apportioned no part of the fee therefrom; and

**b.** See also Hill, Ethics for the Unelected, 68 A.B.A. J. 950 (1982); Address of Sen. Wm. E. Borah, 2 A.B.A. J. 779 (1916).

In Georgia Department of Human Resources v. Sistrunk, 249 Ga. 543, 291 S.E.2d 524 (1982), a lawyer-legislator, in his private practice, represented a client in seeking a writ of habeas corpus against a state department. The department sought to disqualify him asserting that his appearance conflicted with his duties as a legislator. The Georgia Supreme Court agreed with the lawyer that the CPR did not disqualify him, but held that the Georgia Constitution did so when it provided, "Public officers are the trustees and servants of the people, and at all times amenable to them." After examining the duties of trustees generally, the court concluded:

"Specifically concerning legislators, may one trustee of the people—in whose office are vested the powers of enhancement, diminution, and destruction of the office of another trustee of the people—as attorney and for his own financial gain act in a manner to hinder or frustrate the discharge by such other trustee of the duties of their common trust?

"No."

Three justices dissented.

For an example of gross abuse of power and position by a lawyer-legislator to secure pardons and paroles, see State v. Catlin, 2 Wis.2d 240, 85 N.W.2d 857 (1957). Cf. In re Becker, 16 Ill.2d 488, 158 N.E.2d 753 (1959); ABA Formal Opinion 306 (1962); ABA Formal Opinion 296 (1959).

(2) written notice is promptly given to the appropriate government agency to enable it to ascertain compliance with the provisions of this rule.

(b) Except as law may otherwise expressly permit, a lawyer having information that the lawyer knows is confidential government information about a person acquired when the lawyer was a public officer or employee, may not represent a private client whose interests are adverse to that person in a matter in which the information could be used to the material disadvantage of that person. A firm with which that lawyer is associated may undertake or continue representation in the matter only if the disqualified lawyer is screened from any participation in the matter and is apportioned no part of the fee therefrom.

* * *

(d) As used in this Rule, the term "matter" includes:

(1) any judicial or other proceeding, application, request for a ruling or other determination, contract, claim, controversy, investigation, charge, accusation, arrest or other particular matter involving a specific party or parties; and

(2) any other matter covered by the conflict of interest rules of the appropriate government agency.

(e) As used in this Rule, the term "confidential government information" means information which has been obtained under governmental authority and which, at the time this Rule is applied, the government is prohibited by law from disclosing to the public or has a legal privilege not to disclose, and which is not otherwise available to the public.[a]

**a.** See also RPC 1.12, which specifies:

**"RULE 1.12 Former Judge or Arbitrator**

"(a) Except as stated in paragraph (d), a lawyer shall not represent anyone in connection with a matter in which the lawyer participated personally and substantially as a judge or other adjudicative officer, arbitrator or law clerk to such a person, unless all parties to the proceeding consent after disclosure.

"(b) A lawyer shall not negotiate for employment with any person who is involved as a party or as attorney for a party in a matter in which the lawyer is participating personally and substantially as a judge or other adjudicative officer, or arbitrator. A lawyer serving as a law clerk to a judge, other adjudicative officer or arbitrator may negotiate for employment with a party or attorney involved in a matter in which the clerk is participating personally and substantially, but only after the lawyer has notified the judge, other adjudicative officer or arbitrator.

"(c) If a lawyer is disqualified by paragraph (a), no lawyer in a firm with which that lawyer is associated may knowingly undertake or continue representation in the matter unless:

(1) the disqualified lawyer is screened from any participation in the matter and is apportioned no part of the fee therefrom; and

(2) written notice is promptly given to the appropriate tribunal to enable it to ascertain compliance with the provisions of this rule.

"(d) An arbitrator selected as a partisan of a party in a multi-member arbitration panel is not prohibited from subsequently representing that party."

Compare the following CPR provisions:

**"DR 9-101 Avoiding Even the Appearance of Impropriety**

"(A) A lawyer shall not accept private employment in a matter upon the merits of which he has acted in a judicial capacity.

"(B) A lawyer shall not accept private employment in a matter in which he had substantial responsibility while he was a public employee."

### *Comment*

Attorneys commonly enter government service, particularly at the federal level, not only for the remuneration and the gratification experienced from rendering public service, but also to develop professional skills in a particular field and to become specialists in that field on later entering private practice. The Internal Revenue Service, the Labor Department, the Securities and Exchange Commission are examples that offer this kind of attraction.

The government also gains in attracting superior talent that might not otherwise be available.

On leaving government service and entering private practice, the attorney faces some ethical problems. The *Kessenich* case which follows is an example.

## KESSENICH v. COMMODITY FUTURES TRADING COMMISSION

684 F.2d 88 (D.C.Cir.1982).

PER CURIAM:

[Kessenich filed a complaint with the respondent commission (CFTC) charging Rosenthal & Company with unauthorized commodity options transactions in Kessenich's account. Following CFTC's reparations award, the parties cross-appealed and in the appellate court Kessenich moved to disqualify Rosenthal's attorney.]

Kessenich has * * * moved to disqualify Clinton Burr, general counsel of Rosenthal & Company, from acting in this court as attorney for Rosenthal. Although there is little or no indication that Kessenich has been or will be prejudiced by the continuation of Burr as attorney for Rosenthal, we grant the motion in light of the uncertainty surrounding the situation and the effect continued representation may have on public confidence in the CFTC.

Burr was an attorney with the Commodity Futures Trading Commission from 1975 to 1978. He was assigned to the Division of Enforcement from December 1976 until he resigned in May 1978. One of his responsibilities was the review of reparation complaints to ensure that they were complete and stated an appropriate claim. He received Kessenich's letter complaint on March 6, 1977, and apparently forwarded notice of the complaint to Rosenthal. Because the facts were in dispute and the parties did not settle the matter between them, the case was docketed in the Office of Hearings and Appeals on August 1, 1977, past which point Burr had no responsibility for the matter.

Kessenich argues that this participation in the incipient case should disqualify Burr from acting as attorney for Rosenthal in this court. Kessenich relies on a criminal statute, the regulations of the CFTC, and the American Bar Association's Code of Professional Responsibility. The CFTC * * * urges disqualification in order to protect the integrity of the Commission. Burr responds that his participation was merely ministerial and neither created a conflict of interest nor made him privy to confidential information which he could use to the detriment of Kessenich. In fact, Burr claims to have no direct memory of the case.

Kessenich first relies on 18 U.S.C. § 207 (Supp.IV 1980), which makes it a crime for a former government employee to represent any interest but the United States in a matter in which he had "participated personally and substantially" as a government employee. [The court quoted the relevant earlier version of § 207, noting that it was "not substantially different in relevant part" from the current statute. Current § 207(a) provides for punishment up to $10,000 or two years or both for:

> "[w]hoever, having been an officer or employee of the executive branch of the United States Government, [or] of any independent agency of the United States * * *, after his employment has ceased, knowingly acts as agent or attorney for, or otherwise represents, any other person (except the United States), in any formal or informal appearance before, or, with the intent to influence, makes any oral or written communication on behalf of any other person (except the United States) to—
>
> (1) any department, agency, court, court-martial, or any civil, military, or naval commission of the United States or the District of Columbia, or any officer or employee thereof, and
>
> (2) in connection with any judicial or other proceeding, application, request for a ruling or other determination, contract, claim, controversy, investigation, charge, accusation, arrest, or other particular matter involving a specific party or parties in which the United States or the District of Columbia is a party or has a direct and substantial interest, and
>
> (3) in which he participated personally and substantially as an officer or employee through decision, approval, disapproval, recommendation, the rendering of advice, investigation or otherwise, while so employed * * *." [a]]

There is no doubt that Burr was an "employee" of an "independent agency" and he now is attempting to act as an attorney for [a person other than the United States]. The only questions are whether the United States is a party or has a direct and substantial interest and whether Burr had "participated personally and substantially" in the matter as an employee. Our present concern for the integrity of the judicial and administrative process does not require that we determine whether the statute has been violated, and indeed it would be precipitous to do so. It is sufficient to note that there is a real possibility that Burr's representation of Rosenthal may be criminal.

a. For the full text of the § 207, see West Publishing Co., Selected Statutes, Rules and Standards on the Legal Profession 213 (1984).

Kessenich also cites a Commission regulation which would prohibit Burr's representation of Rosenthal before the Commission:

> "(a) *Personal knowledge or consideration of the matter.* No person shall ever appear in a representative capacity before the Commission in a particular matter if such person, or one participating with him in the particular matter, personally considered it or gained nonpublic knowledge of the facts thereof while he was a member or employee of the Commission."

17 C.F.R. § 140.735–10 (1981). Kessenich argues, and the Commission agrees, that this would disable Burr from representing Rosenthal in this case before the Commission. The regulation is not dispositive, however, because it contains no specific disqualification from appearance before other forums. At the least, it does demonstrate the Commission's concern for the integrity of its staff.

Kessenich also cites [DR] 9–101(B) [which] states:

> "A lawyer shall not accept private employment in a matter in which he had substantial responsibility while he was a public employee."

There is no doubt about any of the elements of this prohibition except whether Burr had "substantial responsibility" for the reparation complaint when it was initially filed. * * *

[ABA] Formal Opinion [342 (1975) ] explains the meaning of "substantial responsibility":

> "As used in DR 9–101(B), 'substantial responsibility' envisages a much closer and more direct relationship than that of a mere perfunctory approval or disapproval of the matter in question. It contemplates a responsibility requiring the official to become personally involved to an important, material degree, in the investigative or deliberative processes regarding the transactions of facts in question. Thus, being the chief official in some vast office or organization does not ipso facto give that governmental official or employee the 'substantial responsibility' contemplated by the rule in regard to all the minutiae of facts lodged within that office. Yet it is not necessary that the public employee or official shall have personally and in a substantial manner investigated or passed upon the particular matter, for it is sufficient that he had such a heavy responsibility for the matter in question that it is unlikely he did not become personally and substantially involved in the investigative or deliberative processes regarding that matter. With a responsibility so strong and compelling that he probably became involved in the investigative or decisional processes, a lawyer upon leaving the government service should not represent another in regard to that matter. To do so would be akin to switching sides, might jeopardize confidential government information, and gives the appearance of professional impropriety in that accepting subsequent employment regarding that same matter creates a suspicion

that the lawyer conducted his governmental work in a way to facilitate his own future employment in that matter."

The facts in this case lie at the outer bounds of the "substantial responsibility" required to invoke the disciplinary rule. Burr claims he did little more than accept the Kessenich complaint for filing, and that he has no specific memory of the case. He asserts that his duties were completely ministerial; he had no discretion in the matter, and he was not privy to any confidential information.

The CFTC characterizes his responsibilities very differently. [It noted that Burr's position carried considerable discretionary powers.]

In evaluating whether a violation of the Code of Professional Responsibility has occurred and whether this violation warrants disqualification, it is appropriate to consider the specific societal interests at stake. "A court should be conscious of its responsibility to preserve a reasonable balance between the need to ensure ethical conduct on the part of lawyers appearing before it and other social interests, which include the litigant's right to freely chosen counsel." Woods v. Covington County Bank, 537 F.2d 804, 810 (5th Cir. 1976). Formal Opinion 342 lists the purposes of DR 9–101(B):

> "The policy considerations underlying DR 9–101(B) have been thought to be the following: the treachery of switching sides; the safeguarding of confidential governmental information from future use against the government; the need to discourage government lawyers from handling particular assignments in such a way as to encourage their own future employment in regard to those particular matters after leaving government service; and the professional benefit derived from avoiding the appearance of evil."

See also *Woods* (stating that former government employees are usually disqualified either due to possible conflicts while a government official or due to some improper advantage gained over the adverse party); Board of Education v. Nyquist, 590 F.2d 1241, 1246 (2d Cir. 1979).

An examination of each of these factors indicates that the most concrete danger in this case is the appearance of impropriety which may affect the perceived integrity of the agency. There has been no allegation that Burr has "switched sides" or that any initial investigation was not done from a neutral point of view. There is no indication that he has gained confidential information that might be used to the detriment of the government. Further, there is no claim that he improperly carried out his duties at the CFTC with an eye to future employment. In fact, he promptly notified his superiors after accepting employment with Rosenthal and removed himself from consideration of related cases. There is also no concrete evidence that he has gained any information beyond that contained in the official record which would aid him in the prosecution of this appeal.

The final consideration, the appearance of evil, is clearly implicated. This is a case with which Burr dealt as a government official, and he now represents one of the parties. It is not at all difficult to imagine that he may have gained some advantage from his former connection with the case, even though its exact outlines have not been articulated. The issue is raised whether this is sufficient to disqualify Rosenthal's chosen counsel.

Some courts have at times held that the appearance of impropriety is sufficient in itself to disqualify counsel.[10] See Allied Realty of St. Paul, Inc. v. Exchange Nat'l Bank, 408 F.2d 1099, 1101–02 (8th Cir.), cert. denied, 396 U.S. 823, 90 S.Ct. 64, 24 L.Ed.2d 73 (1969); United States v. Trafficante, 328 F.2d 117, 120 (5th Cir. 1964). In a later case, the Fifth Circuit articulated a different standard: "[W]hile Canon 9 does imply that there need be no proof of actual wrong doing, we conclude that there must be at least a reasonable possibility that some specifically identifiable impropriety did in fact occur." *Woods*, supra, 537 F.2d at 813. In a footnote, the court further explained its standard:

> "We emphasize that an attorney need not be disqualified even where there is a reasonable possibility of improper conduct. As we have seen, a court must also find that the likelihood of public suspicion or obloquy outweighs the social interests which will be served by a lawyer's continued participation in a particular case. Under Canon 9, an attorney should be disqualified only when both of these standards have been satisfied."

Id. at 813 n. 12.

We agree with the implication that counsel should not be disqualified merely because of a hypothetical possibility that an innocuous violation of the Code might have occurred. The more important consideration, however, is the effect of counsel's conduct on the relevant social interests. In this case there is an appearance of impropriety that has an impact beyond its effect on the immediate parties involved. Public confidence in the CFTC's reparation procedures will be undercut if litigants must fear that the public officials who handle their case may one day oppose them in regard to the same matter. This is true even where there is no apparent advantage for the former official. The enforcement of commodity futures trading laws will suffer if laymen are not candid with the investigating personnel of the agency.

Other public considerations militate in favor of disqualification. First, our concern for the integrity of the process before this court suggests we should be wary of allowing Burr to represent Rosenthal in potential contravention of federal criminal proscriptions. Second, the agency itself strongly urges that DR 9–101(B) has been violated. It has encouraged Burr to remove himself from the case, thus indi-

10. The ABA's Formal Opinion calls avoiding the appearance of impropriety "[p]erhaps the least helpful of the seven policy considerations," and it notes that it is not an element of DR 9–101(B), even though it is relevant to its interpretation. See ABA Formal Opinion 342 at n. 17.

cating that it feels the possible problems of public perception outweigh any difficulties such disqualification could cause in the recruiting of new personnel. Finally, there is no allegation that Rosenthal cannot retain other qualified counsel. In fact, Rosenthal was represented by a private law firm before the Commission.

We do not intend to intimate that attorney Burr has not acted with integrity and candor. Instead, our decision rests on considerations beyond the immediate case before us. The integrity, both actual and apparent, of the agency's dispute resolution mechanism is essential to the regulatory enforcement scheme created by Congress. Employees of the Commission who exercise its discretion in a particular case should not later represent one of the parties in the same matter before the courts. This is especially true when the employee's function required the complete confidence of each party, even if no actual secrets revealed are identifiable later on. Public confidence in judicial and quasi-judicial proceedings can best be maintained by steering clear of situations which call into question the regularity of the process.[11]

On at least one occasion in the past, this court has disqualified counsel even though there was no indication of present impropriety. In Yablonski v. United Mine Workers (UMW), 448 F.2d 1175 (D.C.Cir.1971) (per curiam), the court disqualified counsel for the UMW in the district court. The counsel had at first represented both the UMW and its officers and then withdrew as counsel for the individual defendants. The court held that it was not inappropriate for the counsel to continue to represent the union after it withdrew as counsel for the individual defendants. It also found no present evidence of conflict of interest in the counsel's representation of the union officials in other cases which stemmed from the same challenge to the union leadership. Yet the potential for conflict due to these other cases was held sufficient in the context of that case to warrant disqualification, based on the underlying objectives of the federal labor laws and the importance of the particular case. The policy objectives of a federal statutory scheme may necessitate disqualification of a litigant's chosen counsel, even though no present evidence of impropriety exists.

We believe the present case also involves a situation in which counsel should be disqualified even though there is no evidence that Burr abused his public office. The potential detriment to public confidence in the CFTC's dispute resolution mechanism outweighs Rosenthal's

11. For that reason, this court has proscribed such representation by its employees to an even wider extent:

"No one serving as a law clerk or secretary to a member of this Court or employed in any other capacity by this Court shall * * * after separating from that position practice as an attorney in connection with any case pending in this Court during his term of service, permit his name to appear on a brief filed in connection with any such case, or engage in any activity as an attorney or advisor in connection with any such case."

D.C.Cir.R.4. See also D.C.Cir., Handbook of Practice and Internal Procedures 8 (1978) ("No person employed by the Court, after leaving the position, may practice as an attorney in any case pending in the Court during the person's term of service").

interest in retaining its chosen counsel. In addition, the possibility that continued representation may be illegal militates strongly in favor of disqualification in order to maintain the integrity of this court's processes. Therefore we grant the motion to disqualify.[12] * * *

### *Questions*

RPC 1.11(A) states that a lawyer "shall not represent a private client in connection with a matter in which the lawyer participated personally and substantially as a public officer or employee," unless the appropriate agency consents. Neither this provision nor others of the Model Rules appear to deal with the following:

(a) The lawyer's decisions and conduct while with the government agency are intentionally slanted to court attraction and prospective private employment with a business or law firm, without focusing on any particular "matter."[1]

(b) Knowledge of the inner policies and workings of the agency he or she has left can be used to the disadvantage of the government, and to the advantage of new clients.

(c) In representing clients before the agency the lawyer has left, he or she will be dealing with former and persumably friendly colleagues, who may find it difficult to deal objectively with the matter he or she is presenting.

How can these problems be met? If not by ethical Rules, by what other means?[2]

### *Comment*

Attorneys leaving government service frequently join or seek to join, law firms which have important matters pending before the agency the attorney left and in which the attorney had played a substantial part for the agency. The normal rule is that if any member of a law firm is disqualified from representing a particular client, all members of the firm are also disqualified.[3]

This may result in reluctance on the part of law firms to employ former government attorneys and attorneys being hesitant about joining government service. To meet these difficulties, ABA Formal Opinion 342 (1975) took the position that it would be ethically proper

12. We assume that disqualified counsel will take appropriate steps to insulate his successor from both himself and his work product and that he will withdraw his brief already filed with the court.

1. RPC 1.11(c)(2) forbids the government lawyer from negotiating "for private employment with any person who is involved as a party or as attorney for a party in a matter in which the lawyer is participating personally and substantially." See Graceffa, Ethical Considerations of the Federal Lawyer Upon Entering Private Practice, 4 W.New Eng.L.Rev. 199 (1981).

2. See G. Hazard, Ethics in the Practice of Law, ch. 8 (1978); R. Aronson & D. Weckstein, Professional Responsibility in a Nutshell 206–11 (1980); Developments in the Law—Conflicts of Interest in the Legal Profession, 94 Harv.L.Rev. 1244, 1428–39 (1981).

3. See RPC 1.10; DR 5–105(D).

for the law firm to employ the attorney and avoid disqualification of the firm if the disqualified former government lawyer is "screened from any direct or indirect participation in the matter" and from sharing fees therefrom.[4]

This position has been followed by courts,[5] and is adopted in RPC 1.11(a) and (b).

Effective screening would appear to require at least the following:

(1) The former government lawyer must receive no part of the fee received by the firm for services rendered in cases in which the lawyer is disqualified.

(2) No member of the firm must discuss the matter with the lawyer or in the lawyer's presence.

4. The Formal Opinion also required the agency's consent.

5. See Armstong v. McAlpin, 625 F.2d 433 (2d Cir. 1980), vacated on other grounds 449 U.S. 1106, 101 S.Ct. 911, 66 L.Ed.2d 835 (1981), where the court allowed representation subject to screening and agency consent as provided in Formal Opinion 342. Compare Kesselhaut v. United States, 555 F.2d 791 (Ct.Cl.1977), where the court held that a law firm may proceed if the *court* is satisfied with the screening procedure, notwithstanding the government agency's refusal to consent. The court explained:

> "Should an attorney, having left Government * * * ineluctably infect all the members of any firm he joined with all his own personal disqualifications, he would take on the status of a Typhoid Mary, and be reduced to sole practice under the most unfavorable conditions. * * *
>
> "[I]t is the non-delegable responsibility of the court to obtain the adherence of the bar to proper ethical standards in the management of cases before it. Accordingly, the consent of the adverse party would not necessarily compel our assent to a flagrant conflict of interest; nor, on the contrary, should the withholding of consent by the Government, as here, be binding on us."

See generally Comment, The Chinese Wall Defense to Law-Firm Disqualification, 128 U.Pa.L.Rev. 677 (1980), discussing factors courts should consider in determining whether screening should be permitted to prevent firm disqualification.

Morgan, The Evolving Concept of Professional Responsibility, 90 Harv.L.Rev. 702, 729–31 (1977) charges that Formal Opinion 342's construction of DR 9–101(B) "qualified * * * until it is hardly recognizable" the principle that information gained in public service should not be used against the public in a later case, and that the ABA processes which produced that construction "illustrate that the interest of lawyers, not their clients or the public, is given top priority by the Code." Professor Morgan decries the Opinion's permitting use against the government of "sophisticated understanding of agency operations, general enforcement strategy, and the like obtained from confidential discussions between an agency lawyer and his superiors," and responds to the argument that this helps the government to hire able attorneys (by enabling it to "pay lower salaries by providing part of the attorney's compensation in 'experience' which can later be used against it") with the observation that "in no other situation is the lawyer permitted to use client secrets against the client in exchange for charging a lower fee."

See Legal Ethics Forum, 63 A.B.A. J. 724 (1977), setting forth opposing statements by Dean Monroe H. Freedman and Mr. Lloyd N. Cutler and a proposed redraft of DR 9–101 under consideration by the District of Columbia Bar. Dean Freedman asserts that the concept of a government agency waiving the imputed disqualification of a former government lawyer's partners and associates is subject to "three major objections": (1) "no workable standards have ever been suggested," (2) "policing violations of screening once a waiver has been given" is virtually impossible, and (3) "the screening-waiver device seriously compounds the initial conflict of interest" because agency lawyers passing on waiver requests "have a personal incentive to be generous in granting the waiver, because they will themselves be making similar requests when they leave governmental service."

(3) The lawyer must not have access to the files relating to the matter.

(4) The lawyer must not have given any information about the matter to any member of the firm.

# Chapter 6

# COUNSELING AND ADVOCACY

## A. DUTIES TO CLIENT

### MODEL RULES OF PROFESSIONAL CONDUCT

**RULE 1.3 Diligence**

A lawyer shall act with reasonable diligence and promptness in representing a client.

**RULE 1.4 Communication**

(a) A lawyer shall keep a client reasonably informed about the status of a matter and promptly comply with reasonable requests for information.

(b) A lawyer shall explain a matter to the extent reasonably necessary to permit the client to make informed decisions regarding the representation.

**RULE 2.1 Advisor**

In representing a client, a lawyer shall exercise independent professional judgment and render candid advice. In rendering advice, a lawyer may refer not only to law but to other considerations such as moral, economic, social and political factors, that may be relevant to the client's situation.

**RULE 3.1 Meritorious Claims and Contentions**

A lawyer shall not bring or defend a proceeding, or assert or controvert an issue therein, unless there is a basis for doing so that is not frivolous, which includes a good faith argument for an extension, modification or reversal of existing law. A lawyer for the defendant in a criminal proceeding, or the respondent in a proceeding that could result in incarceration, may nevertheless so defend the proceeding as to require that every element of the case be established.

**RULE 3.2 Expediting Litigation**

A lawyer shall make reasonable efforts to expedite litigation consistent with the interests of the client.

**RULE 3.4 Fairness to Opposing Party and Counsel**

A lawyer shall not:

* * *

(d) in pretrial procedure, make a frivolous discovery request or fail to make reasonably diligent effort to comply with a legally proper discovery request by an opposing party * * *.[a]

### *Questions*

(1) You are a lawyer whose wealthy client wants to resist a necessitous widow's meritorious claim on the ground that the statute of limitations has just run out on the claim. What do you do?[1]

a. Compare the following CPR provisions:

"**EC 7–8** * * * In assisting his client to reach a proper decision, it is often desirable for a lawyer to point out those factors which may lead to a decision that is morally just as well as legally permissible. He may emphasize the possibility of harsh consequences that might result from assertion of legally permissible positions. In the final analysis, however, the lawyer should always remember that the decision whether to forego legally available objectives or methods because of non-legal factors is ultimately for the client and not for himself. In the event that the client in a non-adjudicatory matter insists upon a course of conduct that is contrary to the judgment and advice of the lawyer but not prohibited by Disciplinary Rules, the lawyer may withdraw from the employment.

"**EC 7–9** In the exercise of his professional judgment on those decisions which are for his determination in the handling of a legal matter, a lawyer should always act in a manner consistent with the best interests of his client. However, when an action in the best interest of his client seems to him to be unjust, he may ask his client for permission to forego such action."

"**DR 7–101 Representing a Client Zealously**

"(A) A lawyer shall not intentionally:

(1) Fail to seek the lawful objectives of his client through reasonably available means permitted by law and the Disciplinary Rules, except as provided by DR 7–101(B). A lawyer does not violate this Disciplinary Rule, however, by acceding to reasonable requests of opposing counsel which do not prejudice the rights of his client, by being punctual in fulfilling all professional commitments, by avoiding offensive tactics, or by treating with courtesy and consideration all persons involved in the legal process.

(2) Fail to carry out a contract of employment entered into with a client for professional services, but he may withdraw as permitted under DR 2–110, DR 5–102, and DR 5–105.

(3) Prejudice or damage his client during the course of the professional relationship, except as required under DR 7–102(B).

"(B) In his representation of a client, a lawyer may:

(1) Where permissible, exercise his professional judgment to waive or fail to assert a right or position of his client.

(2) Refuse to aid or participate in conduct that he believes to be unlawful, even though there is some support for an argument that the conduct is legal.

"**DR 7–102 Representing a Client Within the Bounds of the Law**

"(A) In his representation of a client, a lawyer shall not:

(1) File a suit, assert a position, conduct a defense, delay a trial, or take other action on behalf of his client when he knows or when it is obvious that such action would serve merely to harass or maliciously injure another.

(2) Knowingly advance a claim or defense that is unwarranted under existing law, except that he may advance such claim or defense if it can be supported by good faith argument for an extension, modification, or reversal of existing law."

1. See Chapman, Lectures on Legal Ethics, 3 Temple L.Q. 409, 413 (1929); Stevens,

(2) A defendant, served with summons and complaint, without employing a lawyer, writes a letter to you as plaintiff's counsel explaining her position, but no formal answer is interposed. What do you do?[2]

(3) Is RPC 3.1 (or DR 7–102(A) (1), (2)) as demanding as F.R.Civ.P. 11 (as amended effective August 1, 1983)? The latter provides:

> "* * * The signature of an attorney * * * constitutes a certificate by him that he has read the pleading, motion, or other paper; that to the best of his knowledge, information, and belief formed after reasonable inquiry it is well grounded in fact and is warranted by existing law or a good faith argument for the extension, modification, or reversal of existing law, and that it is not interposed for any improper purpose, such as to harass or to cause unecessary delay or needless increase in the cost of litigation. If a pleading, motion, or other paper is not signed, it shall be stricken unless it is signed promptly after the omission is called to the attention of the pleader or movant. If a pleading, motion, or other paper is signed in violation of this rule, the court, upon motion or upon its own initiative, shall impose upon the person who signed it, a represented party, or both, an appropriate sanction, which may include an order to pay to the other party or parties the amount of the reasonable expenses incurred because of the filing of the pleading, motion, or other paper, including a reasonable attorney's fee."[3]

Ethics and the Statute of Frauds, 37 Corn.L.Q. 355 (1932).

2. See Lyons v. Paul, 321 S.W.2d 944 (Tex.Civ.App.1958) ("We doubt if [plaintiff's lawyer] owed [defendant the] duty [to file her letter with the clerk of court], but we do think that under all the facts and circumstances [plaintiff's] attorney owed [defendant] the duty to reply immediately to her letter * * * and to return her letter and the enclosures * * * and advise her that he could not represent her in the litigation."). Compare Marcus v. Simotone & Combined Sound & Color Films, Inc., 135 Misc. 228, 237 N.Y.S. 509 (1929) ("[O]rdinary professional courtesy demands that a lawyer should not ask for judgment by default unless * * * satisfied, after communicating with [opposing counsel], that the default is willful or intentional."). Cf. RPC 4.4 ("lawyer shall not use means that have no substantial purpose other than to embarrass, delay, or burden a third person"); DR 7–102(A)(1) (lawyer shall not take action which lawyer knows or it is obvious "would serve merely to harass or maliciously injure another"); F.R.Civ.P. 60(b) (relief from judgment for mistake, inadvertence, or excusable neglect). Compare RPC 4.3 (in dealing with unrepresented person, lawyer "shall not state or imply that the lawyer is disinterested" and, if lawyer knows or reasonably should know that the unrepresented person misunderstands the lawyer's role, "shall make reasonable efforts to correct the misunderstanding") with DR 7–104(A)(2) (lawyer shall not "give advice to [adverse] person who is not represented by a lawyer, other than the advice to secure counsel").

3. See Underwood, Curbing Litigation Abuses: Judicial Control of Adversary Ethics—The Model Rules of Professional Conduct and Proposed Amendments to the Rules of Civil Procedure, 56 St. John's L.Rev. 625, 635–46 (1982).

See also Roadway Express, Inc. v. Piper, 447 U.S. 752, 100 S.Ct. 2455, 65 L.Ed.2d 488 (1980) (attorney fees may be awarded against lawyers for extending court proceedings unreasonably and in bad faith); Nemeroff v. Abelson, 704 F.2d 652 (2d Cir. 1983) (trial court properly awarded $50,000 attorney fees against plaintiff *and plaintiff's lawyers* for bad faith in *continuing* litigation after they should have realized they had no support for their claims); In re Phelps, 637 F.2d 171 (10th Cir. 1981) (two year suspension from practice before federal district court for making statement in new trial motion that witnesses would testify in certain fashion without *reasonable* basis to expect they would so testify); An-

## JOHNS v. SMYTH

176 F.Supp. 949 (E.D.Va.1959).

WALTER E. HOFFMAN, District Judge. Petitioner is a state prisoner serving a life sentence for the murder of one Melvin Childress in accordance with a final judgment of the Circuit Court of the City of Richmond, Virginia, entered on December 17, 1942. * * *

While the petition alleges several points for consideration, it is only necessary to determine whether petitioner had a fair trial by reason of the actions of court-appointed counsel. [O]n the basis of the testimony now given by court-assigned counsel * * * this court has arrived at the conclusion that petitioner's constitutional rights have been invaded.

One of the cardinal principles confronting every attorney in the representation of a client is the requirement of complete loyalty and service in good faith to the best of his ability. In a criminal case the client is entitled to a fair trial, but not a perfect one. These are fundamental requirements of due process under the Fourteenth Amendment. The same principles are applicable in Sixth Amendment cases * * * and suggest that an attorney should have no conflict of interest and that he must devote his full and faithful efforts toward the defense of his client.

With this in mind, let us examine the facts to determine (1) whether the representation afforded petitioner at his murder trial was so totally lacking that it cannot be said that he had a fair trial in the usual sense of the word, and (2) whether the court-appointed attorney was so prejudiced and convinced of his client's guilt of *first degree murder* that he was unable to, and did not, give his client the "undivided allegiance and faithful, devoted service" which the Supreme Court has held to be the right of the accused under the Constitution, and (3) whether the attorney's interest in his client was so diverted by his personal beliefs that there existed a conflict in interest between his duty to his client and his conscience.

not., 50 A.L.R. Fed. 652 (1980) (financial award against lawyer for frivolous appeal). See generally Cann, Frivolous Lawsuits—The Lawyer's Duty to Say "No," 52 U.Colo.L.Rev. 367 (1981).

Compare In re Corace, 390 Mich. 419, 213 N.W.2d 124 (1973), a disciplinary proceeding wherein the lawyer was charged with continuing to include attorney fees as part of the damages claimed for his clients even though, when contested, trial judges had disallowed them as not permissible under state law. The Michigan Supreme Court refused to discipline the lawyer, reasoning that (1) he was under no duty to appeal the adverse decisions of the trial judges, and (2) a federal decision, whether rightly or wrongly decided, lent some support to his position. Therefore, the lawyer had complied with the ethical obligation to represent his clients "zealously within the bounds of the law." The court stated:

"There are a large number of gray areas in the law. When a question is doubtful, the lawyer's obligation to his client permits him to assert the view of the law most favorable to his client's position. * * *

"We agree with Corace that our adversary system 'intends, and expects, lawyers to probe the outer limits of the bounds of the law, ever searching for a more efficacious remedy or a more successful defense'.

"A lawyer may not properly be disciplined for acting without the bounds of the law unless it is established that he knowingly advanced a claim or defense that was unwarranted."

The importance of the attorney's undivided allegiance and faithful service to one accused of crime, irrespective of the attorney's personal opinion as to the guilt of his client, lies in Canon 5 of the American Bar Association Canon of Ethics, in effect during 1942, where it is said:

> "It is the right of the lawyer to undertake the defense of a person accused of crime, regardless of his personal opinion as to the guilt of the accused;[a] otherwise innocent persons, victims only of suspicious circumstances, might be denied proper defense. Having undertaken such defense, the lawyer is bound, by all fair and honorable means, to present every defense that the law of the land permits, to the end that no person may be deprived of life or liberty, but by due process of law."

The difficulty lies, of course, in ascertaining whether the attorney has been guilty of an error of judgment, such as an election with respect to trial tactics, or has otherwise been actuated by his conscience or belief that his client should be convicted in any event. All too frequently courts are called upon to review actions of defense counsel which are, at the most, errors of judgment, not properly reviewable on habeas corpus unless the trial is a farce and a mockery of justice which requires the court to intervene. Diggs v. Welch, 80 U.S.App. D.C. 5, 148 F.2d 667.[b] But when defense counsel, in a truly adverse proceeding, admits that his conscience would not permit him to adopt certain customary trial procedures, this extends beyond the realm of judgment and strongly suggests an invasion of constitutional rights.

Little need be said of the trial. The accused did not testify. No proposed instructions were submitted to the trial judge in behalf of the defendant, although under the law of Virginia it was possible for the defendant to have been convicted of involuntary manslaughter and received a sentence of only five years. The defense attorney agreed

**a.** Compare RPC 1.2(b) (lawyer's representation of client, including representation by appointment, does not constitute endorsement of client's political, economic, social or moral views or activities); RPC 6.2 (lawyer shall not seek to avoid appointment by tribunal to represent person except for good cause, including that client or cause is so repugnant to lawyer as to be likely to impair client-lawyer relationship or lawyer's ability to represent client); EC 2–29 (lawyer's belief that criminal defendant is guilty is not sufficient ground for seeking to be excused from court appointment or bar association request to represent person unable to obtain counsel); EC 2–30 (lawyer should decline employment if intensity of lawyer's personal feeling may impair effective representation).

Regarding defense of persons known to be guilty, see generally D. Mellinkoff, The Conscience of a Lawyer 141–84 (1973); Mitchell, The Ethics of the Criminal Defense Attorney—New Answers to Old Questions, 32 Stan.L.Rev. 293 (1980); Pool, Defending the "Guilty" Client, 64 Mass.L.Rev. 11 (1979).

**b.** The courts have since abandoned the "farce and mockery of justice" standard. See Strickland v. Washington, — U.S. —, 104 S.Ct. 2052, — L.Ed.2d — (1984):

> "As all the Federal Courts of Appeals [and all but a few state courts] have now held, the proper standard for attorney performance is that of reasonably effective assistance. * * *
>
> "Representation of a criminal defendant entails certain basic duties [including] loyalty [and] to bring to bear such skill and knowledge as will render the trial a reliable adversarial testing process.
>
> "[T]he * * * inquiry must be whether counsel's assistance was reasonable considering all the circumstances."

with the prosecutor that the case would be submitted to the jury without argument of counsel. The instructions given by the court were generally acceptable in covering the categories of first and second degree murder, but failed to mention the possibility of a manslaughter verdict.

Standing alone these complaints would have no merit as they may properly be considered as trial tactics. However, when we look at the motivating force which prompted these decisions of trial counsel, it is apparent that "tactics" gave way to "conscience." In explanation of the agreement not to argue the case before the jury, the court-appointed attorney said:

> "I think an argument to the jury would have made me appear ridiculous in the light of the evidence that was offered. * * *
>
> "I had enough confidence in the judgment of the jury to know that they could have drawn an inference, and I would have been a hypocrite and falsifier if I had gone before the jury and argued in the light of what Johns told me that that statement was accurate. * * *
>
> "Well, sir, I did not and I wouldn't be dishonest enough to do it in the light of Mr. Johns' statement to me. You can say what the law is and what the record discloses, but if I asked a client, an accused on defense, to explain some such statement as this and he gives me the explanation that Johns gave me, I consider it dishonest. You can talk about legal duty to client all you wish, but I consider it dishonest for me to get up before a jury and try to argue that the statement that came out from the Commonwealth was true when Johns had told me that it wasn't. The explanation that he gave me was very vague."

Immediately thereafter, the following occurred:

> "Q. That you could not conscientiously argue to the jury that he should be acquitted? A. I definitely could not.
>
> "Q. Regardless of what the law is or what your duty to a client is? A. You can talk about law and you can talk about my duty to clients, I felt it was my—that I couldn't conscientiously stand up there and argue that point in the light of what Johns had told me."

The attorney was then asked whether he ever considered requesting permission to withdraw from the case. He replied in the negative.

No attorney should "frame" a factual defense in any case, civil or criminal, and it is not intimated by this opinion that the attorney should plant the seeds of falsehood in the mind of his client.[c] In the instant case, however, the evidence adduced by the prosecution suggested

c. Compare R. Traver, Anatomy of a Murder 44–46 (1958) (defendant "recalls" blacking out during shooting only after defense counsel reviews all defenses to murder in manner showing that insanity was only feasible defense).

some provocation for the act through the summary of the statement given by the defendant on the day following the killing. When the defendant was interviewed by his court-appointed attorney, the attorney stated that he had reason to doubt the accuracy of the defendant's statement. It was at this time that the attorney's conscience actuated his future conduct which continued throughout the trial. If this was the evidence presented by the prosecution, the defendant was entitled to the faithful and devoted services of his attorney uninhibited by the dictating conscience. The defendant could not be compelled to testify against himself, and if the prosecution saw fit to use the defendant's statement in aid of the prosecution, the attorney was duty bound to exert his best efforts in aid of his client. The failure to argue the case before the jury, while ordinarily only a trial tactic not subject to review, manifestly enters the field of incompetency when the reason assigned is the attorney's conscience. It is as improper as though the attorney had told the jury that his client had uttered a falsehood in making the statment. The right to an attorney embraces effective representation throughout all stages of the trial, and where the representation is of such low caliber as to amount to no representation, the guarantee of due process has been violated. Powell v. State of Alabama, 287 U.S. 45, 53 S.Ct. 55, 77 L.Ed. 158.

The entire trial in the state court had the earmarks of an *ex parte* proceeding. If petitioner had been without the services of an attorney, but had remained mute, it is unlikely that he would have been worse off. The state argues that the defendant may have received a death sentence. Admitting this to be true, it affords no excuse for lack of effective representation.

Holding that the petitioner was not accorded a "fair trial" in the true sense of the word, because of the motivating forces which dictated the actions and decisions of his court-appointed counsel, we turn to the legal problem which has given this court grave concern. It is a general rule of law that a federal court cannot order the release of a state prisoner, grounded upon the lack of effective counsel in the state court proceeding, unless the incompetence and ineffectiveness of the attorney is so obvious that it becomes the duty of the trial judge or prosecutor (both state officers) to intervene and protect the rights of the accused. * * *

If it be necessary to engraft an exception on the general rule, it would appear that one is appropriate here, for indeed it would be a dark day in the history of our judicial system if a conviction is permitted to stand where an attorney, furnished to an indigent defendant, candidly admits that his conscience prevented him from effectively representing his client according to the customary standards prescribed by attorneys and the courts.

Counsel for petitioner will prepare an appropriate order granting the writ of habeas corpus and remanding petitioner to the proper authorities of the State of Virginia for further proceedings on the charge of murder. * * * [d]

## B. CLIENT UNDER DISABILITY

### MODEL RULES OF PROFESSIONAL CONDUCT

**RULE 1.14 Client Under a Disability**

(a) When a client's ability to make adequately considered decisions in connection with the representation is impaired, whether because of minority, mental disability or for some other reason, the lawyer shall, as far as reasonably possible, maintain a normal client-lawyer relationship with the client.

(b) A lawyer may seek the appointment of a guardian or take other protective action with respect to a client, only when the lawyer reasonably believes that the client cannot adequately act in the client's own interest.

COMMENT:

The normal client-lawyer relationship is based on the assumption that the client, when properly advised and assisted, is capable of making decisions about important matters. When the client is a minor or suffers from a mental disorder or disability, however, maintaining the ordinary client-lawyer relationship may not be possible in all respects. In particular, an incapacitated person may have no power to make legally binding decisions. Nevertheless, a client lacking legal competence often has the ability to understand, deliberate upon, and reach conclusions about matters affecting the client's own well-being. Furthermore, to an increasing extent the law recognizes intermediate degrees of competence. For example, children as young as five or six years of age, and certainly those of ten or twelve, are regarded as having opinions that are entitled to weight in legal proceedings concerning their custody. So also, it is recognized that some persons of advanced age can be quite capable of handling routine financial matters while needing special legal protection concerning major transactions.

The fact that a client suffers a disability does not diminish the lawyer's obligation to treat the client with attention and respect. If the person has no guardian or legal representative, the lawyer often must act as de facto guardian. Even if the person does have a legal representative, the lawyer should as far

**d.** See Lessenberry v. Adkisson, 255 Ark. 285, 499 S.W.2d 835 (1973) (lawyer should be allowed to withdraw if "convinced of the defendant's guilt to the extent that he could not properly represent her"); State v. Merchant, 10 Md.App. 545, 271 A.2d 752 (1970) (rape conviction reversed where defense counsel "didn't believe" defendant's account that victim had consented and hence did not raise the defense); Gold, Split Loyalty: An Ethical Problem for the Criminal Defense Lawyer, 14 Clev.-Mar.L.Rev. 65 (1965).

Regarding situations where a defendant claims that counsel was incompetent in acceding to or in not acceding to the defendant's desires to pursue certain strategies or tactics, see infra pp. 496–97.

Regarding discipline of a lawyer for inadequate representation of a criminal defendant, see Holt v. Whelan, 388 Mich. 50, 199 N.W.2d 195 (1972).

Regarding a lawyer's civil malpractice liability to a criminal defendant for inadequate representation, see infra p. 507.

as possible accord the represented person the status of client, particularly in maintaining communication.

If a legal representative has already been appointed for the client, the lawyer should ordinarily look to the representative for decisions on behalf of the client. If a legal representative has not been appointed, the lawyer should see to such an appointment where it would serve the client's best interests. Thus, if a disabled client has substantial property that should be sold for the client's benefit, effective completion of the transaction ordinarily requires appointment of a legal representative. In many circumstances, however, appointment of a legal representative may be expensive or traumatic for the client. Evaluation of these considerations is a matter of professional judgment on the lawyer's part.

If the lawyer represents the guardian as distinct from the ward, and is aware that the guardian is acting adversely to the ward's interest, the lawyer may have an obligation to prevent or rectify the guardian's misconduct. See Rule 1.2(d).

DISCLOSURE OF THE CLIENT'S CONDITION

Rules of procedure in litigation generally provide that minors or persons suffering mental disability shall be represented by a guardian or next friend if they do not have a general guardian. However, disclosure of the client's disability can adversely affect the client's interests. For example, raising the question of disability could, in some circumstances, lead to proceedings for involuntary commitment. The lawyer's position in such cases is an unavoidably difficult one. The lawyer may seek guidance from an appropriate diagnostician.[a]

### *Questions*

(1) Should your ethical duties as a lawyer be different depending upon whether you represent one or another of the following clients:

(a) A mentally ill adult charged in a criminal case, or whose commitment is being sought, or who is suing or is being sued in a civil case?

**a.** Compare the following CPR provisions:

"**EC 7–11** The responsibilities of a lawyer may vary according to the intelligence, experience, mental condition or age of a client, the obligation of a public officer, or the nature of a particular proceeding. Examples include the representation of an illiterate or an incompetent, service as a public prosecutor or other government lawyer, and appearances before administrative and legislative bodies.

"**EC 7–12** Any mental or physical condition of a client that renders him incapable of making a considered judgment on his own behalf casts additional responsibilities upon his lawyer. Where an incompetent is acting through a guardian or other legal representative, a lawyer must look to such representative for those decisions which are normally the prerogative of the client to make. If a client under disability has no legal representative, his lawyer may be compelled in court proceedings to make decisions on behalf of the client. If the client is capable of understanding the matter in question or of contributing to the advancement of his interests, regardless of whether he is legally disqualified from performing certain acts, the lawyer should obtain from him all possible aid. If the disability of a client and the lack of a legal representative compel the lawyer to make decisions for his client, the lawyer should consider all circumstances then prevailing and act with care to safeguard and advance the interests of his client. But obviously a lawyer cannot perform any act or make any decision which the law requires his client to perform or make, either acting for himself if competent, or by a duly constituted representative if legally incompetent."

(b) A juvenile charged in juvenile court with delinquency? Does it make a difference whether the juvenile is 10 or 16 years of age? Or that the parents are absent or hostile? If the parents are present and supportive, who do you represent? To whom do you look for guidance in the case? Do your status and duties change if the case is transferred for adult criminal prosecution?

(c) A child whose custody is in dispute in a divorce or other proceeding? Does the age of the child make a difference?

(d) A child or minor suing or being sued in a civil action?

(2) When is a lawyer under a duty to seek the appointment of a representative for a client who is under disability?

(3) How helpful in finding answers to these quesions are RPC 1.14 or EC 7–11 and 7–12?

## PLATT & FRIEDMAN, THE LIMITS OF ADVOCACY: OCCUPATIONAL HAZARDS IN JUVENILE COURT [a]

116 U.Pa.L.Rev. 1156, 1179 (1968).

Lawyers apply different standards to juvenile clients because they are children, not necessarily because the lawyers have been occupationally constrained to accept the court's welfare policies. A lawyer typically has conscientious reservations about helping a juvenile beat a case [as shown by the following responses of lawyers interviewed]:

> "I am not as careful to avoid disclosure as I am in an adult case. I let the facts out as they are. A child must realize what he did wrong and that he is responsible for the truth."
>
> "If I knew a child was innocent, I would interpose a good rigorous defense. But this has never happened. I have gotten cases where a child was not malicious, or not in the wrong, but never where a child did not participate in the act. I have no objection to having a client put on probation when he did something wrong but was not at fault."
>
> "I tried to impress him with the difference between right and wrong, about church and telling the truth and all that. He denied the charges, but I think he was lying."
>
> "I don't resort to the technical defense that often I know I could raise and perhaps get the child off. My interest is in whether the youngster can be rehabilitated. If he has done something wrong, I point this out to the court. The judges seem to like this approach better." [b]

a. Copyright 1968 by University of Pennsylvania; reprinted with permission.

b. See Heilman, So You're Going to Represent a Juvenile! 6 Pepperdine L.Rev. 783, 792 (1979) ("Face-saving for the juvenile, or letting him think he got away with something * * * is not in the best interests of the juvenile."); Kay & Segal, The Role of the Attorney in Juvenile Court Proceedings: A Non-Polar Approach, 61 Geo.L.J. 1401 (1973) (attorney should take nonadversary approach).

## WELCH, DELINQUENCY PROCEEDINGS—FUNDAMENTAL FAIRNESS FOR THE ACCUSED IN A QUASI-CRIMINAL FORUM

50 Minn.L.Rev. 653, 679–81 (1966).

A further word about the attorney's role in a delinquency hearing seems warranted. Initially he is faced with some difficult ethical and practical problems. Usually he is retained by the child's parents to represent both the child and themselves. This situation has potential difficulties because the interests are separable and possibly conflicting. For example, in the ordinary delinquency case the parents have a legitimate interest in resisting jurisdiction which might result in the court preempting their right of custody. If the child wishes to admit to a petition alleging delinquency, and his attorney has no personal doubts that the allegations are correct, there would be such a conflict. Conflict could also arise where the parents want to retain custody and the child's best interests would be served by placing him in the custody of more responsible adults. An even more extreme case arises when the delinquency alleged is "waywardness," and the attorney becomes convinced that it is really a case of parental neglect. A motion for substitution of a neglect petition against the parents may be the child's only legitimate defense.

In each of these examples shared confidences with either the child or his parents could have occurred before the conflict became apparent. Total withdrawal from the case is the attorney's only way out of this dilemma.

What has been said so far about conflicting interests is premised on the assumption that the child is *entitled* to a status independent of his parents for purposes of the delinquency proceedings. This problem does not exist in criminal prosecutions because resistance is considered the common interest of both parent and juvenile. Nor is there a problem in delinquency cases where parents have originated the petition against their own child. By so doing the parents have waived their parental prerogative of control over the child.

In situations of potential conflict, the parents lose some of their prerogatives to determine the child's best interests while defending against the state's challenge to that prerogative. Parental rights are never so pervasive as to eliminate the child's independent identity in the eyes of the law. Under the fifth and fourteenth amendments the child is entitled to a hearing on the question of delinquency. However, the juvenile does not have those rights if his parents can waive his right to a prima facie showing of delinquency by admitting to the allegations in the petition. Thus the child, or his attorney as guardian ad litem, must make the final decision on matters affecting his constitutional rights to ensure their exercise in the juvenile's best interests.

It is apparent in certain situations an attorney should not represent both the child and his parents. If the parents desire independent representation, the attorney should insist that separate counsel be retained for the child. If he is hired to represent the child, it should be understood that the child's interests alone will guide the course of his representation.

The attorney as guardian ad litem, must decide the scope of his responsibility to make the final decision on matters which affect the child's fundamental rights. When he is convinced that the allegations of delinquency are well-founded and the child needs treatment, should he admit the allegations in the child's behalf even if the juvenile wants to resist? The answer is decidedly "no." In the first place neither the question of delinquency nor the need for treatment is a matter for him to decide. If the allegation is "waywardness," even the juvenile may not know whether he has been delinquent within the statutory definition; this question is for the court. By thus dispensing with the delinquency hearing over his client's objection, the attorney sets himself up as another *parens patriae*—without statutory control.

Secondly, it is quite likely the attorney has become convinced of his client's delinquency partly as a result of confidences which his client has shared with him. The need for a jealously protected attorney-client privilege is as strong in juvenile court as in any other instance. In juvenile court it is especially important that the defendant have complete confidence that his case has been fully presented and that the state's case has been fully tested before any treatment or correction is undertaken.

Finally, the juvenile has a personal right to not lose his freedom on less than a prima facie case. This is the most fundamental element of due process. This right embodies notions of fair play, a guarantee of reliability, and a recognition of the individual's status before the law.[a]

**a.** See Polier, A View From the Bench 55–57 (1964); Isaacs, The Lawyer in the Juvenile Court, 10 Crim.L.Q. 222, 231 (1968); Levin, The Role of the Lawyer in Juvenile Proceedings, 39 Pa.B. Ass'n Q. 427 (1968). Cf. ABA Informal Opinion 1160 (1971) (lawyer should seek full exoneration for juvenile client in most instances).

Lawyers representing mentally ill clients are faced with ethical problems similar to those of lawyers appearing for minors in juvenile court. See Blinick, Mental Disability, Legal Ethics, and Professional Responsibility, 33 Alb.L.Rev. 92 (1968); Gupta, New York's Mental Health Information Service: An Experiment in Due Process, 25 Rutgers L.Rev. 405, 439–41 (1971); Hiday, The Attorney's Role in Involuntary Civil Commitment, 60 N.C.L.Rev. 1027 (1982).

See also Bell v. Wayne County General Hospital, 384 F.Supp. 1085, 1094 (E.D.Mich.1974):

"[W]here an attorney is appointed guardian ad litem, his representation of the prospective patient may be inadequate since in these circumstances he usually sees his role not as defense counsel but as a traditional guardian who determines for himself what is in the best interests of his ward and proceeds on that basis, virtually disregarding the latter's will."

On the ethical problems of defending the mentally ill in criminal cases, see Chernoff & Schaffer, Defending the Mentally Ill: Ethical Quicksand, 10 Am.Crim.L.Rev. 505 (1972), which discusses such problems as whether to assert the defense of insanity and risk confinement of the client, probably without adequate treatment of the illness, for a period much beyond that prescribed for the crime committed; whether to call the court's attention to the client's condition; the extent to which the lawyer should leave to the client decisions which must be left to normal clients; and whether a guilty plea may be entered without the client's consent. The authors conclude: "The proper role of defense counsel in this situation has never been defined—is

### *Problems*

(1) A 17½ year old is charged with armed robbery, for sitting outside and keeping the engine running in a getaway car while a gunman stuck up a store. He claims the gunman threatened to kill him if he did not cooperate, and that the reason he did not drive off while the gunman was in the store was fear. If tried as an adult and convicted, he would get at least five years, as that is the mandatory minimum for robbery. As his lawyer, you have learned that the juvenile court is willing to retain jurisdiction only if your client admits the charge, in which event he would be sent to a juvenile institution until he turns 18. Your client does not want to do this, because he is deathly afraid of going to a juvenile institution, but both his parents are strongly in favor of it because they feel it is certain he would be convicted if tried as an adult. The juvenile court would permit you to admit the petition in your client's behalf. What do you do? [1]

(2) A lawyer's regular client called the lawyer to say his boy was in trouble again. The lawyer said, "Since you have always gone down and gotten the boy out on previous occasions, and since the juvenile court has been lenient on those occasions, your boy has never learned his lesson. If I were you, I would let him sit in jail over the weekend rather than going down to get him out." Was this proper?

(3) May an attorney for a minor properly function also as the minor's guardian ad litem? [2]

he an advocate for his client's desires or is he the legal guardian of his client's interests?"

See also People v. Samuel, 29 Cal.3d 489, 174 Cal.Rptr. 684, 629 P.2d 485 (1981) (counsel representing criminal defendant as to whose competence judge has declared a doubt sufficient to require hearing need not entrust key decisions about fundamental matters to client's apparently defective judgment).

Regarding nondisclosure of a client's mental incapacity, see Goerke v. Vojvodich, 67 Wis.2d 102, 226 N.W.2d 211 (1975) (when vendor seeks rescission of sale of her homestead on grounds of mental incapacity, purchaser cannot get indemnity from lawyer who represented vendor for failing to disclose her mental incapacity unless nondisclosure was for purpose of misleading purchaser).

1. Compare In re M.G.S., 267 Cal.App.2d 329, 72 Cal.Rptr. 808 (1968) (court should not have accepted counsel's admission; juvenile said he could not remember committing robbery); Inst. of Judicial Admin./ABA Joint Comm'n on Juvenile Justice Standards, Standards Relating to Counsel for Private Parties 3.1(b) (ii) (1980) (ordinarily juvenile should decide whether to admit or deny; if juvenile not capable of considered judgment, guardian ad litem should decide; if no guardian ad litem, lawyer should ask that one be appointed; if no appointment, lawyer should inquire thoroughly into all circumstances that careful and competent person in juvenile's position should consider, consult with juvenile and family members or interested persons and either "remain neutral concerning the proceeding, limiting participation to presentation and examination of material evidence or, if necessary * * * adopt the position requiring the least intrusive intervention justified by the juvenile's circumstances"). (Doesn't the latter approach permit the lawyer to forego providing legal services the juvenile needs?)

2. See In re Dobson, 125 Vt. 165, 212 A.2d 620 (1965):

> "An attorney can effectively argue the alternative courses open to a client only to one assumed to be capable of making a discriminating choice. The minor is presumed incapable and under disability, hence, the need of a guardian ad litem to weigh alternatives for him. Yet a lawyer attemping to function as both guardian ad litem and legal counsel is cast in the quandry of acting as both attorney and client, to the detriment of both capacities and the possible jeopardizing of the infant's interests."

Compare In re Westover, 125 Vt. 354, 215 A.2d 498 (1966) (failure to appoint separate guardian does not always require reversal of

# C. PROHIBITION ON COUNSELING OR ASSISTING ILLEGAL CONDUCT

## 1. GENERALLY

### MODEL RULES OF PROFESSIONAL CONDUCT

**RULE 1.2 Scope of Representation**

* * *

(d) A lawyer shall not counsel a client to engage, or assist a client, in conduct that the lawyer knows is criminal or fraudulent, but a lawyer may discuss the legal consequences of any proposed course of conduct with a client and may counsel or assist a client to make a good faith effort to determine the validity, scope, meaning or application of the law.

(e) When a lawyer knows that a client expects assistance not permitted by the rules of professional conduct or other law, the lawyer shall consult with the client regarding the relevant limitations on the lawyer's conduct.

COMMENT:

* * *

A lawyer is required to give an honest opinion about the actual consequences that appear likely to result from a client's conduct. The fact that a client uses advice in a course of action that is criminal or fraudulent does not, of itself, make a lawyer a party to the course of action. However, a lawyer may not knowingly assist a client in criminal or fraudulent conduct. There is a critical distinction between presenting an analysis of legal aspects of questionable conduct and recommending the means by which a crime or fraud might be committed with impunity.[a]

criminal conviction—it depends on whether "the two functions work to the disadvantage and prejudice of a minor," which is an "ever present hazard"). Cf. Gibson v. State, 47 Wis.2d 810, 177 N.W.2d 912 (1970).

**a.** Compare the following CPR provisions

**"EC 7–3** Where the bounds of law are uncertain, the action of a lawyer may depend on whether he is serving as advocate or adviser. A lawyer may serve simultaneously as both advocate and adviser, but the two roles are essentially different. In asserting a position on behalf of his client, an advocate for the most part deals with past conduct and must take the facts as he finds them. By contrast, a lawyer serving as adviser primarily assists his client in determining the course of future conduct and relationships. While serving as advocate, a lawyer should resolve in favor of his client doubts as to the bounds of the law. In serving a client as adviser, a lawyer in appropriate circumstances should give his professional opinion as to what the ultimate decisions of the courts would likely be as to the applicable law."

**"EC 7–6** Whether the proposed action of a lawyer is within the bounds of the law may be a perplexing question when his client is contemplating a course of conduct having legal consequences that vary according to the client's intent, motive, or desires at the time of the action. Often a lawyer is asked to assist his client in developing evidence relevant to the state of mind of the client at a particular time. He may properly assist his client in the development and preservation of evidence of existing motive, intent, or desire; obviously, he may not do anything furthering the creation or preservation of false evidence. In many cases a lawyer may not be certain as to the state of mind of his client, and in those situations he should resolve reasonable doubts in favor of his client."

**"DR 7–102 Representing a Client Within the Bounds of the Law**

"(A) In his representation of a client, a lawyer shall not:

* * *

(2) Knowingly advance a claim or defense that is unwarranted under

### *Questions*

(1) Could a lawyer be disciplined for advising a client who owns a trucking firm that it would be more advantageous to have the firm's drivers speed and pay the fines than to obey the speed limit? Is it relevant that a lawyer could not be disciplined for the lawyer's own speeding violations?

(2) How would you as a lawyer advise your client who owns a trucking firm in a state with a 55 m.p.h. speed limit for vehicles generally and a 45 m.p.h. speed limit for trucks over a certain size, if the client wants to test the validity of the truck speed limit, and you feel there is a reasonable although not overwhelming argument that the truck speed limit violates equal protection or the negative implications of the commerce clause? [1]

(3) Would a lawyer be subject to discipline for approving a client's proposal to disobey an immoral but concededly valid law for the purpose of calling attention to the law's unwisdom so that public reaction would produce its repeal? For answering the client's question on what punishment the client might incur for the violation? [2]

(4) Would a lawyer be subject to discipline for answering a client's question about what countries do not have extradition treaties with the United States? About whether the penalty for armed robbery is greater if an automatic weapon is used? [3]

(5) A client wishes to so arrange her business and property affairs as to avoid paying more than the least possible taxes. To what extent, if any, may you as a lawyer assist her in accomplishing this aim? [4]

existing law, except that he may advance such claim or defense if it can be supported by good faith argument for an extension, modification, or reversal of existing law.

(3) Conceal or knowingly fail to disclose that which he is required by law to reveal.

* * *

(7) Counsel or assist his client in conduct that the lawyer knows to be illegal or fraudulent."

1. Compare ABA Standards for Criminal Justice 4–3.7(c) (2d ed. 1980), which states:

"It is unprofessional conduct for a lawyer to agree in advance of the commission of a crime that the lawyer will serve as counsel for the defendant, except as part of a bona fide effort to determine the validity, scope, meaning or application of the law, or where the defense is incident to a general retainer for legal services to a person or enterprise engaged in legitimate activity."

See also ABA Formal Opinion 281 (1952) (improper to accept retainer from organization known to be unlawful and agree in advance to defend its members when from time to time they are accused of crime arising out of its unlawful activities).

2. See Cowen, The Lawyer's Role in Civil Disobedience, 47 N.C.L.Rev. 587, 592–93 (1969).

3. See M. Freedman, Lawyers' Ethics in an Adversary System 59–61 (1975).

4. See B. Bittker, Professional Responsibility in Federal Tax Practice (1970); B. Wolfman & J. Holden, Ethical Problems in Federal Tax Practice (1981); Darrell, The Tax Practitioner's Duty to His Client and His Government, 7 Prac. Law. 23 (Mar. 1961); Paul, The Lawyer as a Tax Adviser, 25 Rocky Mt.L.Rev. 412 (1953); Sellin, Professional Responsibility of the Tax Practitioner, 52 Taxes 584 (1974); Walters, Ethical and Professional Responsibilities of Tax Practitioners, 17 Gonzaga L.Rev. 23 (1981); Young, Tax Ethics: Some Practical Dilemmas, 12 Prac.Law. 15 (May 1966). Cf. ABA Formal Opinion 346 (1982) (ethical standards for lawyers who issue tax shelter opinions).

Regarding a lawyer's duties as to evidence of crime, see supra pp. 118–27.

## 2. PERJURY

### MODEL RULES OF PROFESSIONAL CONDUCT

**RULE 3.3 Candor Toward the Tribunal**

(a) A lawyer shall not knowingly:

(1) make a false statement of material fact or law to a tribunal;

(2) fail to disclose a material fact to a tribunal when disclosure is necessary to avoid assisting a criminal or fraudulent act by the client;

* * *

(4) offer evidence that the lawyer knows to be false. If a lawyer has offered material evidence and comes to know of its falsity, the lawyer shall take reasonable remedial measures.

(b) The duties stated in paragraph (a) continue to the conclusion of the proceeding, and apply even if compliance requires disclosure of information otherwise protected by rule 1.6.

(c) A lawyer may refuse to offer evidence that the lawyer reasonably believes is false.

* * *

COMMENT:

* * *

FALSE EVIDENCE

When evidence that a lawyer knows to be false is provided by a person who is not the client, the lawyer must refuse to offer it regardless of the client's wishes.

When false evidence is offered by the client, however, a conflict may arise between the lawyer's duty to keep the client's revelations confidential and the duty of candor to the court. Upon ascertaining that material evidence is false, the lawyer should seek to persuade the client that the evidence should not be offered or, if it has been offered, that its false character should immediately be disclosed. If the persuasion is ineffective, the lawyer must take reasonable remedial measures.

Except in the defense of a criminal accused, the rule generally recognized is that, if necessary to rectify the situation, an advocate must disclose the existence of the client's deception to the court or to the other party. Such a disclosure can result in grave consequences to the client, including not only a sense of betrayal but also loss of the case and perhaps a prosecution for perjury. But the alternative is that the lawyer cooperate in deceiving the court, thereby subverting the truth-finding process which the adversary system is designed to implement. See Rule 1.2(d). Furthermore, unless it is clearly understood that the lawyer will act upon the duty to disclose the existence of false evidence, the client can simply reject the lawyer's advice to reveal the false evidence and insist that the lawyer keep silent. Thus the client could in effect coerce the lawyer into being a party to fraud on the court.

PERJURY BY A CRIMINAL DEFENDANT

Whether an advocate for a criminally accused has the same duty of disclosure has been intensely debated. While it is agreed that the lawyer should seek to persuade the client to refrain from perjurious testimony, there has been dispute concerning the lawyer's duty when that persuasion fails. If the confrontation with the client occurs before trial, the lawyer ordinarily can withdraw. Withdrawal before trial may not be possible, however, either because trial is imminent, or because the confrontation with the client does not take place until the trial itself, or because no other counsel is available.

The most difficult situation, therefore, arises in a criminal case where the accused insists on testifying when the lawyer knows that the testimony is perjurious. The lawyer's effort to rectify the situation can increase the likelihood of the client's being convicted as well as opening the possibility of a prosecution for perjury. On the other hand, if the lawyer does not exercise control over the proof, the lawyer participates, although in a merely passive way, in deception of the court.

Three resolutions of this dilemma have been proposed. One is to permit the accused to testify by a narrative without guidance through the lawyer's questioning. This compromises both contending principles; it exempts the lawyer from the duty to disclose false evidence but subjects the client to an implicit disclosure of information imparted to counsel. Another suggested resolution, of relatively recent origin, is that the advocate be entirely excused from the duty to reveal perjury if the perjury is that of the client. This is a coherent solution but makes the advocate a knowing instrument of perjury.

The other resolution of the dilemma is that the lawyer must reveal the client's perjury if necessary to rectify the situation. A criminal accused has a right to the assistance of an advocate, a right to testify and a right of confidential communication with counsel. However, an accused should not have a right to assistance of counsel in committing perjury. Furthermore, an advocate has an obligation, not only in professional ethics but under the law as well, to avoid implication in the commission of perjury or other falsification of evidence. See Rule 1.2(d).

### Remedial Measures

If perjured testimony or false evidence has been offered, the advocate's proper course ordinarily is to remonstrate with the client confidentially. If that fails, the advocate should seek to withdraw if that will remedy the situation. If withdrawal will not remedy the situation or is impossible, the advocate should make disclosure to the court. It is for the court then to determine what should be done—making a statement about the matter to the trier of fact, ordering a mistrial or perhaps nothing. If the false testimony was that of the client, the client may controvert the lawyer's version of their communication when the lawyer discloses the situation to the court. If there is an issue whether the client has committed perjury, the lawyer cannot represent the client in resolution of the issue, and a mistrial may be unavoidable. An unscrupulous client might in this way attempt to produce a series of mistrials and thus escape prosecution. However, a second such encounter could be construed as a deliberate abuse of the right to counsel and as such a waiver of the right to further representation.

### Constitutional Requirements

The general rule—that an advocate must disclose the existence of perjury with respect to a material fact, even that of a client—applies to defense counsel in criminal cases, as well as in other instances. However, the definition of the lawyer's ethical duty in such a situation may be qualified by constitutional provisions for due process and the right to counsel in criminal cases. In some jurisdictions these provisions have been construed to require that counsel present an accused as a witness if the accused wishes to testify, even if counsel knows the testimony will be false. The obligation of the advocate under these Rules is subordinate to such a constitutional requirement. * * *

REFUSING TO OFFER PROOF BELIEVED TO BE FALSE

Generally speaking, a lawyer has authority to refuse to offer testimony or other proof that the lawyer believes is untrustworthy. Offering such proof may reflect adversely on the lawyer's ability to discriminate in the quality of evidence and thus impair the lawyer's effectiveness as an advocate. In criminal cases, however, a lawyer may, in some jurisdictions, be denied this authority by constitutional requirements governing the right to counsel.

### RULE 3.4 Fairness to Opposing Party and Counsel

A lawyer shall not:

* * *

(b) falsify evidence, counsel or assist a witness to testify falsely, or offer an inducement to a witness that is prohibited by law * * *.[a]

## PEOPLE v. SCHULTHEIS

638 P.2d 8 (Colo. 1981).

ERICKSON, Justice.

We granted certiorari to review People v. Schultheis, Colo.App., 618 P.2d 710 (1980), which held that defense counsel has an affirmative duty to withdraw when an accused demands that defense counsel call

a. Compare the following CPR provisions:

"**EC 7-26** The law and Disciplinary Rules prohibit the use of fradulent, false, or perjured testimony or evidence. A lawyer who knowingly participates in introduction of such testimony or evidence is subject to discipline. A lawyer should, however, present any admissible evidence his client desires to have presented unless he knows, or from facts within his knowledge should know, that such testimony or evidence is false, fraudulent, or perjured.

"**DR 7-102 Representing a Client Within the Bounds of the Law**

"(A) In his representation of a client, a lawyer shall not:

* * *

(4) Knowingly use perjured testimony or false evidence.

(5) Knowingly make a false statement of law or fact.

(6) Participate in the creation or preservation of evidence when he knows or it is obvious that the evidence is false.

(7) Counsel or assist his client in conduct that the lawyer knows to be illegal or fraudulent.

(8) Knowingly engage in other illegal conduct or conduct contrary to a Disciplinary Rule.

"(B) A lawyer who receives information clearly establishing that:

(1) His client has, in the course of the representation, perpetrated a fraud upon a person or tribunal shall promptly call upon his client to rectify the same, and if his client refuses or is unable to do so, he shall reveal the fraud to the affected person or tribunal, except when the information is protected as a privileged communication.

(2) A person other than his client has perpetrated a fraud upon a tribunal shall promptly reveal the fraud to the tribunal."

witnesses to present perjured alibi testimony. The court of appeals also held that, under such circumstances, the trial court must grant defense counsel's motion to withdraw. We reverse and remand to the court of appeals with directions to affirm the defendant's conviction for first-degree murder.

While incarcerated at the Denver County Jail, Glen O. Schultheis was charged with murder and sexual assault of one of his fellow inmates. The victim, Joseph C. Dodrill, was dubbed a "snitch" by other inmates. Schultheis agreed to kill Dodrill for $75. However, he waived the fee with the understanding that he would "have some fun" with the victim before he killed him. A plan was made to lead Dodrill back to his cell with Schultheis shortly before 7:00 p. m. on June 10, 1977, when jail cells were automatically locked for approximately two hours. During that time, Dodrill was strangled, his throat was cut, and he was stabbed repeatedly in the head and back. The words "Life is really a trip you know" were carved on the victim's back and buttocks. The body was discovered with a homemade knife implanted in the victim's back. Schultheis subsequently described the grisly homicide to several inmates, and said that he had sodomized Dodrill before he killed him. Some of the inmates saw Schultheis in the cell with Dodrill shortly after 7:00 p. m. Apart from the physical evidence, a number of inmates, after being granted immunity, testified as to the agreement made by Schultheis to kill Dodrill and as to the events which occurred after Schultheis and Dodrill were locked in the same cell together.

The defendant initially tendered a plea of not guilty by reason of insanity. He was then examined by two court-appointed psychiatrists, and admitted his culpability to both. When both psychiatrists reported that Schultheis was sane, the initial plea was withdrawn and Schultheis entered a plea of not guilty.

On the morning of trial, Schultheis * * * asked for a continuance, and announced that he would not proceed to trial because his defense counsel was inadequate and unprepared. He asserted that his lawyer refused to subpoena two alibi witnesses who would testify that he was not in the cell with Dodrill at the time of the homicide. After some discussion, court-appointed defense counsel stated that he "refused to affirmatively put on evidence that [he knew] was fabricated." Counsel then asked to make a record outside the presence of the prosecutor and the trial judge, and moved to withdraw from the case on the grounds of irreconcilable differences. The court granted counsel the right to make a record, but denied the motions for continuance and for withdrawal.

Schultheis and his counsel made a record out of the presence of the trial judge and the prosecutor to establish the basis of their disagreement. The record showed that, two days before trial, the defendant asked his counsel to call certain witnesses from the Denver County Jail to testify in his behalf. Counsel refused, declaring that he would not call the prisoners as witnesses because he "knew their testimony would be fabricated" and that, as a lawyer, he had an ethical duty to refrain from presenting perjured testimony. Defense counsel, according to the record, knew that the witnesses would lie because of his own conversations with Schultheis and because of a prior conversation Schultheis had with one of the examining psychiatrists.[2]

After defense counsel made his record, he proceeded to represent Schultheis at the trial. The two alibi witnesses were not called to testify, and Schultheis was convicted of first-degree murder.

Schultheis appealed to the court of appeals, which reversed his conviction. The court of appeals held that a lawyer has an affirmative duty to withdraw from a case in which his client is intent upon presenting perjured witness testimony, and, under such circumstance, the court must grant the lawyer's motion to withdraw. The court of appeals also held that a lawyer who withdraws from such a situation may not state the factual basis for the motion to withdraw. In its view, if counsel knows that his continued employment will result in a disciplinary violation, he must refer to the specific provisions of the Code of Professional Responsibility that prohibit a lawyer from using perjured testimony or false evidence. We granted certiorari, and for the reasons set forth in this opinion, we reverse the court of appeals.

I.

We first address the court of appeals' holding that a lawyer has an affirmative duty to withdraw from a case when his client insists upon presenting perjured testimony through alibi witnesses. In reaching its decision, the court of appeals concluded that Schultheis was denied effective assistance of counsel because his lawyer acted as an *amicus curiae* rather than as an active advocate. See generally, Anders v. California, 386 U.S. 738, 87 S.Ct. 1396, 18 L.Ed.2d 493 (1967). We disagree and conclude that, in this instance, the concepts of professional ethics and effective representation of a client are not inconsistent.[3]

A.

The American adversary system of criminal justice is not inquisitorial, but accusatorial. It consists of the presentation of evidence to the judge or jury by trained advocates, according to established rules, so that conflicting factual issues may be resolved to arrive at the truth. The integrity of the adversary system can be maintained only if both prosecution and defense counsel present reliable evidence

2. The defendant described to one of the examining psychiatrists, in great detail, how he had killed the victim. This description was contained in the psychiatrist's report to the court.

3. At this juncture, we must distinguish this case from one where the accused client insists upon testifying in his own defense and makes known to counsel his intent to commit perjury. See Erickson, The Prejurious Defendant: A Proposed Solution to the Defense Lawyer's Conflicting Ethical Obligations to the Court and to His Client, 59 Den.L.J. 75 (1981).

to guide the trier of fact. Honesty and candor are essential to the fair and impartial administration of justice. Consequently, a lawyer has a professional duty not to perpetrate a fraud upon the court by knowingly presenting perjured testimony or other false evidence. See DR 7–102(A)(4), EC 7–26; ABA, Standards Relating to the Defense Function § 4–7.5(a) (2d ed. 1980) (hereinafter cited as ABA Defense Standards). It is unprofessional conduct for a lawyer, while representing a client, to perpetrate or aid in the perpetration of a crime or a dishonest act. See DR 7–102(A)(7), (8). A lawyer who presents a witness knowing that the witness intends to commit perjury thereby engages in the subornation of perjury. We will not permit the truth-finding process to be deflected by the presentation of false evidence by an officer of the court. Therefore, we hold that a lawyer may not offer testimony of a witness which he knows is false, fraudulent, or perjured.

A lawyer's belief that a witness intends to offer false testimony, however, must be based upon an independent investigation of the evidence or upon distinct statements by his client or the witness which support that belief. A mere inconsistency in the client's story is insufficient in and of itself to support the conclusion that a witness will offer false testimony. In this case, the record shows a substantial basis for defense counsel's knowledge that the alibi witnesses would present perjured testimony. The reports of the examining psychiatrists and the defendant's own conversations with his lawyer are inconsistent with the allegation that defense counsel was usurping the province of the jury by judging the credibility of the proposed alibi witnesses. Accordingly, counsel was correct in refusing to call the witnesses which the defendant located to support his spurious defense of alibi.

B.

The court of appeals concluded that defense counsel departed from his role as an advocate and became an *amicus curiae* by continuing to represent Schultheis in light of their disagreement over calling the alibi witnesses. In its view, the continued representation deprived the defendant of the effective assistance of counsel guaranteed by the United States and Colorado Constitutions. The weight of authority does not support such a conclusion. Defense counsel is not the alter ego or mouthpiece of the accused, but is a trained advocate charged with representing an accused within the parameters of the Code of Professional Responsibility and according to his obligations and duties as an officer of the court. ABA Defense Standards § 4–1.1, Commentary at 4.9; Johnson v. United States, 360 F.2d 844 (D.C.Cir.1966) (Burger, J. concurring). It is the function of defense counsel, and not the defendant, to determine what witnesses will be called to support the defense case:

> "The decisions on what witnesses to call, whether and how to conduct cross-examination, what jurors to accept or strike, what trial

motions should be made, and all other strategic and tactical decisions are the exclusive province of the lawyer after consultation with the client." ABA Defense Standards § 4–5.2(b). See also, ABA Defense Standards § 4–3.1(b).

The defendant, therefore, could not compel his counsel to call witnesses to present a fabricated alibi.[6] When defense counsel makes an informed and intelligent decision as to the witnesses who are to be called, it is not error that the decision was based on ethical considerations.

A refusal to call a particular witness because of an obedience to ethical standards which prohibit the presentation of fabricated testimony does not constitute ineffective assistance of counsel. See, e.g., Martinez v. People, supra, quoting United States v. Gutterman, 147 F.2d 540 (2d Cir. 1945). The defendant's constitutional right to the effective assistance of counsel does not include the right to require his lawyer to perpetrate a fraud on the court. While a lawyer must protect and defend the interests of his client with all his skill and energy, he must always comply with his ethical obligations to the court. State v. Henderson, 205 Kan. 231, 468 P.2d 136 (1970). The high ethical standards required of defense counsel are not inconsistent with the zealous representation which is guaranteed an accused. Instead, they are designed to exemplify the truth-finding goal of our legal system. Unless trial counsel is deficient in the competent and professional representation of the accused, no constitutional infirmity exists.

An examination of the record in this case reveals no such deficiency. Defense counsel competently and zealously defended Schultheis despite the accusations of inadequacy and lack of preparation which the defendant made against his appointed counsel. We therefore conclude that the defendant was not deprived of his constitutional right to the effective assistance of counsel.

C.

Contrary to the court of appeals' decision, the foregoing analysis does not contemplate that a lawyer has an affirmative duty to withdraw from a case whenever his client desires to present perjured testimony through alibi witnesses. Regardless of the client's wishes, defense counsel must refuse to present the testimony of a witness that he knows

6. See State v. Robinson, 290 N.C. 56, 224 S.E.2d 174 (1976). According to ABA Defense Standards § 4–5.2(a), the accused has the exclusive right to make three decisions regarding the conduct of his case:

"(a) Certain decisions relating to the conduct of the case are ultimately for the accused and others are ultimately for defense counsel. The decisions which are to be made by the accused after full consultation with counsel are:

(i) what plea to enter;

(ii) whether to waive jury trial; and

(iii) whether to testify in his or her own behalf."

[Eds.] Accord, RPC 1.2(a). Compare EC 7–7 (client to make decisions affecting merits of the cause or substantially affecting client's rights, e.g., what plea to enter and whether to appeal). See generally infra pp. 483–97.

is fabricated, and his continued role as defense counsel does not result in an ethical violation. When a serious disagreement arises between defense counsel and the accused, and counsel is unable to dissuade his client from insisting that fabricated testimony be presented by a witness, counsel should request permission to withdraw from the case in accordance with the procedures set forth in part II of this opinion.[7] If the motion to withdraw is denied, however, he must continue to serve as defense counsel. So long as counsel performs competently as an advocate, the accused is represented effectively and the integrity of the adversary system of justice is not compromised.

II.

The court of appeals concluded that, in order to protect the confidentiality of privileged communications between defendant and counsel, a lawyer who seeks to withdraw from a case in which his client demands to present perjured testimony by a witness may not state the factual basis for the withdrawal. Instead, the court of appeals directed the lawyer to refer to the specific provisions of the Code of Professional Responsibility that prohibit the use of perjured testimony or false evidence,[8] and held that the trial court must grant the lawyer's motion to withdraw.

We disagree with the court of appeals and conclude that, when the accused insists that counsel present fabricated testimony of a witness, counsel should not reveal to the trial judge the specific reasons for his motion to withdraw. In our view, the court of appeals also erred by imposing the requirement that the trial court grant a motion to withdraw; such a rule provides no safeguards against the wholesale manipulation of the judicial system by an unscrupulous defendant.

A.

In part I of this opinion, we addressed the duties of defense counsel when he is unable to dissuade his client from insisting that fabricated testimony of a witness be presented. Even when counsel makes a motion to withdraw, however, the defendant is always entitled to an impartial trial judge, untainted by accusations that the defendant had insisted upon presenting fabricated testimony. Therefore, we hold that defense counsel, in a motion to withdraw, should never be required to cite the specific provisions of the Code of Professional Responsibility which prohibit the use of perjured testimony or false evidence. The

7. This procedure is consistent with DR 2–110(C)(1)(c) which provides that a lawyer may request permission to withdraw when his client "insists that the lawyer pursue a course of conduct that is illegal or that is prohibited under the Disciplinary Rules."

[Eds.] See RPC 1.16(b)(1) (unless court orders lawyer to continue representation, lawyer may withdraw if client persists in course of action involving lawyer's service that lawyer reasonably believes is criminal or fraudulent).

8. In this case, the court of appeals did not specify which rules would have been correct to cite. However, DR 7–102(A)(4) and DR 4–101 seem most appropriate to this situation.

court of appeals' rule is tantamount to a full disclosure to the court, since citing specific ethical provisions enables the court to determine that the factual basis for the motion to withdraw is the defendant's intention to present false alibi testimony. We do not approve of such a rule. Defense counsel should not, in any way, be required to divulge a privileged communication to the trial court during trial. See DR 4–101.

When confronted with a client who insists upon presenting perjured testimony as to an alibi, counsel may only state, in the motion to withdraw, that he has an irreconcilable conflict with his client. An "irreconcilable conflict" may mean a conflict of interest, a conflict of personality, a conflict as to trial strategy, or a conflict regarding the presentation of false evidence. The integrity of the trial proceedings is thereby preserved.

Any disagreement between counsel and the accused on a decision to be made before or during trial, however, may be the subject of postconviction proceedings questioning the effectiveness of the lawyer's performance. It is not sufficient to determine the matter solely on the strength of the memories of the lawyer and client, which are invariably in conflict if the issue arises. Therefore, although no record of disagreement is required for the trial judge, counsel should proceed with a request for a record out of the presence of the trial judge and the prosecutor if the court denies the motion to withdraw:

> "If a disagreement on significant matters of tactics or strategy arises between the lawyer and the client, the lawyer should make a record of the circumstances, the lawyer's advice and reasons, and the conclusion reached. The record should be made in a manner which protects the confidentiality of the lawyer-client relationship." ABA Defense Function Standards § 4–5.2(c).

Appellate review of the private record [is] adequate * * * to protect the accused against counsel's unwarranted judgment that the proposed testimony by a witness is false.

In this case, we recognize that counsel, by wrongfully disclosing to the trial court the nature of his disagreement with Schultheis, did not follow the procedure which we recommend. We do not endorse counsel's comments to the trial court. In the discourse between the trial judge, defense counsel, and Schultheis, counsel was at first vague in describing his refusal to call the witnesses requested by the defendant. It was only after counsel requested the defendant's permission to reveal to the court the basis of his decision not to call the alibi witnesses that he stated his refusal to put on evidence he knew was fabricated. Counsel thereafter sought and received permission to make a private record to reveal the specific factual basis underlying the disagreement. The entire discourse was out of the presence of the jury. Although counsel is generally not permitted to disclose information imparted to him by the client or acquired during the professional relationship, we do not believe that, under the circumstances, there was a breach of the attorney-client privilege. Further, as discussed in part I of this opinion, counsel's conduct did not deprive the defendant of the effective assistance of counsel.

B.

The court of appeals also erred in requiring the trial court to grant a lawyer's motion to withdraw when counsel and the defendant disagree over the presentation of alibi testimony. Such a conclusion is replete with dire practical consequences. A mandatory withdrawal before trial may not be possible because the confrontation with the client does not occur until the time of trial, or because other counsel cannot be obtained without continuing the trial date. In addition, if each successive lawyer was faced with an ethical disagreement with the accused, mandatory withdrawal would always allow the defendant an unlimited number of continuances. This situation could ultimately result in a perpetual cycle of eleventh-hour motions to withdraw.[9] If the trial court was required to grant every motion to withdraw, new counsel might fail to recognize the problem of fabricated testimony by alibi witnesses, and false evidence would be presented to the court. Or, counsel may view his ethical obligation as requiring neither a withdrawal nor any indication that the problem of potential false evidence exists. We cannot sanction either result, for in both cases, fraud is committed upon the court.

A decision as to whether counsel should be permitted to withdraw must lie within the sound discretion of the trial judge. As long as the trial court has a reasonable basis for believing that the lawyer-client relation has not deteriorated to the point where counsel is unable to give effective aid in the fair presentation of a defense, the court is justified in refusing to appoint new counsel. State v. Henderson, supra; People v. Williams, 2 Cal.3d 894, 471 P.2d 1008, 88 Cal.Rptr. 208 (1970). Therefore, a disagreement between defense counsel and the accused concerning counsel's refusal to call certain witnesses is not sufficient to require the trial judge to grant the motion to withdraw and replace defense counsel. See State v. Robinson, 290 N.C. 56, 224 S.E.2d 174 (1976); People v. Williams, supra. Under the circumstances, the denial of the motion to withdraw did not deprive the accused of the effective assistance of counsel. People v. Durham, 70 Cal.2d 171, 449 P.2d 198, 74 Cal.Rptr. 262 (1969).

In making the decision whether to grant counsel permission to withdraw, the trial court must balance the need for the orderly administration of justice with the fact that an irreconcilable conflict exists between counsel and the accused. In doing so, the court must consider the timing of the motion, the inconvenience to witnesses, the period of time elapsed between the date of the alleged offense and trial, and

9. The trial judge recognized these practical problems and stated, in denying defense counsel's motion to withdraw, that no matter who else he could have appointed, the same predicament would occur in the future.

the possibility that any new counsel will be confronted with the same irreconcilable conflict. The decision of the trial court to deny a motion to withdraw will not be disturbed absent a clear abuse of discretion.

The primary responsibility of the court is the orderly administration of justice. Under the circumstances in this case, the trial court did not abuse its discretion by requiring counsel to remain as the defendant's advocate.

Accordingly, we reverse the judgment of the court of appeals, and remand to the court of appeals with directions to affirm the defendant's conviction for first-degree murder.[a]

### *Comment*

(1) *Refusal to call witness other than criminal defendant.* Other courts agree that counsel should refuse to call a witness (other than the defendant in a criminal case[1]) who counsel knows will commit perjury, and that such a refusal does not violate a criminal defendant's constitutional right to competent counsel.[2]

(2) *Revealing client's desire to call perjurious witness.* The *Schultheis* court's ruling that counsel seeking to withdraw should not apprise the court of the client's desire to call a perjurious witness seems correct under both the CPR and the RPC:

(a) DR 4–101(C)(3) permits revelation of the client's intent to commit a crime and the information necessary to prevent the crime, but if withdrawal is denied the client will not be able to commit the crime of suborning perjury because the lawyer will refuse to call the perjurious witness. Only if the court grants withdrawal would DR 4–101(C)(3) *permit* the lawyer to reveal the client's desire to call a perjurious witness because only then would the client be able to commit the crime of suborning perjury.

(b) Nor would revelation be allowed under the Rules of Professional Conduct. RPC 1.6(b)(1) only permits revelation regarding

**a.** Compare State v. Robinson, 290 N.C. 56, 224 S.E.2d 174 (1976); State v. Trapp, 52 Ohio App.2d 189, 368 N.E.2d 1278 (1977). In each case, counsel moved to withdraw because accused desired to call perjurious witness(es) and to testify perjuriously himself, and the trial court denied withdrawal but relieved counsel of the responsibility to question the perjurious witness(es) and to assist accused in testifying (if accused chose to take the stand). In *Robinson,* the court held that it denied due process for the trial court to do this *without giving accused the option of proceeding without counsel.* In *Trapp,* the court held that absent a competent waiver of counsel, it violated the accused's constitutional right to counsel to leave a significant portion of the defense to be carried out by the accused without the assistance of counsel.

**1.** Regarding perjurious criminal defendants, see the next principal case and Comments following it infra.

**2.** See Cornell v. Maryland, 396 F.Supp. 1092 (D.Md.1975); In re Branch, 70 Cal.2d 200, 74 Cal.Rptr. 238, 449 P.2d 174 (1969) ("an attorney who attempts to benefit his client through the use of perjured testimony may be subject to criminal prosecution as well as severe disciplinary action"); Herbert v. United States, 340 A.2d 802 (D.C.App.1975); State v. Lloyd, 48 Md.App. 535, 429 A.2d 244 (1981); Smothers v. State, 614 S.W.2d 20 (Mo.App.1981).

Regarding discipline for allowing perjured testimony by a witness (including one's client in a civil case), see Committee on Professional Ethics v. Crary, 245 N.W.2d 298 (Iowa 1976); Annot., 40 A.L.R.3d 169, 179–80 (1971).

a crime likely to result in imminent death or substantial bodily harm. RPC 3.3(a)(4) requires the lawyer to take "reasonable remedial measures" (which the Comment says can include revelation of the existence of perjury) only when the lawyer *"has offered"* evidence and has come to know of its falsity.

### PEOPLE v. SALQUERRO

107 Misc.2d 155, 433 N.Y.S.2d 711 (1980).

PATRICK W. McGINLEY, Judge:

Defense counsel, appointed to represent the defendant, moves to withdraw from further representation of the defendant and to recuse the trial judge.

Defendant Salquerro was indicted on February 5, 1980 for attempted murder and robbery. He stands accused of beating the victim with a blunt instrument and of stabbing him with an ice pick during the commission of the robbery. * * * On October 6, 1980, the day before trial was to commence, defense counsel spoke with his client concerning his anticipated defense. During this discussion, the defendant unequivocally informed counsel that he intended to lie when he testified in his own behalf. Upon learning of his client's intention, counsel immediately informed both the court and the assistant district attorney. Neither the nature nor substance of any anticipated false testimony was communicated to the court.

In a letter submitted October 8, 1980, defense counsel expressed concern over his decision to reveal his client's perjurious intention. Counsel's motion to withdraw was prompted by this disclosure which he feels may have "destroyed totally the necessary confidence that a client must have in his attorney in order to receive the effective assistance of counsel which the Sixth Amendment guarantees."

The question of defense counsel's obligation when his client informs him that he is going to commit perjury is a troublesome one. However, there can never be a real conflict between the attorney's obligation to provide a zealous defense and his moral duties to himself and the court.

The starting point in our examination of the issues raised herein is the * * * Code of Professional Responsibility * * *. No definitive rule is provided by the Code. However, Disciplinary Rule (DR) 7–102(A)(4) states that "In his representation of a client, a lawyer shall not: * * * Knowingly use perjured testimony or false evidence." An attorney who does use such testimony is subject to disciplinary sanctions.

In addition, DR 7–102(B)(1) states that:

> "A lawyer who receives information clearly establishing that: His client has, in the course of the representation, perpetrated a fraud upon a person or tribunal shall promptly call upon his client to rectify the same, and if his client refuses or is unable to do so,

he shall reveal the fraud to the affected person or tribunal, except when the information is protected as a [confidence or secret]."

"Fraud on the court * * * can be characterized as a scheme to interfere with the judicial machinery performing the task of impartial adjudication * * * A finding of fraud on the court is justified only by the most egregious misconduct directed to the court itself, such as * * * fabrication of evidence by counsel * * *" (Pfizer v. International Rectifier Corp., 538 F.2d 180 [8th Cir. 1976]). An attorney who knowingly presents perjured testimony is practicing a fraud on the tribunal (Norman Lefstein, The Criminal Defendant who Proposes Perjury: Rethinking the Defense Lawyer's Dilemma, 6 Hofstra L.Rev. 665 [1978]).

Implicit in counsel's dilemma is the concern that he may have violated Canon 4's duty to preserve the confidences and secrets of his client. However, the information revealed herein by counsel was not a protected "confidence or secret," since according to DR 4–101(C)(3), "a lawyer may reveal: * * * The intention of his client to commit a crime and the information necessary to prevent the crime." Clearly, defense counsel did not violate Canon 4 because he revealed his client's intention to commit the crime of perjury.

Counsel, in the first instance evidently did not seek to dissuade his client from going through with his stated intention to commit perjury. However, it cannot be assumed that counsel will not attempt to dissuade the defendant from committing perjury between now and the date of trial. In any event, counsel's decision to inform the court of the defendant's plan was highly laudable and in conformity with standards announced by bar associations, courts of sister states, and commentators.[1]

The question of whether or not to grant a criminal defense attorney's motion to withdraw in this situation is not without difficulty. * * * In this case, if the attorney is permitted to withdraw, the problem of the anticipated perjury and resultant fraud upon the court will not be resolved.

If the motions to withdraw and recuse are granted, substitution of court and counsel, unaware of the possibility of perjury, may overtly facilitate, or appear to condone, a fraud upon the court. Such substitution procedures would effectively cloak the problem; however, this ostrich-like approach would do little to resolve it.

1. See the American Bar Association Committee on Ethics and Professional Responsibility, Informal Opinion No. 1314 (March 25, 1975); comment to [January 30, 1980 Discussion Draft of RPC 3.3]; Carter v. Bordenkircher, W.Va., 226 S.E.2d 711 (1976); Thornton v. United States, 357 A.2d 429 (D.C.App.1976); State v. Henderson, 205 Kan. 231, 468 P.2d 136 (1970); Charles W. Wolfram, Client Perjury, 50 So.Cal.L.Rev. 809 (1976–77). However, see Monroe Freedman, Professional Responsibility of the Criminal Defense Lawyer: The Three Hardest Questions, 64 Mich.L.Rev. 1469 (1966). Professor Freedman, in a much criticized article, proposes that the defense attorney in a criminal case refrain from revealing his client's intention to commit perjury.

A defendant inclined to commit perjury may find another attorney who lacks the ethical standards possessed by his present attorney, and who may readily present his client's falsified story, or who at the very least would not impede its telling. Such a defendant may even be less candid with a new attorney and keep his perjurious intentions to himself. Alternatively, bolstered by the success of his first disclosure in postponing trial, such defendant might be equally frank with a new attorney, in order to further delay the proceedings.

If the motion to withdraw is denied, certain problems remain for the attorney, i.e., how to prevent the perjury and still preserve the defendant's right to take the witness stand in his own defense. These problems are manageable, however; they relate to trial practice and may be addressed as any other procedure or evidentiary matter at the appropriate time.

If at trial there remains a chance of perjured testimony, formulas have been proposed which preserve the sanctity of the tribunal and the ethical standards that counsel, as an officer of the court, has vowed to uphold. Under such a formula, the responsibility for committing or not committing a fraud on the tribunal lies with the defendant, and not with his attorney, and the jury, as the ultimate trier of fact, will decide the issue of whether the defendant's testimony is credible.

One possible solution involves a two-step process: First, as this counsel has done, the attorney should inform the court of the client's intention to commit perjury, as suggested by Informal Opinion 1314. In the second step, the attorney may follow the procedure set out in section 7.7(c) of the American Bar Association Project on Standards for Criminal Justice: The Defense Function (1971).[a] This section states:

> "If withdrawal from the case is not feasible or is not permitted by the court, or if the situation arises during the trial and the defendant insists upon testifying falsely in his own behalf, it is unprofessional conduct for the lawyer to lend his aid to the perjury or use the perjured testimony. Before the defendant takes the stand in these circumstances, the lawyer should make a record of the fact that the defendant is taking the stand against the advice of counsel in some appropriate manner without revealing the fact to the court. The lawyer must confine his examination to iden-

a. ABA Standards, The Defense Function 7.7(a) and (b) (1971) state:

"(a) If the defendant has admitted to his lawyer facts which establish guilt and the lawyer's independent investigation establishes that the admissions are true but the defendant insists on his right to trial, the lawyer must advise his client against taking the witness stand to testify falsely.

"(b) If, before trial, the defendant insists that he will take the stand to testify falsely, the lawyer must withdraw from the case, if that is feasible, seeking leave of the court if necessary."

Defense Function Standard 7.7 was not included in the 1980 Second Edition of the ABA Standards for Criminal Justice. The Editorial Note explains that "the question of what should be done in situations dealt with by the standard has been deferred until the ABA Commission on Evaluation of Professional Standards [which drafted the RPC] reports its final recommendations."

tifying the witness as the defendant and permitting him to make his statement to the trier or the triers of the facts; the lawyer may not engage in direct examination of the defendant as a witness in the conventional manner and may not later argue the defendant's known false version of facts to the jury as worthy of belief and he may not recite or rely upon the false testimony in his closing argument."

Under this procedure, a defendant is afforded his right to speak to the jury under oath. The constitutional right to assistance of counsel is also preserved, but the defense attorney is protected from participation in the fraud. (Commentary to section 7.7, The Defense Function, supra.)

The determination of whether or not to grant a motion to withdraw rests within the sound discretion of the trial court. (State v. Henderson, supra.) In *Henderson,* the defendant told his court-appointed attorney, four days before trial, that he was going to lie on the witness stand. Counsel then informed the prosecutor and judge that he would be unable to represent the defendant. The judge denied his motion to withdraw. The trial court held that the attorney had acted in an ethical manner since counsel is not "required to stultify himself by tendering evidence or making any statement which he knows to be false, as a matter of fact in an attempt to obtain an acquittal at any cost." The court held that as long as the trial court reasonably believed that the attorney could continue to provide effective assistance in the presentation of a defense, the trial court's action in refusing to appoint new counsel was justified. This court finds that counsel herein can provide effective assistance in the presentation of a defense.[2]

"It is axiomatic that the right of a client to effective counsel in any case (criminal or civil) does not include the right to compel counsel to knowingly assist or participate in the commission of perjury or the creation of false evidence." (ABA Informal Opinion, 1314, supra.) It is equally clear that the defendant is not entitled to appointment of a new attorney in order to be assisted in any possible perjury. Accordingly, the motion of defense counsel to withdraw, is denied.

The motion to have this court disqualify itself from this case is also denied. Section 14 of the Judiciary Law provides for disqualification of a judge when he is connected with a case as a party or prior counsel, or by financial interest or consanguinity. "Prior knowledge of the issues or the parties acquired as a Judge, or even prior ruling on the very issues, is no ground for disqualification." (Matter of Diana A., 65 Misc.2d 1034, 319 N.Y.S.2d 691 [1971]). It should be noted that this trial is to be conducted as a jury trial, with the jury rendering the final decision as to whether the People have proved defendant's guilt beyond a reasonable doubt.

2. After the attorney in *Henderson* made his opening statement, presented witnesses and informed the defendant of his right to take the stand and "tell his story," the defendant declined to do so. There is no way of knowing at this time what the defendant in this case will do during trial.

The principal argument raised in support of granting the motion to recuse the trial judge is that since it is the judge's function to sentence the defendant, it is likely that the judge will be prejudiced against him because of his knowledge that the defendant stated an unlawful intention at one point. Of course, it would be improper for this court to assume that the defendant will go through with his proposal. Moreover, any succeeding judge, who would preside at sentencing, would undoubtedly be apprised of the fact and nature of this motion from court records or probation investigation.

Similarly, there are many pretrial proceedings where past conduct or incriminating statements of the defendant are brought before the trial judge but which do not require his disqualification. In motions to suppress, for example, the judge is regularly informed of incriminating statements or evidence which may later be excluded at trial. Nevertheless, the judge, although aware of the existence of such evidence, upon conviction, is not thereby disqualified from imposing sentence upon the defendant.

For the above-stated reasons, defense counsel's motions are denied.[b]

### *Comment*

(1) *Moving to withdraw when accused intends to commit perjury.* Other courts have agreed with the *Salquerro* court that a criminal defense lawyer confronted with a client who insists upon taking the stand to commit perjury in a jury case should seek to withdraw.[1] Similarly, ABA Informal Opinion 1314 (1975) takes the position that a lawyer who knows in advance that a criminal defendant client intends to commit perjury can avoid violation of the Disciplinary Rules against using, participating in, or assisting perjury only by advising the client that the lawyer must either (1) withdraw or (2) inform the court of the testimony's falsity, if the client insists on committing perjury. However, it should be noted that ABA Standards, The Defense Function 7.7(b) (1971) (not included in the 1980 Second Edition of the ABA Standards for Criminal Justice) requires the lawyer to seek withdrawal only if the client's insistence on committing perjury occurs before trial and if withdrawal is "feasible."

(2) *Informing judge in jury trial of accused's intent to commit perjury.* Although Defense Function Standard 7.7(c) (not included in the 1980 Second Edition) states that counsel "should make a record of the fact that the defendant is taking the stand against the advice of counsel

b. See generally Wolfram, Client Perjury: The Kutak Commission and the Association of Trial Lawyers on Lawyers, Lying Clients and the Adversary System, 1980 Am.B. Found.Research J. 966.

1. See State v. Henderson, 205 Kan. 231, 468 P.2d 136, 64 A.L.R.3d 375 (1970) (pretrial request to withdraw was consistent with "the moral and ethical obligations required of * * * a member of the legal profession"); State v. Robinson, 290 N.C. 56, 224 S.E.2d 174 (1976) (pretrial request "commendable"); State v. Trapp, 52 Ohio App.2d 189, 368 N.E.2d 1278 (1977) (withdrawal request made at trial was in line with lawyer's duty).

in some appropriate manner *without revealing the fact to the court,"* courts have agreed with *Salquerro* that it is appropriate for defense counsel to apprise the judge in a jury trial of the accused's intent to commit perjury.[2] Doing so is at least *permissible* under the CPR, but it raises questions under the RPC:

(a) DR 4–101 (C) (3) permits the disclosure by allowing a lawyer to reveal a client's intent to commit a crime and the information necessary to prevent the crime. ABA Informal Opinion 1314 (1975) (without mentioning Defense Function Standard 7.7!) takes the position that a lawyer who knows in advance that the accused intends to commit perjury can avoid violation of DR 7–102 (A) (4), (6) and (7)'s proscriptions on using, participating in, or assisting perjury, only by advising the client that the lawyer must either withdraw or inform the court of the testimony's falsity if the client insists on committing perjury.

(b) The Model Rules are quite unclear on this issue. RPC 1.6 (b) (1) only permits revelation regarding a crime likely to result in imminent death or substantial bodily harm. RPC 3.3 (a) (4) requires the lawyer to take "reasonable remedial measures" (which the Comment says can include revelation of the existence of perjury) only when the lawyer *"has offered"* evidence and has come to know of its falsity. But RPC 3.3's Comment refers with apparent approval to the idea that the lawyer should reveal an accused's perjury "if necessary to rectify the situation" in order to "avoid implication in the commission of perjury" because "an accused should not have a right to assistance of counsel in committing perjury." However, under RPC 1.2 (a) and numerous authorities[3] it is for the accused,

2. See State v. Henderson, 205 Kan. 231, 468 P.2d 136, 64 A.L.R.3d 375 (1970) (pretrial withdrawal request); State v. Robinson, 290 N.C. 56, 224 S.E.2d 174 (1976) (pretrial withdrawal request). Cf. People v. McGalvin, 55 Ill.2d 161, 302 N.E.2d 342 (1973) (informing judge that accused wanted to take stand against counsel's advice did not violate accused's rights, but possibly it would have been preferable to have recorded the fact in a different manner under Defense Function Standard 7.7), cert. denied 416 U.S. 909, 94 S.Ct. 1618, 40 L.Ed.2d 114 (1974); Commonwealth v. Wilson, 381 Mass. 90, 407 N.E.2d 1229 (1980) (disclosure during trial to prevent future allegations counsel had suborned perjury was not shown to have prejudiced defendants at sentencing).

But see In re Goodwin, 305 S.E.2d 578 (S.C.1983) (counsel moving to withdraw because accused intends to take stand to commit perjury "cannot violate the attorney-client privilege to disclose the specific conflict").

Compare United States ex rel. Wilcox v. Johnson, 555 F.2d 115, 122 (3d Cir. 1977) (violates accused's rights for counsel to inform judge in jury trial of counsel's belief that accused intends to commit perjury "without possessing a firm factual basis for that belief").

It would seem a lawyer must resolve in favor of the client any doubts about whether testimony will be perjured. See generally M. Freedman, Lawyers' Ethics in an Adversary System, ch. 5 (1975).

3. See ABA Standards for Criminal Justice 4–5.2 (a) (iii) (2d ed. 1980); State v. Martin, 102 Ariz. 142, 426 P.2d 639 (1967) (conviction reversed because counsel refused to let accused testify); United States ex rel. Wilcox v. Johnson, 555 F.2d 115 (3d Cir. 1977) (habeas granted because accused was prevented from testifying by trial court ruling that if accused testified it would grant counsel's withdrawal request and accused would have to represent himself for rest of trial).

A number of other courts have generally recognized the accused's right to testify contrary to counsel's advice. See, e.g., Hughes v. State, 513 P.2d 1115, 1119 (Alaska 1973); People v. Robles, 2 Cal.3d 205, 214–15, 85 Cal.Rptr. 166, 172, 466 P.2d 710, 716 (1970); Ingle v. State, 92 Nev. 104, 546 P.2d 598

not counsel, to decide whether the accused will testify. Would it be an unduly tortured construction of the Model Rules to at least *permit* the lawyer to apprise the judge in a jury trial of the accused's intent to commit perjury?

(3) *Informing fact-finder of accused's intent to commit perjury.* Several courts have held that in bench trials, as distinguished from jury trials, apprising the judge of a criminal defendant's intent to commit perjury violates the defendant's constitutional rights.[4] Thus, in the Ninth Circuit case of Lowery v. Cardwell,[5] defendant was being tried for murder without a jury. The state's evidence showed that the victim was shot twice at close range while sitting in a parked car, and that the accused had been seen walking to the car with the victim and standing near the car while the victim entered, at which time sounds similar to the popping of fire crackers were heard. When accused took the stand she denied walking outside with the victim or going to the car or shooting him. Thereupon defense counsel requested and was granted a recess, after which he moved to withdraw but declined to state the reason. The trial court denied the withdrawal motion. Counsel stated he had no further questions of defendant. In closing argument, he made no reference to defendant's testimony that she had not accompanied the victim to the car or shot him, but rather argued that the state's case was subject to reasonable doubt and that if the court should find that defendant had pulled the trigger, still the case was not one of first degree murder. The trial court found defendant guilty of second degree murder. The Ninth Circuit ordered the defendant released on habeas on the ground that she was deprived of a fair trial by her lawyer's requesting withdrawal in a

(1976). But see State v. Whiteside, 272 N.W.2d 468 (Iowa 1978) (counsel properly refused to permit accused to testify in view of evidence indicating the testimony would be perjurious).

In Harris v. New York, 401 U.S. 222, 225, 91 S.Ct. 643, 645, 28 L.Ed.2d 1 (1971), holding that an accused could be impeached with statements obtained in violation of *Miranda*, the Court stated that an accused's privilege to testify in his own defense "cannot be construed to include the right to commit perjury." But it should be noted that the Court authorized only impeachment, not prevention, of the accused's testimony.

Compare United States v. Von Roeder, 435 F.2d 1004, 1008–10 (10th Cir.) (accused's rights not violated by counsel's *dissuading* accused from taking the stand), vacated on other grounds 404 U.S. 67, 92 S.Ct. 326, 30 L.Ed.2d 222 (1971).

4. See State v. Jefferson, 126 Ariz. 341, 615 P.2d 638 (1980) (counsel at probation revocation proceeding requested withdrawal because accused insisted on testifying and counsel felt accused could not testify for reasons counsel could not reveal because of attorney-client privilege; this amounted to announcement of counsel's disbelief in client's testimony); Butler v. United States, 414 A.2d 844 (D.C.App.1980) (due process violated when counsel before trial informed judge accused intended to commit perjury and judge later heard case without jury; case should have been transferred to different judge).

Compare United States v. Campbell, 616 F.2d 1151 (9th Cir.) (although counsel should not have informed court in jury's presence that accused was testifying against counsel's advice, this did not deny fair trial to accused with previous robbery record since the "jury, which is generally not alert to the ethical problems faced by an attorney, could have interpreted counsel's actions as a desire to keep [accused] off the stand so that [his] prior robbery convictions would not be used for impeachment purposes"), cert. denied 447 U.S. 910, 100 S.Ct. 2998, 64 L.Ed.2d 861 (1980).

5. 575 F.2d 727 (9th Cir. 1978).

manner that clearly apprised the judge in a non-jury trial that counsel thought she had testified falsely. The court said:

"The * * * question * * * is whether the motion to withdraw, made when it was and under the circumstances then existing, served to deprive appellant of fair trial. We conclude that it did.

"The problem presented is that which arises when defense counsel, in the course of a criminal trial, forms the belief that his client's defense is based on false testimony. We start with the basic proposition that if, under these circumstances, counsel informs the fact finder of his belief he has, by that action, disabled the fact finder from judging the merits of the defendant's defense. Further, he has by his action openly placed himself in opposition to his client upon her defense. The consequences of such action on the part of counsel, in our judgment, are such as to deprive the defendant of a fair trial. If in truth the defendant has committed perjury (a fact we do not know in this case) she does not by that falsehood forfeit her right to fair trial.

"The question presented, then, is whether what here occurred amounted to such an unequivocal announcement to the fact finder as to deprive appellant of due process. In our judgment it must be said that it did. The judge, and not a jury, was the fact finder. From the testimony of appellant * * *, from the fact that the examination of appellant ceased abruptly * * * with a request for a recess, from the making of a motion to withdraw and counsel's statement to the court that he could not state the reason for his motion, the only conclusion that could rationally be drawn by the judge was that in the belief of her counsel appellant had falsely denied shooting the deceased.

"The result on these unusual facts is not inconsistent with the principles of professional responsibility under ethical standards as they are generally recognized today[1] and does not expose counsel to a charge of subornation of perjury. The American Bar Association Code of Professional Responsibility states only that 'In his representation of a client, a lawyer shall not * * * knowingly use perjured testimony or false evidence.' Disciplinary Rule 7–102 (A) (4). The ABA Defense Function Standards[2] cast light on the rule and deal with the subject at greater length, although they do not deal specifically with trial before a judge without a jury or

1. Much has been written on the subject of counsel's professional responsibilities when confronted with client perjury or intent to commit perjury, and scholars differ strongly on some of the questions presented. See Wolfram, Client Perjury, 50 So.Cal.L.Rev. 809 (1977) (and articles cited therein). However, we feel that the ABA standards set forth in the ABA Project on Standards for Criminal Justice, Standards Relating to the Prosecution Function and the Defense Function (Approved Draft 1971) (hereinafter the "Defense Function Standards"), discussed infra, can be said to represent an authoritative consensus.

2. The Standards were adopted by the ABA House of Delegates in 1971 and are designed to be compatible with the Code. See Wolfram, supra, at 824.

with the case where counsel is surprised by perjury in the course of examination of his client.[3]

"The Standards, in brief, would appear to require that when, in the course of trial, counsel is surprised by his client's perjury he should not act to advance it. However, there is no requirement that he seek to withdraw, since, during trial, that course is likely not to be feasible. The Standards seem quite sensibly to assume that counsel will not be expected to act in such a fashion as to disclose his quandary to the fact finder.[4]

"Thus it does not follow from our holding that a passive refusal to lend aid to what is believed to be perjury in accordance with the Defense Function Standards would violate due process. In our view, mere failure to pursue actively a certain course of defense, which counsel ethically is precluded from actively pursuing, cannot be said to constitute denial of fair trial. While a knowledgeable judge or juror, alert to the ethical problems faced by attorneys and the manner in which they traditionally are met, might infer perjury from inaction, counsel's belief would not appear in the clear and unequivocal manner presented by the facts here. There may be many reasons for failure actively to pursue a particular line of defense. And in the weighing of competing values in which we are engaged * * * the integrity of the judicial process must be allowed to play a respectable role; the concept of due process must allow room for it.

"The distinction we draw is between a passive refusal to lend aid to perjury and such direct action as we find here—the addressing of the court in pursuit of court order granting leave to withdraw. By calling for a judicial decision upon counsel's motion in a case in which the judge served as fact finder, this conduct affirmatively and emphatically called the attention of the fact finder to the problem counsel was facing.[5]

3. [Quotation of Defense Function Standard 7.7 (1971).]

4. An ABA panel, which included then Circuit Judge Warren E. Burger, in commenting on a hypothetical case submitted to it in 1966, anticipated the Standards on the question of the proper method of dealing with the client who insists on taking the stand to commit perjury. Judge Burger states:

> "If in those circumstances the lawyer's immediate withdrawal from the case is either not feasible, or if the judge refuses to permit withdrawal, the lawyer's course is clear: He may not engage in direct examination of his client to facilitate known perjury. He should confine himself to asking the witness to identify himself and to make a statement, but he cannot participate in the fraud by conventional direct examination. Since this informal procedure is not uncommon with witnesses, there is no basis for saying that this tells the jury the witness is lying. A judge may infer that such is the case but lay jurors will not."

Burger, Standards of Conduct: A Judge's Viewpoint, 5 Am.Crim.Law Q. 11, 13 (1966).

5. The attorney may justifiably desire to establish a record for his own protection in the event that his professional conduct is later questioned. Especially in a case tried to the court, and even in a jury trial:

> "* * * if the trial judge is informed of the situation, the defendant may be unduly prejudiced * * * and the lawyer may feel he is caught in a dilemma between protecting himself by making such a record and prejudicing his client's case by making it with the court. The dilemma can be avoided in most instances by making the record in

"That this is an unhappy result cannot be denied. Trial counsel is to be commended for his attention to professional responsibility.[6] * * * We are acutely aware of the anomaly presented when mistrial must result from counsel's bona fide efforts to avoid professional irresponsibility. We find no escape, however, from the conclusion that fundamental requisites of fair trial have been irretrievably lost. Whether a just result nevertheless was reached would be a futile and irrelevant inquiry."

Hufstedler, C. J., concurred on Sixth Amendment grounds. She stated:

"Although I do not disagree with the majority's due process analysis, I would rest the decision on the petitioner's Sixth Amendment right to effective assistance of counsel. The petitioner sustained her burden of proving that counsel failed to render reasonably effective assistance and that failure resulted in the denial of fundamental fairness.

"Under the circumstances * * *, when defense counsel moved to withdraw, he ceased to be an active advocate of his client's interests. Despite counsel's ethical concerns, his actions were so adverse to petitioner's interests as to deprive her of effective assistance of counsel. No matter how commendable may have been counsel's motives, his interest in saving himself from potential violation of the canons was adverse to his client, and the end product was his abandonment of a diligent defense."

(4) *Refraining from examining in conventional manner or arguing perjurious version.* A number of courts agree with *Salquerro* and *Lowery* that defense counsel still in the case after learning that the accused intends to commit perjury should follow the Defense Function Standard 7.7(c) procedure of refraining from examining the accused in the conventional manner or arguing the accused's false version in closing argument.[7] Thus, in In re Goodwin[8] the South Carolina Supreme

some other appropriate manner, for example, by having the defendant subscribe to a file notation, witnessed, if possible, by another lawyer."

ABA Defense Function Standards § 7.7 Commentary at 277.

6. Problems of ethics are not before us. Our sole concern relates to the requisites of due process and fair trial. Thus, we do not reach such questions as the extent to which counsel should satisfy himself that the testimony of his client is false, or the extent to which he should confer with his client before passively refusing to lend aid to her defense. Of course, we do not condone such misconduct as a deliberate and strategic causing of mistrial.

7. But see M. Freedman, Lawyers' Ethics in an Adversary System 31 (1975) (if accused insists on taking stand after lawyer advises that the proposed testimony is unlawful, lawyer should proceed in normal fashion in presenting the testimony and arguing to the jury because "any other course would be a betrayal of the assurances of confidentiality given by the attorney in order to induce the client to reveal everything").

See ABA Standards for Criminal Justice 4–3.1(a) (defense counsel should explain the necessity of full disclosure of all facts and the obligation of confidentiality which makes privileged accused's disclosures relating to case); id. 3.2(a) (lawyer should probe for all legally relevant information without seeking to influence the direction of client's responses); id. 3.2(b) (unprofessional conduct to instruct or intimate that client should not be candid in revealing facts so as to afford lawyer free rein to take action which would be precluded by

Court recently ruled that when the trial court denied a public defender's motion to withdraw (made as soon as the public defender learned that her criminal defendant client intended to take the stand to commit perjury), the defender should not have disobeyed the trial court's order to proceed with the case, but should have proceeded as outlined in Defense Function Standard 7.7. The court reasoned:

> "Under [Standard 7.7], the defendant who intends to commit perjury may take the stand and deliver his statement in narrative form [and] the lawyer does not examine the defendant or use the false testimony in * * * closing argument. With an acute awareness that any practice we endorse will draw criticism, we approve this procedure as an acceptable method of balancing the conflicting interests, as it allows the lawyer to refrain from actively participating in the presentation of the false testimony while affording the defendant the assistance of counsel.
>
> "The record reveals [counsel was] aware of this procedure at the time of trial, but rejected it because [she] felt it denied the defendant the *effective* assistance of counsel. We think the deprivation of counsel occasioned by this practice is substantially less prejudicial to the defendant than complete abandonment in mid-trial. Moreover, the defendant's right to counsel does not include the right to insist that counsel assist him in presenting fraudulent testimony."

Similarly, courts relying upon standard 7.7 have held that it does not violate an accused's rights for defense counsel:

(a) after informing the judge that the accused wants to take the stand against counsel's advice and that counsel is uncertain as to the specifics of what the accused will say and receiving permission for the accused to testify in the narrative form, to ask the accused on direct only his name, age, place of birth, what he remembers about the date in question, and (after the accused finished) if he remembers anything else about the fight, and not ask the defendant any questions on redirect,[9] or

(b) after unsuccessfully requesting a pretrial judge to allow withdrawal on the ground that the accused intends to commit perjury and advising the trial judge that the accused is taking the stand against counsel's advice, to ask the accused only to tell the jury

lawyer's knowing such facts). Compare RPC 1.2(e) (when lawyer knows client expects assistance not permitted by RPC or other law, lawyer shall consult with client regarding the relevant limitations on the lawyer's conduct).

8. 305 S.E.2d 578 (S.C. 1983).

Cf. State v. Lowery, 111 Ariz. 26, 523 P.2d 54 (1974) (quoting Standard 7.7 and Commentary with apparent approval).

9. People v. Lowery, 52 Ill.App.3d 44, 9 Ill.Dec. 41, 366 N.E.2d 155 (1977) ("We fail to understand how the actions of an attorney which closely parallels [Standard 7.7] can establish incompetence sufficient to constitute a denial of defendant's right to effective representation").

where he was and what he did at the time in question and thereafter only limited questions like "Then what happened?"[10]

Even though Standard 7.7 was not included in the 1980 Second Edition of the ABA Standards for Criminal Justice, it would seem safe for a lawyer whose criminal defendant client insists upon taking the stand to commit perjury to follow Standard 7.7 inasmuch as it was held out as the ABA's official policy from 1971 to 1979 and a number of courts have expressed approval of its approach.

It should be emphasized that the Standard 7.7 "free narrative" approach applies only to the criminal defendant, because it is for the accused, not counsel, to decide whether the accused will testify.[11] The approach has no application where a criminal defendant (or civil litigant) desires to call a *witness* to testify perjuriously or where a civil litigant desires to take the stand personally to commit perjury—in those situations the answer is that the lawyer must refuse to allow the witness or litigant to take the stand.[12]

(5) *Unanticipated client perjury.* The CPR and the RPC differ on whether the lawyer should blow the whistle when a client unexpectedly commits, and refuses to rectify, what the lawyer knows is perjury:

(a) Under DR 4–101 and 7–102 (B) (1), the lawyer should not tell the judge if the lawyer's knowledge that the testimony was perjurious is from information gained in the professional relationship. DR 7–102 (B) (1), as amended in 1974, specifies that if a lawyer receives information clearly establishing that the client, in the course of the representation, perpetrated a fraud upon a person or tribunal and the client refuses to rectify it, the lawyer must reveal the fraud "except when the information is protected as a privileged communication," and ABA Formal Opinion 341 (1975) construes "privileged communication" to include both "confidences" and "secrets." (It should be noted that many states did not adopt the 1974 amendment adding the quoted language to DR 7–102 (B)(1).[13])

10. Thornton v. United States, 357 A.2d 429 (D.C.App.), cert. denied 429 U.S. 1024, 97 S.Ct. 644, 50 L.Ed.2d 626 (1976) ("Throughout, defense counsel followed the course delineated in ABA Standard 7.7(c)").

11. See Comment (2)(b) and footnote 3 thereto.

12. See People v. Schultheis and Comment (1) following it, above.

13. See Brazil, Unanticipated Client Perjury and the Collision of Rules of Ethics, Evidence, and Constitutional Law, 44 Mo.L.Rev. 601, 604–06 n.6 (1979).

Compare In re Malloy, 248 N.W.2d 43 (N.D. 1976) (in case arising before 1974 amendment where client unexpectedly committed perjury in deposition, lawyer should have *withdrawn* but had no duty to disclose perjury because of DR 4–101's conflict with DR 7–102 (B) (1)); In re King, 7 Utah 2d 258, 322 P.2d 1095 (1958) (six month suspension for failing to disclose civil litigant client's perjury at trial).

For cases of discipline where the lawyer's knowledge that the client's testimony was perjured came elsewhere than from a privileged confidential communication from the client, see In re Carroll, 244 S.W.2d 474 (Ky. 1951) (divorce defendant asserted opposite in other proceeding); In re Mendelsohn, 150 App.Div. 445, 135 N.Y.S. 438 (1912) (tort plaintiff asserted opposite in other proceedings).

(b) RPC 3.3 (a) (4) specifies that "[i]f a lawyer has offered material evidence and comes to know of its falsity, the lawyer shall take reasonable remedial measures," RPC 3.3 (b) states that this duty applies "even if compliance requires disclosure of information otherwise protected by Rule 1.6," and the Comment specifies that if remonstrance fails and withdrawal will not remedy the situation or is impossible, the lawyer has a duty to disclose unless that duty is "qualified by constitutional provisions for due process and the right to counsel in criminal cases."

The cases cited in Comment (3) above bar a lawyer from apprising the judge of a criminal defendant client's perjury, *if the judge is the fact-finder.* By their approval of Standard 7.7, those cases, as well as those cited in Comment (4) above, may indicate that defense counsel is barred from apprising the judge of the accused's perjury even in a jury trial.[14]

On the other hand, as indicated in Comment (2) above, several courts have ruled that it is appropriate to apprise the judge in a jury case of the accused's *intent* to commit perjury, and this may apply as well to a revelation that the accused *has* committed perjury. In the 1967 case of McKissick v. United States,[15] the Fifth Circuit held that if in the midst of a jury trial accused tells counsel that accused's testimony had been perjured, it is appropriate for counsel to apprise the trial judge of accused's admission and request withdrawal. The court reasoned:

> "If appellant told his attorney that he had committed perjury, that offense was in effect a continuing one so long as allowed to remain in the record to influence the jury's verdict. Whether appellant did or did not specifically authorize or direct his attorney to make it known to the court, or even directed it not be made known, he could not abrogate the attorney's discharge of his professional, ethical and public duty to report it. The statement was good cause to the attorney to withdraw from the case, and he would have been subject to discipline had he continued in the defense without making a report to the court. The attorney not only could, but was obligated to, make such disclosure to the court as necessary to withdraw the perjured testimony from the consideration of the jury. This was essential for good judicial administration and to protect the public."[16]

For cases of discipline where the lawyer relied upon the civil litigant client's perjured testimony, effectively assisting the client to commit a fraud, see People ex rel. Attorney General v. Beattie, 137 Ill. 553, 27 N.E. 1096 (1891); In re Hardenbrook, 135 App.Div. 634, 121 N.Y.S. 250 (1909), affirmed 199 N.Y. 539, 92 N.E. 1086 (1910).

**14.** In fact, the court in In re Goodwin, 305 S.E.2d 578 (S.C. 1983), expressly stated that "counsel cannot violate the attorney-client privilege to disclose the specific conflict" when requesting withdrawal.

**15.** 379 F.2d 754 (5th Cir. 1967).

**16.** Compare Gold, Split Loyalty: An Ethical Problem for the Criminal Defense Lawyer, 14 Clev.-Mar.L.Rev. 65, 69 (1965) (unable to find case in which criminal defense lawyer was required to disclose client's lack of veracity; argument that perjury is prospective rather than past crime "seems to be

(6) *Unanticipated perjury by witness.* Revelation that a *witness* (other than the client) has committed perjury is clearly required under both RPC 3.3 (a) (4)'s requirement of "reasonable remedial measures" and DR 7-102 (B) (2)'s requirement that a lawyer who receives information clearly establishing that a person other than the client has perpetrated a fraud upon a tribunal shall promptly reveal the fraud to the tribunal, which requirement does *not* append DR 7-102 (B) (1)'s "except when the information is protected as a privileged communication." [17]

### *Question*

Your criminal defendant client admits to you that he committed the crime, and your investigation establishes that to be true. Part of the state's evidence is a flashlight belonging to defendant and bearing his fingerprints which was found at the scene of the crime (where defendant told you he dropped it). May you put on the stand witnesses who will testify truthfully that someone stole a flashlight from defendant three days before defendant's alleged offense? [18]

## D. EXAMINATION AND ARGUMENT

### MODEL RULES OF PROFESSIONAL CONDUCT

**RULE 3.3 Candor Toward the Tribunal**

(a) A lawyer shall not knowingly:

(1) make a false statement of material fact or law to a tribunal * * *.

**RULE 3.4 Fairness to Opposing Party and Counsel**

A lawyer shall not:

* * *

(e) in trial, allude to any matter that the lawyer does not reasonably believe is relevant or that will not be suported by admissible evidence, assert personal knowledge of facts in issue except when testifying as a witness, or state a personal opinion as to the justness of a cause, the credibility of a witness, the culpability of a civil litigant or the guilt or innocence of an accused * * *.

**RULE 4.4 Respect for Rights of Third Persons**

In representing a client, a lawyer shall not use means that have no substantial purpose other than to embarrass, delay, or burden a third per-

a tortured extension of the exception to the privilege").

17. For the view that a lawyer should not be required to reveal the fact that a *criminal defendant's* witness committed perjury when the lawyer knows it was perjury because of a privileged communication, see Gold, supra note 16, at 69.

18. See Cornell v. Maryland, 396 F.Supp. 1092 (D.Md.1975) (defendant's right to competent counsel not violated: since he "specifically told his trial counsel that he had dropped the flashlight at the scene of the crime, any testimony about the theft of *a* flashlight from [defendant] three days before the crime would have been misleading at the very least").

son, or use methods of obtaining evidence that violate the legal rights of such a person.[a]

## HEISE, CHEMICAL TESTS FOR INTOXICATION—SCIENTIFIC BACKGROUND AND PUBLIC ACCEPTANCE

41 Marq.L.Rev. 296, 297–98 (1958).

When the police called upon me to examine an obvious drunk, I cheerfully examined a man whose condition would have been recognized by a child. Then, at a later time I was called to court to testify as to my findings. The details still rankle, but this is what happened as taken from the court records:

> Attorney for the Defense: "Doctor, did you say that my client staggered when you examined him on January 1?"
>
> Answer: "Yes."
>
> Question: "Did that prove that he was intoxicated?"
>
> Answer: "No, that was just one of many symptoms."
>
> Question: "Doctor, is there anything besides alcohol that might cause staggering?"
>
> Answer: "Yes."
>
> Question: "Will you name some of these conditions?"
>
> Answer: "A blow on the head, a tumor of the brain, multiple sclerosis and many more."
>
> Attorney: "Then there are many conditions besides alcohol that can cause the abnormalities you have described."
>
> Answer: "Yes."

He then proceeded to have me admit that all of the symptoms of intoxication could have been duplicated by conditions other than the effects of alcohol. Then he propounded his coup de grace: "Doctor, now consider all of the symptoms that you have been telling us about, his gait, coordination, balance, his speech, his appearance; could such findings have been caused by some condition other than alcohol?"

a. Compare DR 7–106(C), which specifies:

"In appearing in his professional capacity before a tribunal, a lawyer shall not:

(1) State or allude to any matter that he has no reasonable basis to believe is relevant to the case or that will not be supported by admissible evidence.

(2) Ask any question that he has no reasonable basis to believe is relevant to the case and that is intended to degrade a witness or other person.

(3) Assert his personal knowledge of the facts in issue, except when testifying as a witness.

(4) Assert his personal opinion as to the justness of a cause, as to the credibility of a witness, as to the culpability of a civil litigant, or as to the guilt or innocence of an accused; but he may argue, on his analysis of the evidence, for any position or conclusion with respect to the matters stated herein.

(5) Fail to comply with known local customs of courtesy or practice of the bar or a particular tribunal without giving to opposing counsel timely notice of his intent not to comply.

(6) Engage in undignified or discourteous conduct which is degrading to a tribunal.

(7) Intentionally or habitually violate any established rule of procedure or of evidence."

Answer (reluctantly): "Yes." (At the time, I was unaware that there were at least a hundred ailments that might produce symptoms resembling those of alcoholic intoxication). And then I made the mistake of staying in the courtroom while the attorney for the defense made his final plea. Take my advice. Get out of the courtroom when you can. This is what I heard: "Ladies and Gentlemen of the Jury. You have heard this doctor testify that my client was intoxicated on the night of January 1. And when I asked this doctor whether he knew of any symptom of intoxication he couldn't name one single symptom. And he had to admit that everything that he said about my client was probably due to some illness. And now, ladies and gentlemen of the jury, having heard this doctor testify, I leave it to you. Who on the night of January the first was under the influence of alcohol, this client of mine, or this doctor!" The verdict: "Not guilty. Costs on the County."

After this experience, I refused to examine persons suspected of being drunk, particularly since I had learned that "odor of alcohol on the breath" was not proof of drinking alcohol.[a]

### *Questions*

(1) Does Dr. Heise's description indicate any possibly improper defense counsel conduct?

(2) *Role of criminal defense counsel.* Are the following quotations reconcilable?

(a) Mr. Justice White, dissenting in part in the 1967 case of United States v. Wade[1]:

> "Law enforcement officers have the obligation to convict the guilty and to make sure they do not convict the innocent. They must be dedicated to making the criminal trial a procedure for the ascertainment of the true facts surrounding the commission of the crime. To this extent, our so-called adversary system is not adversary at all; nor should it be. But defense counsel has no comparable obligation to ascertain or present the truth. Our system assigns him a different mission. He must be and is interested in preventing the conviction of the innocent, but, absent a voluntary plea of guilty, we also insist that he defend his client whether he is innocent or guilty. The State has the obligation to present the evidence. Defense counsel need present nothing, even if he knows what the truth is. He need not furnish any witnesses to the police, or reveal any confidences of his client, or furnish any other information to help the prosecution's case. If he can confuse a witness, even a truthful one, or make him appear at a disadvantage, unsure

a. Dr. Carl Binger, a psychiatrist who testified for the defense in the Alger Hiss case, was subjected to similar cross-examination by the prosecution. His reaction and conclusions were similar to those of Dr. Heise, conclusions still held 15 years later. Slovenko, Witness Psychology and the Credibility of Testimony, 19 U.Fla.L.Rev. 1, 11 (1966).

1. 388 U.S. 218, 87 S.Ct. 1926, 18 L.Ed.2d 1149 (1967) (defendant entitled to presence of counsel at police line-up).

or indecisive, that will be his normal course. Our interest in not convicting the innocent permits counsel to put the State to its proof, to put the State's case in the worst possible light, regardless of what he thinks or knows to be the truth. Undoubtedly there are some limits which defense counsel must observe but more often than not, defense counsel will cross-examine a prosecution witness, and impeach him if he can, even if he thinks the witness is telling the truth, just as he will attempt to destroy a witness who he thinks is lying. In this respect, as part of our modified adversary system and as part of the duty imposed on the most honorable defense counsel, we countenance or require conduct which in many instances has little, if any, relation to the search for truth."

(b) The Oklahoma Court of Criminal Appeals in the 1912 case of Ostendorf v. State [2]:

"It appears that upon the trial of this case counsel relied alone upon a technical defense, without regard to the guilt or innocence of his client. He interposed objections to everything that was done in the trial court. He demurred to the information, which was overruled. When the case was tried, he objected to the introduction of any testimony, upon the ground that the information did not charge any offense against the laws of Oklahoma. Every conceivable objection was offered to each question asked every witness in the case. * * *

"As long as [some lawyers] continue to insist upon trying their cases on the basis of technicalities, without reference to merit or justice, this court will be forced to continue to condemn such practices, and the longer this practice is continued the stronger our condemnation will become, it matters not who the lawyers may be. In fact, this is not practicing law; it is practicing quibbling, and courts are to be blamed for permitting it to be done. It lowers the standard of the profession and brings courts into disrepute with intelligent and justice-loving people." [3]

(3) *Cross-examining truthful witness.* Is ABA Standards for Criminal Justice 4–7.6 (b)[4] appropriate? It specifies:

"A lawyer's belief or knowledge that the witness is telling the truth does not preclude cross-examination, but should, if possible,

2. 8 Okl.Cr. 360, 128 P. 143 (1912).

3. Compare Professional Responsibility: Report of the Joint Conference, 44 A.B.A. J. 1159, 1162 (1958):

"[P]artisan advocacy is a form of public service so long as it aids the process of adjudication; it ceases to be when it hinders that process, when it misleads, distorts and obfuscates, when it renders the task of the deciding tribunal not easier, but more difficult * * *. The primary responsibility for preserving adjudication as a meaningful and useful social institution rests ultimately with the practicing legal profession."

4. (2d ed. 1980). Compare id. 3–5.7(b), the parallel provision applicable to prosecutors, which specifies:

"The prosecutor's belief that the witness is telling the truth does not preclude cross-examination, but may affect the method and scope of cross-examination. A prosecutor should not use the power of cross-examination to discredit or undermine a witness

be taken into consideration by counsel in conducting the cross-examination."

The "History of Standard" explains:

"This standard has been changed[a] to make clear that it is permissible, if necessary, for defense counsel to cross-examine vigorously witnesses who are believed or known to be testifying truthfully. There are some cases where, unless counsel challenges the prosecution's known truthful witnesses, there will be no opposition to the prosecution's evidence and the defendant will be denied an effective defense. However, lawyers are encouraged in paragraph (b) to take into consideration in conducting cross-examination the fact that the state's witness is testifying truthfully."

The Commentary elaborates:

"The mere fact that defense counsel can, by use of impeachment, impair or destroy the credibility of an adverse witness does not impose on counsel a duty to do so. Cross-examination and impeachment are legal tools that are a monopoly of licensed lawyers, given primarily for the purpose of exposing falsehood. A prosecution witness, for example, may testify in a manner that confirms precisely what the defense lawyer has learned from the defendant and has substantiated by investigation. But defense counsel may believe that the temperament, personality, or inexperience of the witness provide an opportunity, by adroit cross-examination, to confuse the witness and undermine the witness's testimony in the eyes of the jury. If defense counsel can provide an effective defense for the accused and also avoid confusion or embarrassment of the witness, counsel should seek to do so.

"Another example of a situation where restraint may be called for is where a witness whose testimony the lawyer believes to be truthful is subject to impeachment by revealing to the jury that the witness was convicted of a crime many years earlier. The use of

if the prosecutor knows the witness is testifying truthfully."

The Commentary to the latter Standard states:

"A question of long standing is whether a prosecutor, in cross-examining a witness, should be restrained by the belief that the witness has testified truthfully. Generally, a lawyer is not required to substitute personal opinion for the available fact-finding processes of the trial and may, therefore, properly invoke the usual cross-examination techniques to test the witness's capacity and opportunity for observation and the witness's ability to recall. However, it is sometimes argued that the manner and tenor of cross-examination ought to be restricted where examining counsel believes in the truthfulness of the testimony given by the witness.

"Where the prosecutor knows that the testimony of the witness is accurate, paragraph (b) adopts the view that the power of cross-examination may not be invoked to destroy or undermine the truth. In this regard, it is believed that the duty of the prosecutor differs from that of the defense lawyer, who on occasion may be required to challenge known truthful witnesses of the prosecution in order to put the state to its proof."

**a.** Before the change, the Defense Function Standard was substantially identical to the Prosecution Function Standard quoted in the preceding footnote. See ABA Standards, The Defense Function 7.6(b) (1971).

this conventional method of impeachment against a witness who has testified truthfully should be avoided, if it is possible for defense counsel to do so without jeopardizing the defense of the accused. In deciding whether to use such impeachment, counsel undoubtedly will want to consider the tactical implications, since the jury may recognize the undue humiliation to the witness and thus react adversely to the lawyer.

"There also is a public policy factor underlying restraint in use of impeachment powers vested in a lawyer. The policy of the law is to encourage witnesses to come forward and give evidence in litigation. If witnesses are subjected to needless humiliation when they testify, the existing human tendency to avoid 'becoming involved' will be increased.

"Notwithstanding the foregoing comments, there unquestionably are many cases where defense counsel cannot provide the accused with a defense at all if counsel is precluded from engaging in vigorous cross-examination of witnesses either believed or known to have testified truthfully. For example, where the defendant has admitted guilt to the lawyer and does not plan to testify, and the lawyer simply intends to put the state to its proof and raise a reasonable doubt, skillful cross-examination of the prosecution's witnesses is essential. Indeed, were counsel in this circumstance to forgo vigorous cross-examination of the prosecution's witnesses, counsel would violate the clear duty of zealous representation that is owed to the client. Justice White, in a 1967 Supreme Court opinion, addressed the sometimes professional obligation of defense counsel to impeach truthful witnesses: [Quotation of matter set forth above]."

Compare Jethro Lieberman's view:

"[The client] is not entitled to acquittal at any cost. That the client is in an unenviable position does not excuse the harm that the lawyer's forensic brilliance can cause the witness. [The contrary view] is a little like supposing you are hired as a bodyguard for an important person and find him in a situation where you can save him only by throwing someone else in front to catch the bullet. Is this permissible? I think not." [5]

(4) *Improper argument.* To what extent would conduct violative of the following ABA Standards for Criminal Justice[6] be grounds for discipline? [7]

5. J. Lieberman, Crisis at the Bar 160 (1978).

See generally Freedman, Lawyers' Ethics in an Adversary System, ch. 4 (1975); Burger, Standards for Prosecution and Defense Personnel: A Judge's Viewpoint, 5 Am.Crim.L.Q. 11, 14–15 (1966).

6. ABA Standards for Criminal Justice 3–5.5, 3–5.8 and 3–5.9 (2d ed. 1980), applicable to prosecutors, are substantially identical.

7. See ABA Standards for Criminal Justice 3–1.1(e), 4–1.1(f) (2d ed. 1980) ("As used in this chapter, the term 'unprofessional conduct' denotes conduct which, in either identical or similar language, is or should be made subject to disciplinary sanctions pursuant to codes of professional responsibility * * *. Where other terms are used, the standard is intended as a guide to honorable professional conduct and performance.")

**"4–7.4 Opening Statement**

"The lawyer's opening statement should be confined to a brief statement of the issues in the case and evidence the lawyer intends to offer which the lawyer believes in good faith will be available and admissible. It is unprofessional conduct to allude to any evidence unless there is a good faith and reasonable basis for believing such evidence will be tendered and admitted in evidence.

**"4–7.8 Argument to the Jury**

"(a) In closing argument to the jury the lawyer may argue all reasonable inferences from the evidence in the record. It is unprofessional conduct for a lawyer intentionally to misstate the evidence or mislead the jury as to the inferences it may draw.

"(b) It is unprofessional conduct for a lawyer to express a personal belief or opinion in his or her client's innocence or personal belief or opinion in the truth or falsity of any testimony or evidence, or to attribute the crime to another person unless such an inference is warranted by the evidence.

"(c) A lawyer should not make arguments calculated to inflame the passions or prejudices of the jury.

"(d) A lawyer should refrain from argument which would divert the jury from its duty to decide the case on the evidence by injecting issues broader than the guilt or innocence of the accused under the controlling law or by making predictions of the consequences of the jury's verdict.

"(e) It is the responsibility of the court to ensure that final argument to the jury is kept within proper, accepted bounds."

**"4–7.9 Facts Outside the Record**

"It is unprofessional conduct for a lawyer intentionally to refer to or argue on the basis of facts outside the record, unless such facts are matters of common public knowledge based on ordinary human experience or matters of which the court can take judicial notice."

In addition to professional discipline and contempt of court citation, courts have sought to remedy improper argument by instructing the jury to disregard it, immediately declaring a mistrial, or granting a new trial upon post-trial motion or appeal.[8] What are the strengths

8. See Alschuler, Courtroom Misconduct by Prosecutors and Trial Judges, 50 Tex.L.Rev. 629, 644–74 (1972). See, e.g., Gordon v. Nall, 379 So.2d 585 (Ala. 1980) (new trial for argument that corporation "doesn't have a soul, it has a board of directors"); Norlin Music, Inc. v. Keyboard "88" Inc., 425 A.2d 74 (R.I. 1981) (new trial for argument comparing plaintiff and defendant corporations to David and Goliath; error not shown to be cured by instruction to disregard); Annot., 40 L.Ed.2d 886 (1975) (new trial for improper argument by prosecutor).

See generally Annot., 41 A.L.R.Fed. 10 (1979) and annotations cited (improper argument by prosecutors); Annot., 16 A.L.R.4th 810 (1982) and annotations cited (improper argument in criminal cases); Annot., 15 A.L.R.3d 1101 (1967) and annotations cited (improper argument in civil cases); Annot., 96 A.L.R.2d 9 (1964) (argument attacking opposing counsel).

In Ferguson v. Moore, 98 Tenn. 342, 39 S.W. 341 (1897), a colorful statement appears that it is the right of counsel to shed tears

and weaknesses of each remedy, as respects the opposing party, the client, and the efficient and fair administration of justice? How does each remedy apply to criminal defense counsel? The prosecutor? Civil defendant's counsel? Plaintiff's counsel? Should there be more disciplinary proceedings for improper argument?

(5) *Preparation of witness.* In a 1969 Illinois case, People v. McGuirk,[9] the prosecutrix in a rape prosecution was a nine-year-old child:

> "In cross-examination, following her testimony in chief, the prosecutrix testified that the prosecutor had read something to her [a transcript of her testimony before the grand jury] and told her to say the same thing that was on the paper. She also answered 'yes' to the following questions:
>
> > 'And you want to do what the nice man says, do you not, honey?'
> >
> > 'Did he tell you that he [McGuirk] would be the only colored man that was sitting at the table?'
> >
> > 'And he told you to point out the colored man, did he not, is that right, honey?'
> >
> > 'And you would do what the man says, would you not, honey, because he is a good man?'
> >
> > 'Whatever he says you are to say you would say, is that not right honey?'
>
> On re-direct examination she reaffirmed that the prosecutor had told her 'some to say' and that he had said that the man she was to identify would be seated at the table."

What do you think of the conduct attributed to the prosecuting attorney? [10]

and, if he can produce them, his duty to do so in the course of his argument. But this is hardly more than a product of frontier concepts of justice and is inconsistent with the prohibition on a lawyer's asserting his or her personal opinion as to the client's innocence or in the justice of the client's cause. People v. McGrane, 12 A.D.2d 465, 207 N.Y.S.2d 88 (1960). The tears shed by the prosecuting attorney for the victim of the crime led to a reversal in People v. Dukes, 12 Ill.2d 334, 146 N.E.2d 14, 67 A.L.R.2d 724 (1957).

**9.** 106 Ill.App.2d 266, 245 N.E.2d 917, cert. denied 396 U.S. 972, 90 S.Ct. 459, 24 L.Ed.2d 439 (1969).

**10.** Upholding McGuirk's rape conviction, the court said:

> "An attorney is bound by the testimony of his witnesses and there is nothing improper in refreshing their memories before they take the stand. Reviewing their testimony before trial makes for better direct examination, facilitates the trial and lessens the possibility of irrelevant and perhaps prejudicial interpolations. It is particularly advisable in a sex case to prepare a prosecutrix for the ordeal she will face in the courtroom. A State's attorney must go over her story with her, ease her embarrassment, familiarize himself with the sexual terms she uses and perhaps suggest others. There is nothing wrong with this if the witness' essential testimony is neither altered nor colored by emphasis or suggestion."

The court regarded telling the child "some to say" and to identify the colored man at the counsel table as raising a more serious question but found no reversible error since the record failed to show what she was told to say or that it was untruthful and there was overwhelming independent evidence of identification.

See Hamdi & Ibrahim Mango Co. v. Fire Association, 20 F.R.D. 181, 183 (S.D.N.Y.1957)

(6) *Misleading conduct.* Would it be proper without trial court permission to have someone other than the accused sit at counsel table in the hope that the prosecution's witnesses will identify that person as the perpetrator? Several courts have held in the negative, upholding contempt convictions for defense counsel who did this.

In the Ninth Circuit case of United States v. Thoreen,[11] defendant was charged with fishing violations. Counsel had next to him at counsel table a person who resembled defendant dressed in jeans, heavy shoes, a plaid shirt, and a jacket-vest. Defendant, attired in a business suit and large round glasses, sat behind the rail in a row normally reserved for the press. Throughout the trial, counsel gestured to the person next to him as though he were the client. He gave him a yellow pad on which to take notes and conferred with him. Counsel did not correct the court when it referred to the person next to counsel as the defendant and caused the record to show identification of that person as the defendant. Two government witnesses identified the person next to counsel as the perpetrator. Following the government's case, counsel called the person sitting next to him as a witness and disclosed the substitution. The court allowed the government to reopen its case, whereupon the government recalled one of the witnesses, who identified the defendant. The defendant was convicted and counsel was found in criminal contempt.

Upholding the contempt conviction, the Ninth Circuit reasoned that counsel's conduct was inappropriate because, contrary to DR 7–106(C)(5),[12] it violated the court custom that only counsel and parties sit at counsel table without special permission, and that it obstructed justice because it delayed the proceedings by requiring the recalling and reexamination of the identification witness and impeded the court's ability to ascertain the truth. The court concluded that "[t]he [trial] court's

("The line is not easily drawn between proper review of the facts and refreshment of the recollection of a witness and putting words in the mouth of the witness or ideas in his mind"); State v. McCormick, 298 N.C. 788, 259 S.E.2d 880 (1979) (preparation is proper as long as lawyer is preparing witness to give *the witness'* testimony as opposed to testimony lawyer has placed in witness' mouth).

Cf. Shedlock v. Marshall, 186 Md. 218, 46 A.2d 349 (1946) (talking to witness during testimony, although during lunch recess, questioned).

Regarding preparation of the *client* as a witness, see M. Freedman, Lawyers' Ethics in an Adversary System, ch. 6 (1975). Cf. Geders v. United States, 425 U.S. 80, 96 S.Ct. 1330, 47 L.Ed.2d 592 (1976) (trial court's ordering criminal defendant not to consult with counsel during overnight recess during his testimony violated sixth amendment right to assistance of counsel); United States v. Conway, 632 F.2d 641 (5th Cir. 1980) (same regarding brief daytime recess); Potashnick v. Port City Construction Co., 609 F.2d 1101, 54 A.L.R.Fed. 825 (5th Cir.) (barring *civil* litigant from consulting with lawyer during breaks and recesses in litigant's testimony violated due process), cert. denied 449 U.S. 820, 101 S.Ct. 78, 66 L.Ed.2d 22 (1980); Cartin v. Continental Homes, 134 Vt. 362, 360 A.2d 96 (1976) (preventing consultation in civil case was at least abuse of discretion, and perhaps unconstitutional).

**11.** 653 F.2d 1332 (9th Cir. 1981), cert. denied 455 U.S. 938, 102 S.Ct. 1428, 71 L.Ed.2d 648 (1982).

**12.** DR 7–106(C)(5) specifies, "In appearing in his professional capacity before a tribunal, a lawyer shall not * * * [f]ail to comply with known local customs of courtesy or practice of the bar or a particular tribunal without giving to opposing counsel timely notice of his intent not to comply."

ire and this criminal contempt conviction could have been avoided easily and the admirable goal of representing his client zealously preserved if only [counsel] had given the court and opposing counsel prior notice and sought the court's consent," and noted:

"If identification is at issue, an attorney could test a witness's credibility by notifying the court and counsel that it is and by seeking the court's permission to (1) seat two or more persons at counsel table without identifying the defendant; (2) have no one at counsel table; (3) hold an in-court lineup."

In Miskovsky v. State ex rel. Jones,[13] an Oklahoma court upheld a contempt conviction for similar conduct, saying that although counsel never referred to the substitute as being the defendant, counsel's actions "were *designed* to create that mistaken assumption" and "indicated a disrespectful attitude for the judicial process, in that he felt it necessary to resort to deception and misrepresentation to protect his client's interest" rather than informing the court of his intentions.

Quite analogous to these "counsel table" cases is the 1931 disciplinary case of In re Metzger.[14] In that case, a 2–1 Hawaii Supreme Court imposed a ten-day suspension on a murder case defense counsel for secretly (albeit with witnesses) substituting a writing prepared by himself for a court exhibit which a prosecution expert witness had testified came from the same hand as other court exhibits. The court reasoned:

"There can be no doubt that it was the right and the duty of the respondent, who was entrusted with the defense of two men who were on trial for their lives, to expose if he could what he believed to be a lack of ability and a lack of credibility or accuracy on the part of the witness who had testified as an expert on handwriting; but there was a limitation upon that right and that duty and the limitation was that the test and the exposure must be accomplished by fair and lawful means, free from falsehood and misrepresentation. The so-called 'necessities of the case,' the keenness of the desire of the attorney to defend the accused to the best of his ability, cannot in our judgment justify falsehood or misrepresentation by the attorney to a witness or to the clerk of the court, whether that falsehood or misrepresentation be expressed in direct language or be conveyed by artful subterfuge. We are unwilling to certify to the younger attorneys who are beginning their experience at the bar of this court, or to any of the attorneys of this Territory, that it is lawful and proper for them to defend men, even though on trial for their lives, by the use of falsehood and misrepresentation, direct or indirect. The conduct of the respondent was unethical and unprofessional."

The dissenting justice protested:

"[Counsel] testified that having had considerable experience in chirography he believed that the writing on the [exhibits] was not by

13. 586 P.2d 1104 (Okl.Crim.App.1978).

14. 31 Hawaii 929 (1931).

the same person * * *. His purpose therefore was not the evil one of misleading the jury as to a fact which he knew existed but the laudable one of exposing what he believed to be an erroneous opinion. This was in the interest of justice and not against it. [Counsel] also testified that he had been unable after a long cross-examination of [the witness] to discredit his opinion and that there was no other handwriting expert available whom he could consult or to whose opinion he could submit the writings. His only alternative therefore was in some way to lead [the witness] to disclose his own fallibility. The question that remains is whether the means he used to accomplish his purpose were unethical.

"I do not think that his treatment of the witness was unfair. A cross-examiner is certainly under no professional obligation to warn an expert witness, whose opinion he wishes to test, of the pit which has been dug for him and into which he will fall unless he has sufficient technical learning to discover and avoid it. Nor do I think it a violation of legal ethics to withhold from such witness a fact which, if he knew it, would enable him to discover the pit independently of his technical knowledge. It is a principle peculiar to the cross-examination of expert witnesses that in order to evaluate their opinions things may be assumed as facts which are not facts. This is all that [counsel] really did."

## E. DEALING WITH OPPONENTS

### MODEL RULES OF PROFESSIONAL CONDUCT

**RULE 4.1 Truthfulness in Statements to Others**

In the course of representing a client a lawyer shall not knowingly:

(a) make a false statement of material fact or law to a third person; or

(b) fail to disclose a material fact to a third person when disclosure is necessary to avoid assisting a criminal or fraudulent act by a client, unless disclosure is prohibited by Rule 1.6.

**RULE 4.2 Communication With Person Represented by Counsel**

In representing a client, a lawyer shall not communicate about the subject of the representation with a party the lawyer knows to be represented by another lawyer in the matter, unless the lawyer has the consent of the other lawyer or is authorized by law to do so.

**RULE 4.3 Dealing With Unrepresented Person**

In dealing on behalf of a client with a person who is not represented by counsel, a lawyer shall not state or imply that the lawyer is disinterested. When the lawyer knows or reasonably should know that the unrepresented person misunderstands the lawyer's role in the matter, the lawyer shall make reasonable efforts to correct the misunderstanding.

**RULE 4.4 Respect for Rights of Third Persons**

In representing a client, a lawyer shall not use means that have no substantial purpose other than to embarrass, delay, or burden a third person, or use methods of obtaining evidence that violate the legal rights of such a person.[a]

### *Questions*

(1) Defendant was charged with aggravated assault on an elderly woman. Defense counsel learned that the victim would die shortly. Without disclosing this to the prosecuting attorney, knowing the latter was ignorant of it, the two consummated a plea bargain which was carried out. Subsequently the victim died and a murder prosecution was started. The plea bargain was held a bar. Did defense counsel act properly?[1]

(2) You are a lawyer representing a defendant who has authorized you to settle for any amount under $100,000. Plaintiff's lawyer says, "I think $90,000 will settle this case. Will your client give $90,000?" What do you say?[2]

Is RPC 4.1(a)'s Comment sound in specifying as follows?

"This Rule refers to statements of fact. Whether a particular statement should be regarded as one of fact can depend on the cir-

a. Compare the following CPR provisions:

**"DR 7-102 Representing a Client Within the Bounds of the Law**

"(A) In his representation of a client, a lawyer shall not:

(1) File a suit, assert a position, conduct a defense, delay a trial, or take other action on behalf of his client when he knows or when it is obvious that such action would serve merely to harass or maliciously injure another.

* * *

(3) Conceal or knowingly fail to disclose that which he is required by law to reveal.

* * *

(5) Knowingly make a false statement of law or fact.

* * *

**"DR 7-104 Communicating With One of Adverse Interest**

"(A) During the course of his representation of a client a lawyer shall not:

(1) Communicate or cause another to communicate on the subject of the representation with a party he knows to be represented by a lawyer in that matter unless he has the prior consent of the lawyer representing such other party or is authorized by law to do so.

(2) Give advice to a person who is not represented by a lawyer, other than the advice to secure counsel, if the interests of such person are or have a reasonable possibility of being in conflict with the interests of his client.

**"DR 7-105 Threatening Criminal Prosecution**

"(A) A lawyer shall not present, participate in presenting, or threaten to present criminal charges solely to obtain an advantage in a civil matter."

1. In State v. Thomas, 61 N.J. 314, 294 A.2d 57 (1962), holding the assault conviction a bar to the murder prosecution, the court noted that the prosecution could have discovered the victim's condition and said that "it forms no part of the duties of defense counsel to alert the State to imminent pitfalls or warn of possible missteps."

Compare Spaulding v. Zimmerman, 263 Minn. 346, 116 N.W.2d 704 (1962) (while no canon of ethics or legal obligation required civil defendant's lawyers, before settling for $6500, to disclose that defendant's lawyer had found plaintiff to have an aneurysm apparently caused by the accident, this opened the way for the court later to vacate the settlement).

Regarding prosecutors, see infra p. 367, Problem (2).

2. See White, Machiavelli and the Bar: Ethical Limitations on Lying in Negotiation, 1980 Am.B.Found.Research J. 926, 932–33.

cumstances. *Under generally accepted conventions in negotiation, certain types of statements ordinarily are not taken as statements of material fact. Estimates of price or value* placed on the subject of a transaction *and a party's intentions as to an acceptable settlement of a claim are in this category*, and so is the existence of an undisclosed principal except where nondisclosure of the principal would constitute fraud."[3]

## PEOPLE v. GREEN

405 Mich. 273, 274 N.W.2d 448 (1979).

COLEMAN, Chief Justice [joined by RYAN, J.] (to affirm).

The defendant appeals his conviction of first-degree murder. The question presented is whether voluntary statements made by the defendant to a detective and an assistant prosecuting attorney after knowingly and understandingly waiving his right to an attorney and his right to remain silent must nonetheless be suppressed if the assistant prosecuting attorney violated Disciplinary Rule 7–104(A)(1) * * * which states:

> "During the course of his representation of a client a lawyer shall not:
>
> "(1) Communicate or cause another to communicate on the subject of the representation with a party he knows to be represented by a lawyer in that matter unless he has the prior consent of the lawyer representing such other party or is authorized by law to do so."

The Court of Appeals ruled, one judge dissenting, that an ethics violation alone does not warrant or require the suppression of voluntary statements.

We affirm.

### I

On October 19, 1974 at approximately 8:30 p. m., the victim left her home and drove to a nearby market to purchase some milk. * * *

The victim's whereabouts remained unknown until the late afternoon of October 21 when some hunters found her body floating in a nearby river. An autopsy performed the next day revealed that she had been stabbed once in the back and once in the chest. * * *

On October 24 the police arrested the defendant and booked him for murder. The detective in charge of the case then drove the defendant to the area where the victim's body had been found and advised the defendant of his *Miranda* rights * * *. The defendant indi-

3. Emphasis added.

Compare Curtis, The Ethics of Advocacy, 4 Stan.L.Rev. 3 (1951) (lawyer sometimes warranted and perhaps obligated to lie for client) with Drinker, Some Remarks on Mr. Curtis' "The Ethics of Advocacy," 4 Stan.L.Rev. 349 (1952) (that view is inconsistent with profession's obligations and ideals).

cated that he understood his rights and would waive them. He then denied having any knowledge of the murder.

On October 28 the defendant sent a message to the detective asking to speak with him. The defendant complained that the guards at the jail were harassing him. That afternoon the detective visited the defendant at the jail. After hearing his *Miranda* rights and again waiving them, the defendant proffered a statement concerning his supposed whereabouts on the night of the crime and again denied having any knowledge of the murder. * * *

On October 31, counsel was appointed to represent the defendant. * * *

Sometime during the middle of November, the defendant again sent word to the detective, asking to speak with him. The detective and the assistant prosecuting attorney assigned to the case visited the defendant at the jail. However, when the detective advised the defendant of his *Miranda* rights, the defendant indicated that he wanted to speak with his attorney before talking further about the case. The discussion ceased immediately at that point.

Near the end of January, 1975, the defendant again sent word to the authorities expressing a desire to talk. On January 29 the detective and the assistant prosecuting attorney * * * visited the defendant at the jail. They did not communicate with the defendant's attorney. The detective advised the defendant of his *Miranda* rights. The defendant waived his rights and said that he wanted to talk to the authorities without his attorney present. The detective asked about the murder and the defendant proceeded to tell an exculpatory story about driving to a store on the night of the crime to purchase some wine and meeting a man who revealed a large knife and said something about "killing this bitch". The defendant said he gave this man a ride to a bar and later discovered that the man had managed to slip the knife underneath the defendant's coat in the back seat of the defendant's car. * * * He refused to identify the man. At the end of this story, the assistant prosecuting attorney, who, up to that point, had only been taking notes, asked the defendant if he was telling the whole truth. The defendant said that he was.

Prior to trial * * * defense counsel objected to the admission of the January 29 statements * * *. The trial judge overruled the objection and the statements were ultimately admitted into evidence at trial.

The jury convicted the defendant of first-degree premeditated murder.

II

On appeal the defendant has not argued that his statements were involuntary or that the authorities failed to comply with the *Miranda* requirements. Instead he contends that the statements should have been suppressed because the assistant prosecuting attorney violated DR 7–104(A)(1). Alternatively he contends that the statements should have been suppressed because the assistant prosecuting attorney's conduct was so fundamentally unfair and shocking to the sensibilities of reasonable persons that it violated general notions of due process of law.

The state responds that there was no violation of DR 7–104(A)(1) in this case because the defendant initiated the January 29 discussion, waived his right to counsel and indicated that he wanted to talk to the authorities without his attorney present. Further, the state argues that the assistant prosecuting attorney played only a minor role in the discussion listening to the defendant and taking notes, and that there was no overreaching of any kind. Alternatively the state contends that the exclusionary rule does not apply to violations of the Code of Professional Responsibility. The proper action is disciplinary proceedings against the offending attorney. Finally, the state argues that if the admission of the defendant's statements at trial was error, it was harmless.

III

The threshold question is whether the assistant prosecuting attorney violated DR 7–104(A)(1). * * *

The state has conceded in its brief that prosecuting attorneys are not exempt from the strictures of DR 7–104(A)(1). * * *

The argument that the defendant's request to speak out of the presence of his attorney obviates the necessity of notifying the defendant's attorney and obtaining his or her consent is contrary to opinions by both the American Bar Association and Michigan State Bar Association Committees on Professional Ethics.

In ABA Formal Opinion 108 issued in 1934, the Committee was asked to interpret the forerunner of DR 7–104(A)(1), old Canon 9 * * *. The question before the committee was whether the plaintiff's attorney in a civil case could ethically interview the defendant in the absence of the defendant's attorney if the defendant was willing to discuss the case. The committee unanimously answered in the negative and, after quoting Canon 9, stated:

> "The reasons for such a prohibition are equally clear. They arise out of the nature of the relation of attorney and client and are equally imperative in the right and interest of the adverse party and of his attorney. To preserve the proper functioning of the legal profession as well as to shield the adverse party from improper approaches the Canon is wise and beneficent and should be obeyed." * * *

The quotation from ABA Formal Opinion 108 set forth above indicates that there is more to this ethical prohibition than just the prevention of overreaching. The rights and interests of the adverse party's attorney and the proper functioning of the legal system are involved as well.

Ethical Consideration 7–18 * * * emphasizes the importance of this ethical prohibition to the functioning of the legal system:

"The legal system in its broadest sense functions best when persons in need of legal advice or assistance are represented by their own counsel. For this reason a lawyer should not communicate on the subject matter of the representation of his client with a person he knows to be represented in the matter by a lawyer, unless pursuant to law or rule of court or unless he has the consent of the lawyer for that person."

Other authorities have not exempted prosecuting attorneys from the strictures of DR 7–104(A)(1) in fact situations where the defendant requested an interview or was willing to speak and where there was no overreaching.[12] * * *

We hold that while this defendant's initiative and willingness to speak and the lack of overreaching by the assistant prosecuting attorney are factors to be considered in mitigation, they do not excuse compliance with the standard of professional conduct prescribed by DR 7–104(A) (1).

IV

Our resolution of the question above brings us to the principal dispute in this appeal—whether the voluntary statements made by the defendant after knowingly and understandingly waiving his *Miranda* rights must nonetheless be suppressed solely because the assistant prosecuting attorney violated DR 7–104(A)(1). * * *

The defendant has argued that the violation of DR 7–104(A)(1) was a violation of his rights and that unless his statements are suppressed, he will have no effective remedy to redress the wrong done to him.

This argument rests upon a basic misconception of the Code of Professional Responsibility. The provisions of the code are not constitutional or statutory rights guaranteed to individual persons. They are instead self-imposed internal regulations prescribing the standards of conduct for members of the bar. Although it is true that the principal purpose of many provisions is the protection of the public, the remedy for a violation has traditionally been internal bar disciplinary action against the offending attorney. The sanctions available are by no means trivial. The attorney faces permanent disbarment. In these respects the provisions of the code are no different from the provisions found in the codes of conduct for other professions, such as medicine or architecture. They are all self-governing in-house regulations.

12. See, for example, United States v. Carlson, 423 F.2d 431, 442 (CA 9, 1970), cert. den. 400 U.S. 847, 91 S.Ct. 94, 27 L.Ed.2d 84 (1970); United States v. Four Star, 428 F.2d 1406, 1407 (CA 9, 1970), cert. den. 400 U.S. 947, 91 S.Ct. 255, 27 L.Ed.2d 253 (1970); United States v. Springer, 460 F.2d 1344, 1353–1354 (CA 7, 1972), cert. den. 409 U.S. 873, 93 S.Ct. 205, 34 L.Ed.2d 125 (1972); and United States v. Thomas, 474 F.2d 110, 111–112 (CA 10, 1973), cert. den. 412 U.S. 932, 93 S.Ct. 2758, 37 L.Ed.2d 160 (1973).

The admissibility of evidence in a court of law, on the other hand, is normally determined by reference to relevant constitutional and statutory provisions, applicable court rules and pertinent common-law doctrines. Codes of professional conduct play no part in such decisions.

Few courts have mixed the standard of conduct found in DR 7–104(A)(1) or any other provision of a code of professional responsibility into questions concerning the admissibility of evidence in criminal or civil cases. Even the courts which have embraced this novel concept have linked their decisions to do so with constitutional doctrines or statutory provisions not recognized or present in Michigan's jurisprudence. See, for example, People v. Hobson, 39 N.Y.2d 479, 384 N.Y.S.2d 419, 348 N.E.2d 894 (1976).

The defendant also has argued that if his statements are not suppressed this Court would in effect give its stamp of approval to unethical conduct. As this opinion clearly indicates in part III above, such a conclusion is unsupported. To the contrary, part III reflects a commitment by the Court to insure that future violations do not occur.

The facts in the case at bar provide a good example why a violation of DR 7–104(A)(1) standing alone should be dealt with by bar disciplinary action rather than by withholding relevant and material evidence from the jury.

The defendant had a story he wanted to tell to the authorities, presumably to clear himself of the murder charge lodged against him. He sent word to the authorities and asked to speak with them. He waived his *Miranda* rights with full knowledge of what he was doing. He specifically stated that he wanted to talk without his attorney present. The assistant prosecuting attorney and the detective did little except listen to what the defendant had to say and take notes. The defendant's statements were completely voluntary and there was no overreaching of any kind. When asked if he was telling the whole truth, defendant said that he was.

Reversal of the conviction and grant of a new trial (if in fact the witnesses and evidence presented in 1975 could be obtained for a second trial) solely because of this less than consequential violation of DR 7–104(A)(1) would constitute reprehensible "overkill".

In cases such as this, bar disciplinary action directed against the offending attorney would be a more appropriate response and would serve as a more effective deterrent than the indirect sanction of the exclusionary rule. Although the presence of a prosecuting attorney is still one factor to be considered in assessing the "totality of the circumstances" in order to determine whether a defendant's statements are constitutionally admissible, we find no unconstitutional intrusion in this factual situation.

This resolution makes it unnecessary to consider the state's argument that if admission of the defendant's statements at trial was error, it was harmless.

V

The final question is whether the assistant prosecuting attorney's conduct was so fundamentally unfair and shocking to the sensibilities of reasonable persons that it rises to the level of a violation of due process of law. We find that it does not.

As noted above, the assistant prosecuting attorney's conduct, although a violation of DR 7–104(A)(1), was relatively innocuous. It pales in comparison to the cases in which a due process violation has been found. See, for example, Rochin v. California, 342 U.S. 165, 72 S.Ct. 205, 96 L.Ed. 183 (1952).

This is not a case in which the authorities used deception or force to extract a confession from an ignorant and helpless defendant. At most they acquiesced in a course of conduct initiated by a defendant who knew precisely what he was doing after they offered him the right to have counsel present and after that right was refused. We do not find this so unfair or so shocking that the defendant's conviction must be reversed.

We affirm.

WILLIAMS, Justice [joined by WILLIAMS and FITZGERALD, JJ.] (concurring in part; dissenting in part).

I concur with my sister Coleman's opinion that the prophylactic exclusionary rule need not, and should not, be extended to cover this case. However, while I agree that the assistant prosecuting attorney's action did not rise to the level of a violation of due process of law, I disagree that his action was "innocuous." I would affirm but order the Clerk to report this matter to bar grievance authorities for appropriate action.

The "prophylactic exclusionary rule" is an indirect method to deter wrongful police action. Since the courts have no effective direct method of disciplining police officers, this indirect method, which costs the public a retrial, has been justified.

However, with respect to attorneys, including prosecuting attorneys, the courts do have a direct method of discipline to deter their wrongful action. Attorneys can be disciplined by the bar grievance authorities, and the courts can refer attorneys to them for appropriate action.

Therefore, to deter future action as here committed, without burdening the public criminal justice system with a retrial, and to directly reach the alleged wrongdoer, I would order the Clerk to report the assistant prosecuting attorney's action in this matter to the grievance authorities for appropriate action.

KAVANAGH, Justice [joined by LEVIN, J.] (concurring in part; dissenting in part).

I concur in the holding that the prosecutor violated DR 7–104(A)(1) when he took part in the questioning of Ernest Green without first notifying defense counsel. I do not agree that the defendant's statements should be admissible.

The opinion for affirmance sets forth the conventional view that disciplinary action under the established grievance procedure is an adequate method of dealing with violations of disciplinary rules. Violation of such rules, it is asserted, does not affect the admissibility of evidence.

The opinion also rejects the defendant's argument that without suppression of his statements he will have no redress for the wrong done to him.

I am convinced both the opinion and the defendant's argument misperceive the error and ignore this Court's duty to supervise the procedure of trial as well as the practice of law.

Here the evidence sought to be introduced was obtained in violation of one of this Court's established rules of practice.

This action by the prosecutor is an affront to the whole profession for it diminishes the effectiveness of the attorney-client relationship, and enfeebles defendant's Fifth and Sixth Amendment rights.

But we should not here be diverted by consideration of any violation of defendant's rights. We should treat the affront to this Court and the procedure it has established. I would apply the exclusionary rule for the purpose of deterring unacceptable practice of the type involved in this case.

The evidence should be suppressed to give unmistakable notice that, in addition to exposure to disciplinary action, disregard of our rules will in no way assist an attorney in the performance of professional duty.

MOODY, Justice (concurring in part; dissenting in part).

I concur in the holding that the prosecutor violated DR 7–104(A)(1) when he took part in the questioning of Ernest Green without first notifying defense counsel. Under the circumstances of this case, I do not agree that the defendant's statements should be admissible.

The prosecutor was a direct participant in the preparation for and the conducting of this interview. The influence of the prosecutor's presence upon the defendant is immeasurable. Defense counsel's presence could have substantially altered the interrogation. Furthermore, the prosecutor twice accompanied the detective to interrogate Green without notification to defense counsel. * * *

LEVIN, Justice (dissenting). * * *

We all agree that [DR 7–104(A)(1)] was violated and that it is applicable in criminal as well as in civil cases. We disagree whether the statement should be suppressed. * * *

A primary purpose of the rule is to protect persons represented by a lawyer from harming their cases by statements to opposing lawyers.

Only suppression of a statement obtained in violation of the rule will vindicate that interest which the rule was designed to protect. * * *

I

The concept that persons are benefited by retention of and active representation by a lawyer is deeply ingrained in our legal system. The status we afford this belief is most evident in the development of the Sixth-Amendment right to counsel in criminal proceedings. * * * [The concept of] protecting a litigant, not only from the approaches of his adversary's lawyer, but from the folly of his own well-meaning initiatives and the generally unfortunate consequences of his ignorance * * * is reflected in DR 7–104(A)(1).[10]

II

The lead opinion states that the Code of Professional Responsibility and the Disciplinary Rules are designed to protect "attorney[s]," the "proper functioning of the legal system" and "the public." The opinion avoids acknowledging that any citizen, any plaintiff, any defendant, any individual human being who is not a lawyer has an interest protected by the Code. Having failed to acknowledge that anyone other than a lawyer has a protected interest, it need not come to grips with the effective protection of that interest.

A primary purpose of the rule is to "shield the adverse party," not, as the lead opinion states, the "adverse party's attorney":

> "The reasons for such a prohibition are equally clear. They arise out of the nature of the relation of attorney and client and are equally imperative in the right and interest of the adverse party and of his attorney. To preserve the proper functioning of the legal profession as well as *to shield the adverse party* from improper approaches the canon is wise and beneficent and should be obeyed." ABA Committee on Professional Ethics, Formal Opinion 108 (1934) (emphasis supplied).

The emphasis on the protection of people goes beyond abstract concerns about the public reputation of the bar and general harm to society; the Code recognizes that individuals can be concretely harmed by violations of ethical standards. * * *

The public is not an abstract entity; it consists of individuals who are the intended beneficiaries of the Court's actions in regulating the conduct of the bar. It would be anomalous for the Court to claim to be acting for the "protection of the public" and in the interest of "the administration of justice" and then refuse in individual cases to assure that particular persons are not harmed by unethical practices; the Court cannot protect the public except by protecting individuals.

10. " * * * DR 7–104 * * * protects a party against himself by ensuring that contacts with opposing attorneys will take place only through the party's own counsel or in his presence." Note, DR 7–104 of the Code of Professional Responsibility Applied to the Government "Party", 61 Minn.L.Rev. 1007, 1012 (1977).

The Code's purpose of protecting individuals from becoming the victims of unethical behavior has led courts to assume an active role in its enforcement, going beyond mere review of disciplinary proceedings that may reach the courts. Rather than sit by and await possible disciplinary proceedings, the courts have exercised their supervisory power in particular cases to undo the damage caused individual human beings.

Courts have required counsel, on the authority of the disciplinary rules and canons, to choose between withdrawing from the case and having his otherwise admissible testimony on behalf of his client barred.

Courts have also acted pursuant to the disciplinary rules and canons, in both civil and criminal cases, to protect a former client when his lawyer subsequently represents an adverse interest. Lawyers have been disqualified in such circumstances, and judgments in favor of the lawyer's new client have been reversed.

In criminal cases, courts have found the Code of Professional Responsibility an independent basis for disqualifying a prosecutor from handling a case because of a personal or other relationship with the accused making it inappropriate for him to prosecute. Also, indictments have been quashed or dismissed, and convictions reversed or habeas corpus relief granted. * * *

III

I have not found a single civil case in any jurisdiction in which a court has suggested that disciplinary proceedings are the only appropriate and available "remedy" for a party who has been directly harmed by conduct violative of DR 7–104(A)(1). In civil cases, the courts have acted to protect individuals who would otherwise have been victimized by violations of the rule.[23]

* * * Since the stakes in criminal cases are generally higher, and incarceration tends to put defendants under pressure to seek out

23. In Mitton v. State Bar of California, 71 Cal.2d 525, 78 Cal.Rptr. 649, 455 P.2d 753 (1969), plaintiff's lawyer in an automobile accident case was accused of violating professional ethics by conferring with a defendant represented by a lawyer concerning defendant's motion for a new trial after a jury verdict against her. It appears that with no notice given to defendant's lawyer, plaintiff's lawyer in conjunction with defendant drew up a declaration stating that the motion for a new trial was without defendant's consent and against her wishes. Defendant signed this declaration. The declaration was offered at the time the motion for new trial was set for hearing. The hearing judge not only called this incident to the attention of the state bar, but refused to accept or consider the declaration because defendant's lawyer had not been notified or consulted.

In Obser v. Adelson, 96 N.Y.S.2d 817 (Sup.Ct.1949), aff'd 276 App.Div. 999, 95 N.Y.S.2d 757 (1950), a motion to suppress evidence was at issue. An action was brought on behalf of an infant injured as a result of alleged negligence. The infant's father retained a lawyer who advised defendants of the infant's claim. Defendants' lawyer was also notified of the claim by plaintiff's lawyer. Subsequently, a representative of defendants' lawyer obtained a statement from the infant's mother. The court directed that the statement be "suppressed and that the defendants be not permitted to use the same for any purpose whatsoever." See, also, Chilcutt v. Baker, 355 S.W.2d 338 (Mo., St. Louis Ct.App.1962).

the prosecutorial authorities in a generally hapless effort to extricate themselves, the need for protecting defendants in criminal cases is most compelling. Both the Michigan and ABA ethics committees have refused to draw any distinction between violations of the rule in criminal and civil cases.[25]

The heart of the matter is that if the rule's purpose of protecting people is to be achieved, evidence obtained in violation of the rule must be suppressed. Disciplinary proceedings against a prosecuting attorney do not undo the harm caused an individual who otherwise might not have been convicted.

Further, it is uncertain what, if any, grievance action will be taken. It will often be left to the defendant or his attorney to report ethical violations and initiate disciplinary proceedings. It flies in the face of reason to expect a defendant to risk a prosecutor's actual or imagined displeasure by instituting proceedings that cannot directly benefit him. The defendant may not unreasonably believe such action will adversely affect his case in subsequent proceedings at the trial, on appeal or at a retrial following an appeal, or his later chances for parole.

It is unlikely that a defendant has any cause of action for damages against a prosecutor.[26] Even if a defendant has such a remedy, few will think that a loss of liberty can be adequately compensated, especially, as here, where the defendant has been imprisoned for life.

* * * The Court cannot justify promulgation of DR 7–104(A)(1), designed to protect people, often from themselves, but, when actual abuse occurs, failure to enforce that protection in a meaningful manner.

An excuse is sometimes offered that the overriding importance of disclosing the truth justifies a court's failure to suppress illicitly obtained evidence. But our legal system operates on the principle that the goal is the ascertainment of truth within the limitations imposed by law. Lawyers—prosecutors especially—play an important role in the administration of justice and thus the Code of Professional Responsibility regulating their conduct in relation to those who encounter

**25.** * * * In Informal Opinion 1373 (1976) the ABA committee considered the propriety of a prosecuting attorney mailing a plea offer to both a defendant and his lawyer. The committee concluded:

"In the view of the committee, the sending of a copy of the offer to the defendant is unethical in that it violates DR 7–104(A)(1). * * *

"The committee had occasion recently in Informal Opinion 1348 to consider the rule in the context of a civil matter. The committee held that it was improper to send a copy of a settlement offer to the other party (the original going to the attorney) * * *. *We see no valid reason for a different result in criminal matters. In fact, there are perhaps stronger policy considerations in criminal cases.* A copy of a letter such as the sample furnished could have the effect of influencing a defendant to plead guilty to a crime for which no indictment might ever be returned. The defendant should have the advice of his counsel at hand when such an offer is transmitted to him." (Emphasis supplied.)

**26.** Cf. Mallen & Levit, Legal Malpractice (1977), § 117; see, e.g., Merritt-Chapman & Scott Corp. v. Elgin Coal, Inc., 358 F.Supp. 17 (E.D.Tenn. 1972); Spencer v. Burglass, 337 So.2d 596 (La.App.1976); Noble v. Sears, Roebuck & Co., 33 Cal.App.3d 654, 109 Cal.Rptr. 269 (1973); Tingle v. Arnold, Cate & Allen, 129 Ga.App. 134, 199 S.E.2d 260 (1973).

the system is part of the very fabric of the law. There can be no ordered system of law if those for whose protection the Code has been promulgated are not effectively protected from harm caused by its violation. No lawyer should be permitted to advance his client's cause with evidence obtained from another lawyer's client in violation of a rule designed as a safeguard against that very violation.

Courts have suppressed evidence in criminal cases where a violation of DR 7–104(A)(1) has occured.

In United States v. Thomas, 474 F.2d 110, 112 (CA 10, 1973),[a] a written statement was obtained from the defendant in the absence of and without the knowledge of his lawyer. The statement was obtained at an interview requested by the defendant at which he read and signed a *Miranda*-type waiver of rights form. The court held that the ethical violation required suppression of the statement:

> "[O]nce a criminal defendant has either retained an attorney or had an attorney appointed for him by the court, any statement obtained by interview from such defendant may not be offered in evidence for any purpose unless the accused's attorney was notified of the interview which produced the statement and was given a reasonable opportunity to be present. *To hold otherwise, we think, would be to overlook conduct which violated both the letter and the spirit of the canons of ethics.* This is obviously not something which the defendant alone can waive." (Emphasis supplied.)[b]

The New York Court of Appeals in People v. Hobson, 39 N.Y.2d 479, 384 N.Y.S.2d 419, 348 N.E.2d 894 (1976), held that New York's constitutional protections prevented a defendant in custody, represented by a lawyer, from waiving his right to counsel in the absence of his lawyer. The Court said that apart from the constitutional violation, the statements should have been excluded under the Code of Professional Responsibility:

> "Moreover, an attempt to secure a waiver of the right of counsel in a criminal proceeding in the absence of a lawyer, already retained or assigned, would constitute a breach of professional ethics, as it would be in the least-consequential civil matter (see DR 7–104[A] [1]) * * *. Since the Code of Professional Responsibility is applicable, *it would be grossly incongruous for the courts to blink its violation in a criminal matter.*"

The Court then explained why it is important to enforce DR 7–104(A)(1):

> "[T]he principle is not so much, important as that is, to preserve the civilized decencies, but to protect the individual, often ignorant and uneducated, and always in fear, when faced with the coercive

a. Cert. denied 412 U.S. 932, 93 S.Ct. 2758, 37 L.Ed.2d 160 (1973).

b. However, the *Thomas* court went on to hold that "[a] violation of the canon * * * need not be remedied by a reversal" of the conviction.

police power of the State. *The right to the continued advice of a lawyer, already retained or assigned, is his real protection against an abuse of power by the organized State.* It is more important than the preinterrogation warnings given to defendants in custody. These warnings often provide only a feeble opportunity to obtain a lawyer, because the suspect or accused is required to determine his need, unadvised by anyone who has his interests at heart. The danger is not only the risk of unwise waivers of the privilege against self incrimination and of the right to counsel, but the more significant risk of inaccurate, sometimes false, and inevitably incomplete descriptions of the events described." ([E]mphasis supplied).[28]

## IV

I do not believe that the Court intends to circumscribe its powers to the extent that it cannot enforce the Code of Professional Responsibility except through disciplinary proceedings. * * *

28. In both *Thomas* and *Hobson* the statement was made to a police officer and the government's lawyer was not present. The courts nevertheless concluded that the disciplinary rule had been violated, and that the statement should be suppressed. The rationale is that the police, after commencement of prosecution, are acting as investigators for the prosecutor. See ABA Opinion 95 and People v. Patterson, 39 Mich.App. 467, 475, 198 N.W.2d 175 (1972) (Levin, P. J., dissenting). [Eds.: Compare United States v. Kenny, 645 F.2d 1323, 1339 (9th Cir.) (no violation where prosecutor arranged for informant to tape phone conversation *before* represented defendant's arrest or commencement of prosecution), cert. denied 452 U.S. 920, 101 S.Ct. 3059, 69 L.Ed.2d 425 (1981).]

See United States v. Wedra, 343 F.Supp. 1183 (S.D.N.Y.1972), where the defendant was questioned in the absence of and without the knowledge of his attorney. After being given *Miranda* warnings, the defendant was asked if he cared to make a statement. He replied in the negative, but did answer a series of questions. * * * The court suppressed, finding that defendant did not waive his constitutional right to counsel and to remain silent. The court offered as an independent ground * * * its supervisory power to suppress statements unethically obtained. [T]he court said:

> "I see little point in well-intentioned utterances denouncing in-custody interrogation of an accused person known to be represented by counsel without affording counsel an opportunity to be present, or in condemning prosecuting attorneys who take part in such interrogation in violation of professional ethics and then allowing the government to become the beneficiary of the condemned conduct. The only effective way to terminate this unfair and at times unethical practice is to prohibit the government from using its illicit fruits."

See, also, United States v. Brown, [569 F.2d 236, 240 (5th Cir. 1978)] (Simpson, J., dissenting); Coughlan v. United States, [391 F.2d 371, 372 (9th Cir. 1968)] (Hamley, J., dissenting).

See, also, United States v. Springer, [460 F.2d 1344 (7th Cir.), cert. denied 409 U.S. 873, 93 S.Ct. 205, 34 L.Ed.2d 125 (1972)]; and United States v. Smith, [379 F.2d 628 (7th Cir.), cert. denied 389 U.S. 993, 88 S.Ct. 491, 19 L.Ed.2d 486 (1967)], where the courts recognized that they had the authority to exclude evidence obtained in violation of old Canon 9 but chose not to.

But see Reinke v. United States, 405 F.2d 228 (CA 9, 1968); State v. Yatman, 320 So.2d 401 (Fla.App.1975); State v. McConnell, 529 S.W.2d 185 (Mo.App.1975). In State v. Richmond, 114 Ariz. 186, 560 P.2d 41 (1976), cert. den. 433 U.S. 915, 97 S.Ct. 2988, 53 L.Ed.2d 1101 (1977); and State v. Nicholson, 77 Wash.2d 415, 463 P.2d 633 (1969), the courts refused in criminal cases to suppress unethically obtained evidence, finding that DR 7–104 is designed to afford protection only to civil litigants. In United States v. Crook, [502 F.2d 1378 (3d Cir. 1974)], the court held that it was precluded from exercising its supervisory power to exclude evidence unethically obtained in a criminal case by the Omnibus Crime Control and Safe Streets Act of 1968, P.L. 90–351; 18 U.S.C. § 3501(a), which provides that "[i]f the trial judge determines that the confession was voluntarily made it shall be admitted in evidence * * *."

Adoption of such a limiting rule of law might prevent, for example, a court granting relief to an individual charged an excessive contingent fee * * *.

* * * This Court should effectuate [DR 7–104(A)(1)'s] protection in the only way which would be meaningful in this case—by reversing Green's conviction and ordering a new trial at which his statement would be suppressed.[c]

### *Comment*

(1) *"Authorized by law."* In Nai Cheng Chen v. Immigration & Naturalization Service,[1] the First Circuit held that an Immigration and Naturalization Service Investigator did not violate DR 7–104(A)(1) because he was "authorized by law" (8 U.S.C.A. § 1357) to interrogate an alien as to his right to be in the United States, and hence was not required to notify the alien's lawyer although notification was "better practice."

(2) *"Party."* Although RPC 4.2 (like DR 7–104(A)(1)) on its face only restricts communicating with a "party," and not with employees or others connected with a party, RPC 4.2's Comment states:

> "In the case of an organization, this Rule prohibits communications by a lawyer for one party concerning the matter in repre-

**c.** See United States v. Batchelor, 484 F.Supp. 812 (E.D.Pa. 1980) (prosecutor's interviewing defendant without defense counsel's consent required new trial "where significant prejudice may have flowed from the [DR 7–104(A)(1)] breach").

Compare State v. Britton, 157 W.Va. 711, 203 S.E.2d 462 (1974) (due process denied when prosecutor tried case after defendant consulted him about the case following indictment, where prosecutor knew defendant had counsel: "the prosecutor may have gained some information useful to him in securing the subsequent conviction of the accused").

Regarding disqualification because of improper communication with adverse party, see Meat Price Investigators Association v. Spencer Foods, Inc., 448 F.Supp. 1 (S.D.Iowa 1977), affirmed 572 F.2d 163 (8th Cir. 1978); Chronometrics, Inc. v. Sysgen, Inc., 110 Cal.App.3d 597, 168 Cal.Rptr. 196 (1980).

For cases involving discipline for direct dealing with an adverse party, see Abeles v. State Bar, 9 Cal.3d 603, 108 Cal.Rptr. 359, 510 P.2d 719 (1973) (improper even though adverse party said lawyer of record did not in fact represent him); In re Schwabe, 242 Or. 169, 408 P.2d 922 (1965) (lawyer contacted adverse party to check on other lawyer's claim that adverse party had employed him); Annot., 1 A.L.R.3d 1113 (1965).

Compare In re Mauch, 107 Wis.2d 557, 319 N.W.2d 877 (1982), where the court refused to discipline a prosecutor for communicating with a defendant under unique circumstances. When informed that the defendant insisted upon meeting with him, the prosecutor asked the defendant's lawyer for permission. The defendant's lawyer said he neither objected to nor condoned the proposed meeting. The prosecutor invited an associate of defendant's lawyer to attend, but the associate declined. The prosecutor concluded that the defendant had made a conscious decision not to be involved with his court-appointed lawyer, and required that the defendant waive his right to have his lawyer present, which the defendant freely and voluntarily did. The court concluded, "Under the circumstances, nothing more was required of the [prosecutor] in order to enter into a discussion with the defendant, and the [prosecutor's] conduct in this matter was proper."

See also In re Murray, 287 Or. 633, 601 P.2d 780 (1979) (where lawyer gave client papers for opponent to review with his own counsel and sign, no DR 7–104(A) violation where client never delivered papers).

It should be noted that while RPC 4.2 does not include DR 7–104(A)(1)'s language that a lawyer shall not "cause another to communicate" with an unrepresented party and RPC 4.2's Comment specifies that "parties to a matter may communicate directly with each other," RPC 8.4(a) prohibits a lawyer to "violate or attempt to violate the Rules of Professional conduct * * * through the acts of another."

**1.** 537 F.2d 566 (1st Cir. 1976).

sentation with persons having a managerial responsibility on behalf of the organization, and with any other person whose act or omission in connection with that matter may be imputed to the organization for purposes of civil or criminal liability or whose statement may constitute an admission on the part of the organization. If an agent or employee of the organization is represented in the matter by his or her own counsel, the consent by that counsel to a communication will be sufficient for purposes of this Rule."

Similarly, there is authority for construing DR 7–104(A)(1) to restrict communication with certain principals of a corporate, organizational, or governmental "party." Thus, although ABA Formal Opinion 117 (1934) held it permissible for a slip-and-fall plaintiff's lawyer to interview the defendant department store's employees,[2] ABA Informal Opinion 1410 (1979) held that a plaintiff's lawyer could not, without opposing counsel's consent, communicate with any "officer or employee of [the defendant] corporation with the power to commit the corporation in the particular situation," reasoning that such persons "as the alter egos of the corporation, are parties for purposes of DR 7–104(A)(1)."[3] Compare In re FMC Corp.,[4] where a federal district court held that United States attorney and Environmental Protection Agency lawyers investigating a corporation for violation of criminal statutes could, without corporate counsel's consent, interview any of the corporation's people except its president, board chairman, and plant managers.[5]

RPC 4.2's Comment also calls for a broad interpretation of the term "party" by specifying that the Rule "covers any person, whether or not a party *to a formal proceeding*, who is represented by counsel concerning the matter in question."[6]

(3) *Dealing with unrepresented person.* In the Second Circuit case of W. T. Grant v. Haines,[7] plaintiff's lawyer made misleading indications to an unrepresented not-yet-served defendant that candid answers to the lawyer's questions might clear the defendant's name and that the results of his taking a lie detector test might be considered in plaintiff's determining whether to fire him, and said "I think this would be the best way for you to help the company" in requesting defendant's signature on authorizations to obtain confidential infor-

2. See Vega v. Bloomsburgh, 427 F.Supp. 593 (D.Mass. 1977) (plaintiff's lawyer may interview defendant public officials' employees).

3. See ABA Informal Opinion 1377 (1977) (same approach for municipal officer). Compare ABA Informal Opinion 1362 (1976) (plaintiff's lawyer may not, without opposing counsel's consent, communicate with members of defendant professional association's 150-member governing council or of the council's task force).

4. 430 F.Supp. 1108 (S.D.W.Va. 1977).

5. See generally Leubsdorf, Communicating with Another Lawyer's Client: The Lawyer's Veto and the Client's Interests, 127 U.Pa.L.Rev. 683, 694–96 (1979); Note, DR 7–104 of the Code of Professional Responsibility Applied to the Government "Party," 61 Minn.L.Rev. 1007 (1977). Compare supra pp. 260–62.

6. Emphasis added.

7. 531 F.2d 671 (2d Cir. 1976).

mation. The court held that even if the lawyer violated DR 7–104(A)(2)'s prohibition on giving advice (other than to secure counsel) to an unrepresented person whose interests are or reasonably may be in conflict with the client's, the trial court properly refused to impose the sanction of disqualifying the lawyer from representing plaintiff. The court said:

> "The business of the court is to dispose of litigation and not to act as a general overseer of the ethics of those who practice here unless the questioned behavior taints the trial of the cause before it. [Defendant] has failed to establish that taint here in our judgment. If the [lawyer] is guilty of professional misconduct, as to which we express no view, the appropriate forum is the Grievance Committee of the bar association."

It should be noted that RPC 4.3 does not include DR 7–104(A)(2)'s ban on giving an unrepresented person of (possibly) adverse interests advice other than to secure counsel; it merely prohibits stating or implying that the lawyer is disinterested and requires the lawyer who reasonably should know that the person misunderstands the lawyer's role to make reasonable efforts to correct that misunderstanding. But RPC 8.4(c), like DR 1–102(A) (4), prohibits "conduct involving dishonesty, fraud, deceit or misrepresentation."

The Model Rules also include no provision paralleling DR 7–105's specification that a lawyer "shall not present, participate in presenting, or threaten to present criminal charges solely to obtain an advantage in a civil matter," under which a number of lawyers have been disciplined.[8] But RPC 8.4(b) provides that it is professional misconduct for a lawyer to "commit a criminal act that reflects adversely on the lawyer's honesty, trustworthiness or fitness as a lawyer in other respects," and using the threat of criminal prosecution to enforce a private claim may amount to the crime of compounding a felony, compromising a crime, blackmail, bribery, coercion, or extortion. Thus in the 1918 case of People v. Beggs,[9] the California Supreme Court

8. See, e.g., People ex rel. Gallagher v. Hertz, 198 Colo. 522, 608 P.2d 335 (1980) (six month suspension; rejecting claim threat not *solely* to obtain settlement of civil matter); In re Charles, 290 Or. 127, 618 P.2d 1281 (1980) (reprimand for threatening that client would press criminal charges; rejecting claim threat not *solely* in attempt to obtain settlement of civil case). Cf. Bluestein v. State Bar, 13 Cal.3d 162, 118 Cal.Rptr. 175, 529 P.2d 599 (1975) (discipline for offering to drop assault charge against reconciled divorce client's husband if he paid attorney fee); People ex rel. Brundage v. Blakemore, 309 Ill. 311, 141 N.E. 138 (1923) (disbarment for threatening to publicize and publicizing charges of immorality to enforce claim).

Compare Decato's Case, 117 N.H. 885, 379 A.2d 825 (1977) (no discipline absent proof that mention of possibly filing criminal charges was *solely* to gain leverage in collection suit).

Regarding tort liability, see Kinnamon v. Staitman & Snyder, 66 Cal.App.3d 893, 136 Cal.Rptr. 321 (1977) (lawyers' threat of criminal prosecution to obtain advantage in civil case gives rise to intentional infliction of emotional distress claim). Compare Lucas v. Ludwig, 313 So.2d 12 (La.App.1975), (lawyer's inducing police to go to home of landlady who had seized client's property for nonpayment of rent constituted unreasonable and actionable invasion of landlady's privacy or tortious attempt to coerce her to release property), review denied 318 So.2d 42 (La.1975).

9. 178 Cal. 79, 172 P. 152 (1918).

upheld a lawyer's extortion conviction, saying, "The plain import of the language of our code is that to threaten a thief with an accusation and prosecution based thereon, unless he pays the value of property stolen, and which by reason of fear induced by such threat he does pay, is extortion within the meaning of section 518 of the Penal Code; and this without reference to the exercise of good faith in exacting the amount justly due."

Professor Livermore has argued that lawyers should be prohibited from threatening, not just criminal prosecution, but any legal action which is unavailable to the client or which is questionable or obviously excessive.[10]

In the 1975 Kansas case of State v. Zeigler,[11] a lawyer was suspended indefinitely for, inter alia, sending the following letters in behalf of clients:

"OH! THE JOY OF BEING SUED!!

---

---

"How do you explain to the neighbors and the kids when the Sheriff's car pulls up front and an officer hands you the summons?

"OR, how do you explain a garnishment to the boss, and the other fellows at work???

"I don't know, but I guess you do; at least you didn't bother to answer my letter. You do not need to send me your check immediately to pay your account, because I am not going to bother you any more — but the Sheriff will. Oh yes, I will see you in court.

"You owe ________ $ ________

"PAY ME NOW! ! !"

"WRITTEN NOTICE OF GARNISHMENT

"Dr. Sippy

vs

"Charles Loughlin [sp]
RR #1 Box 208 A
Stilwell, Kansas

"Since you have refused to pay this debt voluntarily or to keep your arrangements for payment:

"Court action is now required.

"Therefore be advised, your wages will be garnished. Twenty-five percent (25%) thereof will be taken for the payment of this bill unless the entire balance of $143.00 is paid immediately to Wayne L. Zeigler."

The court found that "use of 'The Joy of Being Sued' letter set forth herein reveals a lack of sound professional judgment and violated DR 1–102(A)(6) (conduct that adversely reflects on fitness to practice law)"[12]

10. Livermore, Lawyer Extortion, 20 Ariz.L.Rev. 402 (1978).

11. 217 Kan. 748, 538 P.2d 643, 93 A.L.R.3d 869 (1975).

12. Compare RPC 8.4(b) (*criminal act* that reflects adversely on lawyer's honesty, trustworthiness or fitness as a lawyer in other respects).

and that the lawyer "simulated legal process by drafting and sending the 'Notice of Garnishment' letter in violation of DR 1–102(A)(4)" (conduct involving deceit and misrepresentation).[13]

### *Question*

Professor Leubsdorf has argued that the current prohibition on communicating with a represented party without counsel's consent fosters roundabout communications and higher attorney fees, makes it easier for lawyers to neglect or deceive clients, and increases inequality and dehumanization in the lawyer-client relationship. He concluded that clients would be protected adequately and served better if the area governed by RPC 4.2 and 4.3 and DR 7–104 were covered by a provision specifying:

"A lawyer who communicates directly with a party he does not represent during the course of his representation of a client shall:

"(A) Disclose his capacity as an attorney of another party.

"(B) Inform an unrepresented party of his right to secure counsel before initiating communication.

"(C) When the party is represented by counsel in that matter:

"1. Send counsel a simultaneous copy of any written communication he makes to the party.

"2. Notify counsel in writing of the terms of any settlement with the party a reasonable time before it is executed.

"3. Honor the party's written request that any future communication be with counsel.

"4. Notify counsel before engaging in any conversation with the party; except that this last provision shall not apply to a conversation with an employee of a party, without independent counsel, who is interviewed solely to obtain his testimony."[14]

What do you think of Professor Leubsdorf's proposal?

## F. PROSECUTORS

### MODEL RULES OF PROFESSIONAL CONDUCT

**RULE 3.8 Special Responsibilities of a Prosecutor**

The prosecutor in a criminal case shall:

(a) refrain from prosecuting a charge that the prosecutor knows is not supported by probable cause;

13. See In re Dows, 168 Minn. 6, 209 N.W. 627, 47 A.L.R. 265 (1926) (six month suspension for simulating legal process). Compare ABA Standards for Criminal Justice 3–3.1(d) (2d ed. 1980) (unprofessional conduct for prosecutor to secure persons' attendance for interviews by using communication with appearance or color of subpoena or similar judicial process unless so authorized by law).

Regarding debt collection methods as grounds for discipline generally, see Annot., 93 A.L.R.3d 880 (1979).

14. Leubsdorf, Communicating with Another Lawyer's Client: The Lawyer's Veto and the Client's Interests, 127 U.Pa.L.Rev. 683, 704 (1979).

(b) make reasonable efforts to assure that the accused has been advised of the right to, and the procedure for obtaining, counsel and has been given reasonable opportunity to obtain counsel;

(c) not seek to obtain from an unrepresented accused a waiver of important pretrial rights, such as the right to a preliminary hearing;

(d) make timely disclosure to the defense of all evidence or information known to the prosecutor that tends to negate the guilt of the accused or mitigates the offense, and, in connection with sentencing, disclose to the defense and to the tribunal all unprivileged mitigating information known to the prosecutor, except when the prosecutor is relieved of this responsibility by a protective order of the tribunal; and

(e) exercise reasonable care to prevent investigators, law enforcement personnel, employees or other persons assisting or associated with the prosecutor in a criminal case from making an extrajudicial statement that the prosecutor would be prohibited from making under Rule 3.6.

COMMENT:

A prosecutor has the responsibility of a minister of justice and not simply that of an advocate. This responsibility carries with it specific obligations to see that the defendant is accorded procedural justice and that guilt is decided upon the basis of sufficient evidence. Precisely how far the prosecutor is required to go in this direction is a matter of debate and varies in different jurisdictions. Many jurisdictions have adopted the ABA Standards of Criminal Justice Relating to Prosecution Function, which in turn are the product of prolonged and careful deliberation by lawyers experienced in both criminal prosecution and defense. See also Rule 3.3(d), governing ex parte proceedings, among which grand jury proceedings are included. Applicable law may require other measures by the prosecutor and knowing disregard of those obligations or a systematic abuse of prosecutorial discretion could constitute a violation of Rule 8.4.

Paragraph (c) does not apply to an accused representing himself with the approval of the tribunal. Nor does it forbid the lawful questioning of a suspect who has knowingly waived his rights to counsel and silence.

The exception in paragraph (d) recognizes that a prosecutor may seek an appropriate protective order from the tribunal if disclosure of information to the defense could result in substantial harm to an individual or to the public interest.[a]

a. Compare the following CPR provisions: "**EC 7–13** The responsibility of a public prosecutor differs from that of the usual advocate; his duty is to seek justice, not merely to convict. This special duty exists because: (1) the prosecutor represents the sovereign and therefore should use restraint in the discretionary exercise of governmental powers, such as in the selection of cases to prosecute; (2) during trial the prosecutor is not only an advocate but he also may make decisions normally made by an individual client, and those affecting the public interest should be fair to all; and (3) in our system of criminal justice the accused is to be given the benefit of all reasonable doubts. With respect to evidence and witnesses, the prosecutor has responsibilities different from those of a lawyer in private practice: the prosecutor should make timely disclosure to the defense of available evidence known to him, that tends to negate the guilt of the accused, mitigate the degree of the offense, or reduce the punishment. Further, a prosecutor should not intentionally avoid pursuit of evidence merely be-

## UNITED STATES v. AGURS

427 U.S. 97, 96 S.Ct. 2392, 49 L.Ed.2d 342 (1976).

MR. JUSTICE STEVENS delivered the opinion of the Court.

* * *

I

At about 4:30 p. m. on September 24, 1971, respondent, who had been there before, and Sewell, registered in a motel as man and wife. They were assigned a room without a bath. Sewell was wearing a bowie knife in a sheath, and carried another knife in his pocket. Less than two hours earlier, according to the testimony of his estranged wife, he had had $360 in cash on his person.

About 15 minutes later three motel employees heard respondent screaming for help. A forced entry into their room disclosed Sewell on top of respondent struggling for possession of the bowie knife. She was holding the knife; his bleeding hand grasped the blade; according to one witness he was trying to jam the blade into her chest. The employees separated the two and summoned the authorities. Respondent departed without comment before they arrived. Sewell was dead on arrival at the hospital.

Circumstantial evidence indicated that the parties had completed an act of intercourse, that Sewell had then gone to the bathroom down the hall, and that the struggle occurred upon his return. The contents of his pockets were in disarray on the dresser and no money was found; the jury may have inferred that respondent took Sewell's money and that the fight started when Sewell re-entered the room and saw what she was doing.

On the following morning respondent surrendered to the police. She was given a physical examination which revealed no cuts or bruises of any kind, except needle marks on her upper arm. An autopsy of Sewell disclosed that he had several deep stab wounds in his chest and

cause he believes it will damage the prosecutor's case or aid the accused.

**"DR 7–103 Performing the Duty of Public Prosecutor or Other Government Lawyer**

"(A) A public prosecutor or other government lawyer shall not institute or cause to be instituted criminal charges when he knows or it is obvious that the charges are not supported by probable cause.

"(B) A public prosecutor or other government lawyer in criminal litigation shall make timely disclosure to counsel for the defendant, or to the defendant if he has no counsel, of the existence of evidence, known to the prosecutor or other government lawyer, that tends to negate the guilt of the accused, mitigate the degree of the offense, or reduce the punishment."

Cf. ABA Standards for Criminal Justice 3-3.9(a) (2d ed. 1980) (instituting or permitting continued pendency of charges: *unprofessional conduct* if known not supported by probable cause; *should not* be done absent sufficient admissible evidence to support conviction); id. 3-3.9(e) (should not bring or seek charges greater in number or degree than can reasonably support with evidence at trial); id. 3-3.11(a) (unprofessional conduct intentionally to fail to disclose to defense, at earliest feasible opportunity, existence of evidence tending to negate guilt or reduce punishment), id. 3-3.11(c) (unprofessional conduct intentionally to avoid pursuing evidence because of belief it will damage prosecution's case or aid accused).

abdomen, and a number of slashes on his arms and hands, characterized by the pathologist as "defensive wounds."

Respondent offered no evidence. Her sole defense was the argument made by her attorney that Sewell had initially attacked her with the knife, and that her actions had all been directed toward saving her own life. The support for this self-defense theory was based on the fact that she had screamed for help. Sewell was on top of her when help arrived, and his possession of two knives indicated that he was a violence-prone person. It took the jury about 25 minutes to elect a foreman and return a verdict.

Three months later defense counsel filed a motion for a new trial asserting that he had discovered (1) that Sewell had a prior criminal record that would have further evidenced his violent character; [and] (2) that the prosecutor had failed to disclose this information to the defense * * * . Sewell's prior record included a plea of guilty to a charge of assault and carrying a deadly weapon in 1963, and another guilty plea to a charge of carrying a deadly weapon in 1971. Apparently both weapons were knives. * * *

The District Court denied the motion. It rejected the Government's argument that there was no duty to disclose material evidence unless requested to do so,[4] assumed that the evidence was admissible, but held that it was not sufficiently material. The District Court expressed the opinion that the prior conviction shed no light on Sewell's character that was not already apparent from the uncontradicted evidence, particularly the fact that he carried two knives; the court stressed the inconsistency between the claim of self-defense and the fact that Sewell had been stabbed repeatedly while respondent was unscathed.

The Court of Appeals reversed. The court found * * * no misconduct by the prosecutor in this case. It held, however, that the evidence was material, and that its nondisclosure required a new trial because the jury might have returned a different verdict if the evidence had been received.

II

The rule of Brady v. Maryland, 373 U.S. 83, 83 S.Ct. 1194, 10 L.Ed.2d 215 [1963], arguably applies in three quite different situations. Each involves the discovery, after trial, of information which had been known to the prosecution but unknown to the defense.

In the first situation, typified by Mooney v. Holohan, 294 U.S. 103, 55 S.Ct. 340, 79 L.Ed. 791 [1935], the undisclosed evidence demonstrates that the prosecution's case includes perjured testimony and that the prosecution knew, or should have known, of the perjury. In a series of subsequent cases, the Court has consistently held that a conviction obtained by the knowing use of perjured testimony is fun-

4. "THE COURT: What are you saying? How can you request that which you don't know exists. * * * "

damentally unfair, and must be set aside if there is any reasonable likelihood that the false testimony could have affected the judgment of the jury. * * * In those cases the Court has applied a strict standard of materiality, not just because they involve prosecutorial misconduct, but more importantly because they involve a corruption of the truth-seeking function of the trial process. Since this case involves no misconduct, and since there is no reason to question the veracity of any of the prosecution witnesses, the test of materiality followed in the *Mooney* line of cases is not necessarily applicable to this case.

The second situation, illustrated by the *Brady* case itself, is characterized by a pretrial request for specific evidence. * * *

Brady was found guilty of murder in the first degree. Since the jury did not add the words "without capital punishment" to the verdict, he was sentenced to death. At his trial Brady did not deny his involvement in the deliberate killing, but testified that it was his accomplice, Boblit, rather than he, who had actually strangled the decedent. This version of the event was corroborated by one of several confessions made by Boblit but not given to Brady's counsel despite an admittedly adequate request. * * *

This Court [affirmed the state court's] holding that the suppression of exculpatory evidence violated Brady's right to due process [and] that [Brady] should receive a new trial on the issue of punishment but not on the issue of guilt or innocence. The Court [reasoned that] the confession could not have affected the outcome on the issue of guilt but could have affected Brady's punishment. * * *

The test of materiality in a case like *Brady* in which specific information has been requested by the defense is not necessarily the same as in a case in which no such request has been made. * * *

In *Brady* the request was specific. It gave the prosecutor notice of exactly what the defense desired. Although there is, of course, no duty to provide defense counsel with unlimited discovery of everything known by the prosecutor, if the subject matter of such a request is material, or indeed if a substantial basis for claiming materiality exists, it is reasonable to require the prosecutor to respond either by furnishing the information or by submitting the problem to the trial judge. When the prosecutor receives a specific and relevant request, the failure to make any response is seldom, if ever, excusable.

In many cases, however, exculpatory information in the possession of the prosecutor may be unknown to defense counsel. In such a situation he may make no request at all, or possibly ask for "all *Brady* material" or for "anything exculpatory." Such a request really gives the prosecutor no better notice than if no request is made. If there is a duty to respond to a general request of that kind, it must derive from the obviously exculpatory character of certain evidence in the hands of the prosecutor. But if the evidence is so clearly supportive of a claim of innocence that it gives the prosecution notice of a duty to produce, that duty should equally arise even if no request is made. Whether we focus on the desirability of a precise definition of the prosecutor's duty or on the potential harm to the defendant, we conclude that there is no significant difference between cases in which there has been merely a general request for exculpatory matter and cases, like the one we must now decide, in which there has been no request at all. The third situation in which the *Brady* rule arguably applies, typified by this case, therefore embraces the case in which only a general request for "*Brady* material" has been made.

We now consider whether the prosecutor has any constitutional duty to volunteer exculpatory matter to the defense, and if so, what standard of materiality gives rise to that duty.

III

We are not considering the scope of discovery authorized by the Federal Rules of Criminal Procedure, or the wisdom of amending those Rules to enlarge the defendant's discovery rights. We are dealing with the defendant's right to a fair trial mandated by the Due Process Clause * * * .

The problem arises in two principal contexts. First, in advance of trial, and perhaps during the course of a trial as well, the prosecutor must decide what, if anything, he should voluntarily submit to defense counsel. Second, after trial a judge may be required to decide whether a nondisclosure deprived the defendant of his right to due process. Logically the same standard must apply at both times. For unless the omission deprived the defendant of a fair trial, there was no constitutional violation requiring that the verdict be set aside; and absent a constitutional violation, there was no breach of the prosecutor's constitutional duty to disclose.

Nevertheless, there is a significant practical difference between the pretrial decision of the prosecutor and the post-trial decision of the judge. Because we are dealing with an inevitably imprecise standard, and because the significance of an item of evidence can seldom be predicted accurately until the entire record is complete, the prudent prosecutor will resolve doubtful questions in favor of disclosure. But to reiterate a critical point, the prosecutor will not have violated his constitutional duty of disclosure unless his omission is of sufficient significance to result in the denial of the defendant's right to a fair trial.

The Court of Appeals appears to have assumed that the prosecutor has a constitutional obligation to disclose any information that might affect the jury's verdict. That statement of a constitutional standard of materiality approaches the "sporting theory of justice" which the Court expressly rejected in *Brady*.[15] For a jury's appraisal of a case

15. "In the present case a unanimous Court of Appeals has said that nothing in the suppressed confession 'could have reduced the appellant Brady's offense below murder in the first degree.' We read that statement as a ruling on the admissibility of the confession on the issue of innocence or guilt. A sporting theory of justice might assume that if the sup-

"might" be affected by an improper or trivial consideration as well as by evidence giving rise to a legitimate doubt on the issue of guilt. If everything that might influence a jury must be disclosed, the only way a prosecutor could discharge his constitutional duty would be to allow complete discovery of his files as a matter of routine practice.

Whether or not procedural rules authorizing such broad discovery might be desirable, the Constitution surely does not demand that much. * * *[16] The mere possibility that an item of undisclosed information might have helped the defense, or might have affected the outcome of the trial, does not establish "materiality" in the constitutional sense.

Nor do we believe the constitutional obligation is measured by the moral culpability, or the willfulness, of the prosecutor. If evidence highly probative of innocence is in his file, he should be presumed to recognize its significance even if he has actually overlooked it. Conversely, if evidence actually has no probative significance at all, no purpose would be served by requiring a new trial simply because an inept prosecutor incorrectly believed he was suppressing a fact that would be vital to the defense. If the suppression of evidence results in constitutional error, it is because of the character of the evidence, not the character of the prosecutor.

[T]here are situations in which evidence is obviously of such substantial value to the defense that elementary fairness requires it to be disclosed even without a specific request. For though the attorney for the sovereign must prosecute the accused with earnestness and vigor, he must always be faithful to his client's overriding interest that "justice shall be done." He is the "servant of the law, the twofold aim of which is that guilt shall not escape or innocence suffer." Berger v. United States, 295 U.S. 78, 88, 55 S.Ct. 629, 633, 79 L.Ed. 1314 [1935]. This description of the prosecutor's duty illuminates the standard of materiality that governs his obligation to disclose exculpatory evidence.

On the one hand, the fact that such evidence was available to the prosecutor and not submitted to the defense places it in a different category than if it had simply been discovered from a neutral source after trial. For that reason the defendant should not have to satisfy the severe burden of demonstrating that newly discovered evidence

pressed confession had been used at the first trial, the judge's ruling that it was not admissible on the issue of innocence or guilt might have been flouted by the jury just as might have been done if the court had first admitted a confession and then stricken it from the record. But we cannot raise that trial strategy to the dignity of a constitutional right * * *." 373 U.S., at 90–91.

16. In his opinion concurring in the judgment in Giles v. Maryland, 386 U.S. 66, 98, 87 S.Ct. 793, 809, 17 L.Ed.2d 737 [1967], Mr. Justice Fortas stated:

"This is not to say that convictions ought to be reversed on the ground that information merely repetitious, cumulative, or embellishing of facts otherwise known to the defense or presented to the court, or without importance to the defense for purposes of the preparation of the case or for trial was not disclosed to defense counsel. It is not to say that the State has an obligation to communicate preliminary, challenged, or speculative information."

probably would have resulted in acquittal. If the standard applied to the usual motion for a new trial based on newly discovered evidence were the same when the evidence was in the State's possession as when it was found in a neutral source, there would be no special significance to the prosecutor's obligation to serve the cause of justice.

On the other hand, since we have rejected the suggestion that the prosecutor has a constitutional duty routinely to deliver his entire file to defense counsel, we cannot consistently treat every nondisclosure as though it were error. It necessarily follows that the judge should not order a new trial every time he is unable to characterize a nondisclosure as harmless under the customary harmless-error standard. Under that standard when error is present in the record, the reviewing judge must set aside the verdict and judgment unless his "conviction is sure that the error did not influence the jury, or had but very slight effect." Kotteakos v. United States, 328 U.S. 750, 764, 66 S.Ct. 1239, 1248, 90 L.Ed. 1557 [1946]. Unless every nondisclosure is regarded as automatic error, the constitutional standards of materiality must impose a higher burden on the defendant.

The proper standard of materiality must reflect our overriding concern with the justice of the finding of guilt. Such a finding is permissible only if supported by evidence establishing guilt beyond a reasonable doubt. It necessarily follows that if the omitted evidence creates a reasonable doubt that did not otherwise exist, constitutional error has been committed. This means that the omission must be evaluated in the context of the entire record.[21] If there is no reasonable doubt about guilt whether or not the additional evidence is considered, there is no justification for a new trial. On the other hand, if the verdict is already of questionable validity, additional evidence of relatively minor importance might be sufficient to create a reasonable doubt.

This * * * is * * * the standard which the trial judge applied in this case. He evaluated the significance of Sewell's prior criminal record in the context of the full trial which he recalled in detail. Stressing in particular the incongruity of a claim that Sewell was the aggressor with the evidence of his multiple wounds and respondent's unscathed condition, the trial judge indicated his unqualified opinion that respondent was guilty. He noted that Sewell's prior record did not contradict any evidence offered by the prosecutor, and was largely cumulative of the evidence that Sewell was wearing a bowie knife in

21. "If, for example, one of only two eyewitnesses to a crime had told the prosecutor that the defendant was definitely not its perpetrator and if this statement was not disclosed to the defense, no court would hesitate to reverse a conviction resting on the testimony of the other eyewitness. But if there were fifty eyewitnesses, forty-nine of whom identified the defendant, and the prosecutor neglected to reveal that the other, who was without his badly needed glasses on the misty evening of the crime, had said that the criminal looked something like the defendant but he could not be sure as he had only had a brief glimpse, the result might well be different." Comment, [Brady v. Maryland and The Prosecutor's Duty to Disclose], 40 U.Chi.L.Rev. [112,] 125 [1972].

a sheath and carrying a second knife in his pocket when he registered at the motel.

Since the arrest record was not requested and did not even arguably give rise to any inference of perjury, since after considering it in the context of the entire record the trial judge remained convinced of respondent's guilt beyond a reasonable doubt, and since we are satisfied that his firsthand appraisal of the record was thorough and entirely reasonable, we hold that the prosecutor's failure to tender Sewell's record to the defense did not deprive respondent of a fair trial as guaranteed by the Due Process Clause * * *.

Reversed.

MR. JUSTICE MARSHALL, with whom MR. JUSTICE BRENNAN joins, dissenting.

The Court today holds that the prosecutor's constitutional duty to provide exculpatory evidence to the defense is not limited to cases in which the defense makes a request for such evidence. But once having recognized the existence of a duty to volunteer exculpatory evidence, the Court so narrowly defines the category of "material" evidence embraced by the duty as to deprive it of all meaningful content.

[T]he Court observes:

"If the standard applied to the usual [F.R.Crim.P. 33] motion for a new trial based on newly discovered evidence were the same when the evidence was in the State's possession as when it was found in a neutral source, there would be no special significance to the prosecutor's obligation to serve the cause of justice."

I agree completely.

The Court, however, seemingly forgets these precautionary words when it comes time to state the proper standard of materiality to be applied in cases involving neither the knowing use of perjury nor a specific defense request for an item of information. In such cases, the prosecutor commits constitutional error, the Court holds, "if the omitted evidence creates a reasonable doubt that did not otherwise exist." As the Court's subsequent discussion makes clear, the defendant challenging the prosecutor's failure to disclose evidence is entitled to relief, in the Court's view, only if the withheld evidence actually creates a reasonable doubt as to guilt in the judge's mind. The burden thus imposed on the defendant is at least as "severe" as * * * the burden he generally faces on a Rule 33 motion. Surely if a judge is able to say that evidence actually creates a reasonable doubt as to guilt in his mind (the Court's standard), he would also conclude that the evidence "probably would have resulted in acquittal" (the general Rule 33 standard). In short, in spite of its own salutary precaution, the Court treats the case in which the prosecutor withholds evidence no differently from the case in which evidence is newly discovered from a neutral source. The "prosecutor's obligation to serve the cause of justice" is reduced to a status, to borrow the Court's words, of "no special significance."

* * * One of the most basic elements of fairness in a criminal trial is that available evidence tending to show innocence, as well as that tending to show guilt, be fully aired before the jury; more particularly, it is that the State in its zeal to convict a defendant not suppress evidence that might exonerate him. This fundamental notion of fairness does not pose any irreconcilable conflict for the prosecutor, for as the Court reminds us, the prosecutor "must always be faithful to his client's overriding interest that 'justice shall be done.'" No interest of the State is served, and no duty of the prosecutor advanced, by the suppression of evidence favorable to the defendant. On the contrary, the prosecutor fulfills his most basic responsibility when he fully airs all the relevant evidence at his command. * * *

Under today's ruling, if the prosecution has not made knowing use of perjury, and if the defense has not made a specific request for an item of information, the defendant is entitled to a new trial only if the withheld evidence actually creates a reasonable doubt as to guilt in the judge's mind. [This] rule creates little, if any, incentive for the prosecutor conscientiously to determine whether his files contain evidence helpful to the defense. Indeed, the rule reinforces the natural tendency of the prosecutor to overlook evidence favorable to the defense, and creates an incentive for the prosecutor to resolve close questions of disclosure in favor of concealment.

More fundamentally, the Court's rule usurps the function of the jury as the trier of fact in a criminal case. The Court's rule explicitly establishes the judge as the trier of fact with respect to evidence withheld by the prosecution. * * *

* * * The prevailing view in the federal courts of the standard of materiality for cases involving neither a specific request for information nor other indications of deliberate misconduct * * * is quite different. It is essentially the following: If there is a significant chance that the withheld evidence, developed by skilled counsel, would have induced a reasonable doubt in the minds of enough jurors to avoid a conviction, then the judgment of conviction must be set aside. * * *

The Court approves—but only for a limited category of cases—a standard virtually identical to the one I have described as reflecting the prevailing view. In cases in which "the undisclosed evidence demonstrates that the prosecution's case includes perjured testimony and that the prosecution knew, or should have known, of the perjury," the judgment of conviction must be set aside "if there is any reasonable likelihood that the false testimony could have affected the judgment of the jury." This lesser burden on the defendant is appropriate, the Court states, primarily because the withholding of evidence contradicting testimony offered by witnesses called by the prosecution "involve[s] a corruption of the truth-seeking function of the trial process." But surely the truth-seeking process is corrupted by the withholding of evidence favorable to the defense, regardless of whether the evidence is directly contradictory to evidence offered by the prosecution. * * *

* * * Leaving open the question whether a different rule might appropriately be applied in cases involving deliberate misconduct, I would hold that the defendant in this case had the burden of demonstrating that there is a significant chance that the withheld evidence, developed by skilled counsel, would have induced a reasonable doubt in the minds of enough jurors to avoid a conviction. This is essentially the standard applied by the Court of Appeals, and I would affirm its judgment.[a]

### *Problems*

(1) Defendant is being prosecuted for robbery of a grocery store, inasmuch as the victim picked his picture out of a book of mug shots. The victim of another grocery store robbery a month earlier on the other side of town also picked Defendant's picture, but Defendant was not charged with that one because he was in jail when it was committed. Defendant has other grocery store robberies on his record. Must the prosecutor disclose to the defense the fact that Defendant's picture was picked for the robbery committed while Defendant was in jail?

(2) Must a prosecutor about to conclude a plea agreement tell the defense that the prosecution's key witness has just died?

In People v. Jones,[1] New York's highest court held that the defendant was not denied due process by the prosecutor's failure during plea negotiations to disclose that the complaining witness had died four days before the defendant pleaded guilty. The court said:

> "The circumstance that the testimony of the complaining witness was no longer available to the prosecution was not evidence at all. Further, to the extent that proof of the fact of the death of this witness might have been admissible on trial, it would not have constituted exculpatory evidence—i.e., evidence favorable to an accused where the evidence is material either to guilt or to punishment. Accordingly, it does not fall within the doctrine enunciated by the Supreme Court of the United States in Brady v. Maryland (and cf. United States v. Agurs). * * * Rather * * * the death of [complaining witness] would merely have been one of the

**a.** See Note, The Prosecutor's Duty to Disclose after United States v. Agurs, 1977 U.Ill.L.F. 690; Annot., 34 A.L.R.3d 16 (1970). Cf. Note, A Prosecutor's Duty to Disclose Promises of Favorable Treatment Made to Witnesses for the Prosecution, 94 Harv.L.Rev. 887 (1981).

Compare Imbler v. Pachtman, 424 U.S. 409, 96 S.Ct. 984, 47 L.Ed.2d 128 (1976), where the Court, holding that prosecutors are immune from damage suits under 42 U.S.C. § 1983 for conduct in initiating prosecution or presenting the state's case, emphasized that they remain subject to professional discipline as well as criminal prosecution. See Brown v. Dayton Hudson Corp., 314 N.W.2d 210 (Minn.1981) (prosecutor's refusal to investigate criminal defendant's claim of mistaken identity was within scope of absolute immunity).

**1.** 44 N.Y.2d 76, 404 N.Y.S.2d 85, 375 N.E.2d 41, cert. denied 439 U.S. 846, 99 S.Ct. 145, 58 L.Ed.2d 148 (1978).

factors—though a most significant factor—to be weighed by defendant in reaching his decision whether, as a matter of tactics in light of the strength of the People's case against him, to interpose a negotiated plea of guilty.

" * * * Analytically the issue is not whether this defendant was entitled to evidence in the possession of the prosecution; the question before us on this appeal is whether the pretrial conduct of the prosecutor in the course of plea negotiation was such as to constitute a denial of due process to defendant in the circumstances disclosed in this record.

" * * * Defendant notes that, as the basis for announcing the case ready, the prosecutor had represented to the court and to defense counsel that the complaining witness had been located and would therefore be available to testify at trial. Defendant adds that the prosecutor knew, or at least was chargeable with knowledge, that the plea for which defendant had negotiated was predicated principally on the availability of the [complaining witness'] testimony. * * *

"[N]otwithstanding that the responsibilities of a prosecutor for fairness and open-dealing are of a higher magnitude than those of a private litigant, no prosecutor is obliged to share his appraisal of the weaknesses of his own case (as opposed to specific exculpatory evidence) with defense counsel. [T]he courts will allow a defendant to withdraw a guilty plea when the prosecution has * * * persuaded him by affirmative deceit to enter a guilty plea. All the reported instances of deceitful persuasion appear to have involved positive misstatement or misrepresentations; none has considered the effect to be accorded silence only. Consistent with legal principles recognized elsewhere in our jurisprudence, it would seem that silence should give rise to legal consequences only if it may be concluded that the one who was silent was under an affirmative duty to speak. Whether and to what extent the courts, in the absence of statute or possible rule of court would impose such an affirmative duty on a prosecutor would necessarily be dependent on the circumstances of the individual case. Thus, we do not decide what the rule might be where in the course of plea negotiation a particular defendant staunchly and plausibly maintains his innocence but states explicitly and creditably that as a matter of balanced judgment in the light of the apparent strength of the People's proof he wishes to interpose a negotiated plea to reduced charges to avoid the risk of a more severe sentence likely to attend conviction after trial; failure of the prosecutor to reveal the death of a critical complaining witness might then call for a vacatur of the plea. Silence in such circumstances might arguably be held to be so subversive of the criminal justice process as to offend due process.

"[In] the present case, we hold that there was no obligation on the part of the prosecutor to reveal * * *. Defendant does not protest his innocence; on the contrary he testified to the factual basis for the charge to which he pleaded." [2]

### *Comment*

(1) *Prosecutor's role.* In the 1935 *Berger* case to which the *Agurs* Court referred,[3] the Court stated:

> "The United States Attorney is the representative not of an ordinary party to a controversy, but of a sovereignty whose obligation to govern impartially is as compelling as its obligation to govern at all; and whose interest, therefore, in a criminal prosecution is not that it shall win a case, but that justice shall be done. As such, he is in a peculiar and very definite sense the servant of the law, the twofold aim of which is that guilt shall not escape or innocence suffer. He may prosecute with earnestness and vigor—indeed, he should do so. But, while he may strike hard blows, he is not at liberty to strike foul ones. It is as much his duty to refrain from improper methods calculated to produce a wrongful conviction as it is to use every legitimate means to bring about a just one.
>
> "It is fair to say that the average jury, in a greater or less degree, has confidence that these obligations, which so plainly rest upon the prosecuting attorney, will be faithfully observed. Consequently, improper suggestions, insinuations, and, especially, assertions of personal knowledge are apt to carry much weight against the accused when they should properly carry none." [4]

(2) *Prosecutorial vindictiveness.* In In re Rook,[5] the Oregon Supreme Court gave a prosecutor a public reprimand for refusing, because of personal animosity toward two lawyers, to plea bargain with any criminal defendants they represented. The court held that this constituted conduct "prejudicial to the administration of justice" under DR 1–102(A)(5) [6] and conduct serving "merely to harass or maliciously injure another" under DR 7–102(A)(1).[7]

But in Bordenkircher v. Hayes,[8] a 6–3 United States Supreme Court found no due process denial in a prosecutor's bringing a habitual of-

2. See Symposium, Professional Responsibility in the Practice of Criminal Law: The Murky Divide between Right and Wrong, in N. Galston, ed., Professional Responsibility of the Lawyer 49, 62–65 (1977).

Compare supra p. 340, Question (1). See also Virzi v. Grand Trunk Warehouse & Cold Storage Co., 571 F.Supp. 507 (E.D.Mich.1983) (plaintiff's lawyer has ethical obligation, prior to concluding settlement in personal injury action, to disclose fact client has died).

3. Berger v. United States, 295 U.S. 78, 55 S.Ct. 629, 79 L.Ed. 1314 (1935).

4. See Civiletti, The Prosecutor as Advocate, 25 N.Y.L.Sch.L.Rev. 1 (1979).

Compare Justice White's observations about the criminal defense lawyer's role, supra pp. 331–32.

5. 276 Or. 695, 556 P.2d 1351 (1976).

6. See RPC 8.4(d).

7. Compare RPC 4.4 (lawyer shall not use means that have no substantial purpose other than to embarrass, delay or burden a third person).

8. 434 U.S. 357, 98 S.Ct. 663, 54 L.Ed.2d 604 (1978).

fender indictment against a defendant because the defendant refused to plead guilty to the same unenhanced charge.[9]

(3) *Impartiality.* In People v. Superior Court,[10] the California Supreme Court, rejecting a separation-of-executive-and-judicial-powers agrument, held that the trial court properly disqualified the district attorney in a murder case because his impartiality might be undermined by the fact that the victim's mother was a discovery clerk in the DA's office, and was assigned to the very office where the murder prosecution was being handled. The court said that a trial court need not first determine that failure to disqualify the prosecutor would permit a violation of the defendant's constitutional rights—it has "discretion to prevent even the possibility of their violation." The court continued:

> "A fair and impartial trial is a fundamental aspect of the right of accused persons not to be deprived of liberty without due process of law.
>
> "It is the obligation of the prosecutor, as well as of the court, to respect this mandate. Nor is the role of the prosecutor in this regard simply a specialized version of the duty of any attorney not to overstep the bounds of permissible advocacy. The prosecutor is a public official vested with considerable discretionary power to decide what crimes are to be charged and how they are to be prosecuted. * * *
>
> "[B]ecause the prosecutor enjoys such broad discretion * * * the public he serves and those he accuses may justifiably demand that he perform his functions with the highest degree of integrity and impartiality, and with the appearance thereof. One of the reasons often cited for the institution of public prosecutions is that 'Americans believed that an office in a position of public trust could make decisions more impartially than could the victims of crimes or other private complainants,' persons who often brought prosecutions under the older English system of criminal justice. This advantage of public prosecution is lost if those exercising the discretionary duties of the district attorney are subject to conflicting personal interests which might tend to compromise their impartiality."

Similarly, in United States v. Gold,[11] a federal district court in Illinois dismissed an indictment because the "Special Attorney for the Department of Justice presenting the government's case to the grand

9. See generally Recent Developments, Prosecutorial Vindictiveness: An Examination of Divergent Lower Court Standards and a Proposed Framework for Analysis, 34 Vand.L.Rev. 431 (1981); 70 Geo.L.J. 1051 (1982).

10. 19 Cal.3d 255, 137 Cal.Rptr. 476, 561 P.2d 1164 (1977).

11. 470 F.Supp. 1336 (N.D.Ill.1979).

jury * * * was at the same time on the staff of the Environmental Protection Agency, the complaining party in the criminal charges being investigated" and "the duty he owed his EPA superiors led to disregard of the duties he owed as a Special Attorney for the United States Department of Justice, and to the defendants in this case." [12]

(4) *Law enforcement motive for misconduct.* In the Illinois case of In re Friedman,[13] the prosecuting attorney directed police officers to secure evidence of bribery by defense lawyers in two separate cases, and if necessary to give false information to the court to secure the dismissals of cases which the lawyers sought in return for the proposed bribes. Pursuant to these instructions, the officer in one of the cases falsely informed the court that an essential witness was unavailable. In the other case, the officer testified falsely under oath that the complaining witness did not wish to prosecute. As a result, the charge in each case was dismissed and the lawyers paid the bribes. One of the lawyers was later suspended from practice for two years,[14] and the other was convicted of bribery.[15] The *Friedman* court held that the prosecutor had violated DR 7–102(A)(4) ("knowingly us[ing] perjured testimony or false evidence") and DR 7–109(B) (causing person to be unavailable as witness), but (with two dissents on this point) withheld discipline because the prosecutor "acted without the guidance of precedent or settled opinion and because there is apparently considerable belief * * * that he acted properly in conducting the investigations" and because the prosecutor acted "not out of self-interest, but from a sincere, if misguided, desire to bring corrupt attorneys to justice."

Should violation of professional conduct provisions be condoned when the motive is laudable and the results commendable?

12. Compare MacDonald v. Musick, 425 F.2d 373 (9th Cir. 1970), cert. denied 400 U.S. 852, 91 S.Ct. 54, 27 L.Ed.2d 90, wherein the court held that a prosecutor may not condition agreement to dismissal of a charge upon the defendant's stipulating that there was probable cause for the arrest. The court reasoned that "[i]t is no part of the proper duty of a prosecutor to use a criminal prosecution to forestall a civil proceeding by the defendant against policemen," and found prosecutors as bound as other lawyers by DR 7–105's prohibition on presenting criminal charges solely to obtain an advantage in a civil matter.

A lawyer who has defended a person may not later prosecute the person on the same charge. Corbin v. Broadman, 6 Ariz.App. 436, 433 P.2d 289 (1967); Young v. State, 177 So.2d 345 (Fla.App.1965). See Ex parte Spain, 589 S.W.2d 132 (Tex.Crim.App.1979) (probation revocation sought by prosecutor who as defense counsel represented defendant when pleading guilty). But RPC 1.11(c) does not extend this disqualification to other prosecutors in the same office. Accord, United States v. Caggiano, 660 F.2d 184 (6th Cir. 1981), cert. denied 454 U.S. 1149, 102 S.Ct. 1015, 71 L.Ed.2d 303 (1982); ABA Formal Opinion 342 (1975). But see State v. Cooper, 63 Ohio Misc. 1, 409 N.E.2d 1070 (1980). Cf. State ex rel. Meyers v. Tippecanoe County Court, 432 N.E.2d 1377 (Ind.1982) (office disqualified where it was chief prosecutor, with administrative control over entire staff, who previously represented defendant).

13. 76 Ill.2d 392, 30 Ill.Dec. 288, 392 N.E.2d 1333 (1979).

14. In re Howard, 69 Ill.2d 343, 14 Ill.Dec. 360, 372 N.E.2d 371 (1978).

15. People v. Powell, 72 Ill.2d 50, 18 Ill.Dec. 318, 377 N.E.2d 803 (1978), cert. denied 440 U.S. 907, 99 S.Ct. 1214, 59 L.Ed.2d 455 (1979).

## G. WITNESSES

### MODEL RULES OF PROFESSIONAL CONDUCT

**RULE 3.4 Fairness to Opposing Party and Counsel**

A lawyer shall not:

(a) unlawfully obstruct another party's access to evidence or unlawfully alter, destroy or conceal a document or other material having potential evidentiary value. A lawyer shall not counsel or assist another person to do any such act;

(b) falsify evidence, counsel or assist a witness to testify falsely, or offer an inducement to a witness that is prohibited by law;

* * *

(f) request a person other than a client to refrain from voluntarily giving relevant information to another party unless:

(1) the person is a relative or an employee or other agent of a client; and

(2) the lawyer reasonably believes that the person's interests will not be adversely affected by refraining from giving such information.[a]

### GREGORY v. UNITED STATES

369 F.2d 185 (D.C.Cir. 1966).

J. SKELLY WRIGHT, Circuit Judge: * * *

The prosecutor embarrassed and confounded the accused in the preparation of his defense by advising the witnesses to the robberies and murder not to speak to anyone unless he were present. Six days before the trial began, defense counsel and the prosecutor, Mr. Weitzel, appeared before a motions judge. Defense counsel asked for the judge's assistance because two eye witnesses to the murder and robbery had

**a.** Compare the following CPR provisions:

**"EC7–28** Witnesses should always testify truthfully and should be free from any financial inducements that might tempt them to do otherwise. A lawyer should not pay or agree to pay a non-expert witness an amount in excess of reimbursement for expenses and financial loss incident to his being a witness; however, a lawyer may pay or agree to pay an expert witness a reasonable fee for his services as an expert. But in no event should a lawyer pay or agree to pay a contingent fee to any witness. A lawyer should exercise reasonable diligence to see that his client and lay associates conform to these standards."

**"DR 7–109 Contact With Witnesses**

"(A) A lawyer shall not suppress any evidence that he or his client has a legal obligation to reveal or produce.

"(B) A lawyer shall not advise or cause a person to secrete himself or to leave the jurisdiction of a tribunal for the purpose of making him unavailable as a witness therein.

"(C) A lawyer shall not pay, offer to pay, or acquiesce in the payment of compensation to a witness contingent upon the content of his testimony or the outcome of the case. But a lawyer may advance, guarantee, or acquiesce in the payment of:

(1) Expenses reasonably incurred by a witness in attending or testifying.

(2) Reasonable compensation to a witness for his loss of time in attending or testifying.

(3) A reasonable fee for the professional services of an expert witness."

declined "to talk to me unless Mr. Weitzel is present or unless Mr. Weitzel authorizes him to talk to me." Defense counsel asked the judge to direct Mr. Weitzel to allow the witnesses to talk to him. The court ruled: "I can't direct the Government to permit you to talk to a Government witness."

On the day the trial opened, defense counsel asked for the assistance of the trial judge with respect to his difficulty in interviewing the witnesses to the events on trial. Defense counsel stated to the court that the witnesses had refused to talk to him because "the United States Attorney told them not to talk to us." At this point the prosecutor, Mr. Weitzel, stated: "I instructed all the witnesses that they were free to speak to anyone they like. However, it was my advice that they not speak to anyone about the case unless I was present." Mr. Weitzel further advised the trial court that defense counsel's motion had already been denied by a motions judge, whereupon the trial court stated: "Well, I think that disposes of the matter."

After the prosecutor had completed his opening statement, defense counsel called to the court's attention the fact that, according to the opening statement, several witnesses on the list of witnesses provided defense counsel as required by 18 U.S.C.A. § 3432 would not be called by the Government. Apparently thinking that if the Government had no use for these witnesses he might have, defense counsel again pointed out that he had not been able to interview these witnesses because "they have been told not to talk to us," and asked the court's assistance at least with reference to interviewing the witnesses on the list the Government would not use. The court stated: "There is nothing I can do about it."

The purpose of 18 U.S.C.A. § 3432 requiring that in capital cases the defendant be furnished a list of the names and addresses of the witnesses to be called by the Government is to assist defense counsel in preparing the defense by interviewing the witnesses. Witnesses, particularly eye witnesses, to a crime are the property of neither the prosecution nor the defense. Both sides have an equal right, and should have an equal opportunity, to interview them. Here the defendant was denied that opportunity which, not only the statute, but elemental fairness and due process required that he have. It is true that the prosecutor stated he did not instruct the witnesses not to talk to defense counsel. He did admit that he advised the witnesses not to talk to anyone unless he, the prosecutor, were present.

We accept the prosecutor's statement as to his advice to the witnesses as true. But we know of nothing in the law which gives the prosecutor the right to interfere with the preparation of the defense by effectively denying defense counsel access to the witnesses except in his presence. Presumably the prosecutor, in interviewing the witnesses, was unencumbered by the presence of defense counsel, and there seems to be no reason why defense counsel should not have an equal opportunity to determine, through interviews with the witnesses, what they know about the case and what they will testify to.
* * *

We do not, of course, impugn the motives of the prosecutor in giving his advice to the witnesses. Tampering with witnesses and subornation of perjury are real dangers, especially in a capital case. But there are ways to avert this danger without denying defense counsel access to eye witnesses to the events in suit unless the prosecutor is present to monitor the interview. We cannot indulge the assumption that this tactic on the part of the prosecution is necessary. Defense counsel are officers of the court. And defense counsel are not exempted from prosecution under the statutes denouncing the crimes of obstruction of justice and subornation of perjury. In fact, the Government's motivation in disallowing defense counsel to interview witnesses apparently stems from factors other than fear of tampering. Recent records in this court reveal that the same policy followed in this case is followed even when the witness involved is a member of the police force.

A criminal trial, like its civil counterpart, is a quest for truth. That quest will more often be successful if both sides have an equal opportunity to interview the persons who have the information from which the truth may be determined. The current tendency in the criminal law is in the direction of discovery of the facts before trial and elimination of surprise at trial. A related development in the criminal law is the requirement that the prosecution not frustrate the defense in the preparation of its case. Information favorable to the defense must be made available to the defense. Brady v. State of Maryland, 373 U.S. 83, 83 S.Ct. 1194, 10 L.Ed.2d 215 (1963). Reversals of convictions for suppression of such evidence, and even for mere failure to disclose, have become commonplace. It is not suggested here that there was any direct suppression of evidence. But there was unquestionably a suppression of the means by which the defense could obtain evidence. The defense could not know what the eye witnesses to the events in suit were to testify to or how firm they were in their testimony unless defense counsel was provided a fair opportunity for interview. In our judgment the prosecutor's advice to these eye witnesses frustrated that effort and denied appellant a fair trial.

[Reversed on this and another ground.][a]

**a.** See Annot., 90 A.L.R.3d 1231 (1979) (prosecution interference with defense right to interview witnesses before trial). Cf. Annot., 14 A.L.R.3d 652 (1967) (defense right to interview witness held in public custody).

Compare Corbett v. Patterson, 272 F.Supp. 602, 610 (D.Colo.1967) (not error for prosecutor to advise witnesses they do not *have* to speak to anyone); Commonwealth v. McLaughlin, 352 Mass. 218, 224 N.E.2d 444, cert. denied, 389 U.S. 916, 88 S.Ct. 250, 19 L.Ed.2d 268 (1967) (similar).

ABA Standards for Criminal Justice 3–3.1(c) (2d ed. 1980) states:

"A prosecutor should not discourage or obstruct communication between prospective witnesses and defense counsel. It is unprofessional conduct for the prosecutor to advise any person or cause any person to be advised to decline to give to the defense information which such person has the right to give."

See id. 4–4.3(c) (same for defense counsel except last sentence specifies any person "other than a client").

Regarding interviewing of opponent's employees, see supra p. 353 Comment (2).

### *Comment*

(1) *Discipline.* Lacking RPC 3.4(f)'s specific restriction on requesting a person to refrain from giving information to another party, disciplinary proceedings under the CPR have relied upon DR 1–102(A)(5)'s prohibition of conduct prejudicial to the administration of justice or DR 7–104's restrictions on communicating with persons of adverse interest. Thus, in the Kansas case of State v. Martindale,[1] a lawyer defending a criminal case accidentally met two prosecution witnesses who were not subpoenaed. They asked him if they had to appear. He said no, and reminded them that his client would go to prison if they testified. Upon disciplinary proceedings, the lawyer was censured. The Kansas Supreme Court said that although the lawyer's conduct did not violate DR 7–109(B) (advising person to secrete self or leave jurisdiction for purpose of making the person unavailable as witness), it violated DR 1–102(A)(5) (conduct prejudicial to the administration of justice).[2]

Similarly, in In re Blatt,[3] a lawyer representing a public official involved in a corruption investigation advised other involved persons to be uncooperative and say as little as possible when questioned by government authorities. The New Jersey Supreme Court found that this constituted "conduct prejudicial to the administration of justice" in violation of DR 1–102(A)(5).

In In re Russell,[4] another New Jersey Supreme Court case, the court cited DR 7–104 (communicating with one of adverse interest) in severely reprimanding a lawyer for advising two grand jury witnesses to invoke the fifth amendment, contrary to the advice of the witnesses' own attorney.

(2) *Compensating witnesses.* Instead of setting forth DR 7–109(C)'s specific restrictions on compensating witnesses, RPC 3.4(b) merely prohibits a lawyer to "offer an inducement to a witness that is prohibited by law," and observes in the Comment:

> "[I]t is not improper to pay a witness's expenses or to compensate an expert witness on terms permitted by law. The common law rule in most jurisdictions is that it is improper to pay an occurrence witness any fee for testifying and that it is improper to pay an expert witness a contingent fee."

Compare the following ABA Standards for Criminal Justice (2d ed.1980)[5]:

1. 215 Kan. 667, 527 P.2d 703 (1974).

2. It would seem the conduct also could have been found violative of DR 7–104(A)(2) (giving advice to person not represented by lawyer other than advice to secure counsel, if person's interests are or have reasonable possibility of being in conflict with client's interests).

Regarding discipline for procuring absence of witnesses, see Annot., 40 A.L.R.3d 169, 190–91 (1971). Regarding discipline for suppression of evidence, see id. at 191–96.

3. 65 N.J. 539, 324 A.2d 15 (1974).

4. 59 N.J. 315, 282 A.2d 42 (1971).

5. Id. 3–3.2(a) and 3–3.3 (2d ed.1980) impose identical restrictions upon prosecutors.

"**Standard 4-4.3 Relations With Prospective Witnesses**

"(a) It is unprofessional conduct to compensate a witness, other than an expert, for giving testimony, but it is not improper to reimburse a witness for the reasonable expenses of attendance upon court, including transportation and loss of income, attendance for depositions pursuant to statute or court rule, or attendance for pretrial interviews, provided there is no attempt to conceal the fact of reimbursement.

* * *

"**Standard 4-4.4 Relations With Expert Witnesses**

"(a) A lawyer who engages an expert for an opinion should respect the independence of the expert and should not seek to dictate the formation of the expert's opinion on the subject. To the extent necessary, the lawyer should explain to the expert his or her role in the trial as an impartial witness called to aid the fact finders and the manner in which the examination of witnesses is conducted.

"(b) It is unprofessional conduct for a lawyer to pay an excessive fee for the purpose of influencing the expert's testimony or to fix the amount of the fee contingent upon the testimony the expert will give or the result in the case."

Lawyers have been disciplined for offering, making or acquiescing in payments to occurrence witnesses of amounts other than expenses,[6] or to any witnesses of contingent fees,[7] notwithstanding that the witnesses threatened otherwise to withhold their testimony[8] or to testify unfavorably.[9] Thus, in the New York case of In re Robinson,[10] a lawyer's participation, or at least acquiescence in, a client's systematic attempts to create a friendly attitude toward the client's cases on the part of witnesses and court officials led to the lawyer's disbarment. The court explained:

"To procure the testimony of witnesses, it is often necessary to pay the actual expenses of a witness in attending court and a reasonable compensation for the time lost. It is often necessary to pay a reasonable fee to an expert in preparing to testify for a party in an action. And there are many incidental expenses in relation to the prosecution or defense of an action at law which can with propriety be paid by a party to the action. But, on the other hand,

6. See In re Shamy, 59 N.J. 319, 282 A.2d 401 (1971) (lawyer made loan to prospective witness in order to keep witness available; absence of improper motive on lawyer's part did not preclude discipline).

7. See People v. Belfor, 197 Colo. 223, 591 P.2d 585 (1979) (lawyer offered occurrence witness remuneration contingent upon favorable testimony).

8. See In re O'Keefe, 49 Mont. 369, 142 P. 638 (1911) (lawyer promised to pay witnesses who threatened otherwise to withhold testimony $250 contingent upon favorable judgment).

9. See In re Schapiro, 144 A.D. 1, 128 N.Y.S. 852 (1911) (lawyer promised doctor, who threatened otherwise to testify unfavorably, percentage of amount recovered).

10. 151 A.D. 589, 136 N.Y.S. 548 (1912).

the payment of a sum of money to a witness to testify in a particular way, the payment of money to prevent a witness's attendance at a trial, the payment of money to a witness to make him 'sympathetic' with the party expecting to call him. These are all payments which are absolutely indefensible, and which are really included in the general definition of subornation of perjury. The payment of a sum of money to a witness to 'tell the truth' is as clearly subversive of the proper administration of justice as to pay him to testify to what is not true. The prevalence of perjury is a serious menace to the administration of justice, to prevent which no means have as yet been satisfactorily devised. But there certainly can be no greater incentive to perjury than to allow a party to make payments to its opponent's witnesses under any guise or on any excuse, and at least attorneys, who are officers of the court to aid it in the administration of justice, must keep themselves clear of any connection which in the slightest degree tends to induce witnesses to testify in favor of their clients."

The constitutionality of barring *expert* witness fees from being contingent *upon the case's outcome* was challenged by a New York lawyer in Person v. Association of the Bar.[11] The federal *district* court ruled that application of DR 7–109(C) was unconstitutional, finding that it prevented the lawyer, who represented ten antitrust plaintiffs, from obtaining needed accounting and economic testimony because of the clients' lack of funds, and discerning no rational basis for outlawing an expert witness fee arrangement, reasonable in amount and not contingent *upon content of testimony*, merely because the fee will not be paid if the client loses the case. The district court reasoned:

"The interests involved are *first*, the interest of plaintiff and every other lawyer in being able freely to seek out and, on his clients' behalf, contract on a contingent fee basis with qualified experts where that is the only way in which the client can afford to engage the expert's services or the way which is otherwise appropriate, and *second*, the client litigant's interest in having genuine access to the courts. * * *

"The purpose of the prohibition, to remove an incentive to untruthful testimony, is not likely to be achieved by the Rule, and, to the extent achieved, would be gained at too great a loss in fundamental fairness. * * *

"[T]o treat contingency of payment as in and of itself improper is too irrational to survive Fourteenth Amendment analysis. The interest in access to the courts on a basis of equality may not exact redress of every imbalance that disparity of means can produce, but it is of such fundamental importance that it cannot be subjected to a constraint that is not adapted to effective achievement of its

11. 414 F.Supp. 144 (E.D.N.Y.1976), reversed 554 F.2d 534 (2d Cir.), cert. denied 434 U.S. 924, 98 S.Ct. 403, 54 L.Ed.2d 282 (1977).

professed goal and which exacts a sacrifice which must, in any case, be disproportionate to the merely conjectured probability of occurrence of the wrong aimed at."

But the Second Circuit reversed the district court's judgment and upheld DR 7–109(C)'s applicability to expert witness fees contingent upon outcome, reasoning:

"Here we have no denial of access—[plaintiff's clients] are in court and have already engaged in extensive litigation. Their claim is that the rules place an insuperable obstacle in the way of successful presentation of their position on trial. It may be conceded that litigation of difficult and complex matters by persons with small individual stakes in the outcome may be aided and encouraged by elimination of the prohibition against the hiring of experts whose fees may be contingent upon the results. We are not convinced, however, that there is no danger of the inducement of false expert testimony by such contingency arrangements.

"[New York] has made a judgment that the need for discouragement of contingent fee arrangements outweighs the obstacle to financing litigation which a ban on contingent fees may create. We cannot say that this legislative judgment is irrational. The extent of the obstacle and the weight to be given its existence when balanced against the likelihood of false testimony and unfair results from permitting the procurement of expert testimony by the offer of a stake in the outcome are matters of judgment best confided to legislative and judicial bodies of the state. * * *

"New York Disciplinary Rule 7–109[C] does not affect a fundamental right nor create a suspect classification. We hold that it has a sufficient rational basis to withstand a constitutional challenge under the equal protection and due process clauses of the fourteenth amendment." [12]

## H. TRIAL PUBLICITY

### MODEL RULES OF PROFESSIONAL CONDUCT

**RULE 3.6 Trial Publicity**

(a) A lawyer shall not make an extrajudicial statement that a reasonable person would expect to be disseminated by means of public communi-

12. Compare Seigal v. Merrick, 619 F.2d 160 (2d Cir. 1980), where the court held that an expert witness fee was not contingent in violation of DR 7–109(C) merely because the litigant would likely be unable to pay and the witness would likely forebear pressing the litigant's lawyer for full payment if the litigant lost. The court said that "if New York law prohibited the employment of an expert witness unless a party realistically expected to pay a substantial fee even in the event of failure, our *Person* decision indicates that a serious constitutional question might arise."

See generally Comment, Contingent Fees for Expert Witnesses in Civil Litigation, 86 Yale L.J. 1680 (1977), which argues that expert witness contingent fees should be permitted when set in reasonable amount by the trial court.

cation if the lawyer knows or reasonably should know that it will have a substantial likelihood of materially prejudicing an adjudicative proceeding.

(b) A statement referred to in paragraph (a) ordinarily is likely to have such an effect when it refers to a civil matter triable to a jury, a criminal matter, or any other proceeding that could result in incarceration, and the statement relates to:

(1) the character, credibility, reputation or criminal record of a party, suspect in a criminal investigation or witness, or the identity of a witness, or the expected testimony of a party or witness;

(2) in a criminal case or proceeding that could result in incarceration, the possibility of a plea of guilty to the offense or the existence or contents of any confession, admission, or statement given by a defendant or suspect or that person's refusal or failure to make a statement;

(3) the performance or results of any examination or test or the refusal or failure of a person to submit to an examination or test, or the identity or nature of physical evidence expected to be presented;

(4) any opinion as to the guilt or innocence of a defendant or suspect in a criminal case or proceeding that could result in incarceration;

(5) information the lawyer knows or reasonably should know is likely to be inadmissible as evidence in a trial and would if disclosed create a substantial risk of prejudicing an impartial trial; or

(6) the fact that a defendant has been charged with a crime, unless there is included therein a statement explaining that the charge is merely an accusation and that the defendant is presumed innocent until and unless proven guilty.

(c) Notwithstanding Paragraph (a) and (b)(1–5), a lawyer involved in the investigation or litigation of a matter may state without elaboration:

(1) the general nature of the claim or defense;

(2) the information contained in a public record;

(3) that an investigation of the matter is in progress, including the general scope of the investigation, the offense or claim or defense involved and, except when prohibited by law, the identity of the persons involved;

(4) the scheduling or result of any step in litigation;

(5) a request for assistance in obtaining evidence and information necessary thereto;

(6) a warning of danger concerning the behavior of a person involved, when there is reason to believe that there exists the likelihood of substantial harm to an individual or to the public interest; and

(7) in a criminal case:

(i) the identity, residence, occupation and family status of the accused;

(ii) if the accused has not been apprehended, information necessary to aid in apprehension of that person;

(iii) the fact, time and place of arrest; and

(iv) the identity of investigating and arresting officers or agencies and the length of the investigation.

## RULE 8.2 Judicial and Legal Officials

(a) A lawyer shall not make a statement that the lawyer knows to be false or with reckless disregard as to its truth or falsity concerning the qualifications or integrity of a judge, adjudicatory officer or public legal officer, or of a candidate for election or appointment to judicial or legal office.[a]

**a.** Compare the following CPR provisions:

**"DR 7–107 Trial Publicity**

"(A) A lawyer participating in or associated with the investigation of a criminal matter shall not make or participate in making an extrajudicial statement that a reasonable person would expect to be disseminated by means of public communication and that does more than state without elaboration:

(1) Information contained in a public record.

(2) That the investigation is in progress.

(3) The general scope of the investigation including a description of the offense and, if permitted by law, the identity of the victim.

(4) A request for assistance in apprehending a suspect or assistance in other matters and the information necessary thereto.

(5) A warning to the public of any dangers.

"(B) A lawyer or law firm associated with the prosecution or defense of a criminal matter shall not, from the time of the filing of a complaint, information, or indictment, the issuance of an arrest warrant, or arrest until the commencement of the trial or disposition without trial, make or participate in making an extrajudicial statement that a reasonable person would expect to be disseminated by means of public communication and that relates to:

(1) The character, reputation, or prior criminal record (including arrests, indictments, or other charges of crime) of the accused.

(2) The possibility of a plea of guilty to the offense charged or to a lesser offense.

(3) The existence or contents of any confession, admission, or statement given by the accused or his refusal or failure to make a statement.

(4) The performance or results of any examinations or tests or the refusal or failure of the accused to submit to examinations or tests.

(5) The identity, testimony, or credibility of a prospective witness.

(6) Any opinion as to the guilt or innocence of the accused, the evidence, or the merits of the case.

"(C) DR 7–107(B) does not preclude a lawyer during such period from announcing:

(1) The name, age, residence, occupation, and family status of the accused.

(2) If the accused has not been apprehended, any information necessary to aid in his apprehension or to warn the public of any dangers he may present.

(3) A request for assistance in obtaining evidence.

(4) The identity of the victim of the crime.

(5) The fact, time and place of arrest, resistance, pursuit, and use of weapons.

(6) The identity of investigating and arresting officers or agencies and the length of the investigation.

(7) At the time of seizure, a description of the physical evidence seized, other than a confession, admission, or statement.

(8) The nature, substance, or text of the charge.

(9) Quotations from or references to public records of the court in the case.

(10) The scheduling or result of any step in the judicial proceedings.

(11) That the accused denies the charges made against him.

## IN RE HINDS

90 N.J. 604, 449 A.2d 483 (1982).

HANDLER, J. * * *

I

* * * Hinds has been a member of the New Jersey Bar since 1973. He has been active and prominent as a lawyer in civil rights causes and has a national reputation for his work as Director of the National Conference of Black Lawyers (hereinafter "NCBL"), a capacity in which he served for five years until 1978. In 1973 Joanne Chesimard, a black woman reputed to be a militant radical, was accused

"(D) During the selection of a jury or the trial of a criminal matter, a lawyer or law firm associated with the prosecution or defense of a criminal matter shall not make or participate in making an extra-judicial statement that a reasonable person would expect to be disseminated by means of public communication and that relates to the trial, parties, or issues in the trial or other matters that are reasonably likely to interfere with a fair trial, except that he may quote from or refer without comment to public records of the court in the case.

"(E) After the completion of a trial or disposition without trial of a criminal matter and prior to the imposition of sentence, a lawyer or law firm associated with the prosecution or defense shall not make or participate in making an extrajudicial statement that a reasonable person would expect to be disseminated by public communication and that is reasonably likely to affect the imposition of sentence.

"(F) The foregoing provisions of DR 7–107 also apply to professional disciplinary proceedings and juvenile disciplinary proceedings when pertinent and consistent with other law applicable to such proceedings.

"(G) A lawyer or law firm associated with a civil action shall not during its investigation or litigation make or participate in making an extrajudicial statement, other than a quotation from or reference to public records, that a reasonable person would expect to be disseminated by means of public communication and that relates to:

(1) Evidence regarding the occurrence or transaction involved.

(2) The character, credibility, or criminal record of a party, witness, or prospective witness.

(3) The performance or results of any examinations or tests or the refusal or failure of a party to submit to such.

(4) His opinion as to the merits of the claims or defenses of a party, except as required by law or administrative rule.

(5) Any other matter reasonably likely to interfere with a fair trial of the action.

"(H) [Provision on administrative proceedings similar to subdivision (G).]

"(I) The foregoing provisions of DR 7–107 do not preclude a lawyer from replying to charges of misconduct publicly made against him or from participating in the proceedings of legislative, administrative, or other investigative bodies.

"(J) A lawyer shall exercise reasonable care to prevent his employees and associates from making an extrajudicial statement that he would be prohibited from making under DR 7–107."

**"DR 8–102 Statements Concerning Judges and Other Adjudicatory Officers**

* * *

"(B) A lawyer shall not knowingly make false accusations against a judge or other adjudicatory officer."

See also ABA Code of Judicial Conduct, Canon 3(A)(6), which specifies:

"A judge should abstain from public comment about a pending or impending proceeding in any court, and should require similar abstention on the part of court personnel subject to his direction and control. This subsection does not prohibit judges from making public statements in the course of their official duties or from explaining for public information the procedures of the court."

of killing a New Jersey State trooper. Following her arrest, Chesimard was brought to trial after a long series of delays. Hinds represented Chesimard during this pretrial period in several federal civil actions concerning the legality and general conditions of her incarceration by the State. Hinds apparently did not, however, represent Chesimard at her criminal trial.

Chesimard finally went on trial for murder in 1977 in the Superior Court, Law Division, in New Brunswick. After observing the initial phases of the trial and while the jury was still being impaneled, Hinds called a press conference at his New Brunswick office on January 20, 1977. In an article appearing January 21, 1977, in the *New York Daily News* under the headline, "Joanne Loses 2 Rounds in Trial Transfer," it was reported that:

> "* * * [Lennox] Hinds, an attorney also representing Mrs. Chesimard, said the defense team wanted the case moved to another court because in New Brunswick 'what we are seeing is legalized lynching.'
>
> "He said he was speaking for the defense team because its members were 'gagged' by [the trial judge] whom he accused of asking prospective jurors self-serving questions which he said were leading to 'the creation of a hangman's court.' "

An article appearing in the *Newark Star-Ledger* on the same date reported that Hinds had referred to the Chesimard trial as "a travesty." The article further quoted Hinds as saying that the trial judge "does not have the judicial temperament or the racial sensitivity to sit as an impartial judge" in Chesimard's trial, and that "[i]t was only after the trial began that we began to have fears that what we are seeing is a legalized lynching."

Also, a television reporter covering the press conference for the New Jersey Public Broadcasting Authority (Channel 52) recorded the following exchange:

> Hinds: "We feel that it is a kangaroo—it will be a kangaroo court unless the judge recluses [sic] himself and that will be the very minimum." * * *

* * * Chesimard was eventually convicted of murder in the first degree and sentenced to a mandatory term of life imprisonment. [After a disciplinary authority's investigation, Hinds was] charged with violating two disciplinary rules: DR 1–102(A)(5), which prohibits attorneys from "[e]ngag[ing] in conduct * * * prejudicial to the administration of justice"[a]; and DR 7–107(D), which provides that

> "[d]uring the selection of a jury or a trial of a criminal matter, a lawyer or law firm associated with the prosecution or defense of a criminal matter shall not make or participate in making an extrajudicial statement that he expects to be disseminated by means of

a. Accord, RPC 8.4(d).

public communication and that relates to the trial, parties, or issues in the trial or other matters that are reasonably likely to interfere with a fair trial * * *."

* * * Instead of responding * * * Hinds filed a suit in federal court on February 10, 1978, seeking to enjoin the State disciplinary proceedings and to obtain a judgment declaring these particular disciplinary rules unconstitutional. * * *

This court, on its own motion, * * * ordered certification of the complaint against Hinds, pursuant to R. 2:12–1, and directed that "the entire record, including but not limited to, the constitutional challenges to DR 1–102 and DR 7–197(D) raised by respondent, be considered by this Court." * * *

* * * In a decision dated June 21, 1982, the [United States] Supreme Court [held] that the federal courts should abstain from interfering with this State's ongoing disciplinary proceedings. Middlesex Ethics Comm. v. Garden St. Bar Ass'n [Casebook p. 72]. * * *

II

* * * Hinds claims that DR 7–107(D) is unconstitutionally vague and overbroad under the First Amendment. He asserts that the rule can be applied to restrict speech only when an attorney's out-of-court statements create a "clear and present danger" to the trial and that, applying this constitutional standard to these facts, his remarks regarding the conduct of the judge at the Chesimard trial did not violate the disciplinary rule or otherwise warrant sanction.

We note at the outset that the freedom to engage in robust public debate is at the very heart of the First Amendment. The Constitution unquestionably guarantees the right of citizens to criticize public officials, including judges. * * *

In their unique and special capacity as judicial officers, lawyers differ from ordinary citizens. This was aptly expressed by Justice Frankfurter in his dissent in In re Sawyer [360 U.S. 622, 666, 79 S.Ct. 1376, 1397, 3 L.Ed.2d 1473, 1499–1500 (1959)]:

> "Of course, a lawyer is a person and he too has a constitutional freedom of utterance and may exercise it to castigate courts and their administration of justice. But a lawyer actively participating in a trial, particularly an emotionally charged criminal prosecution, is not merely a person and not even merely a lawyer * * *. He is an intimate and trusted and essential part of the machinery of justice, an 'officer of the court' in the most compelling sense."

[The] interest in trial fairness is particularly acute in the criminal context. There, the problem of preserving the basic fairness and integrity of the proceeding is of constitutional dimension because the defendant's right to a fair trial is guaranteed in the Sixth Amendment of the federal Constitution. Some courts, including the Supreme Court, have even held that the criminal defendant's constitutional right to a fair trial must take precedence over free speech. See, e.g., Estes v. Texas, 381 U.S. 532, 540, 85 S.Ct. 1628, 1632, 14 L.Ed.2d 543, 549 (1965) (defendant's right to a fair trial is "the most fundamental of all freedoms"); [Chicago Council of Lawyers v.] Bauer, 522 F.2d [242,] 248 [(7th Cir. 1975), cert. denied, 427 U.S. 912, 96 S.Ct. 3201, 49 L.Ed.2d 1204 (1976)]; [United States v.] Tijerina, 412 F.2d [661,] 667 [10th Cir. 1969]; Hirschkop v. Virginia State Bar, 421 F.Supp. 1137, 1146–47 (E.D.Va. 1976) [aff'd sub nom. Hirschkop v. Snead, 594 F.2d 356 (4th Cir. 1979)].

DR 7–107(D) clearly seeks to effectuate this important and substantial governmental interest in trial fairness. The difficult question is whether this disciplinary rule is broader than necessary or essential to protect that governmental interest. * * *

Ordinarily, speech restrictions will withstand constitutional scrutiny only if they are limited to prohibiting that speech which creates a "clear and present danger" of threatening some substantial governmental interest unrelated to the suppression of expression. See Brandenburg [v. Ohio], 395 U.S. 444, 89 S.Ct. 1827, 33 L.Ed.2d 430 [1969]; Bridges [v. California], 314 U.S. 252, 62 S.Ct. 190, 86 L.Ed. 192 [1941]. However, attorney extrajudicial speech in the criminal trial setting presents special concerns. * * *

In Sheppard [v. Maxwell, 384 U.S. 333, 361–63, 86 S.Ct. 1507, 1521–22, 16 L.Ed.2d 600, 619–20 (1966) (dictum) ], the Supreme Court observed:

> "Effective control of [counsel]—concededly within the court's power—might well have prevented the divulgence of inaccurate information, rumors, and accusations that made up much of the inflammatory publicity * * *.
>
> "[W]here there is a reasonable likelihood that prejudicial news prior to trial will prevent a fair trial, the judge should continue the case until the threat abates, or transfer it to another county not so permeated with publicity * * *. If publicity during the proceedings threatens the fairness of the trial, a new trial should be ordered. But we must remember that reversals are but palliatives; the cure lies in those remedial measures that will prevent the prejudice at its inception. The courts must take such steps by rule and regulation that will protect their processes from prejudicial outside interferences. Neither prosecutors, counsel for defense, the accused, witnesses, court staff nor enforcement officers coming under the jurisdiction of the court should be permitted to frustrate its function. Collaboration between counsel and the press as to information affecting the fairness of a criminal trial is not only subject to regulation, but is highly censurable and worthy of disciplinary measures."

Thus, the Supreme Court targeted the evil as public speech that creates "a reasonable likelihood * * * [of] prevent[ing] a fair trial." * * *

Many courts have upheld the constitutional validity of the "reasonable likelihood" standard for limiting lawyer extrajudicial comments during criminal trials. See, e.g., *Hirschkopj Tijerina;* Younger v. Smith, 30 Cal.App.3d 138, 106 Cal.Rptr. 225 (1973); People v. Dupree, 88 Misc.2d 780, 388 N.Y.S.2d 203 (Sup.Ct.1976). Cf. State v. Ross, 36 Ohio App.2d 185, 304 N.E.2d 396 (Ct.App.1973), appeal dismissed, 415 U.S. 904, 94 S.Ct. 1397, 39 L.Ed.2d 461 (1974) (court refused to grant attorney permission to appear *pro hac vice* in criminal trial because the attorney said he would only limit his public comments to those not creating a "clear and present danger" to the proceedings); Widoff v. Disciplinary Board, 54 Pa.Commw.Ct. 124, 420 A.2d 41 (1980), aff'd sub nom. Cohen v. Disciplinary Board, 494 Pa. 129, 430 A.2d 1151 (1981), appeal dismissed, 455 U.S. 914, 102 S.Ct. 1266, 71 L.Ed.2d 454 (1982) ("reasonable likelihood" standard applied in context of administrative hearing).

Other courts have rejected the "reasonable likelihood" test and have applied a traditional First Amendment analysis, holding that the Constitution protects an attorney's right to make extrajudicial statements, except when those comments create a "clear and present danger" or a "serious and imminent threat" to the administration of justice. See, e.g., *Bauer;* In re Oliver, 452 F.2d 111 (7 Cir. 1971); Chase v. Robson, 435 F.2d 1059 (7 Cir. 1970); United States v. Garcia, 456 F.Supp. 1354 (D.P.R.1978); Hamilton v. Municipal Court for Berkeley-Albany Judicial District, 270 Cal.App.2d 797, 76 Cal.Rptr. 168, cert. denied 396 U.S. 985, 90 S.Ct. 479, 24 L.Ed.2d 449 (1969). See also Model Rules of Professional Conduct, ABA Commission of Evaluation of Professional Standards at 270, 275 (Alt.Draft 1981) (recommending change in standard to proscribe only those comments that have a "substantial likelihood of materially prejudicing" the trial, with change intended to incorporate "clear and present danger" test); ABA Standards [for Criminal Justice 8–1.1 (2d ed. 1980) (using] "clear and present danger" test and suggesting constitutional invalidity of present standard).

In addressing the issue of prejudicial out-of-court statements by attorneys in *Sawyer*, the Supreme Court refused to endorse the clear and present danger test. There, an attorney was suspended from the practice of law for making an out-of-court speech in which she allegedly maligned the judge before whom she was appearing as defense counsel in a pending conspiracy case. Although five members of the Court voted to overturn the suspension because of insufficient evidence of professional misconduct, four dissenting justices, joined by concurring Justice Stewart, questioned the applicability of the clear and present danger test to situations involving attorneys who make extrajudicial statements about ongoing cases in which they are participating.

We are satisfied that the clear and present danger formulation is not constitutionally compelled when the subject of the restriction is the extrajudicial speech of attorneys participating in criminal trials. The clear and present danger test is neither more precise nor more certain in meaning than is the reasonable likelihood test. While the clear and present danger test may be stricter than the reasonable likelihood standard, strictness does not import more precision or imply greater clarity. * * *

* * * Whether a particular utterance creates a reasonable likelihood of affecting trial fairness will depend upon the special circumstances of each case. This inquiry involves a careful balancing and consideration of all relevant factors. These factors can include such matters as the nature of the statement, the timing of the statement, the extent to which the information has been publicized, the nature of the proceeding and its vulnerability to prejudicial influence, the attorney's status in the case, the lawyer's unique position as an informed and accurate source of information in the case, and the effect of unrestricted comment on the interest of the litigants and the integrity of the proceeding.[4] See Note, "A Constitutional Assessment of Court Rules Restricting Lawyer Comment on Pending Litigation," 65 Cornell L.Rev. 1106, 1120–21 (1980).

In terms of whether the reasonable likelihood standard is overbroad, we agree with Hinds that this test is not as narrow or limited in its reach as the clear and present danger standard. We must decide, however, not whether this test is broader than another possible standard but whether it is no broader than necessary and essential to protect the substantial governmental interest involved.

We find the reasonable likelihood test to be a permissible standard for restricting free speech in this special context. We are impelled to this conclusion because of both the nature of the governmental interest involved and the status and role of attorneys in effectuating

4. We note that Hinds faced these charges because of his association with the *defense* in a criminal trial. The status of an attorney as defense counsel, as opposed to prosecutor, is a relevant factor to consider in imposing speech restrictions. There are clear differences between the two that affect their respective abilities to influence the proceedings through extrajudicial statements.

Several commentators have suggested that criminal defense attorneys should not be subject to the same strict speech limitations as prosecutors. See, e.g., Freedman and Starwood, "Prior Restraints on Freedom of Expression by Defendants and Defense Attorneys: Ratio Decidendi v. Obiter Dictum," 29 Stan.L.Rev. 607 (1977); Hirst, "Silence Orders—Preserving Political Expression by Defendants and Their Lawyers," 6 Harv.Civ.Rts.—Civ.Lib.L.Rev. 595, 604, 606–08 (1976); Isaacson, "Fair Trial and Free Press: An Opportunity for Coexistence," 29 Stan.L.Rev. 561, 568–70 (1977); Kaplan, "Of Babies and Bathwater," 29 Stan.L.Rev. 621, 625 n.13 (1977); Comment, "Professional Ethics and Trial Publicity: Another Constitutional Attack on DR 7–107—Hirschkop v. Snead," 14 U.Rich.L.Rev. 231, 225–236 (1979). These commentators essentially reason that the constitutional guarantee of a fair trial belongs to the defendant alone, not the prosecution. See U.S.Const., Amends. IV, V, VI. Thus, regulations restricting free speech in this context should be tailored to advance the defendant's constitutionally protected interest in a fair trial. Moreover, they point out that "the scales of justice * * * are weighed extraordinarily heavy against an accused after his indictment." *Bauer*, 522 F.2d at 250, quoted in Freedman and Starwood, 29 Stan.L.Rev. at 611. Therefore, they conclude that the defendant and his counsel need access to the public to combat the stigma of an indictment.

When extrajudicial statements of defense attorneys are prohibited, the interest sought to be protected is not simply the right of the accused to a fair trial. Defense attorneys are also silenced because of the government's interest in the "fair administration of justice" and basic "integrity of judicial processes." *Hirschkop*, 594 F.2d at 362, 376. As we have noted, this is a significant interest which justifies speech restrictions on attorneys associated with the case, whether as prosecutor or defense counsel.

that interest. Society has an important stake in the proper administration of criminal justice. The reconciliation of intersecting values in the administration of criminal justice—the rights of an accused and society's needs for safety and protection—constitutes one of the most difficult and sensitive tasks of government. The State's concern for an effective, efficient, fair and balanced system of criminal justice is unquestioned. It has been accorded a high priority in terms of government's responsibility to its citizens. The significance of this governmental obligation justifies scrupulous and conscientious measures to assure its fulfillment.

Furthermore, attorneys perform a unique service in the criminal justice system. While the administration of criminal justice is a governmental responsibility, [its] proper functioning depends upon all who participate in the process. It utilizes adversarial, not inquisitorial, techniques. Lawyers in criminal cases represent opposing parties and conflicting interests. They must, therefore, discharge their professional responsibilities ethically as well as skillfully. They must do so according to carefully prescribed rules within a procedural framework designed to assure due process and fairness to both the accused and the public. The sole objective of this system is to secure justice. The benchmark of its success is the reaching of a just result based solely on properly adduced, competent evidence that is relevant to the truth of the criminal charges.

These considerations, in our view, require ethical constraints upon attorneys. These must include reasonable restrictions upon their extrajudicial speech to discourage and prevent extraneous matters from being insinuated into a criminal case. Such outside influences, if left unchecked, could divert the search for truth and wreck the intricate machinery of the criminal justice system. The reasonable likelihood test expressed in DR 7–107(D) is necessary and essential to the achievement of these objectives and, therefore, does not suffer from constitutional overbreadth.[5]

5. An overbreadth analysis also necessarily involves consideration of whether the government's substantial interest could be adequately protected through some means other than a speech restriction. If an alternative form of regulation would combat the danger without infringing upon First Amendment rights, then a speech restriction would be unnecessary and, therefore, unconstitutional. A variety of alternatives to attorney speech restrictions exist for protecting a fair trial, including: (1) exclusion of the public from those hearings during trial held in the absence of jury; (2) continuances; (3) change of venue; (4) jury waiver; (5) searching voir dire; (6) selection of jury from locality outside area of extensive news coverage; (7) sequestration of jury; (8) admonitions to jury to avoid news reports relating to trial (9) cautionary instructions to media regarding critical matters; (10) examination of jurors regarding possible exposure to prejudicial information during trial; (11) declaring a mistrial, and (12) granting a new trial.

These other options, taken singly or together, do not preclude the imposition of attorney free speech restrictions because, in the criminal trial setting, courts have an overriding obligation to "prevent * * * prejudice at its inception," *Sheppard*, rather than to wait until after the fact to attempt remedial action. Certain of these measures, such as change of venue, continuances and searching voir dire, simply are not effective alternatives. Moreover, ready resort to these alternative steps might impinge upon other constitutional guarantees, such as the defendant's right to a speedy trial or trial by jury. Thus, while alternative approaches to dealing with the problem of prejudicial publicity exist, they do not obviate the need for properly fashioned restrictions on the extrajudicial speech of attorneys participating in criminal trials.

The question next presented is whether Hinds' remarks were reasonably likely to interfere with a fair trial such that they violated the standard of DR 7–107(D). On this ultimate question there has been no adequate factual record developed. The Ethics Committee never conducted a hearing on this or any other issue. * * *

Even if the record below * * * were capable of being canvassed for factfindings, the Ethics Committee could not have known to resolve this issue by applying the balancing test that we have enunciated for the first time in this opinion. We reiterate that this balancing process for determining when an attorney's extrajudicial remarks are reasonably likely to affect a fair trial entails careful consideration of such factors as the status of the attorney, the nature and content of the statement, the timing of the statement, and the context in which it was uttered. The reasonable likelihood standard requires a showing by clear and convincing evidence that an attorney's extrajudicial speech truly jeopardized trial fairness, a determination that can be reached only by thoroughly balancing all relevant considerations.

III

* * * The prohibition of DR 7–107(D) does not apply unless the speech is made by an attorney "associated with" the criminal trial.[b] Hinds contends that this aspect of the rule also suffers from constitutional vagueness and overbreadth.

In dealing with this contention as a facial attack upon the rule, we accept the notion that by restricting the extrajudicial speech of attorneys, DR 7–107(D) was adopted in order to "stop * * * prejudice at its inception," *Sheppard*. The rule seeks to prevent attorneys with a special status in the case from making disclosures that are prejudicial to the trial process.

Attorneys of record clearly fall within the class of lawyers who have a special connection with the case. * * *

The question remains whether an attorney who is not an attorney of record but is closely "associated with" the trial in other ways can be subject to the rule's sanctions. * * *

We are satisfied that DR 7–107(D) was intended to be applied to attorneys who have such an association with the defense of a criminal trial that extrajudicial statements made by them about the proceedings have a unique capacity for prejudicial impact upon the trial process. Accordingly, we now hold that under DR 7–107(D) an attorney who cooperates with the defense of a criminal prosecution on a regular and continuing basis, provides legal assistance in connection with the defense of a criminal charge, and holds himself out to be a member of the defense team is to be considered "associated with" the defense for purposes of invoking this disciplinary rule.

**b.** Compare RPC 3.6.

So interpreted, we conclude that the rule is neither vague nor overbroad. While the rule does not define the term "associated with," it is not an esoteric or abstruse expression. It fairly imports a common sense meaning and is susceptible to a simple interpretation in accordance with common experience and ordinary understanding. The term is, therefore, adequate to inform and forewarn attorneys who potentially may be subject to the strictures of the rule. Consequently, the rule is not impermissibly vague in its application to attorneys associated with the defense of a criminal case.

Extending the coverage of the rule to include not only attorneys of record but also attorneys associated with the defense of a criminal prosecution does not constitute overreaching. Attorneys falling into both categories possess special knowledge and information relating to the criminal action. They are readily perceived as authoritative persons whose remarks carry the mark of reliability, authority and accuracy. Comments made by such attorneys about ongoing trials can carry significant weight in the minds of members of the public, including potential jurors, witnesses and others who may have a role to play in the trial. Restrictions upon the attorneys' freedom to comment about the case are necessary to assure that the fairness of the criminal trial will not be jeopardized. We are thus satisfied that DR 7–107(D) is constitutional as applied to this class of individuals.

IV

Although we determine that DR 7–107(D) is constitutional, under the circumstances of this case, we conclude that Hinds should not be found in violation of the rule. We do so for two reasons. First, there is sufficient doubt as to the underlying facts regarding Hinds' relationship with the Chesimard defense to prevent an ultimate conclusion from being drawn on this important issue. That factual question was never conclusively resolved. The Ethics Committee conducted no hearing * * *. Therefore, the extent of Hinds' association with the defense team is not entirely clear or free from dispute.

Our second and primary reason for refusing to apply DR 7–107(D) in this instance is based on elementary fairness. This is the first time we have addressed the question of whether an attorney in Hinds' position would be considered "associated with" a case for purposes of falling within the rule's coverage. Furthermore, as already pointed out, this decision also constitutes the first time we have explained the balancing test to be applied for determining whether the extrajudicial speech of an attorney associated with an ongoing criminal trial is reasonably likely to interfere with a fair trial. We therefore deem it appropriate that DR 7–107(D) be applied prospectively only and that Hinds be given the benefit of this ruling.

In terms of the propriety of sanctions, we are not engaged in the enforcement of the State's criminal laws. Rather, we are addressing disciplinary rules governing the professional conduct of attorneys.

Our major concern is the ethics lesson to be extracted from this case and the prophylactic effect of our decision in explaining the appropriate ethics principle. Our purpose is not to punish but to enlighten and improve the profession for the benefit of the public. Furthermore, we are dealing here not with unethical conduct which bespeaks corruption, fraud, breach of trust, professional negligence or some form of criminality. The problematic conduct in this case is speech, an activity protected under the First Amendment. While such speech may under limited circumstances constitute unprofessional conduct, we should not rush to impose sanctions upon expressional activity unless that course of action is clear and unavoidable. In this instance we find the imposition of punishment unnecessary to promote our ethical aims and, therefore, refrain from doing so.

V

Since we have determined that DR 7–107(D), as construed by us in this decision, is to be given prospective effect only and, therefore, should not be applied to Hinds, the question arises whether he can nevertheless be punished under DR 1–102(A)(5). This disciplinary rule sanctions attorney conduct that is "prejudicial to the administration of justice." Hinds contends that application of that rule to these facts would constitute a violation of his free speech rights under the First Amendment because the rule is impermissibly vague and overbroad.

DR 1–102(A)(5) is framed in broad language and gives the appearance of an aspirational standard, rather than a disciplinary rule. Courts have held that a broad disciplinary rule may acquire constitutional certitude when examined in light of traditions in the profession and established patterns of application. See Parker v. Levy, 417 U.S. 733, 94 S.Ct. 2547, 41 L.Ed.2d 439 (1974); In re Ruffalo, 390 U.S. 544, 88 S.Ct. 1222, 20 L.Ed.2d 117 (1968); In re Bithoney, 486 F.2d 319 (1 Cir. 1973) (dictum).

Attorney disciplinary rules have long been framed in general, rather sweeping language. The legal profession's cardinal ethical edict—"to avoid even the appearance of impropriety"—suggests that a lawyer should refrain from acting if there is any basis for suggesting that his conduct might be questioned. See Canon 9 of the Code of Professional Responsibility. As one court explained in affirming the constitutionality of DR 1–102(A)(5): "[T]he rule was written by and for lawyers. The language of a rule setting guidelines for members of the bar need not meet the precise standards of clarity that might be required of rules of conduct for laymen." In re Keiler, 380 A.2d 119, 126 (D.C.1977). See State v. Martindale, 215 Kan. 667, 527 P.2d 703 (1979).

Moreover, unlike DR 7–107, which has rarely been applied, DR 1–102(A)(5) has regularly been invoked in disciplinary actions. The New Jersey cases disclose a pattern of applying DR 1–102(A)(5) in conjunction with other more specific disciplinary rules to sanction attorney misconduct. See, e.g., In re Clark, 83 N.J. 458, 416 A.2d 851 (1980) (also violating DR 6–101, 9–102); Wilson, 81 N.J. 451, 409 A.2d 1153 (also violating DR 9–102). And on those few occasions when the rule has served as the sole basis for discipline, it has been applied only in situations involving conduct flagrantly violative of accepted professional norms. See, e.g., In re Schleimer, 78 N.J. 317, 394 A.2d 359 (1978) (false swearing). Thus, the rule's broad language proscribing acts "prejudicial to the administration of justice" takes on sufficient definition to pass constitutional muster, given these prior judicial determinations narrowing its scope to particularly egregious conduct. See Committee on Professional Ethics v. Durham, 279 N.W.2d 280 (Iowa 1979).

Several considerations militate against the application of DR 1–102(A)(5) under the circumstances of this case. Such a determination would require a factual inquiry similar to that involved in the application of DR 7–107, the primary rule governing attorney extrajudicial speech. The effect or impact of the attorney's speech upon the criminal case and the attorney's status in the case would also be relevant in determining whether the attorney's conduct was prejudicial to the administration of justice under DR 1–102(A)(5). Because the record in this case is inadequate to demonstrate whether Hinds was "associated with" the Chesimard case or whether his remarks were reasonably likely to interfere with the criminal trial for purposes of applying DR 7–107(D), we are satisfied that the record is similarly deficient for purposes of applying DR 1–102(A)(5).

It seems quite certain that, in the separate application of this disciplinary rule, the First Amendment would require a higher standard than the reasonable likelihood formulation of DR 7–107. The critical distinction in the application of the two disciplinary rules hinges upon the status of the attorney whose speech is subject to scrutiny. As already shown, an attorney who is specially connected with an ongoing criminal trial under DR 7–107 may be subject to the broader restraints of the reasonable likelihood standard. In contrast, DR 1–102(A)(5) would come into play when the attorney is not particularly or specially connected with or involved in a pending criminal matter. In that context, there would appear to be no reason cognizable under First Amendment principles for distinguishing such an attorney from other citizens. An attorney with no supervening professional responsibilities in a pending criminal case would seemingly enjoy the same free speech rights as any other citizen.[9]

9. Inconsistencies in the case law also suggest the need for a strict standard. Courts in other jurisdictions have reached widely divergent results in deciding whether to impose sanctions in situations such as this one, where the attorney's speech consisted of mere criticism of judges. For cases imposing sanctions for criticizing judges, see, e.g., Eisenberg v. Boardman, 302 F.Supp. 1360 (D.Wis. 1969) (attorney circulated statement designed to humilate judge); In re Lacey, 283 N.W.2d 250 (S.D.1979) (attorney quoted in press as saying "state courts were incompetent and sometimes downright crooked"); In re Raggio, 87 Nev. 369, 487 P.2d 499 (1970) (attorney wrote magazine article criticizing judges in intemperate terms). See also In re Friedland, 268 Ind. 536, 376 N.E.2d 1126 (1978)

Because DR 1–102(A)(5) applies to an attorney in his capacity as an ordinary citizen, the standard for invoking the rule's sanctions against speech should be that of a "clear and present danger" or, to use an alternative formulation, a "serious and imminent threat" to the fairness and integrity of the judicial system. While we recognize the absence of an adequate record in this case, the facts that have thus far been presented do not suggest that Hinds' statements created a "clear and present danger" of prejudicing the administration of justice such that he could be found to have committed an ethical violation. If we were called upon to address that proposition, we would have to "be on guard against confusing offenses to [our] sensibilities with obstruction to the administration of justice." Brown [v. United States], 356 U.S. [148,] 153, 78 S.Ct. [622,] 625, 2 L.Ed.2d [589,] 596 [1958].

We need not further discuss the need for additional proceedings or the significant question of whether the First Amendment requires the application of a stricter standard than the reasonable likelihood test under DR 1–102(A)(5). The reasons which have deterred us from reaching a determination of the issues posed by the charges under DR 7–107(D) apply as well to DR 1–102(A)(5). Since our ruling on the meaning and application of DR 7–107(D) will be given prospective effect only, it is unnecessary, if not unwarranted, to attempt to discipline Hinds under DR 1–102(A)(5).

VI

Thus, we conclude that the reasonable likelihood standard of DR 7–107(D) is constitutional as applied to the extrajudicial statements of an attorney who is associated with a criminal trial, where the statements are about the trial and are intended to be disseminated publicly.

We limit this holding to the criminal context only. With the personal liberty of the defendant at stake and the need to reach the right result so vital, a criminal case presents unique problems of trial fairness that compel us to take every step possible to protect the integrity of that process.[10] Therefore, our decision today should not be inter-

(attorney suspended for referring to paternity hearing as "ordeal," "travesty," and "the biggest farce I've ever seen"); In re Paulsrude, 311 Minn. 303, 248 N.W.2d 747 (1979) (attorney disbarred for in-court remarks, which included calling the judge a "horse's ass" after an adverse ruling and labelling the proceedings a "kangaroo court"). For cases not disciplining attorneys for criticizing judges, see, e.g., State v. Nelson, 210 Kan. 637, 504 P.2d 211 (1972) (no discipline imposed where attorney made only general accusations and was speaking as losing party in litigation); Justices of Appellate Division v. Erdmann, 33 N.Y.2d 559, 301 N.E.2d 426, 347 N.Y.S.2d 441 (1973) (attorney not subject to discipline even though he called appellate judges "whores who become madams," and claimed that the only way to become a judge was "to be in politics or to buy it"); State Bar v. Semaan, 508 S.W.2d 429 (Tex.Civ.App.1974) (no discipline imposed against attorney who wrote letters to newspapers critical of a judge's qualifications to hold office). See generally Annot. "Attorney's Criticism of Judicial Acts as Ground for Disciplinary Action," 12 A.L.R.3d 1408 (1967).

**10.** As previously noted, the preservation of trial fairness is a significant and, indeed, compelling State interest in the criminal context. However, civil cases present very different considerations. Civil actions sometimes take years to complete and often involve

preted as approving of the reasonable likelihood standard to restrict attorney speech in any other context but a criminal trial.

We decline, however, to find Hinds in violation of any ethical rule. We do so for several reasons. First, because the District Ethics Committee conducted no hearing on this case, we are presented with an inadequate factual record on which to base a decision. Second, because this case involves the application of an ethical precept rather than a criminal law, we view the decision itself as a sufficient explanation of the ethical responsibility of attorneys and find no need for punishment. Third, because this opinion represents the first opportunity we have had to define the proper scope of DR 7–107(D), the primary disciplinary rule sought to be applied in this case, we deem it appropriate to give that rule prospective effect only. Finally, there being no present basis for imposing discipline under DR 7–107(D), the related charges under DR 1–102(A)(5) should likewise be dismissed.

Accordingly, the charges against Hinds are dismissed.[c]

SCHREIBER, J., dissenting. * * *

I agree with the majority that DR 7–107(D) is constitutional. * * * The policy underlying this Disciplinary Rule is that the defendant and the State are entitled to and should have a fair trial. The attorney's right to speak is not completely prohibited. He may make appropriate argument in the courtroom. He may after the case has been completed properly comment on the matter. What he may not do is intentionally disseminate to the public statements relating to the trial which are "reasonably likely to interfere with a fair trial."

The majority contends that the charge should be dismissed for two reasons, neither of which is valid. First it claims that its interpretation of DR 7–107(D) involves some new concept. I submit that application of the stated test—reasonably likely to interfere with a fair trial—does not involve any new or unforeseen dogma. The so-called "balancing test" referred to by the majority, is nothing more than the usual weighing which any fact finder must do when evaluating facts to reach a conclusion. * * *

The second reason advanced is even more curious. It is that the charge should be dismissed because the factual dispute concerning the respondent's relationship to the defendant has never been resolved.

crucial issues of public importance. *Hirschkop; Bauer.* Moreover, there is far less evidence that statements by lawyers involved in civil trials can prejudice such proceedings. *Hirschkop.* Therefore, the two federal Circuit Courts which have addressed this issue have found the "reasonable likelihood" standard unconstitutional as applied to attorneys associated with a civil case. *Hirschkop; Bauer.*

In addition to sections (A) through (E), DR 7–107 also contains provisions dealing with civil trials, (G), administrative actions, (H), disciplinary actions, (F), and juvenile hearings, (F). Since we are faced in this case with a criminal trial situation, we need not consider the constitutionality of the "reasonable likelihood" test in these other contexts and refrain from doing so.

c. Justices Pashman and Clifford filed concurring opinions.

Thus the respondent has successfully evaded a hearing to resolve whether he was "associated with the * * * defense" by instituting a constitutional attack—which the Court finds is unsuccessful.[2]

Lastly, I disagree with the majority's opinion that it seems quite certain that the First Amendment would require application of a "clear and present danger" standard to conduct under DR 1–102(A)(5). * * * This Disciplinary Rule on its face requires that the conduct must be shown to be prejudicial. There must be clear and convincing evidence that the attorney's conduct did in fact hinder, block or obstruct the administration of justice. I envisage no constitutional impediment to that standard. Assuredly attorneys whether directly related or not to an ongoing trial should not be permitted to frustrate a fair trial. In truth it is conceivable that an attorney who is not associated with the defense may have such standing in the community that his words may have a substantially greater impact on the fairness of a trial than those of the attorney of record. This is not to say that attorneys may not criticize courts, judges, their decisions, and the judicial system. There is a proper time and place for such criticism. * * *[d]

### *Comment*

(1) *Kinds of proceedings covered.* In the Hirschkop v. Snead case cited in *Hinds*, although the Fourth Circuit upheld DR 7–107's prohibition respecting *criminal jury trials* of specified statements "reasonably likely to interfere with a fair trial," it held DR 7–107 unconstitutional insofar as it extended to civil, administrative, disciplinary, or non-jury criminal, juvenile, or sentencing proceedings. Regarding civil proceedings, the court said:

> "Civil litigation is often more protracted than criminal prosecution because of broader civil discovery rules, the complexity of many civil controversies, and the priority given criminal cases. Thus, it is not unlikely that the rule could prohibit comment over a period of several years from the time investigation begins until the appellate proceedings are completed.
>
> "Civil actions may also involve questions of public concern such as the safety of a particular stretch of highway, the need of the government to exercise its power of eminent domain, or the means of racially integrating schools and colleges. The lawyers involved in such cases can often enlighten public debate. It is no answer to say that the comments can be made after the case is concluded,

2. I also do not agree with the Court's very restrictive definition of what "associated with" means. It has limited the concept to any attorney who (1) cooperates with the defendant on a regular and continuing basis, (2) provides legal assistance *and* (3) holds himself out to be a member of the defense team. An attorney could escape the effect of the rule by eliminating any one condition.

**d.** Regarding discipline or contempt proceedings against lawyers for trial publicity, see Annot., 11 A.L.R.3d 1104 (1967).

Regarding gag orders directed to counsel as well as parties and witnesses, see Annot., 33 A.L.R.3d 1041 (1970); Annot., 5 A.L.R.Fed. 948 (1970).

for it is well established that the first amendment protects not only the content of speech but also its timeliness.

"[T]his record contains no empirical data that restrictions on lawyers' speech are needed to protect the fairness of civil trials. *Sheppard* and the other prejudicial publicity cases involved criminal proceedings. No decision reversing the judgment in a civil action because of prejudicial publicity has been called to our attention * * *."

"The dearth of evidence that lawyers' comments taint civil trials and the courts' ability to [issue protective orders covering trade secrets and other] confidential information establish that [DR 7–107(G)'s] restrictions on freedom of speech are not esential to fair civil trials. We therefore conclude that this provision of the rule is invalid because it is overbroad."[1]

The court similarly found it unlikely that lawyers' comments could threaten the fairness of administrative or disciplinary proceedings or non-jury criminal, juvenile, or sentencing proceedings.

On the other hand, as indicated in *Hinds*, DR 7–107(H), construed to prohibit only communications "reasonably likely to interfere with a fair [administrative] hearing," was upheld in the Pennsylvania case of Widoff v. Disciplinary Board.[2] And in the Chicago Council of Lawyers v. Bauer case cited in *Hinds*, the Seventh Circuit, although declaring DR 7–107 unconstitutional regarding sentencing proceedings, held that if it were construed to apply only to statements posing a serious and imminent threat of interfering with the fair administration of justice, certain of its provisions could validly apply to non-jury as well as jury criminal trials and to civil litigation.[3]

(2) *Persons covered.* It would seem that first amendment objections available to defense lawyers and other private individuals would not be available to prosecutors or other government officers acting as such, since constitutional rights (as opposed to powers) are not conferred upon government.[4]

1. Accord, Shadid v. Jackson, 521 F.Supp. 85 (E.D.Tex. 1981).

2. Compare In re Richmond, 285 Or. 469, 591 P.2d 728 (1979) (DR 7–107's restriction on publicity regarding administrative proceedings, construed narrowly to avoid constitutional difficulties, did not apply to lawyer's letter to governor with copies to editors about zoning appeal).

3. Compare Ruggieri v. Johns-Manville Products Corp., 503 F.Supp. 1036 (D.R.I.1980) (lawyer's TV interview comments alleged to violate DR 7–107(G) were protected by first amendment absent proof of "serious and imminent threat" to fair trial); In re Porter, 268 Or. 417, 521 P.2d 345 (reprimand for violating DR 7–107(G) by statements made while investigating and litigating civil case), cert. denied 419 U.S. 1056, 95 S.Ct. 639, 42 L.Ed.2d 653 (1974).

4. See T. Emerson, The System of Freedom of Expression 463, 700 (1970); Ely, Flag Desecration: A Case Study in the Roles of Categorizing and Balancing in First Amendment Analysis, 88 Harv.L.Rev. 1482, 1505 (1975).

Compare Chicago Council of Lawyers v. Bauer, 522 F.2d 242 (7th Cir. 1975), cert. denied 427 U.S. 912, 96 S.Ct. 3201, 49 L.Ed.2d 1204 (1976) (DR 7–107(A)'s restrictions on persons "participating in or associated with" criminal investigation vague and overbroad as applied to lawyers other than prosecutors; provision may be used as presumption of se-

(3) *Criticizing court.* Regarding criticism of courts, in addition to footnote 9 in *Hinds* and the U.S. Supreme Court In re Sawyer case discussed in *Hinds*, see Konigsberg v. State Bar,[5] where the United States Supreme Court reversed California's refusal to admit Konigsberg to the bar, saying:

> "In 1950 Konigsberg wrote a series of editorials for a local newspaper. In these editorials he severely criticized, among other things, * * * this Court's decisions in Dennis (Dennis v. U. S., 341 U.S. 494, 71 S.Ct. 857, 95 L.Ed. 1137) and other cases.[27] When read in the light of the ordinary give-and-take of political controversy the editorials Konigsberg wrote are not unusually extreme and fairly interpreted only say that certain officials were performing their duties in a manner that, in the opinion of the writer, was injurious to the public. We do not believe that an inference of bad moral character can rationally be drawn from these editorials. Because of the very nature of our democracy such expressions of political views must be permitted. Citizens have a right under our constitutional system to criticize government officials and agencies. Courts are not, and should not be, immune to such criticism. Government censorship can no more be reconciled with our national constitutional standard of freedom of speech and press when done in the guise of determining 'moral character,' than if it should be attempted directly."[6]

rious and imminent threat only as to lawyers working for government); In re Lasswell, 296 Or. 121, 673 P.2d 855 (1983) (no discipline absent proof prosecutor intended or was knowingly indifferent to risk that remarks would seriously prejudice potential jurors); In re Burrows, 290 Or. 131, 618 P.2d 1283 (1980) (prosecutor's reading to high school class defendant's letter expressing sorrow for actions did not violate DR 7-107(B)(3) because it was not kind of communication likely to prejudice jurors or even to reach news media or persons likely to be jurors).

Regarding reversal of conviction because of prosecutor's pretrial statements, see 22 A.L.R.Fed. 556 (1975).

5. 353 U.S. 252, 77 S.Ct. 722, 1 L.Ed.2d 810 (1957).

27. For example, petitioner wrote:

"When the Supreme Court of these benighted states can refuse to review the case of the Hollywood Ten thus making that high tribunal an integral part of the cold war machine directed against the American people—then the enemies of democracy have indeed won a major victory. When the commanders of the last legal bulwark of our liberties sell out to the enemy, then the fascists have gone far, much farther than most people think. He who cannot see the dangerous damnable parallel to what happened in Germany is willfully blind."

6. See also Garrison v. Louisiana, 379 U.S. 64, 85 S.Ct. 209, 13 L.Ed.2d 125 (1964), where the Court reversed a district attorney's criminal libel conviction for charging state criminal court judges with inefficiency, laziness, and hampering his investigation of vice, on the ground there was no showing of "false statements made with [a] high degree of awareness of their probable falsity."

Regarding discipline for criticism of courts in appellate briefs, see Ramirez v. State Bar, 28 Cal.3d 402, 169 Cal.Rptr. 206, 619 P.2d 399 (1980).

Regarding discipline for criticism of courts in communications to clients, see In re Chopak, 160 F.2d 886 (2d Cir.), cert. denied 331 U.S. 835, 67 S.Ct. 1516, 91 L.Ed. 1848 (1947) (three-year suspension; dissent questioned whether this violated free speech rights); In re Bull, 123 F.Supp. 389 (D.Nev. 1954) (letter seized from convicted prisoner could not be used since seizure violated constitutional right to consult with counsel).

# I. COURTROOM CONDUCT

## MODEL RULES OF PROFESSIONAL CONDUCT

**RULE 3.4 Fairness to Opposing Party and Counsel**

A lawyer shall not:

* * *

(c) knowingly disobey an obligation under the rules of a tribunal except for an open refusal based on an assertion that no valid obligation exists * * *.

**RULE 3.5 Impartiality and Decorum of the Tribunal**

A lawyer shall not:

* * *

(c) engage in conduct intended to disrupt a tribunal.

COMMENT:

* * *

The advocate's function is to present evidence and argument so that the cause may be decided according to law. Refraining from abusive or obstreperous conduct is a corollary of the advocate's right to speak on behalf of litigants. A lawyer may stand firm against abuse by a judge but should avoid reciprocation; the judge's default is no justification for similar dereliction by an advocate. An advocate can present the cause, protect the record for subsequent review and preserve professional integrity by patient firmness no less effectively than by belligerence or theatrics.[a]

**a.** Compare the following CPR provisions:

**"DR 7-106 Trial Conduct**

"(A) A lawyer shall not disregard or advise his client to disregard a standing rule of a tribunal or a ruling of a tribunal made in the course of a proceeding, but he may take appropriate steps in good faith to test the validity of such rule or ruling.

* * *

"(C) In appearing in his professional capacity before a tribunal, a lawyer shall not:

* * *

(5) Fail to comply with known local customs of courtesy or practice of the bar or a particular tribunal without giving to opposing counsel timely notice of his intent not to comply.

(6) Engage in undignified or discourteous conduct which is degrading to a tribunal.

(7) Intentionally or habitually violate any established rule of procedure or of evidence."

See ABA Standards for Criminal Justice 4-7.1(a)-(d) (2d ed. 1980) (to which id. 3-5.2(a)-(d) applicable to prosecutors is substantially identical), providing:

"Standard 4-7.1 Courtroom decorum

"(a) As an officer of the court the lawyer should support the authority of the court and the dignity of the trial courtroom by strict adherence to the rules of decorum and by manifesting an attitude of professional respect toward the judge, opposing counsel, witnesses, jurors, and others in the courtroom.

"(b) When court is in session defense counsel should address the court and should not address the prosecutor directly on any matter relating to the case.

"(c) It is unprofessional conduct for a lawyer to engage in behavior or tactics purposefully calculated to irritate or annoy the court or the prosecutor.

## COMMONWEALTH v. GARRISON

478 Pa. 356, 386 A.2d 971 (1978).

ROBERTS, Justice.

While representing a defendant accused of rape, statutory rape, and corruption of a minor, appellant Bruce Sagel, Esquire, was twice summarily held in criminal contempt. The trial court, Judge James T. McDermott, fined appellant $200 for the first offense and $50 for the second. Appellant contends that his contempt convictions are not supported by sufficient evidence. We agree, [reverse] judgments of sentence and discharge appellant.[2]

Appellant, an attorney for the Defender Association of Philadelphia, acted as defense counsel for Floyd Garrison in a trial held from March 24, 1976 to March 29, 1976. The Commonwealth sought to prove that Garrison had raped the 13 year-old daughter of the woman with whom Garrison had been living. Several times during the first day of trial, the court accused appellant of misconduct, but did not hold him in contempt until the complainant's mother took the witness stand. At that time, the district attorney requested that the court order Garrison to stand:

"MR. CUNNINGHAM: Would the court instruct the defendant to stand? * * *

THE COURT: Very well. Have the defendant stand.

(The defendant rose).

DIRECT EXAMINATION BY MR. CUNNINGHAM:

Q. * * * do you know this man standing now in this courtroom, to my left?

MR. SAGEL: Judge, that is absurd. That is absurd.

"(d) The lawyer should comply promptly with all orders and directives of the court, but the lawyer has a duty to have the record reflect adverse rulings or judicial conduct which the lawyer considers prejudicial to his or her client's legitimate interests. The lawyer has a right to make respectful requests for reconsiderations of adverse rulings."

See also ABA Code of Judicial Conduct, Canon 3(A)(2)–(4), providing:

"(2) A judge should maintain order and decorum in proceedings before him.

"(3) A judge should be patient, dignified, and courteous to litigants, jurors, witnesses, lawyers, and others with whom he deals in his official capacity, and should require similar conduct of lawyers, and of his staff, court officials, and others subject to his direction and control.

"(4) A judge should accord to every person who is legally interested in a proceeding, or his lawyer, full right to be heard according to law * * *."

2. In view of our disposition, we do not consider appellant's assertion that both summary convictions for criminal contempt denied him due process because (1) the contempt charge did not sufficiently specify the underlying facts to permit review of the first conviction; (2) appellant denied the court's statement of the facts underlying the first conviction; (3) impermissibly long delay occurred between the second alleged contemptuous conduct and imposition of contempt; (4) the convictions were without hearing, notice or other elements of due process; and (5) the trial court was so deeply embroiled in, and personally offended by, the alleged misconduct that it could not impartially impose the convictions.

A. Yes.

MR. SAGEL: That is absurd, and I object.

THE COURT: You're going to continue shouting at me, aren't you?

MR. SAGEL: I was not shouting, your Honor.

THE COURT: Don't tell me what you were doing. That is not the proper way to interpose an objection, by suggesting something to be absurd. Will you follow the rules or not?

(No response)

THE COURT: Are you going to follow the rules or not?

MR. SAGEL: Yes, sir.

THE COURT: I suggest you do so.

MR. SAGEL: May I be heard on my objection?

THE COURT: No, *be seated.*

MR. SAGEL: *May my client be seated as well?*

THE COURT: *Did you hear what I said?*

MR. SAGEL: *May my client be seated as well, or is he to be flagellated in front of the jury?*

THE COURT: What was that sir?

MR. SAGEL: Is he to just stand, as if they don't know each other, then to be identified to the Jury?

THE COURT: Take the jurors out.

(The Jury was removed from the Courtroom at 2:19 P.M.)

THE COURT: Come to the bar of the Court, sir. You're in contempt of this Court, sir. You are fined $200. Take him into custody. We will recess.

MR. SAGEL: May I please be heard your Honor, on the record?

THE COURT: You will not be heard sir, by me in the fashion you choose to address me. You conducted yourself in a most unprofessional manner. You have been sitting here all morning shouting at this Court. I have all regard for your zealousness. You are entitled to struggle on behalf of your client, if you choose. But we have certain rules here you are apparently not familiar with. If you have an objection to interpose, you do so, the Court rules on it, you be quiet after that. *You are not to suggest to the Court that your client is being flagellated before the jury. You are in contempt, sir,* and consequently you have been fined. Take him into custody.

(Counsel was taken into custody. Recessed at 2:20 P.M.)."

(Emphasis supplied)

Although there was obvious friction between the court and appellant during the next two days, the court did not hold appellant in contempt again until the third day of trial when a district attorney, Mr. Henry, was cross-examining a defense investigator. The subject of this cross-examination was an interview the district attorney thought the witness had conducted with the complainant. Appellant sought to point out that the interview had been conducted by Joseph Block, Esquire, another attorney of the Defender Association:

"MR. HENRY: This conversation that took place, how long did it take; five seconds?

A. I guess maybe fifteen minutes; I suppose twenty minutes.

MR. HENRY: You said you were out there twenty minutes—ten minutes and just before on direct examination didn't you tell the jury—

MR. SAGEL: No your Honor, I think he's mistaken—

THE COURT: Do you have an objection.

MR. SAGEL: I have an objection.

THE COURT: It is overruled.

MR. SAGEL: Mr. Block said that. He's mistaken.

MR. HENRY: If that's the case, I'll withdraw that.

MR. SAGEL: Thank you.

THE COURT: The sun is setting, Mr. Sagel."

At the end of the day, after excusing the jury, the court summarily held appellant in contempt for these statements. In its opinion in support of the contempt citations, the court concluded:

"That counsel persisted despite warnings and instruction cannot be read less than contempt * * * overzealousness that disrupts a trial is a gross immaturity in all who practice or indulge it. To permit this individual to shout down a Court, or indulge epicene outbursts of anger while he performs some arcane mating dance with the jury or the audience is simply to give license to childish effrontery. We believe his conduct was deliberate contempt, that in fact obstructed the orderly process of trial. We believe his contempt was designed not only to disrupt the Court, but to obstruct the trial in an effort to present or avoid issues and inferences otherwise beyond the scope of the rules. More, we believe his conduct, particularly in light of the many warnings, a deliberate attempt to poison the record with his conduct so as to ultimately vitiate the proceedings."

I

Courts unquestionably have inherent power to punish willful misconduct which obstructs a fair and orderly trial. * * *

"The court has inherent power to punish any contempt in order to protect the rights of the defendant and the interests of the public by assuring that the administration of criminal justice shall not be thwarted. The trial judge has the power to cite and, if necessary, punish summarily anyone who, in [the judge's] presence in open court, willfully obstructs the course of criminal proceedings."

[ABA Standards for Criminal Justice 6–4.1 (2d ed. 1980).[a]]

When acting to uphold its authority, however, a court must use the least possible power and should first consider less severe remedies such as civil contempt before imposing summary criminal contempt. Shillitani v. United States, 384 U.S. 364, 86 S.Ct. 1531, 16 L.Ed.2d 622 (1966); [ABA Standards for Criminal Justice 6–3.5 (2d ed. 1980)]. Following the principle of *Shillitani* and the ABA Standards, appellate courts have reversed convictions for summary criminal contempt where a cautionary instruction to the jury would have restored order or negated any ill effects of counsel's behavior, where civil or nonsummary criminal contempt would have served the trial court's purpose, or where some other effective sanction was available. [S]ee generally United States v. Fisher, 477 F.2d 300 (4th Cir. 1973) (trial court may control lawyers by censuring them); [ABA Standards for Criminal Justice 6–3.5 (2d ed. 1980)] (listing sanctions available).

The power to impose summary criminal contempt is available only for

> "such conduct as created an open threat to the orderly procedure of the court and such flagrant defiance of the person and presence of the judge before the public that, if not instantly suppressed and punished, demoralization of the court's authority will follow."

Jessup v. Clark, 490 F.2d 1068, 1071 (3rd Cir. 1973) (quotation marks omitted); accord, Cooke v. United States, 267 U.S. 517, 536, 45 S.Ct. 390, 394–95, 69 L.Ed. 767 (1925). Only in such circumstances may a court subject a contemner to punishment without the procedural protections otherwise accorded the criminally accused.

In this Commonwealth, the power of courts to inflict summary contempts is carefully limited. The Act of June 16, 1836, P.L. 784, § 23, 17 P.S. § 2041 (1962) provides:

> "The power of the several courts of this commonwealth to * * * inflict summary punishments for contempts of court shall be restricted to the following cases, to-wit:
>
> "I. To the official misconduct of the officers of such courts respectively;
>
> "II. To disobedience or neglect by officers, parties, jurors or witnesses of or to the lawful process of the court;
>
> "III. To the misbehavior of any person in the presence of the court, thereby obstructing the administration of justice."[5]

a. Throughout this opinion, references to the ABA Standards are updated to refer to the 1980 Second Edition.

5. Likewise, the Congress of the United States has restricted the power of the federal courts to impose summary criminal contempt. 18 U.S.C. § 401 (1969) provides:

"A court of the United States shall have power to punish by fine or imprisonment, at its discretion, such contempt of its authority, and none other, as—

"(1) Misbehavior of any person in its presence or so near thereto as to obstruct the administration of justice;

"(2) Misbehavior of any of its officers in their official transactions;

"(3) Disobedience or resistance to its lawful writ, process, order, rule, decree, or command."

Each of these subsections is designed to reach a particular type of conduct.

A.

* * * A lawyer is not an "officer" subject to punishment by contempt under [subsection I]. Cammer v. United States, [350 U.S. 399,] 407–08, 76 S.Ct. [456,] 460–01, [100 L.Ed. 474 (1956)].

B.

Under subsection II, * * * conviction of contempt for violation of a court order can be sustained only if the order or decree was "definite, clear, specific and left no doubt or uncertainty" in the mind of the person to whom it was addressed of the conduct prohibited. Richmond Black Police Officers v. City of Richmond, Va., 548 F.2d 123, 129 (4th Cir. 1977). "The long-standing salutary rule in contempt cases is that ambiguities and omissions in orders redound to the benefit of the person charged with contempt." Ford v. Kammerer, 450 F.2d 279, 280 (3rd Cir. 1971) (contempt reversed because court order contained "no prohibitory language explicitly addressed" to the appellant's act).

Contempt under subsection II is justified only if the contemner had notice of the specific order or decree, the act constituting the violation was volitional, and the contemner acted with wrongful intent. [T]his Court has adopted the standard of intent prevailing in the federal courts that the contemner "knows or should reasonably be aware that his conduct is wrongful." Commonwealth v. Washington, 470 Pa. [199,] 203, 368 A.2d [263,] 265 [1977]; see [ABA Standards for Criminal Justice 6–4.1 (2d ed. 1980)] (judge has power to punish willful obstructions) and [id. 6–4.2] (contempt available for "willfully contemptuous" conduct).

Contempt convictions for willful violations of court orders, obstructing a judicial proceeding, have been upheld where an attorney failed to appear as directed at a hearing. See United States v. Lespier, 558 F.2d 624 (1st Cir. 1977); United States v. Marx, [553 F.2d 874 (4th Cir. 1977)]; Douglas v. First National Realty Corp., 177 U.S.App.D.C. 409, 543 F.2d 894 (1976); compare In re Niblack, 155 U.S.App.D.C. 174, 476 F.2d 930, cert. denied, 414 U.S. 909, 94 S.Ct. 229, 38 L.Ed.2d 147 (1973) (willfulness demonstrated by disregard of explicit warnings and previous noncompliance) with Commonwealth v. Washington, 470 Pa. 199, 368 A.2d 263 (1977) (no willful misconduct in failure to appear where judge knew that attorney had conflicting court engagement and record did not show that attorney received notice of expected appearance) and Commonwealth v. Washington, 466 Pa. 506, 353 A.2d 806 (1976) (contempt reversed where late appearance was caused by neglect to set alarm). * * *

By F.R.Crim.Pro. 42(a), this contempt power may be exercised summarily. Because the federal statute is identical in all material respects to the Pennsylvania contempt statute, this Court looks to federal decisions for guidance in interpreting 17 P.S. § 2041.

C.

Finally, misconduct occurring in or near the courtroom falls under subsection III * * *.

Subsection III, like its federal counterpart, 18 U.S.C. § 401(1), requires proof beyond a reasonable doubt of (1) misconduct, (2) in the presence of the court, (3) committed with intent to obstruct the proceedings, which (4) obstructs the administration of justice. In re Johnson, 467 Pa. [552,] 557, 359 A.2d [739,] 742, [1976]; United States v. Seale, [461 F.2d 345,] 366–67 [7th Cir. 1972]. No satisfactory definition of contemptuous misconduct has been developed. Perhaps the best definition is that misconduct is behavior that is inappropriate to the role of the actor. United States v. Seale, supra. An attorney engages in misconduct if his behavior is calculated to hinder the search for truth. In re Dellinger, 461 F.2d 389, 400 (7th Cir. 1972); see United States v. Schiffer, 351 F.2d 91 (6th Cir. 1965), cert. denied, 384 U.S. 1003, 86 S.Ct. 1914, 16 L.Ed.2d 1017 (1966) (contempt upheld where attorney attempted to pressure court into ruling favorably by accusing court of being a tool of the government). * * * A contemner acts with wrongful intent if he "knows or should reasonably be aware that his conduct is wrongful." United States v. Seale, supra at 368 (same standard for subsection II). An obstruction of the administration of justice is a significant disruption of judicial proceedings. See In re Johnson, supra; [ABA Standards for Criminal Justice 6–3.5 (2d ed. 1980)]. What is required is a showing of actual, imminent prejudice to a fair proceeding or to preservation of the court's authority. In re Johnson, supra (no contempt where counsel's statement to jury that judge and prosecutor shared signal system caused no disruption); United States v. Seale, supra at 370. This danger "must not be remote or even probable; it must immediately imperil." In re Little, 404 U.S. 553, 555, 92 S.Ct. 659, 660, 30 L.Ed.2d 708 (1972); accord, In re McConnell, [370 U.S. 230, 82 S.Ct. 1288, 8 L.Ed.2d 434 (1962)] (contempt reversed where attorney failed to carry out threat to disobey court order); United States v. Seale, supra at 370.

Courts require a high likelihood of imminent disruption because a lesser standard would deter vigorous courtroom advocacy. In re Dellinger, supra at 398. "It is also essential to a fair administration of justice that lawyers be able to make honest good-faith efforts to present their client's cases." In re McConnell, supra, 370 U.S. at 236, 82 S.Ct. at 1292. In Bloom Discipline Case, 423 Pa. 192, 223 A.2d 712 (1966), this Court stated that under the Canons of Professional Responsibility

> " 'The lawyer owes "entire devotion to the interest of the client, warm zeal in the maintenance and defense of his rights and the exertion of his utmost learning and ability," to the end that nothing be taken or withheld from him, save by the rules of law, legally applied. *No fear of judicial disfavor* or public unpopularity should restrain him from full discharge of his duty. * * * ' "

Id. at 196, 223 A.2d at 714 (emphasis in original). Thus, that remarks are injudicious, an affront to the dignity or sensibility of the court, or even disrespectful or insulting, will not, without more, justify conviction for summary criminal contempt.

> "The 'heat of courtroom debate' may prompt statements which are ill-considered and might later be regretted. In Re Hallinan, 71 Cal.2d 1179, 81 Cal.Rptr. 1, 459 P.2d 255 (1969). Substantial free dom of expression should be tolerated in this area since '[J]udges are supposed to be men of fortitude, able to thrive in a hardy climate.' Craig v. Harney, 331 U.S. 367, 376, 67 S.Ct. 1249, 1255, 91 L.Ed. 1546."

In re Dellinger, supra at 400. Only in an atmosphere where counsel feels secure in actively and zealously presenting his client's cause can a fair and thorough proceeding be assured. "Attorneys have a right to be persistent, vociferous, contentious, and imposing, even to the point of appearing obnoxious, when acting in their client's behalf." In re Dellinger, supra at 400.

II

Before examining whether sufficient evidence exists to sustain the convictions, we must determine which subsection of 17 P.S. § 2041 the court relied upon in imposing each conviction. We must make this determination because the trial court failed to specify any statutory provision either at the time it imposed the convictions or in its opinion. This omission raises a problem of due process, for a criminally accused is entitled to fair notice of the charges against him. Commonwealth v. Mayberry, 459 Pa. 91, 327 A.2d 86 (1974); accord, Taylor v. Hayes, 418 U.S. 488, 94 S.Ct. 2697, 41 L.Ed.2d 897 (1974); [ABA Standards for Criminal Justice 6–4.4 (2d ed. 1980)]. If the court did not give appellant sufficient notice of the charges to enable him to present an argument in response, due process would require this Court to reverse the convictions. Because the court did not specify the charges against appellant, we must search the record to determine which subsection formed the authority for the convictions and if appellant can reasonably be said to have understood that he had been charged under that subsection.

The court could not have acted under subsection I because that provision does not extend to attorneys. * * *

When imposing the first contempt, the court could not have been acting under subsection II because appellant had not violated any order or ruling of the court. Thus, the only possible statutory authority for the first conviction was subsection III. We therefore will consider the legality of the first conviction only on the basis of that provision.

In imposing the second conviction, the court could have acted under either subsection II or subsection III because appellant had allegedly violated a ruling of the court. At the close of the third day of trial, the court held a short hearing at which it convicted appellant of the second contempt. At that hearing, the court stated that it was fining appellant because he had refused "to acquiesce in the rules of the court and your conduct is bordering the absolutely unprofessional." At other times during the hearing, the court again referred to appellant's alleged violation of the rules of the court and his alleged misconduct. From these comments, we cannot determine whether the court relied upon subsection II or subsection III. The court's reference to a refusal to acquiesce in the rules of the court suggests that the court had subsection II in mind, but the references to misconduct indicate that subsection III formed the basis of the second conviction.

In its opinion, the court once more stated that appellant had refused to obey rulings of the court, but the clear emphasis was on appellant's purported misbehavior. The court charged appellant with conduct of a "continuous, abusive nature," referred to "overzealousness that disrupts a trial," asserted that appellant had attempted to "shout down the court," unleashed an "epicene outburst of anger" and engaged in "childish effrontery." The court concluded that appellant's conduct "obstructed the orderly process of trial," was "designed to disrupt the Court" and to "obstruct the trial" and was "a deliberate attempt to poison the record with his conduct so as to ultimately vitiate the proceedings." Thus, it appears that the court viewed subsection III, which reaches misconduct obstructing the administration of justice, as the statutory source of authority for the second contempt conviction as well as for the first.

Several other considerations compel this conclusion. Appellant apparently believed that he had been charged in both contempts under subsection III, for the primary argument in his brief was that his conduct did not cause an obstruction of the proceedings and that he lacked intent to cause any such obstruction. Moreover, the Commonwealth in its brief did not challenge appellant's assumption. To the contrary, the Commonwealth, which failed to specify the relevant subsection, also appeared to believe that the relevant subsection was subsection III, for its argument was that the court acted to quell a disruption. In short, the court did not specify the statutory source of its authority to impose contempt, the language of the court was ambiguous but indicated that it relied upon subsection III, appellant apparently believed that he had been charged under that subsection, and the Commonwealth did not alert this Court to the proper statutory authority and appeared to acquiesce in appellant's assumption. In these circumstances, to test the convictions under subsection II would reward the obscurity of the trial court and the Commonwealth while subjecting appellant to review under a provision he reasonably did not believe was at issue. Perhaps most importantly, because an offense under subsection II contains different elements from those of subsection III, we would deprive appellant of due process if we sustained the contempt convictions under subsection II when the trial court did not give appellant notice of charges under that provision. By reviewing the second conviction under subsection III, we avoid the risk of such a violation of due process.

Therefore, both of appellant's convictions must be tested according to the standards of 17 P.S. § 2041(III).

III

With the standards of subsection III in mind, we do not believe that appellant's statement triggering the first contempt citation was misconduct punishable under subsection III. Appellant had objected to the court's direction that the defendant stand to be identified by the mother. The court overruled the objection and stated, "be seated." The defendant rose and was identified by the complainant's mother. Appellant then asked whether his client could also be seated, and inquired, "is he to be flagellated in front of the jury?" The court requested appellant to repeat his comment, to which appellant replied, "Is he just to stand, as if they don't know each other, then to be identified to the jury?" Although appellant rephrased his remark in unemotional terms, the court dismissed the jury and held appellant in contempt.

Appellant engaged in misconduct under subsection III only if his expression, "is he to be flagellated in front of the jury?" exceeded the bounds of zealous advocacy. In In re Johnson, supra, defense counsel asserted in closing argument that the court and the district attorney employed a system of signals, and, when asked by the court how long his summation would be, responded, "I don't know how long I will be judge, I will speak as long as necessary." We held that these statements were not misconduct punishable under subsection III. In *Bloom Discipline Case*, supra, this Court reversed a conviction for criminal contempt where counsel had objected to the court's disposition of the proceedings as unfair and disputed a fact asserted by the court, because we could not say that the statements were misconduct. In McMillan v. Mountain Laurel Racing, Inc., [467 Pa. 266, 356 A.2d 742 (1976)], counsel, when admonished that the court "will hear no more comment," replied, "I will not operate under an ultimatum like that." This Court held that counsel's statement was not misconduct obstructing the administration of justice.

Other jurisdictions have reached the same result on comparable facts. In United States ex rel. Robson v. Oliver, [470 F.2d 10 (7th Cir. 1972)], counsel in a trial involving charges of mutilation of draft records asked a witness if he had seen a sign at the end of the hall proclaiming, "Abandon Ye All Hope Who Enter Here," provoking laughter, applause and shouts. Although it described this question as provocative and inflammatory, the court held that counsel had not engaged in misbehavior supporting contempt. In In re Hallinan, 71 Cal.2d 1179, 81 Cal.Rptr. 1, 459 P.2d 255 (1969), defense counsel stated that "the restrictions that have been imposed upon the evidence are unfair to the defendant." The California Supreme Court reversed counsel's conviction for summary criminal contempt imposed by the trial court. Similarly, in In re Carrow, 40 Cal.App.3d 924, 115 Cal.Rptr. 601 (1974), counsel objected, "Your Honor, I submit this trial is becoming a joke." The appellate court found these words "ill-chosen," but not contemptuous misbehavior. Appellant's conduct was less offensive than the statements made in these decisions where convictions of contempt were reversed on appeal.

The contrast between these cases and appellant's comments, and those cases where courts have upheld determinations of misbehavior, is clear. In United States v. Schiffer, supra, counsel's accusation that the court was a tool of the government and otherwise unfair carried the imminent risk that the court might be pressured into awarding favorable rulings to the defense. Accord, In re Buckley, 10 Cal.3d 237, 110 Cal.Rptr. 121, 514 P.2d 1201 (1973), cert. denied, 418 U.S. 910, 94 S.Ct. 3202, 41 L.Ed.2d 1156 (1974) (counsel's charge during trial that "This Court obviously doesn't want to apply the law" created imminent threat to court's authority by alleging judicial dishonesty).

Appellant's conduct does not rise to the level of the misbehavior in United States v. Schiffer, supra, and In re Buckley, supra. Appellant's statement did not exceed the "outermost limits of his proper role" and "[hinder] rather than facilitate the search for truth." In re Dellinger, supra at 400; see D. Dobbs, Contempt of Court, 56 Corn.L.Rev. 183, 188 (1971). We therefore reverse appellant's first conviction of summary criminal contempt.[7]

## IV

When held in contempt on the first day of trial, appellant had been instructed by the court that the procedure for objections was to rise, announce an objection and silently await the court's ruling. Counsel was not to offer any reasons for his objection unless the court specifically so requested.[8] Appellant was held in contempt a second time when, after the court overruled his objection to a line of cross-examination, he explained why he was protesting. Appellant's per-

7. Because we reverse on this ground, we do not consider whether appellant's conduct caused an obstruction to the administration of justice or whether appellant intended to obstruct justice.

8. We note that the court's rule of procedure for objections prohibiting statement of the grounds for objections except by permission, is contrary to recommended standards. [ABA Standards for Criminal Justice 6–2.4 (2d ed. 1980)] provides:

> "Duty of judge on counsel's objections and requests for rulings.
>
> "The trial judge should respect the obligation of counsel to present objections to procedures and to admissibility of evidence, to request rulings on motions, to make offers of proof, and to have the record show adverse rulings and reflect conduct of the judge which counsel considers prejudicial. Counsel should be permitted to state succinctly the grounds of his [or her] objections or requests; but the judge should nevertheless control the length and manner of argument."

The Commentary to this section notes that "This standard is intended to admonish the trial judge to exercise self-restraint and fairness in permitting counsel for the prosecution and for the defense to perform their duties," and that "the standard affirms the right of counsel * * * to make known the grounds of the objection." The reason for this rule is that general objections are disfavored, and that "it is through such colloquy that the judge may recognize his mistake and prevent error from infecting the record." In re Dellinger, supra at 399.

sistence, however, did not cause any obstruction of the orderly process of trial or create an imminent threat of significant disruption. Thus, the second conviction for contempt must also fall.

It is well established under subsection III that "the mere showing of noncompliance with a court order * * * is never sufficient, alone, to prove contempt." Commonwealth v. Haefner, 470 Pa. 392, 396, 368 A.2d 686, 688 (1977); see McMillan v. Mountain Laurel Racing, Inc., supra (contempt reversed despite counsel's violation of court order to proceed); Jessup v. Clark, supra (contempt reversed despite counsel's violation of court order to appear at designated time). Under this subsection, allegedly contemptuous conduct will not justify imposition of summary criminal contempt except where it causes an obstruction of the administration of justice.

Appellant's conduct did not cause any obstruction of justice. There was no disruption or delay in the proceedings or an imminent threat of such disruption. In fact, the district attorney admitted that he was in error and withdrew the disputed question. Because the court waited until the end of the day to impose the contempt, there was no delay in the proceedings. It is even unclear whether the trial court thought appellant's statements were contemptuous when uttered, for the court at that time said only, "Mr. Sagel, the sun is setting," and waited until the end of the day to inform appellant that he was in contempt of court. Compare In re Johnson, supra (contempt reversed where counsel's statement that the district attorney and the judge shared a signal system was brief, caused no disruption or delay, was neither an assault on the authority of the court nor a vicious personal attack on the judge and the jury was not improperly influenced) with Commonwealth v. Mayberry, 434 Pa. 478, 255 A.2d 131 (1969) (plurality opinion), vacated on other grounds, 400 U.S. 455, 91 S.Ct. 499, 27 L.Ed.2d 532 (1971) (contempt upheld where defendant interrupted proceedings by interfering with charge to jury, called trial judge a "hatchet man for the State," "a dirty S.O.B.," and a "bum," and asserted judge suffered mental illness).

In McMillan v. Mountain Laurel Racing, Inc., supra, counsel and the court engaged in a dispute over counsel's course of cross-examination. The court twice warned counsel that if he did not proceed with the questioning as ordered, the court would impose sanctions. When counsel refused to comply, the court summarily held him in criminal contempt. This Court reversed because counsel's conduct did not obstruct the administration of justice even though it had caused a slight delay in the proceedings. * * *

Two federal decisions illustrate the line which separates advocacy from obstruction under subsection III. In In re Dellinger, 370 F.Supp. 1304 (N.D.Ill. 1973), counsel continued to argue after the court had overruled an objection. Despite three specific orders to cease argument, counsel continued to press his point. On remand from the court of appeals, the district court held that counsel's failure to obey the court's ruling and orders to proceed was not an obstruction of the proceedings. By contrast, in Pennsylvania v. Local 542, [Int'l Union of Operating Eng'rs, 552 F.2d 498 (3d Cir.), cert. denied, 434 U.S. 822, 98 S.Ct. 67, 54 L.Ed.2d 79 (1977)], the court of appeals upheld convictions where counsel was twice summarily adjudged in contempt. The trial court imposed the first conviction after counsel persisted in stating the reason for his objection after the court overruled the objection and directed counsel not to state his reason. Before the court summarily held counsel in criminal contempt, it had specifically directed him seven times not to state the reason for the objection, had specifically warned him four times that if he failed to comply he would be held in contempt and had delayed the proceedings to speak with counsel in chambers. Here, appellant caused no delay and exhibited no defiance to the court. Appellant did not cross the line which separates In re Dellinger, 370 F.Supp. 1304, supra, from Pennsylvania v. Local 542, supra, and therefore appellant's second conviction must be reversed.[11]

In reversing appellant's convictions for summary criminal contempt, we emphasize that in a proper case a court retains the power to impose summary criminal contempts. Further, for those situations not justifying this drastic sanction, less severe sanctions, such as civil contempt and nonsummary criminal contempt, are available. See United States v. Shillitani, supra; [ABA Standards for Criminal Justice 6–3.3, 6–3.5 (2d ed. 1980)].

Neither of appellant's convictions of contempt is supported by sufficient evidence. We therefore reverse appellant's convictions and discharge him.

Judgments reversed and appellant discharged.[b]

POMEROY, Justice, concurring.

* * * There * * * was no need for the trial court to hold Mr. Sagel in contempt in order to vindicate its authority.[6]

11. Because we reverse on this ground, we need not consider whether appellant engaged in misconduct and, if so, whether he did so with intent to obstruct the proceedings.

b. Chief Justice Eagen and Justices O'Brien and Nix concurred in the result. Justice Packel did not participate.

6. I agree with Mr. Justice Roberts that the trial judge is not to be commended for his practice of forbidding counsel to state on the record his reasons for an objection to a question, an answer or a ruling. Ante n. 8. But cf. Pennsylvania v. Local 542, International U. Of Operating Engrs., 552 F.2d 498 (3d Cir. 1977). Worth repeating, however, is the admonition of Mr. Justice Jackson in Sacher v. United States, 343 U.S. 1, 9, 72 S.Ct. 451, 96 L.Ed. 717 (1952), quoted with approval in In re Dellinger, 461 F.2d 389, 398 (7th Cir. 1972):

> "Of course, it is the right of counsel for every litigant to press his claim, even if it appears farfetched and untenable, to obtain the court's considered ruling. Full enjoyment of that right, with due allowance for the heat of controversy, will be protected by appellate courts when infringed by trial courts. But if the ruling is adverse, it is not counsel's right to resist it or to insult the judge—his right is only respectfully to preserve his point for appeal."

Moreover, neither *Dellinger* nor In re McConnell, 370 U.S. 230, 82 S.Ct. 1288, 8 L.Ed.2d 434 (1962), also relied upon the plurality opinion, stand for the proposition that a lawyer is given "a grant of immunity for all conduct undertaken in good faith" on behalf of his client. 461 F.2d at 398.

Because I agree that the record reveals insufficient evidence for contempt convictions under any part of the Act of 1836, I concur in the result.

MANDERINO, Justice, concurring.

I join in the opinion of the Court; however, I do not endorse the holding of all cases from other jurisdictions cited therein. In some of those cases, conduct which clearly did not constitute contempt was held to be contemptuous. * * * [c]

### *Comment*

(1) *Gallagher.* In Gallagher v. Municipal Court,[1] the California Supreme Court set aside a lawyer's contempt conviction, saying:

> "An attorney has the duty to protect the interests of his client. He has a right to press legitimate argument and to protest an erroneous ruling. It is reported in Oswald on Contempt of Court that the following interchange occurred between Erskine and Buller, J. 'At length Erskine said, "I stand here as an advocate for a brother citizen, and I desire that the word 'only' be recorded;" whereupon Buller, J., said, "Sit down, sir! remember your duty or I shall be obliged to proceed in another manner,"—to which Erskine retorted, "Your Lordship may proceed in whatever manner you think fit. I know my duty as well as your Lordship knows yours. I shall not alter my conduct." The Judge took no notice of this reply. Lord Campbell speaks of the conduct of Erskine as "a noble stand for the independence of the Bar." ' Oswald, 3rd Ed., pp. 51, 52."

The court also pointed out that the fact that the lawyer is in error in the contentions the lawyer vigorously presses is not a basis for contempt proceedings.

(2) *Hawk.* Compare Hawk v. Superior Court,[2] wherein a California court, relying upon various provisions of the CPR and ABA Stan-

c. See N. Dorsen & L. Friedman, Disorder in the Court (1973); Annot., 58 A.L.R.Fed. 22 (1982) (lawyer's conduct as contempt); Annot., 68 A.L.R.3d 314 (1976) (conduct in making objections as contempt); Annot., 68 A.L.R.3d 273 (1976) (insulting remarks to judge during trial as contempt). Cf. Annot., 13 A.L.R.4th 122 (1982) (failure to attend or tardiness in attending court as contempt); Annot., 8 A.L.R.4th 1181 (1981) (delaying or obstructing discovery as contempt); Annot., 70 A.L.R.3d 797 (1976) (affidavit or motion to disqualify judge as contempt).

Regarding due process requisites where the judge does not act immediately but waits until the end of the trial during which the lawyer's contumaceous conduct was committed, see Taylor v. Hayes, 418 U.S. 488, 94 S.Ct. 2697, 41 L.Ed.2d 897 (1974) and cases cited.

Compare Cannon v. Commission on Judicial Qualifications, 14 Cal.3d 678, 122 Cal.Rptr. 778, 537 P.2d 898 (1975) (outrageous behavior in using powers of contempt against lawyers led to judge's removal).

Regarding court regulation of courtroom attire, see Annot., 73 A.L.R.3d 353 (1976). See also Annot., 84 A.L.R.3d 1143 (1978) (lawyer-member of clergy wearing clerical garb in courtroom).

1. 31 Cal.2d 784, 192 P.2d 905 (1948).

2. 42 Cal.App.3d 108, 116 Cal.Rptr. 713 (1974), cert. denied, 421 U.S. 1012, 95 S.Ct. 2417, 44 L.Ed.2d 680 (1975).

dards, The Defense Function, upheld contempt judgments for the following defense counsel conduct in the Juan Corona multiple murder case:

(a) Instructing the defendant not to provide handwriting exemplars as ordered by the court.

(b) During voir dire examination of a prospective juror, saying:

"Now, he [the prosecutor] made some reference to a psychologist being here, and this man sitting here, his name is Harvey Ross from Los Angeles. He is a psychologist. Do you have any objection to someone coming up from Los Angeles for a couple of days free of charge to Mr. Corona to help Mr. Corona select a jury because he believes Mr. Corona is innocent?"

(c) During voir dire, indicating that the prosecution intended to introduce into evidence photographs of a gruesome or revolting nature depicting deceased human bodies or portions thereof, that these were not necessary to be introduced in evidence, and that he would attempt to keep such photographs from being admitted into evidence, and asking a prospective juror, "Now, understanding what our position is, do you see any reason in the world why you should look at all these gory photographs?"

(d) During voir dire, in the hearing of prospective jurors, saying:

"Your Honor, for the record, I want to say that they [the prosecution] passed that woman one time and now they exercise their peremptory challenge; and to me that's an act of absolute white racism. I would like the record to show that the District Attorney is trying to systematically exclude minority groups. He excluded Mrs. Bailey because her husband is black; and now he excludes Mrs. Jackson, who is black also. I think it is improper."

(e) In his opening statement, despite having been warned during voir dire that it was improper for him to refer to defendant by his first name and to refer to his friendship for his client, saying:

"Let me tell you about the man that I smuggled cupcakes into his cell up in Yuba City on his birthday in February of 1971 contrary to the Sheriff's office regulations about bringing in foodstuffs, which I did anyway. * * * Let me tell you about Juan, the Christian."

(f) In his opening statement, referring to information in an affidavit for search warrants being "passed out to the press, where Mr. Corona was stripped of his presumption of innocence by the press with the help of the Sheriff's office."

(g) With reference to a witness' alleged inability to determine directions on an exhibit, examining the witness as follows:

Q "Have you ever done any flying?"

A "No."

Q "I recommend that you don't."

(h) Persisting, over objections by the prosecution, in asking questions about certain tire tracks, after objections to such questions had been sustained.

(i) Stating, in the presence of the jury:

"Your honor, in view of [the Deputy District Attorney's] statement that he has reasonable doubt as to Juan Corona's guilt [interruption]."

(j) While cross-examining a prosecution witness, engaging in the following colloquy:

DEFENSE COUNSEL: "No, I am trying to point out the fact that he gave a phony address. He lives at the Yuba City Jail."

PROSECUTOR: "I will object. That's improper."

DEFENSE COUNSEL: "I can't show where he lives?"

THE COURT: "[What] is the purpose of it, to show what?"

DEFENSE COUNSEL: "I am asking if this is where he is living at the current time."

THE COURT: "As an inmate?"

DEFENSE COUNSEL: "Yes, he is a thief; he is doing a year in jail. I am entitled to show that."

(k) In the presence of the jury, saying with reference to the prosecutor, "I am sorry if I offended the high-priced lawyer."

(*l*) While cross-examining a prosecution witness, engaging in the following colloquy:

DEFENSE COUNSEL: "Was an investigation ever conducted of Ray Duron to find out where his whereabouts were on the critical dates?"

PROSECUTOR: "Objection, your honor, that goes beyond the scope of direct examination."

THE COURT: "Sustained."

DEFENSE COUNSEL: "It is not beyond the scope of common sense."

### *Problems*

(1) During an informal pretrial conference in chambers attended by the two lawyers and the judge, one of the lawyers rose from his chair, turned to opposing counsel, and said, "Mr. Jones, I'm sick and tired of your lies and I don't intend to take any more of them." The judge promptly held the lawyer in contempt, $10 or two days. On appeal, what result?[3]

3. In In re Chaifetz, 68 A.2d 228 (D.C.1949), the court affirmed, saying:

"To call another a liar in the presence of the court and while the court is in session amounts to contempt of court. * * *

" '[I]n the presence of the court' generally means any place set apart for the use of any constituent part of the court while in session and includes such places as the courtroom itself, the judge's chambers, jury rooms, and

(2) A judge in open court told a lawyer he thought it was a dirty trick and a sneaky practice to try to get a certain matter handled by an ex parte order, and said he wished to hear nothing further. The lawyer said:

> "Your Honor's remarks are unwarranted, uncalled for and not appreciated and I would like to be heard."

The judge said he would hold the lawyer in contempt if he took any more of the court's time. The lawyer said he had a right to be heard on the judge's comments, whereupon the judge held him in contempt, $50 or ten days. On appeal, what result?[4]

## J. CANDOR TOWARD TRIBUNAL

### MODEL RULES OF PROFESSIONAL CONDUCT

**RULE 3.3 Candor Toward the Tribunal**

(a) A lawyer shall not knowingly:

* * *

(2) fail to disclose a material fact to a tribunal when disclosure is necessary to avoid assisting a criminal or fraudulent act by the client;

(3) fail to disclose to the tribunal legal authority in the controlling jurisdiction known to the lawyer to be directly adverse to the position of the client and not disclosed by opposing counsel * * *.

* * *

(d) In an ex parte proceeding, a lawyer shall inform the tribunal of all material facts known to the lawyer which will enable the tribunal to make an informed decision, whether or not the facts are adverse.[a]

the immediate vicinity such as hallways. Consequently any act of conduct revealing disrespect for the dignity and authority of the court, or which tends to embarrass the administration of justice in such places is 'in the presence of the court.'

"Here the trial judge was attempting to settle the case, in an informal type of pre-trial or conciliation proceeding. * * * Although only the judge and the two attorneys were actually present, the judge was acting in his judicial capacity * * *."

Regarding *discipline* for verbal abuse of other lawyer, see Annot., 87 A.L.R.3d 351 (1978).

4. In In re Abse, 251 A.2d 655 (D.C.App.1969), the court reversed saying:

"We are not here concerned with the correctness of either the judge's position or the lawyer's position with respect to the propriety of the submission of the proposed ex parte order.

"In the representation of a client in court * * *, if the court's ruling is adverse, the lawyer has no right to persist in pressing his claim. His right is only to preserve his point for appeal and thus protect his client's interest. * * * The situation here is quite different. The court made no ruling adversely affecting the attorney's client. The attorney was personally charged by the judge with unprofessional conduct and no appeal could be taken from the judge's remarks. * * *

"A charge that an attorney is guilty of unprofessional conduct is a serious charge and is even more serious and damaging when made by a judge in open court. Fundamental fairness requires that the attorney be given reasonable opportunity to answer such a charge. [I]t is not contempt of court for the attorney to insist on being heard. Of course the attorney does not have unlimited time to be heard and his answer must be in a respectful manner, but he does have the right to be heard and should not be penalized for attempting to exercise that right."

**a.** Compare the following RPC provisions:

**"EC 7–23** The complexity of law often makes it difficult for a tribunal to be fully informed unless the pertinent law is pre-

## WEINSTEIN, JUDICIAL NOTICE AND THE DUTY TO DISCLOSE ADVERSE INFORMATION

51 Iowa L.Rev. 807, 810–14 (1966).[b]

It may be useful to recall that the lawyers' responsibility to the court on questions of law is one fixed by a substantial tradition. The Year Books show the sergeants (respected court officers) discussing legal points with the judges as adversaries representing clients and yet as persons responsible for the proper development of the law. A common-law tradition where individual decisions strongly affect the development of legal doctrine for future cases almost necessarily implies a reasoning together of bench and bar and a candid and thorough exploration of the legal issues and precedents.

Even if we were to ignore, as do the critics of the rule on disclosure of adverse law, the moral and historical questions, their conclusions seem doubtful on tactical grounds. The dual responsibilities of the advocate—to his client and the court—present the most tantalizing and vexing problems. Often there is no fixed line to separate situations where the duty is clearly to the one or to the other. But in the area of questions of law, the balance usually appears to favor candor, on purely pragmatic grounds.

We may put to the side the special position of the government attorney, whose obligation to his specific client is tempered by the fact that he has a deeper obligation to the public, which his client represents, and to the enforcement of justice generally. His duty to disclose seems quite clear.

The advocate who practices regularly before the court and who is retained by other lawyers for this purpose also presents a special case. His chief stock-in-trade is the reputation he enjoys in the court for reliability. It is for this reason, for example—as well as because he will tend to be a craftsman with pride in his work—that the skilled appellate lawyer will spend inordinate amounts of time methodically checking the statement of facts in his brief against the record, and the accuracy of his citations and quotations. Anyone retaining him should understand that he will defend his standing—and that of his clients—in the court by protecting the judges before whom he practices against

sented by the lawyers in the cause. A tribunal that is fully informed on the applicable law is better able to make a fair and accurate determination of the matter before it. The adversary system contemplates that each lawyer will present and argue the existing law in the light most favorable to his client. Where a lawyer knows of legal authority in the controlling jurisdiction directly adverse to the position of his client, he should inform the tribunal of its existence unless his adversary has done so; but, having made such disclosure, he may challenge its soundness in whole or in part.

**"DR 7–106 Trial Conduct**

* * *

"(B) In presenting a matter to a tribunal, a lawyer shall disclose:

(1) Legal authority in the controlling jurisdiction known to him to be directly adverse to the position of his client and which is not disclosed by opposing counsel."

overlooking cases that they should be aware of in making their decisions. The bench may come to rely in some measure upon the research of the candid advocate it trusts. The judges may also be more inclined to favor the "reputable," "skilled," and "candid" advocate's distinguishing of adverse decisions. The benefits of such a reputation obviously redound to the client.

The practiced advocate may not, however, protect his own standing to the injury of a particular client in exceeding acceptable limits of candor by, for example, stating that his client is wrong in taking the appeal. If that is his view, he should not have accepted the case.

We deal then with the occasional advocate who is motivated solely by the desire to increase the probability of his client's success. If there is a specific, freshly-minted, and thoroughly considered case by the highest court in the jurisdiction on the only point in question which absolutely forecloses the matter, then, of course, the best thing that the attorney can do for his client is to advise him that there is no point in going forward. The same advice is to be expected if there is an absolutely unavoidable binding statute, ordinance, or administrative ruling.

If the case or statute appears to be both adverse and controlling but can be neutralized or explained away, then the attorney assumes an unwarranted risk for his client by failing to reveal the difficulties explicitly and by failing to demonstrate to the court how the precedent should be dealt with. For, should the court itself discover the case, then he has foreclosed himself from presenting argument explaining why the ruling is not decisive.

There may, of course, be instances where, all things considered, purely pragmatic analysis argues in favor of nondisclosure as providing a somewhat lesser risk to the client; here ethics and tradition come into play and require disclosure. That is to say, immediate practical considerations do not supply the whole answer to the advocate; if they could, there would be no reason for the canons of ethics.

If an adverse precedent is not really distinguishable on the facts, the advocate then has no alternative but to meet the problem head on and to argue on grounds of policy, principle, and subsequent decisions for a modification of the doctrine in a way helpful to his client. * * *

As a tactical-psychological matter of dealing with the courts, it is useful, particularly in appellate argument, to state candidly that there is an apparent difficulty with the case. One of the chief problems of the advocate is to obtain the full attention of the court so that it focuses on his client's position. There is hardly a better way to gain that attention than to state the problem frankly. Indeed, it is a standard ploy in appellate argument to give the appearance of this position by setting up a straw man.

The bench today, on the whole, recognizes its obligation to modify case law and to interpret statutes reasonably. Judges who will mechanically apply the precedents despite the fact that they make no sense are becoming rarer. Judges, like lawyers, are interested in establishing a good name; they know that an acceptable way to achieve a reputation as a jurist is by writing learned opinions, clearing away objectionable law and establishing a sound basis for future litigation. A well-written brief and good argument, making it easy for the court to write a good opinion, will be welcomed by most members of the bench and will tend to assist the client.

In short, the tactic of non-disclosure of adverse cases seems based upon two dubious assumptions. They are, first, that judges are ignorant and indolent, and, second, that the legal system is moribund, designed to follow worn-out precedent, and likely to use prior decisions mechanically. It is doubtful that these unflattering conclusions about our judicial system are acted upon by our most successful litigators. * * *

Nevertheless, and accepting what has been written above, there are shadowy areas of very considerable significance where the lawyer's obligation, even as to matters of "law," seems to favor protection of his client. For example, if the trial judge rules improperly on admissibility or exclusion of evidence, most lawyers in whose favor the ruling was made would feel no obligation to correct the judge. Nor would they feel obligated to inform the other side that the law permits an objection to evidence—although evidence should not be offered which is clearly inadmissible. If the judge charges improperly in a way favorable to a client, the bar would see no ethical obligation to correct him or to suggest an exception to an opponent to preserve the question for appeal even though the error may become "law of the case" upon appeal. Perhaps the justification for these positions is that such a mistake affects only the instant litigation, has no effect on the future development of the law, and enhances the effectiveness of the adversarial system which, in turn, insures an effective judicial system. But this rationale is disquieting, for it suggests that preserving the honor of an abstract concept of justice and law is more important than doing right to particular individual litigants—a proposition inconsistent with our society's concern for the individual. Some would argue that the opponent chose his lawyer and if the lawyer makes mistakes, the client can only blame himself. But a profession dedicated to justice cannot so easily shrug off responsibility for its individual member's competence.[c]

c. See Katris v. Immigration & Naturalization Service, 562 F.2d 866 (2d Cir. 1977) (costs taxed against lawyer for failing to cite controlling adverse decision in case in which the lawyer personally participated); Shaeffer v. State Bar, 26 Cal.2d 739, 747, 160 P.2d 825, 829 (1945) (no discipline for same where lawyer thought statement in previous case was dictum and had not intentionally attempted to mislead court); Freedman, Arguing the Law in an Adversary System, 16 Ga.L.Rev. 833 (1982); Hazard, Arguing the Law: The Advocate's Duty and Opportunity, 16 Ga.L.Rev. 821 (1982); Uviller, Zeal and Frivolity: The Ethical Duty of the Appellate Advocate to Tell the Truth About the Law, 6 Hofstra L.Rev. 729 (1978).

Compare Stare v. Tate, 21 Cal.App.3d 432, 98 Cal.Rptr. 264 (1971) (property settlement agreement reformed because of defendant's

# K. IMPROPER INFLUENCES

## MODEL RULES OF PROFESSIONAL CONDUCT

### RULE 3.5 Impartiality and Decorum of the Tribunal

A lawyer shall not:

(a) seek to influence a judge, juror, prospective juror or other official by means prohibited by law;

(b) communicate ex parte with such a person except as permitted by law * * *

COMMENT:

Many forms of improper influence upon a tribunal are proscribed by criminal law. Others are specified in the ABA Model Code of Judicial Conduct, with which an advocate should be familiar. A lawyer is required to avoid contributing to a violation of such provisions.[a]

lawyer's failure to point out plaintiff's lawyer's math mistake); Marcus v. State, 249 Ga. 345, 290 S.E.2d 470 (1982) (no criminal conviction for lawyer's presenting bail order to deputy sheriff knowing it had typographical error specifying "$300,00.00" instead of "$300,000.00" so that client got out on $30,000 bail; "behavior which might be unethical and might even subject an attorney to discipline * * * does not necessarily rise to the level of criminal conduct"); State v. White, 94 Wash.2d 498, 617 P.2d 998 (1980) ("if at the trial setting, defendant's counsel was aware that the trial date fixed was beyond the 60-day [speedy trial provision] limit, he had a duty to so advise the court").

**a.** Compare the following CPR provisions:

"**EC 7–36** [A lawyer] should avoid undue solicitude for the comfort or convenience of judge or jury and should avoid any other conduct calculated to gain special consideration.

"**DR 7–108 Communication With or Investigation of Jurors**

"(A) Before the trial of a case a lawyer connected therewith shall not communicate with or cause another to communicate with anyone he knows to be a member of the venire from which the jury will be selected for the trial of the case.

"(B) During the trial of a case:

(1) A lawyer connected therewith shall not communicate with or cause another to communicate with any member of the jury.

(2) A lawyer who is not connected therewith shall not communicate with or cause another to communicate with a juror concerning the case.

"(C) DR 7–108(A) and (B) do not prohibit a lawyer from communicating with veniremen or jurors in the course of official proceedings.

"(D) After discharge of the jury from further consideration of a case with which the lawyer was connected, the lawyer shall not ask questions of or make comments to a member of that jury that are calculated merely to harass or embarrass the juror or to influence his actions in future jury service.

"(E) A lawyer shall not conduct or cause, by financial support or otherwise, another to conduct a vexatious or harassing investigation of either a venireman or a juror.

"(F) All restrictions imposed by DR 7–108 upon a lawyer also apply to communications with or investigations of members of a family of a venireman or a juror.

"(G) A lawyer shall reveal promptly to the court improper conduct by a venireman or a juror, or by another toward a venireman or a juror or a member of his family, of which the lawyer has knowledge.

"**DR 7–110 Contact With Officials**

"(A) A lawyer shall not give or lend anything of value to a judge, official, or employee of a tribunal except as permitted by Section C(4) of Canon 5 of the Code of Judicial Conduct, but a lawyer may make a contribution to the campaign fund of a candidate for judicial office in conformity with Section

## ABA CODE OF JUDICIAL CONDUCT

**CANON 3(A)(4):**

A judge should * * * except as authorized by law, neither initiate nor consider *ex parte* or other communications concerning a pending or impending proceeding. A judge, however, may obtain the advice of a disinterested expert on the law applicable to a proceeding before him if he gives notice to the parties of the person consulted and the substance of the advice, and affords the parties reasonable opportunity to respond.

**CANON 5(C)(4):**

Neither a judge nor a member of his family residing in his household should accept a gift, bequest, favor, or loan from anyone except as follows:

(a) a judge may accept a gift incident to a public testimonial to him; books supplied by publishers on a complimentary basis for official use; or an invitation to the judge and his spouse to attend a bar-related function or activity devoted to the improvement of the law, the legal system, or the administration of justice;

(b) a judge or a member of his family residing in his household may accept ordinary social hospitality; a gift, bequest, favor, or loan from a relative; a wedding or engagement gift; a loan from a lending institution in its regular course of business on the same terms generally available to persons who are not judges; or a scholarship or fellowship awarded on the same terms applied to other applicants;

(c) a judge or a member of his family residing in his household may accept any other gift, bequest, favor, or loan only if the donor is not a party or other person whose interests have come or are likely to come before him, and, if its value exceeds $100, the judge reports it in the same manner as he reports compensation in Canon 6C.

**CANON 7(B)(2):**

A candidate, including an incumbent judge, for a judicial office that is filled by public election between competing candidates should not himself solicit or accept campaign funds, or solicit publicly stated support, but he may establish committees of responsible persons to secure and manage the expenditure of funds for his campaign and to obtain public statements of support for his candidacy. Such committees are not prohibited from soliciting campaign contributions and public support from lawyers. A

B(2) under Canon 7 of the Code of Judicial Conduct.

"(B) In an adversary proceeding, a lawyer shall not communicate, or cause another to communicate, as to the merits of the cause with a judge or an official before whom the proceeding is pending, except:

(1) In the course of official proceedings in the cause.

(2) In writing if he promptly delivers a copy of the writing to opposing counsel or to the adverse party if he is not represented by a lawyer.

(3) Orally upon adequate notice to opposing counsel or to the adverse party if he is not represented by a lawyer.

(4) As otherwise authorized by law, or by Section A(4) under Canon 3 of the Code of Judicial Conduct."

candidate's committees may solicit funds for his campaign no earlier than [90] days before a primary election and no later than [90] days after the last election in which he participates during the election year. A candidate should not use or permit the use of campaign contributions for the private benefit of himself or members of his family.

## ELISOVSKY v. STATE

592 P.2d 1221, 19 A.L.R.4th 1196 (Alaska 1979).

BOOCHEVER, Justice.

Walter Elisovsky appeals his conviction of the crime of assault with a dangerous weapon in violation of AS 11.15.220. Issues are raised pertaining to the failure of the trial court to give a lesser included offense instruction as to careless use of a firearm; the jurors making an unauthorized inspection of the scene of the offense; an instruction authorizing jurors to use their past experience in considering the evidence and the fact that jurors decided to consider prior bad conduct of the defendant which the court had excluded; * * * and the imposition of a fine of $100.00 on defense counsel for securing affidavits from jurors and not promptly notifying the court.

Subsequent to the trial of this case, we ruled that a requested lesser included offense instruction of careless use of a firearm is required under circumstances similar to those involved in this case. That rule, which we find applicable to this case, is dispositive of Elisovsky's appeal. The failure to give the instruction requires a reversal and remand. Since the other instruction issue may arise on retrial, it will be discussed, as will the separate appeal of attorney Suddock from the imposition of a sanction. We regard the remaining issues as moot.[3]

### Statement of Facts

On September 14, 1976, Walter and Jackie Elisovsky went out for the evening in Cordova to celebrate their wedding anniversary. After a period of celebration, the Elisovsky couple had an argument over the control of the car keys. When Elisovsky refused to give the car keys to his wife, she telephoned the Cordova police. As the police arrived, Elisovsky was taking his rifle and gear out of the rear of the couple's station wagon. Both police officers testified that Walter pointed the rifle at them and that Jackie pushed the muzzle of the gun to the ground. Elisovsky testified that he was taking the rifle and other gear out of the car for the purpose of spending the night on a friend's boat and was merely planning to stand the rifle beside the car. Jackie testified that she had grabbed the barrel of the rifle to push it down, but believed that Elisovsky was only brandishing the gun and had not pointed it at anyone. Elisovsky was charged with assault with a dangerous weapon.

3. The state does not seriously question that the bailiff permitting the jurors to take an unauthorized view of the scene, at which they attempted to recreate the occurrence, was error. The only real issue is whether such error was harmless. * * *

At trial, the court refused to give a requested instruction that careless use of a firearm was a lesser included offense of the charged crime. The court also instructed, over defense objection, that:

> "When you think about the evidence in this case and discuss it in the jury room you do not have to set aside the things you have seen and experienced in the affairs of life but you do in fact have a right to consider all the evidence in the light of things you have seen and experienced."

Defense counsel had objected on the grounds that, in a small community such as Cordova, such an instruction authorized the use of extrinsic evidence. Elisovsky's prior convictions of possession of marijuana, driving while intoxicated and disorderly conduct were covered by a protective order; similarly, a prior suicide attempt on Elisovsky's part and an acquittal on a fishing violation were not to be used. No information on any of these incidents was presented to the jury during the trial.

The jury returned a verdict of guilty of assault with a dangerous weapon on December 10, 1976. The court after the verdict authorized the jurors to speak about their deliberations should they be approached by one of the attorneys.[7] Rodger James, one of the jurors, encountered defense counsel John Suddock at a Cordova hotel on Saturday the day after the verdict was received, and invited Suddock over to his table. The following day, Suddock contacted Arlot Hall, the jury foreman, and juror Dennis Bain. From these conversations, Suddock learned that the jurors had made an unauthorized trip to the scene of the incident and had also made a formal decision to discuss events in Walter's history which were not introduced into evidence.

Suddock prepared affidavits relating to this information[8] and submitted them on December 23, 1976, along with a motion for a new trial.

7. The judge stated:

"Lawyers who practice in courts before juries very often find it helpful, or think they find it helpful at least, to speak to the jurors after a case is over, to find out perhaps how their style affects the jury, how their witnesses affect the jury—things that might help them become better trial lawyers. If you wish—you are not required to, but if you wish, and if you are approached by either of these gentlemen, you are authorized to speak to them about the case and how their presentation might have affected you, or things of this nature—questions to educate them, to help them sharpen their skills if they wish to do that. As I say, you're not required to do that; you may do that—you may respond to their questions if you wish. They are not authorized to talk to you about what went on in the jury room—in other words, to inquire into your deliberative process. * * * [I]f you—if these gentlemen do ask to speak to you and you do decide to speak to them, you must be very careful to speak accurately and not say anything which would tend to impeach your verdict, that is to say, raise some question. You all decided tonight, now. It might even be—you know, tomorrow or the next day, if somebody were to talk to you, you might have a kind of a different slant from what you had tonight. And you—I caution you, if you do talk to counsel, that you must be cautious, I think, not to say anything that would give rise to a suggestion that your verdict would be impeached—because that would be improper for them to question you in that area."

8. Dennis Bain's affidavit indicated that the jury requested the bailiff to take them to the scene of the incident and that, upon arriving at the Alaskan Bar, some jurors attempted to recreate the scene. Also, Bain indicated that after considering Instruction No. 2, "our decision was that under that instruction, those of us with knowledge about Walter

A hearing was held on the motion for a new trial, and ten of the twelve jurors appeared at the request of the court. They were collectively asked a series of questions.[9] The motion for a new trial was denied.

On March 3, 1977, the state filed a motion to censure defense counsel for securing juror affidavits "for the purpose of impeaching the jury's verdict in this case." A hearing was held in Anchorage on May 4, 1977, at which the court told Suddock:

> "I find that your failure [to notify the court immediately upon finding information of apparently improper jury conduct] but to go ahead and secure affidavits—and secure them in support of a motion for a new trial, and not to apply to the court for its assistance and its supervision in the jury-inquiry process is improper."

The court imposed a fine of $100.00 * * *.

INSTRUCTION OF JURORS TO USE PAST EXPERIENCE

* * * Elisovsky objected to the instruction on the ground that it would encourage the jurors who lived in a small community where most people knew him to consider rumors and prior conduct which had been excluded from evidence. The jurors' affidavits indicated that they did consider the extrinsic evidence.

* * * In view of the possibility of the questioned portion of the instruction being misunderstood, it should not be given upon retrial of this case.

THE FINE IMPOSED ON COUNSEL

The state filed a motion requesting censure of defense counsel and disapproval of his actions in securing affidavits for the purpose of impeaching the jury's verdict in this case. At the hearing, the court found Mr. Suddock's failure immediately to inform the court of the jurors' alleged improper conduct and his decision to secure affidavits without applying to the court for its assistance and supervision to be improper. This was the apparent basis for the imposition of the fine of $100.00.

But Mr. Suddock was not given notice that he was being subjected to a possible fine for failing promptly to inform the court of the jurors'

could give the information to the other jurors, and that we had the right to consider such information in deciding the case, and did not have to set it aside." Bain also swore that the jury discussed the fact that Walter had recently attempted suicide by stabbing himself, and that one juror told the group that he had seen Jackie Elisovsky after she had been beaten up, presumably by her husband.

Rodger James' and Arlot Hall's affidavits were of generally similar content.

9. When asked to respond in writing, nine jurors wrote down that they had not considered general character information in reaching their verdict. All ten of the jurors present indicated that the verdict would have been the same without any discussion of character. All ten also indicated that the unauthorized jury view of the scene of the incident did not cause them to disregard evidence presented, and that to a "reasonable certainty," there would not have been a different verdict without the jury view. Suddock objected to the questions as leading and also objected that all of the jurors were not present. Jury Foreman Arlot Hall was not present.

alleged misconduct. The state's motion to censure referred to the securing of the affidavits, not the failure promptly to report juror misconduct. We believe that this circumstance violated Mr. Suddock's right to be informed of the specific charges against him and his right to prepare a response to such charges.

The court did not specify the source of its power in imposing the fine. Conceivably, the proceeding could have been in the nature of contempt, for conduct occurring outside the presence of the court. Civil Rule 90(b) establishes the procedure to be followed for such instances.

Civil Rule 95(b) authorizes the imposition of a fine, not to exceed $500.00, for failure to comply with any rules promulgated by the supreme court. In Davis v. Superior Court, 580 P.2d 1176, 1179 (Alaska 1978), we held that the trial court has the power to impose fines under this section for a violation of the disciplinary rules when necessary for the orderly and efficient operation of the courtroom. Alaska Bar Rule 11 specifies that acts or omissions by an attorney which violate the Code of Professional Responsibility of the American Bar Association shall constitute misconduct and grounds for discipline.

Disciplinary Rule 7–108(G) of the Code of Professional Responsibility requires that:

> "A lawyer shall reveal promptly to the court improper conduct by a venireman or a juror, or by another toward a venireman or a juror or a member of his family, of which the lawyer has knowledge." [a]

Obviously, immediate notice is required of knowledge of such improper conduct learned during the course of trial. "Promptly" is a flexible term and we do not express an opinion as to the time for presenting such information learned after a trial, except to state that reasonable diligence is required.

Under either Civil Rule 90(b) or 95(b), notice and an opportunity to be heard are required. * * * Here no adequate notice was given to Mr. Suddock that he might be subject to a fine for failure promptly to reveal improper conduct by jurors.

**a.** Note that the Rules of Professional Conduct do not include this requirement. Compare RPC 8.3 (duty to report lawyer or judge misconduct raising substantial question as to fitness).

As to DR 7–108(G), see In re Kozlov, 79 N.J. 232, 398 A.2d 882 (1979) (under circumstances not necessary for lawyer to identify client who in confidence disclosed information regarding misconduct of juror in case involving neither lawyer nor client); In re R., 276 Or. 365, 554 P.2d 522 (1976) (lawyer must reveal knowledge that client had inadvertently picked up juror as hitchhiker during client's trial although lawyer did not learn this until after trial).

The Rules of Professional Conduct also include no counterpart to DR 7–108(F)'s extension of the restrictions to members of a juror's or prospective juror's family. See In re Two Anonymous Members of the South Carolina Bar, 278 S.C. 477, 298 S.E.2d 450 (1982) (reprimand for communicating with sister not living in home of prospective juror about latter's attitudes).

We therefore must reverse the order imposing a fine of $100.00 on Mr. Suddock and remand for further hearing on proper notice to be conducted in the discretion of the trial court. On remand, the trial court may determine whether Mr. Suddock failed to report promptly to the court improper juror conduct and whether such failure, in the circumstances of this case, would be grounds for imposing disciplinary sanctions.

Since a new proceeding might again involve the issue of conferring with jurors, we note that it would be improper to sanction Mr. Suddock for talking to the jurors in the absence of a showing that he harassed them. The court specifically authorized jurors to talk to counsel. The American Bar Association Ethical Considerations permit such communications.[20] Disciplinary Rule 7–108(D) of the Code of Professional Responsibility provides:

> "After discharge of the jury from further consideration of a case with which the lawyer was connected, the lawyer shall not ask questions of or make comments to a member of that jury that are calculated merely to harass or embarrass the juror or to influence his actions in future jury service."

In Irving v. Bullock, 549 P.2d 1184, 1188 n. 10 [Alaska 1976], we stated in part:

> "However, interrogation of jurors for the purpose of discovering 'errors' which are not grounds for impeaching the verdict deprives jurors of the protection from harassment which the rule seeks to give them. See DR 7–108, EC 7–29. The Ninth Circuit Court of Appeals has declared it unethical even to interview jurors about the course of their deliberations. Northern Pacific Railway v. Mely, 219 F.2d 199, 202 (9th Cir. 1954). Henceforth, an attorney wishing to obtain evidence concerning the behavior of jurors in the performance of their duty should first file a motion in the trial court for leave to do so, stating in detail the reasons [therefor]. The trial court shall weigh such applications with great care, granting leave to make such an inquiry only where it appears that there is a strong likelihood that an obstruction of justice may have occurred. If the motion is granted, the court shall specify the manner in which such evidence [is] to be obtained."

We now find that the *Irving* directive requires some modification. As indicated in the American Bar Association Ethical Consideration 7–29:

> "Were a lawyer to be prohibited from communicating after trial with a juror, he could not ascertain if the verdict might be subject to legal challenge, in which event the invalidity of a verdict might go undetected."

20. See [EC 7–29, stating in part, "After the trial, communication by a lawyer with jurors is permitted so long as he refrains from asking questions or making comments that tend to harass or embarrass the juror or to influence actions of the juror in future cases."]

The proposed Alaska Rule of Evidence 606(b), which is similar to the like numbered Federal Rule of Evidence, provides:

> "(b) *Inquiry into validity of verdict or indictment.* Upon an inquiry into the validity of a verdict or indictment, a juror may not testify as to any matter or statement occurring during the course of the jury's deliberations or to the effect of any matter or statement upon his or any other juror's mind or emotions as influencing him to assent to or dissent from the verdict or indictment or concerning his mental processes in connection therewith, except that a juror may testify on the question whether extraneous prejudicial information was improperly brought to the jury's attention or whether any outside influence was improperly brought to bear upon any juror. Nor may his affidavit or evidence of any statement by him concerning a matter about which he would be precluded from testifying be received for these purposes." [b]

We approve of the proposed rule and believe that it sets forth the proper standard for determining permissible inquiry into jury conduct. Inquiry should not be made into subjects about which a juror may not testify. This standard may also be used in part in ascertaining whether inquiries of jurors exceed the authorized contacts so as to constitute harassment.

The securing of affidavits from jurors after inquiry presents a more delicate problem. If the attorney wishes to secure affidavits, he may do so without filing a formal motion before the court, but the affidavits must not exceed the permissible scope of inquiry under proposed Alaska Rule of Evidence 606(b).[21] Again, the standard delineated therein may be used to determine if the attorney's conduct in securing jurors' affidavits amounts to harassment.

To summarize, we are no longer requiring that before counsel can make inquiry of jurors, an order must be obtained. Counsel are generally authorized to make inquiry within the contours set forth in proposed Alaska Rule of Evidence 606(b). In the event counsel discovers alleged juror misconduct, he must promptly reveal this information to

**b.** Compare ABA Standards for Criminal Justice 15–4.7 (2d ed. 1980), which specifies:

**"Standard 15–4.7 Impeachment of the Verdict**

"(a) Upon an inquiry into the validity of a verdict, no evidence shall be received to show the effect of any statement, conduct, event, or condition upon the mind of a juror or concerning the mental processes by which the verdict was determined.

"(b) The limitations in paragraph (a) shall not bar evidence concerning whether the verdict was reached by lot.

"(c) Subject to the limitations in paragraph (a), a juror's testimony or affidavit shall be received when it concerns:

(i) whether matters not in evidence came to the attention of one or more jurors, under circumstances which would violate the defendant's constitutional right to be confronted with the witnesses against him or her; or

(ii) any other misconduct for which the jurisdiction permits jurors to impeach their verdict."

See also id. Commentary.

**21.** After being informed of the alleged juror misconduct, the court may, upon its own motion, regulate the manner in which evidence is to be obtained.

the trial court. In the event counsel wishes to secure an affidavit from a juror, he may do so without prior court order subject to the limitations of Rule 606(b). The court, however, may, on its own motion, after being informed of alleged prior misconduct, regulate the manner in which evidence is to be obtained.

Reversed and Remanded.[c]

### *Comment*

(1) *Communication during trial.* Regarding communication with jurors during the trial, see Johnson v. Trueblood,[1] wherein a federal district court in Pennsylvania withdrew pro hac vice permission because the lawyer, among other misconduct, smiled, waved, and told the jurors to "have a nice weekend" as they were leaving the courtroom, and Omaha Bank for Cooperatives v. Siouxland Cattle Cooperative,[2] wherein the Iowa Supreme Court reversed a defendant's judgment because the trial court had refused to replace a juror with an alternate after defendant's lawyers had allowed the juror, who happened to see them in a bar, to buy them a drink.[3]

(2) *Communication after trial.* Although the ABA Standards for Criminal Justice,[4] ABA Formal Opinion 319 (1967), and the Kansas Supreme Court case of State v. Blocker[5] support the Alaska court's current approach of allowing post-trial juror interviewing without court permission or supervision, a number of courts follow its former approach of allowing it only with court permission upon a showing of cause.[6]

**c.** Justice Connor concurred in part and dissented in part.

**1.** 476 F.Supp. 90 (E.D.Pa. 1979), vacated on other grounds 629 F.2d 302 (3d Cir. 1980), cert. denied 450 U.S. 999, 101 S.Ct. 1704, 68 L.Ed.2d 200 (1981).

**2.** 305 N.W.2d 458 (Iowa 1981).

**3.** Compare In re Shon, 262 App.Div. 225, 28 N.Y.S.2d 872 (1941) (nondisclosure of friendship with two jurors one of several grounds for disbarment).

**4.** ABA Standards for Criminal Justice 4–7.3(c) (2d ed. 1980) (lawyer who believes verdict may be subject to legal challenge may, if no statute or rule prohibits, communicate with jurors to determine whether challenge may be available).

**5.** 211 Kan. 185, 505 P.2d 1099 (1973).

**6.** See, e.g., United States v. Sanchez, 380 F.Supp. 1260 (N.D.Tex.1973), affirmed 508 F.2d 388 (5th Cir. 1975) ("This Court does not permit the disgusting practice of unbridled interrogation of jurors about their deliberations"); Brassell v. Brethauer, 305 So.2d 217 (Fla.App.1974) (interviewing permissible only with court order upon showing of cause); Baker v. Gile, 257 N.W.2d 376 (Minn. 1977) (evidence of jury misconduct obtained by questioning jurors may be used as grounds for new trial only if the questioning occurred in a proceeding granted by and conducted before trial court); Annot., 19 A.L.R.4th 1209 (1983).

# Chapter 7

# THE CONTRACT OF EMPLOYMENT

## A. FEES

### 1. ANTITRUST RESTRICTIONS

#### GOLDFARB v. VIRGINIA STATE BAR

421 U.S. 773, 95 S.Ct. 2004, 44 L.Ed.2d 572 (1975)

Mr. Chief Justice BURGER delivered the opinion of the Court.

We granted certiorari to decide whether a minimum fee schedule for lawyers published by the Fairfax County Bar Association and enforced by the Virginia State Bar violated § 1 of the Sherman Act, 15 U.S.C.A. § 1. * * *

I

In 1971 petitioners, husband and wife, contracted to buy a home in Fairfax County, Virginia. The financing agency required them to secure title insurance; this required a title examination, and only a member of the Virginia State Bar could legally perform that service. Petitioners therefore contacted a lawyer who quoted them the precise fee suggested in a minimum fee schedule published by respondent Fairfax County Bar Association; the lawyer told them that it was his policy to keep his charges in line with the minimum fee schedule which provided for a fee of 1% of the value of the property involved. Petitioners then tried to find a lawyer who would examine the title for less than the fee fixed by the schedule. They sent letters to 36 other Fairfax County lawyers requesting their fees. Nineteen replied, and none indicated that he would charge less than the rate fixed by the schedule; several stated that they knew of no attorney who would do so.

The fee schedule the lawyers referred to is a list of recommended minimum prices for common legal services. Respondent Fairfax County Bar Association published the fee schedule although, as a purely voluntary association of attorneys, the County Bar has no formal power to enforce it. Enforcement has been provided by respondent Virginia State Bar which is the administrative agency through which the Virginia Supreme Court regulates the practice of law in that State; membership in the State Bar is required in order to practice in Virginia. Although the State Bar has never taken formal disciplinary action to compel adherence to any fee schedule, it has published reports condoning fee schedules, and has issued two ethical opinions indicating fee schedules cannot be ignored. The most recent opinion states that "evidence that an attorney *habitually* charges less than the suggested minimum fee schedule adopted by his local bar association raises a presumption that such lawyer is guilty of misconduct. * * * "[6]

Because petitioners could not find a lawyer willing to charge a fee lower than the schedule dictated they had their title examined by the lawyer they had first contacted. They then brought this class action against the State Bar and the County Bar alleging that the operation of the minimum fee schedule, as applied to fees for legal services relating to residential real estate transactions, constitutes price fixing in violation of § 1 of the Sherman Act. Petitioners sought both injunctive relief and damages.

After a trial solely on the issue of liability the District Court held that the minimum fee schedule violated the Sherman Act. * * *

The Court of Appeals reversed * * * .

II

Our inquiry can be divided into four steps: did respondents engage in price fixing? If so, are their activities in interstate commerce or do they affect interstate commerce? If so, are the activities exempt from the Sherman Act because they involve a "learned profession?" If not, are the activities "state action" within the meaning of Parker v. Brown, 317 U.S. 341, 63 S.Ct. 307, 87 L.Ed. 315 (1943), and therefore exempt from the Sherman Act?

A

The County Bar argues that because the fee schedule is merely advisory, the schedule and its enforcement mechanism do not constitute price fixing. Its purpose, the argument continues, is only to provide legitimate information to aid member lawyers in complying with Virginia professional regulations. Moreover, the County Bar contends that in practice the schedule has not had the effect of producing fixed fees. The facts found by the trier belie these contentions, and nothing in the record suggests these findings lack support.

6. Virginia State Bar Committee on Legal Ethics, Opinion No. 170, May 28, 1971. The parties stipulated that these opinions are a substantial influencing factor in lawyers' adherence to the fee schedules. One reason for this may be because the State Bar is required by statute to "investigate * * * and report * * * the violation of * * * rules and regulations adopted by the [Virginia Supreme Court] to a court of competent jurisdiction for such proceedings as may be necessary. * * * " Therefore any lawyer who contemplated ignoring the fee schedule must have been aware that professional sanctions were possible, and that an enforcement mechanism existed to administer them.

A purely advisory fee schedule issued to provide guidelines, or an exchange of price information without a showing of an actual restraint on trade, would present us with a different question. The record here, however, reveals a situation quite different from what would occur under a purely advisory fee schedule. Here a fixed, rigid price floor arose from respondents' activities: every lawyer who responded to petitioners' inquiries adhered to the fee schedule, and no lawyer asked for additional information in order to set an individualized fee. The price information disseminated did not concern past standards, but rather minimum fees to be charged in future transactions, and those minimum rates were increased over time. The fee schedule was enforced through the prospect of professional discipline from the State Bar, and the desire of attorneys to comply with announced professional norms * * *; the motivation to conform was reinforced by the assurance that other lawyers would not compete by underbidding. This is not merely a case of an agreement that may be inferred from an exchange of price information * * *, for here a naked agreement was clearly shown, and the effect on prices is plain.

Moreover, in terms of restraining competition and harming consumers like petitioners the price-fixing activities found here are unusually damaging. A title examination is indispensable in the process of financing a real estate purchase, and since only an attorney licensed to practice in Virginia may legally examine a title, consumers could not turn to alternative sources for the necessary service. All attorneys, of course, were practicing under the constraint of the fee schedule. The County Bar makes much of the fact that it is a voluntary organization; however, the ethical opinions issued by the State Bar provide that any lawyer, whether or not a member of his county bar, may be disciplined for "*habitually* charg[ing] less than the suggested minimum fee schedule adopted by his local bar Association. * * *" These factors coalesced to create a pricing system that consumers could not realistically escape. On this record respondent's activities constitute a classic illustration of price fixing.

B

* * * As the District Court found, "a significant portion of funds furnished for the purchasing of homes in Fairfax County comes from without the State of Virginia," and "significant amounts of loans on Fairfax County real estate are guaranteed by the United States Veterans Administration and Department of Housing and Urban Development, both headquartered in the District of Columbia." Thus in this class action the transactions which create the need for the particular legal services in question frequently are interstate transactions. The necessary connection between the interstate transactions and the restraint of trade provided by the minimum fee schedule is present because, in a practical sense, title examinations are necessary in real estate transactions to assure a lien on a valid title of the borrower.

* * * Given the substantial volume of commerce involved, and the inseparability of this particular legal service from the interstate aspects of real estate transactions we conclude that interstate commerce has been sufficiently affected.

The fact that there was no showing that home buyers were discouraged by the challenged activities does not mean that interstate commerce was not affected. Otherwise, the magnitude of the effect would control, and our cases have shown that, once an effect is shown, no specific magnitude need be proved. Nor was it necessary for petitioners to prove that the fee schedule raised fees. Petitioners clearly proved that the fee schedule fixed fees and thus "deprive[d] purchasers or consumers of the advantages which they derive from free competition."

Where, as a matter of law or practical necessity, legal services are an integral part of an interstate transaction, a restraint on those services may substantially affect commerce for Sherman Act purposes. Of course, there may be legal services that involve interstate commerce in other fashions, just as there may be legal services that have no nexus with interstate commerce and thus are beyond the reach of the Sherman Act.

C

The County Bar argues that Congress never intended to include the learned professions within the terms "trade or commerce" in § 1 of the Sherman Act, and therefore the sale of professional services is exempt from the Act. No explicit exemption or legislative history is provided to support this contention, rather the existence of state regulation seems to be its primary basis. Also, the County Bar maintains that competition is inconsistent with the practice of a profession because enhancing profit is not the goal of professional activities; the goal is to provide services necessary to the community.[16] That, indeed, is the classic basis traditionally advanced to distinguish professions from trades, businesses, and other occupations, but it loses some of its force when used to support the fee control activities involved here.

In arguing that learned professions are not "trade or commerce," the County Bar seeks a total exclusion from antitrust regulation. Whether state regulation is active or dormant, real or theoretical, lawyers would be able to adopt anticompetitive practices with impunity. We cannot find support for the proposition that Congress intended any such sweeping exclusion. The nature of an occupation, standing alone, does not provide sanctuary from the Sherman Act * * * nor is

16. The reason for adopting the fee schedule does not appear to have been wholly altruistic. The first sentence in respondent State Bar's 1962 Minimum Fee Schedule Report states:

"The lawyers have slowly, but surely, been committing economic suicide as a profession."

the public service aspect of professional practice controlling in determining whether § 1 includes professions. Congress intended to strike as broadly as it could in § 1 of the Sherman Act, and to read into it so wide an exemption as that urged on us would be at odds with that purpose.

* * * Whatever else it may be, the examination of a land title is a service; the exchange of such a service for money is "commerce" in the most common usage of that word. It is no disparagement of the practice of law as a profession to acknowledge that it has this business aspect,[17] and § 1 of the Sherman Act "[o]n its face shows a carefully studied attempt to bring within the Act every person engaged in business whose activities might restrain or monopolize commercial intercourse among the states." United States v. South-Eastern Underwriters Assn., 322 U.S. 533, 553, 64 S.Ct. 1162, 1174. * * *

D

In Parker v. Brown, 317 U.S. 341, 63 S.Ct. 307, 87 L.Ed. 315 (1943), the Court held that an anticompetitive marketing program "which derived its authority and efficacy from the legislative command of the state" was not a violation of the Sherman Act because the Act was intended to regulate private practices and not to prohibit a State from imposing a restraint as an act of government. Respondent State Bar and respondent County Bar both seek to avail themselves of this so-called state action exemption.

Through its legislature Virginia has authorized its highest court to regulate the practice of law.[18] That court has adopted ethical codes which deal in part with fees and far from exercising state power to authorize binding price-fixing, explicitly directed lawyers not "to be controlled" by fee schedules.[19] The State Bar, a state agency by law,

17. The fact that a restraint operates upon a profession as distinguished from a business is, of course, relevant in determining whether that particular restraint violates the Sherman Act. It would be unrealistic to view the practice of professions as interchangeable with other business activities, and automatically to apply to the professions antitrust concepts which originated in other areas. The public service aspect, and other features of the professions, may require that a particular practice, which could properly be viewed as a violation of the Sherman Act in another context, be treated differently. We intimate no view on any other situation than the one with which we are confronted today.

18. Virginia Code § 54–48 (1972 Repl. Vol.) * * * In addition, the Supreme Court of Virginia, has inherent power to regulate the practice of law in that State. Button v. Day, 204 Va. 547, 132 S.E.2d 292 (1960). See Lathrop v. Donohue, 367 U.S. 820, 81 S.Ct. 1826, 6 L.Ed.2d 1191 (1961).

19. In 1938 the Supreme Court of Virginia adopted Rules for the Integration of the Virginia State Bar, and Rule II, § 12 dealt with the procedure for setting fees. Among six factors that court directed to be considered in setting a fee were "the customary charges of the Bar for similar services." The court also directed that "[i]n determining the customary charges of the Bar for similar services, it is proper for a lawyer to consider a schedule of minimum fees adopted by a Bar Association, but *no lawyer should permit himself to be controlled* thereby or to follow it as his sole guide in determining the amount of his fee." (Emphasis supplied.) In 1970 the Virginia Supreme Court amended the 1938 rules in part, and adopted the Code of Professional Responsibility, effective January 1, 1971. Certain of its provisions also dealt with the fee setting procedure. In EC 2–18 lawyers were told again that fees vary according to many factors, but that "[s]uggested fee schedules and economic reports of state and local bar associations provide some guidance on the

argues that in issuing fee schedule reports and ethical opinions dealing with fee schedules it was merely implementing the fee provisions of the ethical codes. The County Bar, although it is a voluntary association and not a state agency, claims the ethical codes and the activities of the State Bar "prompted" it to issue fee schedules and thus its actions too are state action for Sherman Act purposes.

The threshold inquiry in determining if an anticompetitive activity is state action of the type the Sherman Act was not meant to proscribe is whether the activity is required by the State acting as sovereign. * * * Here we need not inquire further into the state action question because it cannot fairly be said that the State of Virginia through its Supreme Court Rules required the anticompetitive activities of either respondent. Respondents have pointed to no Virginia statute requiring their activities; state law simply does not refer to fees, leaving regulation of the profession to the Virginia Supreme Court; although the Supreme Court's ethical codes mention advisory fee schedules they do not direct either respondent to supply them, or require the type of price floor which arose from respondents' activities. Although the State Bar apparently has been granted the power to issue ethical opinions there is no indication in this record that the Virginia Supreme Court approves the opinions. Respondents' arguments, at most, constitute the contention that their activities complemented the objective of the ethical codes. In our view that is not state action for Sherman Act purposes. It is not enough that, as the County Bar puts it, anticompetitive conduct is "prompted" by state action; rather, anticompetitive activities must be compelled by direction of the State acting as a sovereign.

The fact that the State Bar is a state agency for some limited purposes does not create an antitrust shield that allows it to foster anticompetitive practices for the benefit of its members.[21] The State Bar, by providing that deviation from County Bar minimum fees may lead to disciplinary action, has voluntarily joined in what is essentially a private anticompetitive activity, and in that posture cannot claim it is beyond the reach of the Sherman Act.[22] Its activities resulted in a

subject of reasonable fees." [Eds.: The ABA removed this from EC 2–18 in 1974.] In DR 2–106(B)(3), which detailed eight factors that should be considered in avoiding an excessive fee, one of the factors was "the fee customarily charged in the locality for similar legal services." [Eds.: Accord, RPC 1.5(a)(3).]

21. The District Court stated that the State Bar acted in only a "minor role" as far as the price-fixing was concerned * * *. Of course, an alleged participant in a restraint of trade may have so insubstantial a connection with the restraint that liability under the Sherman Act would not be found; however, that is not the case here. The State Bar's fee schedule reports provided the impetus for the County Bar, on two occasions, to adopt minimum fee schedules. More important, the State Bar's ethical opinions provided substantial reason for lawyers to comply with the minimum fee schedules. Those opinions threatened professional discipline for habitual disregard of fee schedules, and thus attorneys knew their livelihood was in jeopardy if they did so. Even without that threat the opinions would have constituted substantial reason to adhere to the schedules because attorneys could be expected to comply in order to assure that they did not discredit themselves by departing from professional norms, and perhaps betraying their professional oaths.

22. The State Bar also contends that it is protected by the Eleventh Amendment. Petitioners dispute this contention, and the Dis-

rigid price floor from which petitioners, as consumers, could not escape if they wished to borrow money to buy a home.

III

We recognize that the States have a compelling interest in the practice of professions within their boundaries, and that as part of their power to protect the public health, safety, and other valid interests they have broad power to establish standards for licensing practitioners and regulating the practice of professions. We also recognize that in some instances the State may decide that "forms of competition usual in the business world may be demoralizing to the ethical standards of a profession." United States v. Oregon State Medical Society, 343 U.S. 326, 336, 72 S.Ct. 690, 697, 96 L.Ed. 978 (1952). The interest of the States in regulating lawyers is especially great since lawyers are essential to the primary governmental function of administering justice, and have historically been "officers of the courts." In holding that certain anticompetitive conduct by lawyers is within the reach of the Sherman Act we intend no diminution of the authority of the State to regulate its professions. * * *

Reversed and remanded.[a]

### *Questions*

(1) Would the Sherman Act be violated if a bar association published an advisory fee schedule, making clear that it was purely advisory, and the state disciplinary authority made it clear that no one could be disciplined for charging less than the fee schedule specified?[1] If a bar association published the results of a comparative study of billable hours and hourly fees of partners and associates with varying degrees of experience and from various areas?[2] If it published tables indicating

trict Court had no occasion to reach it in view of its holding. Given the record before us we intimate no view on the issue, leaving it for the District Court on remand.

**a.** Powell, J., took no part. Many bar associations had already stopped issuing fee schedules before the *Goldfarb* case was decided. See In re Tierney, 70 Wis.2d 438, 234 N.W.2d 357 (1975).

**1.** See In re Tierney, 70 Wis.2d 438, 234 N.W.2d 357 (1975); Green, The Gross Legal Product: "How Much Justice Can You Afford?" in R. Nader & M. Green, Verdicts on Lawyers 63, 65–69 (1976).

**2.** In the course of his separate opinion in Bates v. State Bar, supra p. 541, Chief Justice Burger argued that the public interest would not be served as well by allowing lawyer advertising as it would be "by permitting the organized bar to experiment with, and perfect programs which would announce to the public the probable *range* of fees for specifically defined services and thus give putative clients some idea of potential cost liability when seeking out legal assistance." He noted that "The publication of such information by the organized bar would create no conflict with our holding in Goldfarb v. Va. State Bar so long as attorneys were under no obligation to charge within the range of fees described."

Branca & Steinberg, Attorney Fee Schedules and Legal Advertising: The Implications of Goldfarb, 24 U.C.L.A.L.Rev. 475 (1977), suggests that the Sherman Act would not prohibit the dissemination of statistical information about lawyers' charges, and asserts that this might even increase competition among lawyers.

See generally, Morgan, Where Do We Go from Here with Fee Schedules? 59 A.B.A.J. 1403 (1973). Compare Jeffers, Goldfarb v. Virginia: A Narrow Decision, 38 Texas B.J. 701 (1975).

hourly fees that would have to be charged to produce various annual incomes with various numbers of billable hours and various overhead percentages? If there was discussion at bar association meetings regarding what annual income the average lawyer should be able to earn?

(2) Is the Sherman Act violated by a bar association lawyer referral service's specifying a *maximum* fee for the first consultation? In Arizona v. Maricopa County Medical Society,[3] a 4–3 United States Supreme Court held that it constituted a *per se* Sherman Act violation for doctors, who belonged to a medical association–organized foundation, to establish maximum fees they could charge for patients covered by certain health plans. The doctors claimed they did this in order to provide the community with a competitive alternative to existing health insurance plans.

(a) The court held that the *per se* rule against price fixing agreements applied even though the agreements fixed *maximum* prices, explaining:

> "The *per se* rule is grounded on faith in price competition as a market force [and not] on a policy of low selling prices at the price of eliminating competition. Rahl, Price Competition and the Price Fixing Rule—Preface and Perspective, 57 Nw.U.L.Rev. 137, 142 (1962). In this case the rule is violated by a price restraint that tends to provide the same economic rewards to all practitioners regardless of their skill, their experience, their training, or their willingness to employ innovative and difficult procedures in individual cases. Such a restraint also may discourage entry into the market and may deter experimentation and new developments by individual entrepreneurs. It may be a masquerade for an agreement to fix uniform prices, or it may in the future take on that character."

(b) The court refused to exempt the agreements from the *per se* rule because they were among members of a profession, saying:

> "In [footnote 17 of] *Goldfarb*, we stated that the public service aspect, and other features of the professions, may require that a particular practice, which could properly be viewed as a violation of the Sherman Act in another context, be treated differently." See National Society of Professional Engineers v. United States, 435 U.S. 679, 696, 98 S.Ct. 1355, 1367, 55 L.Ed.2d 637 (1978).[a] The price fixing agreements in this case, however, are not premised on public service or ethical norms."

(c) Finally, the Court refused to exempt the agreements because of their alleged procompetitive justifications, saying that under the *per se* concept, "The anticompetitive potential inherent in all price

3. 457 U. S. 332, 102 S.Ct. 2466, 73 L.Ed.2d 48 (1982).

a. In *Professional Engineers*, the Court held that the engineers' society's canon of ethics prohibiting competitive bidding violated the Sherman Act.

fixing agreements justifies their facial invalidation even if procompetitive justifications are offered for some." The court pointed out that although it may be desirable for maximum medical fees to be established so that a patient can be assured that the insurance will cover the whole cost and so that insurance premiums can be held down, it is not necessary for the *doctors* to establish the maximum fees; rather *insurers* are perfectly capable of not only setting maximum reimbursable amounts but obtaining doctors' agreements not to charge more than those amounts.

How does *Maricopa* bear upon the lawyer referral service maximum fee situation?

(3) Is the Sherman Act violated by a state supreme court *itself* adopting a rule specifying maximum percentage contingent fees that may charged (absent specific court approval) in tort cases? [4]

In Bates v. State Bar,[5] the United States Supreme Court held that a state supreme court's adoption of restrictions on lawyer advertising was within the Sherman Act's state-action exemption because, as distinct from *Goldfarb*, the challenged restraint was the "affirmative command" of the state supreme court, "the ultimate body wielding the State's power over the practice of law," because the state had an "independent regulatory interest" in restricting lawyer advertising, and because the state supreme court's action was not merely acquiescence in an anticompetitive program instigated by the persons regulated.

***Comment***

(1) *Action of state supreme court itself.* In Hoover v. Ronwin,[6] an Arizona bar applicant brought an antitrust action against the state lawyer admission committee, alleging that it set bar exam grading so that it would pass only a predetermined number of persons. A 4-3 U.S. Supreme Court held the action barred by the state-action exemption since the state supreme court had plenary authority over bar admission—its rules required the committee to submit its grading formula to the court before giving the exam and, after grading, to submit its recommendations for admission to the court, which made the final decision to grant or deny admission, and an applicant could petition the state supreme court for individualized review of an adverse committee recommendation. The U.S. Supreme Court, per Justice Powell, recognized that when an action is not directly that of a state legislature or supreme court, but is carried out by others under state authorization, there must be a showing that the conduct is pursuant to a clearly articulated and affirmatively expressed state policy to replace competition with regulation, and the degree to which the state legislature or supreme court actively supervises its representative is relevant. However, when the action is that of the state legislature or supreme

4. See infra pp. 448–51.

5. 433 U.S. 350, 97 S.Ct. 2691, 53 L.Ed.2d 810 (1977). The first amendment aspects of *Bates* are set forth infra p. 541.

6. — U.S. —, 104 S.Ct. 1989, — L.Ed.2d — (1984).

court itself, the issues of "clear articulation" and "active supervision" need not be addressed.[7]

(2) *State bar action required by state supreme court.* In Surety Title Insurance Agency, Inc. v. Virginia State Bar,[8] a title insurer brought a federal court challenge to the process by which a state bar committee issued unauthorized practice opinions which deterred lawyers from participating in any real estate transaction involving title insurance effectuated without a lawyer's examining title. A Virginia Supreme Court rule required the Bar committee to render, at the request of a lawyer, an advisory opinion on contemplated professional conduct. There was no provision for nonlawyer input or court review.

The federal district court granted the title insurer summary judgment on the issue of liability, finding that this process whereby "advisory opinions are issued by lawyers in response to questions submitted by lawyers and no provision is made to inject the participation of non-interested parties into the process" was an antitrust violation to which the state-action exemption did not apply. Although the Virginia Supreme Court *required* the Bar committee to issue the opinions, this process which put "attorneys in the unique position of being able to define the extent of their own monopoly" was not "sufficiently related to [the state's] interests to justify its anticompetitive effects."

But the Fourth Circuit vacated the district court's order because the Virginia Supreme Court's role in the process was not clear and because that issue would be clarified in a state court proceeding the Virginia Attorney General had commenced charging the title insurer with unauthorized practice. The court directed the district court to "withhold further action until final decision by the Supreme Court of Virginia in the case filed by the Attorney General of Virginia * * *, unless the Attorney General is responsible for unreasonable delay in such decision."[9]

(3) *Drafting of professional codes.* In June 1976, the Justice Department's Antitrust Division filed a civil complaint charging the ABA with a combination and conspiracy in unreasonable restraint of trade in adopting, publishing, and distributing "a Code of Professional Responsibility containing provisions prohibiting lawyers from engaging in price advertising and other advertising about the availability and

7. Justice Stevens, joined by Justices White and Blackman, dissented.

Justices Rehnquist and O'Connor took no part.

8. 431 F.Supp. 298 (E.D.Va.1977), vacated 571 F.2d 205 (4th Cir.), cert. denied 436 U.S. 941, 98 S.Ct. 2838, 56 L.Ed.2d 781 (1978).

9. In July 1978, the Virginia Supreme Court amended its rules to allow the governor and state legislators as well as lawyers to request an unauthorized practice opinion, to provide an opportunity for any interested persons to submit comments to be considered before the bar recommends the opinion, to require the attorney general to file an analysis of the economic effect on competition of any restraint the opinion may cause, and to have the opinion take effect only when approved by the Virginia Supreme Court as a rule of court. Rules of Court, 219 Va. 367 (1978). See Little & Rush, Resolving the Conflict Between Professional Ethics Opinions and Antitrust Laws, 15 Ga.L.Rev. 341 (1981); New UPL Process Set to Begin in Virginia, 65 A.B.A.J. 542 (1979).

See generally, Note, The Antitrust Liability of Professional Associations after Goldfarb: Reformulating the Learned Professions Exemptions in the Lower Courts, 1977 DukeL.J. 1047.

cost of legal services" which ABA members obeyed and which the ABA and its members policed.[10]

The ABA responded that the ABA itself "has no power to restrain advertising [but] merely promulgates a model code of professional conduct for consideration by the state bodies regulating the practice of law,"[11] and that its actions "in recommending a model Code of Professional Responsibility * * * for adoption by courts and governmental agencies are protected by the First Amendment to the United States Constitution, and to enjoin or otherwise interfere with such actions would unconstitutionally deprive the ABA and its members of their rights to freedom of speech, press, assembly, and association as well as their right to petition the Government."[12]

In August 1978 the Justice Department secured a voluntary dismissal without prejudice, reasoning that since the Supreme Court had now found constitutional protection for lawyer advertising, the ABA had revised and liberalized its Code and terminated certain practices, and all states now permitted lawyer advertising under a variety of approaches, the interests of the parties and the public would not be served by continuing the lawsuit.[13]

(4) *Accrediting paralegal schools.* In Paralegal Institute, Inc. v. ABA,[14] a federal district court found no Sherman Act violation in the ABA's program for accrediting paralegal schools. The program involved inspection by an evaluation team comprising an ABA committee member, a director from a non-competing paralegal training program, and a practicing paralegal, followed by ABA committee review of the inspection team's report and ABA committee recommendation to the

10. Justice Department Charges Code Advertising Provisions Violate Federal Antitrust Laws, 62 A.B.A.J. 979 (1976). The ABA membership application form used to include a provision whereby the applicant agreed to abide by the ABA Code of Professional Responsibility, but it has been stated that "steps were taken to remove the statement before the Antitrust Division's lawsuit was filed, and even at the time it was removed it was of no practical consequence." White, Why Did the Antitrust Division Dismiss the Case? 64 A.B.A.J. 1667, 1670 (1978). See ABA Informal Opinion 1420, 64 A.B.A.J. 1173 (1978). The application form was actually changed half a year after the suit was commenced. Compare 63 A.B.A.J. 111 (Jan.1977) with 63 A.B.A.J. 239 (Feb.1977).

11. Press Statement of President Walsh, 62 A.B.A.J. 981 (1976). The ABA subsequently started referring to its code as the "Model" Code of Professional Responsibility. Compare ABA Formal Opinion 343 (December 23, 1977) and ABA Informal Opinion 1429 (Sept. 12, 1978) with ABA Informal Opinion 1430 (Jan. 8, 1979) and ABA Formal Opinion 345 (July 12, 1979).

12. Association Files Answer in Civil Antitrust Suit Brought by the United States, 62 A.B.A.J. 1179 (1976). See United Mine Workers v. Pennington, 381 U. S. 657, 85 S.Ct. 1585, 14 L.Ed.2d 626 (1965); Eastern Railroad Presidents Conference v. Noerr Motor Freight, Inc., 365 U.S. 127, 81 S.Ct. 523, 5 L.Ed.2d 464 (1961).

13. Justice Department Dismisses Antitrust Suit against American Bar Association, 64 A.B.A.J. 1538 (1978).

Compare American Medical Association v. FTC, 638 F.2d 443 (2d Cir. 1980), affirmed by equally divided court 455 U.S. 676, 102 S.Ct. 1744, 71 L.Ed.2d 546 (1982) (Blackmun, J., not participating) (FTC properly required AMA to cease and desist from promulgating, implementing and enforcing restraints on, *inter alia*, advertising and solicitation other than false or deceptive practices or "uninvited, in-person solicitation of actual or potential patients who, because of their particular circumstances, are vulnerable to undue influence").

14. 475 F.Supp. 1123 (E.D.N.Y.1979), affirmed mem. 622 F.2d 575 (2d Cir. 1980).

ABA House of Delegates for final action. ABA approval was not legally required, but could be advertised in recruiting students. The court found no group boycott in that there was no evidence of a concerted refusal to deal with non-accredited schools; indeed the ABA corresponded with them and invited them to conferences on paralegal education. The program passed muster under the "rule of reason" as it used reasonable minimum standards, did not favor certain schools over others, did not prevent any schools from operating, and actually stimulated rather than retarded development of paralegal programs.

## 2. KIND AND AMOUNT OF FEE

### MODEL RULES OF PROFESSIONAL CONDUCT

**RULE 1.5 Fees**

(a) A lawyer's fee shall be reasonable. The factors to be considered in determining the reasonableness of a fee include the following:

(1) the time and labor required, the novelty and difficulty of the questions involved, and the skill requisite to perform the legal service properly;

(2) the likelihood, if apparent to the client, that the acceptance of the particular employment will preclude other employment by the lawyer;

(3) the fee customarily charged in the locality for similar legal services;

(4) the amount involved and the results obtained;

(5) the time limitations imposed by the client or by the circumstances;

(6) the nature and length of the professional relationship with the client;

(7) the experience, reputation, and ability of the lawyer or lawyers performing the services; and

(8) whether the fee is fixed or contingent.

(b) When the lawyer has not regularly represented the client, the basis or rate of the fee shall be communicated to the client, preferably in writing, before or within a reasonable time after commencing the representation.

(c) A fee may be contingent on the outcome of the matter for which the service is rendered, except in a matter in which a contingent fee is prohibited by paragraph (d) or other law. A contingent fee agreement shall be in writing and shall state the method by which the fee is to be determined, including the percentage or percentages that shall accrue to the lawyer in the event of settlement, trial or appeal, litigation and other expenses to be deducted from the recovery, and whether such expenses are to be deducted before or after the contingent fee is calculated. Upon conclusion of a contingent fee matter, the lawyer shall provide the client with a written statement stating the outcome of the matter and, if there is a recovery, showing the remittance to the client and the method of its determination.

(d) A lawyer shall not enter into an arrangement for, charge, or collect:

(1) any fee in a domestic relations matter, the payment or amount of which is contingent upon the securing of a divorce or upon the amount of alimony or support, or property settlement in lieu thereof; or

(2) a contingent fee for representing a defendant in a criminal case.

* * *

### RULE 1.8 Conflict of Interest: Prohibited Transactions

* * *

(j) A lawyer shall not acquire a proprietary interest in the cause of action or subject matter of litigation the lawyer is conducting for a client, except that the lawyer may:

* * *

(2) contract with a client for a reasonable contingent fee in a civil case.[a]

**a.** Compare the following CPR provisions:

"**EC 2–19** As soon as feasible after a lawyer has been employed, it is desirable that he reach a clear agreement with his client as to the basis of the fee charges to be made. Such a course will not only prevent later misunderstanding but will also work for good relations between the lawyer and the client. It is usually beneficial to reduce to writing the understanding of the parties regarding the fee, particularly when it is contingent. A lawyer should be mindful that many persons who desire to employ him may have had little or no experience with fee charges of lawyers, and for this reason he should explain fully to such persons the reasons for the particular fee arrangement he proposes.

"**EC 2–20** Contingent fee arrangements in civil cases have long been commonly accepted in the United States in proceedings to enforce claims. The historical bases of their acceptance are that (1) they often, and in a variety of circumstances, provide the only practical means by which one having a claim against another can economically afford, finance, and obtain the services of a competent lawyer to prosecute his claim, and (2) a successful prosecution of the claim produces a *res* out of which the fee can be paid. Although a lawyer generally should decline to accept employment on a contingent fee basis by one who is able to pay a reasonable fixed fee, it is not necessarily improper for a lawyer, where justified by the particular circumstances of a case, to enter into a contingent fee contract in a civil case with any client who, after being fully informed of all relevant factors, desires that arrangement. Because of the human relationships involved and the unique character of the proceedings, contingent fee arrangements in domestic relation cases are rarely justified. In administrative agency proceedings contingent fee contracts should be governed by the same consideration as in other civil cases. Public policy properly condemns contingent fee arrangements in criminal cases, largely on the ground that legal services in criminal cases do not produce a *res* with which to pay the fee."

"**DR 2–106 Fees for Legal Services**

"(A) A lawyer shall not enter into an agreement for, charge, or collect an illegal or clearly excessive fee.

"(B) A fee is clearly excessive when, after a review of the facts, a lawyer of ordinary prudence would be left with a definite and firm conviction that the fee is in excess of a reasonable fee. Factors to be considered as guides in determining the reasonableness of a fee include the following:

"(1) The time and labor required, the novelty and difficulty of the questions involved, and the skill requisite to perform the legal service properly.

"(2) The likelihood, if apparent to the client, that the acceptance of the particular employment will preclude other employment by the lawyer.

"(3) The fee customarily charged in the locality for similar legal services.

"(4) The amount involved and the results obtained.

## FLORIDA BAR v. MORIBER

314 So.2d 145 (Fla.1975).

PER CURIAM. [T]he respondent entered into a written employment agreement with one Theodore Pietz, whose mother had recently died. Under the terms of the agreement, the respondent was to collect all moneys due to Pietz as a result of his mother's death. In return, the respondent was to be paid a contingent fee of 33⅓% of the gross recovery if the matter were settled without suit and 40% of this sum if suit were filed. The respondent had knowledge there was approximately $20,000.00 of assets due the client from a mutual trust fund in which the client was the sole named beneficiary. By his own admission, the respondent believed that there was no will or estate to be probated.

The respondent proceeded to process for collection a $23,126.10 certificate issued by the mutual fund. He also collected $444.00 from Blue Cross, $255.00 from Social Security, and $124.31 from a savings and loan association account. In total, the respondent collected funds in the amount of $23,949.41 without the necessity of instituting suit and without objection by any other parties regarding the payment of these funds to Mr. Pietz. Respondent calculated the amount due him for his legal work on Mr. Pietz' behalf to be $7,983.14 [and] advised * * * that he would send Mr. Pietz $13,468.05 upon request, provided Mr. Pietz would first execute a general release in favor of the

"(5) The time limitations imposed by the client or by the circumstances.

"(6) The nature and length of the professional relationship with the client.

"(7) The experience, reputation, and ability of the lawyer or lawyers performing the services.

"(8) Whether the fee is fixed or contingent.

"(C) A lawyer shall not enter into an arrangement for, charge, or collect a contingent fee for representing a defendant in a criminal case."

"**EC 5–7** The possibility of an adverse effect upon the exercise of free judgment by a lawyer on behalf of his client during litigation generally makes it undesirable for the lawyer to acquire a proprietary interest in the cause of his client or otherwise to become financially interested in the outcome of the litigation. * * * Although a contingent fee arrangement gives a lawyer a financial interest in the outcome of litigation, a reasonable contingent fee is permissible in civil cases because it may be the only means by which a layman can obtain the services of a lawyer of his choice. But a lawyer, because he is in a better position to evaluate a cause of action, should enter into a contingent fee arrangement only in those instances where the arrangement will be beneficial to the client."

* * *

"**DR 5–103 Avoiding Acquisition of Interest in Litigation**

"(A) A lawyer shall not acquire a proprietary interest in the cause of action or subject matter of litigation he is conducting for a client, except that he may: * * *

"(2) Contract with a client for a reasonable contingent fee in a civil case."

See Kizer v. Davis, 174 Ind.App. 559, 369 N.E.2d 439 (1977) (EC 2–23, stating that lawyer "should not sue a client unless necessary to prevent fraud or gross imposition by the client," is aspirational only and is not legal bar to suit); Annot., 91 A.L.R.3d 583 (1979) (discipline for using extortionate, fraudulent or otherwise improper means to collect fees).

See also former Canon 12, which concluded, "In fixing fees it should never be forgotten that the profession is a branch of the administration of justice and not a mere money-getting trade."

respondent. [T]he respondent persisted in this requirement long after he had been advised that Mr. Pietz was contesting the matter of the fee.

The Bar filed its complaint against the respondent alleging that the above fee was "clearly excessive" and therefore violative of Disciplinary Rule 2–106 of the Code of Professional Responsibility. * * * The respondent admitted that he had entered into the employment agreement but contended that it was thoroughly discussed and explained to the client prior to execution; that respondent had advised the client that he need not employ respondent if he did not so desire; and that the client had executed the agreement and employed the respondent with knowledge of these facts. The respondent also alleged that he had flown from Miami to the client's place of employment in Newark, New Jersey, where he presented the closing statement to the client. The client allegedly accepted this statement and approved all disbursements, including the attorney's fee. * * *

Few, if any, areas of attorney discipline are as subject to differing interpretations as the matter of what constitutes an excessive attorney's fee. The answer turns upon multiple factors including the difficulty of the case; the contingencies, if any, upon which the fee is based; the novelty of the legal issues presented; the experience of the attorney; the quality of his work product; and the amount of time spent in preparation and litigation. See DR 2–106(B).

Examining the factors pertinent to the respondent in this case, it is clear that the case was not difficult, a fact of which the respondent was well aware. It frankly could have easily been performed by a layman since the major asset of over $23,000.00 in an investors' variable payment fund passed to the client by operation of law. This was not a novel legal issue requiring specialized legal knowledge or experience. The respondent devoted relatively little time thereto. The record reflects that he wrote approximately seven letters, completed a few forms, and made some telephone calls on behalf of his client, all this in little more than a month. He also undertook a one-day trip to New York for his client * * *.

The respondent contends that excessiveness cannot be charged absent a showing of fraud or dishonesty. This argument is answered by Rule 11.02(4) of the Integration Rule of The Florida Bar, which provides:

> "* * * Controversies as to the amount of fees are not grounds for disciplinary proceedings unless the amount demanded is *clearly excessive,* extortionate *or* the demand is fraudulent." [Emphasis supplied] [a]

a. Under former Canon 12, which said, "In fixing fees, lawyers should avoid charges which overestimate their advice and services * * *," courts generally did not view the charging of an excessive fee as sufficient, standing alone, to warrant discipline, unless it was so clearly excessive under the circumstances that it could not have been charged in good faith. See Annot., 70 A.L.R.2d 962, 964 (1960), superseded by Annot., 11 A.L.R.4th 133 (1982).

Respondent attaches considerable significance to the fact that his client asked him to keep the case in the strictest of confidence. We fail to see the relationship between the degree of secrecy requested (strict confidence being required in every attorney-client relationship) and the size of the fee. * * *

Finally, the respondent relies on the fact that he fully informed the client of the contingency fee arrangement and subsequently discussed all details of the disbursement with him. The client was a night clerk who worked in a New York motel. Presumably, he was not aware of the fees typically charged by attorneys to represent an estate. In any event, even if we presume that the client were an educated and experienced party dealing at arm's length with the respondent, it is our view that an attorney may still be disciplined for overreaching where the fees charged are grossly disproportionate to the services rendered. The arguments presented by the respondent are without merit.

We hold that the total fee of $7,983.14 charged the client in this case was not merely excessive, but was so "clearly excessive" as to constitute a violation of DR 2–106 and to warrant the imposition of appropriate disciplinary measures.

The Referee's initial recommendation was that the respondent be disciplined by this Court only if he failed to reimburse the client the difference between $2,500.00 plus expenses and the $7,983.14 actually charged the client. This was a lenient disciplinary measure.

Notwithstanding the reasonableness of the Referee's recommendations, the respondent to date has not reimbursed the client one penny of the $7,983.14 fee charged and has ignored two supplemental reports of the Referee. The sole mitigating circumstance we find in the record of this case is the absence of any prior disciplinary proceedings against the respondent.

The final recommendation contained in the Referee's second supplemental report was that the respondent be suspended from the practice of law for forty-five days. Apparently, the prospect of such punishment has failed to shake the respondent's patent disregard for applicable rules of professional ethics as well as his own promise given under oath to reimburse his client.

We find, therefore, that if the Referee's final recommendation of discipline erred at all, it was on the side of leniency. * * *

Accordingly, it is ordered that the respondent be suspended from the practice of law for a period of forty-five (45) days effective [July 1], 1975, thereby giving respondent an opportunity to close out his practice and take the necessary steps to protect his clients, and it is further

Ordered that the suspension continue thereafter until he shall pay the following sums to Theodore Pietz and to The Florida Bar respectively: (1) $7,983.14 less a reasonable fee of $2,500.00 and costs incurred by the respondent in processing collection of the client's funds; and (2) $445.35 for costs of these proceedings. * * *[b]

### *Comment*

(1) *Excessive fees.* One commentator has concluded that "for every case in which a one-third fee is justified, there are dozens where that amount is excessive by any standard of reasonableness."[1]

(2) *Refusal to enforce fee.* A Colorado court refused to enforce a one-third contingent fee for collecting life insurance proceeds where the dispute was caused by confusion concerning the date of decedent's enlistment in the military and "little skill or effort was required to obtain the correct information."[2] The court said that far from sounding the death knell of the contingent fee arrangement, "curtailing abuses thereof * * * will serve to answer critics and will help assure its continued use in proper cases to the benefit of litigants, the bar, and the ends of justice."[3]

(3) *Fee arbitration.* The New Jersey Supreme Court has upheld the constitutionality of a court rule that requires a lawyer, upon client request, to submit a fee dispute to and be bound by the decision of a fee arbitration committee.[4]

(4) *Sua sponte reduction.* Although courts recognize their power to reduce agreed-upon fees in class actions[5] and in cases brought in behalf of minors,[6] they are not unanimous on whether absent client request courts may reduce excessive but agreed-upon fees in other

**b.** Boyd, J., dissented.

See Westchester County Bar Association v. St. John, 43 A.D.2d 218, 350 N.Y.S.2d 737 (1974) (one-year suspension for charging one-third fee for approximately 20 hours of work in prosecuting claim for accidental death under $100,000 insurance policy).

Cf. In re Kutner, 78 Ill.2d 157, 35 Ill.Dec. 674, 399 N.E.2d 963, 11 A.L.R.4th 123 (1979) (censure for charging $5,000 fixed fee for representation in routine battery prosecution that was dismissed before trial and that involved no more than ten hours of work); In re Marine, 82 Wis.2d 602, 264 N.W.2d 285 (1978) (discipline for charging $5,000 for divorce representation involving 54 hours of work); Annot., 11 A.L.R.4th 133 (1982).

**1.** Grady, Some Ethical Questions About Percentage Fees, 2 Litigation 20, 26 (Summer 1976).

**2.** Anderson v. Kenelly, 37 Colo.App. 217, 547 P.2d 260 (1975).

**3.** For further detail on judicial refusal to enforce excessive contingent fees, see infra Comment (4) and Question (1).

**4.** In re LiVolsi, 85 N.J. 576, 428 A.2d 1268, 17 A.L.R.4th 972 (1981). Cf. Hargarten & Ardisson, Fine Tuning California's Mandatory Attorney Fee Arbitration Statute, 16 U.S.F.L.Rev. 411 (1982); Attorney-Client Arbitration Committee Report, 28 Bench & B. of Minn. 8 (May–June 1972) (voluntary arbitration boards of one lawyer and two non-lawyers).

**5.** See Dunn v. Porter, 602 F.2d 1105 (3d Cir. 1979); Prandini v. National Tea Co., 557 F.2d 1015 (3d Cir. 1977); Kiser v. Miller, 364 F.Supp. 1311 (D.D.C. 1973), affirmed in part and remanded in part on other grounds sub nom. Pete v. UMW Welfare Retirement Fund, 517 F.2d 1275 (D.C.Cir. 1975) (en banc); 1979 Det.C.L.Rev. 765.

**6.** See Rosquist v. Soo Line Railroad, 692 F.2d 1107 (7th Cir. 1982) (fee reduced from ⅓—$813.57 per hour—to $350 per hour); Hoffert v. General Motors Corp., 656 F.2d 161 (5th Cir. 1981) (fee reduced to 20%), cert. denied 456 U.S. 961, 102 S.Ct. 2037, 72 L.Ed.2d 485 (1982); Knupp v. Schmelzer, 87 Misc.2d 641, 386 N.Y.S.2d 339 (1976) (fee reduced to 25%).

cases. Several decisions hold that they may,[7] but in the 1983 Seventh Circuit case of United States v. Vague,[8] a 2–1 court held that a trial court should not reduce an excessive fee to which the client does not object, but rather should report the lawyer's overcharging to the appropriate disciplinary authority.

(5) *Denial for outrageous request.* In certain circumstances, a prevailing litigant's attorney fees may be recoverable from another party.[9] But in the 1980 case of Brown v. Stackler,[10] the Seventh Circuit upheld a district court's refusal to award any attorney fees to a prevailing civil rights plaintiff on the ground that the plaintiff had requested an "outrageously unreasonable" fee. The court pointed out that although 42 U.S.C. § 1988 specifies that the court "may" award reasonable attorney fees to the prevailing party in a civil rights case, "denial is an entirely appropriate, and hopefully effective, means of encouraging counsel to maintain adequate records and submit reasonable, carefully calculated, and conscientiously measured claims when seeking statutory counsel fees."

(6) *Structured settlements.* The Minnesota Supreme Court has ruled that where a fee agreement specified a fee of "one third (⅓) of the total amount recovered," and a "structured settlement" was concluded giving the client $45,000 "front money" plus periodic payments totalling $110,800 over ten years, the lawyer could recover only $15,000 and ⅓ of each periodic payment as it was made; the court rejected the lawyer's claim to ⅓ of the total recovery's discounted value ($39,054.33) out of the $45,000 front money.[11] The court reasoned that absent "an explicit agreement with the client governing the time and manner of payment of [the] fees," the word "recovered" in the fee agreement must be construed to mean "received" in view of EC 2–19's stating that a lawyer should "reach a clear agreement with [the] client as to the basis of the fee charges to be made."

### *Questions*

(1) As a lawyer, what contingent fee would you seek for representing a personal injury plaintiff whom the defendant refused to offer

7. See Allen v. United States, 606 F.2d 432 (4th Cir. 1979); Coffelt v. Shell, 577 F.2d 30 (8th Cir. 1978). Cf. Krause v. Rhodes, 640 F.2d 214 (6th Cir.) (court limited attorney fees and expenses to $75,000 out of $675,000 settlement in line with condition in settlement offer) cert. denied 454 U.S. 836, 102 S.Ct. 140, 70 L.Ed.2d 117 (1981); Note, Judicial Power Over Contingent Fee Contracts: Reasonableness and Ethics, 30 Case W.Res.L.Rev. 523 (1980).

8. 697 F.2d 805 (7th Cir. 1983).

9. Alyeska Pipeline Service Co. v. Wilderness Society, 421 U.S. 240, 95 S.Ct. 1612, 44 L.Ed.2d 141 (1975) (where (a) provided by statute or enforceable contract, (b) litigant is trustee or party preserving or recovering fund for benefit of others and seeks to recover attorney fees from the fund, property or other parties enjoying the benefit, (c) court assesses attorney fees as part of fine levied on adversary for willful disobedience of court order, or (d) adversary has acted in bad faith, vexatiously, wantonly, or for oppressive reasons).

10. 612 F.2d 1057 (7th Cir. 1980).

11. Cardenas v. Ramsey County, 322 N.W.2d 191 (Minn. 1982).

anything where it appears (a) plaintiff's recovery, if plaintiff prevails, will be about $12,000, (b) plaintiff has about a two-thirds chance of prevailing, and (c) you will put in time for which you would charge $2,000 if you were doing the case on a time basis? Would you accept all of this fee if the case resulted in a $20,000 verdict? If it resulted in a $12,000 settlement after you have put only four hours into the case? [12]

(2) Would a flat-amount contingent fee rather than a percentage contingent fee sometimes be appropriate? [13] If a percentage fee is used, should a higher percentage apply to the first so many dollars than the next so many? [14] Should a lower percentage apply if the case is settled, a higher if it goes to trial, and a still higher if it is appealed? [15] (Note that under the latter scheme, "One small step for the lawyer means one giant leap for his fee." [16]) Should the percentage(s) apply only to the amount by which the recovery exceeds what the client could have obtained before retaining counsel?

(3) Are RPC 1.5 and DR 2–106[17] sufficiently restrictive as to situations in which contingent fees may be used? One commentator has summarized the criticisms and justifications of the contingent fee system as follows:

"Among the more frequently expressed [criticisms by detractors of the contingent fee system] are the following:

"(1) The contingent fee stirs up litigation for it encourages nuisance claims.

12. Compare Dombey, Tyler, Richards & Grieser v. Detroit Toledo & Ironton Railway, 351 F.2d 121 (6th Cir. 1965) (upholding 25% recovery where lawyer interviewed client, opened file, and made one or two phone calls before $50,000 settlement) with McInerney v. Massasoit Greyhound Association, 359 Mass. 339, 269 N.E.2d 211 (1971) (refusing to enforce one-third fee agreement as "excessive and unreasonable as a matter of law" and in violation of DR 2–106, court rejected "notion that * * * permits a complete dichotomy between a fee which is reasonable in the light of hindsight and one which is permissible at the outset").

See Note, Contingent Fee Contracts: Validity, Controls and Enforceability, 47 Iowa L.Rev. 942, 950–51 (1962) (courts ruling on enforceability of contingent fee agreements are not agreed on whether reasonableness should be determined as of time contract was made or after services are performed); Note, The Contingent Fee: Disciplinary Rule, Ethical Consideration, or Free Competition? 1979 Utah L.Rev. 547, 559 (Code *should* require lawyer, before entering contingent fee agreement, to inform client of amount of time lawyer expects to spend on case, expected recovery, degree of risk, and fixed fee lawyer would charge; after recovery lawyer should voluntarily reduce fee rather than accept unexpected windfall).

See generally Grady, Some Ethical Questions About Percentage Fees, 2 Litigation 20 (Summer 1976).

13. See Note, 47 Iowa L.Rev. 942, 947 & n. 25 (1962); Note, 1979 Utah L.Rev. 547, 560. Compare Magids v. Dorman, 430 S.W.2d 910 (Tex.Civ.App.1968) (lawyer not on contingent fee representing client whose $14,000 claim resulted in a $500 recovery held entitled to $1500 fee).

14. See Note, 47 Iowa L.Rev. 942, 947 (1962).

In Foshee v. Lloyds, New York, 643 F.2d 1162 (5th Cir. 1981), the court upheld an agreement to pay two lawyers 100% of the first $50,000, 50% of the next $100,000, and 20% of anything over $150,000, in addition to paying a third lawyer 10% of anything over $50,000, which yielded $95,000 fees out of a $125,000 verdict. The court emphasized that the fee was solely the idea of the client, who had expected his recovery to be about $1,000,000 or nothing.

15. See Note, 47 Iowa L.Rev. 942, 948 (1962).

16. Clermont & Currivan, Improving on the Contingent Fee, 63 Cornell L.Rev. 529, 595 (1978).

17. Compare EC 2–20, 5–7.

"(2) The attorney becomes a partner and not a counsellor and thus is less able to render impartial advice. He is tempted to reach for success in the litigation at all costs. Perhaps this criticism purports to be an aspect of the idea that a man who serves as his own lawyer has a fool for a client.

"(3) This method of compensation leads to overreaching in fee setting for payment of the contingent fee does not seem a problem to the client when the contract is made.

"(4) It leads the attorney to try to settle the case quickly, whether or not this is to the advantage of the client, when it will maximize the lawyer's average hourly compensation for the work he does.

"(5) It equates successful outcome of litigation with the successful practice of law.

"(6) Setting a percentage of the recovery as a fee makes it appear to the client that there is no relation between the fees charged and the services rendered.

"After attempting to rebut these objections supporters of the system point out:

"(1) It allows all people with a meritorious claim to pursue their claim with competent legal assistance.

"(2) It encourages accident victims to seek legal advice early and thus be fully aware of their rights. As well, early retention of a lawyer will increase the plaintiff's chances for a just settlement for the attorney immediately begins to gather facts about the controversy—a task which is much harder to do well as the interval between the occurrence and the investigation lengthens.

"(3) This notion that lawyers are not in some respects businessmen is nonsense and payment by commission is legitimate.

"(4) Most of the criticisms levelled at the contingent fee are not of things inherent in the system; e.g., excessive fees are but a function of the percentage charged." [18]

(4) In an article in the Cornell Law Review, Clermont and Currivan make a good case for using a hybrid "contingent hourly-percentage" fee.[19] This fee is payable only in the event of recovery and is computed by adding (a) the lawyer's time charge for the hours worked and (b) a small percentage (possibly 5% or 10%) of the amount by which the recovery exceeds the time charge. Clermont and Currivan show that this kind of fee neutralizes the economic conflict of interest inhering in the straight hourly fee (where the lawyer is tempted to maximize the number of hours) and the straight percentage fee (where the lawyer is tempted to accept an early settlement or otherwise minimize the number of hours expended), and that it measures the value of legal services more accurately than a pure hourly or percentage fee. In the situation specified in Question (1) above, would it be appropriate

18. Youngwood, The Contingent Fee—Reasonable Alternative? 28 Mod.L.Rev. 330, 333 (1965).

19. Clermont & Currivan, Improving on the Contingent Fee, 63 Cornell L.Rev. 529 (1978).

to use a contingent fee of (a) $50 per hour plus (b) 10% of the amount by which the proceeds exceed (a)? Would this produce a reasonable fee in the event of a $12,000 verdict after 40 hours of work on the case? A $20,000 verdict after 40 hours of work on the case? A $12,000 settlement after four hours of work on the case?

(5) If it does not produce an excessive fee, may a lawyer properly agree to defend a well-to-do person against a damage claim for a fee of one-third of the *difference* between what his adversary claims and what he ends up having to pay?

Not if the claim is *unliquidated*, according to the Iowa Supreme Court. In the 1980 case of Wunschel Law Firm, P.C. v. Clabaugh,[20] the lawyer informed the client that the fee to defend against a defamation suit would be $50 per hour. Upon being asked if an alternative arrangement were possible, the lawyer said the client could be charged one-third of the amount saved under the $17,500 prayer in the defamation complaint. Although the lawyer advised that it may cost more than the hourly fee, the client agreed to the contingent arrangement. The defamation verdict was $1,750, and the lawyer (upon suing the client) was awarded $5,250, one-third of the difference between $17,500 and $1,750.

The Iowa Supreme Court reversed, holding that a defense contingent fee agreement for a percentage of the difference between a complaint's *unliquidated* damage claim and the amount awarded is void as against public policy. Distinguishing the case from decisions upholding contingent fees for defending against *liquidated* claims, the court pointed out that (a) complaints' unliquidated damage claims, often made hastily and with little reflection, may bear no logical relationship to the amount ultimately awarded, (b) the defendant-client may not appreciate this, and (c) it is hard to believe that a truly knowledgeable defendant-client would agree to a fee measured by the difference between an unliquidated claim and the ultimate award. The court concluded:

> "[A] contingent fee contract is unreasonable when it provides for determination of the fee by factors having no logical relationship to the value of the services. * * *
>
> " * * * We do not decide whether the fee charged in the present case is reasonable or not. We simply hold that contracts of this type are likely to result in unreasonable fees in too many cases and thus are contrary to sound public policy."

The court remanded the case for determination of the fee on a quantum meruit (reasonable value) basis.[21]

20. 291 N.W.2d 331, 9 A.L.R.4th 181 (Iowa 1980).

21. In fixing a "reasonable fee," courts look to factors like those in RPC 1.5(a) and DR 2–106(B). See Hensley v. Eckerhart, — U.S. —, 103 S.Ct. 1933, 76 L.Ed.2d 40 (1983); Annot., 57 A.L.R.3d 475 (1974). Cf. Berger, Court Awarded Attorneys' Fees: What is "Reasonable"? 126 U.Pa.L.Rev. 281 (1977) (court should award hours justifiably expended times market hourly rate times factor reflecting risk of nonrecovery); Leubsdorf, The Contingency Factor in Attorney Fee

A commentator has asserted that *Wunschel* should not be viewed as hostile to all types of defense contingent fee contracts and that those containing nonspeculative provisions should be allowed.[22] Another commentator urges adaptation of contingent fees to the defense of cases on the ground that this would reduce expense, paper and delay by making defense lawyers result-oriented rather than time-oriented.[23]

(6) Where a fee agreement is made after the lawyer has commenced representing the client and the lawyer sues for the fee or the client sues for its return, most courts treat the agreement as presumptively unfair or invalid and put the burden on the lawyer to prove its fairness.[24] Thus the court in a New York case refused to enforce the agreement and limited the lawyer to a quantum meruit recovery on the ground that "when an agreement is consummated after the relationship has been established, and trust and confidence have been reposed in the attorney by the client * * * the burden of proving that the arrangement for compensation was fair and reasonable and fully comprehended by the client rests with the attorney." [25] Does this mean that in a *disciplinary proceeding* a lawyer will have the burden of proving that a fee was reasonable under RPC 1.5(a) or was not clearly excessive under DR 2–106(A) if the agreement for it was made after the lawyer commenced the client's representation? Does it indicate that a lawyer would be wise to make the fee agreement *before* commencing the representation, rather than within a reasonable time after commencing it, as permitted by RPC 1.5(b) and EC 2–19?

Awards, 90 Yale L.J. 473 (1981) (factor reflecting risk of nonrecovery should be standardized rather than calculated separately in each case).

22. Comment, Toward a Valid Defense Contingent Contract: A Comparative Analysis, 67 Iowa L.Rev. 373 (1982). Cf. Annot., 9 A.L.R.4th 191 (1981).

23. Kreindler, The Contingent Fee: Whose Interests Are Actually Being Served? 14 Forum 406 (1979).

24. Annot., 13 A.L.R.3d 701, 731–34 (1967). Some courts say this is so only if the client, by pleading or otherwise, raises the question of the agreement's validity. Id. at 735. Others say it is so only if the client presents some evidence of undue influence, overreaching, or other inequitable conduct by the lawyer. Id. at 735–36. A few courts refuse to put the burden of proof on the lawyer. Id. at 737; see Kittler and Hedelson v. Sheehan Properties, Inc., 295 Minn. 232, 203 N.W.2d 835 (1973) (while "agreements made after services have been rendered should be closely scrutinized to see that there has been no overreaching and that the client was fully informed," lawyer does not have burden of proving contract was fair and reasonable). See generally 1 S. Speiser, Attorneys' Fees § § 1:25–:34 (1973).

Fee agreements made *before* accepting a matter are generally treated as arms-length transactions. See Setzer v. Robinson, 57 Cal.2d 213, 18 Cal.Rptr. 524, 368 P.2d 124 (1962) ("The presumption of 'insufficient consideration' and 'undue influence' * * * is not applicable to a contract by which the relation of attorney and client is originally created"; here lawyer "did not agree or undertake to act as * * * attorney until the agreement for a fee had been arrived at between them"); Kent v. Fishblate, 247 Pa. 361, 93 A. 509 (1915); Note, 47 Iowa L.Rev. 942, 946 (1962).

Compare Note, 1979 Utah L.Rev. 547, 555 (better view would be to apply fiduciary principles without regard to when agreement was made—"It is doubtful that the client is in any better position to negotiate the few minutes before a lawyer-client relationship exists than after.").

25. In re Schanzer's Estate, 7 A.D.2d 275, 182 N.Y.S.2d 475 (1959), affirmed mem. 8 N.Y.2d 972, 204 N.Y.S.2d 349, 169 N.E.2d 11 (1960).

(7) Should ability to pay be a factor in setting a fee?[26] Former Canon 12 stated in part, "A client's ability to pay cannot justify a charge in excess of the value of the service, though his poverty may require a less charge, or even none at all."

## AMERICAN TRIAL LAWYERS ASSOCIATION v. NEW JERSEY SUPREME COURT

126 N.J.Super. 577, 316 A.2d 19, affirmed 66 N.J. 258, 330 A.2d 350 (1974).

KOLOVSKY, P.J.A.D. On December 21, 1971 the New Jersey Supreme Court adopted a rule, to be effective January 31, 1972, regulating "contingent fee arrangements" in tort litigation. R. 1:21–7. Plaintiffs * * * instituted an action * * * challenging the validity of the rule * * *.

[The trial court held the rule invalid.]

The contingent fee rule, R. 1:21–7, as clarified by a directive issued by the Supreme Court on April 13, 1972, applies to all matters, whether the case is to be litigated in the state or federal courts in New Jersey, in which the client's claim for damages is based upon the alleged tortious conduct of another, including products liability claims. It does not apply when the client is a subrogee. Nor does it "apply to 'business torts' such as fraud or conspiracy to interfere with contractual relationships." It does include "all typical negligence cases, such as auto accidents, product liability and 'slip and fall.' " * * *

Paragraph (b) of the rule provides:

> "An attorney shall not enter into a contingent fee arrangement without first having advised the client of the right and afforded the client an opportunity to retain him under an arrangement whereby he would be compensated on the basis of the reasonable value of his services."

Paragraph (c) provides that in cases to which the rule is applicable

"* * * an attorney shall not contract for, charge, or collect a contingent fee in excess of the following limits:

"(1) 50% on the first $1000 recovered;

"(2) 40% on the next $2000 recovered;

"(3) 33⅓% on the next $47,000 recovered;

"(4) 20% on the next $50,000 recovered;

"(5) 10% on any amount recovered over $100,000; and

"(6) where the amount recovered is for the benefit of an infant or incompetent and the matter is settled without trial the foregoing limits shall apply, except that the fee on any amount recovered up to $50,000 shall not exceed 25%." * * *

26. See 1 S. Speiser, Attorneys' Fees § 8:12 (1973); Annot., 57 A.L.R.3d 475, 522-27 (1974).

Paragraph (d) of the rule provides for computation of the contingent fee on the net sum recovered "after deducting [specified] disbursements in connection with the institution and prosecution of the claim * * *." No deduction need be made for hospital and medical liens or similar items. The paragraph concludes:

> "The permissible fee shall include legal services rendered on any appeal or review proceeding or on any retrial, but this shall not be deemed to require an attorney to take an appeal."

Paragraph (f) deals with the situation where the attorney deems the fee permitted by paragraph (c) to be inadequate and provides:

> "If at the conclusion of a matter an attorney considers the fee permitted by paragraph (c) to be inadequate, an application on written notice to the client may be made to the Assignment Judge for the hearing and determining of a reasonable fee in light of all the circumstances. * * * This rule shall not preclude the exercise of a client's existing right to a court review of the reasonableness of an attorney's fee."

Paragraph (g) requires that the contingent fee agreement be in writing and that a signed duplicate thereof be delivered to the client. Pursuant to an administrative directive, any provision reserving the right to the attorney to proceed for a greater fee under R. 1:21–7(f) must be included in the writing. Upon successful conclusion of the litigation, a signed closing statement, in the form prescribed by the Administrative Director of the Courts, must be delivered to the client.

The rule thus defines the outer limits of permissible contingent fees in tort litigation, at the same time providing, by paragraph (f), a procedure by which attorneys who deem the circumstances of a particular case to reasonably warrant a fee greater than that authorized by the rule, to apply for court approval of the larger fee. * * *

We are convinced that the power * * * vested in the Supreme Court to regulate the practice of the law includes the power to adopt a reasonable rule establishing the outer limits of permissible contingent fees in tort litigation. Gair v. Peck, [6 N.Y.2d 97, 188 N.Y.S.2d 491, 160 N.E.2d 43, 77 A.L.R.2d 390 (1959), cert. denied 361 U.S. 374, 80 S.Ct. 401, 4 L.Ed.2d 380 (1960)]; Schlesinger v. Teitelbaum, [475 F.2d 137 (3d Cir.), cert. denied 414 U.S. 1111, 94 S.Ct. 840, 38 L.Ed.2d 738 (1973)]. [a]

In Gair v. Peck, supra, the New York Court of Appeals upheld the power of the Appellate Division, First Department, in the exercise of "their long standing 'power and control over attorneys and counselors-at-law and all persons practicing or assuming to practice law,' "

**a.** In the latter case, the court upheld a federal district court rule establishing a schedule of contingent fees for use in personal injury actions brought by seamen and providing that any fees in excess of the schedule shall constitute the exaction of unreasonable compensation in violation of the CPR unless a showing is made justifying higher compensation based on unusual circumstances.

to adopt a rule embodying a schedule of reasonable fees relating to "Contingent Fees in Claims and Actions for Personal Injury and Wrongful Death." In doing so, the court said:

> "The rule-making power is not limited to prescribing only the specific case after the event. The idea that imposition by lawyers on their clients, oppressive and unconscionable fee agreements or similar conduct is beyond the rule-making power of the court has no shadow of foundation. The idea is frivolous that disciplinary power over attorneys is unrelated to the exaction of excessive fees. Nor are the Appellate Divisions so helpless as to be denied the power to censure or of taking more incisive disciplinary action to curb the practice of excessive exactions against clients merely for the reason that the client himself has not elected to contest payment of the fee. The duty and function of the Appellate Divisions to keep the house of the law in order does not hinge upon whether clients, worn down by injuries, delay, financial need and counsel holding the purse strings of settlement, knowing little about law or lawyers, have had the stamina to resist in court by hiring other lawyers to be paid out of the other half of the recovery for defending against the first lawyer." * * *

While contingent fees are permitted in New Jersey, they always have been subject to strict supervision by the courts.

Leaving for later consideration the question of the reasonableness of the percentages set out in R. 1:21–7, we are satisfied that the rule is a permissible method of exercising the court's power over fee arrangements between attorneys and their clients by a rule of general application which provides advance notice to the Bar of the maximum fee the court deems to be fair under ordinary circumstances and at the same time provides protection to the client from overreaching more expeditiously than through case by case review of individual fees.

Plaintiffs next contend that even if the Supreme Court has the power to adopt a rule regulating contingent fee arrangements, an evidentiary hearing is a prerequisite to a valid promulgation thereof. * * * The argument is without substance. * * *

No evidentiary hearing and findings of fact based thereon—or indeed even a legislative type hearing such as the Supreme Court did hold on November 6, 1971—was required, any more than, as plaintiffs concede, it would have been required had the subject matter thereof been within the jurisdiction of the Legislature and the substance thereof embodied in a statute enacted by the Legislature.

[T]here is no support in the record for the trial court's determinations that R. 1:21–7(c) is unreasonable and violates a right of freedom of contract protected by the New Jersey Constitution. Attorneys have never had the right to enforce contractual provisions for more than a fair and reasonable fee. They are not businessmen entitled to charge what the traffic will bear. * * *

Plaintiffs next contend that the rule "denies the equal protection of the laws to lawyers and their clients" in violation of the New Jersey and United States Constitutions. They argue that the rule is unconstitutionally discriminatory because (1) "it singles out contingent fees from among the varieties of fee arrangements," (2) "it singles out contingent fees in negligence cases," and (3) it excludes subrogation claims from the control of the rule. * * *

As the cases have recognized, contingent fee arrangements involve unique problems in the attorney-client relationship, including those arising from the establishment by contract of a method for compensation which bears no direct relationship either to the effort expended by the attorney or the actual value of the services. The separate treatment thereof is clearly justified; the classification is not arbitrary; it does not deny the equal protection of the law.

Nor is the classification improper because the rule applies only to negligence claims, the area in which contingent fee arrangements are most commonly used.

The exclusion of subrogation claims from the operation of the rule is an obvious recognition of the fact that the client in the subrogation case is an insurance company whose bargaining strength, unlike that of individual clients, is sufficiently strong to eliminate the possibility of the imposition of excessive fees.

The added suggestion by plaintiffs in their argument that the rule somehow discriminates against the poor is frivolous and unsupported by the record.[b]

Finally, we find no merit to plaintiffs' contention that the rule impairs the obligation of contingent fee contracts made and partly performed prior to January 31, 1972. Apart from the fact that, as noted above, it has long been recognized that attorney's fee arrangements are subject to judicial scrutiny, "every contract is made subject to the implied condition that its fulfillment may be frustrated by a proper exercise of the police power." The stated rule is fully applicable to fee contracts between an attorney and his client.

Moreover, the lack of substance in the contention that the retroactive application of R. 1:21–7 impairs the obligation of contract is underscored by the fact that any attorney who believes that the rule operates unfairly as to him may proceed, under R. 1:21–7(f), to seek court approval of a fee in an amount greater than that permitted by R. 1:21–7(c).

We are satisfied that, on the record here, it is clear that the challenged rule is valid and constitutional. The judgment of the Law Division is reversed.[c]

**b.** In affirming, the New Jersey Supreme Court at footnote 4 of its opinion rejected the contention that because "legal service to the poor is frequently available only through the contingent fee device * * * any limitation thereon [carries] with it an invidious reduction in the scope or delivery of such service."

**c.** Regarding the validity of statutes establishing maximum fee schedules for representing medical malpractice claimants, see Annot., 12 A.L.R.4th 23 (1982).

### *Comment*

Commentators assert that the decreasing scale maximum fee schedule (exemplified in the principal case) does not respond to the contingent fee's poor accuracy in measuring the value of legal services nor the economic conflict of interest tempting the lawyer to settle early, and that, with most cases involving relatively small recoveries, it usually allows a greater amount than the prevailing one-third fee.[1] It also is contended that lawyers may reject meritorious cases rather than bother to seek the court's permission to vary from the schedule, and that the schedule may lead some lawyers to charge more than they otherwise would believing a fee's permissibility under the schedule will insulate it from question.[2]

## 3. DIVIDING FEES

### MODEL RULES OF PROFESSIONAL CONDUCT

**RULE 1.5 Fees**

* * *

(e) A division of fee between lawyers who are not in the same firm may be made only if:

(1) the division is in proportion to the services performed by each lawyer or, by written agreement with the client, each lawyer assumes joint responsibility for the representation;

(2) the client is advised of and does not object to the participation of all the lawyers involved; and

(3) the total fee is reasonable.[a]

### *Question*

Is RPC 1.5(e) sound in rejecting DR 2–107(A)'s requirement that division of fees between lawyers not in the same firm be in proportion to *both* services performed and responsibility assumed? Compare Pro-

1. See Clermont & Currivan, Improving on the Contingent Fee, 63 Cornell L.Rev. 529, 593–94 (1978).

2. See Note, The Contingent Fee: Disciplinary Rule, Ethical Consideration, or Free Competition? 1979 Utah L.Rev. 547, 557–58.

a. Compare the following CPR provision:

**"DR 2–107 Division of Fees Among Lawyers**

"(A) A lawyer shall not divide a fee for legal services with another lawyer who is not a partner in or associate of his law firm or law office, unless:

(1) The client consents to employment of the other lawyer after a full disclosure that a division of fees will be made.

(2) The division is made in proportion to the services performed and responsibility assumed by each.

(3) The total fee of the lawyers does not clearly exceed reasonable compensation for all legal services they rendered the client.

"(B) This Disciplinary Rule does not prohibit payment to a former partner or associate pursuant to a separation or retirement agreement."

Regarding the restrictions on sharing fees with nonlawyers, see RPC 5.4(a); DR 3–102.

fessor Morgan's view that banning referral fees inhibits referrals to lawyers who can better meet clients' needs[1] with Professor Bayles' view that "charging in excess of services rendered cannot be justified; it is simple theft."[2]

## B. WITHDRAWAL AND DISCHARGE

### MODEL RULES OF PROFESSIONAL CONDUCT

**RULE 1.16 Declining or Terminating Representation**

(a) Except as stated in paragraph (c), a lawyer shall not represent a client or, where representation has commenced, shall withdraw from the representation of a client if:

(1) the representation will result in violation of the rules of professional conduct or other law;

(2) the lawyer's physical or mental condition materially impairs the lawyer's ability to represent the client; or

(3) the lawyer is discharged.

(b) Except as stated in paragraph (c), a lawyer may withdraw from representing a client if withdrawal can be accomplished without material adverse effect on the interests of the client, or if:

(1) the client persists in a course of action involving the lawyer's services that the lawyer reasonably believes is criminal or fraudulent;

(2) the client has used the lawyer's services to perpetrate a crime or fraud;

(3) a client insists upon pursuing an objective that the lawyer considers repugnant or imprudent;

(4) the client fails substantially to fulfill an obligation to the lawyer regarding the lawyer's services and has been given reasonable warning that the lawyer will withdraw unless the obligation is fulfilled;

(5) the representation will result in an unreasonable financial burden on the lawyer or has been rendered unreasonably difficult by the client; or

(6) other good cause for withdrawal exists.

(c) When ordered to do so by a tribunal, a lawyer shall continue representation notwithstanding good cause for terminating the representation.

1. Morgan, The Evolving Concept of Professional Responsibility, 90 Harv.L.Rev. 702, 720, 727 (1977). Cf. Moran v. Harris, 131 Cal.App.3d 913, 182 Cal.Rptr. 519 (1982), decided under a California provision allowing division of fees other than in proportion to services performed.

2. M. Bayles, Professional Ethics 35 (1981). See Palmer v. Breyfogle, 217 Kan. 128, 535 P.2d 955 (1975) decided under DR 2–107(A), where the court rejected a lawyer's reliance upon the "customary one-third forwarding fee" and held the lawyer entitled to *no* part of an $87,473 fee for getting the case and having several conversations with the client, as the case proceeded, to keep her happy.

(d) Upon termination of representation, a lawyer shall take steps to the extent reasonably practicable to protect a client's interests, such as giving reasonable notice to the client, allowing time for employment of other counsel, surrendering papers and property to which the client is entitled and refunding any advance payment of fee that has not been earned. The lawyer may retain papers relating to the client to the extent permitted by other law.[a]

**a.** Compare the following CPR provisions:

**"DR 2–110 Withdrawal From Employment**

"(A) In general.

"(1) If permission for withdrawal from employment is required by the rules of a tribunal, a lawyer shall not withdraw from employment in a proceeding before that tribunal without its permission.

"(2) In any event, a lawyer shall not withdraw from employment until he has taken reasonable steps to avoid foreseeable prejudice to the rights of his client, including giving due notice to his client, allowing time for employment of other counsel, delivering to the client all papers and property to which the client is entitled, and complying with applicable laws and rules.

"(3) A lawyer who withdraws from employment shall refund promptly any part of a fee paid in advance that has not been earned.

"(B) Mandatory withdrawal.

A lawyer representing a client before a tribunal, with its permission if required by its rules, shall withdraw from employment, and a lawyer representing a client in other matters shall withdraw from employment, if:

"(1) He knows or it is obvious that his client is bringing the legal action, conducting the defense, or asserting a position in the litigation, or is otherwise having steps taken for him, merely for the purpose of harassing or maliciously injuring any person.

"(2) He knows or it is obvious that his continued employment will result in violation of a Disciplinary Rule.

"(3) His mental or physical condition renders it unreasonably difficult for him to carry out the employment effectively.

"(4) He is discharged by his client.

"(C) Permissive withdrawal.

If DR 2–110(B) is not applicable, a lawyer may not request permission to withdraw in matters pending before a tribunal, and may not withdraw in other matters, unless such request or such withdrawal is because:

"(1) His client:

"(a) Insists upon presenting a claim or defense that is not warranted under existing law and cannot be supported by good faith argument for an extension, modification, or reversal of existing law.

"(b) Personally seeks to pursue an illegal course of conduct.

"(c) Insists that the lawyer pursue a course of conduct that is illegal or that is prohibited under the Disciplinary Rules.

"(d) By other conduct renders it unreasonably difficult for the lawyer to carry out his employment effectively.

"(e) Insists, in a matter not pending before a tribunal, that the lawyer engage in conduct that is contrary to the judgment and advice of the lawyer but not prohibited under the Disciplinary Rules.

"(f) Deliberately disregards an agreement or obligation to the lawyer as to expenses or fees.

"(2) His continued employment is likely to result in a violation of a Disciplinary Rule.

"(3) His inability to work with co-counsel indicates that the best interests of the client likely will be served by withdrawal.

"(4) His mental or physical condition renders it difficult for him to carry out the employment effectively.

"(5) His client knowingly and freely assents to termination of his employment.

"(6) He believes in good faith, in a proceeding pending before a tribunal, that the tribunal will find the existence of other good cause for withdrawal."

ABA FORMAL OPINION 88 (1932)

A prospective client gives an attorney a statement of facts which if true, constitute a cause of action. The attorney accepted a retainer and prepared to bring suit. He did a very considerable amount of work in preparing the petition for the suit, and, in the course of that preparation, made an independent investigation of the facts which convinced him beyond any doubt, that his client's story was untrue, and that in his opinion his client had no cause of action. He thereupon advised the client that he would not bring the suit. He asks whether, under such circumstances, he should refund the entire retainer which he received, or whether he is entitled to charge against it a sum which would reasonably compensate him for his work in the matter. * * *

The withdrawal of the attorney from the employment is warranted * * * and his right to keep enough of the retainer to properly compensate him seems clear.

Insofar as the situation is disclosed by the question, this attorney proceeded in a thorough and prudent manner to discharge his duty. Before filing suit, he made an independent and apparently a thorough investigation and thereby discovered, first, that controlling facts were not as his client had represented them, and second, that the client really had no cause of action. The client was then notified that the attorney would not bring the suit. That it was proper, and also wholesome, to thus investigate the case is immediately manifest. If the attorney's legal conclusion was correct, then the client was saved, or at least had the opportunity of saving himself, the embarrassment and expense of bringing a foundationless lawsuit. He should be glad to pay well the attorney whose diligence and knowledge of the law thus protected him; and the attorney is obviously entitled to compensation. The retainer was paid to apply upon services to be thereafter rendered, and it follows that the attorney may, without professional impropriety, retain therefrom a reasonable amount for his services so rendered.[a]

### *Comment*

(1) *Consequences of improper withdrawal.* Improper withdrawal may result in loss of the lawyer's right to compensation[1] and liability for damages resulting from the ensuing neglect of the case.[2]

(2) *Client's nonpayment of fee.* Although courts *sometimes* recognize the client's failure or refusal to pay the lawyer's fee as justifying withdrawal,[3] lawyers have been disciplined who, without withdrawing,

**a.** See Annot., 88 A.L.R.3d 246 (1978) (lawyer entitled to compensation upon withdrawal consented to by client or for justifiable cause).

**1.** See Annot., 88 A.L.R.3d 246 (1978).

**2.** See Annot., 6 A.L.R.4th 342 (1981).

**3.** See Annot., 88 A.L.R.3d 246, 264–67 (1978). Cf. RPC 1.16(b)(4),(5); DR 2–110(C)(1)(f). Compare United States v. Maines, 462 F.Supp. 15 (E.D.Tenn.1978) (denial of criminal defense counsel's request to withdraw because of client's nonpayment and noncooperation; by accepting employment, lawyer impliedly stipulated he would represent defendant in matter to conclusion); Kriegsman v. Kriegsman, 150 N.J.Super. 474, 375 A.2d 1253 (1977) (withdrawal request properly denied although after divorce client

withheld services in order to induce a client to pay a fee,[4] and a lawyer was held in contempt for failing to appear for trial because he had not been paid.[5]

(3) *Action upon withdrawal.* It has been held that when withdrawing a lawyer may not undo what he or she has already done, e.g., by withdrawing a pleading, to the harm of the client,[6] and that the lawyer is under a duty to give the client such information as he or she has obtained in the course of the employment bearing on its subject matter.[7]

(4) *Court permission to withdraw.* Court permission to withdraw has been withheld on the ground that the request therefor was too close to trial,[8] and on the ground that the client was a corporation and could, therefore, only appear by counsel, substitution being the proper procedure in such a case.[9] The fact that defendant insured, although notified, failed to appear at trial has been held insufficient to require the granting of insurer-provided defense counsel's request to withdraw.[10]

But it has been held that insurer-provided defense counsel's pretrial request to withdraw because diligent search failed to locate the insured must be granted where plaintiff did not show the withdrawal delayed the case's disposition,[11] and timely withdrawal by such counsel has been

paid $2000 partial fee, case became unusually complicated and client went on welfare and could not pay more).

In United States v. Martinez, 385 F.Supp. 323 (W.D.Tex.1974), affirmed mem. 522 F.2d 1279 (5th Cir. 1975), cert. denied 425 U.S. 906, 96 S.Ct. 1498, 47 L.Ed.2d 756 (1976), the court held that where paying his private lawyer's fee for representation at trial rendered the defendant destitute and that fee substantially exceeded what would have been allowed to an appointed lawyer, the lawyer would be ordered to continue representing the defendant on appeal and to bear the expenses thereof. See EC 2–31:

> "Full availability of legal counsel requires both that persons be able to obtain counsel and that lawyers who undertake representation complete the work involved. Trial counsel for a convicted defendant should continue to represent his client by advising whether to take an appeal and, if the appeal is prosecuted, by representing him through the appeal unless new counsel is substituted or withdrawal is permitted by the appropriate court."

**4.** See Hulland v. State Bar, 8 Cal.3d 440, 105 Cal.Rptr. 152, 503 P.2d 608 (1972); State v. Mayes, 216 Kan. 38, 531 P.2d 102 (1975); In re Daggs, 384 Mich. 729, 187 N.W.2d 227 (1971); Dayton Bar Association v. Weiner, 40 Ohio St.2d 7, 317 N.E.2d 783 (1974), cert. denied 420 U.S. 976, 95 S.Ct. 1400, 43 L.Ed. 2d 656 (1975); In re Thomsen, 262 Or. 496, 499 P.2d 815 (1972). Cf. In re Hunoval, 294 N.C. 740, 247 S.E.2d 230 (1977) (appointed criminal defense counsel suspended for one year for refusing to file petition for certiorari because he believed he would not be compensated for doing so).

**5.** United States v. Marx, 553 F.2d 874 (4th Cir. 1977).

**6.** Sterling v. Jones, 255 La. 842, 233 So.2d 537 (1970).

**7.** American Casualty Co. v. Glorfield, 216 F.2d 250, 253 (9th Cir. 1954) (insurer-provided lawyer on withdrawing failed to inform client of offer of settlement—insurer held liable).

**8.** United States v. Maines, 462 F.Supp. 15 (E.D.Tenn.1978); Roediger v. Sapos, 217 N.C. 95, 6 S.E.2d 801 (1940).

**9.** Laskowitz v. Shellenberger, 107 F.Supp. 397 (S.D.Cal.1952).

**10.** Cascella v. Jay James Camera Shop, Inc., 147 Conn. 337, 160 A.2d 899 (1960).

**11.** Schmittinger v. Grogan, 182 Pa.Super. 399, 128 A.2d 114 (1956).

allowed where the insurer's operations had been suspended and the insured failed to respond to counsel's letters.[12]

Counsel has been held entitled to withdraw on the ground that "counsel's judgment and advice has been disdained as incorrect and improvident and, at least by inference, counsel, if they continue, will be required to maintain cross-claims they believe to be wanting in merit."[13]

In Fisher v. State,[14] the Florida Supreme Court appeared to recognize a greater degree of freedom to withdraw than courts generally have perceived, stating that, absent special circumstances, a lawyer has the same right as the client to terminate the relationship.[15] The lawyer was defending an insured at the instance of the insurer when the insurer became insolvent. When the trial court directed the lawyer to continue in the case, the lawyer refused and was held in contempt. This was held error, no adverse effects on the litigation appearing from the withdrawal. The court stressed this was a civil action rather than a criminal one.[16]

In Riley v. District Court,[17] the Colorado Supreme Court reversed the trial court's refusal to grant a defendant's and his public defenders' request to permit the defenders to withdraw and to appoint other counsel, where defendant sought to withdraw his guilty plea on the ground his counsel had misadvised him. The court held that the public defenders must be permitted to withdraw in the circumstances; otherwise "they would be in the inconsistent position of attempting to defend their own conduct while representing a client who is contending that he was not properly advised as to his plea."

## ROSENBERG v. LEVIN

409 So.2d 1016 (Fla. 1982).

OVERTON, Justice.

* * * Levin hired Rosenberg and Pomerantz to perform legal services pursuant to a letter agreement which provided for a $10,000 fixed fee, plus a contingent fee equal to fifty percent of all amounts recovered in excess of $600,000. Levin later discharged Rosenberg and Pomerantz without cause before the legal controversy was resolved and subsequently settled the matter for a net recovery of

12. Jacobs v. Pendel, 98 N.J.Super. 252, 236 A.2d 888 (1967).

13. Goldsmith v. Pyramid Communications, Inc., 362 F.Supp. 694 (S.D.N.Y. 1973).

14. 248 So.2d 479 (Fla. 1971).

15. Compare RPC 1.16(b), (c) with DR 2–110(C).

16. Compare Lessenberry v. Adkisson, 255 Ark. 285, 499 S.W.2d 835 (1973), involving withdrawal in a criminal case:

"[I]t goes without saying that an attorney has the right to withdraw from his contract with a client when he does so with the client's consent and approval and when the rights of others, or the administration of justice, are not affected by such action."

17. 181 Colo. 90, 507 P.2d 464 (1973).

$500,000. Rosenberg and Pomerantz sued for fees based on a "quantum meruit" evaluation of their services. After lengthy testimony, the trial judge concluded that quantum meruit was indeed the appropriate basis for compensation and awarded Rosenberg and Pomerantz $55,000. The district court also agreed that quantum meruit was the appropriate basis for recovery but lowered the amount awarded to $10,000, stating that recovery could in no event exceed the amount which the attorneys would have received under their contract if not prematurely discharged.

The issue submitted to us for resolution is whether the terms of an attorney employment contract limit the attorney's quantum meruit recovery to the fee set out in the contract. This issue requires, however, that we answer the broader underlying question of whether in Florida quantum meruit is an appropriate basis for compensation of attorneys discharged by their clients without cause where there is a specific employment contract. The Florida cases which have previously addressed this issue have resulted in confusion and conflicting views.
* * *

There are two conflicting interests involved in the determination of the issue presented in this type of attorney-client dispute. The first is the need of the client to have confidence in the integrity and ability of his attorney and, therefore, the need for the client to have the ability to discharge his attorney when he loses that necessary confidence in the attorney. The second is the attorney's right to adequate compensation for work performed. To address these conflicting interests, we must consider three distinct rules.

### CONTRACT RULE

The traditional contract rule adopted by a number of jurisdictions holds that an attorney discharged without cause may recover damages for breach of contract under traditional contract principles. The measure of damages is usually the full contract price, although some courts deduct a fair allowance for services and expenses not expended by the discharged attorney in performing the balance of the contract. E.g., Bockman v. Rorex, 212 Ark. 948, 208 S.W.2d 991 (1948) (fixed fee contract); Tonn v. Reuter, 6 Wis.2d 498, 95 N.W.2d 261 (1959) (contingency fee contract); see generally 1 S. Speiser, Attorneys' Fees §§ 4:24–:36 (1973).[a] Some jurisdictions following the contract rule also permit an alternative recovery based on quantum meruit so that an attorney can elect between recovery based on the contract or the reasonable value of the performed services. See 1 S. Speiser, Attorneys' Fees § 4:36 (1973).

a. See also Anderson v. Gailey, 100 Idaho 796, 606 P.2d 90 (1980) (first lawyer may recover 40% contingent fee minus value of being relieved of obligation to complete the representation; in determining latter deduction court may look to services performed by second lawyer that did not duplicate services already performed by first lawyer).

Support for the traditional contract theory is based on: (1) the full contract price is arguably the most rational measure of damages since it reflects the value that the parties placed on the services; (2) charging the full fee prevents the client from profiting from his own breach of contract; and (3) the contract rule is said to avoid the difficult problem of setting a value on an attorney's partially completed legal work.

### QUANTUM MERUIT RULE

To avoid restricting a client's freedom to discharge his attorney, a number of jurisdictions in recent years have held that an attorney discharged without cause can recover only the reasonable value [of] services rendered prior to discharge.[b] See, e.g., Covington v. Rhodes, 38 N.C.App. 61, 247 S.E.2d 305 (1978), cert. denied, 296 N.C. 410, 251 S.E.2d 468 (1979); Johnson v. Long, 15 Ill.App.3d 506, 305 N.E.2d 30 (1973); State Farm Mutual Insurance Co. v. St. Joseph's Hospital, 107 Ariz. 498, 489 P.2d 837 (1971). See generally 1 S. Speiser, §§ 4:28, :35–:36. This rule was first announced in Martin v. Camp, 219 N.Y. 170, 114 N.E. 46 (1916), where the New York Court of Appeals held that a discharged attorney could not sue his client for damages for breach of contract unless the attorney had completed performance of the contract. The New York court established quantum meruit recovery for the attorney on the theory that the client does not breach the contract by discharging the attorney. Rather, the court reasoned, there is an implied condition in every attorney-client contract that the client may discharge the attorney at any time with or without cause. With this right as part of the contract, traditional contract principles are applied to allow quantum meruit recovery on the basis of services performed to date. Under the New York rule, the attorney's cause of action accrues immediately upon his discharge by the client, under the reasoning that it is unfair to make the attorney's right to compensation dependent on the performance of a successor over whom he has no control. See Tillman v. Komar, 259 N.Y. 133, 135–36, 181 N.E. 75, 76 (1932).

The California Supreme Court, in Fracasse v. Brent, 6 Cal.3d 784, 494 P.2d 9, 100 Cal.Rptr. 385 (1972), also adopted a quantum meruit rule. That court carefully analyzed those factors which distinguish the attorney-client relationship from other employment situations and concluded that a discharged attorney should be limited to a quantum meruit recovery in order to strike a proper balance between the client's

b. See Salem Realty Co. v. Matera, 10 Mass.App.Ct. 571, 410 N.E.2d 716 (1980), affirmed 426 N.E.2d 384 Mass. 803, 1160 (1981), wherein the court reasoned:

"If it is bootless to make an opera singer sing, Lumley v. Wagner, 42 Eng.Rep. 687, 693 (1852), it makes still less sense in a civil case to require that a lawyer advocate and a client take advice once they have had a falling out. Not only is contractual yoking of lawyer and client impractical; it would diminish the integrity of the bar and undermine public confidence in it."

right to discharge his attorney without undue restriction and the attorney's right to fair compensation for work performed. The *Fracasse* court sought both to provide clients greater freedom in substituting counsel and to promote confidence in the legal profession while protecting society's interest in the attorney-client relationship.

Contrary to the New York rule, however, the California court also held that an attorney's cause of action for quantum meruit does not accrue until the happening of the contingency, that is, the client's recovery. If no recovery is forthcoming, the attorney is denied compensation. The California court offered two reasons in support of its position. First, the result obtained and the amount involved, two important factors in determining the reasonableness of a fee, cannot be ascertained until the occurrence of the contingency. Second, the client may be of limited means and it would be unduly burdensome to force him to pay a fee if there was no recovery. The court stated that: "[S]ince the attorney agreed initially to take his chances on recovering any fee whatever, we believe that the fact that the success of the litigation is no longer under his control is insufficient to justify imposing a new and more onerous burden on the client."

QUANTUM MERUIT RULE LIMITED BY THE CONTRACT PRICE

The third rule is an extension of the second that limits quantum meruit recovery to the maximum fee set in the contract. This limitation is believed necessary to provide client freedom to substitute attorneys without economic penalty. Without such a limitation, a client's right to discharge an attorney may be illusory and the client may in effect be penalized for exercising a right.

The Tennessee Court of Appeals in Chambliss, Bahner & Crawford v. Luther, 531 S.W.2d 108 (Tenn.Ct.App.1975), expressed the need for limitation on quantum meruit recovery, stating: "It would seem to us that the better rule is that because a client has the unqualified right to discharge his attorney, fees in such cases should be limited to the value of the services rendered or the contract price, whichever is less." In rejecting the argument that quantum meruit should be the basis for the recovery even though it exceeds the contract fee, that court said:

> "To adopt the rule advanced by Plaintiff would, in our view, encourage attorneys less keenly aware of their professional responsibilities than Attorney Chambliss, * * * to induce clients to lose confidence in them in cases where the reasonable value of their services has exceeded the original fee and thereby, upon being discharged, reap a greater benefit than that for which they had bargained."

Other authorities also support this position.*

* For example, Corbin on Contracts, in the chapter dealing with restitution, cites the quantum meruit rule with this limitation with approval. Contracts § 1102 (1980 Supp.) at

Conclusion

* * * It is our opinion that it is in the best interest of clients and the legal profession as a whole that we adopt the modified quantum meruit rule which limits recovery to the maximum amount of the contract fee in all premature discharge cases involving both fixed and contingency employment contracts. The attorney-client relationship is one of special trust and confidence. The client must rely entirely on the good faith efforts of the attorney in representing his interests. This reliance requires that the client have complete confidence in the integrity and ability of the attorney and that absolute fairness and candor characterize all dealings between them. These considerations dictate that clients be given greater freedom to change legal representatives than might be tolerated in other employment relationships. We approve the philosophy that there is an overriding need to allow clients freedom to substitute attorneys without economic penalty as a means of accomplishing the broad objective of fostering public confidence in the legal profession. Failure to limit quantum meruit recovery defeats the policy against penalizing the client for exercising his right to discharge. However, attorneys should not be penalized either and should have the opportunity to recover for services performed.

Accordingly, we hold that an attorney employed under a valid contract who is discharged without cause before the contingency has occurred or before the client's matters have concluded can recover only the reasonable value of his services rendered prior to discharge, limited by the maximum contract fee. We reject both the traditional contract rule and the quantum meruit rule that allow recovery in excess of the maximum contract price because both have a chilling effect on the client's power to discharge an attorney. Under the contract rule in a contingent fee situation, both the discharged attorney and the second attorney may receive a substantial percentage of the client's final recovery. Under the unlimited quantum meruit rule, it is possible, as the instant case illustrates, for the attorney to receive a fee greater than he bargained for under the terms of his contract. Both these results are unacceptable to us.

We further follow the California view that in contingency fee cases, the cause of action for quantum meruit arises only upon the successful occurrence of the contingency. If the client fails in his recovery, the

207–08. Another commentator stated: "The protection afforded to the client becomes illusory if the discharged attorney's recovery on *quantum meruit* exceeds the contract price." Note Limiting the Wrongfully Discharged Attorney's Recovery to Quantum Meruit—Fracasse v. Brent, 24 Hastings L.Rev. 771, 774 (1973). This comment also appeared in a recent article:

"In New York, discharge of an attorney cancels the contract of employment. Thus an attorney can recover the full value of his services, even if it exceeds the contract price. This holding defeats the policy against penalizing the client for exercising his right to discharge an attorney, because he essentially is forced to pay damages for exercising a right."

Note, Attorney's Right to Compensation When Discharged Without Cause From a Contingent Fee Contract—Covington v. Rhodes, 678 Wake Forest L.Rev. 677, 689–90 (1979).

discharged attorney will similarly fail and recover nothing. We recognize that deferring the commencement of a cause of action until the occurrence of the contingency is a view not uniformly accepted. Deferral, however, supports our goal to preserve the client's freedom to discharge, and any resulting harm to the attorney is minimal because the attorney would not have benefited earlier until the contingency's occurrence. There should, of course, be a presumption of regularity and competence in the performance of the services by a successor attorney.

In computing the reasonable value of the discharged attorney's services, the trial court can consider the totality of the circumstances surrounding the professional relationship between the attorney and client. Factors such as time, the recovery sought, the skill demanded, the results obtained, and the attorney-client contract itself will necessarily be relevant considerations.

We conclude that this approach creates the best balance between the desirable right of the client to discharge his attorney and the right of an attorney to reasonable compensation for his services. * * * We find the district court of appeal was correct in limiting the quantum meruit award to the contract price, and its decision is approved.[c]

### *Comment*

(1) *Limitation of successive contingent fees.* The Louisiana Supreme Court has adopted a novel approach to successive contingent fees, differing from both the traditional contract rule and the modern quantum meruit rule.[1] Rejecting a discharged lawyer's claim that the client owed him the agreed-upon one-third (in addition to the one-third the client agreed to pay the second lawyer), the court ruled:

> "[O]nly one contingency fee should be paid by the client, the amount of the fee to be determined according to the highest ethical contingency percentage to which the client contractually agreed in any of the contingency fee contracts which he executed. Further, that fee should in turn be allocated between or among the various attorneys involved in handling the claim in question, such fee apportionment to be on the basis of factors which are set forth in the Code of Professional Responsibility. * * *
>
> "On remand of these proceedings the trial court should require that the second attorney be joined as an indispensable party for a full and proper adjudication of this entire matter.
>
> "[I]f the second attorney has already collected his contingent fee, and if the client * * * asserts his right to recover from the second attorney the money paid to which the attorney is not entitled, that second attorney should be ordered to restore the same

c. Adkins and McDonald, JJ., dissented.

See Plaza Shoe Store, Inc. v. Hermel, Inc., 636 S.W.2d 53 (Mo.1982); Annot., 92 A.L.R.3d 690 (1979); 10 Fla.St.U.L.Rev. 167.

1. Saucier v. Hayes Dairy Products, Inc., 373 So.2d 102 (La.1978).

to [the client] as having been a payment of a thing not due. The second attorney, along with the first attorney, will then be accorded the opportunity to establish his right to receive an appropriate apportionment of the one contingent fee owed by [the client] for legal services rendered in connection with his claim." [2]

(2) *Completed performance.* Where the lawyer has completed all or substantially all services under the contingent fee contract before being discharged, even quantum meruit rule courts usually require the client to pay the full contracted-for fee.[3] But in the New York case of In re Krooks,[4] a lawyer whose fee in a condemnation case was to have been "all moneys in excess of $38,000" was limited to quantum meruit although not discharged until after the court issued a memorandum stating that it was awarding the client $46,500.[5]

(3) *Third party interference.* In certain circumstances, a lawyer may recover damages on grounds of tortious interference with contractual or business relationship from a third party who wrongfully induces a client to discharge a lawyer.[6]

(4) *Employment for period of time.* Some courts which limit a lawyer to quantum meruit upon discharge under a contingent fee contract refuse to do so regarding a contract employing the lawyer for a particular period of time.[7] But in LaRocco v. Bakwin,[8] an Illinois court

2. The West Virginia Supreme Court subsequently adopted a similar approach to allocate compensation between the second lawyer and the first lawyer who voluntarily withdrew without good cause (because the client had refused to follow the lawyer's recommendation to settle) but whose withdrawal followed appropriate procedures and did not prejudice the client. See May v. Seibert, 264 S.E.2d 643 (W.Va.1980) (allocating fee on basis of time spent by each lawyer). It should be noted that many courts deny any compensation to a lawyer who voluntarily withdraws without good cause. See Annot., 88 A.L.R.3d 246 (1978).

3. See Annot., 92 A.L.R.3d 690, 709–11 (1979).

4. 257 N.Y. 329, 178 N.E. 548 (1931).

5. See Also Demov, Morris, Levin & Shein v. Glantz, 53 N.Y.2d 553, 444 N.Y.S.2d 55, 428 N.E.2d 387 (1981) (lawyer may not recover contract amount as opposed to quantum meruit on ground of client's alleged fraud in making contract with intent not to allow lawyer to complete representation).

6. Compare State Farm Mutual Insurance Co. v. St. Joseph's Hospital, 107 Ariz. 498, 489 P.2d 837 (1971) (insurer which unjustifiably induced plaintiffs to discharge lawyers may be held liable for tort of intentional interference with contractual relationship); Herron v. State Farm Mutual Insurance Co., 56 Cal.2d 202, 14 Cal.Rptr. 294, 363 P.2d 310 (1951) (same); LaRocco v. Bakwin, 108 Ill.App.3d 723, 64 Ill.Dec. 286, 439 N.E.2d 537 (1982) (person may be liable for interference with business relationship between lawyer and client notwithstanding relationship was terminable at will); Walsh v. O'Neill, 350 Mass. 586, 215 N.E.2d 915, 26 A.L.R.3d 673 (1966) (no liability if lawyer's relationship not founded on contract). See Restatement (Second) of Torts §§ 766–774A (1979) (including § 766B, "Intentional Interference with Prospective Contractual Relation"); Prosser, Torts §§ 129, 130 (4th ed. 1971) (interference with contractual relations; interference with prospective advantage).

See also Adler, Barish, Daniels, Levin & Creskoff v. Epstein, 482 Pa. 416, 393 A.2d 1175, 1 A.L.R.4th 1144 (1978), appeal dismissed 442 U.S. 907, 99 S.Ct. 2817, 61 L.Ed.2d 272 (1979) (injunction against associates who induced clients on whose cases they had worked to discharge law firm and retain new firm the associates were forming). Cf. supra p. 44–45 Comment (2).

7. See Alpern v. Hurwitz, 644 F.2d 943 (2d Cir. 1981); Annot., 54 A.L.R.2d 604, 628–31 (1957); Annot., 43 A.L.R.2d 677, 680 (1955).

Regarding discharge under a contract specifying a flat sum fee for a particular service, see Annot., 54 A.L.R.2d 604, 607–28 (1957).

8. 108 Ill.App.3d 723, 439 N.E.2d 537 (1982).

held that the client's right to terminate was implicit in an agreement to employ a lawyer for life as long as he provided adequate legal services—upon being discharged the lawyer could recover only on the basis of quantum meruit for services performed up to the time of discharge. And in Taylor v. Board of Education,[9] a New Jersey court held that a school board could discharge its attorney without regard to the good cause or hearing requirements of veteran's tenure statutory provisions. The court reasoned that application of the veteran's tenure provisions to a lawyer-employee was superseded by DR 2–110(B)(4)'s requirement (continued in RPC 1.16(a)(3) ) that a lawyer shall withdraw from employment if discharged by the client.

(5) *Refunding part of retainer.* In Jacobson v. Sassower,[10] a New York court held that a lawyer who had expended ten hours at $100 per hour before she was discharged without cause had to return $1500 of what the retainer agreement called a "non-refundable retainer of $2500." The retainer agreement specified that the retainer was to be credited against the lawyer's $100 per hour charges. The court said:

> "In my opinion, the practice of charging advance 'non-refundable' fees is a bald attempt to circumvent the rule limiting an attorney's recovery upon discharge to *quantum meruit.* * * *
>
> "A retainer fee ordinarily constitutes a payment in advance to cover future services in connection with a specific legal matter until further provision is made. This is commonly known as a 'special retainer'. While its acceptance obligates the attorney to refuse adversary employment, that is not its intention. On the other hand, payment of a preliminary fee may be made solely to receive whatever professional services a client may request during a fixed period. This is called a 'true', or 'general retainer,' and is intended to remunerate the attorney for being deprived of the opportunity to act for another. I Speiser, Attorneys' Fees sec. 1:4; L'Estrange and Turner, 'Fee Agreements,' 27 Prac.Law. 11 (April 1981).
>
> "When an attorney hired pursuant to a general retainer is discharged without cause, the client is liable for the entire contract price.[a]
>
> "Nothing in this agreement indicates that the parties intended a general retainer. [It] provides for an hourly fee, and * * * states that accumulating charges are to be offset against the $2,500 advance payment. * * *
>
> "The defendant's contention that provision for nonrefundability of advance fees furnishes assurance of the client's commitment to his own cause is * * * without merit. I fail to see why a client should have to assume the risk of forfeiture as proof to the

9. 187 N.J.Super. 546, 455 A.2d 552 (1983).

10. 113 Misc.2d 279, 452 N.Y.S.2d 981 (1982).

a. See Jacobs v. Holston, 70 OhioApp.2d 55, 434 N.E.2d 738 (1980) (lawyer specifically explained that $2500 was nonrefundable and not to be credited toward charge of $75 per hour).

attorney that he is sincere about asserting a legitimate claim or defense. * * *

"It is significant that retention of the retainer fee by the defendant would violate an important ethical duty owed by lawyers to their clients. * * * DR 2–110(A) provides that '* * * (3) A lawyer who withdraws from employment shall refund promptly any part of a fee paid in advance that has not been earned.'[b]"[11]

## C. CLIENT FUNDS AND PROPERTY

### MODEL RULES OF PROFESSIONAL CONDUCT

**RULE 1.8 Conflict of Interest: Prohibited Transactions**

* * *

(j) A lawyer shall not acquire a proprietary interest in the cause of action or subject matter of litigation the lawyer is conducting for a client, except that the lawyer may:

(1) acquire a lien granted by law to secure the lawyer's fee or expenses * * *.

**RULE 1.15 Safekeeping Property**

(a) A lawyer shall hold property of clients or third persons that is in a lawyer's possession in connection with a representation separate from the lawyer's own property. Funds shall be kept in a separate account maintained in the state where the lawyer's office is situated, or elsewhere with the consent of the client or third person. Other property shall be identified as such and appropriately safeguarded. Complete records of such account funds and other property shall be kept by the lawyer and shall be preserved for a period of [five years] after termination of the representation.

(b) Upon receiving funds or other property in which a client or third person has an interest, a lawyer shall promptly notify the client or third person. Except as stated in this rule or otherwise permitted by law or by agreement with the client, a lawyer shall promptly deliver to the client or third person any funds or other property that the client or third person is entitled to receive and, upon request by the client or third person, shall promptly render a full accounting regarding such property.

(c) When in the course of representation a lawyer is in possession of property in which both the lawyer and another person claim interests, the property shall be kept separate by the lawyer until there is an accounting and severance of their interests. If a dispute arises concerning their respective interests, the portion in dispute shall be kept separate by the lawyer until the dispute is resolved.

**b.** See RPC 1.16(d).

**11.** See Jersey Land & Development Corp. v. United States, 342 F.Supp. 48, (D.N.J.1972) ("Judged in the light of common experience of mankind in this area of attorneys fees, it is most improbable that [client] agreed to pay [lawyer] $5,000 *merely* to assure availability of future legal services.").

**RULE 1.16 Declining or Terminating Representation**

* * *

(d) Upon termination of representation, a lawyer shall take steps to the extent reasonably practicable to protect a client's interests, such as giving reasonable notice to the client, allowing time for employment of other counsel, surrendering papers and property to which the client is entitled and refunding any advance payment of fee that has not been earned. The lawyer may retain papers relating to the client to the extent permitted by other law.[a]

## BRAUER v. HOTEL ASSOCIATES, INC.

40 N.J. 415, 192 A.2d 831 (1963).

HANEMAN, J. On November 23, 1960 Hotel Associates, Inc. (the corporation) was adjudged insolvent and a statutory receiver was appointed for it. The New Jersey law firm of Shanley and Fisher (Shanley & Fisher) filed a proof of claim with the receiver in the sum of $7,494.61 representing disbursements and professional services ren-

a. Compare the following CPR provisions:

**"DR 2–110 Withdrawal from Employment**

"(A) In general. * * *

"(2) [A] lawyer shall not withdraw from employment until he has taken reasonable steps to avoid foreseeable prejudice to the rights of his client, including * * * delivering to the client all papers and property to which the client is entitled * * *.

"(3) A lawyer who withdraws from employment shall refund promptly any part of a fee paid in advance that has not been earned."

**"DR 5–103 Avoiding Acquisition of Interest in Litigation**

"(A) A lawyer shall not acquire a proprietary interest in the cause of action or subject matter of litigation he is conducting for a client, except that he may:

"(1) Acquire a lien granted by law to secure his fee or expenses."

**"DR 9–102 Preserving Identity of Funds and Property of a Client**

"(A) All funds of clients paid to a lawyer or law firm, other than advances for costs and expenses, shall be deposited in one or more identifiable bank accounts maintained in the state in which the law office is situated and no funds belonging to the lawyer or law firm shall be deposited therein except as follows:

"(1) Funds reasonably sufficient to pay bank charges may be deposited therein.

"(2) Funds belonging in part to a client and in part presently or potentially to the lawyer or law firm must be deposited therein, but the portion belonging to the lawyer or law firm may be withdrawn when due unless the right of the lawyer or law firm to receive it is disputed by the client, in which event the disputed portion shall not be withdrawn until the dispute is finally resolved.

"(B) A lawyer shall:

"(1) Promptly notify a client of the receipt of his funds, securities, or other properties.

"(2) Identify and label securities and properties of a client promptly upon receipt and place them in a safe deposit box or other place of safekeeping as soon as practicable.

"(3) Maintain complete records of all funds, securities, and other properties of a client coming into the possession of the lawyer and render appropriate accounts to his client regarding them.

"(4) Promptly pay or deliver to the client as requested by a client the funds, securities, or other properties in the possession of the lawyer which the client is entitled to receive."

dered in behalf of the corporation prior to insolvency, from January 1960 to October 1960. Shanley & Fisher also asserted an attorneys' retaining lien upon all the documents and books of the corporation in its possession, for the full amount of its bill.

The receiver filed a petition with the Chancery Division requesting an order that Shanley & Fisher be required to show cause why it should not "turn over all books and records pertaining to the operation of the * * * corporation to your petitioner, same being necessary and required by your petitioner in examination of claims, accounts, and processing of any claims for and against the said corporation." The order to show cause was issued, and, after a hearing, the Chancery Division entered an order directing Shanley & Fisher to "relinquish possession of all of the books and records of Hotel Associates, Inc. as the same pertain to the affairs of that corporation and that said books and records be surrendered and turned over to [the receiver]." The court orally held in abeyance for later consideration the determination of the question of Shanley & Fisher's alleged lien and its possible entitlement to a priority in payment over general creditors. After the requested documents were surrendered to the receiver, through J. William Barba, Esq., the registered agent of the corporation and a member of Shanley & Fisher, a further hearing was held in the Chancery Division. At that hearing, the receiver argued that Shanley & Fisher did not have an attorneys' retaining lien on the books and records of the corporation (for reasons stated and discussed below), so that its undisputed charge of $7,494.61 was a general claim against the corporation, entitled to no priority of payment. The Chancery Division rejected this argument and entered an order that a retaining lien did exist and that Shanley & Fisher was entitled to a right of priority for the full amount of its claim, as an administration expense. The receiver appealed this order * * *.

The basic questions are whether Shanley & Fisher has a retaining lien, since Barba, a member of that firm, was the registered agent of the corporation, and if the answer to this query is in the affirmative, whether such a lien survives the appointment of a receiver.

The common law retaining lien attaches to all papers, books, documents, securities, moneys, and property of the client which come into the possession of the attorney in the course of, and with reference to, his professional employment. It is a general lien which gives an attorney the right to retain possession of his client's property until the entire balance due him for legal services, as well as for costs and disbursements, is paid. It is termed a "passive" lien since it cannot be actively enforced through legal proceedings, and rests wholly upon the right to retain possession until the bill is paid. The retaining lien is distinguishable from the common-law special or charging lien which an attorney may have for services rendered in a particular cause of action and which attaches to the judgment in the cause for which the services were rendered. The charging lien may be actively enforced and does not rest upon possession. Its scope was enlarged by N.J.S. 2A:13–

5, N.J.S.A. It is, however, only the common-law general or retaining lien with which we are herein concerned.

The attorney's retaining lien can only attach to property that comes into the possession of the attorney in the course of, and with respect to, his professional employment. It cannot arise if possession of the property is maintained for a special purpose inconsistent with his claim to a lien. Ideal Tile Corp. v. N. T. Investment Co., 111 N.J.Eq. 241, 162 A. 111 (Ch. 1932).[a] Thus, counsel for the receiver argues that the books and records were not in the possession of Shanley & Fisher in the course of, and with respect to, its performance of professional services for the corporation, but pursuant to Barba's statutory capacity of registered agent. However, Shanley & Fisher's undisputed affidavit in support of its charges indicates that it rendered services in the formation of the corporation and attended the meetings of its stockholders and directors in the capacity of counsel for the corporation. * * *

It is further contended that the insolvency of the corporation and the appointment of a receiver should dissolve any retaining lien which Shanley & Fisher may have acquired. It has been held that if the services to the insolvent corporation were rendered subsequent to the appointment of a receiver, or possession of the property was acquired at that time, the receiver's interest in the corporation and its property would be paramount to the attorney's right to a lien. However, it has been firmly established that a trustee in bankruptcy takes only such title as the bankrupt has, subject to all liens and equities existing upon or against the property, including an attorney's retaining lien for services rendered *prior* to the bankruptcy proceedings. This rule is equally applicable to situations identical with the present case, where an insolvency receiver has been appointed for a corporate debtor. Consequently, the attorneys' retaining lien is as effective against the statutory receiver herein as it was against the corporation prior to the receiver's appointment.

The receiver additionally attacks Shanley & Fisher's right to a lien upon the ground that the corporate documents were of no intrinsic value. The cases, cited above do not distinguish between the intrinsic worth or worthlessness of the property upon which the attorney asserts his lien, even when receivership proceedings are involved. The receiver's argument would lead to the conclusion that the attorney's fees and disbursements only need to be satisfied up to the value of the property retained. But to so hold would dilute the general quality of the lien, viz., the retention of the client's property until *all* the fees

**a.** Money came into lawyer's possession in trust for client's creditors.

See United States v. J.H.W. & Gitlitz Deli & Bar, Inc., 499 F.Supp. 1010 (S.D.N.Y. 1980) (no retaining lien on funds deposited in escrow for payment to others unless escrow agreement specifically authorizes payment of lawyer's fees from escrow fund); Akers v. Akers, 233 Minn. 133, 46 N.W.2d 87 (1951) (no retaining lien on valuable property divorce plaintiff delivered to lawyer to prevent husband from reaching it during pendency of proceeding).

and disbursements of the attorney are satisfied. It is not the value of the property itself which measures the effectiveness of the lien. Rather, the effectiveness of the lien is proportionate to the inconvenience of the client in being denied access to his property. The focal point is not upon the objective worth of the property, but upon its subjective worth, to the client and those who represent him. If the property loses this latter value, the attorney's possession becomes meaningless, and his passive lien, to all effects, worthless. Therefore, it is the inconvenience suffered by the client which determines the value of the lien, and if the client or his representative considers the elimination of this inconvenience to be as valuable as the amount of the attorney's charges, then the client will satisfy the charges, the lien will dissolve, and the client's property will be returned. The nature of the lien thus evokes the conclusion that the intrinsic value of the property is immaterial. * * *

Judgment affirmed.

### *Comment*

(1) *Retaining lien.* In jurisdictions where the retaining lien is recognized, courts generally will require a substituted lawyer to turn over the former client's papers only if the former client pays or furnishes adequate security for payment of the substituted lawyer's fee.[1] But a New York court has held that in a criminal case the constitutional right to assistance of counsel requires that defendant's new counsel be allowed to examine and copy papers in the first lawyer's possession.[2] The Alaska Supreme Court has enumerated the following as some of the "factors to be weighed in determining what security, if any, should be required for release of files":

"(a) Whether there was just cause for discharging the attorney;

"(b) Whether the attorney initiated the withdrawal;

"(c) The client's ability to provide security or to pay the fee;

"(d) The importance of the files to the client;

"(e) The ethical obligations of an attorney;

"(f) Whether the fee is disputed, and, if so, the reasonable amount of any lien to be charged;

"(g) Whether the amount due the attorney is contingent or fixed;

"(h) Whether part of the sum due is for costs advanced by the attorney which may justify reimbursement before ordering release of the files."[3]

1. See, e.g., Jenkins v. Weinshienk, 670 F.2d 915 (10th Cir. 1982); Upgrade Corp. v. Michigan Carton Co., 87 Ill.App.3d 662, 43 Ill.Dec. 159, 410 N.E.2d 159 (1980).

2. People v. Altvater, 78 Misc.2d 24, 355 N.Y.S.2d 736 (1974). Cf. ABA Informal Opinion 1461 (1980) (lawyer should forego retaining lien if asserting it would prejudice client's ability to defend against criminal charge or to protect similarly important personal liberty or if client is unable to pay amount owing).

3. Miller v. Paul, 615 P.2d 615 (Alaska 1980).

Some jurisdictions do not recognize retaining liens. For example, in Academy of California Optometrists, Inc. v. Superior Court,[4] a California court rejected a discharged lawyer's attempt to force payment of a disputed fee by a contracted-for retaining lien on pleadings, depositions and other papers essential to the client's pending case. The court held that there is no attorney's retaining lien at common law in California and that an agreement for such a lien is void as against public policy at least "where the subject matter * * * is of no economic value to him, but is used only to extort disputed fees from his client." "The client's cause, sacred as it is to a member of the legal profession, may not be so abused," said the court, citing DR 2–110(A) (2) (requiring lawyer on withdrawal to take "reasonable steps to avoid foreseeable prejudice to the rights of his client, including * * * delivering to the client all papers and property to which the client is entitled").[5] Similarly, after the state legislature repealed Minnesota's statutory retaining lien, that state's disciplinary board issued a formal opinion stating:

> "It is professional misconduct for an attorney to assert a retaining lien on the files and papers of a client. This prohibition applies to all retaining liens, whether they be statutory, common law, contractual, or otherwise."[6]

(2) *Lien on judgment.* "Attorneys also possess a special or charging lien for their fees and costs on any judgment fund which is the fruit of their labor. This lien * * * has been accepted as part of the common law by most but not all of the courts which have passed upon the question. Today the lien exists, either by statute or decision, in nearly every jurisdiction. * * *

"Generally the lien only attaches to a money judgment which has been recovered for the client. In most but not all states there can

4. 51 Cal.App.3d 999, 124 Cal.Rptr. 668 (1975).

5. Cf. RPC 1.16(d).

6. See Hoover, Lawyers Professional Responsibility Board Report, 36 Bench & B. of Minn. 43 (Dec. 1979).

For further detail on retaining liens, see Wentworth, Attorneys' Liens—A Survey and Proposal, 35 Conn.B.J. 191, 191–95 (1961); Note, Attorney's Retaining Liens Over Former Client's Papers, 65 Colum.L.Rev. 296 (1965); Annot., 3 A.L.R.2d 148 (1949). Cf. Adams, George, Lee, Schulte & Ward, P.A. v. Westinghouse Electric Corp., 597 F.2d 570 (5th Cir. 1979) (retaining lien on settlement money received for client may be asserted only on amount lawyer claims as fee); People ex rel. MacFarlane v. Harthun, 195 Colo. 38, 581 P.2d 716 (1978) (disbarred or suspended lawyer may not assert retaining lien).

On priority of attorneys' liens, see Note, Priority of Attorney's Liens, 45 Iowa L.Rev. 147 (1959). See also In re Washington Square Slum Clearance, 5 N.Y.2d 300, 184 N.Y.S.2d 585, 157 N.E.2d 587 (1959), cert. denied 363 U.S. 841, 80 S.Ct. 1606, 4 L.Ed.2d 1726 (1960) (over federal tax lien); Plumb, Federal Liens and Priorities—Agenda for the Next Decade II, 77 Yale L.J. 605, 682 (1968).

In Antaya v. Majett, 12 Misc.2d 585, 177 N.Y.S.2d 242 (1958), the court held that neither the retaining nor charging lien can be used to secure repayment of the lawyer's loans to the client, but left open the question whether there may be an equitable (as opposed to attorney's) lien where the client agreed that the loans were to be repaid from the action's proceeds.

be no lien on specific real or personal property which has been either recovered for the client or successfully protected from adverse claims in the absence of a statute or special agreement. No lien can be asserted in most states against public funds. Since the lien operates only on the judgment and not on the cause of action, settlements made prior to judgment are not affected by any lien. But settlements made for the purpose of defrauding counsel may be set aside by the court and in some states the attorney will then be allowed to prosecute the claim to a judgment."[7]

(3) *Lien on cause of action.* Attorneys' liens have been expanded substantially by statute.[8] A common provision gives a claimant's lawyer a lien upon the cause of action.[9] Thus, N.Y. Judiciary Law § 475 grants the lien from the commencement of an action or other proceeding.[10] Under this lien, a defendant with notice of the plaintiff's lawyer's rights[11] must, in paying the plaintiff's claim, ensure that the plaintiff's lawyer receives his or her fee. This is typically done by making the check payable to both plaintiff and plaintiff's lawyer.[12]

7. Wentworth, supra note 6, at 195–96.

See Levine v. Levine, 206 Misc. 884, 135 N.Y.S.2d 304 (1954) (public policy precludes recognizing alimony award as subject to lien on judgment); Ross v. Scannell, 97 Wn.2d 598, 647 P.2d 1004 (1982) (Washington's statutory lien on judgment does not extend to real estate constituting fruits of judgment). Cf. Northwestern National Bank v. Kroll, 306 N.W.2d 104 (Minn.1981) (statutory lien on interest of client in property affected by action does not attach to homestead property).

Courts are divided on whether a party's lawyer has an enforceable lien on a judgment where that judgment is subject to being set off against the opponent's larger judgment. Compare Hobson Construction Co. v. Max Drill, Inc., 158 N.J.Super. 263, 385 A.2d 1256 (1978) ("The judgment or fund * * * is zero * * * and thus there is absent the precondition of the imposition of the statutory lien") with Forrest Currell Lumber Co. v. Thomas, 82 N.M. 789, 487 P.2d 491 (1971) ("modern trend is to protect the attorney against such a set-off by holding his charging lien to be superior").

8. For descriptions of attorneys' lien statutes, see Stevens, Our Inadequate Attorney's Lien Statutes—A Suggestion, 31 Wash.L.Rev. 1, 3–7 (1956); Wentworth, supra note 6, at 199–202.

9. See Note, Attorneys: Recovering the Attorney's Fee, 16 Okla.L.Rev. 91 (1963).

A *discharged* lawyer's lien on the cause of action may be enforced against a settlement obtained after the lawyer was discharged. Skelton v. Spencer, 102 Idaho 69, 625 P.2d 1072, 23 A.L.R.4th 315 (1981) (may be enforced by court without jury upon discharged lawyer's motion in client's original action), cert. denied 454 U.S. 894, 102 S.Ct. 390, 70 L.Ed.2d 208 (1981); Plaza Shoe Store, Inc. v. Hermel, Inc., 636 S.W.2d 53 (Mo.1982) (same). But where the lien attaches not to the cause of action but to the *judgment* at the time it is rendered, a discharged lawyer has been held to have no lien against a judgment obtained after the discharge, on the ground that "[a]t the time when this purported charging lien would have attached, the time of judgment * * * the judgment was not a fund recovered by [the lawyer's] aid, as he had been discharged." Covington v. Rhodes, 38 N.C.App. 61, 247 S.E.2d 305 (1978), discretionary review denied 296 N.C. 410, 251 S.E.2d 468 (1979). Compare Pearlmutter v. Alexander, 97 Cal.App.3d Supp. 16, 158 Cal.Rptr. 762 (1979) (where defendant settles without regard to lien of plaintiff's former lawyer who had properly withdrawn, latter may recover from defendant, defendant's lawyer, and plaintiff's new lawyer for tortious interference with prospective economic advantage).

10. Section 475–a creates the lien prior to the action's commencement on service of a prescribed notice.

11. See Annot., 85 A.L.R.2d 859 (1962). Cf. Downs v. Hodge, 413 S.W.2d 519 (Mo.App.1967) (defendant's insurer subject to lien).

12. Hafter v. Farkas, 498 F.2d 587 (2d Cir. 1974) (lawyer may not insist it be made out to lawyer alone).

(4) *Direct settlement between parties.* Although the decision whether and at what amount to settle is the client's,[13] and the lawyer cannot bar a client from settling without the lawyer's consent,[14] if the parties settle between themselves in disregard of the plaintiff's lawyer's lien on the cause of action, the defendant remains liable to plaintiff's lawyer[15] for an amount depending upon the terms of the statute, the terms and effect of the lawyer's contract of employment, and the nature of the defendant's liability.[16]

If the plaintiff's lawyer was proceeding under a percentage contingent fee agreement and the direct settlement was in good faith and not for the fraudulent purpose of defeating the lawyer's compensation, many courts hold the defendant liable for the specified percentage applied to the settlement amount.[17] Most courts do not hold the defendant liable for a greater amount for having induced the plaintiff to agree to a settlement which the lawyer regards as inadequate.[18]

**13.** See RPC 1.2(a); EC 7-7; Whittier Union High School v. Superior Court, 66 Cal.App.3d 504, 136 Cal.Rptr. 86 (1977); Cohen v. Goldman, 85 R.I. 434, 132 A.2d 414 (1957); May v. Siebert, — W.Va. —, 264 S.E.2d 643 (1980).

**14.** See Singleton v. Foreman, 435 F.2d 962 (5th Cir. 1970); Note, Contingent Fee Contracts: Validity, Controls, and Enforceability, 47 Iowa L.Rev. 942, 951–52 (1962).

**15.** There is a conflict, turning partly on statutory terms, on whether the lawyer in enforcing this liability has an option to continue to judgment the action settled by the parties or bring an independent action against the defendant. See Hendricks v. Superior Court, 197 Cal.App.2d 586, 17 Cal.Rptr. 364 (1961) (independent action required); Davis v. Great Northern Railway, 128 Minn. 354, 151 N.W. 128 (1915) (either permitted); Fischer-Hansen v. Brooklyn Heights Railroad, 173 N.Y. 492, 66 N.E. 395 (1903) (independent action preferred); Smelker v. Chicago & Northwestern Railway, 106 Wis. 135, 81 N.W. 994 (1900) (independent action not permitted).

There is also disagreement on whether the lawyer in enforcing the lien on the settled cause of action must establish the merits of the client's claim against the defendant. In Slayton v. Russ, 205 Ark. 474, 169 S.W.2d 571, 146 A.L.R. 64 (1943), the court held that the lawyer need not, since "the defendant, by compromising and settling, has recognized the attorney's absolute right to recover a fee of some amount" and distinguished cases to the contrary on statutory or other grounds.

See Annot., 146 A.L.R. 67 (1943).

**16.** See Annot., 40 A.L.R. 1529 (1926); Annot., 3 A.L.R. 472 (1919).

**17.** See McGlynn & McGlynn v. Louisville & Nashville Railroad, 313 Ill.App. 396, 40 N.E.2d 539, reversed on other grounds 381 Ill. 55, 44 N.E.2d 841 (1942); Davis v. Great Northern Railway, 128 Minn. 354, 151 N.W. 128 (1915); Downs v. Hodge, 413 S.W.2d 519 (Mo.App.1967); Fischer-Hansen v. Brooklyn Heights Railroad, 173 N.Y. 492, 66 N.E. 395 (1903). Compare Gerritzen v. Louisville & Nashville Railroad, 115 S.W.2d 44 (Mo.App.1938) (where direct settlement was with understanding defenddant would pay plaintiff's lawyer's fee and there was 50% contingent fee agreement, defendant is liable to plaintiff's lawyer for same amount as defendant paid plaintiff).

**18.** See, e.g., Krause v. Hartford Accident & Indemnity Co., 331 Mich. 19, 49 N.W.2d 41 (1951).

But see Fuessel v. Cadillac Bar Corp., 63 N.J.Super. 430, 164 A.2d 821 (1960), certification denied, 34 N.J. 65, 167 A.2d 54 (1961), where the court ruled that the defendant could be held liable for the reasonable value of the plaintiff's lawyer's services up to, but not exceeding, the full amount of the settlement. The court reasoned that an agreement for a percentage "of the amount collected" refers to "the amount *the attorney collects*," so that a direct settlement "renders impossible the execution of the contingency formula for fixing the lien, and it will then be set at the fair value of the services rendered," but that defendant's liability cannot exceed the amount received by the plaintiff in good faith because the settlement "liquidates the claim" and thereby places a "maximum valuation upon the subject of the lien beyond which the remedy given by [the] statute does not purport to go."

But if the direct settlement was not in good faith, the plaintiff's lawyer may recover more than the specified percentage of the settlement amount, although there is disagreement on whether the fee should be determined on a quantum meruit basis[19] or by applying the specified percentage to the true value of the client's claim.[20]

## ABA FORMAL OPINION 348 (1982)

Programs are being developed in a number of states to provide financial support for law-related public service projects from interest earned on lawyers' trust accounts in depository institutions. The committee has been asked for its opinion whether it is ethically permissible for lawyers to participate in these programs.

As the organized bar has investigated the feasibility of these programs, attention also has focused on establishing guidelines for placing clients' funds in interest-bearing accounts for the benefit of individual clients. This raises some ethical issues which also are related to the question presented to the committee. Before expressing an opinion on the ethical propriety of a lawyer participating in programs which use interest earned on lawyers' trust accounts for law-related public service projects, the committee will address the following related questions: Does the Model Code of Professional Responsibility permit lawyers to place clients' funds in interest-bearing accounts? Are there circumstances under which a lawyer must place a client's funds at interest for the client's benefit? If an interest-bearing account is used for a client's funds, what duties does the model code impose on the lawyer respecting the account? Does the model code permit lawyers to retain interest earned on client funds in lawyers' trust accounts to offset operating costs, including the cost of administering the trust account?

### Background

Historically, client funds entrusted to lawyers in the United States have been placed in noninterest bearing bank checking accounts maintained by the lawyers separate from their own funds. Typically these funds are held temporarily for use in a particular transaction in behalf of the client and must be readily available for this purpose. Because of the impracticability of establishing a separate account for each client, all client funds generally are commingled in the lawyer's trust account.

**19.** See Fuessel v. Cadillac Bar Corp., 63 N.J.Super. 430, 164 A.2d 821 (1960) (quantum meruit recovery may even exceed full amount of settlement if settlement was in bad faith).

**20.** See State Farm Fire Insurance Co. v. Gregory, 184 F.2d 447 (4th Cir. 1950) (percentage applied to face amount of fire policy rather than lesser amount for which defendant induced plaintiff to settle to avoid lawyer's fee); Desaman v. Butler Brothers, 118 Minn. 198, 136 N.W. 747 (1912) (after $3000 judgment, defendant by overreaching of necessitous plaintiff induced plaintiff to settle directly for $700; defendant liable to plaintiff's lawyer on 50% contingent fee for $1500); Griggs v. Chicago, Rock Island & Pacific Railway, 104 Neb. 301, 177 N.W. 185 (1920) (similar). Cf. Frear v. Lewis, 201 App.Div. 660, 195 N.Y.S. 3 (1922).

Since it also is impracticable to calculate interest on each client's funds when commingled with the funds of other clients, the lawyer's trust account is left uninvested. For years clients have accepted this practice, apparently recognizing that the earnings potential of their funds in relation to the administrative costs would not justify investing the funds. As a consequence, the depository institutions have had the use of the funds without payment of any interest. Occasionally a client's funds are deposited in a separate account at interest for the benefit of the client where the amount and expected holding period make it obvious that the interest earned will exceed the administrative costs of placing the funds at interest for the client.

### May Lawyers Place Clients' Funds in Interest-Bearing Accounts?

* * *

It is clear * * * that nothing in the model code prohibits a lawyer from placing clients' funds in interest-bearing accounts so long as the * * * requirements of DR 9–102 are met.[a]

### Are There Circumstances Where a Lawyer Must Place a Client's Funds at Interest for the Benefit of the Client?

In addition to expenses created by the notification, recordkeeping, and accounting requirements of DR 9–102(B), lawyers may incur other costs in attempting to place clients' funds at interest. Income tax filings may be necessary to enable the client to report the interest earned on the funds, and bank handling fees may further reduce the potential return. It is evident, therefore, that in many—if not most—instances, the accounting and administrative costs, plus any bank charges, will more than offset the potential gains to the client. Thus, while no ethical rule proscribes placing client funds at interest for the benefit of an individual client, administrative costs and practical considerations often will make it self-defeating for the lawyer to attempt to obtain interest on small sums or even on large amounts of clients' funds held for short periods of time.[3]

In apparent recognition of these practical difficulties, the [CPR] does not specify that a lawyer has the duty to invest clients' nominal or short-term funds entrusted to the lawyer. The thrust of DR 9–102 is that lawyers must neither misuse a client's funds nor impede their prompt delivery. The focus is on safekeeping, accounting, and delivery, and not on investment of the funds.

a. DR 9–102's requirements are discussed later in the opinion.

3. Electronic subaccount techniques that track earnings and report them on a multitude of small accounts are being offered by a few depository institutions in some states. But even were these accounts widely available, bank charges and other costs of administering the accounts, such as accounting to the client and income tax reporting, usually would make their use infeasible in most circumstances.

The law of agency and trusts governs when a lawyer has a fiduciary duty to invest a client's funds. A trustee may be liable for lost earnings on funds left with the trustee for investment and kept uninvested for an unreasonably long time. See 2 Scott, The Law of Trusts, Sections 180.3, 181 (3d ed. 1967 and supp. 1981). Where, however, circumstances show that the trustee "was not under a duty to invest trust money but merely to safeguard it, he is not liable for interest because of this failure to invest." Id. at 1464.

This latter exception applies to most instances where a lawyer is entrusted with client funds. However, where the amount of funds held for a specific client and the expected holding period make it obvious that the interest which would be earned would exceed the lawyer's administrative costs and the bank charges, the lawyer should consult the client and follow the client's instructions as to investing. In the case of an extreme violation of the lawyer's fiduciary duty to invest a client's funds amounting to gross neglect of a client's matter, moreover, the model code would provide a basis for professional discipline. See DR 6–101(A)(3) (neglect); DR 6–101(A)(1) (competence); and DR 7–101(A)(1) (zealous representation).[b]

### What Duties Does the [CPR] Impose When an Interest-Bearing Account Is Used?

To comply with the requirements which DR 9–102 establishes with respect to the handling of funds entrusted to a lawyer, the lawyer must: (a) promptly notify a client of the receipt of the client's funds (DR 9–102(B)(1)); (b) maintain complete records of all funds of a client coming into the possession of the lawyer and render appropriate accounts to the client regarding the funds (DR 9–102(B)(3)); and (c) promptly pay to the client as requested by the client the funds in the possession of the lawyer which the client is entitled to receive (DR 9–102(B)(4)).[c] These notification, recordkeeping, and payment requirements apply to the interest generated by a separate bank account established by a lawyer for an individual client because that interest, when posted to the client's account, becomes funds of the client.

Not treated as funds of the client within the purview of these requirements, however, is the interest earned on bank accounts in which are deposited clients' funds, nominal in amount or to be held for short periods of time, under state-authorized programs providing for the interest to be paid to tax-exempt organizations. As explained in the section of this opinion addressing the ethical propriety of participation in these programs, the interest earned is treated as funds of the recipient tax-exempt organization and not as funds of any client. These programs provide mechanisms ensuring accountability, recordkeeping,

b. See RPC 1.1 (competence); 1.3 (diligence).

c. See RPC 1.15.

notification, and payment to the tax-exempt recipient in a manner consistent with the purposes of DR 9–102(B).

### MAY LAWYERS RETAIN INTEREST EARNED ON CLIENTS' FUNDS WHERE ADMINISTRATIVE COSTS WOULD EXCEED THE INTEREST EARNED?

* * *

Although DR 9–102 does not carry forward the precise language from [former] Canon 11 that "money of the client * * * should not under any circumstances * * * be used by" the lawyer, the disciplinary rule, when read in its entirety, clearly continues the strict requirements for notice, accounting, and prompt payment of funds to the client. The committee perceives no intention by the drafters of the model code to relax in any manner the long-standing restrictions on a lawyer's use of client funds. Moreover, retention of interest earned on clients' funds inevitably would create a conflict between the financial interests of the lawyer and those of the client, requiring client consent after full disclosure (DR 5–104).[d]

For these reasons, the opinion of the committee is that the model code does not permit the lawyer to use interest earned on client funds to defray the lawyer's own operating expenses without the specific and informed consent of the client. * * *

### MAY LAWYERS PARTICIPATE IN PROGRAMS USING INTEREST ON LAWYERS' TRUST ACCOUNTS FOR LAW-RELATED PUBLIC SERVICE PROJECTS?

Successful programs using the interest on lawyers' trust accounts for law-related public service projects in Canadian provinces and several British Commonwealth countries have inspired bar groups in the United States to consider the creation of similar programs. Several recent developments have caused the use of this untapped resource to

**d.** DR 5–104(A) provides:

"A lawyer shall not enter into a business transaction with a client if they have differing interests therein and if the client expects the lawyer to exercise his professional judgment therein for the protection of the client, unless the client has consented after full disclosure."

Compare RPC 1.8, which states:

"A lawyer shall not enter into a business transaction with a client or knowingly acquire an ownership, possessory, security or other pecuniary interest adverse to a client unless:

(1) The transaction and terms on which the lawyer acquires the interest are fair and reasonable to the client and are fully disclosed and transmitted in writing to the client in a manner which can be reasonably understood by the client;

(2) The client is given a reasonable opportunity to seek the advice of independent counsel in the transaction; and

(3) The client consents in writing thereto."

See also DR 5–101(A) (except with client's consent after full disclosure, lawyer shall not accept employment if exercise of professional judgment on behalf of client will or reasonably may be affected by lawyer's own financial, business, property, or personal interests); RPC 1.7(b) (lawyer shall not represent client if representation may be materially limited by lawyer's own interests unless lawyer reasonably believes representation will not be adversely affected and client consents after consultation).

become desirable and feasible. The availability of public funds for law-related public service uses, such as legal services for the indigent, has been reduced. The Internal Revenue Service has ruled that income generated under the circumstances of one program is not taxable to the client. A ruling of the Federal Reserve System has been obtained authorizing the use of negotiable order of withdrawal (NOW) accounts in connection with one of the programs. As a consequence, Florida has a program authorized by supreme court rule, California and Maryland have legislated programs, and numerous other states are in various stages of developing similar programs.

The programs being implemented vary in detail but have certain elements in common. All strive to have the pooled funds generate income for remittance to tax-exempt organizations where it will be applied to underwrite law-related public service activities. Under most plans, participation is at the option of the lawyer.[e] Included are funds nominal in amount or to be held for a short period of time; all other funds are outside the scope of the programs. The decision as to what funds will be included is left to the sound discretion of the lawyer to whom the funds are entrusted, and the lawyer's reasonable exercise of discretion often is protected by either judicial or legislative statement.[6] Prior client consent is not required. Notice to clients also is not required but is encouraged where practicable. The funds are placed in interest-bearing accounts in conventionally insured depository institutions and can be withdrawn on request. The banks are directed to remit earnings net of handling charges to a designated receiving entity, usually a bar foundation or similar tax-exempt organization, and to report account activity periodically to both the organization and the participating lawyer. The tax-exempt organizations generally segregate and strictly account for the funds and apply them as directed by governing boards to law-related uses compatible with Section 501(c)(3) of the Internal Revenue Code.

The viability of these programs depends on the answer to a question of law: whether the client has a constitutionally protected property right in the interest earned on these client funds. The Florida Supreme Court has addressed the question and has concluded that "no client has a 'property interest,' in the constitutional sense, which is being taken from him by this program." In re Interest on Trust Accounts, 402 So.2d [389,] 396 [Fla.1981]. Distinguishing Webb's Fab-

e. The Colorado, Florida, Idaho, Illinois, Maryland, Nevada, New Hampshire, Oklahoma, Oregon and Virginia programs are voluntary, but the California and Minnesota programs are mandatory. See Rivlin, IOLTA Gains Momentum Nationwide, 69 A.B.A.J. 1036 (1983).

6. In re Interest on Trust Accounts, supra note 4 at 394; 1982 Md. Laws ch. 839 authorizes placing client funds in commingled accounts at interest, with the interest paid to the Maryland Legal Services Corporation (created by 1982 Md. Laws ch. 829) where the funds are "too small in amount or are reasonably expected to be held for too short a period of time to generate at least $50 of interest or such larger amount of interest as in the judgment of the attorney" equals administration costs of an account for the client. See also Cal.Bus. & Prof. Code, art. 14, § 6211(A) (West, 1981).

ulous Pharmacies, Inc. v. Beckwith, 449 U.S. 155 (1980), the Florida court noted that under the Florida program "no client is compelled to part with 'property' by reason of a state directive, since the program creates income where there had been none before, and the income thus created would never benefit the client under any set of circumstances." Id. at 395.[f] The court also observed that the Florida program, unlike the situation in *Webb's*, "is volitional not only from the perspective of attorneys but, in the most practical sense, from the will of clients, for no attorney or firm will participate in the program * * * in the face of a strenuous objection from its clients." The court expressed "doubt that client concerns will prohibit broad participation in the program since only clients with nominal funds or those to be held for short durations—that is, clients who cannot themselves benefit from investing—are in effect providing the pooled income source." Id. at 396.

The Internal Revenue Service has ruled that interest earned on clients' nominal and short-term funds held by lawyers under a program like Florida's is not includable in the gross income of the clients under the Internal Revenue Code. Rev. Rul. 81–209, 26 C.F.R. § 1.61–7 (1981). This ruling, based largely on severance of the earned income from control or use by the client, has removed a major impediment to implementing these programs in the United States.[7]

The [CPR] does not establish whether it is ethically permissible for lawyers to participate in these programs. In the opinion of the committee, however, the rationale for the ethical acceptability of these programs is the same as the premise for acceptability in constitutional law and tax law. The client has no right under the circumstances to require the payment of any interest on the funds to himself or herself because the amount of interest which the funds could earn is likely to be less than the appropriate charges for administering the earnings. The practical effect of implementing these programs is to shift a part of the economic benefit from depository institutions to tax-exempt organizations. There is no economic injury to any client. The program creates income where there was none before. For these reasons, the

f. See Note, Minnesota's New Interest on Lawyer Trust Accounts Program, 67 Minn.L.Rev. 1286, 1299 (1983), wherein it is stated:

> "[T]he fifth amendment has never protected inchoate, unilateral expectations of property. Interest which does not exist and cannot economically be created without implementing the IOLTA program is merely an expectation of property. The *Webb's* Court recognized that 'a mere unilateral expectation or an abstract need is not a property interest entitled to protection.' "

But see Baker & Wood, "Taking" a Constitutional Look at the State Bar of Texas Proposal to Collect Interest on Attorney-Client Trust Accounts, 14 Tex.Tech.L.Rev. 327 (1983).

7. Another obstacle has been the lack of a readily available banking mechanism for the programs. The Florida Bar Foundation has obtained from the Federal Reserve System a ruling permitting the use of negotiable order of withdrawal (NOW) accounts as the banking vehicle for the Florida program. See letters from Florida Attorney General and Office of General Counsel, Board of Governors, Federal Reserve System, reprinted in Middlebrooks, The Interest on Trust Accounts Program, Mechanics of its Operation, 56 Fla.B.J. 115, 116–17 (1982). * * *

interest is not client funds in the ethical sense any more than the interest is client property in the constitutional sense or client income in the tax law sense. Therefore, assuming that either a court or a legislature has authorized a program with the attributes described above and thus, either implicitly or explicitly, has made a determination that the interest earned is not the clients' property, participation in the program by lawyers is ethical.

For several reasons, participation in these programs differs significantly from the lawyer's use of interest earned on clients' funds to defray the lawyer's own operating expenses, a practice which, as noted above, is prohibited by the [CPR] unless the client consents after full disclosure.

First, retention by a lawyer of interest earned on clients' funds inevitably places the lawyer's own financial interests in conflict with those of the client. The lawyer who retains the interest has an incentive to delay disbursement of the funds. That is why client consent after full disclosure is a prerequisite to such lawyer activity. In contrast, a state-authorized program, by requiring payment of the interest to tax-exempt organizations not selected by the lawyer, poses no conflict between the financial interest of the client and that of the lawyer.

Second, the state-authorized programs are subject to public scrutiny and accountability. Precise standards for use of interest earned on lawyer trust accounts are set by state legislatures and state supreme courts. As circumstances may warrant, the programs may be altered by law. Any direct use by a lawyer of interest on clients' funds, on the other hand, would be virtually unsupervised and, in most states, subject to public review only on complaint of a client.

Third, lawyer participation in these programs involves no commingling of funds belonging to the client and the lawyer. Since all the interest is payable to the charitable organization, interest earned on the account is not even arguably the lawyer's property. In contrast, the lawyer's personal retention of interest on client trust funds would lead inevitably to some commingling, could lead to disputes between the lawyer and client, and might subject the account to claims made by the lawyer's creditors.

The [CPR] also imposes no duty to obtain prior consent or to notify clients of the application of their funds in the programs described above. Although keeping the client informed about the program is laudatory, here, as a practical matter, the client's funds cannot be placed at interest for the benefit of the individual client. Therefore, the lawyer has no ethical responsibility to advise the client that the interest earned will be used toward funding law-related public service projects. In re Interest on Trust Accounts, 402 So.2d at 396.[g] Fur-

g. But see In re Interest on Lawyers' Trust Accounts, 279 Ark. 84, 648 S.W.2d 480 (1983), where the court refused to adopt an IOLTA program because it did not require notice to and approval by clients whose funds are used. The court urged efforts to change the tax laws or their interpretation to allow a notice requirement.

thermore, it is ethically proper without the client's consent to allow the application of a portion of the earnings on these funds to reasonable bank charges, as distinguished from the law firm's own expenses, for performing the additional computerization, transfer, and reporting called for in the programs.

The committee recognizes that the bar long has been sensitive to its role in the careful stewardship of clients' monies entrusted to lawyers. The committee finds no conflict with the principle of careful stewardship when a lawyer participates in the state-authorized programs described. Canon 8 of the [CPR] says "[a] lawyer should assist in improving the legal system." This standard of conduct is advanced when a lawyer participates in a program which puts idle funds to law-related public uses. Moreover, by focusing attention on the earnings potential of lawyer trust accounts, these programs have the added benefit of encouraging lawyers to earn interest for clients on trust funds where the expected interest is more than the cost of administering the account.

### *Comment*

(1) *Account paying interest to client.* In the 1979 Fifth Circuit case of Adams, George, Lee, Schulte & Ward, P.A. v. Westinghouse Electric Corp.,[1] a law firm put a $300,000 settlement it received for its client into the firm's non-interest bearing trust account and asserted a retaining lien against the entire $300,000 to secure payment of the $75,000 it claimed as its "reasonable" fee. After upholding a fee of only $55,000, the court held that the firm should have asserted the retaining lien against only the $75,000 claimed as fee, not the entire $300,000, and that therefore the firm owed the client interest on $225,000 from the time of the client's demand. The court went on to deny the firm's claim for interest on the $55,000 fee, saying:

> "The [lawyers] also claim that under [governing] law, attorney fees, unlike other unliquidated demands, bear interest from the date payment is due to the date of judgment * * *. The difficulty with [lawyers'] position is that they had the funds in their possession during the entire period of time and [under governing law] it would have been entirely proper for the [lawyers] to have retained the amount they claimed for their attorneys' fees in an interest bearing account pending final resolution of the correctness of the claim. The [lawyers] having unilaterally taken custody of the funds, it would be wholly illogical to determine that the client should pay them interest for the amount ultimately established as being due them."

(2) *Discipline for misappropriation and commingling.* A survey found that approximately 1/25 of 1% of lawyers were disciplined annually for misappropriating clients' funds.[2] The importance of proper book-

1. 597 F.2d 570 (5th Cir. 1979).

2. Standing Comm. on Clients' Security Fund Report, 97 A.B.A.Rep. 645, 646 (1972). See Comment, Attorney Misappropriation of Clients' Funds: A Study in Professional Responsibility, 10 U.Mich.J.L.Ref. 415, 418–23 (1977); Annot., 94 A.L.R.3d 846 (1979).

keeping cannot be overstressed. It is not a defense that commingling of a client's funds was due to careless office supervision or inadequate bookkeeping.[3] Evidence of dishonest motives is unnecessary for discipline.[4]

(3) *Civil liability*. A lawyer has been held personally liable where the bank failed after he deposited in his personal account a check received for his client.[5]

(4) *Client security funds*. Almost all states have client security funds, which pay compensation to clients whose lawyers have misappropriated their money.[6] In some states lawyers are assessed for the fund pursuant to legislation[7] or court rule.[8] But in most states a bar association-funded approach is used:

> "Certain basic principles are common to the funds in this country. Briefly they may be summarized as follows:
>
> "1. Clients' Security Fund by its nature relates only to acts of defalcation and misappropriation, not to negligent acts or conduct.
>
> "2. The defalcation must have occurred in the attorney-client relationship.
>
> "3. Payment out of the fund is a matter of grace, not of right.
>
> "4. Disbarment, suspension or disciplinary action, death or mental incompetence, or voluntary resignation of the attorney are commonly conditions precedent to payment (although some funds lodge a broader discretion in the administrators of the fund).
>
> "5. Payments are made annually. In their initial states some funds limit the amounts to be paid on claims in any one year.
>
> "6. Subrogation of the fund to the claim against the defalcating attorney is customary, with requirement in some cases of previous degrees of effort by the client to obtain reimbursement.
>
> "Other provisions than the foregoing are sometimes included, depending upon the extent of detail to which the association seeks to go in the adoption of rules and regulations."[9]

Regarding discipline for failure to notify the client promptly upon receiving client money or property, see Annot., 91 A.L.R.3d 975 (1979).

3. See Vaughn v. State Bar, 6 Cal.3d 847, 100 Cal.Rptr. 713, 494 P.2d 1257 (1972); In re Banner, 31 N.J. 24, 155 A.2d 81 (1959).

4. See In re Clayter, 78 Ill.2d 276, 35 Ill.Dec. 790, 399 N.E.2d 1318 (1980); State v. Hilton, 217 Kan. 694, 538 P.2d 977 (1975); State v. Aldrich, 71 Wis.2d 206, 237 N.W.2d 689 (1976); Annot., 94 A.L.R.3d 846, 863–65 (1979).

5. Wangsness v. Berdahl, 69 S.D. 586, 13 N.W.2d 293 (1944).

6. Comment, 10 U.Mich.J.L.Ref. 415, 417 n.13 (1977).

7. See Hersh v. State Bar, 7 Cal.3d 241, 101 Cal.Rptr. 833, 496 P.2d 1201 (1972); Bennett v. Oregon State Bar, 256 Or. 37, 470 P.2d 945, 53 A.L.R.3d 1291 (1970) (upholding legislation).

8. See In re Member of Bar, 257 A.2d 382 (Del.1969) (upholding constitutionality), appeal dismissed for want of substantial federal question 396 U.S. 274, 90 S.Ct. 562, 24 L.Ed.2d 464 (1970); Folly Farms I, Inc. v. Trustees of Clients' Security Trust Fund, 282 Md. 659, 387 A.2d 248 (1978). Amster, Clients' Security Funds: The New Jersey Story, 62 A.B.A.J. 1610 (1976).

9. Special Comm. on Clients' Security Fund Report, 91 A.B.A.Rep. 596, 599 (1966). See also Comment, 10 U.Mich.J.L.Ref. 415, 423–33 (1977); Comment, Pennsylvania Clients'

Before adopting its client security fund, Iowa "initially considered bonding lawyers, but rejected that idea when we discovered that surety companies would in effect be deciding who could practice law" and that "the lowest quotation we were able to obtain for a $100,000 surety bond per lawyer was $200 per year."[10] (Client security fund assessments often run as low as $10 or $15 per year.[11])

(5) *Audits.* Several states have inaugurated provisions for auditing lawyers' trust accounts,[12] and the ABA Standing Committee on Clients' Security Fund has supported the concept of regular and surprise audits as a means of discouraging misappropriations.[13]

(6) *Summary proceedings.* "Our concern is the alleged misconduct of the attorneys themselves, who are the court's own officers. * * *.

" 'A proceeding of this character, to compel the attorney to pay over money received by him, and which belongs to the client, may be entertained, and is within the power of the court. The principle upon which this exceptional remedy, in such cases, is based, is the power which the court has over its own officers to prevent them from or punish them for committing acts of dishonesty or impropriety calculated to bring contempt upon the administration of justice. In such case the court, in vindication of its own dignity, or for the relief of the client when clearly wronged, may entertain summary proceedings by attachment against any of its officers, and may, in its discretion, direct the payment of money, or punish them by fine or imprisonment. When an application is made to the court for the exercise of its powers to compel an attorney to pay over money received for and belonging to the client, the ground of the jurisdiction is the misconduct of its own officer. It has been said that this power should always be exercised with great prudence and caution, and a sedulous regard for the rights of the client on the one hand, and of the attorney on the other. It is not an absolute right that the client has, to invoke this severe and summary remedy against the attorney, but one always subject to discretion. It is for the court to say when and under what circumstances it will entertain such proceedings against its officers upon application of the client, and a refusal to proceed is not the denial of any legal right.' "[14]

Security Fund—How Secure is the Public? 22 Vill.L.Rev. 452 (1977); Note, The Disenchanted Client v. The Dishonest Lawyer: Where Does the Legal Profession Stand? 42 Notre Dame Law. 382 (1967).

**10.** Neiman, Lawyer Audits: A Matter of Trust, 17 Judges J. 10, 10 (Fall 1978).

**11.** See, e.g., id. at 13; Amster, Clients' Security Funds: The New Jersey Story 1610, 1610 (1976); Comment, 10 U.Mich.J.L.Ref. 415, 423 n.52 (1977).

**12.** See Nieman, supra note 10, at 10 (describing Iowa's system of random audits); Comment, 10 U.Mich.J.L.Ref. 415, 440–45 (1977) (describing various states' systems). Cf. Doyle v. State Bar, 32 Cal.3d 12, 184 Cal.Rptr. 720, 648 P.2d 942 (1982); Andresen v. Bar Association, 269 Md. 313, 305 A.2d 845, cert. denied 414 U.S. 1065, 94 S.Ct. 572, 38 L.Ed.2d 470 (1973).

**13.** See reports of that Committee in 98 A.B.A.Rep. 564 (1973); 97 A.B.A.Rep. 645, 647 (1972).

**14.** In re Long, 287 N.Y. 449, 40 N.E.2d 247, 141 A.L.R. 651 (1942). See People's Savings Bank v. Chesley, 138 Maine 353, 26 A.2d 632 (1942); Maljak v. Murphy, 385 Mich. 210, 188 N.W.2d 539 (1971); Akers v. Akers, 233 Minn. 133, 46 N.W.2d 87 (1951); Cox v. Scott, 10 A.D.2d 32, 197 N.Y.S.2d 60 (1960).

# D. ALLOCATION OF AUTHORITY

## MODEL RULES OF PROFESSIONAL CONDUCT

### RULE 1.2 Scope of Representation

(a) A lawyer shall abide by a client's decisions concerning the objectives of representation, subject to paragraphs (c), (d) and (e),[a] and shall consult with the client as to the means by which they are to be pursued. A lawyer shall abide by a client's decision whether to accept an offer of settlement of a matter. In a criminal case, the lawyer shall abide by the client's decision, after consultation with the lawyer, as to a plea to be entered, whether to waive jury trial and whether the client will testify.[b]

COMMENT:

Both lawyer and client have authority and responsibility in the objectives and means of representation. The client has ultimate authority to determine the purposes to be served by legal representation, within the limits imposed by law and the lawyer's professional obligations. Within those limits, a client also has a right to consult with the lawyer about the means to be used in pursuing those objectives. At the same time, a lawyer is not required to pursue objectives or employ means simply because a client may wish that the lawyer do so. A clear distinction between objectives and means sometimes cannot be drawn, and in many cases the client-lawyer relationship partakes of a joint undertaking. In questions of means, the lawyer should assume responsibility for technical and legal tactical issues, but should defer to the client regarding such questions as the expense to be incurred and concern for third persons who might be adversely affected. Law defining the lawyer's scope of authority in litigation varies among jurisdictions.

In a case in which the client appears to be suffering mental disability, the lawyer's duty to abide by the client's decisions is to be guided by reference to Rule 1.14.[c]

**a.** RPC 1.2(c), (d) and (e) provide:

"(c) A lawyer may limit the objectives of the representation if the client consents after consultation.

"(d) A lawyer shall not counsel a client to engage, or assist a client, in conduct that the lawyer knows is criminal or fraudulent, but a lawyer may discuss the legal consequences of any proposed course of conduct with a client and may counsel or assist a client to make a good faith effort to determine the validity, scope, meaning or application of the law.

"(e) When a lawyer knows that a client expects assistance not permitted by the rules of professional conduct or other law, the lawyer shall consult with the client regarding the relevant limitations on the lawyer's conduct."

**b.** Compare EC 7–7, which provides:

"In certain areas of legal representation not affecting the merits of the cause or substantially prejudicing the rights of a client, a lawyer is entitled to make decisions on his own. But otherwise the authority to make decisions is exclusively that of the client and, if made within the framework of the law, such decisions are binding on his lawyer. As typical examples in civil cases, it is for the client to decide whether he will accept a settlement offer or whether he will waive his right to plead an affirmative defense. A defense lawyer in a criminal case has the duty to advise his client fully on whether a particular plea to a charge appears to be desirable and as to the prospects of success on appeal, but it is for the client to decide what plea should be entered and whether an appeal should be taken."

**c.** Regarding client under disability, see supra pp. 297–302.

## ABA STANDARDS FOR CRIMINAL JUSTICE

### 4–5.2 Control and Direction of the Case

(a) Certain decisions relating to the conduct of the case are ultimately for the accused and others are ultimately for defense counsel. The decisions which are to be made by the accused after full consultation with counsel are: (i) what pleas to enter; (ii) whether to waive jury trial; (iii) whether to testify in his or her own behalf.

(b) The decisions on what witnesses to call, whether and how to conduct cross-examination, what jurors to accept or strike, what trial motions should be made, and all other strategic and tactical decisions are the exclusive province of the lawyer after consultation with the client.

(c) If a disagreement on significant matters of tactics or strategy arises between the lawyer and his client, the lawyer should make a record of the circumstances, the lawyer's advice and reasons, and the conclusion reached. The record should be made in a manner which protects the confidentiality of the lawyer-client relation.

---

## JONES v. BARNES

— U.S. —, 103 S.Ct. 3308, 77 L.Ed.2d 987 (1983).

Chief Justice BURGER delivered the opinion of the Court.

We granted certiorari to consider whether defense counsel assigned to prosecute an appeal from a criminal conviction has a constitutional duty to raise every nonfrivolous issue requested by the defendant.

In 1976, Richard Butts was robbed at knifepoint by four men in the lobby of an apartment building; he was badly beaten and his watch and money were taken. Butts informed a Housing Authority Detective that he recognized one of his assailants as a person known to him as "Froggy," and gave a physical description of the person to the detective. The following day the detective arrested respondent David Barnes, who is known as "Froggy."

Respondent was charged with first and second degree robbery, second degree assault, and third degree larceny. The prosecution rested primarily upon Butts' testimony and his identification of respondent. During cross-examination, defense counsel asked Butts whether he had ever undergone psychiatric treatment; however, no offer of proof was made on the substance or relevance of the question after the trial judge *sua sponte* instructed Butts not to answer. At the close of trial, the trial judge declined to give an instruction on accessorial liability requested by the defense. The jury convicted respondent of first and second degree robbery and second degree assault.

The Appellate Division of the Supreme Court of New York, Second Department, assigned Michael Melinger to represent respondent on appeal. Respondent sent Melinger a letter listing several claims that he felt should be raised. Included were claims that Butts' identification testimony should have been suppressed, that the trial judge improperly excluded psychiatric evidence, and that respondent's trial counsel was ineffective. Respondent also enclosed a copy of a *pro se* brief he had written.

In a return letter, Melinger accepted some but rejected most of the suggested claims, stating that they would not aid respondent in obtaining a new trial and that they could not be raised on appeal because they were not based on evidence in the record. Melinger then listed seven potential claims of error that he was considering including in his brief, and invited respondent's "reflections and suggestions" with regard to those seven issues. The record does not reveal any response to this letter.

Melinger's brief to the Appellate Division concentrated on three of the seven points he had raised in his letter to respondent: improper exclusion of psychiatric evidence, failure to suppress Butts' identification testimony, and improper cross-examination of respondent by the trial judge. In addition, Melinger submitted respondent's own *pro se* brief. Thereafter, respondent filed two more *pro se* briefs, raising three more of the seven issues Melinger had identified.

At oral argument, Melinger argued the three points presented in his own brief, but not the arguments raised in the *pro se* briefs. On May 22, 1978, the Appellate Division affirmed by summary order. The New York Court of Appeals denied leave to appeal.

[O]n March 31, 1980, [respondent] filed a petition in the New York Court of Appeals for reconsideration of that court's denial of leave to appeal. In that petition, respondent for the first time claimed that his *appellate* counsel, Melinger, had provided ineffective assistance.[a] The New York Court of Appeals denied the application * * *.

Respondent then [proceeded in] United States District Court * * * with a petition for habeas corpus based on the claim of ineffective assistance by appellate counsel. The District Court * * * dismissed the petition, holding that the record gave no support to the claim of ineffective assistance of appellate counsel on "any * * * standard which could reasonably by applied." * * *

A divided panel of the Court of Appeals reversed, 665 F.2d 427 (CA2 1981). Laying down a new standard, the majority held that when "the appellant requests that [his attorney] raise additional colorable points [on appeal], counsel *must argue the additional points to the full extent of his professional ability.*" In the view of the majority, this conclusion followed from Anders v. California, 386 U.S. 738, 87 S.Ct. 1396, 18 L.Ed.2d 493 (1967). In *Anders*, this Court held that an appointed attorney must advocate his client's cause vigorously and may not withdraw from a nonfrivolous appeal.[b] The Court of

**a.** Regarding such claims in general, see Annot., 15 A.L.R.4th 582 (1982); Annot., 26 A.L.R.Fed. 218, 279–81 (1976).

**b.** The *Anders* court held that appellate counsel's withdrawal request was not warranted by his mere conclusion that the appeal

Appeals majority held that, since *Anders* bars counsel from abandoning a nonfrivolous appeal, it also bars counsel from abandoning a nonfrivolous issue on appeal.

> "[A]ppointed counsel's unwillingness to present particular arguments at appellant's request functions not only to abridge defendant's right to counsel on appeal, but also to limit the defendant's constitutional right of equal access to the appellate process. * * *" Ibid.

The Court of Appeals went on to hold that, "[h]aving demonstrated that appointed counsel failed to argue colorable claims at his request, an appellant need not also demonstrate a likelihood of success on the merits of those claims."

The court concluded that Melinger had not met the above standard in that he had failed to press at least two nonfrivolous claims: the trial judge's failure to instruct on accessory liability and ineffective assistance of trial counsel. The fact that these issues had been raised in respondent's own *pro se* briefs did not cure the error, since "[a] pro se brief is no substitute for the advocacy of experienced counsel." The court reversed and remanded, with instructions to grant the writ of habeas corpus unless the State assigned new counsel and granted a new appeal.

Circuit Judge Meskill dissented, stating that the majority had overextended *Anders*. In his view, *Anders* concerned only whether an attorney must pursue nonfrivolous *appeals*; it did not imply that attorneys must advance all nonfrivolous *issues*.

We granted certiorari, and we reverse.

In announcing a new *per se* rule that appellate counsel must raise every nonfrivolous issue requested by the client, the Court of Appeals relied primarily upon Anders v. California. There is, of course, no constitutional right to an appeal, but in Griffin v. Illinois, 351 U.S. 12, 18, 76 S.Ct. 585, 590, 100 L.Ed. 891 (1955), and Douglas v. California, 372 U.S. 353, 83 S.Ct. 814, 9 L.Ed.2d 811 (1963), the Court held that if an appeal is open to those who can pay for it, an appeal must be provided for an indigent. It is also recognized that the accused has the ultimate authority to make certain fundamental decisions regarding the case, as to whether to plead guilty, waive a jury, testify in his or her own behalf, or take an appeal, see Wainwright v. Sykes, 433 U.S. 72, 93 n.1, 97 S.Ct. 2497, 2509 n.1, 53 L.Ed.2d 594 (1977) (Burger, C.J., concurring); ABA Standards for Criminal Justice 4–5.2, 21–2.2 (2d ed. 1980). In addition, we have held that, with some limitations, a defendant may elect to act as his or her own advocate, Faretta v.

*lacked merit;* it said counsel should request withdrawal only upon finding the appeal *wholly frivolous* and even then the withdrawal request "must be accompanied by a brief referring to anything in the record that might arguably support the appeal."

See ABA Standards for Criminal Justice 4–8.3 (2d ed. 1980) ("Appellate counsel should not seek to withdraw from a case solely on the basis of his or her own determination that the appeal lacks merit.").

California, 422 U.S. 806, 95 S.Ct. 2525, 45 L.Ed.2d 562 (1975). Neither *Anders* nor any other decision of this Court suggests, however, that the indigent defendant has a constitutional right to compel appointed counsel to press nonfrivolous points requested by the client, if counsel, as a matter of professional judgment, decides not to present those points.

This Court, in holding that a State must provide counsel for an indigent appellant on his first appeal as of right, recognized the superior ability of trained counsel in the "examination into the record, research of the law, and marshalling of arguments on [the appellant's] behalf," Douglas v. California, 372 U.S., at 358, 83 S.Ct., at 817. Yet by promulgating a *per se* rule that the client, not the professional advocate, must be allowed to decide what issues are to be pressed, the Court of Appeals seriously undermines the ability of counsel to present the client's case in accord with counsel's professional evaluation.

Experienced advocates since time beyond memory have emphasized the importance of winnowing out weaker arguments on appeal and focusing on one central issue if possible, or at most on a few key issues. Justice Jackson, after observing appellate advocates for many years, stated:

> "One of the first tests of a discriminating advocate is to select the question, or questions, that he will present orally. Legal contentions, like the currency, depreciate through over-issue. The mind of an appellate judge is habitually receptive to the suggestion that a lower court committed an error. But receptiveness declines as the number of assigned errors increases. Multiplicity hints at lack of confidence in any one. * * * [E]xperience on the bench convinces me that multiplying assignments of error will dilute and weaken a good case and will not save a bad one." Jackson, Advocacy Before the Supreme Court, 25 Temple L.Q. 115, 119 (1951).

Justice Jackson's observation echoes the advice of countless advocates before him and since. An authoritative work on appellate practice observes:

> "Most cases present only one, two, or three significant questions. * * * Usually, * * * if you cannot win on a few major points, the others are not likely to help, and to attempt to deal with a great many in the limited number of pages allowed for briefs will mean that none may receive adequate attention. The effect of adding weak arguments will be to dilute the force of the stronger ones." R. Stern, Appellate Practice in the United States 266 (1981).

There can hardly be any question about the importance of having the appellate advocate examine the record with a view to selecting the most promising issues for review. This has assumed a greater importance in an era when oral argument is strictly limited in most courts—often to as little as 15 minutes—and when page limits on briefs are widely imposed. See, e.g., Fed. Rules App. Proc. 28(g); McKinney's 1982 New York Rules of Court §§ 670.17(g)(2), 670.22. Even in a court that imposes no time or page limits, however, the new *per se* rule laid down by the Court of Appeals is contrary to all experience and logic. A brief that raises every colorable issue runs the risk of burying good arguments—those that, in the words of the great advocate John W. Davis, "go for the jugular," Davis, The Argument of an Appeal, 26 A.B.A.J. 895, 897 (1940)—in a verbal mound made up of strong and weak contentions. See generally, e.g., Godbold, Twenty Pages and Twenty Minutes—Effective Advocacy on Appeal, 30 Sw.L.J. 801 (1976).[6]

This Court's decision in *Anders*, far from giving support to the new *per se* rule announced by the Court of Appeals, is to the contrary. *Anders* recognized that the role of the advocate "requires that he support his client's appeal to the best of his ability." Here the appointed counsel did just that. For judges to second-guess reasonable professional judgments and impose on appointed counsel a duty to raise every "colorable" claim suggested by a client would disserve the very goal of vigorous and effective advocacy that underlies *Anders*. Nothing in the Constitution or our interpretation of that document requires such a standard.[7] The judgment of the Court of Appeals is accordingly

Reversed.

Justice BLACKMUN, concurring in the judgment.

I do not join the Court's opinion, because I need not decide in this case whether there is or is not a constitutional right to a first appeal of a criminal conviction, and because I agree with Justice Brennan, and the American Bar Association, ABA Standards for Criminal Justice, Criminal Appeals, Standard 21–3.2, Comment, p. 21–42 (2d ed., 1980), that, as an *ethical* matter, an attorney should argue on appeal all nonfrivolous claims upon which his client insists. Whether or not

6. The ABA Model Rules of Professional Conduct provide:

> "A lawyer shall abide by a client's decisions concerning the objectives of representation * * * and shall consult with the client as to the means by which they are to be pursued. * * * In a criminal case, the lawyer shall abide by the client's decision, * * * *as to a plea to be entered, whether to waive jury trial and whether the client will testify.*"

With the exception of these specified fundamental decisions, an attorney's duty is to take professional responsibility for the conduct of the case, after consulting with his client.

Respondent points to the ABA Standards for Criminal Appeals, which appear to indicate that counsel should accede to a client's insistence on pressing a particular contention on appeal, see ABA Standards for Criminal Justice 21–3.2, at 21–42 (2d ed. 1980). The ABA Defense Function Standards provide, however, that, with the exceptions specified above, strategic and tactical decisions are the exclusive province of the defense counsel, after consultation with the client. See ABA Standards for Criminal Justice 4–5.2 (2d ed. 1980). In any event, the fact that the ABA may have chosen to recognize a given practice as desirable or appropriate does not mean that that practice is required by the Constitution.

7. The only question presented by this case is whether a criminal defendant has a constitutional right to have appellate counsel raise every nonfrivolous issue that the defendant requests. The availability of federal habeas corpus to review claims that counsel declined to raise is not before us, and we have no occasion to decide whether counsel's refusal to raise requested claims would constitute "cause" for a petitioner's default within the meaning of Wainwright v. Sykes, 433 U.S. 72, 97 S.Ct. 2497, 53 L.Ed.2d 594 (1977).

one agrees with the Court's view of legal strategy, it seems to me that the lawyer, after giving his client his best opinion as to the course most likely to succeed, should acquiesce in the client's choice of which nonfrivolous claims to pursue.

Certainly, Anders v. California, 386 U.S. 738, 87 S.Ct. 1396, 18 L.Ed.2d 493 (1967), and Faretta v. California, 422 U.S. 806, 95 S.Ct. 2525, 45 L.Ed.2d 562 (1975), indicate that the attorney's usurpation of certain fundamental decisions can violate the Constitution. I agree with the Court, however, that neither my view, nor the ABA's view, of the ideal allocation of decisionmaking authority between client and lawyer necessarily assumes constitutional status where counsel's performance is "within the range of competence demanded of attorneys in criminal cases," McMann v. Richardson, 397 U.S. 759, 771, 90 S.Ct. 1441, 1449, 25 L.Ed.2d 763 (1970), and "assure[s] the indigent defendant an adequate opportunity to present his claims fairly in the context of the State's appellate process," Ross v. Moffitt, 417 U.S. 600, 616, 94 S.Ct. 2437, 2446, 41 L.Ed.2d 341 (1974). I agree that both these requirements were met here.

But the attorney, by refusing to carry out his client's express wishes, cannot forever foreclose review of nonfrivolous constitutional claims. As I noted in Faretta v. California, 422 U.S. 806, 848, 95 S.Ct. 2525, 2547, 45 L.Ed.2d 562 (1975) (dissenting opinion), "[f]or such overbearing conduct by counsel, there is a remedy" * * *. The remedy, of course, is a writ of habeas corpus. Thus, while the Court does not reach the question, ante, at n.7, I state my view that counsel's failure to raise on appeal nonfrivolous constitutional claims upon which his client has insisted must constitute "cause and prejudice" for any resulting procedural default under state law. See Wainwright v. Sykes, 433 U.S. 72, 97 S.Ct. 2497, 53 L.Ed.2d 594 (1977).

Justice BRENNAN, with whom Justice MARSHALL joins, dissenting.

The Sixth Amendment provides that "[i]n all criminal prosecutions, the accused shall enjoy the right * * * to have the *Assistance* of counsel for his defence" (emphasis added). I find myself in fundamental disagreement with the Court over what a right to "the assistance of counsel" means. The import of words like "assistance" and "counsel" seems inconsistent with a regime under which counsel appointed by the State to represent a criminal defendant can refuse to raise issues with arguable merit on appeal when his client, after hearing his assessment of the case and his advice, has directed him to raise them. * * *

* * * In recognizing the right to counsel on appeal, we have expressly relied not only on the Fourteenth Amendment's Equal Protection Clause, which in this context prohibits disadvantaging indigent defendants in comparison to those who can afford to hire counsel themselves, but also on its Due Process Clause and its incorporation of Sixth

Amendment standards. * * * A State may not incarcerate a person, whether he is indigent or not, if he has not had (or waived) the assistance of counsel at all stages of the criminal process at which his substantial rights may be affected. Argersinger v. Hamlin, 407 U.S. 25, 92 S.Ct. 2006, 32 L.Ed.2d 530 (1972). In my view, that right to counsel extends to one appeal, provided the defendant decides to take an appeal and the appeal is not frivolous.[2]

The Constitution does not on its face define the phrase "assistance of counsel," but surely those words are not empty of content. No one would doubt that counsel must be qualified to practice law in the courts of the State in question,[3] or that the representation afforded must meet minimum standards of effectiveness. See Powell v. Alabama, 287 U.S. 45, 71, 53 S.Ct. 55, 65, 77 L.Ed. 158 (1932). To satisfy the Constitution, counsel must function as an advocate for the defendant, as opposed to a friend of the court. Anders v. California, 386 U.S., at 744, 87 S.Ct., at 1400. Admittedly, the question in this case requires us to look beyond those clear guarantees. What is at issue here is the relationship between lawyer and client—who has ultimate authority to decide which nonfrivolous issues should be presented on appeal? I believe the right to "the assistance of counsel" carries with it a right, personal to the defendant, to make that decision, against the advice of counsel if he chooses.

If all the Sixth Amendment protected was the State's interest in substantial justice, it would not include such a right. However, in Faretta v. California, 422 U.S. 806, 95 S.Ct. 2525, 45 L.Ed.2d 562 (1975), we decisively rejected that view of the Constitution, ably advanced by Justice BLACKMUN in dissent. Holding that the Sixth Amendment requires that defendants be allowed to represent themselves, we observed:

> "It is undeniable that in most criminal prosecutions defendants could better defend with counsel's guidance than by their own unskilled efforts. But where the defendant will not voluntarily accept representation by counsel, the potential advantage of a lawyer's training can be realized, if at all, only imperfectly. To force a lawyer on a defendant can only lead him to believe that the law contrives against him. * * * Personal liberties are not rooted in the law of averages. The right to defend is personal. The defendant, and not his lawyer or the State, will bear the personal consequences of a conviction. It is the defendant, therefore, who must be free personally to decide whether in his particular case counsel is to his advantage. And although he may conduct his own

2. Both indigents and those who can afford lawyers have this right. However, with regard to issues involving the allocation of authority between lawyer and client, courts may well take account of paying clients' abililty to specify at the outset of their relationship with their attorneys what degree of control they wish to exercise, and to avoid attorneys unwilling to accept client direction.

3. Of course, a State may also allow properly supervised law students to represent indigent defendants. See Argersinger v. Hamlin, 407 U.S. 25, 40–41, 92 S.Ct. 2006, 2014, 32 L.Ed.2d 530 (1972) (Brennan, J., concurring).

defense ultimately to his own detriment, his choice must be honored out of 'that respect for the individual which is the lifeblood of the law.' Illinois v. Allen, 397 U.S. 337, 350–351, 90 S.Ct. 1057, 1064, 25 L.Ed.2d 353 (Brennan, J., concurring)." 422 U.S., at 834, 95 S.Ct., at 2540.

*Faretta* establishes that the right to counsel is more than a right to have one's case presented competently and effectively. It is predicated on the view that the function of counsel under the Sixth Amendment is to protect the dignity and autonomy of a person on trial by *assisting* him in making choices that are his to make, not to make choices for him, although counsel may be better able to decide which tactics will be most effective for the defendant. Anders v. California also reflects that view. Even when appointed counsel believes an appeal has no merit, he must furnish his client a brief covering all arguable grounds for appeal so that the client may "raise any points that he chooses." 386 U.S., at 744, 87 S.Ct., at 1400.

The right to counsel as *Faretta* and *Anders* conceive it is not an all-or-nothing right, under which a defendant must choose between forgoing the assistance of counsel altogether or relinquishing control over every aspect of his case beyond its most basic structure (i.e., how to plead, whether to present a defense, whether to appeal). A defendant's interest in his case clearly extends to other matters. Absent exceptional circumstances, he is bound by the tactics used by his counsel at trial and on appeal. Henry v. Mississippi, 379 U.S. 443, 451, 85 S.Ct. 564, 569, 13 L.Ed.2d 408 (1963). He may want to press the argument that he is innocent, even if other stratagems are more likely to result in the dismissal of charges or in a reduction of punishment. He may want to insist on certain arguments for political reasons. He may want to protect third parties. This is just as true on appeal as at trial, and the proper role of counsel is to *assist* him in these efforts, insofar as that is possible consistent with the lawyer's conscience, the law, and his duties to the court.

I find further support for my position in the legal profession's own conception of its proper role. The American Bar Association has taken the position that

"[W]hen, in the estimate of counsel, the decision of the client to take an appeal, *or the client's decision to press a particular contention on appeal*, is incorrect[, c]ounsel has the professional duty to give to the client fully and forcefully an opinion concerning the case and its probable outcome. *Counsel's role, however, is to advise. The decision is made by the client.*" ABA Standards for Criminal Justice, Criminal Appeals, Standard 21–3.2, Comment, at 21–42 (1980) (emphasis added).[4]

4. Cf. ABA Code of Professional Responsibility (1980) EC7–7 ("the authority to make decisions is exclusively that of the client" except for decisions "not substantially affecting the merits of the cause or substantially prejudicing the rights of a client"); id., EC7–8 ("the lawyer should always remember that the decision whether to forego legally available objectives or methods because of non-legal factors is ultimately for the client").

The Court disregards this clear statement of how the profession defines the "assistance of counsel" at the appellate stage of a criminal defense by referring to standards governing the allocation of authority between attorney and client at trial. See ante, at n.6; ABA Standards for Criminal Justice, The Defense Function, Standard 4–5.2 (1980). In the course of a trial, however, decisions must often be made in a matter of hours, if not minutes or seconds. From the standpoint of effective administration of justice, the need to confer decisive authority on the attorney is paramount with regard to the hundreds of decisions that must be made quickly in the course of a trial. Decisions regarding which issues to press on appeal, in contrast, can and should be made more deliberately, in the course of deciding whether to appeal at all.

[T]he Court argues that good appellate advocacy demands selectivity among arguments. That is certainly true—the Court's advice is good. It ought to be taken to heart by every lawyer called upon to argue an appeal in this or any other court, and by his client. It should take little or no persuasion to get a wise client to understand that, if staying out of prison is what he values most, he should encourage his lawyer to raise only his two or three best arguments on appeal, and he should defer to his lawyer's advice as to which are the best arguments. The Constitution, however, does not require clients to be wise, and other policies should be weighed in the balance as well.

It is no secret that indigent clients often mistrust the lawyers appointed to represent them. There are many reasons for this, some perhaps unavoidable even under perfect conditions—differences in education, disposition, and socioeconomic class—and some that should (but may not always) be zealously avoided. A lawyer and his client do not always have the same interests. Even with paying clients, a lawyer may have a strong interest in having judges and prosecutors think well of him, and, if he is working for a flat fee—a common arrangement for criminal defense attorneys—or if his fees for court appointments are lower than he would receive for other work, he has an obvious financial incentive to conclude cases on his criminal docket swiftly. Good lawyers undoubtedly recognize these temptations and resist them, and they endeavor to convince their clients that they will. It would be naive, however, to suggest that they always succeed in either task. A constitutional rule that encourages lawyers to disregard their clients' wishes without compelling need can only exacerbate the clients' suspicion of their lawyers. As in *Faretta,* to force a lawyer's *decisions* on a defendant "can only lead him to believe that the law conspires against him." In the end, what the Court hopes to gain in effectiveness of appellate representation by the rule it imposes today may well be lost to decreased effectiveness in other areas of representation.

[T]oday's ruling denigrates the values of individual autonomy and dignity central to many constitutional rights, especially those Fifth and Sixth Amendment rights that come into play in the criminal process. Certainly a person's life changes when he is charged with a crime and brought to trial. He must, if he harbors any hope of success, defend himself on terms—often technical and hard to understand—that are the State's, not his own. As a practical matter, the assistance of counsel is necessary to that defense. Yet, until his conviction becomes final and he has had an opportunity to appeal, any restrictions on individual autonomy and dignity should be limited to the minimum necessary to vindicate the State's interest in a speedy, effective prosecution. The role of the defense lawyer should be above all to function as the instrument and defender of the client's autonomy and dignity in all phases of the criminal process. * * *

The Court subtly but unmistakably adopts a different conception of the defense lawyer's role—he need do nothing beyond what the State, not his client, considers most important. In many ways, having a lawyer becomes one of the many indignities visited upon someone who has the ill fortune to run afoul of the criminal justice system.

I cannot accept the notion that lawyers are one of the punishments a person receives merely for being accused of a crime. Clients, if they wish, are capable of making informed judgments about which issues to appeal, and when they exercise that prerogative their choices should be respected unless they would require lawyers to violate their consciences, the law, or their duties to the court. On the other hand, I would not presume lightly that, in a particular case, a defendant has disregarded his lawyer's obviously sound advice. The Court of Appeals, in reversing the District Court, did not address the factual question whether respondent, having been advised by his lawyer that it would not be wise to appeal on all the issues respondent had suggested, actually insisted in a timely fashion that his lawyer brief the nonfrivolous issues identified by the Court of Appeals. If he did not, or if he was content with filing his *pro se* brief, then there would be no deprivation of the right to the assistance of counsel. I would remand for a hearing on this question.

### *Comment*

(1) *Lawyer may decide.* In Nelson v. California,[1] the Ninth Circuit rejected a criminal defendant's habeas claim where the public defender for tactical reasons declined, despite defendant's request, to object to the introduction of seized evidence. The court said:

> "Our reasons are that only counsel is competent to make such a decision, that counsel must be the manager of the lawsuit, that if such decisions are to be made by the defendant, he is likely to do himself more harm than good, and that a contrary rule would seriously impair the constitutional guaranty of the right to counsel. One of the surest ways for counsel to lose a lawsuit is to permit his client to run the trial. We think that few competent counsel would

1. 346 F.2d 73 (9th Cir. 1965).

accept retainers, or appointments * * *, to defend criminal cases, if they were to have to consult the defendant, and follow his views, on every issue of trial strategy that might, often as a matter of hindsight, involve some claim of constitutional right."

Similarly, in a civil case a party may be bound by counsel at trial withdrawing previous objections to exhibits and stipulating to proposed findings of fact.[2]

(2) *Lawyer may not decide—generally.* In Linsk v. Linsk,[3] the California Supreme Court held that where proceedings ended in a mistrial because of the trial judge's disability, a lawyer could not validly stipulate over the client's express objection that the case would be decided by a different judge solely on the record previously made. The court reasoned, with extensive citations, as follows:

> "The attorney is authorized by virture of his employment to bind the client in procedural matters arising during the course of the action but he may not impair the client's substantial rights or the cause of action itself. The extent of an attorney's powers in this regard has been aptly described as follows: 'In retaining counsel for the prosecution or defense of a suit, the right to do many acts in respect to the cause is embraced as ancillary, or incidental to the general authority conferred, and among these is included the authority to enter into stipulations and agreements in all matters of procedure during the progress of the trial. Stipulations thus made, so far as they are simply necessary or incidental to the management of the suit, and which affect only the procedure or remedy as distinguished from the cause of action itself, and the essential rights of the client, are binding on the client.'
>
> "Under the foregoing concept it has been held that an attorney may refuse to call a witness even though his client desires that the witness testify; may abandon a defense he deems to be unmeritorious; may stipulate that the trial judge could view the premises, that a witness, if called, would give substantially the same testimony as a prior witness and that the testimony of a witness in a prior trial be used in a later action; and he may waive the late filing of a complaint.
>
> "On the other hand, an attorney may not, by virtue of his general authority over the conduct of the action, stipulate that his client's premises constituted an unsafe place to work where such a stipulation would dispose of the client's sole interest in the premises, nor may he stipulate to a matter which would eliminate an essential defense. He may not agree to the entry of a default judgment against his client, may not compromise his client's claim, or stipulate that only nominal damages may be awarded, and he cannot agree to an increase in the amount of the judgment against his

2. United States v. Texas, 523 F.Supp. 703 (E.D.Tex.1981).

3. 70 Cal.2d 272, 74 Cal.Rptr. 544, 449 P.2d 760 (1969).

client. Likewise an attorney is without authority to waive findings so that no appeal can be prosecuted, or agree that a judgment may be made payable in gold coin rather than in legal tender.

"An attorney is also forbidden without authorization to stipulate that the opposing party's failure to comply with a statute would not be pleaded as a defense, or to write a letter to a creditor asking it to join in a bankruptcy petition where he has been employed only to institute bankruptcy proceedings, and he may not bind his client by a statement that it stands ready to pay a stated sum or that if the jury finds for plaintiff the amount of the verdict would constitute a landlord's lien against livestock.

"The dichotomy in the foregoing cases appears to relate to whether the attorney has relinquished a substantial right of his client in entering into a stipulation on his behalf. If counsel merely employs his best discretion in protecting the client's rights and achieving the client's fundamental goals, his authority to proceed in any appropriate manner has been unquestioned. On the other hand, if counsel abdicates a substantial right of the client contrary to express instructions, he exceeds his authority.

"It seems incontrovertible that the right of a party to have the trier of fact observe his demeanor, and that of his adversary and other witnesses, during examination and cross-examination is so crucial to a party's cause of action that an attorney cannot be permitted to waive by stipulation such right as to all the testimony in a trial when the stipulation is contrary to the express wishes of his client. Indeed it has been held that the very right to trial contemplates the 'right to be present at and to participate in every phase of the trial.' "[4]

(3) *Lawyer may not decide—settlements.* "The rule is almost universal that an attorney who is clothed with no other authority than that arising from his employment in that capacity has no implied power by virture of his general retainer to compromise and settle his client's claim or cause of action."[5] Accordingly, a number of courts have held that a lawyer's unauthorized making of (and absconding with) a settlement does not affect the client's right to continue pressing the claim against the defendant.[6] But the Rhode Island Supreme Court, while

4. See also Graves v. P.J. Taggares Co., 94 Wn.2d 298, 616 P.2d 1223 (1980) (defendant's lawyer may not validly without defendant's consent make stipulations admitting vicarious liability, admitting the nature and extent of plaintiff's injuries, and withdrawing a jury demand).

Regarding authority to dismiss or otherwise terminate action, see Annot., 56 A.L.R.2d 1290 (1957).

5. Annot., 30 A.L.R.2d 944, 945 (1953).

An exception exists where the lawyer is confronted with an emergency which requires prompt action to protect the client's interest and consultation with the client is impossible. Id. at 950; see Bates v. Bates, 66 Minn. 131, 68 N.W. 845 (1896).

6. See Nehleber v. Anzalone, 345 So.2d 822 (Fla.App.1977); Miotk v. Rudy, 4 Kan.App. 296, 605 P.2d 587 (1980); Henderson v. Great Atlantic & Pacific Tea Co., 374 Mich. 142, 132 N.W.2d 75 (1965); Gibson v. Nelson, 111 Minn. 183, 126 N.W. 731 (1910); Annot., 30 A.L.R. 944, 954–55 (1953).

agreeing that the lawyer had no *implied* authority to make and collect the settlement, found *apparent* authority to bar the client's continued pressing of the defendant.[7] And a California court has held that although neither implied nor ostensible authority barred plaintiffs from continuing to press their suit against defendant, who had paid $30,000 to plaintiffs' faithless lawyer, plaintiffs had to credit the $30,000 against any recovery.[8]

(4) *Client may decide.* The Alabama Supreme Court has held that counsel did not act incompetently in acceding to the defendant's insistence on a plea of alibi over the lawyer's advice that self-defense was the only chance, on the ground that the issue of the defense to assert is for the defendant to decide.[9]

(5) *Client may not decide.* A federal district court in Alaska has held that a stipulation extending time to answer signed by the plaintiff rather than the plaintiff's lawyer was void.[10] The court, with voluminous citations of authority, said:

> "The cause of action, the claim or demand sued upon, the subject-matter of the litigation, are within the exclusive control of the client; and the attorney may not impair, compromise, settle, surrender, or destroy them without the client's consent. But all the proceedings in court to enforce the remedy, to bring the claim, demand, cause of action, or subject-matter of the suit to hearing, trial, determination, judgment, and execution, are within the exclusive control of the attorney. 'All acts, in and out of court, necessary or incidental to the prosecution or management of the suit, and which affect the remedy only, and not the cause of action,' are to be performed by the attorney."

(6) *Permitting client to decide.* In People v. Hunt,[11] an Illinois court rejected a defendant's claim that his conviction should be reversed because the trial court acceded to defendant's insistence, against counsel's advice, upon calling defendant's brother as a witness. Before the brother was called, counsel informed the court outside the jury's presence that he had spoken with the brother about the possible testimony and that he believed admitting the testimony was against his professional judgment and the client's best interest. Defendant nevertheless wanted the brother to testify, and so informed the court. The court allowed the brother's testimony, which indicated a different

7. Cohen v. Goldman, 85 R.I. 434, 132 A.2d 414 (1957).

8. Whittier Union High School District v. Superior Court, 66 Cal.App.3d 504, 136 Cal.Rptr. 86 (1977). The court went on to say that it was possible that defendants in a separate action could recover the $30,000 from plaintiffs as principal of the faithless lawyer, from the banks that negotiated the check with forged endorsements, or, derivatively to plaintiffs' rights, from the state clients' security fund.

9. Taylor v. State, 291 Ala. 756, 287 So.2d 901 (1973).

10. Bonnifield v. Thorp, 71 F. 924 (D.Alaska 1896), error dismissed 83 F. 1022 (9th Cir. 1898).

11. 100 Ill.App.3d 553, 55 Ill.Dec. 894, 426 N.E.2d 1268 (1981).

alibi than that just testified to by defendant's other witness. Sustaining the conviction, the appellate court concluded:

> "[W]e hold that [ABA Standards for Criminal Justice 4–5.2] should not be used to absolve the overzealous defendant who intrudes into this area of professional discretion by insisting on a contrary course of action after counsel has explained the possible disadvantages of the insisted tactic. [W]e hold that where counsel has explained on the record the consequences of a particular tactic but the defendant still insists on taking such action, he is estopped from claiming on appeal that the ruling countenancing the tactic which was made upon his insistence constituted prejudicial error even though such insistence invaded the province normally reserved for defense counsel." [12]

(7) *Court's, adverse party's, and client's interests.* Professor Spiegel concludes that the results in the settlement, trial tactics, and attorney default cases "seem more easily explained by a theory focusing on the interests of affected third parties—the court and the adverse party—than by the * * * subject-matter/procedure distinction." [13] He goes on to argue in favor of increasing the client's decisionmaking role through an informed consent approach similar to the one that lawyers have created for doctors. He would have the client decide matters as to which the client's values are likely to be implicated or as to which there is a danger of divergence between the lawyer's and client's interests.

## E. NEGLECT AND MISHANDLING

### MODEL RULES OF PROFESSIONAL CONDUCT

**RULE 1.1 Competence**

A lawyer shall provide competent representation to a client. Competent representation requires the legal knowledge, skill, thoroughness and preparation reasonably necessary for the representation.

**RULE 1.3 Diligence**

A lawyer shall act with reasonable diligence and promptness in representing a client.

**RULE 1.4 Communication**

(a) A lawyer shall keep a client reasonably informed about the status of a matter and promptly comply with reasonable requests for information.

12. Compare Freedman, A Lawyer Doesn't Always Know Best, 7 Human Rights 28, 51 (1978) ("At issue is not the lawyer's day in court, but the defendant's—the defendant's right to trial, right to due process of law, and right to counsel.").

13. Spiegel, Lawyering and Client Decisionmaking: Informed Consent and the Legal Profession, 128 U.Pa.L.Rev. 41 (1979).

(b) A lawyer shall explain a matter to the extent reasonably necessary to permit the client to make informed decisions regarding the representation.

**RULE 1.8 Conflict of Interest: Prohibited Transactions**

* * *

(h) A lawyer shall not make an agreement prospectively limiting the lawyer's liability to a client for malpractice unless permitted by law and the client is independently represented in making the agreement, or settle a claim for such liability with an unrepresented client or former client without first advising that person in writing that independent representation is appropriate in connection therewith.[a]

## TOGSTAD v. VESELY, OTTO, MILLER & KEEFE

291 N.W.2d 686 (Minn. 1980).

PER CURIAM.

This is an appeal by the defendants from a judgment of the Hennepin County District Court involving an action for legal malpractice. The jury found that the defendant attorney Jerre Miller was negligent and that, as a direct result of such negligence, plaintiff John Togstad sustained damages in the amount of $610,500 and his wife, plaintiff Joan Togstad, in the amount of $39,000. Defendants (Miller and his law firm) appeal * * *. We affirm.

In August 1971, John Togstad began to experience severe headaches and on August 16, 1971, was admitted to Methodist Hospital where tests disclosed that the headaches were caused by a large aneurism[1] on the left internal carotid artery.[2] The attending physician, Dr. Paul Blake, a neurological surgeon, treated the problem by applying a Selverstone clamp to the left common carotid artery. The clamp was surgically implanted on August 27, 1971, in Togstad's neck to allow the gradual closure of the artery over a period of days.

**a.** Compare the following CPR provisions:

**"EC 6–3** While the licensing of a lawyer is evidence that he has met the standards then prevailing for admission to the bar, a lawyer generally should not accept employment in any area of the law in which he is not qualified. However, he may accept such employment if in good faith he expects to become qualified through study and investigation, as long as such preparation would not result in unreasonable delay or expense to his client. * * *"

**"DR 6–101 Failing to Act Competently**

"(A) A lawyer shall not:

(1) Handle a legal matter which he knows or should know that he is not competent to handle, without associating with him a lawyer who is competent to handle it.

(2) Handle a legal matter without preparation adequate in the circumstances.

(3) Neglect a legal matter entrusted to him.

**"DR 6–102 Limiting Liability to Client**

"(A) A lawyer shall not attempt to exonerate himself from or limit his liability to his client for his personal malpractice."

**1.** An aneurism is a weakness or softening in an artery wall which expands and bulges out over a period of years.

**2.** The left internal carotid artery is one of the major vessels which supplies blood to the brain.

The treatment was designed to eventually cut off the blood supply through the artery and thus relieve the pressure on the aneurism, allowing the aneurism to heal. It was anticipated that other arteries, as well as the brain's collateral or cross-arterial system would supply the required blood to the portion of the brain which would ordinarily have been provided by the left carotid artery. The greatest risk associated with this procedure is that the patient may become paralyzed if the brain does not receive an adequate flow of blood. In the event the supply of blood becomes so low as to endanger the health of the patient, the adjustable clamp can be opened to establish the proper blood circulation.

In the early morning hours of August 29, 1971, a nurse observed that Togstad was unable to speak or move. At the time, the clamp was one-half (50%) closed. Upon discovering Togstad's condition, the nurse called a resident physician, who did not adjust the clamp. Dr. Blake was also immediately informed of Togstad's condition and arrived about an hour later, at which time he opened the clamp. Togstad is now severely paralyzed in his right arm and leg, and is unable to speak.

Plaintiff's expert, Dr. Ward Woods, testified that Togstad's paralysis and loss of speech was due to a lack of blood supply to his brain. Dr. Woods stated that the inadequate blood flow resulted from the clamp being 50% closed and that the negligence of Dr. Blake and the hospital precluded the clamp's being opened in time to avoid permanent brain damage. Specifically, Dr. Woods claimed that Dr. Blake and the hospital were negligent for (1) failing to place the patient in the intensive care unit or to have a special nurse conduct certain neurological tests every half-hour; (2) failing to write adequate orders; (3) failing to open the clamp immediately upon discovering that the patient was unable to speak; and (4) the absence of personnel capable of opening the clamp.

Dr. Blake and defendants' expert witness, Dr. Shelly Chou, testified that Togstad's condition was caused by blood clots going up the carotid artery to the brain. They both alleged that the blood clots were not a result of the Selverstone clamp procedure. In addition, they stated that the clamp must be about 90% closed before there will be a slowing of the blood supply through the carotid artery to the brain. Thus, according to Drs. Blake and Chou, when the clamp is 50% closed there is no effect on the blood flow to the brain.

About 14 months after her husband's hospitalization began, plaintiff Joan Togstad met with attorney Jerre Miller regarding her husband's condition. Neither she nor her husband was personally acquainted with Miller or his law firm prior to that time. * * *

Mrs. Togstad had become suspicious of the circumstances surrounding her husband's tragic condition due to the conduct and statements of the hospital nurses shortly after the paralysis occurred. One nurse told Mrs. Togstad that she had checked Mr. Togstad at 2 a. m. and he was fine; that when she returned at 3 a. m., by mistake, to give him someone else's medication, he was unable to move or speak; and that if she hadn't accidentally entered the room no one would have discovered his condition until morning. Mrs. Togstad also noticed that the other nurses were upset and crying, and that Mr. Togstad's condition was a topic of conversation.

Mrs. Togstad testified that she told Miller "everything that happened at the hospital," including the nurses' statements and conduct which had raised a question in her mind. She stated that she "believed" she had told Miller "about the procedure and what was undertaken, what was done, and what happened." She brought no records with her. Miller took notes and asked questions during the meeting, which lasted 45 minutes to an hour. At its conclusion, according to Mrs. Togstad, Miller said that "he did not think we had a legal case, however, he was going to discuss this with his partner." She understood that if Miller changed his mind after talking to his partner, he would call her. Mrs. Togstad "gave it" a few days and, since she did not hear from Miller, decided "that they had come to the conclusion that there wasn't a case." No fee arrangements were discussed, no medical authorizations were requested, nor was Mrs. Togstad billed for the interview.

Mrs. Togstad denied that Miller had told her his firm did not have expertise in the medical malpractice field, urged her to see another attorney, or related to her that the statute of limitations for medical malpractice actions was two years. She did not consult another attorney until one year after she talked to Miller. Mrs. Togstad indicated that she did not confer with another attorney earlier because of her reliance on Miller's "legal advice" that they "did not have a case."

On cross-examination, Mrs. Togstad was asked whether she went to Miller's office "to see if he would take the case of [her] husband * * *." She replied, "Well, I guess it was to go for legal advice, what to do, where shall we go from here? That is what [I] went for." Again in response to defense counsel's questions, Mrs. Togstad testified as follows:

> "Q And it was clear to you, was it not, that what was taking place was a preliminary discussion between a prospective client and lawyer as to whether or not they wanted to enter into an attorney-client relationship?
>
> "A I am not sure how to answer that. It was for legal advice as to what to do.
>
> "Q And Mr. Miller was discussing with you your problem and indicating whether he, as a lawyer, wished to take the case, isn't that true?
>
> "A Yes."

On re-direct examination, Mrs. Togstad acknowledged that when she left Miller's office she understood that she had been given a "qualified, quality legal opinion that [she and her husband] did not have a malpractice case."

Miller's testimony was different in some respects from that of Mrs. Togstad. Like Mrs. Togstad, Miller testified that * * * the meeting * * * lasted about 45 minutes. According to Miller, Mrs. Togstad described the hospital incident, including the conduct of the nurses. He asked her questions, to which she responded. Miller testified that "[t]he only thing I told her [Mrs. Togstad] after we had pretty much finished the conversation was that there was nothing related in her factual circumstances that told me that she had a case that our firm would be interested in undertaking."

Miller also claimed he related to Mrs. Togstad "that because of the grievous nature of the injuries sustained by her husband, that this was only my opinion and she was encouraged to ask another attorney if she wished for another opinion" and "she ought to do so promptly." He testified that he informed Mrs. Togstad that his firm "was not engaged as experts" in the area of medical malpractice, and that they associated with the Charles Hvass firm in cases of that nature. Miller stated that at the end of the conference he told Mrs. Togstad that he would consult with Charles Hvass and if Hvass's opinion differed from his, Miller would so inform her. Miller recollected that he called Hvass a "couple days" later and discussed the case with him. It was Miller's impression that Hvass thought there was no liability for malpractice in the case. Consequently, Miller did not communicate with Mrs. Togstad further.

On cross-examination, Miller testified as follows:

"Q Now, so there is no misunderstanding, and I am reading from your deposition, you understood that she was consulting with you as a lawyer, isn't that correct?

"A That's correct.

"Q That she was seeking legal advice from a professional attorney licensed to practice in this state and in this community?

"A I think you and I did have another interpretation or use of the term 'Advice.' She was there to see whether or not she had a case and whether the firm would accept it.

"Q We have two aspects; number one, your legal opinion concerning liability of a case for malpractice; number two, whether there was or wasn't liability, whether you would accept it, your firm, two separate elements, right?

"A I would say so. * * * "

Kenneth Green, a Minneapolis attorney, was called as an expert by plaintiffs. He stated that in rendering legal advice regarding a claim of medical malpractice, the "minimum" an attorney should do would be to request medical authorizations from the client, review the hospital records, and consult with an expert in the field. John McNulty, a Minneapolis attorney, and Charles Hvass testified as experts on behalf of the defendants. McNulty stated that when an attorney is consulted as to whether he will take a case, the lawyer's only responsibility in refusing it is to so inform the party. He testified, however, that when a lawyer is asked his legal opinion on the merits of a medical malpractice claim, community standards require that the attorney check hospital records and consult with an expert before rendering his opinion.

Hvass stated that he had no recollection of Miller's calling him in October 1972 relative to the Togstad matter. He testified that:

> "A * * * when a person comes in to me about a medical malpractice action, based upon what the individual has told me, I have to make a decision as to whether or not there probably is or probably is not, based upon that information, medical malpractice. And if, in my judgment, based upon what the client has told me, there is not medical malpractice, I will so inform the client."

Hvass stated, however, that he would never render a "categorical" opinion. In addition, Hvass acknowledged that if he were consulted for a "legal opinion" regarding medical malpractice and 14 months had expired since the incident in question, "ordinary care and diligence" would require him to inform the party of the two-year statute of limitations applicable to that type of action.

This case was submitted to the jury by way of a special verdict form. The jury found that Dr. Blake and the hospital were negligent and that Dr. Blake's negligence (but not the hospital's) was a direct cause of the injuries sustained by John Togstad; that there was an attorney-client contractual relationship between Mrs. Togstad and Miller; that Miller was negligent in rendering advice regarding the possible claims of Mr. and Mrs. Togstad; that, but for Miller's negligence, plaintiffs would have been successful in the prosecution of a legal action against Dr. Blake; and that neither Mr. nor Mrs. Togstad was negligent in pursuing their claims against Dr. Blake. The jury awarded damages to Mr. Togstad of $610,500 and to Mrs. Togstad of $39,000. * * *

In a legal malpractice action of the type involved here, four elements must be shown: (1) that an attorney-client relationship existed; (2) that defendant acted negligently or in breach of contract; (3) that such acts were the proximate cause of the plaintiffs' damages; (4) that but for defendant's conduct the plaintiffs would have been successful in the prosecution of their medical malpractice claim. See, Christy v. Saliterman, 288 Minn. 144, 179 N.W.2d 288 (1970).

This court first dealt with the element of lawyer-client relationship in the decision of Ryan v. Long, 35 Minn. 394, 29 N.W. 51 (1886). The *Ryan* case involved a claim of legal malpractice and on appeal it was argued that no attorney-client relation existed. This court, without stating whether its conclusion was based on contract principles or a tort theory, disagreed:

> "[I]t sufficiently appears that plaintiff, for himself, called upon defendant, as an attorney at law, for 'legal advice,' and that defendant

> assumed to give him a professional opinion in reference to the matter as to which plaintiff consulted him. Upon this state of facts the defendant must be taken to have acted as plaintiff's legal adviser, at plaintiff's request, and so as to establish between them the relation of attorney and client."

More recent opinions of this court, although not involving a detailed discussion, have analyzed the attorney-client consideration in contractual terms. See, Ronnigen v. Hertogs, 294 Minn. 7, 199 N.W.2d 420 (1972); Christy v. Saliterman, supra. For example, the *Ronnigen* court, in affirming a directed verdict for the defendant attorney, reasoned that "[u]nder the fundamental rules applicable to contracts of employment * * * the evidence would not sustain a finding that defendant either expressly or impliedly promised or agreed to represent plaintiff * * *." The trial court here, in apparent reliance upon the contract approach utilized in *Ronnigen* and *Christy*, supra, applied a contract analysis in ruling on the attorney-client relationship question. This has prompted a discussion by the *Minnesota Law Review*, wherein it is suggested that the more appropriate mode of analysis, at least in this case, would be to apply principles of negligence, i.e., whether defendant owed plaintiffs a duty to act with due care. 63 Minn.L.Rev. 751 (1979).

We believe it is unnecessary to decide whether a tort or contract theory is preferable for resolving the attorney-client relationship question raised by this appeal. The tort and contract analyses are very similar in a case such as the instant one,[4] and we conclude that under either theory the evidence shows that a lawyer-client relationship is present here. The thrust of Mrs. Togstad's testimony is that she went to Miller for legal advice, was told there wasn't a case, and relied upon this advice in failing to pursue the claim for medical malpractice. In addition, according to Mrs. Togstad, Miller did not qualify his legal opinion by urging her to seek advice from another attorney, nor did Miller inform her that he lacked expertise in the medical malpractice area. Assuming this testimony is true, as this court must do, we believe a jury could properly find that Mrs. Togstad sought and received legal advice from Miller under circumstances which made it reasonably foreseeable to Miller that Mrs. Togstad would be injured if the advice were negligently given. Thus, under either a tort or contract analysis, there is sufficient evidence in the record to support the existence of an attorney-client relationship.

4. Under a negligence approach it must essentially be shown that defendant rendered legal advice (not necessarily at someone's request) under circumstances which made it reasonably foreseeable to the attorney that if such advice was rendered negligently, the individual receiving the advice might be injured thereby. See, e.g., Palsgraf v. Long Island R. Co., 248 N.Y. 339, 162 N.E. 99, 59 A.L.R. 1253 (1928). Or, stated another way, under a tort theory, "[a]n attorney-client relationship is created whenever an individual seeks and receives legal advice from an attorney in circumstances in which a reasonable person would rely on such advice." 63 Minn.L.Rev. 751, 759 (1979). A contract analysis requires the rendering of legal advice pursuant to another's request and the reliance factor, in this case, where the advice was not paid for, need be shown in the form of promissory estoppel. See, 7 C.J.S., Attorney and Client, § 65; Restatement (Second) of Contracts, § 90.

Defendants argue that even if an attorney-client relationship was established the evidence fails to show that Miller acted negligently in assessing the merits of the Togstads' case. They appear to contend that, at most, Miller was guilty of an error in judgment which does not give rise to legal malpractice. Meagher v. Kavli, 256 Minn. 54, 97 N.W.2d 370 (1959). However, this case does not involve a mere error of judgment. The gist of plaintiffs' claim is that Miller failed to perform the minimal research that an ordinarily prudent attorney would do before rendering legal advice in a case of this nature. The record, through the testimony of Kenneth Green and John McNulty, contains sufficient evidence to support plaintiffs' position.

[T]here is adequate evidence supporting the claim that Miller was also negligent in failing to advise Mrs. Togstad of the two-year medical malpractice limitations period * * *.

There is also sufficient evidence in the record establishing that, but for Miller's negligence, plaintiffs would have been successful in prosecuting their medical malpractice claim. Dr. Woods, in no uncertain terms, concluded that Mr. Togstad's injuries were caused by the medical malpractice of Dr. Blake. Defendants' expert testimony to the contrary was obviously not believed by the jury. Thus, the jury reasonably found that had plaintiff's medical malpractice action been properly brought, plaintiffs would have recovered. * * *

Defendants also contend that the trial court erred by refusing to instruct the jury that plaintiffs' damages should be reduced by the amount of attorney fees plaintiffs would have paid defendants had Miller prosecuted the medical malpractice action. In *Christy*, supra, the court was presented with this precise question, but declined to rule on it because the issue had not been properly raised before the trial court. The *Christy* court noted, however:

> "[T]he record would indicate that, in the trial of this case, the parties probably proceeded upon the assumption that the element of attorneys' fees, which plaintiff might have had to pay defendant had he successfully prosecuted the suit, was canceled out by the attorneys' fees plaintiff incurred in retaining counsel to establish that defendant failed to prosecute a recoverable action."

Decisions from other states have divided in their resolution of the instant question. The cases allowing the deduction of the hypothetical fees do so without any detailed discussion or reasoning in support thereof. McGlone v. Lacey, 288 F.Supp. 662 (D.S.D.1968); Sitton v. Clements, 257 F.Supp. 63 (E.D.Tenn. 1966), aff'd 385 F.2d 869 (6th Cir. 1967); Childs v. Comstock, 69 App.Div. 160, 74 N.Y.S. 643 (1902). The courts disapproving of an allowance for attorney fees reason, consistent with the *dicta* in *Christy*, supra, that a reduction for lawyer fees is unwarranted because of the expense incurred by the plaintiff in bringing an action against the attorney. Duncan v. Lord, 409 F.Supp. 687 (E.D.Pa.1976) (citing *Christy*); Winter v. Brown, 365 A.2d 381 (D.C.App.1976) (citing *Christy*); Benard v. Walkup, 272 Cal.App.2d 595, 77 Cal.Rptr. 544 (1969).

We are persuaded by the reasoning of the cases which do not allow a reduction for a hypothetical contingency fee, and accordingly reject defendants' contention. * * *

Affirmed.[a]

### *Comment*

(1) *Discipline.* Neglect and mishandling of cases and failure to communicate adequately with clients are common causes of lawyer discipline.[1] The fact that a case's unpleasantness causes the lawyer to have a psychological block is no excuse for neglecting the client's case.[2] That the misconduct is attributable to dire necessity or financial misfortune is not a defense to disciplinary proceedings.[3] Nor is the fact that the misconduct is attributable to mental illness,[4] although there is a tendency to recognize that because conduct caused by mental illness bears no culpability it warrants no more than suspension from practice until the lawyer shows he has recovered.[5] A similar approach has been applied regarding conduct caused by alcoholism.[6]

(2) *Relevance of professional conduct provisions in malpractice actions.* Professor Wolfram makes a good case for the relevance of the CPR in malpractice actions.[7] He emphasizes the Code's similarity to criminal statutes, violation of which is evidence of lack of due care if the injured party is within the statute's intended area of protection, and to customs or work practices, which show standards of care. He says that the CPR Preliminary Statement's declaration that the Code does not "undertake to define standards for civil liability of lawyers for professional conduct" should be read as neutrality, not hostility, and that lawyers can hardly claim that the Code was drafted without

**a.** Regarding admissibility and necessity of expert testimony on standards of care in lawyer malpractice cases, see Olfe v. Gordon, 93 Wis.2d 173, 286 N.W.2d 573 (1980); Annot., 17 A.L.R.3d 1442 (1968).

Regarding malpractice insurance, see Annot., 84 A.L.R.3d 187 (1978). See also Schneyer, Mandatory Malpractice Insurance for Lawyers in Wisconsin—and Elsewhere, 1979 Wis.L.Rev. 1019; Comment, Should Legal Malpractice Insurance Be Mandatory? 1978 B.Y.U.L.Rev. 102.

**1.** See Annot., 80 A.L.R.3d 1240 (1977) (failure to communicate); Annot., 96 A.L.R.2d 823 (1964) (neglect and mishandling).

**2.** In re Rosenblatt, 60 N.J. 505, 291 A.2d 369 (1972).

**3.** In re Rosenberg, 413 Ill. 567, 110 N.E.2d 186 (1953); In re Park, 45 Wn.2d 383, 274 P.2d 1006 (1954). Compare Annot., 96 A.L.R.2d 823, 855–56 (1964) (mitigating factors).

**4.** Grove v. State Bar, 66 Cal.2d 680, 58 Cal.Rptr. 564, 427 P.2d 164 (1967); Louisiana State Bar Association v. Theard, 222 La. 328, 62 So.2d 501 (1953); In re Chmelik, 203 Minn. 156, 280 N.W. 283 (1938).

**5.** In re Bourgeois, 25 Ill.2d 47, 182 N.E.2d 651, 96 A.L.R.2d 735 (1962); In re Sherman, 66 Wn.2d 718, 404 P.2d 978 (1965). See Annot., 96 A.L.R.2d 739 (1964).

**6.** See In re Evans, 94 S.C. 414, 78 S.E. 227 (1913); 69 W.Va.L.Rev. 341 (1967).

**7.** Wolfram, The Code of Professional Responsibility as a Measure of Attorney Liability in Civil Litigation, 30 S.C.L.Rev. 281 (1979). See Lipton v. Boesky, 110 Mich.App. 589, 313 N.W.2d 163 (1981); R. Mallen & V. Levit, Legal Malpractice §§ 122, 153–56, 256 (2d ed. 1981); Morgan, Conflicts of Interest and the Former Client in the Model Rules of Professional Conduct, 1980 Am.B.Found. Research J. 993, 1001 (argument CPR is not relevant to malpractice is "nonsense"). Compare Dahlquist, The Code of Professional Responsibility and Civil Actions Against Attorneys, 9 Ohio N.U.L.Rev. 1 (1982).

sufficient consideration of their interests. Compare RPC Scope, which states:

"Violation of a Rule should not give rise to a cause of action nor should it create any presumption that legal duty has been breached. The Rules are designed to provide guidance to lawyers and to provide a structure for regulating conduct through disciplinary agencies. They are not designed to be a basis for civil liability. Furthermore, the purpose of the Rules can be subverted when they are invoked by opposing parties as procedural weapons. The fact that a Rule is a just basis for a lawyer's self-assessment, or for sanctioning a lawyer under the administration of a disciplinary authority, does not imply that an antagonist in a collateral proceeding or transaction has standing to seek enforcement of the Rule. Accordingly, nothing in the Rules should be deemed to augment any substantive legal duty of lawyers or the extra-disciplinary consequences of violating such a duty."

(3) *Duty to refer to specialist.* A California court upheld the following jury instruction in a malpractice case notwithstanding the fact that the state did not have a specialty certification program at the time of the alleged malpractice:

"It is the duty of an attorney who is a general practitioner to refer his client to a specialist or recommend the assistance of a specialist if under the circumstances a reasonably careful and skillful practitioner would do so.

"If he fails to perform that duty and undertakes to perform professional services without the aid of a specialist, it is his further duty to have the knowledge and skill ordinarily possessed, and exercise the care and skill ordinarily used by specialists in good standing in the same or similar locality and under the same circumstances.

"A failure to perform any such duty is negligence."[8]

(4) *Informing client of one's negligence.* Does a lawyer have an affirmative duty to inform the client of the lawyer's negligence in handling the client's case? In Troy's Stereo Center, Inc. v. Hodson,[9] a North Carolina court held a genuine issue of material fact precluded summary judgment because:

"Plaintiff argues that defendant served in a fiduciary relationship * * *, that defendant had an affirmative duty to disclose to the plaintiff his own negligence in the handling of the case and

8. Horne v. Peckham, 97 Cal.App.3d 404, 158 Cal.Rptr. 714 (1979). See R. Mallen & V. Levit, Legal Malpractice § 253 (2d ed. 1981).

Regarding the court's "locality" reference, see id. § 254, asserting that the locality element merely requires lawyers to have knowledge of local considerations essential to a client's representation, noting that several states employ statewide standards, and observing that a national standard may be appropriate for some specialties.

Regarding specialization, see supra pp. 47–49.

9. 39 N.C.App. 591, 251 S.E.2d 673 (1979).

that his failure to do so during the four and one half years subsequent to his original negligent act should bar him from asserting a plea of the [three year] statute of limitations." [10]

(5) *Civil liability of appointed criminal defense counsel.* In Ferri v. Ackerman,[11] the United States Supreme Court held that *federal* law does not give a lawyer appointed by a federal court to represent an indigent federal criminal defendant absolute immunity in a state court malpractice suit. The Court said:

> "The narrow issue presented to this Court is whether federal law in any way pre-empts the freedom of a State to decide the question of immunity in this situation in accord with its own law. * * *
>
> "In a sense a lawyer who is appointed to represent an indigent defendant in a federal judicial proceeding is * * * a federal officer. Since other federal officers—the judge, the prosecutor, and the grand jurors—enjoy immunity by virtue of their office, arguably that immunity should be shared by appointed counsel. There is however, a marked difference between the nature of counsel's responsibilities and those of other officers of the court. * * * The point of immunity for such officials is to forestall an atmosphere of intimidation that would conflict with their resolve to perform their designated functions in a principled fashion.
>
> "In contrast, the primary office performed by appointed counsel parallels the office of privately retained counsel. * * * The fear that an unsuccessful defense of a criminal charge will lead to a malpractice claim does not conflict with performance of that function. If anything, it provides the same incentive for appointed and retained counsel to perform that function competently."

State courts also generally deny public defenders and appointed criminal defense counsel immunity from malpractice liability under *state* law.[12]

10. See R. Mallen & V. Levit, Legal Malpractice § 714 (2d ed. 1981) (malpractice insurance cooperation clause usually provides that, except at insured's own cost, insured shall not voluntarily make a payment or settlement or assume an obligation).

11. 444 U.S. 193, 100 S.Ct. 402, 62 L.Ed.2d 355 (1979).

12. See Donigan v. Finn. 95 Mich.App. 28, 290 N.W.2d 80 (1980) (appointed counsel); Annot., 6 A.L.R.4th 744 (1981) (public defenders). See Malloy v. Sullivan, 387 So.2d 169 (Ala. 1980), cert. denied 459 U.S. 974, 103 S.Ct. 308, 74 L.Ed.2d 288 (1982) (allowing state court malpractice action against federal court appointed counsel without mentioning immunity issue). Compare Walker v. Kruse, 484 F.2d 802 (7th Cir. 1973) (Illinois law may give immunity to appointed criminal defense counsel); Nakles, Criminal Defense Lawyer: The Case for Absolute Immunity from Civil Liability, 81 Dick.L.Rev. 229 (1977) (all criminal defense counsel, appointed and retained, should have malpractice immunity).

In Polk County v. Dodson, 454 U.S. 312, 102 S.Ct. 445, 70 L.Ed.2d 509 (1981), the Court precluded 42 U.S.C. § 1983 from being used for malpractice actions against public defenders by ruling that public defenders' representation of clients is not conduct "under color of state law" covered by § 1983.

Regarding criminal defense counsel's malpractice liability in general, see Kaus & Mallen, The Misguiding Hand of Counsel—Reflections on "Criminal Malpractice," 21 U.C.L.A.L.Rev. 1191 (1974); Comment, Criminal Malpractice: Threshold Barriers to Recovery Against Negligent Criminal Counsel, 1981 Duke L.J. 542; Annot., 53 A.L.R.3d 731 (1973).

## PELHAM v. GRIESHEIMER

92 Ill.2d 13, 64 Ill.Dec. 544, 440 N.E.2d 96 (1982).

RYAN, Chief Justice:

Plaintiffs appeal the dismissal of their amended complaint for failure to state a cause of action for legal malpractice against the defendant, Ronald Griesheimer. The circuit court of Lake County held that there was no attorney-client relationship between the plaintiffs and the defendant and that therefore no cause of action for legal malpractice was stated. The appellate court affirmed. We granted plaintiffs leave to appeal.

Plaintiffs' amended complaint alleges that the defendant was retained to represent Loretta Ray in a divorce action against her husband, George Ray. The plaintiffs herein are the children of Loretta and George Ray, all of whom were minors at the time the divorce was granted in June 1971. The divorce decree contained a provision requiring George Ray to "maintain all four of his children as the prime beneficiaries in his life insurance policies." George Ray had a $10,000 life insurance policy through his employer at the time the divorce decree was entered. After the divorce decree was entered, he remarried and named his second wife the beneficiary of the insurance policy. She received the proceeds after his death in 1976.

The complaint also alleges that the defendant owes the plaintiffs "the duty to exercise a reasonable degree of professional care and skill, as an attorney, with reference to seeing that the plaintiffs became the prime beneficiaries in all life insurance policies which insured George J. Ray." The complaint also alleges that the defendant breached that duty by "negligently and carelessly," *inter alia*, failing to notify George Ray's employer, or the insurance company, of the divorce-decree provision and failing to advise Loretta Ray to notify her ex-husband's employer or insurance company of the provision. Finally, the amended complaint alleges that "as a direct and proximate result of the negligent acts or omissions of the defendant" the plaintiffs have suffered monetary damage.

Plaintiffs argue that their complaint states a cause of action for breach of contract. The plaintiffs maintain that this complaint should be construed to allege that the children are direct third-party beneficiaries of the contract between their mother, Loretta Ray, and her attorney, the defendant. The defendant argues that the complaint fails to allege that a contract was entered into for the direct benefit of the plaintiffs and that, in any event, the plaintiffs herein could not have been intended beneficiaries of the contract. * * *

The amended complaint herein clearly fails to state a cause of action for breach of contract. The amended complaint fails to allege, legally or factually, that a contract was entered into for the direct benefit of the plaintiffs, which is an indispensable element of a third-party beneficiary theory of recovery.

* * * If plaintiffs' amended complaint states a cause of action at all, it is in tort, rather than contract.

A complaint for negligence, to be legally sufficient, must set out facts that establish the existence of a duty owed by the defendant to the plaintiff, a breach of that duty, and an injury proximately resulting from the breach. The determination of the duty—whether the defendant and the plaintiffs stood in such a relationship to one another that the law imposed upon the defendant an obligation of reasonable conduct for the benefit of the plaintiffs—is an issue of law for the determination of the court.

In concluding that the plaintiffs' complaint failed to state a cause of action, the appellate court relied on the fact that no attorney-client relationship—no privity—existed between the plaintiffs and the defendant and, therefore, no duty existed. We consider that privity is not an indispensable prerequisite to establishing a duty of care between a non-client and an attorney in a suit for legal malpractice. In this case, however, we find that no duty existed between the parties to this lawsuit.

The traditional, general rule has been that the attorney is liable only to his client, not to third persons. (National Savings Bank v. Ward (1880), 100 U.S. 195, 25 L.Ed. 621.) The concept of privity has long protected attorneys from malpractice claims by nonclients. * * * In Bloomer Amusement Co. v. Eskenazi (1979), 75 Ill.App.3d 117, 31 Ill.Dec. 100, 394 N.E.2d 16, the contract seller of certain realty brought an action against the attorney for the contract purchaser, alleging negligence in the attorney's failure to record the real estate contract. In affirming the trial court's granting of summary judgment for the attorney, the court quoted from National Savings Bank v. Ward (1880), 100 U.S. 195, 200, 25 L.Ed. 621, 623, that "the general rule is that the obligation of the attorney is to his client and not to a third party," absent fraud or collusion.

* * * Though *Bloomer* arose under substantially different factual circumstances than the case at bar, [it] recognized the traditional requirement of privity for a nonclient to recover from an attorney. See annot., 45 A.L.R.3d 1181 (1972).

The trend in tort law has been to abolish privity of contract (Rozny v. Marnul (1969), 43 Ill.2d 54, 252 N.E.2d 656) as a prerequisite to establishing a duty. In *Rozny*, the plaintiffs purchased a house and lot which was described in a plat of an admittedly inaccurate survey prepared by defendant for S&S Builders. In discussing the tort of misrepresentation the court stated:

> "This process of adhering to or eliminating the privity requirement has proved to be an unsatisfactory method of establishing the scope of tort liability to third persons. * * * To eliminate any uncertainty still remaining after Suvada v. White Motor Co., 32 Ill.2d 612, 617, 210 N.E.2d 182, we emphasize that lack of direct contractual relationship between the parties is not a defense in a

tort action in this jurisdiction. Thus, tort liability will henceforth be measured by the scope of the duty owed rather than the artificial concepts of privity."

While privity of contract has been abolished in many areas of tort law, the concern is still that liability for negligence not extend to an unlimited and unknown number of potential plaintiffs. In the area of legal malpractice the attorney's obligations to his client must remain paramount. In such cases the best approach is that the plaintiffs must allege and prove facts demonstrating that they are in the nature of third-party intended beneficiaries of the relationship between the client and the attorney in order to recover in tort. (See Clagett v. Dacy (1980), 47 Md.App. 23, 420 A.2d 1285; R. Mallen & V. Levit, Legal Malpractice sec. 80, at 156–59 (2d ed. 1981); cf. Marker v. Greenberg (Minn.1981), 313 N.W.2d 4; Brody v. Ruby (Iowa 1978), 267 N.W.2d 902.) By this we mean that to establish a duty owed by the defendant attorney to the nonclient the nonclient must allege and prove that the intent of the client to benefit the nonclient third party was the primary or direct purpose of the transaction or relationship. Note, Attorney's Liability to Third Parties for Malpractice: The Growing Acceptance of Liability in the Absence of Privity, 21 Washburn L.J. 48, 59 (1981).

Analogizing the scope of the duty to the concept of a third-party direct beneficiary serves the purpose of limiting the scope of the duty owed by an attorney to nonclients. The key consideration is the attorney's acting at the direction of or on behalf of the client to benefit or influence a third party. (Probert & Hendricks, Lawyer Malpractice: Duty Relationships Beyond Contract, 55 Notre Dame Law. 708, 728 (1980).) In Clagett v. Dacy (1980), 47 Md.App. 23, 29, 420 A.2d 1285, 1289, a legal malpractice action, the court stated:

> "Whether the action is based upon a contract (express or implied), to which the traditional rules relating to third party beneficiaries may apply, or more on a theory of negligence—the violation of a duty not founded exclusively upon contract—there still must be shown (i.e., alleged and shown) that the plaintiff, if not the direct employer/client of the defendant attorney, is a person or part of a class of persons specifically intended to be the beneficiary of the attorney's undertaking."

We conclude that, for a nonclient to succeed in a negligence action against an attorney, he must prove that the primary purpose and intent of the attorney-client relationship itself was to benefit or influence the third party. Under such proof, recovery may be allowed, provided that the other elements of a negligence cause of action can be proved. Comment, Liability of Lawyers to Third Parties for Professional Negligence in Oregon, 60 Or.L.Rev. 375 (1981).

The analogy to third-party direct beneficiaries to determine the duty owed to a nonclient by an attorney in a negligence action provides for a broader scope of liability than privity, but a narrower scope of liability than the balancing approach used in California. (R. Mallen

& V. Levit, Legal Malpractice sec. 81, at 161 (2d ed. 1981).) In Biakanja v. Irving (1958), 49 Cal.2d 647, 320 P.2d 16, the California Supreme Court held that whether in a specific case the defendant will be liable to a third person not in privity is a matter of policy and involves the balancing of various factors. The factors are the extent to which the transaction was intended to affect the plaintiff, the foreseeability of harm to him, the degree of certainty that the plaintiff suffered injury, the closeness of the connection between the defendant's conduct and the injury suffered, the moral blame attached to the defendant's conduct and the policy of preventing future harm. However, even under the California balancing test, the predominant inquiry has generally resolved to one criterion: Were the services intended to benefit the plaintiff? R. Mallen & V. Levit, Legal Malpractice sec. 80, at 157 (2d ed. 1981).

It would appear that courts are more willing to apply the balancing test to extend an attorney's duty to nonclients in cases in which the attorney's representation of his client has essentially been of a nonadversarial nature, such as drafting wills for the benefit of intended beneficiaries thereunder. Garcia v. Borelli (1982), 129 Cal.App.3d 24, 180 Cal.Rptr. 768; Heyer v. Flaig (1969), 70 Cal.2d 223, 449 P.2d 161, 74 Cal.Rptr. 225; Biakanja v. Irving (1958), 49 Cal.2d 647, 320 P.2d 16.

Where a client's interest is involved in a proceeding that is adversarial in nature, the existence of a duty of the attorney to another person would interfere with the undivided loyalty which the attorney owes his client and would detract from achieving the most advantageous position for his client. (R. Mallen & V. Levit, Legal Malpractice sec. 80, at 159 (2d ed. 1981).) Our code of professional responsibility requires that a lawyer represent his client with undivided fidelity, and Canon 7 provides that a lawyer should represent a client zealously within the boundaries of the law. In cases of an adversarial nature, in order to create a duty on the part of the attorney to one other than a client, there must be a clear indication that the representation by the attorney is intended to directly confer a benefit upon the third party.

Applying the "intent to directly benefit" test to the facts alleged in the complaint, it is clear that the plaintiffs herein are not in the nature of direct third-party beneficiaries. The attorney was hired primarily for the purpose of obtaining a divorce, property settlement, and custody of the minor children for Loretta Ray, not to represent her children's interest. The plaintiffs herein are, at best, only incidental beneficiaries in this situation. That George Ray name the children as beneficiaries of the policy cannot be described as the primary reason that Loretta Ray retained the defendant to be her attorney.

Dissolution proceedings are, for the most part, adversarial in nature. To conclude that an attorney representing one of the spouses also owes a legal duty to the children of the two litigants would clearly create conflict-of-interest situations. (R. Mallen & V. Levit, Legal Malpractice sec. 447 (2d ed. 1981).) In this case, a conflict could possibly have arisen between the plaintiffs' right to support or the proceeds of the insurance policy versus the wife's interest in a property settlement and maintenance. The same conflict could arise in all dissolution proceedings when minor children's support issues arise. In this case, if the wife was the beneficiary of the insurance policy in question before the divorce, and the husband insisted on naming the children as beneficiaries, or the court so decreed, then the wife's interest would conflict with the children's interest. We refuse to create such a wide range of potential conflicts by imposing such duties upon an attorney in favor of a nonclient, unless the intent to benefit the third party is clearly evident.

We believe a different situation would confront us if this complaint had alleged sufficient facts to show that the defendant had undertaken a duty to notify the insurance company or the husband's employer of the provision in the divorce decree. In that situation, the attorney may have a duty to exercise reasonable care because his client and the plaintiffs herein could have justifiably relied on that undertaking. Schwartz v. Greenfield, Stein & Weisinger (1977), 90 Misc.2d 882, 396 N.Y.S.2d 582; Steward v. Sbarro (1976), 142 N.J.Super. 581, 362 A.2d 581.

In cases where it appears that the interest of a minor requires separate representation, we note that section 506 of the Illinois Marriage and Dissolution of Marriage Act (Ill.Rev.Stat.1979, ch. 40, par. 506) provides for representation of minor children by an attorney and a guardian *ad litem*. This provision was not in effect when the decree in this case was entered. However, courts have always had the inherent equitable power to appoint a guardian *ad litem* for minors interested in litigation. * * * Thus, the rights of the minor children of the parties in this case could have been protected without compromising the undivided loyalty of either spouse's attorney.

Under the facts as pleaded, we hold that no duty in negligence was owed by the wife's attorney to his client's children; hence, no cause of action was stated. In this case, to establish a duty, the plaintiffs must plead and prove that the relationship between the attorney and his client was entered into for the primary and direct benefit of the plaintiffs, plus the other traditional elements of negligence. Also, the allegations of this complaint do not state a cause of action in contract for the reasons heretofore stated. * * *

Judgment affirmed.[a]

**a.** See Page v. Frazier, 388 Mass. 55, 445 N.E.2d 148 (1938) (bank's lawyer not liable to land purchaser for negligent examination of title where purchaser signed mortgage application saying bank's lawyer represented bank's interests and purchaser could retain own lawyer).

Compare Needham v. Hamilton, 459 A.2d 1060 (D.C.App.1983) (testator's lawyer liable to intended beneficiary for negligent drafting of will); Bradford Securities Processing Services, Inc. v. Plaza Bank & Trust, 653 P.2d 188 (Okl.1982) (bond counsel who knew opinion would appear on bond certificates liable to

### *Comment*

(1) *Defendant asserting plaintiff's lawyer's failure to investigate adequately before bringing action.* The courts uniformly refuse to entertain a defendant's claim that plaintiff's lawyer was negligent in failing to investigate adequately before suing the defendant.[1] They reason that recognizing a duty to the client's adversary would create an unacceptable conflict of interest which would seriously hamper the lawyer's effectiveness as the client's counsel, and that the nature of the adversary system precludes a party's relying upon the opponent's lawyer.

(2) *Former lawyer asserting current lawyer's negligence.* In Gibson, Dunn & Crutcher v. Superior Court,[2] a 2–1 California appellate court held that when Lawyer I is sued for malpractice by Client, now represented by Lawyer II, Lawyer I may not cross claim for partial indemnity against Lawyer II for alleged negligence in extricating Client from the situation Lawyer I's negligence created.

Lawyer I represented Client in a transaction wherein Client guaranteed repayment of Debtor's loan, for which Debtor purportedly furnished certain security interests. Debtor defaulted, so Client had to repay the loan. When Client tried to enforce the security interests, Debtor went into bankruptcy proceedings, where Debtor's other creditors challenged the security interests' validity. Client hired Lawyer II, who helped Client settle with the other creditors, but the settlement was about $1,000,000 less than Client would have received if the security interests had been valid. Then Client, through Lawyer II, sued Lawyer I for malpractice for failing to discover and warn Client of the security interests' shortcomings. Lawyer I, proceeding under comparative negligence standards, filed not only an answer asserting that Client was contributorily negligent in settling with Debtor's other creditors, but a cross-complaint against Lawyer II claiming Lawyer II was negligent in not doing more to enforce the security interests and in not getting more in the settlement with the other creditors.

The appellate court upheld Lawyer II's demurrer to the cross-complaint. Recognizing that in medical malpractice cases a doctor who caused an injury could get partial indemnification from a doctor whose subsequent negligence aggravated it, the court stated:

> "The * * * distinction * * * is the effect the cross-complaint for indemnification may have upon the relationship be-

bond purchasers for negligence in giving opinion on bonds' legality and tax exempt status).

See generally Note, Attorneys' Negligence and Third Parties, 57 N.Y.U.L.Rev. 126 (1982) (liability to third parties should be expanded to enforce standards of care and conduct more adequately and to compensate deserving plaintiffs).

1. Beecy v. Pucciarelli, 387 Mass. 589, 441 N.E.2d 1035 (1982); Mallen & Roberts, The Liability of a Litigation Attorney to a Party Opponent, 14 Willamette L.J. 387 (1978).

Cf. Allied Financial Services, Inc. v. Easley, 676 F.2d 422 (10th Cir. 1982) (no liability for negligently garnishing when appeal had suspended authority to do so).

2. 94 Cal.App.3d 347, 156 Cal.Rptr. 326 (1979).

tween the injured party and the law firm (Lawyer II) chosen by that party to extricate him from the condition created by the cross-complainant (who need not have been a lawyer, but who, for convenience, we call Lawyer I)."

The court went on to acknowledge that the present case was factually distinguishable from Goodman v. Kennedy,[3] where the California Supreme Court had held that a lawyer for a seller of stock owed no duty to the buyers regarding the sale's conformity with SEC regulations. The present case was not based upon any alleged duty to anyone other than the client—there was no claim that Lawyer II owed a duty to Lawyer I, and Lawyer I asked only that Lawyer II contribute to any damages awarded to Client to the extent that Lawyer II's negligence harmed Client. But the court said:

> "However, the reasoning of *Goodman* is not based entirely upon the absence of any duty owed by the attorney to the plaintiff. The [*Goodman* court also pointed] out an important policy consideration. That is, to expose the attorney to actions for negligence brought by parties other than the client, 'would inject undesirable self-protective reservations into the attorney's counselling role' and tend to divert the attorney from single-minded devotion to his client's interests."

Then the *Gibson* court quoted the following to explain the inapplicability of the medical malpractice cases:

> "In the situation of successive acts of negligence by a tortfeasor and treating physician, the possibility that he may be sued by the original tortfeasor for indemnity in no way inhibits the performance of the professional duty by the physician. Whatever may be the effect of exposure to malpractice suits upon the performance of good medicine, it exists irrespective of the indemnity potential. Where, however, an attorney is retained to represent the interests of his client against persons who are actual or potential adversaries, the possibility that one of those adversaries may seek indemnity from the attorney if he is held liable to the client can impinge upon the undivided loyalty owed by counsel."

Finally, the court responded to Lawyer I's argument that permitting the cross-complaint would not impinge upon Lawyer II's duty to Client because the cross-complaint did not expand Lawyer II's duty, but only sought to protect and enforce Lawyer II's duty to Client, and that a lawyer who fully performed his or her duty to a client need not fear any cross-complaint. The court said:

> "This argument misses the vice of the Lawyer I versus Lawyer II cross-complaint. The problem is not that Lawyer II may be found liable to his client for malpractice. It is that in satisfying the needs and desires of his client, Lawyer II may be exposing

3. 18 Cal.3d 335, 134 Cal.Rptr. 375, 556 P.2d 737 (1976).

himself to the not insubstantial cost of defending an action by his client's opponent.

"* * * Lawyer II should not be required to face a potential conflict between the course which is in his client's best interest and the course which would minimize his exposure to the cross-complaint of Lawyer I. * * *

"Counsel for [Lawyer I] have argued that a suit for malpractice is one of the risks of professional life and should not be regarded as a serious inhibition upon professional loyalty and objectivity. With respect to malpractice claims of dissatisfied clients, that philosophy may be appropriate. But the effect is different if the attorney is exposed to negligence claims by parties who are his client's adversaries. The teaching of [the] cases * * * is that exposure to the client's potential adversaries ' "would prevent him from devoting his entire energies to his client's interest." ' "

Justice Jefferson dissented, saying:

"It is my view that there is no rational basis for not applying the principles of [comparative indemnity] to the case at bench. When Lawyer II made the decision to represent [Client] in connection with the problems created by Lawyer I's prior representation of [Client], Lawyer II certainly had every reason to believe that Lawyer I would seek to hold him liable for any malpractice on his part which might increase the amount of damages which [Client] would undoubtedly seek to recover from Lawyer I.

"I consider the principle sound that, since privity with a negligent attorney is no longer a prerequisite to an action for legal malpractice, an attorney ought to be held liable for his negligence to anyone who foreseeably may be damaged by such negligence. * * * I see no sound public policy reasons for carving out an exception to the principles of [comparative indemnity] in order to protect a negligent lawyer. * * *

"The alleged public policy of insuring that an attorney will devote his full energies to his client's interests * * * simply evaporates under the circumstances of the instant case. The rule of law of comparative-fault principles * * * is supported by a much stronger public policy than a rule of law which protects a lawyer from liability for negligence to a person who deals with the lawyer's client.

"Under the facts presented by the instant case, it is tenuous and speculative at best to conclude that permitting cross-complaints by Lawyer I against Lawyer II in a malpractice action against Lawyer I will distort and adversely affect Lawyer II's ability to devote his best efforts to serving his client. The * * * rationale rests on an unexamined and unpersuasive hypothesis, namely, the belief that the possibility of an attorney's liability to third parties for negligence in advising a client will inhibit an attorney's best representation of his client even in a situation where there is no conflict between the interest of the client and the third party.

"To impose a duty of due care on Lawyer II in favor of Lawyer I in the case at bench represents no addition or conflict in the duties imposed upon Lawyer II, since the duty imposed is already the very same duty owed by Lawyer II to his client to exercise due care. If Lawyer II does not exercise due care with respect to his client who is also a former client of Lawyer I and, as a result, increases the damages suffered by the client from Lawyer I's negligence, why shouldn't Lawyer II be liable for the increased damages resulting from his negligence? My answer to this question is simple. He should be liable."

In a perceptive article,[4] Jerome Braun argues that *Gibson* was wrongly decided. He says that the court's mistake was not in recognizing the importance of the policy goal of avoiding the potentially adverse effects of the "consultative conflict" (based on the assumption that Lawyer II is more likely to be sued upon advising Client to sue Lawyer I than upon advising other alternatives); rather it was in seeing that goal as irreconcilable with the equitable loss distribution goal of comparative indemnity. He points out that since general agency principles impute Lawyer II's acts to Client, disallowing the cross-complaint does not really make much difference to Lawyer I—under comparative negligence, Lawyer I can use Lawyer II's negligence defensively to reduce Client's recovery. He notes that *Gibson* did not really eliminate the problem of consultative conflict, but merely changed the focus of Lawyer II's self-interest from avoiding Lawyer I's cross claim to avoiding (1) Lawyer I's defensive use of Lawyer II's negligence and (2) Client's later malpractice suit. Finally, he observes that allowing Lawyer I's cross-complaint actually benefits Client, by immediately alerting Client to Client's possible claims against Lawyer II and by saving the expense and inconvenience of a separate malpractice action against Lawyer II.

(3) *Corporate securities lawyers.* Regarding corporate securities lawyers' liability to non-clients, see pages 269–71 above.

4. Braun, Gibson, Dunn & Crutcher v. Superior Court Revisited: A Critical Analysis and Proposal Respecting an Attorney Malpractice Defendant's Right to Cross-Complain for Comparative Indemnity Against the Former Client's Present Attorney, 22 Santa Clara L.Rev. 1 (1982).

# Chapter 8

# MAKING LEGAL SERVICES AVAILABLE

## A. GENERALLY

### MODEL RULES OF PROFESSIONAL CONDUCT

**RULE 6.1 Pro Bono Publico Service**

A lawyer should render public interest legal service. A lawyer may discharge this responsibility by providing professional services at no fee or a reduced fee to persons of limited means or to public service or charitable groups or organizations, by service in activities for improving the law, the legal system or the legal profession, and by financial support for organizations that provide legal services to persons of limited means.

COMMENT:

The ABA House of Delegates has formally acknowledged "the basic responsibility of each lawyer engaged in the practice of law to provide public interest legal services" without fee, or at a substantially reduced fee, in one or more of the following areas: poverty law, civil rights law, public rights law, charitable organization representation and the administration of justice. This Rule expresses that policy but is not intended to be enforced through disciplinary process.

* * *

**RULE 6.2 Accepting Appointments**

A lawyer shall not seek to avoid appointment by a tribunal to represent a person except for good cause, such as:

(a) representing the client is likely to result in violation of the rules of professional conduct or other law.

(b) representing the client is likely to result in an unreasonable financial burden on the lawyer; or

(c) the client or the cause is so repugnant to the lawyer as to be likely to impair the client-lawyer relationship or the lawyer's ability to represent the client.[a]

**a.** Compare the following CPR provisions: "**EC 2–25** Historically, the need for legal services of those unable to pay reasonable fees has been met in part by lawyers who donated their services or accepted court appointments on behalf of such individuals.

## FERREN, THE LAWYER'S PROFESSIONAL RESPONSIBILITY TO THE LEGAL SYSTEM

55 Wis.B.Bull. 10 (Sept.1982).

I begin from the premise that, as a matter of public and professional conscience, we should not deny legal assistance to anyone with a credible civil claim or defense, simply because that person cannot afford a lawyer's fee. * * * My premise, in short, is equal access to the legal system. Equal access to justice.

Obviously, a statement like that suggests a number of questions:

- Who has the obligation to provide lawyers for indigents in civil cases: the society-at-large through the government, or the legal profession itself, or both?
- How do we define a legal problem worthy of subsidized assistance?
- If we do not have the resources to provide a lawyer for every indigent person who needs one, how do we allocate the subsidies we do have, in the absence of a market mechanism?
- If government funds should be made available, what government: federal? Or state or local?

The basic responsibility for providing legal services for those unable to pay ultimately rests upon the individual lawyer, and personal involvement in the problems of the disadvantaged can be one of the most rewarding experiences in the life of a lawyer. Every lawyer, regardless of professional prominence or professional workload, should find time to participate in serving the disadvantaged. The rendition of free legal services to those unable to pay reasonable fees continues to be an obligation of each lawyer, but the efforts of individual lawyers are often not enough to meet the need. Thus it has been necessary for the profession to institute additional programs to provide legal services. Accordingly, legal aid offices, lawyer referral services, and other related programs have been developed, and others will be developed, by the profession. Every lawyer should support all proper efforts to meet this need for legal services.

"**EC 2–26** A lawyer is under no obligation to act as adviser or advocate for every person who may wish to become his client; but in furtherance of the objective of the bar to make legal services fully available, a lawyer should not lightly decline proffered employment. The fulfillment of this objective requires acceptance by a lawyer of his share of tendered employment which may be unattractive both to him and the bar generally.

"**EC 2–27** History is replete with instances of distinguished and sacrificial services by lawyers who have represented unpopular clients and causes. Regardless of his personal feelings, a lawyer should not decline representation because a client or a cause is unpopular or community reaction is adverse.

"**EC 2–28** The personal preference of a lawyer to avoid adversary alignment against judges, other lawyers, public officials, or influential members of the community does not justify his rejection of tendered employment.

"**EC 2–29** When a lawyer is appointed by a court or requested by a bar association to undertake representation of a person unable to obtain counsel, whether for financial or other reasons, he should not seek to be excused from undertaking the representation except for compelling reasons. Compelling reasons do not include such factors as the repugnance of the subject matter of the proceeding, the identity or position of a person involved in the case, the belief of the lawyer that the defendant in a criminal proceeding is guilty, or the belief of the lawyer regarding the merits of the civil case.

"**EC 2–30** [A] lawyer should decline employment if the intensity of his personal feeling, as distinguished from a community attitude, may impair his effective representation of a prospective client. * * *"

• What kinds of legal service providers should the government supply: full-time poverty lawyers, or private practitioners under a Judicare or contract model?

• If the legal profession itself has a responsibility to help subsidize the need, is it an institutional—a bar association—responsibility, or a personal one for every lawyer? Or is it both?

• Is it a responsibility to give time, or will money do?

• If the organized bar, especially a unified bar, has a responsibility here, can the bar properly require its members to give time, or money—or neither?

• What about persons of moderate income: how can we be sure they will have lawyers?

• If we cannot cover all legal problems of indigent and moderate income persons with some form of subsidized legal assistance, should we begin to redefine and narrow the practice of law, so that lay persons may provide some kinds of advice and representation traditionally performed by lawyers?

• Should we try to cut down on the need for lawyers by making informal dispute resolution through mediation or arbitration, without lawyers, a precondition of access to the courts in some kinds of cases?

• Or should we simplify certain laws to encourage more self-help?

• Or should we eliminate certain rights and duties in order to cut down the number of acknowledged legal problems?

It is hard to know where to stop. You probably can think of other questions. But although every one of these questions is legitimate and must be addressed, there is at least one danger in doing so: all of us are bound to disagree on the answers. * * *

As to legal services to the poor, for example, I have heard some lawyers say:

• It is up to the federal government, not the bar; and if the government won't do it, the bar should not bail out the government; or

• It is up to the bar, not the government; but unless there is a system requiring every lawyer to do *pro bono* work, I won't either; or

• Not all these divorce and landlord-tenant and consumer disputes belong in court; the courts are too clogged already. Just because the rich overuse the courts doesn't mean the poor should be subsidized to do so also; or

• Lay persons ought to be allowed to handle many of these cases; it's a waste of valuable resources to ask lawyers to give time. So I won't handle simple cases; get a less experienced lawyer to do it.

I have trouble with these attitudes because they judge the system harshly—which is fine as far as it goes—but they also say, "If the system is not as I would have it, I won't help out."

That will not do.

I believe as lawyers, we have two fundamental responsibilities to the legal system. First, each of us has a responsibility, implied by our very expertise, to think through how we would redesign the system to guarantee equal access to justice for rich and poor alike. What should be the respective roles of the government and of the profession in subsidizing legal services? What matters must be handled by lawyers, and which ones can be left to lay advocates? What kinds of disputes definitely belong in the courts, and what sorts should be presented first in alternative forums? We have, in short, a responsibility for long range planning and advocacy.

### *Comment*

At the discussion draft stage, the forerunner of RPC 6.1 specified that a lawyer *shall* render unpaid public interest legal service, and make an annual report concerning such service to the appropriate regulatory authority.[1]

Proponents of mandatory pro bono have asserted that since the profession's monopoly over the practice of law contributes to the problem of unmet legal needs, the profession should be required to take reasonable steps to alleviate them, and only *mandatory* pro bono offers a promise of involving all lawyers,[2] that mandatory pro bono is justifiable as an inherent duty of the lawyer as an officer of the court and as an implied condition of the license to practice,[3] and that only a mandatory requirement will meet the desperate needs of the disadvantaged and disempowered.[4]

On the other hand, mandatory pro bono has been opposed on the grounds that the poor suffer deprivation of *all* sorts and if given five or ten percent of lawyers' *incomes* instead of five or ten percent of lawyers' time, the poor might find better uses for the money, that many lawyers would not be competent in the areas involved in poor persons' legal problems, and that it may violate the thirteenth amendment's proscription of involuntary servitude.[5]

1. ABA Commission on Evaluation of Professional Standards, Model Rules of Professional Conduct 8.1 (Discussion Draft Jan. 30, 1980), 48 U.S.L.W.Supp. (Feb. 19, 1980).

2. Christensen, The Lawyer's Pro Bono Publico Responsibility, 1981 Am.B.Found. Research J. 1.

3. Rosenfeld, Mandatory Pro Bono: Historical and Constitutional Perspectives, 2 Cardozo L.Rev. 255 (1981) (discussing Association of Bar of City of New York proposal as well as RPC Discussion Draft proposal).

4. Spencer, Mandatory Public Service for Attorneys: A Proposal for the Future, 12 Sw.U.L.Rev. 493 (1981).

5. Humbach, Serving the Public Interest: An Overstated Objective, 65 A.B.A.J. 564 (1979). Compare Rosenfeld, supra note 3, at 290–94 (no thirteenth amendment violation under cases upholding military conscription, required alternative service by conscientious objectors, and requirement to do 60 hours county road and bridge work as duty person owes public); Spencer, supra note 4, at 502 & n. 39 (no thirteenth amendment violation because of, inter alia, nonspecific nature of work assignment).

See generally Shapiro, The Enigma of the Lawyer's Duty to Serve, 55 N.Y.U.L.Rev. 735 (1980).

In In re Emergency Delivery of Legal Services to the Poor (Mandatory Pro Bono),[6] the Florida Supreme Court denied a petition to require lawyers to provide 25 hours of free legal service to the poor or, in the alternative, donate $500 to the Florida Bar Foundation or participate in the interest on lawyers' trust accounts program (under which interest from pooled trust accounts is used for public purposes including legal services for the poor[7]). The court said:

"[W]e do not say that members of The Florida Bar have no duty or responsibility to render legal services to the poor. Our emphasis is to the exact opposite. * * *

"[W]hy all the idealistic talk in the Code of Professional Responsibility without a mandatory enforcement of its provisions? Part of the answer to that question lies within the nature of our free society: We have been loathe to coerce involuntary servitude in all walks of life; we do not forceably take property without just compensation; we do not mandate acts of charity. We believe that a person's voluntary service to others has to come from within the soul of that person. Our canons in this area are designed to be directory, to enlighten one's conscience, to focus attention on what is right for lawyers to do, but, historically, have not been meant to force an involuntary act.

"* * * We feel that it would be neither appropriate nor in the best interest of the public or the profession to compel by external means conduct which should be prompted from within each member of our profession."

But judges in El Paso County, Texas, responding to deep cuts in legal services funding, adopted the county bar association's proposal to order every lawyer in the county to take two uncompensated domestic relations cases each year.[8]

### STATE EX REL. WOLFF v. RUDDY

617 S.W.2d 64 (Mo.1981), cert. denied 454 U.S. 1142, 102 S.Ct. 1000, 71 L.Ed.2d 293 (1982).

PER CURIAM:

[R]espondent [judge] advised relator [lawyer] that, unless prohibited by an appellate court, he would, on or before April 15, 1981, appoint relator to defend Joann Williams, in State of Missouri v. Joann Williams, No. 452742, pending in the Circuit Court of the County of St. Louis. As the last sentence of his order, respondent also stated: "Under the present status of the appointed counsel fund, said attorney will not be paid or reimbursed for any of his expenses." * * *

6. 432 So.2d 39 (Fla.1983).

7. See supra pp. 473–80.

8. Pro Bono Mandated for El Paso Lawyers, National Law Journal, Oct. 11, 1982, at 2. See Family Division Trial Lawyers of Superior Court v. Moultrie, 51 U.S.L.W. 2413 (D.D.C. Dec. 20, 1982) (as prerequisite to being on roster for compensated appointments in juvenile cases, lawyer must accept uncompensated appointments to represent parents in neglect and abuse cases).

In State v. Green, 470 S.W.2d 571, 572, 573 (Mo.1971), this Court addressed the question of a lawyer gratuitously furnishing legal services to an indigent accused and said:

> "In 1963, in Gideon v. Wainwright, 372 U.S. 335, 83 S.Ct. 792, 9 L.Ed.2d 799, the United States Supreme Court held that the United States Constitution requires the State of Missouri, and other States, to furnish counsel to an indigent accused of crime. This means, in practical effect, that an indigent accused of crime cannot be prosecuted, convicted, and incarcerated in Missouri unless he is furnished counsel. The lawyers of Missouri, as officers of the Court, have fulfilled this State obligation, without compensation, since we attained statehood, although other persons essential to the administration of criminal justice (e.g. prosecuting attorneys, assistants to the Attorney General, psychiatrists, et al.) have not been asked to furnish services gratuitously. The question is whether the legal profession must continue to bear this burden *alone*." (Emphasis ours.)

The Court held in *Green* that the legal profession need not continue to bear the burden *alone*. The General Assembly of Missouri responded with enactment of Chapter 600, RSMo 1978. It must be said that its response has been less than resolute:

(1) In 1972, the General Assembly declared the public policy of Missouri to be that in cases where counsel, other than public defenders, are appointed to represent indigent defendants "the reimbursement of expenses and the attorney's fee for services shall be paid by the state from funds appropriated for that purpose." § 600.150, RSMo 1978.

(2) In 1977, the General Assembly declared, with certain stated exceptions, the public policy of Missouri to be that when a plea of not guilty is entered by an accused, his trial "shall commence within one hundred eighty days of arraignment." The sanction imposed for failure of compliance is possible dismissal of the charge against the accused. § 545.780, RSMo 1978.

(3) However, in 1980, the General Assembly provided: "Under no circumstances may the expenditures from general revenue for the purposes provided in sections 600.010 to 600.160 exceed the amount, five million dollars, if and when appropriated by the general assembly for such purposes." § 600.160, RSMo Supp. 1980.

(4) And, for the fiscal year ending June 30, 1981, the General Assembly appropriated only a total of $3,475,894 for representation of indigent defendants.

We must recognize that as of the date of this opinion the money appropriated by the General Assembly for the fiscal year ending June 30, 1981, has been spent. The cupboard is bare.

What are we to do? "No money shall be withdrawn from the state treasury except by warrant drawn in accordance with an appropriation made by law * * *." Mo.Const.Art. IV, § 28. We are reminded of our limitations by Alexander Hamilton in The Federalist No. 78: "The executive not only dispenses the honors but holds the sword of the community. The legislature not only commands the purse but prescribes the rules by which the duties and rights of every citizen are to be regulated. The judiciary, on the contrary, has no influence over either the sword or the purse; no direction either of the strength or of the wealth of the society, and can take no active resolution whatever. It may truly be said to have neither force nor will but merely judgment; and must ultimately depend upon the aid of the executive arm even for the efficacy of its judgments." The Federalist Papers 465 (New York: New American Library, 1961). However, we cannot permit the administration of criminal justice in Missouri to grind to a halt.

In these circumstances, we must turn again to the Bar of Missouri. We do so without apology.

The inherent nature of the practice of law has been described as follows:

> "The term 'profession,' it should be borne in mind, as a rule is applied to a group of people pursuing a learned art as a common calling in the spirit of public service where economic rewards are definitely an incidental, though under the existing economic conditions undoubtedly a necessary by-product. In this a profession differs radically from any trade or business which looks upon money-making and personal gain as its primary purpose. * * * "

Anton-Hermann Chroust, 1 The Rise of the Legal Profession in America x–xi (Norman, Oklahoma: University of Oklahoma Press, 1965).

The premise that practice of law "in the spirit of public service" is a *primary* consideration is articulated in EC 2–16:

> "The legal profession cannot remain a viable force in fulfilling its role in our society unless its members receive adequate compensation for services rendered, and reasonable fees should be charged in appropriate cases to clients able to pay them. Nevertheless, persons unable to pay all or a portion of a reasonable fee should be able to obtain necessary legal services, and lawyers should support and participate in ethical activities designed to achieve that objective."

And, the lawyers of Missouri have taken and subscribed, in part, the following oath or affirmation prescribed in Rule 8.11:

> "I do solemnly swear * * *
>
> "That I will never reject, from any consideration personal to myself, the cause of the defenseless or oppressed, or delay any person's cause for lucre or malice. So help me God." * * *

At the present time, the Court is becoming inundated with cases similar in nature involving non-payment of fees for the defense of the indigent. They include cases where accused indigents are being deprived of a reasonable defense by reason of lack of available funds necessary to prepare a proper defense for the accused and cases where lawyers are alleging that they are being denied the right to earn a livelihood for their family or in effect are being placed in involuntary servitude contrary to the thirteenth amendment to the United States Constitution. Because of insufficient funding of the Public Defender Program for the defense of indigents, the problem is currently approaching crisis proportion.

In this background, the Court has concluded that the processing of the voluminous pending and threatened cases concerning representation of the indigent is neither economically desirable for the state nor is it in the best interest of the indigent accused, the legal profession, or the public.

We believe that the best interests of the state of Missouri and the orderly administration of justice require that we at this time declare and establish temporary guidelines for meeting the problem of defense of the indigent accused. We believe our primary obligation is to the people to insure the continued operation of the criminal justice system, for without it, the peace of the community cannot be attained as the guilty cannot be convicted nor the innocent be acquitted. As a necessary part of this system the accused is entitled to counsel and, where indigent, counsel must be provided. It is our first obligation to secure to the indigent accused all of his constitutional rights and guarantees. We also have an obligation to deal fairly and justly with the members of the legal profession who are subject to our supervision. To accomplish these ends, we direct and order that the following temporary guidelines be followed by the judiciary and the members of the legal profession until the problem of defense of the indigent accused can be resolved in an orderly process by the Executive, Legislative, and Judicial branches of our government.

1. In this case or any similar case, the respondent circuit judge is admonished by this Court to hold all accused to a high standard of proof of indigency and to make every effort possible to fully verify indigency.

2. In this and any similar case, the respondent circuit judge should provide relator when requested with an evidentiary hearing as to the propriety of his appointment, taking into consideration his right to earn a livelihood for himself and his family and to be free from involuntary servitude. If respondent judge determines that the appointment will work any undue hardships, he should appoint another attorney. After hearing, we call on all members of the legal profession who may be appointed to accept appointment and to exert their best efforts in the defense of the indigent accused; and to refuse such service only with recognition that such refusal may be the subject of disciplinary action.

3. Non-payment to a lawyer for a period in excess of one hundred and twenty days for any prior appointed service may be deemed by the court to be grounds for excusing the lawyer from additional appointment in other cases.

4. We know of no requirement of either law or professional ethics which requires attorneys to advance personal funds in substantial amounts for the payment of either costs or expenses of the preparation of a proper defense of the indigent accused. If after evidentiary hearing, reasonable and necessary costs ordered advanced by the court are not forthcoming and available for preparation of the proper defense of the indigent within the time required by law for the trial of the accused, § 545.780, RSMo 1978, or where the court is unable to find and appoint counsel for the indigent accused who can prepare for trial within the time required by law, the court should on proper motion where necessary to protect the constitutional rights of the accused, order discharge of the accused.

5. Until further order of this Court, employment by government without further evidence of conflict with the interest of the indigent accused, shall not be deemed to be a bar to appointment by the Court to defend an indigent accused.

6. To assure that this situation shall not become worse and the failure of payment of such services become larger and more intolerable, the Public Defender Commission is requested that from appropriated funds, all approved fees and costs shall be paid in the order certified to and received by the Commission.

7. The Court will continue to urge the co-equal Executive and Legislative branches of government to each assume its share of responsibility for solution of the problem of defense of the indigent accused, realizing that the Court's action of this date is at best only temporary and stop gap because of the limitations upon our own power to make excessive demands upon those whom we are charged with supervising.

8. For a reasonable period of time pending the solution of this problem, the members of the legal profession are advised that in its discretion this Court will decline to hear other than the most extraordinary of applications for writs or extraordinary relief. We expect that each member of the legal profession, as he or she has throughout history, to continue to honor the oath "That I will never reject, from any consideration personal to myself, the cause of the defenseless or the oppressed * * * ", with complete confidence that this Court will do all within its power to protect the rights of indigent accused and to implement the public policy set forth in Chapter 600, RSMo 1978 & Cum.Supp.1980, that those ordered to defend the indigent accused shall be fairly compensated for their expenses and services.

For the present, the preliminary rule in prohibition is ordered quashed, without prejudice to reapply for extraordinary relief at any time that it may appear that the indigent accused is being denied a reasonable defense and a fair trial.[a]

### *Comment*

(1) *Uncompensated appointments.* A large majority of courts uphold the constitutional validity of requiring lawyers to represent indigents without compensation.[1]

(2) *Limited compensation.* Where legislatures have provided compensation for appointed counsel, but specified a per-case dollar maximum, several courts have found it within their inherent powers to direct compensation beyond the maximum, but only in "extraordinary circumstances" where necessary to save appointed counsel from financial ruin or to prevent impairment of the defendant's constitutional right to counsel.[2]

### *Question*

The United States Supreme Court has held that a state may provide that a convicted defendant who may be able to reimburse the state for the cost of counsel appointed for him as an indigent may be placed on probation subject to a requirement that he make such reimbursement if his indigency ends and he can do so without "manifest hardship."[3] Does this mean that assigned counsel may properly extract a promise from his or her indigent client to pay a fee when able to do so?[4]

**a.** See 50 U.M.K.C.L.Rev. 207 (1982) (*Wolff* takes a "drastic step backward" from *Green* by reinstituting "the plight of the Bar to defend indigent defendants gratuitously").

**1.** See Sontag v. State, 629 P.2d 1269 (Okl.Crim.App.1981), cert. denied 454 U.S. 1142, 102 S.Ct. 1001, 71 L.Ed.2d 294 (1982); Note, Court Appointment of Attorneys in Civil Cases: The Constitutionality of Uncompensated Legal Assistance, 81 Colum.L.Rev. 366 (1981); Annot., 21 A.L.R.3d 819 (1968).

But see In re Nine Applications for Appointment of Counsel, 475 F.Supp. 87 (N.D.Ala.1979), vacated 646 F.2d 203 (5th Cir. 1981); 50 U.M.K.C.L.Rev. 207, 215–17 (1982); Annot., 21 A.L.R.3d 819, 830–33 (1968). Cf. Menin v. Menin, 79 Misc.2d 285, 359 N.Y.S.2d 721 (1974), affirmed mem. 48 A.D.2d 904, 372 N.Y.S.2d 985 (1975).

Sometimes courts are able to construe statutes on expenses of proceedings to cover compensation for appointed counsel. See Abodeely v. County of Worcester, 352 Mass. 719, 227 N.E.2d 486 (1967); State v. Rush, 46 N.J. 399, 217 A.2d 441, 21 A.L.R.3d 804 (1966).

**2.** See People ex rel. Conn v. Randolph, 35 Ill.2d 24, 219 N.E.2d 337, 18 A.L.R.3d 1065 (1966); Brown v. Board of County Commissioners, 85 Nev. 149, 451 P.2d 708 (1969). Compare Smith v. State, 118 N.H. 764, 394 A.2d 834, 3 A.L.R. 4th 568 (1978) (statute limiting appointed counsel's compensation violates state constitution's separation of powers and its provision for indigent criminal defendants' counsel at state expense). See generally Annot., 3 A.L.R. 4th 576 (1981).

**3.** Fuller v. Oregon, 417 U.S. 40, 94 S.Ct. 2116, 40 L.Ed.2d 642 (1974). Compare ABA Standards for Criminal Justice 5–6.2 (2d ed.) 1980) (reimbursement should not be required except for fraud in obtaining eligibility determination).

**4.** Compare Oliver v. Mitchell, 14 Utah 2d 9, 376 P.2d 390 (1962) ("Indigents are as legally competent to contract as other men. * * * A promise to pay is to the credit of an indigent defendant for as yet in Utah the court appointed defense attorney receives no compensation by the county") with Hale v. Brewster, 81 N.M. 342, 467 P.2d 8, 43 A.L.R.3d 142 (1970) (defendant's promise lacks consideration). See Annot., 43 A.L.R.3d 1426 (1972). Cf. Coles, Manter & Watson v. Denver District Court, 177 Colo. 210, 493 P.2d

# B. GROUP LEGAL SERVICES

### *Comment*

Three United States Supreme Court cases furnish the background for the next principal case:

(a) NAACP v. BUTTON (1963).[1] NAACP-paid lawyers represented litigants (regardless of NAACP membership) seeking desegregation. The lawyers were selected by the NAACP and had to agree to abide by NAACP's policies, but this essentially amounted only to limiting assistance to cases wherein the litigants sought full desegregation, rather than "separate but equal" facilities, and the lawyers controlled the actual conduct of the assisted litigation. Much of the litigation resulted from the NAACP lawyers speaking at meetings of parents and children where the lawyers explained the steps necessary to achieve desegregation and furnished printed forms which litigants signed to authorize the NAACP lawyers to handle their cases (sometimes blank as to the name of the lawyer authorized to act).

The Court held "that the activities of the NAACP, its affiliates and legal staff shown on this record are modes of expression and association protected by the First and Fourteenth Amendments which Virginia may not prohibit, under its power to regulate the legal profession, as improper solicitation of legal business violative of [statute] and the Canons of Professional Ethics."

(b) BROTHERHOOD OF RAILROAD TRAINMEN v. VIRGINIA STATE BAR (1964).[2] The union selected, on advice of local lawyers and judges, a lawyer or firm for each of its 16 regions and, when a worker was injured or killed, recommended that the Federal Employers Liability Act claim not be settled without seeing a lawyer and that in the union's judgment the best lawyer to consult was the counsel selected. The union also provided a staff, at its own expense, to investigate accidents to help gather evidence for use by the plaintiffs.

The Court held "that the First and Fourteenth Amendments protect the right of the members through their Brotherhood to maintain and carry out their plan for advising workers who are injured to obtain legal advice and for recommending specific lawyers," adding, "*And, of course, lawyers accepting employment under this constitutionally protected plan have a like protection which the State cannot abridge.*"[3] The Court reasoned:

> "It cannot be seriously doubted that the First Amendment's guarantees of free speech, petition, and assembly give railroad workers the right to gather together for the lawful purpose of help-

374 (1972) (unethical but not illegal for public defender, on resigning, to take client for fee); Willcher v. United States, 408 A.2d 67 (D.C.App.1979) (compensated appointed counsel may be prosecuted for soliciting additional payment).

1. 371 U.S. 415, 83 S.Ct. 328, 9 L.Ed.2d 405.

2. 377 U.S. 1, 84 S.Ct. 1113, 12 L.Ed.2d 89.

3. Emphasis added.

ing and advising one another in asserting the rights Congress gave them * * *. The right of members to consult with each other in a fraternal organization necessarily include the right to select a spokesman from their number who could be expected to give the wisest counsel. That is the role played by the members who carry out the legal aid program. And the right of the workers personally or through a special department of their Brotherhood to advise concerning the need for legal assistance—and, most importantly, what lawyer a member could confidently rely on—is an inseparable part of this constitutionally guaranteed right to assist and advise each other.

" * * * Here what Virginia has sought to halt is not a commercialization of the legal profession which might threaten the moral and ethical fabric of the administration of justice. It is not 'ambulance chasing.' The railroad workers, by recommending competent lawyers to each other, obviously are not themselves engaging in the practice of law, nor are they or the lawyers whom they select parties to any soliciting of business. * * *

"A state could not, by invoking the power to regulate the professional conduct of attorneys, infringe in any way the right of individuals and the public to be fairly represented in lawsuits authorized by Congress to effectuate a basic public interest. [F]or [laypersons] to associate together to help one another to preserve and enforce rights granted them under federal laws cannot be condemned as a threat to legal ethics. * * *

"[T]he State again (as in *Button*) has failed to show any appreciable public interest in preventing the Brotherhood from carrying out its plan to recommend the lawyers it selects to represent injured workers."

(c) UNITED MINE WORKERS V. ILLINOIS STATE BAR ASS'N (1967).[4] The union employed a lawyer on an annual salary basis to represent members who desired his services in workers' compensation claims. The arrangement specified that the union would not interfere with the conduct of cases, and that the lawyer's relations would be only with the claimants. When members were injured, the union provided forms and suggested they be sent to the union's legal department.

The Court held "that the freedom of speech, assembly, and petition guaranteed by the First and Fourteenth Amendments gives petitioner the right to hire attorneys on a salary basis to assist its members in the assertion of their legal rights."

Rejecting an attempt to distinguish *Button* as "concerned chiefly with litigation that can be characterized as a form of political expression," the Court said:

"The litigation in question is, of course, not bound up with political matters of acute social moment, as in *Button*, but the First Amend-

4. 389 U.S. 217, 88 S.Ct. 353, 19 L.Ed.2d 426.

ment does not protect speech and assembly only to the extent it can be characterized as political. 'Great secular causes, with small ones, are guarded. The grievances for redress of which the right of petition was insured, and with it the right of assembly, are not solely religious or political ones. And the rights of free speech and a free press are not confined to any field of human interest.' "

The Court similarly refused to distinguish *Trainmen* on the ground it involved statutory rights created by Congress, observing, "[P]etitioner's freedom of speech, petition, and assembly * * * is, of course, as extensive with respect to assembly and discussion related to matters of local as to matters of federal concern."

The main part of the Court's reasoning was as follows:

"The First Amendment would * * * be a hollow promise if it left government free to destroy or erode its guarantees by indirect restraints * * *. We have therefore repeatedly held that laws which actually affect the exercise of these vital rights cannot be sustained merely because they were enacted for the purpose of dealing with some evil within the State's legislative competence, or even because the laws do in fact provide a helpful means of dealing with such an evil.

" * * * Thus in *Button* we * * * held * * * dangers of baseless litigation and conflicting interests between the association and individual litigants far too speculative to justify the broad remedy invoked by the State, a remedy that would have seriously crippled the efforts of the NAACP to vindicate the rights of its members in court. Likewise in the *Trainmen* case there was a theoretical possibility that the union's interests would diverge from that of the individual litigant members, and there was a further possibility that if this divergence ever occurred, the union's power to cut off the attorney's referral business could induce the attorney to sacrifice the interests of his client. Again we ruled that this very distant possibility of harm could not justify a complete prohibition of the Trainmen's efforts to aid one another in assuring that each injured member would be justly compensated for his injuries. * * *

"Nor can the case at bar be distinguished from the *Trainmen* case in any persuasive way. Here, to be sure, the attorney is actually paid by the Union, not merely the beneficiary of its recommendations. But in both situations the attorney's economic welfare is dependent to a considerable extent on the good will of the union, and if the temptation to sacrifice the client's best interests is stronger in the present situation, it is stronger to a virtually imperceptible degree. In both cases, there was absolutely no indication that the theoretically imaginable divergence between the interests of union and member ever actually arose in the context of a particular lawsuit * * *.

"The decree at issue here thus substantially impairs the associational rights of the Mine Workers and is not needed to protect the State's interest in high standards of legal ethics."

## UNITED TRANSPORTATION UNION v. STATE BAR

401 U.S. 576, 91 S.Ct. 1076, 28 L.Ed.2d 339 (1971).

Mr. Justice BLACK delivered the opinion of the Court.

The Michigan State Bar brought this action to enjoin the members of [the Union] from engaging in activities undertaken for the stated purpose of assisting their fellow workers, their widows and families, to protect themselves from excessive fees at the hands of incompetent attorneys in suits for damages under the Federal Employers' Liability Act. [The State Bar complained of the Union's recommending] selected attorneys to its members and their families [and of its securing] a commitment from those attorneys that the maximum fee charged would not exceed 25% of the recovery * * *. The Union * * * admitted that * * * it had recommended, with respect to FELA claims, that injured member employees, and their families, consult attorneys designated by the Union as "Legal Counsel"; that * * * it had informed the injured members and their families that the legal counsel would not charge in excess of 25% of any recovery; and that Union representatives were reimbursed for transporting injured employees, or their families, to the legal counsel offices. * * *

[T]he state trial court * * * issued an order enjoining the Union's activities on the ground that they violated the state statute making it a misdemeanor to "solicit" damage suits * * *. Brotherhood of Railroad Trainmen v. Virginia State Bar [involved] a similar injunction * * *.

In affirming the trial court decree, the material part of which is set out below,[4] the Michigan Supreme Court gave our holding in *Trainmen* the narrowest possible reading, focusing only on the specific literal language of the injunctive provisions challenged in that case rather than the broad range of union activities held to be protected by the First Amendment. * * * The Michigan Supreme Court failed to follow our decisions in *Trainmen, United Mine Workers,* and NAACP v. Button, upholding the First Amendment principle that groups can unite to assert their legal rights as effectively and economically as practicable. When applied, as it must be, to the Union's activities

4. The decree entered by the Michigan trial court permanently restrained and enjoined the Union:

"from giving or furnishing legal advice to its members or their families; from informing any lawyer or lawyers that an accident has been suffered by a member or nonmember of the said Brotherhood and furnishing the name and address of such injured or deceased person for the purpose of obtaining legal employment for any lawyer; from stating or suggesting that a recommended lawyer will defray expenses of any kind or make advances for any purpose to such injured persons or their families pending settlement of their claim; from controlling, directly or indirectly, the fees charged or to be charged by any lawyer; from accepting or receiving compensation of any kind, directly or indirectly, for the solicitation of legal employment for any lawyer, whether by way of salary, commission or otherwise; from sharing in any manner in the legal fees of any lawyer or countenancing the splitting of or sharing in such fees with any layman or lay agency; and from sharing in any recovery for personal injury or death by gift, assignment or otherwise."

reflected in the record of this case, the First Amendment forbids the restraints imposed by the injunction here under review for the following among other reasons.

*First.* The decree approved by the Michigan Supreme Court enjoins the Union from "giving or furnishing legal advice to its members or their families." Given its broadest meaning, this provision would bar the Union's members, officers, agents, or attorneys from giving any kind of advice or counsel to an injured worker or his family concerning his FELA claim. In *Trainmen* we upheld the commonsense proposition that such activity is protected by the First Amendment. Moreover, the plain meaning of this particular injunctive provision would emphatically deny the right of the Union to employ counsel to represent its members, a right explicitly upheld in *United Mine Workers* and NAACP v. Button.

We cannot accept the restricted interpretation of this provision urged by the State Bar, and accepted by our Brother HARLAN, that it only prohibits the Union or its members themselves from "practicing law." The record is devoid of any evidence or allegation of such conduct on the part of the Union or its members. A decree must relate specifically and exclusively to the pleadings and proof. If not so related, the provision, because of its vagueness, will jeopardize the exercise of protected freedoms. This injunction, like a criminal statute, prohibits conduct under fear of punishment. Therefore, we look at the injunction as we look at a statute, and if upon its face it abridges rights guaranteed by the First Amendment, it should be struck down. * * *

*Second.* The decree also enjoins the Union from furnishing to any attorney the names of injured members or information relating to their injuries. The investigation of accidents by Union staff for purposes of gathering evidence to assist the injured worker or his family in asserting FELA claims was part of the Union practice upheld in *Trainmen.* It would seem at least a little strange now to hold that the Union cannot communicate that information to the injured member's attorney.[7]

*Third.* A provision of the decree enjoins the members of the Union from "accepting or receiving compensation of any kind, directly or indirectly, for the solicitation of legal employment for any lawyer,

7. Our Brother Harlan suggests that the injured member should be free to direct the collected information to whatever lawyer he chooses, rather than for the Union to give it to the Union's recommended legal counsel. However, the injunction prohibits the Union from furnishing the information to "any lawyer," apparently including both recommended and nonrecommended counsel alike. The injunction would prohibit the injured member's attorney, regardless of whether or not he was recommended by the Union, from communicating with the Union's representative who investigated the accident, is familiar with the facts, and, other than the injured member himself, is probably the person most qualified to answer the attorney's questions and assist in preparation of the claim. To satisfy the Michigan court's notion that direct communication between the Union and the member's attorney is somehow unlawful, it seems our Brother Harlan would restrict the Union's efforts, which we expressly approved in *Trainmen,* of assisting the injured member in preparing his case for trial, to a written accident report filed with the injured member.

whether by way of salary, commission or otherwise." The Union conceded that prior to 1959, Union representatives were reimbursed for their actual time spent and out-of-pocket expenses incurred in bringing injured members or their families to the offices of the legal counsel. Since the members of a union have a First Amendment right to help and advise each other in securing effective legal representation, there can be no doubt that transportation of injured members to an attorney's office is within the scope of the protected activity. To the extent that the injunction prohibits this practice, it is invalid under *Trainmen, United Mine Workers*, and NAACP v. Button.

*Fourth.* Our Brothers HARLAN and WHITE apparently accept the State Bar contention that the provision prohibiting compensation to Union representatives for solicitation refers to compensation paid by the attorney rather than the Union. And so interpreted, it supplements the two provisions which prohibit the Union from sharing in legal fees received by the recommended counsel. There is no basis for this restraint. Such activity is not even suggested in the complaint. There is not a line of evidence concerning such practice in the record in this case. * * *

Our Brother HARLAN appears to concede that the State Bar has neither alleged nor proved that the Union has engaged in the past, is presently engaging, or plans to engage, in the sharing of legal fees. Nonetheless, he suggests that the injunction against such conduct is justified in order to remove any "temptation" for the Union to participate in such activities. We cannot accept this novel concept of equity jurisdiction that would open the courts to claims for injunctions against "temptation," and would deem potential "temptation" to be a sufficient basis for the issuance of an injunction. Indeed, it would appear that jurisdiction over "temptation" has heretofore been reserved to the churches.

An injunction can issue only after the plaintiff has established that the conduct sought to be enjoined is illegal and that the defendant, if not enjoined, will engage in such conduct. * * *

*Fifth.* Finally, the challenged decree bars the Union from controlling, directly or indirectly, the fees charged by any lawyer. [T]he Union sought to protect its members from excessive legal fees by securing an agreement from the counsel it recommends that the fee will not exceed 25% of the recovery, and that the percentage will include all expenses incidental to investigation and litigation. * * *

*United Mine Workers* upheld the right of workers to act collectively to obtain affordable and effective legal representation. One of the abuses sought to be remedied by the Mine Workers' plan was the situation pursuant to which members "were required to pay forty or fifty per cent of the amounts recovered in damage suits, for attorney fees." The Mine Workers dealt with the problem by employing an attorney on a salary basis, thereby providing free legal representation for its members in asserting their claims before the state workmen's compensation board. The Union in the instant case sought to protect its members against the same abuse by limiting the fee charged by recommended attorneys. It is hard to believe that a court of justice would deny a cooperative union of workers the right to protect its injured members, and their widows and children, from the injustice of excessive fees at the hands of inadequate counsel. Indeed, the Michigan court was foreclosed from so doing by our decision in *United Mine Workers.*[9]

In the context of this case we deal with a cooperative union of workers seeking to assist its members in effectively asserting claims under the FELA. But the principle here involved cannot be limited to the facts of this case. At issue is the basic right to group legal action, a right first asserted in this Court by an association of Negroes seeking the protection of freedoms guaranteed by the Constitution. The common thread running through our decisions in NAACP v. Button, *Trainmen,* and *United Mine Workers* is that collective activity undertaken to obtain meaningful access to the courts is a fundamental right within the protection of the First Amendment. However, that right would be a hollow promise if courts could deny associations of workers or others the means of enabling their members to meet the costs of legal representation. That was the holding in *United Mine Workers, Trainmen,* and NAACP v. Button. The injunction in the present case cannot stand in the face of these prior decisions.

Reversed.

Mr. Justice HARLAN, concurring in part and dissenting in part.
* * *

I agree that, in light of this Court's recent decisions, one portion of the Michigan decree—that prohibiting the union from controlling the fees charged by attorneys—cannot stand. * * * In all other respects I think the decree is consistent with our past decisions and otherwise valid.

* * * I share my Brothers' concern with the problems of providing meaningful access to competent legal advice for persons in the middle and lower economic strata of our society. This is a matter of public concern deserving our best efforts at resolution, a task that the organized bar may be thought to have been too slow in recognizing. Nor do I condone, any more than my Brethren, the nefarious practices that called forth the Brotherhood's plan before us today.

9. The injunction also bars the Union "from stating or suggesting that a recommended lawyer will defray expenses of any kind or make advances for any purpose to such injured persons or their families pending settlement of their claim." The only allegation in the complaint possibly relating to this injunctive provision is that the Union representatives informed the injured members that the 25% fee included all expenses. This provision of the injunction, therefore, is invalid for the same reasons that the provision limiting fees is invalid.

[Eds.] The Court took no note of restrictions on advancements like DR 5-103(B), which allows a lawyer to advance expenses of litigation only if the client remains ultimately liable for such expenses. Compare RPC 1.8(e)(1) (repayment may be contingent on outcome).

But the issue presented for decision is not the desirability of group legal services, or the ways in which the traditional concepts of professional ethics should be modified to take account of the changes in social structure and social needs since the 19th century. The issue, rather, is the scope left by the Federal Constitution for state action in the regulation of the practice of law. Despite the First Amendment implications of denial of access to the courts in other situations, see NAACP v. Button (dissenting opinion), all that is involved here is a combination of purchasers of services seeking to increase their market power. The relationship to First Amendment interest seems to me remote at best. * * *

Mr. Justice WHITE, with whom Mr. Justice BLACKMUN joins, concurring in part and dissenting in part.

The first provision in the decree prohibiting the union from giving or furnishing legal advice to its members or their families is overbroad in light of United Mine Workers v. Illinois Bar Assn. and should be narrowed to prohibit only legal advice by nonlawyers. Also, I agree with the Court that the portion of the decree forbidding the setting of fees by union-lawyer agreement cannot stand. Otherwise, however, I do not read the decree as being inconsistent with our prior cases and I would not now extend them to set aside this decree in its entirety.[a]

### *Comment*

(1) *Background.* Prior to the United States Supreme Court decisions, organizations offering the services of a lawyer to their members were met with the prohibition against unauthorized practice of law. For example, an automobile club could not provide a lawyer to advise its members on traffic laws or make appearances in court,[1] a banking association[2] or a trade association[3] could not engage a lawyer to give legal services to its members, and taxpayers could not organize into a non-profit corporation to engage a lawyer to resist in court taxes imposed on members and deemed unfair.[4] Several authoritative commentators believed these limitations too restrictive, preventing the fulfillment of an important need for more extended legal services to

**a.** Justice Stewart took no part in the decision.

For the latest Supreme Court case on organizational legal service activities, see In re Primus, infra p. 581.

See also Great Western Cities, Inc. v. Binstein, 476 F.Supp. 827 (N.D.Ill.) (allegedly defrauded property buyers have right to band together, retain lawyers, and solicit others similarly situated to join in litigation against seller), affirmed mem. 614 F.2d 775 (7th Cir. 1979).

**1.** In re Maclub of America, 295 Mass. 45, 3 N.E.2d 272, 105 A.L.R. 1360 (1936); Automobile Club v. Hoffmeister, 338 S.W.2d 348 (Mo.App.1960); ABA Formal Opinion 8 (1925).

**2.** ABA Formal Opinion 98 (1933).

**3.** ABA Formal Opinions 158, 162 (1936).

**4.** People ex rel. Courtney v. Association of Real Estate Taxpayers, 354 Ill. 102, 187 N.E. 823 (1933).

those who would otherwise not receive them or receive them inadequately.[5]

(2) *Need for group legal services.* It has been estimated that "the middle 70% of our population" is not being reaching or served adequately by the legal profession because of fear of legal services' cost and unawareness "of what problems are 'legal' and what lawyers can do to solve such problems." [6] The group or prepaid legal services approach has been urged as a means to alleviate this problem.[7] The Report of the American Assembly on Law and the Changing Society[8] declared:

> "Access to legal services must be recognized as a matter of legal right. Legal services provided through conventional law office and lawyer-client relationships are beyond the means of many citizens. * * *
>
> "Group legal service arrangements should be encouraged subject to safeguards that will assure independence of professional judgment and fidelity to the lawyer-client relation. Properly administered, they should reduce the cost of needed legal services, ease the problem of finding a lawyer, and provide the client with a lawyer in whom he has reason to have confidence."

(3) *Open panel v. closed panel.* There has been considerable discussion regarding the relative merits of the "open-panel" approach (where the organization pays whatever lawyer the individual selects) and the "closed-panel" approach (where the organization employs, pays for, or recommends particular counsel),[9] but it seems to have become

5. See E. Cheatham, A Lawyer When Needed 73–86 (1963); H. Drinker, Legal Ethics 161–68 (1953).

6. ABA Revised Handbook on Prepaid Legal Services 2 (2d ed. 1972).

7. B. Christensen, Group Legal Services (1967); Ashe, Group Legal Services—Equal Justice in Fact: A Prognosis for the Seventies, 23 Syracuse L.Rev. 1167 (1972); Cady, The Future of Group Legal Services, 55 A.B.A.J. 420 (1969); Stolz, Sesame Street for Lawyers: A Dramatic Rendition of United Transportation Union v. The State Bar of Michigan, 36 Unauth.Pr.News 14 (Nov.1971); Voorhees, Group Legal Services and the Public Interest, 55 A.B.A.J. 534 (1969); Zimroth, Group Legal Services and the Constitution, 76 Yale L.J. 966 (1967); Comment, Prepaid Legal Services: Obstacles Hampering Its Growth and Development, 47 Fordham L.Rev. 841 (1979). See generally Annot., 93 A.L.R.3d 199 (1979).

But see Weinstein, The Furture of the Legal Profession—Part 2: Salvation Through Prepaid and Other Fictions, 5 Juris Doctor 19 (Sept. 1975), contending that the organized bar has greatly exaggerated the middle class' unmet need and that "what little need really does exist does not by itself justify the bar's suggested remedies—especially in light of what those 'remedies' would do to the profession itself."

8. 54 A.B.A. J. 450, 451 (1968).

9. For arguments in favor of the open panel approach, see Fisher, Future Options of the Private Bar in the Field of Prepaid Legal Services, 58 Mass.L.Q. 243 (1973).

For arguments favoring the closed panel approach, see Baron & Cole, Real Freedom of Choice for the Consumer of Legal Services, 58 Mass.L.Q. 253 (1973); Bartosic & Bernstein, Group Legal Services as a Fringe Benefit: Lawyers for Forgotten Clients Through Collective Bargaining, 59 Va.L.Rev. 410, 427–32 (1973).

For discussion of the most famous open panel plan, see Getman, A Critique of the Report of the Shreveport Experiment, 3 J.Legal Studies 487 (1974); Hallauer, The Shreveport Experiment in Prepaid Legal Services, 2

recognized that the United States Supreme Court cases restrict a state's ability to preclude the closed-panel approach.

(4) *ABA response.* In 1975,[10] the ABA responded to the Supreme Court decisions by inserting exhaustively detailed provisions into DR 2–103 and 2–104 regarding the conditions under which a lawyer could cooperate with an organization's legal services activities.[11]

By contrast, the ABA's 1983 Rules of Professional Conduct include only a few provisions relevant to a lawyer's conduct regarding group legal services:

**MODEL RULES OF PROFESSIONAL CONDUCT**

**RULE 5.4 Professional Independence of a Lawyer**

* * *

(c) A lawyer shall not permit a person who recommends, employs, or pays him to render legal services for another to direct or regulate his professional judgment in rendering such legal services.[a]

(d) A lawyer shall not practice with or in the form of a professional corporation or association authorized to practice law for a profit, if:

(1) a nonlawyer owns any interest therein, except that a fiduciary representative of the estate of a lawyer may hold the stock or interest of the lawyer for a reasonable time during administration;

(2) a nonlawyer is a corporate director or officer thereof; or

J.Legal Studies 223 (1973); Comment, The Shreveport and Columbus Plans of Prepaid Legal Services, 27 Baylor L.Rev. 485 (1975).

For discussion of the various approaches used in California, see Note, Developments in California Private Legal Services Plans, 4 Golden Gate L.Rev. 155 (1974).

See generally Pfennigstorf & Kimball, Legal Service Plans: A Typology, 1976 Am.B. Found. Research J. 411.

10. The ABA's 1975 response was subsequent to 1974 amendments, see House of Delegates Acts on Group Legal Services, Shield Legislation, Court Organization Standards, and Uniform Divorce, 60 A.B.A.J. 446 (1974). The 1974 amendments had been roundly criticized as too restrictive. See Bowler, Prepaid Legal Services and the Alternative Practice of Law, 51 Chi.-Kent L.Rev. 41, 47–48 (1974); Cornish & Cornish, Group Legal Services Today, 14 Washburn L.J. 31 (1975); Gilmore, The Organized Bar and Prepaid Legal Services, 21 Wayne L.Rev. 213, 217–24 (1975); Justice Department and Other Views on Prepaid Legal Services Plans Get an Airing Before the Tunney Subcommittee, 60 A.B.A. J. 791 (1974); Comment, Group Legal Services: From Houston to Chicago, 79 Dick.L.Rev. 621 (1975); Note, Prepaid Legal Services, Ethical Codes, and the Snares of Antitrust, 26 Syracuse L.Rev. 754, 757–58 (1975).

11. The original 1969 CPR basically allowed lawyer cooperation with a nonprofit organization's legal service activities "only in those instances and to the extent that controlling constitutional interpretation at the time of the rendition of the services requires the allowance of such legal service activities." A number of states modified or omitted the group legal services provisions when adopting the CPR. See Bartosic & Bernstein, Group Legal Services as a Fringe Benefit: Lawyers for Forgotten Clients Through Collective Bargaining, 59 Va.L.Rev. 410, 414 n. 9 (1973). The relevant original 1969 provisions, 1974 amendments, 1975 amendments, and comments to 1975 amendments are set forth in parallel columns in a chart prepared by the ABA, reprinted in 11 Tenn.B.J. 36 (May 1975) (but DR 2–103(D)(4)(e) is not set forth as ultimately adopted).

The ABA made minor additional amendments in DR 2–103 and 2–104 in August 1977.

a. Accord, DR 5–107(B).

(3) a nonlawyer has the right to direct or control the professional judgment of a lawyer.[b]

**RULE 7.2 Advertising**

* * *

(c) A lawyer shall not give anything of value to a person for recommending the lawyer's services, except that a lawyer * * * may pay the usual charges of a not-for-profit lawyer referral service or other legal service organization.[c]

**RULE 7.3 Direct Contact With Prospective Clients**

* * *

COMMENT:

* * * General mailings not addressed to recipients involved in a specific legal matter or incident * * * more closely resemble permissible advertising rather than prohibited solicitation.

Similarly, this Rule would not prohibit a lawyer from contacting representatives of organizations or groups that may be interested in establishing a group or prepaid legal plan for its members, insureds, beneficiaries or other third parties for the purpose of informing such entities of the availability of and details concerning the plan or arrangement which he or his firm is willing to offer. This form of communication is not directed to a specific prospective client known to need legal services related to a particular matter. Rather, it is usually addressed to an individual acting in a fiduciary capacity seeking a supplier of legal services for others who may, if they choose, become prospective clients of the lawyer. Under these circumstances, the activity which the lawyer undertakes in communicating with such representatives and the type of information transmitted to the individual are functionally similar to and serve the same purpose as advertising permitted under Rule 7.2.[d]

**b.** Accord, DR 5–107(C). See also RPC 5.4(a) and (b)'s restrictions on sharing legal fees with a nonlawyer and on forming a partnership with a nonlawyer if any of the partnership's activities consist of the practice of law. Accord, DR 3–102, 3–103. Regarding unauthorized practice of law, see supra pp. 77–97.

**c.** See DR 2–103(B).

**d.** In light of RPC 7.3's language and the Comment's context, perhaps the Comment should be understood as countenancing only *mailed*, not face to face or telephonic, communication to organizations about group legal services.

Compare the following CPR provisions:

**"DR 2–103 Recommendation of Professional Employment**

* * *

"(D) A lawyer or his partner or associate or any other lawyer affiliated with him or his firm may be recommended, employed or paid by, or may cooperate with, one of the following offices or organizations that promote the use of his services or those of his partner or associate or any other lawyer affiliated with him or his firm if there is no interference with the exercise of independent professional judgment in behalf of his client:

* * *

(4) Any bona fide organization that recommends, furnishes or pays for legal services to its members or beneficiaries provided the following conditions are satisfied:

(a) Such organization, including any affiliate, is so organized and operated that no profit is derived by it from the rendition of legal services by lawyers, and that, if the organization is organized for profit, the legal services are not rendered by lawyers employed, directed, supervised or

### *Questions*

(1) Are RPC 5.4(d) and DR 2–103(D)(4)(a) and 5–107(C) sound in restricting one's practicing law for a *for-profit* organization in which nonlawyers participate?[1] Is lay commercialization of the practice of law contrary to the public interest because a lay commercial provider of legal services is not, like a lawyer, restricted as to competence, integrity, manner of seeking employment, charging excessive fees, divided loyalties, independent judgment, or maintaining confidential in-

selected by it except in connection with matters where such organization bears ultimate liability of its member or beneficiary.

(b) Neither the lawyer, nor his partner, nor associate, nor any other lawyer affiliated with him or his firm, nor any non-lawyer, shall have initiated or promoted such organization for the primary purpose of providing financial or other benefit to such lawyer, partner, associate or affiliated lawyer.

(c) Such organization is not operated for the purpose of procuring legal work or financial benefit for any lawyer as a private practitioner outside of the legal services program of the organization.

(d) The member or beneficiary to whom the legal services are furnished, and not such organization, is recognized as the client of the lawyer in the matter.

(e) Any member or beneficiary who is entitled to have legal services furnished or paid for by the organization may, if such member or beneficiary so desires, select counsel other than that furnished, selected or approved by the organization for the particular matter involved; and the legal service plan of such organization provides appropriate relief for any member or beneficiary who asserts a claim that representation by counsel furnished, selected or approved would be unethical, improper or inadequate under the circumstances of the matter involved and the plan provides an appropriate procedure for seeking such relief.

(f) The lawyer does not know or have cause to know that such organization is in violation of applicable laws, rules of court and other legal requirements that govern its legal service operations.

(g) Such organization has filed with the appropriate disciplinary authority at least annually a report with respect to its legal service plan, if any, showing its terms, its schedule of benefits, its subscription charges, agreements with counsel, and financial results of its legal service activities or, if it has failed to do so, the lawyer does not know or have cause to know of such failure."

See also DR 2–103(C), 2–104(A)(2), (3); EC 2–33, 5–21 to 5–24.

1. The United States Supreme Court has held that it does not violate due process to prohibit a corporation from engaging in a pursuit unless controlled by licensed practitioners, on the ground that ownership "by people who do not know anything about it" and "divorce between the power of control and knowledge" where the pursuit "calls for knowledge in a high degree" may be seen as an evil. North Dakota State Board v. Snyder's Drug Stores, Inc., 414 U.S. 156, 94 S.Ct. 407, 38 L.Ed.2d 379 (1973) (upholding statute allowing corporation to operate pharmacy only if majority of stock owned by registered pharmacists).

See Cuyahoga County Bar Association v. Gold Shield, Inc., 52 Ohio Misc. 105, 369 N.E.2d 1232 (1975), affirmed by Court of Appeals (for-profit corporation may not operate prepaid legal services plan). See also State ex rel. Norvell v. Credit Bureau, 85 N.M. 521, 514 P.2d 40 (1973) (lay collection agency may not litigate in its own name through lawyers it retained creditors' claims solicited on a percentage contingency fee basis and assigned to agency).

Regarding unauthorized practice of law, see supra pp. 77–97.

formation? Will the profit motive induce the commercial provider to obtain clients by improper advertising and solicitation, accept clients whose needs will not be competently served, ignore their conflicting interests, compromise their confidential information, and overcharge them? Is it relevant that the first amendment accords less protection to commercial activity than noncommercial? [2]

It should be noted that the ABA Commission which drafted the RPC originally proposed that RPC 5.4 permit employment by an organization in which a financial interest is held by a nonlawyer, including a business corporation, insurance company, or legal services organization, provided that the relationship's terms specify in writing that there is no interference with the lawyer's independence of professional judgment or with the client-lawyer relationship, that confidential information is protected as required by RPC 1.6, and that the arrangement does not involve advertising or solicitation prohibited by RPC 7.2 and 7.3 or a fee prohibited by RPC 1.5.[3] But the ABA House of Delegates rejected this at its February 1983 meeting, instead inserting the provisions of DR 3–102, 3–103, and 5–107(B) and (C) into RPC 5.4.[4]

(2) Is DR 2–103(D)(4)(e) appropriate in allowing a lawyer to cooperate with a group legal services organization's plan only if "[a]ny member or beneficiary who is entitled to have legal services furnished or paid for by the organization may, if such member or beneficiary so desires, select counsel other than that furnished, selected or approved by the organization for the particular matter involved; and the legal service plan of such organization provides appropriate relief for any member or beneficiary who asserts a claim that representation by counsel furnished, selected or approved would be unethical, improper or inadequate under the circumstances of the matter involved and the plan provides an appropriate procedure for seeking such relief"?

Does this require in some circumstances that the organization provide reimbursement to those who choose counsel other than that selected by the organization? If so, is it consistent with what the *United Transportation Union* Court called the "First Amendment principle that groups can unite to assert their legal rights as effectively and *economically* as practicable"? With that Court's statement that "*collective* activity undertaken to obtain meaningful access to the courts is a fundamental right"? With what the *Mine Workers* Court called the "right to hire attorneys on a *salary basis* to assist its members"? [5]

2. See infra materials on advertising and solicitation.

3. See Final Draft of Model Rules of Professional Conduct, pullout supplement to November 1982 issue of A.B.A.J.

4. See Midyear Meeting of American Bar Association, 51 U.S.L.W. 2488, 2493 (Feb. 22, 1983).

5. Emphasis added throughout. See Bowler, Prepaid Legal Services and the Alternative Practice of Law, 51 Chi.-Kent L.Rev. 41, 47 n. 41 (1974) (requiring "that a closed panel plan become an open panel plan whenever any member * * * so desires * * * is open to attack on * * * constitutional * * * grounds"); Justice Department and Other Views on Prepaid Legal

(3) If DR 2–103(D)(4)(e) requires reimbursement in some circumstances, can it validly apply as to a plan covered by the Employment Retirement Income Security Act of 1974? That Act covers, among other things, "any plan, fund, or program * * * for the purpose of providing * * * prepaid legal services" maintained by an employer whose activities affect commerce, a union whose members' work affects commerce, or both,[6] and "supersedes" among other things "rules" of a state "agency * * * which purports to regulate, directly *or indirectly*, the terms and conditions" of covered plans "insofar as they * * * relate to" covered plans.[7]

### *Comment*

(1) *Collective bargaining.* Section 302(c) of the Labor Management Relations Act, 29 U.S.C. § 186(c), was amended in 1973 to permit collective bargaining for legal services for employees and their families and dependents as a fringe benefit.[8]

(2) *Income tax.* In 1976, Congress amended sections 120 and 501(c)(20) of the Internal Revenue Code to exclude from an employee's gross income employer contributions to a qualified group legal services plan and the value of legal services provided under such a plan.[9]

(3) *Insurance.* There has been discussion as to whether some or all group or prepaid legal services arrangements constitute "insurance," so as to be subject to regulation by state insurance commissioners.[10]

Services Plans Get an Airing Before the Tunney Subcommittee, 60 A.B.A.J. 791, 796 (1974) (denying "to a group the right to select a plan that is wholly and entirely a closed panel plan" is a "blatant restriction on the freedom of association and petition of closed panel plans").

One might argue that although a lawyer should be prohibited from "unethical" or "inadequate" representation (and already is, see, e.g., DR 5–105 and DR 6–101), a lawyer is not unethical merely because he or she serves a group which has decided that the individual rather than the group should pay for different counsel when selected counsel is ethically precluded from serving.

6. Except government and church employee plans, 29 U.S.C. §§ 1002(1), 1003.

7. 29 U.S.C. § 1144(a), (c) (emphasis added). The supersession provision was substituted for one which would have provided for supersession of state laws "insofar as they * * * relate to the reporting and disclosure responsibilities, and fiduciary responsibilities, of persons acting on behalf of" a covered plan. See 120 Cong.Rec. H1303 (daily ed. Feb. 28, 1974). Cf. Pfennigstorf & Kimball, Employee Legal Services Plans: Conflicts Between Federal and State Regulation 1976 Am.B. Found. Research J. 787; Comment, The Effect of ERISA on Prepaid Legal Services, 27 Baylor L.Rev. 566 (1975); Note, Prepaid Legal Services, Ethical Codes and the Snares of Antitrust, 26 Syracuse L.Rev. 754, 756–57 (1975).

Can DR 2–103(D)(4)(g), regarding filing of reports, validly apply to a plan covered by the Act? DR 2–103(D)(4)(a) (non-profit status) to an employer-provided plan covered by the Act?

8. See 29 U.S.C. § 186(c); Dunne, Prepaid Legal Services Have Arrived, 4 Hofstra L.Rev. 1, 18–19 (1975).

9. See Comment, Prepaid Legal Plans: A Glimpse of the Future, 47 Tenn.L.Rev. 148, 167–70 (1979); Note, Recent Developments in Prepaid Legal Services, 17 Washburn L.J. 290; 307–10 (1978).

10. See State v. Blue Crest Plans, Inc., 72 A.D.2d 713, 421 N.Y.S.2d 579 (1979); Van Hooser, Problems of Regulation and Supervision of Prepaid Legal Services Plans, 9 Docket [Va.Bar Ass'n Young Lawyers' Section] 14 (Winter 1973); Note, 4 Golden Gate L.Rev. 155, 177–79 (1974); Note, supra note 9, at 304–07.

(4) *Antitrust.* There has also been discussion of the antitrust implications of group and prepaid legal services.[11] It would seem that the most critical area would be a group of lawyers' involvement in setting a plan's schedule of payments.[12]

(5) *Conflict of interests.* Regarding conflict of interests issues that may arise as to organizations' legal services plans, see supra p. 252.

## C. ADVERTISING

### BATES v. STATE BAR[a]

433 U.S. 350, 97 S.Ct. 2691, 53 L.Ed.2d 810 (1977).

Mr. Justice BLACKMUN delivered the opinion of the Court. * * *

Appellants John R. Bates and Van O'Steen are attorneys licensed to practice law in the State of Arizona. * * * After admission to the bar in 1972, appellants worked as attorneys with the Maricopa County Legal Aid Society.

In March 1974, appellants left the Society and opened a law office, which they call a "legal clinic," in Phoenix. Their aim was to provide legal services at modest fees to persons of moderate income who did not qualify for governmental legal aid. In order to achieve this end, they would accept only routine matters, such as uncontested divorces, uncontested adoptions, simple personal bankruptcies, and changes of name, for which costs could be kept down by extensive use of paralegals, automatic typewriting equipment, and standardized forms and office procedures. More complicated cases, such as contested divorces, would not be accepted. Because appellants set their prices so as to have a relatively low return on each case they handled, they depended on substantial volume.

After conducting their practice in this manner for two years, appellants concluded that their practice and clinical concept could not survive unless the availability of legal services at low cost was advertised and, in particular, fees were advertised. Consequently, in order to generate the necessary flow of business, that is, "to attract clients," appellants on February 22, 1976, placed an advertisement[b] in the *Arizona Republic*, a daily newspaper of general circulation in the Phoenix metropolitan area. * * *

11. Fisher & Gailey, Antitrust Implications of Prepaid Legal Services in Texas, 27 Baylor L.Rev. 451 (1975); Meeks, Antitrust Aspects of Prepaid Legal Services Plans, 1976 Am.B. Found. Research J. 855; Note, Prepaid Legal Services, Ethical Codes, and the Snares of Antitrust, 26 Syracuse L.Rev. 754 (1975). See also supra note 5 and authorities cited.

12. See Cornish & Cornish, Group Legal Services Today, 14 Washburn L.J. 31, 41–42 (1975). Cf. Goldfarb v. Virginia State Bar, supra p. 426.

a. The antitrust aspects of this case are discussed supra p. 434.

b. The advertisement offered "legal services at very reasonable fees" and listed the fees for certain services.

Appellants concede that the advertisement constituted a clear violation of Disciplinary Rule 2–101(B), embodied in Rule 29(a) of the Supreme Court of Arizona. The disciplinary rule provides in part:

> "(B) A lawyer shall not publicize himself, or his partner, or associate, or any other lawyer affiliated with him or his firm, as a lawyer through newspaper or magazine advertisements, radio or television announcements, display advertisements in the city or telephone directories or other means of commercial publicity, nor shall he authorize or permit others to do so in his behalf."

[Upon disciplinary proceedings, the Arizona Supreme Court censured the two lawyers.]

A

Last Term, in Virginia Pharmacy Board v. Virginia Consumer Council, 425 U.S. 748, 96 S.Ct. 1817, 48 L.Ed.2d 346 (1976), the Court considered the validity under the First Amendment of a Virginia statute declaring that a pharmacist was guilty of "unprofessional conduct" if he advertised prescription drug prices. * * *

Although acknowledging that the State had a strong interest in maintaining professionalism among pharmacists, this Court concluded that the proffered justifications were inadequate to support the advertising ban. High professional standards were assured in large part by the close regulation to which pharmacists in Virginia were subject. And we observed that "on close inspection it is seen that the State's protectiveness of its citizens rests in large part on the advantages of their being kept in ignorance." But we noted the presence of a potent alternative to this "highly paternalistic" approach:

> "That alternative is to assume that this information is not in itself harmful, that people will perceive their own best interests if only they are well enough informed, and that the best means to that end is to open the channels of communication rather than to close them."

The choice between the dangers of suppressing information and the dangers arising from its free flow was seen as precisely the choice "that the First Amendment makes for us."

We have set out this detailed summary of the *Pharmacy* opinion because the conclusion that Arizona's disciplinary rule is violative of the First Amendment might be said to flow *a fortiori* from it. Like the Virginia statutes, the disciplinary rule serves to inhibit the free flow of commercial information and to keep the public in ignorance. Because of the possibility, however, that the differences among professions might bring different constitutional considerations into play, we specifically reserved judgment as to the other professions.

In the instant case we are confronted with the arguments directed explicitly toward the regulation of advertising by licensed attorneys.

B

The issue presently before us is a narrow one. First, we need not address the peculiar problems associated with advertising claims relating to the *quality* of legal services. Such claims probably are not susceptible to precise measurement or verification and, under some circumstances, might well be deceptive or misleading to the public, or even false. Appellee does not suggest, nor do we perceive, that appellants' advertisement contained claims, extravagant or otherwise, as to the quality of services. Accordingly, we leave that issue for another day. Second, we also need not resolve the problems associated with in-person solicitation of clients—at the hospital room or the accident site, or in any other situation that breeds undue influence—by attorneys or their agents or "runners." Activity of that kind might well pose dangers of overreaching and misrepresentation not encountered in newspaper announcement advertising. Hence, this issue also is not before us.

The heart of the dispute before us today is whether lawyers also may constitutionally advertise the *prices* at which certain routine services will be performed. Numerous justifications are proffered for the restriction of such price advertising. We consider each in turn:

1. *The Adverse Effect on Professionalism.* Appellee places particular emphasis on the adverse effects that it feels price advertising will have on the legal profession. The key to professionalism, it is argued, is the sense of pride that involvement in the discipline generates. It is claimed that price advertising will bring about commercialization, which will undermine the attorney's sense of dignity and self-worth. The hustle of the marketplace will adversely affect the profession's service orientation, and irreparably damage the delicate balance between the lawyer's need to earn and his obligation selflessly to serve. Advertising is also said to erode the client's trust in his attorney: once the client perceives that the lawyer is motivated by profit, his confidence that the attorney is acting out of commitment to the client's welfare is jeopardized. And advertising is said to tarnish the dignified public image of the profession.

We recognize, of course, and commend the spirit of public service with which the profession of law is practiced and to which it is dedicated. The present Members of this Court, licensed attorneys all, could not feel otherwise. And we would have reason to pause if we felt that our decision today would undercut that spirit. But we find the postulated connection between advertising and the erosion of true professionalism to be severely strained. At its core, the argument presumes that attorneys must conceal from themselves and from their clients the real-life fact that lawyers earn their livelihood at the bar. We suspect that few attorneys engage in such self-deception. And rare is the client, moreover, even one of modest means, who enlists the aid of an attorney with the expectation that his services will be rendered free of charge. In fact, the American Bar Association advises that an attorney should reach "a clear agreement with his client as to the basis of the fee charges to be made," and that this is to be done "[a]s soon as feasible after a lawyer has been employed." EC 2–19.[c] If the commercial basis of the relationship is to be promptly disclosed on ethical grounds, once the client is in the office, it seems inconsistent to condemn the candid revelation of the same information before he arrives at that office.

Moreover, the assertion that advertising will diminish the attorney's reputation in the community is open to question. Bankers and engineers advertise, and yet these professions are not regarded as undignified. In fact, it has been suggested that the failure of lawyers to advertise creates public disillusionment with the profession. The absence of advertising may be seen to reflect the profession's failure to reach out and serve the community: studies reveal that many persons do not obtain counsel even when they perceive a need because of the feared price of services or because of an inability to locate a competent attorney. Indeed, cynicism with regard to the profession may be created by the fact that it long has publicly eschewed advertising, while condoning the actions of the attorney who structures his social or civic associations so as to provide contacts with potential clients.

It appears that the ban on advertising originated as a rule of etiquette and not as a rule of ethics. Early lawyers in Britain viewed the law as a form of public service, rather than as a means of earning a living, and they looked down on "trade" as unseemly. Eventually, the attitude toward advertising fostered by this view evolved into an aspect of the ethics of the profession. But habit and tradition are not in themselves an adequate answer to a constitutional challenge. In this day, we do not belittle the person who earns his living by the strength of his arm or the force of his mind. Since the belief that lawyers are somehow "above" trade has become an anachronism, the historical foundation for the advertising restraint has crumbled.

2. *The Inherently Misleading Nature of Attorney Advertising.* It is argued that advertising of legal services inevitably will be misleading (a) because such services are so individualized with regard to content and quality as to prevent informed comparison on the basis of an advertisement, (b) because the consumer of legal services is unable to determine in advance just what services he needs, and (c) because advertising by attorneys will highlight irrelevent factors and fail to show the relevant factor of skill.

We are not persuaded that restrained professional advertising by lawyers inevitably will be misleading. Although many services performed by attorneys are indeed unique, it is doubtful that any attorney

c. Compare RPC 1.5(b), which specifies:

"When the lawyer has not regularly represented the client, the basis or rate of the fee shall be communicated to the client, preferably in writing, before or within a reasonable time after commencing the representation."

would or could advertise fixed prices for services of that type. The only services that lend themselves to advertising are the routine ones: the uncontested divorce, the simple adoption, the uncontested personal bankruptcy, the change of name, and the like—the very services advertised by appellants.[26] Although the precise service demanded in each task may vary slightly, and although legal services are not fungible, these facts do not make advertising misleading so long as the attorney does the necessary work at the advertised price.[27] The argument that legal services are so unique that fixed rates cannot meaningfully be established is refuted by the record in this case: the appellee State Bar itself sponsors a Legal Services Program in which the participating attorneys agree to perform services like those advertised by the appellants at standardized rates. Indeed, until the decision of this Court in Goldfarb v. Virginia State Bar [supra p. 426], the Maricopa County Bar Association apparently had a schedule of suggested minimum fees for standard legal tasks. We thus find of little force the assertion that advertising is misleading because of an inherent lack of standardization in legal services.[28]

The second component of the argument—that advertising ignores the diagnostic role—fares little better. It is unlikely that many people go to an attorney merely to ascertain if they have a clean bill of legal health. Rather, attorneys are likely to be employed to perform specific tasks. Although the client may not know the detail involved in performing the task, he no doubt is able to identify the service he desires at the level of generality to which advertising lends itself.

The third component is not without merit: advertising does not provide a complete foundation on which to select an attorney. But it seems peculiar to deny the consumer, on the ground that the information is incomplete, at least some of the relevant information needed to reach an informed decision. The alternative—the prohibition of

**26.** Moreover, we see nothing that is misleading in the advertisement of the cost of an initial half-hour consultation. * * *

**27.** One commentator has observed that "a moment's reflection reveals that the same argument can be made for barbers; rarely are two haircuts identical, but that does not mean that barbers cannot quote a standard price. Lawyers perform countless relatively standardized services which vary somewhat in complexity but not so much as to make each job utterly unique." Morgan, [The Evolving Concept of Professional Responsibility, 90 Harv.L.Rev. 702 (1977)] at 714.

**28.** The Chief Justice and Mr. Justice Powell argue in dissent that advertising will be misleading because the exact services that are included in an advertised package may not be clearly specified or understood by the prospective client. The bar, however, retains the power to define the services that must be included in an advertised package, such as an uncontested divorce, thereby standardizing the "product." We recognize that an occasional client might fail to appreciate the complexity of his legal problem and will visit an attorney in the mistaken belief that his difficulty can be handled at the advertised price. The misunderstanding, however, usually will be exposed at the initial consultation, and an ethical attorney would impose, at the most, a minimal consultation charge or no charge at all for the discussion. If the client decides to have work performed, a fee could be negotiated in the normal manner. The client is thus in largely the same position as he would be if there were no advertising. In light of the benefits of advertising to those whose problem can be resolved at the advertised price, suppression is not warranted on account of the occasional client who misperceives his legal difficulties.

advertising—serves only to restrict the information that flows to consumers.[30] Moreover, the argument assumes that the public is not sophisticated enough to realize the limitations of advertising, and that the public is better kept in ignorance than trusted with correct but incomplete information. We suspect the argument rests on an underestimation of the public. In any event, we view as dubious any justification that is based on the benefits of public ignorance. Although, of course, the bar retains the power to correct omissions that have the effect of presenting an inaccurate picture, the preferred remedy is more disclosure, rather than less. If the naiveté of the public will cause advertising by attorneys to be misleading, then it is the bar's role to assure that the populace is sufficiently informed as to enable it to place advertising in its proper perspective.

3. *The Adverse Effect on the Administration of Justice.* Advertising is said to have the undesirable effect of stirring up litigation.[31] The judicial machinery is designed to serve those who feel sufficiently aggrieved to bring forward their claims. Advertising, it is argued, serves to encourage the assertion of legal rights in the courts, thereby undesirably unsettling societal repose. There is even a suggestion of barratry.[d]

But advertising by attorneys is not an unmitigated source of harm to the administration of justice. It may offer great benefits. Although advertising might increase the use of the judicial machinery, we cannot accept the notion that it is always better for a person to suffer a wrong silently than to redress it by legal action.[32] As the bar acknowledges, "the middle 70% of our population is not being reached or served adequately by the legal profession." American Bar Asso-

**30.** It might be argued that advertising is undesirable because it allows the potential client to substitute advertising for reputational information in selecting an appropriate attorney. Since in a referral system relying on reputation an attorney's future business is partially dependent on current performance, such a system has the benefit both of providing a mechanism for disciplining misconduct and of creating an incentive for an attorney to do a better job for his present clients. Although the system may have worked when the typical lawyer practiced in a small, homogeneous community in which ascertaining reputational information was easy for a consumer, commentators have seriously questioned its current efficacy. The trends of urbanization and specialization long since have moved the typical practice of law from its smalltown setting. Information as to the qualifications of lawyers is not available to many. And, if available, it may be inaccurate or biased.

**31.** It is argued that advertising also will encourage fraudulent claims. We do not believe, however, that there is an inevitable relationship between advertising and dishonesty. Unethical lawyers and dishonest laymen are likely to meet even though restrictions on advertising exist. The appropriate response to fraud is a sanction addressed to that problem alone, not a sanction that unduly burdens a legitimate activity.

**d.** The offense of exciting and stirring up litigation.

**32.** Decided cases reinforce this view. The Court often has recognized that collective activity undertaken to obtain meaningful access to the courts is protected under the First Amendment. [Citing group legal services cases supra pp. 527–34.] It would be difficult to understand these cases if a lawsuit were somehow viewed as an evil in itself. Underlying them was the Court's concern that the aggrieved receive information regarding their legal rights and the means of effectuating them. This concern applies with at least as much force to aggrieved individuals as it does to groups.

ciation, Revised Handbook on Prepaid Legal Services: Papers and Documents Assembled by the Special Committee on Prepaid Legal Services 2 (1972). Among the reasons for this underutilization is fear of the cost, and an inability to locate a suitable lawyer. Advertising can help to solve this acknowledged problem: advertising is the traditional mechanism in a free-market economy for a supplier to inform a potential purchaser of the availability and terms of exchange. The disciplinary rule at issue likely has served to burden access to legal services, particularly for the not-quite-poor and the unknowledgable. A rule allowing restrained advertising would be in accord with the bar's obligation to "facilitate the process of intelligent selection of lawyers, and to assist in making legal services fully available." EC 2–1.

4. *The Undesirable Economic Effects of Advertising*. It is claimed that advertising will increase the overhead costs of the profession, and that these costs then will be passed along to consumers in the form of increased fees. Moreover, it is claimed that the additional cost of practice will create a substantial entry barrier, deterring or preventing young attorneys from penetrating the market and entrenching the position of the bar's established members.

These two arguments seem dubious at best. Neither distinguishes lawyers from others, and neither appears relevant to the First Amendment. The ban on advertising serves to increase the difficulty of discovering the lowest-cost seller of acceptable ability. As a result, to this extent attorneys are isolated from competition, and the incentive to price competitively is reduced. Although it is true that the effect of advertising on the price of services has not been demonstrated, there is revealing evidence with regard to products; where consumers have the benefit of price advertising, retail prices often are dramatically lower than they would be without advertising. It is entirely possible that advertising will serve to reduce, not advance, the cost of legal services to the consumer.[35]

The entry barrier argument is equally unpersuasive. In the absence of advertising, an attorney must rely on his contacts with the community to generate a flow of business. In view of the time nec-

35. On the one hand, advertising does increase an attorney's overhead costs, and, in light of the underutilization of legal services by the public, it may increase substantially the demand for services. Both these factors will tend to increase the price of legal services. On the other hand, the tendency of advertising to enhance competition might be expected to produce pressures on attorneys to reduce fees. The net effect of these competing influences is hard to estimate. We deem it significant, however, that consumer organizations have filed briefs as *amici* urging that the restriction on advertising be lifted. And we note as well that, despite the fact that advertising on occasion might increase the price the consumer must pay, competition through advertising is ordinarily the desired norm.

Even if advertising causes fees to drop, it is by no means clear that a loss of income to lawyers will result. The increased volume of business generated by advertising might more than compensate for the reduced profit per case.

[Eds.] See Muris & McChesney, Advertising and the Price and Quality of Legal Services: The Case for Legal Clinics, 1979 Am.B. Found. Research J. 179, finding that advertising permits legal clinics to provide services at lower fees without sacrificing quality.

essary to develop such contacts, the ban in fact serves to perpetuate the market position of established attorneys. Consideration of entry-barrier problems would urge that advertising be allowed so as to aid the new competitor in penetrating the market.

5. *The Adverse Effect of Advertising on the Quality of Service.* It is argued that the attorney may advertise a given "package" of service at a set price, and will be inclined to provide, by indiscriminate use, the standard package regardless of whether it fits the client's needs.

Restraints on advertising, however, are an ineffective way of deterring shoddy work. An attorney who is inclined to cut quality will do so regardless of the rule of advertising. And the advertisement of a standardized fee does not necessarily mean that the services offered are undesirably standardized. Indeed, the assertion that an attorney who advertises a standard fee will cut quality is substantially undermined by the fixed fee schedule of appellee's own prepaid Legal Services Program. Even if advertising leads to the creation of "legal clinics" like that of appellants'—clinics that emphasize standardized procedures for routine problems—it is possible that such clinics will improve service by reducing the likelihood of error.

6. *The Difficulties of Enforcement.* Finally, it is argued that the wholesale restriction is justified by the problems of enforcement if any other course is taken. Because the public lacks sophistication in legal matters, it may be particularly susceptible to misleading or deceptive advertising by lawyers. After-the-fact action by the consumer lured by such advertising may not provide a realistic restraint because of the inability of the layman to assess whether the service he has received meets professional standards. Thus, the vigilance of a regulatory agency will be required. But because of the numerous purveyors of services, the overseeing of advertising will be burdensome.

It is at least somewhat incongruous for the opponents of advertising to extol the virtues and altruism of the legal profession at one point, and, at another, to assert that its members will seize the opportunity to mislead and distort. We suspect that, with advertising, most lawyers will behave as they always have: they will abide by their solemn oaths to uphold the integrity and honor of their profession and of the legal system. For every attorney who overreaches through advertising, there will be thousands of others who will be candid and honest and straightforward. And, of course, it will be in the latters' interest, as in other cases of misconduct at the bar, to assist in weeding out those few who abuse their trust.

In sum, we are not persuaded that any of the proffered justifications rises to the level of an acceptable reason for the suppression of all advertising by attorneys.

C

In the usual case involving a restraint on speech, a showing that the challenged rule served unconstitutionally to suppress speech would end our analysis. In the First Amendment context, the Court has permitted attacks on overly broad statutes without requiring that the person making the attack demonstrate that in fact his specific conduct was protected. Having shown that the disciplinary rule interferes with protected speech, appellants ordinarily could expect to benefit regardless of the nature of their acts.

The First Amendment overbreadth doctrine, however, represents a departure from the traditional rule that a person may not challenge a statute on the ground that it might be applied unconstitutionally in circumstances other than those before the court. The reason for the special rule in First Amendment cases is apparent: an overbroad statute might serve to chill protected speech. First Amendment interests are fragile interests, and a person who contemplates protected activity might be discouraged by the *in terrorem* effect of the statute. Indeed, such a person might choose not to speak because of uncertainty whether his claim of privilege would prevail if challenged. The use of overbreadth analysis reflects the conclusion that the possible harm to society from allowing unprotected speech to go unpunished is outweighed by the possibility that protected speech will be muted.

But the justification for the application of overbreadth analysis applies weakly, if at all, in the ordinary commercial context. As was acknowledged in Virginia Pharmacy Board v. Virginia Consumer Council, there are "commonsense differences" between commercial speech and other varieties. Since advertising is linked to commercial well-being, it seems unlikely that such speech is particularly susceptible to being crushed by overbroad regulation. Moreover, concerns for uncertainty in determining the scope of protection are reduced; the advertiser seeks to disseminate information about a product or service that he provides, and presumably he can determine more readily than others whether his speech is truthful and protected. Since overbreadth has been described by this Court as "strong medicine," which "has been employed * * * sparingly and only as a last resort," Broadrick v. Oklahoma, 413 U.S., at 613, 93 S.Ct., at 2916, we decline to apply it to professional advertising, a context where it is not necessary to further its intended objective.

Is, then, appellants' advertisement outside the scope of basic First Amendment protection? Aside from general claims as to the undesirability of any advertising by attorneys, a matter considered above, appellee argues that appellants' advertisement is misleading, and hence unprotected, in three particulars: (a) the advertisement makes reference to a "legal clinic," an allegedly undefined term; (b) the advertisement claims that appellants offer services at "very reasonable" prices, and, at least with regard to an uncontested divorce, the advertised price is not a bargain; and (c) the advertisement does not inform the consumer that he may obtain a name change without the services of an attorney. On this record, these assertions are unpersuasive. We suspect that the public would readily understand the term "legal clinic"—if, indeed, it focused on the term at all—to refer to an operation like that of appellants' that is geared to provide standardized and multiple services. In fact, in his deposition the President of the State Bar of Arizona observed that there was a committee of the Bar "exploring the ways in which the legal clinic concept can be properly developed." And the clinical concept in the sister profession of medicine surely by now is publicly acknowledged and understood.

As to the cost of an uncontested divorce, appellee stated at oral argument that this runs from $150 to $300 in the area. Appellants advertised a fee of $175 plus a $20 court filing fee, a rate that seems "very reasonable" in light of the customary charge. Appellee's own Legal Services Program sets the rate for an uncontested divorce at $250. Of course, advertising will permit the comparison of rates among competitors, thus exposing if the rates are reasonable.

As to the final argument—the failure to disclose that a name change might be accomplished by the client without the aid of an attorney—we need only note that most legal services may be performed legally by the citizen for himself. See Faretta v. California, 422 U.S. 806, 95 S.Ct. 2525, 45 L.Ed.2d 562 (1975); EC 3–7. The record does not unambiguously reveal some of the relevant facts in determining whether the nondisclosure is misleading, such as how complicated the procedure is and whether the State provides assistance for laymen. The deposition of one appellant, however, reflects that when he ascertained that a name change required only the correction of a record or the like, he frequently would send the client to effect the change himself.[36]

We conclude that it has not been demonstrated that the advertisement at issue could be suppressed.

In holding that advertising by attorneys may not be subjected to blanket suppression, and that the advertisement at issue is protected, we, of course, do not hold that advertising by attorneys may not be regulated in any way. We mention some of the clearly permissible limitations on advertising not foreclosed by our holding.

Advertising that is false, deceptive, or misleading of course is subject to restraint. Since the advertiser knows his product and has a commercial interest in its dissemination, we have little worry that regulation to assure truthfulness will discourage protected speech. And any concern that strict requirements for truthfulness will undesirably inhibit spontaneity seems inapplicable because commercial speech generally is calculated. Indeed, the public and private benefits from commercial speech derive from confidence in its accuracy and reliability. Thus, the leeway for untruthful or misleading expression that has been allowed in other contexts has little force in the commercial arena. In fact, because the public lacks sophistication concerning legal services, misstatements that might be overlooked or deemed unimportant in other advertising may be found quite inappropriate in

36. The same appellant, however, stated: "[I]t's not my job to inform a prospective client that he needn't employ a lawyer to handle his work."

legal advertising. For example, advertising claims as to the quality of services—a matter we do not address today—are not susceptible to measurement or verification; accordingly, such claims may be so likely to be misleading as to warrant restriction. Similar objections might justify restraints on in-person solicitation. We do not foreclose the possibility that some limited supplementation, by way of warning or disclaimer or the like, might be required of even an advertisement of the kind ruled upon today so to assure that the consumer is not misled. In sum, we recognize that many of the problems in defining the boundary between deceptive and nondeceptive advertising remain to be resolved, and we expect that the bar will have a special role to play in assuring that advertising by attorneys flows both freely and cleanly.

As with other varieties of speech, it follows as well that there may be reasonable restrictions on the time, place, and manner of advertising. Advertising concerning transactions that are themselves illegal obviously may be suppressed. See Pittsburgh Press Co. v. Human Relations Comm'n, 413 U.S. 376, 388, 93 S.Ct. 2553, 37 L.Ed.2d 669 (1973). And the special problems of advertising on the electronic broadcast media will warrant special consideration. Cf. Capital Broadcasting Co. v. Mitchell, 333 F.Supp. 582 (DC 1971), aff'd sub nom. Capital Broadcasting Co. v. Acting Attorney General, 405 U.S. 1000 (1972).

The constitutional issue in this case is only whether the State may prevent the publication in a newspaper of appellants' truthful advertisement concerning the availability and terms of routine legal services. We rule simply that the flow of such information may not be restrained, and we therefore hold the present application of the disciplinary rule against appellants to be violative of the First Amendment.

The judgment of the Supreme Court of Arizona is therefore * * * reversed * * *.

Mr. Justice POWELL, with whom Mr. Justice STEWART joins * * * dissenting * * *.

* * * I cannot join the Court's holding that under the First Amendment "truthful" newspaper advertising of a lawyer's prices for "routine legal services" may not be restrained. * * *

I

[T]he Court [proceeds] on the assumption that what it calls "routine" legal services are essentially no different for purposes of First Amendment analysis from prepackaged prescription drugs. In so holding, the Court fails to give appropriate weight to the two fundamental ways in which the advertising of professional services differs from that of tangible products: the vastly increased potential for deception and the enhanced difficulty of effective regulation in the public interest.

A

It has long been thought that price advertising of legal services inevitably will be misleading because such services are individualized with respect to content and quality and because the lay consumer of legal services usually does not know in advance the precise nature and scope of the services he requires. Although the Court finds some force in this reasoning and recognizes that "many services performed by attorneys are indeed unique," its first answer is the optimistic expression of hope that few lawyers "would or could advertise fixed prices for services of that type." But the Court's basic response in view of the acknowledged potential for deceptive advertising of "unique" services is to divide the immense range of the professional product of lawyers into two categories: "unique" and "routine." The only insight afforded by the opinion as to how one draws this line is the finding that services similar to those in appellants' advertisement are routine: "the uncontested divorce, the simple adoption, the uncontested personal bankruptcy, the change of name, and the like." What the phrase "the like" embraces is not indicated. * * *

This definitional problem is well illustrated by appellants' advertised willingness to obtain uncontested divorces for $195 each. A potential client can be grievously misled if he reads the advertised service as embracing all of his possible needs. A host of problems are implicated by divorce. They include alimony; support and maintenance for children; child custody; visitation rights; interests in life insurance, community property, tax refunds and tax liabilities; and the disposition of other property rights. The processing of court papers—apparently the only service appellants provide for $195—is usually the most straightforward and least demanding aspect of the lawyer's responsibility in a divorce case. More important from the viewpoint of the client is the diagnostic and advisory function: the pursuit of relevant inquiries of which the client would otherwise be unaware, and advice with respect to alternative arrangements that might prevent irreparable dissolution of the marriage or otherwise resolve the client's problem.[5] Although those professional functions are not included within appellants' packaged routine divorce, they frequently fall within the concept of "advice" with which the lay person properly is concerned when he or she seeks legal counsel. The average lay person simply has no feeling for which services are included in the packaged divorce, and thus no capacity to judge the nature of the

5. A high percentage of couples seeking counsel as to divorce desire initially that it be uncontested. They often describe themselves as civilized people who have mutually agreed to separate; they want a quiet, out-of-court divorce without alimony. But experienced counsel knows that the initial spirit of amity often fades quickly when the collateral problems are carefully explored. Indeed, scrupulous counsel—except in the rare case—will insist that the parties have separate counsel to assure that the rights of each, and those of children, are protected adequately. [Eds.: See supra pp. 229–44.] In short, until the lawyer has performed his first duties of diagnosis and advice as to rights, it is usually impossible to know whether there can or will be an uncontested divorce.

advertised product.[6] As a result, the type of advertisement before us inescapably will mislead many who respond to it. In the end, it will promote distrust of lawyers and disrespect for our own system of justice.

The advertising of specified services at a fixed price is not the only infirmity of the advertisement at issue.[7] Appellants also assert that these services are offered at "very reasonable fees." That Court finds this to be an accurate statement since the advertised fee fell at the lower end of the range of customary charges. But the fee customarily charged in the locality for similar services has never been considered the sole determinant of the reasonableness of a fee.[8] This is because reasonableness reflects both the quantity and quality of the service. A $195 fee may be reasonable for one divorce and unreasonable for another; and a $195 fee may be reasonable when charged by an experienced divorce lawyer and unreasonable when charged by a recent law school graduate. For reasons which are not readily apparent, the Court today discards the more discriminating approach which the profession long has used to judge the reasonableness of a fee, and substitutes an approach based on market averages. Whether a fee is "very reasonable" is a matter of opinion, and not a matter of verifiable fact as the Court suggests. One unfortunate result of today's decision is that lawyers may feel free to use a wide variety of adjectives—such as "fair," "moderate," "low-cost," or "lowest in town"—to describe the bargain they offer to the public.

B

* * * The Court's almost casual assumption that its authorization of price advertising can be policed effectively by the Bar reflects a striking underappreciation of the nature and magnitude of the disciplinary problem. The very reasons that tend to make price advertising of services inherently deceptive make its policing wholly impractical. * * *

II

* * * The Court observes, and I agree, that there is nothing inherently misleading in the advertisement of the cost of an initial

6. Similar complications surround the uncontested adoption and the simple bankruptcy.

7. Use of the term "clinic" to describe a law firm of any size is unusual, and possibly ambiguous in view of its generally understood meaning in the medical profession. Appellants defend its use as justified by their plan to provide standardized legal services at low prices through the employment of automatic equipment and paralegals. But there is nothing novel or unusual about the use by law firms of automatic equipment, paralegals, and other modern techniques for serving clients at lower cost. Nor are appellants a public service law firm. They are in the private practice, and though their advertising is directed primarily to clients with family incomes of less than $25,000, appellants do not limit their practice to this income level.

8. For example, the American Bar Association's Code of Professional Responsibility specifies the "[f]actors to be considered as guides in determining the reasonableness of a fee. * * *" DR 2–106(B). * * *

[Eds.] See also RPC 1.5(a).

consultation. Indeed, I would not limit the fee information to the initial conference. * * *

III

Although I disagree strongly with the Court's holding as to price advertisements of undefined—and I believe undefinable—routine legal services, there are reservations in its opinion worthy of emphasis since they may serve to narrow its ultimate reach. First, the Court notes that it has not addressed "the peculiar problems associated with advertisements containing claims as to the *quality* of legal services." * * *

Second, as in *Virginia Pharmacy,* the Court again notes that there may be reasonable restrictions on the time, place, and manner of commercial price advertising. In my view, such restrictions should have a significantly broader reach with respect to professional services than as to standardized products. * * * [12]

Finally, the Court's opinion does not "foreclose the possiblity that some limited supplementation, by way of warning or disclaimer or the like, might be required of even an advertisement of the kind ruled upon today so as to assure that the consumer is not misled." * * *

Mr. Chief Justice BURGER, * * * dissenting * * *.

* * * Because legal services can rarely, if ever, be "standardized" and because potential clients rarely know in advance what services they do in fact need, price advertising can never give the public an accurate picture on which to base its selection of an attorney. Indeed, in the context of legal services, such incomplete information could be worse than no information at all. It could become a trap for the unwary. * * *

Mr. Justice REHNQUIST, dissenting.

* * * I cannot agree that the First Amendment is infringed by * * * regulation of * * * essentially commercial activity * * *.

### *Question*

Which of the six concerns discussed in Part B of the Court's opinion (and found not to justify a *total* ban on lawyer advertising) could constitutionally justify *some* kind of lawyer advertising restriction—which of them relate to a "compelling" government interest which would be served by the particular restriction and could not be adequately served without it?

12. The Court speaks specifically only of newspaper advertising, but it is clear that today's decision cannot be confined on a principled basis to price advertisements in newspapers. No distinction can be drawn between newspapers and a rather broad spectrum of other means, for example, magazines, signs in buses and subways, posters, handbills, and mail circulations. But questions remain open as to time, place, and manner restrictions affecting other media, such as radio and television.

### *Comment*

The ABA responded to *Bates* by adopting extensive amendments to the CPR in August 1977. An ABA Task Force had submitted "Proposal A," which took the approach of specifying the permissible contents of lawyer advertising, and "Proposal B," which generally permitted lawyer advertising that is not false, fraudulent, deceptive or misleading. The ABA's Board of Governors recommended that the House of Delegates amend the ABA's CPR as provided in Proposal A but that both proposals "be circulated to the highest courts of all states and to state regulatory agencies for their consideration." After debate, the House of Delegates adopted these recommendations.[1]

The ABA's 1983 Rules of Professional Conduct take an approach more like that of Proposal B:

## MODEL RULES OF PROFESSIONAL CONDUCT

### RULE 7.1 Communications Concerning a Lawyer's Services

A lawyer shall not make a false or misleading communication about the lawyer or the lawyer's services. A communication is false or misleading if it:

(a) contains a material misrepresentation of fact or law, or omits a fact necessary to make the statement considered as a whole not materially misleading;

(b) is likely to create an unjustified expectation about results the lawyer can achieve, or states or implies that the lawyer can achieve results by means that violate the rules of professional conduct or other law; or

(c) compares the lawyer's services with other lawyers' services, unless the comparison can be factually substantiated.

### RULE 7.2 Advertising

(a) Subject to the requirements of Rule 7.1, a lawyer may advertise services through public media, such as a telephone directory, legal directory, newspaper or other periodical, outdoor, radio or television, or through written communication not involving solicitation as defined in Rule 7.3.

(b) A copy or recording of an advertisement or written communication shall be kept for two years after its last dissemination along with a record of when and where it was used.

1. See House of Delegates Adopts Advertising D.R. and Endorses Package of Grand Jury Reforms, 63 A.B.A. J. 1234 (1977); ABA Code of Professional Responsibility Amendments, 46 U.S.L.W. 1 (1977) (setting forth both proposals).

The states seemed to use the ABA proposals as little more than starting points for their own drafting of Disciplinary Rule amendments to respond to *Bates*. See L. Andrews, Birth of a Salesman: Lawyer Advertising and Solicitation 135–46 (1980); M. Proctor, Code of Professional Responsibility by State (1980); Brosnahan & Andrews, Regulation of Lawyer Advertising: In the Public Interest, 46 Brooklyn L.Rev. 423 (1980).

The ABA made minor additional amendments to DR 2–101 and 2–102 in August 1978, February 1979, and February 1980.

(c) A lawyer shall not give anything of value to a person for recommending the lawyer's services, except that a lawyer may pay the reasonable cost of advertising or written communication permitted by this Rule and may pay the usual charges of a not-for-profit lawyer referral service or other legal service organization.

(d) Any communication made pursuant to this Rule shall include the name of at least one lawyer responsible for its content.

**RULE 7.4 Communication of Fields of Practice**

A lawyer may communicate the fact that the lawyer does or does not practice in particular fields of law. A lawyer shall not state or imply that the lawyer is a specialist except as follows:

(a) a lawyer admitted to engage in patent practice before the United States patent and trademark office may use the designation "patent attorney" or a substantially similar designation;

(b) a lawyer engaged in admiralty practice may use the designation "admiralty," "proctor in admiralty" or a substantially similar designation; and

(c) (provisions on designation of specialization of the particular state).

**RULE 7.5 Firm Names and Letterheads**

(a) A lawyer shall not use a firm name, letterhead or other professional designation that violates Rule 7.1. A trade name may be used by a lawyer in private practice if it does not imply a connection with a government agency or with a public or charitable legal services organization and is not otherwise in violation of Rule 7.1.

(b) A law firm with offices in more than one jurisdiction may use the same name in each jurisdiction, but identification of the lawyers in an office of the firm shall indicate the jurisdictional limitations on those not licensed to practice in the jurisdiction where the office is located.

(c) The name of a lawyer holding a public office shall not be used in the name of a law firm, or in communications on its behalf, during any substantial period in which the lawyer is not actively and regularly practicing with the firm.

(d) Lawyers may state or imply that they practice in a partnership or other organization only when that is the fact.[a]

**a.** See generally Andrews, The Model Rules and Advertising, 68 A.B.A. J. 808 (1982).

Compare the following CPR provisions:

**"DR 2-101 Publicity**

"(A) A lawyer shall not, on behalf of himself, his partner, associate or any other lawyer affiliated with him or his firm, use or participate in the use of any form of public communication containing a false, fraudulent, misleading, deceptive, self-laudatory or unfair statement or claim.

"(B) In order to facilitate the process of informed selection of a lawyer by potential consumers of legal services, a lawyer may publish or broadcast, subject to DR 2-103, the following information in print media distributed or over television or radio broadcasted in the geographic area or areas in which the lawyer resides or maintains offices or in which a significant part of the lawyer's clientele resides, provided that the information disclosed by the lawyer in such publication or broadcast complies with DR 2–101(A), and is presented in a dignified manner:

[25 clauses, specifying in detail items of information that may be included].

"(C) Any person desiring to expand the information authorized for disclosure in DR 2–101(B), or to provide for its dissemination through other forums may apply to [the agency having jurisdiction under state law]. [Detail on procedure omitted.]

"(D) If the advertisement is communicated to the public over television or radio, it shall be prerecorded, approved for broadcast by the lawyer, and a recording of the actual transmission shall be retained by the lawyer.

"(E) If a lawyer advertises a fee for a service, the lawyer must render that service for no more than the fee advertized.

"(F) Unless otherwise specified in the advertisement if a lawyer publishes any fee information authorized under DR 2–101(B) in a publication that is published more frequently than one time per month, the lawyer shall be bound by any representation made therein for a period of not less than 30 days after such publication. [Detail regarding publications not published more than once a month.]

"(G) Unless otherwise specified, if a lawyer broadcasts any fee information authorized under DR 2–101(B), the lawyer shall be bound by any representation made therein for a period of not less than 30 days after such broadcast.

"(H) This rule does not prohibit limited and dignified identification of a lawyer as a lawyer as well as by name:

[5 clauses regarding political advertisements, legal notices, organization reports, legal documents, and legal textbooks and publications].

"(I) A lawyer shall not compensate or give any thing of value to representatives of the press, radio, television, or other communication medium in anticipation of or in return for professional publicity in a news item.

**"DR 2–102 Professional Notices, Letterheads and Offices**

"(A) A lawyer or law firm shall not use or participate in the use of professional cards, professional announcement cards, office signs, letterheads, or similar professional notices or devices, except that the following may be used if they are in dignified form:

[4 clauses on what may be included in professional cards, announcement cards, office signs, and letterheads].

"(B) A lawyer in private practice shall not practice under a trade name, a name that is misleading as to the identity of the lawyer or lawyers practicing under such name, or a firm name containing names other than those of one or more of the lawyers in the firm, except that the name of a professional corporation or professional association may contain 'P.C.' or 'P.A.' or similar symbols indicating the nature of the organization, and if otherwise lawful a firm may use as, or continue to include in, its name the name or names of one or more deceased or retired members of the firm or of a predecessor firm in a continuing line of succession. A lawyer who assumes a judicial, legislative, or public executive or administrative post or office shall not permit his name to remain in the name of a law firm or to be used in professional notices of the firm during any significant period in which he is not actively and regularly practicing law as a member of the firm, and during such period other members of the firm shall not use his name in the firm name or in professional notices of the firm.

"(C) A lawyer shall not hold himself out as having a partnership with one or more other lawyers or professional corporations unless they are in fact partners.

"(D) A partnership shall not be formed or continued between or among lawyers licensed in different jurisdictions unless all enumerations of the members and associates of the firm on its letterhead and in other permissible listings make clear the jurisdictional limitations on those members and associates of the firm not licensed to practice in all listed jurisdictions; however, the same firm name may be used in each jurisdiction.

"(E) Nothing contained herein shall prohibit a lawyer from using or permitting the use of, in connection with his name, an earned degree or title derived therefrom indicating his training in the law."

**"DR 2–105 Limitation of Practice**

"(A) A lawyer shall not hold himself out publicly as a specialist, as practicing in certain areas of law or as limiting his practice permitted under DR 2–101(B), except as follows:

### *Comment*

(1) *R.M.J.* In In re R.M.J.,[1] a lawyer was charged with violating Missouri provisions which, like ABA DR 2-101(B), restricted lawyer advertising to specified categories of information and, in line with ABA DR 2-105(A)(2), provided that a lawyer who listed areas of practice had to choose from 26 specified designations.[2]

Whereas Missouri DR 2-101(B) allowed advertising to include only name, address, telephone number, areas of practice, date and place of birth, schools attended, foreign language ability, office hours, fee for an initial consultation, availability of a schedule of fees, credit arrangements, and the fixed fee to be charged for certain specified "routine" legal services,[3] the St. Louis lawyer's ads disclosed that he was licensed in Missouri and Illinois and, using large capital letters, that he was "Admitted to Practice Before THE UNITED STATES SUPREME COURT." Further, his ads listed areas of practice that diverged from the prescribed designations—e.g., "personal injury" and "real estate" instead of "tort law" and "property law"—and that described areas not covered by the prescribed designations—e.g., "contract," "securities-bonds," "zoning & land use," "communication," and "pension & profit sharing plans."

Reversing the Missouri court's reprimand, a unanimous U.S. Supreme Court, per Justice Powell, reasoned:

> "Commercial speech doctrine, in the context of advertising for professional services, may be summarized generally as follows: Truthful advertising related to lawful activities is entitled to the protections of the First Amendment. But when the particular content or method of the advertising suggests that it is inherently

(1) A lawyer admitted to practice before the United States Patent and Trademark Office may use the designation 'Patents,' 'Patent Attorney,' 'Patent Lawyer,' or 'Registered Patent Attorney' or any combination of those terms, on his letterhead and office sign.

(2) A lawyer who publicly discloses fields of law in which the lawyer or the law firm practices or states that his practice is limited to one or more fields of law shall do so by using designations and definitions authorized and approved by [the agency having jurisdiction of the subject under state law].

(3) A lawyer who is certified as a specialist in a particular field of law or law practice by [the authority having jurisdiction under state law over the subject of specialization by lawyers] may hold himself out as such, but only in accordance with the rules prescribed by that authority."

1. 455 U.S. 191, 102 S.Ct. 929, 71 L.Ed.2d 64 (1982).

2. The latter provision also required a disclaimer, "Listing of the above areas of practice does not indicate any certification of expertise therein." The lawyer did not challenge and the Court did not address the disclaimer requirement's validity.

3. The Missouri provision specified ten "routine" services and authorized an Advisory Committee to approve additions to the list. Although the case did not involve application of this provision, the Court's opinion stated in footnote 11, "Presumably * * * the bar may designate the services that may be considered 'routine.' "

The Missouri provision contained no counterpart to ABA DR 2-101(B)(4) allowing advertising to disclose "date and place of admission to the bar of state and federal courts."

misleading or when experience has proven that in fact such advertising is subject to abuse, the states may impose appropriate restrictions. Misleading advertising may be prohibited entirely. But the states may not place an absolute prohibition on certain types of potentially misleading information, e.g., a listing of areas of practice, if the information also may be presented in a way that is not deceptive. Thus, the Court in *Bates* suggested that the remedy in the first instance is not necessarily a prohibition but preferably a requirement of disclaimers or explanation. Although the potential for deception and confusion is particularly strong in the context of advertising professional services, restrictions upon such advertising may be no broader than reasonably necessary to prevent the deception.[a]

" * * * The use of the words 'real estate' instead of 'property' could scarcely mislead the public. Similarly, the listing of areas such as 'contracts' or 'securities,' that are not found on the * * * list in any form, presents no apparent danger of deception. Indeed * * * in certain respects appellant's listing is more informative than that provided * * *. Because the listing published by the appellant has not been shown to be misleading, and because the Advisory Committee suggests no substantial interest promoted by the restriction, we conclude that this portion of [the provision] is an invalid restriction upon speech as applied to appellant's advertisements.

"Nor has the Advisory Committee identified any substantial interest in a rule that prohibits a lawyer from identifying the jurisdictions in which he is licensed to practice. Such information is not misleading on its face. Appellant was licensed to practice in both Illinois and Missouri. This is factual and highly relevant information particularly in light of the geography of the region in which appellant practiced.

"Somewhat more troubling is appellant's listing, in large boldface type, that he was a member of the bar of the Supreme Court of the United States. The emphasis of this relatively uninformative fact is at least bad taste. Indeed, such a statement could be misleading to the general public unfamiliar with the requirements of admission to the bar of this Court. Yet there is no finding to this effect by the Missouri Supreme Court. There is nothing

**a.** The Court added, "Even when a communication is not misleading, the state retains some authority to regulate. But the state must assert a substantial interest and the interference with speech must be in proportion to the interest served. [Footnote: "See Central Hudson Gas v. Public Service Comm'n, 447 U.S. 557, 566 (1980): 'In commercial speech cases, then, a four-part analysis has developed. At the outset, we must determine whether the expression is protected by the First Amendment. For commercial speech to come within that provision, it at least must concern lawful activity and not be misleading. Next, we ask whether the asserted governmental interest is substantial. If both inquiries yield positive answers, we must determine whether the regulation directly advances the governmental interest asserted, and whether it is not more extensive than is necessary to serve that interest.' * * *"]"

in the record to indicate that the inclusion of this information was misleading. Nor does the Rule specifically identify this information as potentially misleading or, for example, place a limitation on type size or require a statement explaining the nature of the Supreme Court bar."[4]

(2) *Media distinctions.* Compare the statement in footnote 12 of Justice Powell's *Bates* dissent, "No distinction can be drawn between newspapers and a rather broad spectrum of other means, for example, magazines, signs in buses and subways, posters, handbills, and mail circulations,"[5] with that of the Tennessee Supreme Court, "Not only is handbill, circular and billboard advertising beneath the dignity of the profession, such advertising poses insurmountable problems in enforcement and is unnecessary to a proper enjoyment of the constitutional right of commercial speech."[6]

(3) *Informative material.* In State ex rel. Oklahoma Bar Association v. Schaffer,[7] the Oklahoma Supreme Court held that the first amendment precluded disciplining a lawyer for an advertisement specifying:

> "adopt: to love and cherish as your very own. Perhaps you already love and cherish your step-child. * * * Even so, he may be losing certain benefits. A legal adoption may give your step-child many of these benefits while telling your step-child you want him as your very own."

4. See Blackmar, The Missouri Supreme Court and Lawyer Advertising: *RMJ* and Its Aftermath, 47 Mo.L.Rev. 621 (1982) (recap and analysis by RMJ's counsel); Boden, Five Years after Bates: Lawyer Advertising in Legal and Ethical Perspective, 65 Marq.L.Rev. 547, 560–62 (*R.M.J.* sounded death knell for "laundry list" type regulation of lawyer advertising); Howard, Going About Suppressing Speech: A Comment on In the Matter of R.M.J., 26 St. Louis U.L.J. 328 (1982) (provision allowing only specified speech should be held void on its face despite general rule that overbreadth doctrine does not apply to commercial expression).

See generally Andrews, Lawyer Advertising and the First Amendment, 1981 Am.B. Found. Research J. 967, discussing the application of the *Central Hudson* standard to the various states' lawyer advertising restrictions.

Regarding direct mail communication, also addressed in the *R.M.J.* case, see infra 584 Comment (3).

5. See Lovett & Linder, Limited v. Carter, 523 F.Supp. 903 (D.R.I.1981) (state cannot restrict lawyer advertising in telephone directory to "lawyers" heading as opposed to covers).

Compare Comment, The Wisconsin Experience with Advertising Legal Services, 1979 Wis.L.Rev. 1251, 1264 n.67 ("One Madison law office—in addition to newspaper, radio, and extensive television advertising—has used billboards, 'gimmick' business cards, T-shirts, a banner towed behind an airplane, magnetic signs on cars, cartop signs, a hearse advertising low cost wills and sponsorship of a stock car in local races").

6. In re Petition for Rule of Court Governing Lawyer Advertising, 564 S.W.2d 638, 644 (Tenn.1978). See Bishop v. Committee on Professional Ethics, 521 F.Supp. 1219 (S.D. Iowa 1981), vacated as moot 686 F.2d 1278 (8th Cir. 1982); In re Utah State Bar Petition for Approval of Changes in Disciplinary Rules on Advertising, 647 P.2d 991 (1982) (3–2) ("substantial state interest in maintaining the high standards of dignity and professionalism required for officers of the courts" supports prohibition of lawyer advertising on billboards, circulars, matchbooks, and inscribed pencils and pens).

7. 648 P.2d 355 (Okl.1982).

The court reasoned:

"Under *R.M.J.'s* teaching lawyer advertising may be divided into these categories: (1) inherently misleading or proven to be misleading in practice, (2) potentially misleading or (3) not misleading. The first category may warrant absolute state prohibition. As to the second, the regulatory device, as suggested in *Bates*, is not necessarily a total ban but rather a required disclaimer or explanation. The restriction on potentially misleading advertising may be no broader than reasonably necessary to prevent specific deception. Regulation of the third category must be justified by a showing of substantial state interest.

"The Bar does not contend that the [ad is] misleading. * * * The record fails to reflect that in practice ads of [this type] may be misleading or that somebody has in fact been harmed by them. The substantial interest interposed by the state in justification of its restrictive policy * * * rests on the need for protecting an unsophisticated lay public from potential harm from lawyer advertising. We reject the claim as unfounded.

"This advertisement, it is argued, appeals solely to the emotions of the reader. It does not impart knowledge designed to foster informed and reliable decision making for counsel selection. The trial authority described the adoption ad as a form of puffery, i.e., one that, though not deceptive, diverts attention of potential clients from the attorney's qualifications to extraneous and irrelevant matters. The alternative counseled by the trial authority—limiting the ad to the mere listing of the word 'adoption'—would serve only to restrict the information that flows to consumers. The consumer's 'right-to-know' was the basis for bringing lawyer advertising within the protected zone of free speech. The perils of harm to be dealt by professional advertising must be carefully weighed against the benefits from unimpeded flow of information. Advertising can play a meaningful role in aiding consumers' recognition of a legal problem and in gaining better insight into the economics of the law practice. We find this ad free of any information which could potentially deceive or mislead the public. Nor are we persuaded by the argument that a substantial interest of the state is served by the restriction sought to be imposed on this genre of lawyer advertising."[8]

(4) *Promises.* The *Schaffer* court also found first amendment protection for an ad specifying:

"Need a lawyer? 5 days—or free. Within 5 working days after you provide us with the information we need, we will file the necessary court documents, or if filing is not appropriate, begin pro-

8. But see Bishop v. Committee on Professional Ethics, 521 F.Supp. 1219 (S.D. Iowa 1981), vacated as moot 686 F.2d 1278 (8th Cir. 1982).

viding legal services—or our services are free. Good for 30 days. DIVORCE NAME CHANGE WILLS INCORPORATION ADOPTION"

As to this ad, the Oklahoma Supreme Court reasoned:

"The trial authority viewed the self-imposed 5-day limit for promptness * * * as a product guarantee and hence likened it to a lawyer's assurance of service quality. *Bates* left unresolved the continued efficacy of state use of power to curb published lawyer claims of guaranteed quality performance. * * *

"[N]o argument is advanced by the Bar * * * that the ad * * * is either misleading or potentially deceptive. It is only because the advertising genre was found to be closely akin to the potentially impermissible claims of quality that the trial authority thought it fit for regulation. The analogy sought to be drawn is inapposite. A lawyer's * * * guarantee might be deemed potentially or presumably deceptive if it is in the nature of a promise whose fulfillment is clearly beyond the sole control of the promisor. This is not the case here. Respondent's representations cannot be considered excessive because his pledge of prompt-service-delivery-or-free-performance is quite well within his own human means to accomplish.

"Even if we assume that respondent's promise to provide free legal services whenever his performance is not rendered expeditiously bears an analogy to a guaranteed performance of quality work, we nonetheless fail to find a substantial state interest being promoted by the restriction sought to be imposed. The state surely has no demonstrable interest in suppressing delivery of free legal service or in discouraging expeditious lawyer performance. To the contrary, the ad content sought to be condemned appears compatible with public interest. The trial authority's concerns fail to demonstrate a constitutionally permissible basis for restraining free speech." [9]

(5) *Burden of proving ad is false or misleading.* The Wisconsin Supreme Court has held that the disciplinary authority has the burden of proving that a lawyer's ad is false, misleading or deceptive.[10] Rejecting arguments that the traditional burden should be shifted in advertising cases because of the difficulty of enforcing the rule if the

9. Compare In re Hodges, 279 S.C. 128, 303 S.E.2d 89 (ad for "Our GET OUT OF DEBT Service" offering to "stop creditor's harassing calls," "stop foreclosure of home or property," and "stop interest/finance charges from building up" held misleading), cert. denied — U.S. —, 104 S.Ct. 393, 78 L.Ed.2d 336 (1983). See also Mezrano v. Alabama State Bar, 434 So.2d 732 (Ala.1983) (disciplinary rule may require statement that no representation is made regarding quality or expertise and may require advance submission of copy); Kentucky Bar Association v. Gangwish, 630 S.W.2d 66 (Ky.1982) (ad in Chamber of Commerce brochure offering chamber members 20% discount on legal services "misleading in every respect").

10. In re Marcus, 107 Wis.2d 560, 320 N.W.2d 806 (1982) (ads specified "the first thing you'll notice is the high level of legal expertise" and "an average saving of one-half or more").

state has the burden or because requiring lawyers to ascertain the truth of their ads is appropriate in light of their status as officers of the court, the court said:

> "The rule at issue [prohibiting use of a false, misleading, or deceptive ad] does not explicitly allocate the burden of proof. * * *
>
> "Given a choice of reasonable interpretations of a rule, this court should select a construction which renders the rule constitutional. * * *
>
> "The *Bates* decision did not explicitly allocate the burden of proof in disciplinary proceedings arising out of advertisements by attorneys. However, [it] implies that sufficient evidence must be introduced to support a finding that the advertisement is improper in order to justify discipline. * * *
>
> "As in *Bates*, the [*R.M.J.*] Court did not explicitly state which party bore the burden of proving that the advertisements warranted discipline. However, [it] did state that 'the listing published by the appellant *has not been shown to be misleading.*' "[11]

(6) *Areas of practice. R.M.J.* undercuts a federal district court's ruling that a state may bar lawyer advertising referring to specific areas of the law except (a) to specify type(s) of work the lawyer or firm does *not* wish to undertake and (b) to advertise fees for certain routine services.[12]

It probably also undercuts the ruling in In re Mountain Bell Directory Advertising,[13] where the Montana Supreme Court refused to approve telephone company plans to allow lawyers in large cities to purchase listings under 33 categories of practice set forth as subheadings under the heading "lawyers."

### *Questions*

(1) Is RPC 7.4 valid in specifying that a lawyer other than a patent, trademark, admiralty, or state-certified specialist lawyer "shall not state or imply that the lawyer is a specialist"?[14] Is RPC 7.4's *Comment* valid? It specifies:

> "[S]tating that the lawyer is a 'specialist' or that the lawyer's practice 'is limited to' or 'concentrated in' particular fields is not permitted. These terms have acquired a secondary meaning implying formal recognition as a specialist. Hence, use of these terms may be misleading unless the lawyer is certified or recognized in accordance with procedures in the state where the lawyer is licensed to practice."

---

11. Compare Heslin v. Connecticut Law Clinic of Trantolo & Trantolo, 190 Conn. 510, 461 A.2d 938 (1983) (lawyer advertising is subject to state unfair trade practices statute).

12. Lovett & Linder, Limited v. Carter, 523 F.Supp. 903 (D.R.I.1981).

13. 185 Mont. 68, 604 P.2d 760 (1979).

14. See DR 2–105. See generally Boden, Five Years After *Bates*: Lawyer Advertising in Legal and Ethical Perspective, 65 Marq.L.Rev. 547, 564–68 (1982).

See In re Johnson,[15] wherein the Minnesota Supreme Court set aside a lawyer's admonition for listing himself as a "Civil Trial Specialist Certified by the National Board of Trial Advocacy." The court struck down as unconstitutional DR 2–105's prohibition on holding oneself out as a specialist unless state rules permitting this are adopted. The court reasoned:

> "Applying *R.M.J.* * * * to the facts of this case, it appears that [DR 2–105's prohibition] is too restrictive. The rule is designed to prevent misleading an uninformed public by claims of specialization and quality of services. That in and of itself is a meritorious goal. But the method used to achieve that goal is to impose a blanket prohibition on all commercial speech regarding specialization until the Minnesota Supreme Court promulgates rules describing what specialty designations will be accepted and how to get that designation. In view of the overbreadth of the rule, the lack of presentation to this court of proposed rules, and the finding [below] that this advertisement was not misleading or deceptive, there is no basis for upholding the rule in this case."[16]

(2) Is DR 2–102(B) valid in prohibiting a private practitioner from practicing under a trade name?[17]

In Friedman v. Rogers,[18] a 7–2 U.S. Supreme Court held that Texas could prohibit use of trade names by *optometrists*, who may practice only under the name of an optometrist present in the office at least half the hours the office is open or the named optometrist practices, where Texas enacted the prohibition in response to numerous instances of deceptive use of optometric trade names.

After pointing out that a trade name is "a significantly different form of commercial speech from that considered in *Virginia Pharmacy* and *Bates*" because "it has no intrinsic meaning" and "conveys no information about the price and nature of the services * * * until it acquires meaning over a period of time," the *Friedman* Court listed the "numerous" and "significant" possibilities for deception of the public through optometric trade names:

> "The trade name * * * can remain unchanged despite changes in the staff of optometrists * * *. Thus, the public may be

15. 341 N.W.2d 282 (Minn.1983).

16. The court noted that discipline could be imposed under the Code's prohibition of false or misleading statements "if the particular certification advertised was perfunctorily granted by an organization with few or no standards and there was a finding that the advertising was false, fraudulent, misleading or deceptive." But the court observed that the National Board of Trial Advocacy, on the contrary, "applies a rigorous and exacting set of standards and examinations on a national scale before certifying a lawyer as a trial specialist, either criminal or civil or both," and as of spring, 1983, after four years of existence, had certified only 541 lawyers as trial specialists.

Regarding specialty certification, see supra pp. 47–49.

17. Compare RPC 7.5(a): "A trade name may be used by a lawyer in private practice if it does not imply a connection with a government agency or with a public or charitable legal services organization and is not otherwise in violation of Rule 7.1."

18. 440 U.S. 1, 99 S.Ct. 887, 59 L.Ed.2d 100 (1979).

attracted by a trade name that reflects the reputation of an optometrist no longer associated with the practice. A trade name frees an optometrist from dependence on his personal reputation to attract clients, and even allows him to assume a new trade name if negligence or misconduct casts a shadow over the old one. By using different trade names at shops under his common ownership, an optometrist can give the public the false impression of competition among the shops. The use of a trade name also facilitates the advertising essential to large-scale commercial practices with numerous branch offices, conduct the State rationally may wish to discourage while not prohibiting commercial optometrical practice altogether."

Then the Court emphasized that these concerns "were not speculative or hypothetical, but were based on experience in Texas with which the legislature was familiar" and, after discussing the particular instances of deceptive use of optometrical trade names that prompted the Texas prohibition, concluded that in light of the "substantial and well-demonstrated" nature of the state's interest and the "most incidental" nature of the restriction's effect on commercial speech, the trade name ban was constitutional as doing "no more than require that commercial information * * * 'appear in such a form * * * as [is] necessary to prevent its being deceptive.' "[19]

The importance of the fact that the optometrist regulation in *Friedman* responded to problems proven by experience was highlighted in *R.M.J.*, where the Court said that regulation is permissible "where the particular advertising is inherently likely to deceive or where the record indicates that a particular form or method of advertising has in fact been deceptive" and that "in *Friedman*, we held that Texas could prohibit the use of trade names by optometrists particularly in view of the considerable history in Texas of deception and abuse worked upon the consuming public through the use of trade names."

Does a lawyer's practice under a trade name contrary to DR 2–102(B) pose dangers which are "not speculative or hypothetical, but * * * based on experience"?

Is DR 2–101(B)'s trade name prohibition justified by the concerns specified in *Friedman*, given that DR 2–102(B) permits a firm to "use as, or continue to include in, its name the name or names of one or more deceased or retired members of the firm or a predecessor firm in a continuing line of succession"? Given that law firms are not restricted in operating branch offices (as Texas optometrists were by the requirement that the named professional be present in the office at least half the hours the office is open or the professional practices)?

Does DR 2–102(B)'s trade name ban discriminate against legal clinics, since ordinary firms in effect are allowed to use trade names by

19. See In re Oldtowne Legal Clinic, P.A., 285 Md. 132, 400 A.2d 1111 (1979) (legal clinic may not use trade name).

being permitted to use deceased or retired members' names, whereas legal clinics' higher turnover of lawyers frequently precludes this option? [20]

## D. SOLICITATION

### RULES OF PROFESSIONAL CONDUCT

**RULE 7.3 Direct Contact with Prospective Clients**

A lawyer may not solicit professional employment from a prospective client with whom the lawyer has no family or prior professional relationship, by mail, in-person or otherwise, when a significant motive for the lawyer's doing so is the lawyer's pecuniary gain. The term "solicit" includes contact in person, by telephone or telegraph, by letter or other writing, or by other communication directed to a specific recipient, but does not include letters addressed or advertising circulars distributed generally to persons not known to need legal services of the kind provided by the lawyer in a particular matter, but who are so situated that they might in general find such services useful.[a]

**20.** See Comment to RPC 7.5, which states:

"Although the United States Supreme Court has held that legislation may prohibit the use of trade names in professional practice, use of such names in law practice is acceptable so long as it is not misleading. * * * It may be observed that any firm name including the name of a deceased partner is, strictly speaking, a trade name."

Compare Mezrano v. Alabama State Bar, 434 So.2d 732 (Ala.1983) (private lawyer practicing on University Boulevard near a state university using name "University Legal Center" may be disciplined for using misleading name); Florida Bar v. Fetterman, 439 So.2d 835 (Fla.1983) ("The Law Team, Fetterman and Associates" not misleading; not distinguishable from "Legal Clinic of Bates and O'Steen"; however, were lawyer to practice solely under name "The Law Team" without lawyer's name also appearing, it would be inherently misleading because public would not be made aware of who is to be held accountable for firm's actions; court's action should not be taken as invitation to lawyers to experiment with other terminology to attract public's attention—"This appears to be the outer limit allowable").

The *Fetterman* case last cited also held that the firm name could keep specifying "and Associates" when it was down to one associate. Regarding the proper use of the terms "partners," "associates," and "of counsel," see supra pp. 49–52.

Until its February 1980 deletion, DR 2–102(E) provided, "A lawyer who is engaged both in the practice of law and another profession or business shall not so indicate on his letterhead, office sign, or professional card, nor shall he identify himself as a lawyer in any publication in connection with his other profession or business." In a jurisdiction where DR 2–102(E) remains in effect, the first amendment should bar its enforcement on the ground that a lawyer's letterhead, office sign, or professional card's referring to another profession or business is not inherently likely to deceive and has not been shown to have been deceptive in fact, the prohibiting it is not necessary to serve any compelling government interest. See Blackmar, The Missouri Supreme Court and Lawyer Advertising: *RMJ* and its Aftermath, 47 Mo.L.Rev. 621, 653 (1982). But see In re Advisory Committee Opinion No. 447, 86 N.J. 473, 432 A.2d 59 (1981) (provision validly barred lawyer from including CPA designation on letterhead).

**a.** See also RPC 7.1 and 7.2.

Compare the following CPR provisions:

**"DR 2–103 Recommendation of Professional Employment**

"(A) A lawyer shall not, except as authorized in DR 2–101(B), recommend employment as a private practitioner, of himself, his partner, or associate to a layperson who has not sought his advice regarding employment of a lawyer.

"(B) A lawyer shall not compensate or give anything of value to a person or organization to recommend or secure his employment by a client, or as a reward for having made a recommen-

### *Questions*

(1) How would you respond if you were the recipient of "A Letter to a Member of a Grievance Committee" [1] as follows:

> "[W]hat is the matter with solicitation? Every lawyer solicits cases * * *. The difference between lawyers is that some of them are not hypocrites and come out and say frankly that they want the business, and the rest do it indirectly. They solicit by joining everything in sight and getting friendly with a lot of people they don't give a damn about in the hope that they will some day conceivably have some legal work, and then inviting them to dinner when they do. I don't want to get personal, but I don't think it

dation resulting in his employment by a client, except that he may pay the usual and reasonable fees or dues charged by any of the organizations listed in DR 2–103(D).

"(C) A lawyer shall not request a person or organization to recommend or promote the use of his services or those of his partner or associate, or any other lawyer affiliated with him or his firm, as a private practitioner, except as authorized in DR 2–101, and except that

(1) He may request referrals from a lawyer referral service operated, sponsored, or approved by a bar association and may pay its fees incident thereto.

(2) He may cooperate with the legal service activities of any of the offices or organizations enumerated in DR 2–103(D)(1) through (4) and may perform legal services for those to whom he was recommended by it to do such work if:

(a) The person to whom the recommendation is made is a member or beneficiary of such office or organization; and

(b) The lawyer remains free to exercise his independent professional judgment on behalf of his client.

* * *

"(E) A lawyer shall not accept employment when he knows or it is obvious that the person who seeks his services does so as a result of conduct prohibited under this Disciplinary Rule.

**"DR 2–104 Suggestion of Need of Legal Services**

"(A) A lawyer who has given in-person unsolicited advice to a layperson that he should obtain counsel or take legal action shall not accept employment resulting from that advice, except that:

(1) A lawyer may accept employment by a close friend, relative, former client (if the advice is germane to the former employment), or one whom the lawyer reasonably believes to be a client.

(2) A lawyer may accept employment that results from his participation in activities designed to educate laypersons to recognize legal problems, to make intelligent selection of counsel, or to utilize available legal services if such activities are conducted or sponsored by a qualified legal assistance organization.

(3) A lawyer who is recommended, furnished or paid by a qualified legal assistance organization enumerated in DR 2–103(D)(1) through (4) may represent a member or beneficiary thereof, to the extent and under the conditions prescribed therein.

(4) Without affecting his right to accept employment, a lawyer may speak publicly or write for publication on legal topics so long as he does not emphasize his own professional experience or reputation and does not undertake to give individual advice.

(5) If success in asserting rights or defenses of his client in litigation in the nature of a class action is dependent upon the joinder of others, a lawyer may accept, but shall not seek, employment from those contacted for the purpose of obtaining their joinder."

1. American Association of Law Schools, Selected Readings in the Legal Profession 130, 131–33 (1962). The "letter" is hypothetical and its author by request has remained anonymous.

was a sudden and powerful attack of religion that made you give up your Sunday golf and take to ushering in the First Presbyterian Church * * *.

"But the horrible thing about me is supposed to be that I solicit personal injury cases. In other words, instead of playing golf with a lot of business men who never move without a lawyer at their elbows, I go out and offer legal assistance to people who are poor and sick and injured, and who are too helpless or haven't the money or the friends or the education or the intelligence to look after their own interests or even to know that they need a lawyer and what he can do for them. * * *

"They tell me that I am supposed to wait around until he gets well and somebody tells him I am a good personal injury lawyer, and sends him to see me. And what is supposed to be happening to his case in the meantime? You don't win cases without witnesses; and who is going to get the witnesses for him while he is flat on his back with a broken coccyx or one leg off at the knee? You know as well as I do what even twenty-four hours does to the witnesses of an automobile collision and to their memories even if you ever succeed in locating them. Well, what about three weeks or a month? And what is the defendant doing in the meantime? Whenever the street car company has an accident, it gets statements down on paper the same day from everyone within a hundred yards, and follows up the case for a week. Who gets those witnesses for the man lying there with the fractured skull? And what chance has he got a month later of even finding out their names?

"And what about the defendant's claim agent, who arrives as soon as the man is conscious, and talks him into settling the case for ten percent of what it is worth, without the 'expense of a lawyer'? * * * All that I have to say is that if it is legal or ethical for one lawyer to send an agent in to see a helpless man who is crippled for life and take his claim away from him for the smallest amount he can get by with, it is just as legal and ethical for another lawyer to go to him and say 'Don't sign that; you are entitled to more, and I can get it for you.'

"But my solicitation is supposed to be 'organized,' and so I ought to be disbarred. Of course it's organized. It has to be. I need as much of an organization as a liability insurance company, and for a better reason. I have to get to my clients before the claim agents settle with them for as little as they will take; and I have to find their witnesses before the defendants work on them too long. And if I take cases away from other lawyers, at least I offer the client better service than they can, because of that organization." [2]

2. Compare Comment, Ambulance Chasing in Illinois: A Success Story, 1957 U.Ill.L.F. 309, 312:

"The argument of unenforceability assumes that either all solicitation or else no solicitation is reprehensible. If a moderate view is taken, then only that kind of solicitation which carries with it the probability of evil consequences in a specific instance need be condemned. The argument that solicitation protects the victim from claims adjusters admits that at best, such

(2) Under RPC 7.3 or DR 2–103, could you as a lawyer be disciplined for approaching your nonlawyer city council representative and explaining why you would be the best person for the council to appoint as city attorney? Could you be disciplined for seeking employment from a corporation as house counsel? For seeking a position with a law firm?

(3) To be guilty of solicitation through another person, must a lawyer request, compensate, or assist that person to solicit, or is it sufficient that the lawyer acquiesces with knowledge of the person's solicitation? Compare the following from the majority and dissenting opinions in the Pennsylvania Supreme Court case of In re Berlant[3]:

MAJORITY:

"While the court below inferred 'that the solicitors did receive something of value for their time, efforts and expense on [appellant's] behalf,' this inference was unnecessary to sustain a finding of guilt. The Code of Professional Responsibility condemns such conduct without any requirement of compensation. DR 1–102 provides:

'(A) A lawyer shall not: * * *

'(2) Circumvent a Disciplinary Rule through actions of another.'[a]

This section, read in light of the proscription against self-recommendation in DR 2–103, not only condemns the hiring of solicitors by attorneys but also forbids any arrangement between an attorney and solicitor for solicitation purposes or even the acquiescence of the attorney who has knowledge of a solicitor's activities in his behalf. We do not mean to suggest that the casual recommendation of an attorney by a friend or acquaintance is improper. Rather we seek to eliminate the active recruitment of clients and stirring up of litigation by or on behalf of attorneys. * * *

"[T]he facts clearly support the inference that either a solicitation arrangement existed or, at the very least, that appellant knew of the solicitation when he accepted the cases * * *. While proof that the runners were paid for their activity is unnecessary, we would concur in the disciplinary court's inference thereof even if such proof were required."

DISSENT:

"Although NAACP v. Button [and later U. S. Supreme Court cases pp. 527–34] have addressed themselves to the issue of col-

practice is merely a necessary expedient, and does not deny that the conduct itself is unethical. The evil conduct of another forms no ethical justification for one's own wrongful action. It is admitted, however, that the personal injury victim needs protection from unfair conduct of claims adjusters, which might appropriately come in the form of legislative action."

3. 458 Pa. 439, 328 A.2d 471 (1974), cert. denied 421 U.S. 964, 95 S.Ct. 1953, 44 L.Ed.2d 451 (1975).

a. Compare RPC 8.4(a) (professional misconduct for lawyer to "violate or attempt to violate the rules of professional conduct, knowingly assist or induce another to do so, or do so through the acts of another").

lective activity designed to apprise potential clients of their legal right, there is no reason to believe that the scope of the First Amendment protections depends on whether the individual being solicited is in the company of his friends and associates.

"The record in this case does not indicate that appellant ever paid money in exchange for recommendations by those who allegedly acted as 'runners' for him. Such activity would involve a fraud on the consumer who accepted that kind of a 'solicitation.' The state undoubtedly has a substantial interest in protecting the public from fraud and other abuses likely to result if lawyers are given unrestrained freedom to solicit. However, the state's infringement on First Amendment association rights must be narrowly drawn. Any restriction of First Amendment rights must be limited to the minimum extent needed to prevent the abuses at which the regulation is directed." [4]

## OHRALIK v. OHIO STATE BAR ASSOCIATION

436 U.S. 447, 98 S.Ct. 1912, 56 L.Ed.2d 444 (1978).

Mr. Justice POWELL delivered the opinion of the Court.

In *Bates*, this Court held that truthful advertising of "routine" legal services is protected by the First and Fourteenth Amendments against blanket prohibition by a State. The Court expressly reserved the question of the permissible scope of regulation of "in-person solicitation of clients—at the hospital room or the accident site, or in any other situation that breeds undue influence—by attorneys or their agents or 'runners.'" Today we answer part of the question so reserved, and hold that the Bar—acting with state authorization—constitutionally may discipline a lawyer for soliciting clients in person, for pecuniary gain, under circumstances likely to pose dangers that the State has a right to prevent.

### I

Appellant, a member of the Ohio Bar, lives in Montville, Ohio. Until recently he practiced law in Montville and Cleveland. On February 13, 1974, while picking up his mail at the Montville Post Office, appellant learned from the postmaster's brother about an automobile accident that had taken place on February 2 in which Carol McClintock,

4. See also Halverson v. Convenient Food Mart, Inc., 458 F.2d 927, 931 n.6, 16 A.L.R.Fed. 875, 881 n.6 (7th Cir. 1972), where the court, citing DR 2–104(A)(5) and referring to association members asking others to join in a class action and be represented by their lawyer, said:

"An interpretation of the professional ethics code which would restrict communication among association members such as plaintiffs would run afoul of the First Amendment. Brotherhood of Railroad Trainmen v. Virginia ex rel. Virginia State Bar [supra p. 527]."

Compare ABA Standards for Criminal Justice 4–2.3 (2d ed. 1980):

"It is unprofessional conduct for a lawyer to accept referrals by agreement *or as a regular practice* from law inforcement personnel, bondsmen or court personnel."

(Emphasis added.)

a young woman with whom appellant was casually acquainted, had been injured. Appellant made a telephone call to Ms. McClintock's parents, who informed him that their daughter was in the hospital. Appellant suggested that he might visit Carol in the hospital. Mrs. McClintock assented to the idea, but requested that appellant first stop by at her home.

During appellant's visit with the McClintocks, they explained that their daughter had been driving the family automobile on a local road when she was hit by an uninsured motorist. Both Carol and her passenger, Wanda Lou Holbert, were injured and hospitalized. In response to the McClintocks' expression of apprehension that they might be sued by Holbert, appellant explained that Ohio's guest statute would preclude such a suit. When appellant suggested to the McClintocks that they hire a lawyer, Mrs. McClintock retorted that such a decision would be up to Carol, who was 18 years old and would be the beneficiary of a successful claim.

Appellant proceeded to the hospital, where he found Carol lying in traction in her room. After a brief conversation about her condition, appellant told Carol he would represent her and asked her to sign an agreement. Carol said she would have to discuss the matter with her parents. She did not sign the agreement, but asked appellant to have her parents come to see her. Appellant also attempted to see Wanda Lou Holbert, but learned that she had just been released from the hospital. He then departed for another visit with the McClintocks.

On his way appellant detoured to the scene of the accident, where he took a set of photographs. He also picked up a tape recorder, which he concealed under his raincoat before arriving at the McClintocks' residence. Once there, he re-examined their automobile insurance policy, discussed with them the law applicable to passengers, and explained the consequences of the fact that the driver who struck Carol's car was an uninsured motorist. Appellant discovered that the McClintocks' insurance policy would provide benefits of up to $12,500 each for Carol and Wanda Lou under an uninsured motorist clause. Mrs. McClintock acknowledged that both Carol and Wanda Lou could sue for their injuries, but recounted to appellant that "Wanda swore up and down she would not do it." The McClintocks also told appellant that Carol had phoned to say that appellant could "go ahead" with her representation. Two days later appellant returned to Carol's hospital room to have her sign a contract, which provided that he would receive one-third of her recovery.

In the meantime, appellant obtained Wanda Lou's name and address from the McClintocks after telling them he wanted to ask her some questions about the accident. He then visited Wanda Lou at her home, without having been invited. He again concealed his tape recorder and recorded most of the conversation with Wanda Lou.[a] After a

a. See ABA Formal Opinion 337 (1974), 60 A.B.A. J. 1448, holding that, with the possible exception of certain law enforcement situations, recording a conversation without the

brief, unproductive inquiry about the facts of the accident, appellant told Wanda Lou that he was representing Carol and that he had a "little tip" for Wanda Lou: the McClintocks' insurance policy contained an uninsured motorist clause which might provide her with a recovery of up to $12,500. The young woman, who was 18 years of age and not a high school graduate at the time, replied to appellant's query about whether she was going to file a claim by stating that she really did not understand what was going on. Appellant offered to represent her, also, for a contingent fee of one-third of any recovery, and Wanda Lou stated "O.K."[4]

Wanda's mother attempted to repudiate her daughter's oral assent the following day, when appellant called on the telphone to speak to Wanda. Mrs. Holbert informed appellant that she and her daughter did not want to sue anyone or to have appellant represent them, and that if they decided to sue they would consult their own lawyer. Appellant insisted that Wanda had entered into a binding agreement. A month later Wanda confirmed in writing that she wanted neither to sue nor to be represented by appellant. She requested that appellant notify the insurance company that he was not her lawyer, as the company would not release a check to her until he did so.[5] Carol also eventually discharged appellant. Although another lawyer represented her in concluding a settlement with the insurance company, she paid appellant one-third of her recovery[6] in settlement of his lawsuit against her for breach of contract.[7]

consent or prior knowledge of all parties to the conversation, even though legal, violates DR 1–102(A)(4)'s prohibition (identical to that in RPC 8.4(c)) of "conduct involving dishonesty, fraud, deceit, or misrepresentation."

Compare People v. Selby, 198 Colo. 386, 606 P.2d 45 (1979) (disbarment for secretly recording chambers conference with judge and prosecutor, using partial and out-of-context quotations from tape to falsely attribute bias to judge, and testifying falsely in disciplinary proceeding).

4. Appellant told Wanda that she should indicate assent by stating "Okay," which she did. Appellant later testified: "I would say that most of my clients have essentially that much of a communication. * * * I think most of my clients, that's the way I practice law."

In explaining the contingency fee arrangement, appellant told Wanda Lou that his representation would not "cost [her] anything" because she would receive two-thirds of the recovery if appellant were successful in representing her but would not "have to pay [him] anything" otherwise.

5. The insurance company was willing to pay Wanda Lou for her injuries but would not release the check while appellant claimed, and Wanda Lou denied, that he represented her. Before appellant would "disavow further interest and claim" in Wanda Lou's recovery, he insisted by letter that Wanda Lou first pay him the sum of $2,466.66, which represented one-third of his "conservative" estimate of the worth of her claim.

6. Carol recovered the full $12,500 and paid appellant $4,166.66. She testified that she paid the second lawyer $900 as compensation for his services.

7. Appellant represented to the Board of Commissioners at the disciplinary hearing that he would abandon his claim against Wanda Lou Holbert because "the rules say that if a contract has its origin in a controversy, that an ethical question can arise." Yet in fact appellant filed suit against Wanda for $2,466.66 after the disciplinary hearing. Appellant dismissed that suit with prejudice on January 27, 1977, after the decision of the Supreme Court of Ohio had been filed.

[Eds.: Regarding fees upon discharge, see supra pp. 457–65.]

Both Carol McClintock and Wanda Lou Holbert filed complaints against appellant * * *. After a hearing, the [lawyer discipline] Board found that appellant had violated Disciplinary Rules (DR) 2–103(A) and 2–104(A) of the Ohio Code of Professional Responsibility.[b] * * * The Supreme Court of Ohio adopted the findings of the Board * * * and increased the sanction of a public reprimand recommended by the Board to indefinite suspension. * * *

II

* * * The entitlement of in-person solicitation of clients to the protection of the First Amendment differs from that of the kind of advertising approved in *Bates*, as does the strength of the State's countervailing interest in prohibition.

A

* * * In rejecting the notion that [commercial] speech "is wholly outside the protection of the First Amendment," *Virginia Pharmacy*, we were careful not to hold "that it is wholly undifferentiable from other forms" of speech. We have not discarded the "commonsense" distinction between speech proposing a commercial transaction, which occurs in an area traditionally subject to government regulation, and other varieties of speech. To require a parity of constitutional protection for commercial and noncommercial speech alike could invite dilution, simply by a leveling process of the force of the Amendment's guarantee with respect to the latter kind of speech. Rather than subject the First Amendment to such a devitalization, we instead have afforded commercial speech a limited measure of protection, commensurate with its subordinate position in the scale of First Amendment values, while allowing modes of regulation that might be impermissible in the realm of noncommercial expression.

Moreover, "it has never been deemed an abridgment of freedom of speech or press to make a course of conduct illegal merely because the conduct was in part initiated, evidenced, or carried out by means of language, either spoken, written, or printed." Giboney v. Empire Storage & Ice Co., 336 U.S. 490, 502, 69 S.Ct. 684, 691, 93 L.Ed. 834 (1949). Numerous examples could be cited of communications that are regulated without offending the First Amendment, such as the exchange of information about securities, SEC v. Texas Gulf Sulphur Co., 401 F.2d 833 (CA2 1968), cert. denied, 394 U.S. 976, 89 S.Ct. 1454, 22 L.Ed.2d 756 (1969), corporate proxy statements, Mills v. Electric Auto-Lite Co., 396 U.S. 375, 90 S.Ct. 616, 24 L.Ed.2d 593 (1970), the exchange of price and production information among competitors,

**b.** The Ohio provisions were substantially identical to ABA DR 2–103(A)'s prohibition on recommending employment to a nonlawyer who has not sought advice regarding employment of a lawyer and ABA DR 2–104(A)'s restriction on accepting employment resulting from unsolicited advice to a nonlawyer that the nonlawyer should obtain counsel or take legal action.

American Column & Lumber Co. v. United States, 257 U.S. 377, 42 S.Ct. 114, 66 L.Ed. 284 (1921), and employers' threats of retaliation for the labor activities of employees, NLRB v. Gissel Packing Co., 395 U.S. 575, 618, 89 S.Ct. 1918, 1942, 23 L.Ed.2d 547 (1969). Each of these examples illustrates that the State does not lose its power to regulate commercial activity deemed harmful to the public whenever speech is a component of that activity.

In-person solicitation by a lawyer of remunerative employment is a business transaction in which speech is an essential but subordinate component. While this does not remove the speech from the protection of the First Amendment, as was held in *Bates* and *Virginia Pharmacy*, it lowers the level of appropriate judicial scrutiny.

As applied in this case, the disciplinary rules are said to have limited the communication of two kinds of information. First, appellant's solicitation imparted to Carol McClintock and Wanda Lou Holbert certain information about his availability and the terms of his proposed legal services. In this respect, in-person solicitation serves much the same function as the advertisement at issue in *Bates.* But there are significant differences as well. Unlike a public advertisement, which simply provides information and leaves the recipient free to act upon it or not, in-person solicitation may exert pressure and often demands an immediate response, without providing an opportunity for comparison or reflection. The aim and effect of in-person solicitation may be to provide a one-sided presentation and to encourage speedy and perhaps uninformed decisionmaking; there is no opportunity for intervention or counter-education by agencies of the Bar, supervisory authorities, or persons close to the solicited individual. The admonition that "the fitting remedy for evil counsels is good ones" is of little value when the circumstances provide no opportunity for any remedy at all. In-person solicitation is as likely as not to discourage persons needing counsel from engaging in a critical comparison of the "availability, nature, and prices" of legal services, cf. *Bates*; it actually may disserve the individual and societal interest, identified in *Bates*, in facilitating "informed and reliable decisionmaking."

It also is argued that in-person solicitation may provide the solicited individual with information about his or her legal rights and remedies. In this case, appellant gave Wanda Lou a "tip" about the prospect of recovery based on the uninsured motorist clause in the McClintocks' insurance policy, and he explained that clause and Ohio's guest statute to Carol McClintock's parents. But neither of the disciplinary rules here at issue prohibited appellant from communicating information to these young women about their legal rights and the prospects of obtaining a monetary recovery, or from recommending that they obtain counsel. DR 2–104(A) merely prohibited him from using the information as bait with which to obtain an agreement to represent them for a fee. The rule does not prohibit a lawyer from giving unsolicited legal advice; it proscribes the acceptance of employment resulting from such advice.

Appellant does not contend, and on the facts of this case could not contend, that his approaches to the two young women involved political expression or an exercise of associational freedom, "employ[ing] constitutionally privileged means of expression to secure constitutionally guaranteed civil rights." NAACP v. Button [supra p. 527]. Nor can he compare his solicitation to the mutual assistance in asserting legal rights that was at issue in [cases supra pp. 527–34]. A lawyer's procurement of remunerative employment is a subject only marginally affected with First Amendment concerns. It falls within the State's proper sphere of economic and professional regulation. While entitled to some constitutional protection, appellant's conduct is subject to regulation in furtherance of important state interests.

B

The state interests implicated in this case are particularly strong. In addition to its general interest in protecting consumers and regulating commercial transactions, the State bears a special responsibility for maintaining standards among members of the licensed professions. "The interest of the States in regulating lawyers is especially great since lawyers are essential to the primary governmental function of administering justice, and have historically been 'officers of the courts.'" Goldfarb v. Virginia State Bar [p. 426]. While lawyers act in part as "self-employed businessmen," they also act "as trusted agents of their clients, and as assistants to the court in search of a just solution to disputes." Cohen v. Hurley, 366 U.S. 117, 124, 81 S.Ct. 954, 958, 6 L.Ed.2d 156 (1961).

As is true with respect to advertising, it appears that the ban on solicitation by lawyers originated as a rule of professional etiquette rather than as a strictly ethical rule. * * * But the fact that the original motivation behind the ban on solicitation today might be considered an insufficient justification for its perpetuation does not detract from the force of the other interests the ban continues to serve. While the Court in *Bates* determined that truthful, restrained advertising of the prices of "routine" legal services would not have an adverse effect on the professionalism of lawyers, this was only because it found "the postulated connection between advertising and the erosion of *true professionalism* to be severely strained." The *Bates* Court did not question a State's interest in maintaining high standards among licensed professionals. Indeed, to the extent that the ethical standards of lawyers are linked to the service and protection of clients, they do further the goals of "true professionalism."

The substantive evils of solicitation have been stated over the years in sweeping terms: stirring up litigation, assertion of fraudulent claims, debasing the legal profession, and potential harm to the solicited client in the form of overreaching, overcharging, underrepresentation, and misrepresentation. The American Bar Association, as *amicus curiae*, defends the rule against solicitation primarily on three broad grounds: It is said that the prohibitions embodied in Disciplinary Rules 2–103(A) and 2–104(A) serve to reduce the likelihood of overreaching and the exertion of undue influence on lay persons; to protect the privacy of individuals; and to avoid situations where the lawyer's exercise of judgment on behalf of the client will be clouded by his own pecuniary self-interest.[19]

We need not discuss or evaluate each of these interests in detail as appellant has conceded that the State has a legitimate and indeed "compelling" interest in preventing those aspects of solicitation that involve fraud, undue influence, intimidation, overreaching, and other forms of "vexatious conduct." We agree that protection of the public from these aspects of solicitation is a legitimate and important state interest.

III

Appellant's concession that strong state interests justify regulation to prevent the evils he enumerates would end this case but for his insistence that none of those evils was found to be present in his acts of solicitation. He challenges what he characterizes as the "indiscriminate application" of the rules to him and thus attacks the validity of DR 2–103(A) and DR 2–104(A) not facially, but as applied to his acts of solicitation. And because no allegations or findings were made of the specific wrongs appellant concedes would justify disciplinary action, appellant terms his solicitation "pure," meaning "soliciting and obtaining agreements from Carol McClintock and Wanda Lou Holbert to represent each of them," without more. Appellant therefore argues that we must decide whether a State may discipline him for solicitation *per se* without offending the First and Fourteenth Amendments.

We agree that the appropriate focus is on appellant's conduct. And, as appellant urges, we must undertake an independent review of the record to determine whether that conduct was constitutionally protected. But appellant errs in assuming that the constitutional validity of the judgment below depends on proof that his conduct constituted actual overreaching or inflicted some specific injury on Wanda Holbert and Carol McClintock. His assumption flows from the premise that nothing less than actual proven harm to the solicited individual would be a sufficiently important state interest to justify disciplining the attorney who solicits employment in person for pecuniary gain.

Appellant's argument misconceives the nature of the State's interest. The rules prohibiting solicitation are prophylactic measures whose objective is the prevention of harm before it occurs. The rules were

19. A lawyer who engages in personal solicitation of clients may be inclined to subordinate the best interests of the client to his own pecuniary interests. Even if unintentionally, the lawyer's ability to evaluate the legal merit of his client's claims may falter when the conclusion will affect the lawyer's income. A valid claim might be settled too quickly, or a claim with little merit pursued beyond the point of reason. These lapses of judgment can occur in any legal representation, but we cannot say that the pecuniary motivation of the lawyer who solicits a particular representation does not create special problems of conflict of interest.

applied in this case to discipline a lawyer for soliciting employment for pecuniary gain under circumstances likely to result in the adverse consequences the State seeks to avert. In such a situation, which is inherently conducive to overreaching and other forms of misconduct, the State has a strong interest in adopting and enforcing rules of conduct designed to protect the public from harmful solicitation by lawyers whom it has licensed.

The State's perception of the potential for harm in circumstances such as those presented in this case is well-founded. The detrimental aspects of face-to-face selling even of ordinary consumer products have been recognized and addressed by the Federal Trade Commission,[23] and it hardly need be said that the potential for overreaching is significantly greater when a lawyer, a professional trained in the art of persuasion, personally solicits an unsophisticated, injured, or distressed lay person.[24] Such an individual may place his or her trust in a lawyer regardless of the latter's qualifications or the individual's actual need for legal representation, simply in response to persuasion under circumstances conducive to uninformed acquiescence. Although it is argued that personal solicitation is valuable because it may apprise a victim of misfortune of his or her legal rights, the very plight of that person not only makes him or her more vulnerable to influence but also may make advice all the more intrusive. Thus, under these adverse conditions the overtures of an uninvited lawyer may distress the solicited individual simply because of their obtrusiveness and the invasion of the individual's privacy,[25] even when no other harm materializes. Under such circumstances, it is not unreasonable for the State to presume that in-person solicitation by lawyers more often than not will be injurious to the person solicited.

The efficacy of the State's effort to prevent such harm to prospective clients would be substantially diminished if, having proved a solicitation in circumstances like those of this case, the State were required in addition to prove actual injury. Unlike the advertising in *Bates*, in-person solicitation is not visible or otherwise open to public

**23.** The Federal Trade Commission has identified and sought to regulate the abuses inherent in the direct-selling industry. See 37 Fed.Reg. 22934, 22937 (1972). Quoted in the FTC report is an observation by the National Consumer Law Center that " '[t]he door to door selling technique strips from the consumer one of the fundamentals in his role as an informed purchaser, the decision as to when, where, and how he will present himself to the marketplace * * *.' "

**24.** Most lay persons are unfamiliar with the law, with how legal services normally are procured, and with typical arrangements between lawyer and client. To be sure, the same might be said about the lay person who seeks out a lawyer for the first time. But the critical distinction is that in the latter situation the prospective client has made an initial choice of a lawyer at least for purposes of a consultation; has chosen the time to seek legal advice; has had a prior opportunity to confer with family, friends, or a public or private referral agency; and has chosen whether to consult with the lawyer alone or accompanied.

**25.** Unlike the reader of an advertisement, who can "effectively avoid further bombardment of [his] sensibilities simply by averting [his] eyes," Cohen v. California, 403 U.S., at 21, 91 S.Ct., at 1786, the target of the solicitation may have difficulty avoiding being importuned and distressed even if the lawyer seeking employment is entirely well-meaning.

scrutiny. Often there is no witness other than the lawyer and the lay person whom he has solicited, rendering it difficult or impossible to obtain reliable proof of what actually took place. This would be especially true if the lay person were so distressed at the time of the solicitation that he or she could not recall specific details at a later date. If appellant's view were sustained, in-person solicitation would be virtually immune to effective oversight and regulation by the State or by the legal profession, in contravention of the State's strong interest in regulating members of the Bar in an effective, objective, and self-enforcing manner. It therefore is not unreasonable, or violative of the Constitution, for a State to respond with what in effect is a prophylactic rule.

On the basis of the undisputed facts of record, we conclude that the disciplinary rules constitutionally could be applied to appellant. He approached two young accident victims at a time when they were especially incapable of making informed judgments or of assessing and protecting their own interests. He solicited Carol McClintock in a hospital room where she lay in traction and sought out Wanda Lou Holbert on the day she came home from the hospital, knowing from his prior inquiries that she had just been released. Appellant urged his services upon the young women and used the information he had obtained from the McClintocks, and the fact of his agreement with Carol, to induce Wanda to say "O. K." in response to his solicitation. He employed a concealed tape recorder, seemingly to insure that he would have evidence of Wanda's oral assent to the representation. He emphasized that his fee would come out of the recovery, thereby tempting the young women with what sounded like a cost-free and therefore irresistible offer. He refused to withdraw when Mrs. Holbert requested him to do so only a day after the initial meeting between appellant and Wanda Lou and continued to represent himself to the insurance company as Wanda Holbert's lawyer.

The court below did not hold that these or other facts were proof of actual harm to Wanda Holbert or Carol McClintock but rested on the conclusion that appellant had engaged in the general misconduct proscribed by the disciplinary rules. Under our view of the State's interest in averting harm by prohibiting solicitation in circumstances where it is likely to occur, the absence of explicit proof or findings of harm or injury is immaterial. The facts in this case present a striking example of the potential for overreaching that is inherent in a lawyer's in-person solicitation of professional employment. They also demonstrate the need for prophylactic regulation in furtherance of the State's interest in protecting the lay public. We hold that the application of Disciplinary Rules 2–103(A) and 2–104(A) to appellant does not offend the Constitution.

Accordingly, the judgment of the Supreme Court of Ohio is

Affirmed.

Mr. Justice MARSHALL, concurring in part and concurring in the judgments [in *Ohralik* and In re Primus, Comment (1) below].

I agree with the majority that the factual circumstances presented by appellant Ohralik's conduct "pose dangers that the State has a right to prevent," and accordingly that he may constitutionally be disciplined * * *.

* * * The circumstances in which appellant Ohralik initially approached his two clients provide classic examples of "ambulance chasing," fraught with obvious potential for misrepresentation and overreaching. Ohralik, an experienced lawyer in practice for over 25 years, approached two 18-year-old women shortly after they had been in a traumatic car accident. One was in traction in a hospital room; the other had just been released following nearly two weeks of hospital care. Both were in pain and may have been on medication; neither had more than a high school education. Certainly these facts alone would have cautioned hesitation in pressing one's employment on either of these women; any lawyer of ordinary prudence should have carefully considered whether the person was in an appropriate condition to make a decision about legal counsel.

But appellant not only foisted himself upon these clients; he acted in gross disregard for their privacy by covertly recording, without their consent or knowledge, his conversations with Wanda Lou Holbert and Carol McClintock's family. This conduct, which appellant has never disputed, is itself completely inconsistent with an attorney's fiduciary obligation fairly and fully to disclose to clients his activities affecting their interest. And appellant's unethical conduct was further compounded by his pursuing Wanda Lou Holbert, when her interests were clearly in potential conflict with those of his prior-retained client, Carol McClintock.

What is objectionable about Ohralik's behavior here is not so much that he solicited business for himself, but rather the circumstances in which he performed that solicitation and the means by which he accomplished it. Appropriately, the Court's actual holding in *Ohralik* is a limited one: that the solicitation of business, under circumstances—such as those found in this record—presenting substantial dangers of harm to society or the client independent of the solicitation itself, may constitutionally be prohibited by the State. In this much of the Court's opinion in *Ohralik*, I join fully.

* * * While the Court's *Primus* opinion does suggest that the only justification for nonsolicitation rules is their prophylactic value in preventing such evils as actual fraud, overreaching, deception, and misrepresentation, I think it should be made crystal clear that the State's legitimate interests in this area are limited to prohibiting such substantive evils.

Like rules against advertising, rules against solicitation substantially impede the flow of important information to consumers from those most likely to provide it—the practicing members of the Bar. * * *

Not only do prohibitions on solicitation interfere with the free flow of information protected by the First Amendment, but by origin and in practice they operate in a discriminatory manner. As we have noted, these constraints developed as rules of "etiquette" and came to rest on the notion that a lawyer's reputation in his community would spread by word-of-mouth and bring business to the worthy lawyer. * * * If ever this conception were more generally true, it is now valid only with respect to those persons who move in the relatively elite social and educational circles in which knowledge about legal problems, legal remedies and lawyers is widely shared.

The impact of the nonsolicitation rules, moreover, is discriminatory with respect to the suppliers as well as the consumers of legal services. Just as the persons who suffer most from lack of knowledge about lawyers' availability belong to the less privileged classes of society, so the disciplinary rules against solicitation fall most heavily on those attorneys engaged in a single practitioner or small partnership form of practice—attorneys who typically earn less than their fellow practitioners in large, corporate-oriented firms. Indeed, some scholars have suggested that the rules against solicitation were developed by the professional bar to keep recently immigrated lawyers, who gravitated toward the smaller, personal injury practice, from effective entry into the profession. See J. Auerbach, Unequal Justice 42–62, 126–129 (1976). In light of this history, I am less inclined than the majority appears to be to weigh favorably in the balance of the State's interests here the longevity of the ban on attorney solicitation.

By discussing the origin and impact of the nonsolicitation rules, I do not mean to belittle those obviously substantial interests that the State has in regulating attorneys to protect the public from fraud, deceit, misrepresentation, overreaching, undue influence, and invasions of privacy. But where honest, unpressured "commercial" solicitation is involved—a situation not presented in either of these cases—I believe it is open to doubt whether the State's interests are sufficiently compelling to warrant the restriction on the free flow of information which results from a sweeping nonsolicitation rule and against which the First Amendment ordinarily protects. While the State's interest in regulating in-person solicitation may, for reasons explained in *Ohralik*, be somewhat greater than its interest in regulating print advertisements, these concededly legitimate interests might well be served by more specific and less restrictive rules than a total ban on pecuniary solicitation. For example, the Justice Department has suggested that the disciplinary rules be reworded "so as to *permit* all solicitation and advertising except the kinds that are false, misleading, undignified or champertous." * * * [c]

c. Justice Rehnquist concurred in the judgment for the reasons expressed in his dissent in In re Primus, infra Comment (1). Justice Brennan took no part.

### *Comment*

(1) *Primus.* In In re Primus,[1] decided the same day as *Ohralik*, the Court drew a sharp distinction between *non-commercial* solicitation and the type of commercial solicitation involved in *Ohralik*. A 7–1 Court reversed the reprimand of a lawyer who, after a meeting triggered by reports that mothers in a South Carolina county were being sterilized or threatened with sterilization as a condition to continued receipt of Medicaid, wrote one of the attendees that the American Civil Liberties Union would like to file a lawsuit in her behalf against the doctor who had sterilized her. The woman would not be charged a fee, but the ACLU would ask the court to award attorney fees. The Court, per Justice Powell, reasoned:

> "Unlike the situation in *Ohralik* * * * appellant's act of solicitation took the form of a letter to a woman with whom appellant had discussed the possibility of seeking redress for an allegedly unconstitutional sterilization. This was not in-person solicitation for pecuniary gain. Appellant was communicating an offer of free assistance by attorneys associated with the ACLU, not an offer predicated on entitlement to a share of any monetary recovery. And her actions were undertaken to express personal political beliefs and to advance the civil-liberties objectives of the ACLU, rather than to derive financial gain. * * *
>
> "[A]ppellant's conduct implicates interests of free expression and association sufficient to justify the level of protection recognized in *Button* and subsequent cases [supra pp. 527–34]. * * *
>
> " * * * From all that appears, the ACLU and its local chapters, much like the NAACP and its local affiliates in *Button*, 'engage * * * in extensive educational and lobbying activities' and 'also devote * * * much of [their] funds and energies to an extensive program of assisting certain kinds of litigation on behalf of [their] declared purposes.' * * * For the ACLU, as for the NAACP, 'litigation is not a technique of resolving private differences'; it is 'a form of political expression' and 'political association.' * * *[a]

1. 436 U.S. 412, 98 S.Ct. 1893, 56 L.Ed.2d 417 (1978).

a. The Court rejected appellee's attempt to distinguish *Button* on the ground that the ACLU would ask the court to award attorney fees, saying:

> "[T]he ACLU's policy of requesting an award of counsel fees does not take this case outside of the protection of *Button*. [T]here are differences between counsel fees awarded by a court and traditional fee-paying arrangements which militate against a presumption that ACLU sponsorship of litigation is motivated by considerations of pecuniary gain rather than by its widely recognized goal of vindicating civil liberties. Counsel fees are awarded in the discretion of the court; awards are not drawn from the plaintiff's recovery, and are usually premised on a successful outcome; and the amounts awarded often may not correspond to fees generally obtainable in private litigation. * * * Although such benefit to the organization may increase with the maintenance of successful litigation, the same situation obtains with voluntary contributions and foundation support, which also may rise with ACLU victories in important areas of the law. That possibility, standing alone, offers no basis for equating the work of lawyers associated with the ACLU or the NAACP with that of a group that exists for the primary purpose of financial gain through the recovery of counsel fees."

" * * * Where political expression or association is at issue, this Court has not tolerated the degree of imprecision that often characterizes government regulation of the conduct of commercial affairs. The approach we adopt today in *Ohralik*, that the State may proscribe in-person solicitation for pecuniary gain under circumstances likely to result in adverse consequences, cannot be applied to appellant's activity on behalf of the ACLU. Although a showing of potential danger may suffice in the former context, appellant may not be disciplined unless her activity in fact involved the type of misconduct at which South Carolina's broad prohibition is said to be directed.

"The record does not support appellee's contention that undue influence, overreaching, misrepresentation, or invasion of privacy actually occurred in this case. Appellant's letter * * * followed up the earlier meeting—one concededly protected by the First and Fourteenth Amendments—by notifying [attendee] that the ACLU would be interested in supporting possible litigation. The letter imparted additional information material to making an informed decision about whether to authorize litigation, and permitted [attendee] an opportunity, which she exercised, for arriving at a deliberate decision. The letter was not facially misleading; indeed, it offered 'to explain what is involved so you can understand what is going on.' The transmittal of this letter—as contrasted with in-person solicitation—involved no appreciable invasion of privacy;[28] nor did it afford any significant opportunity for overreaching or coercion. Moreover, the fact that there was a written communication lessens substantially the difficulty of policing solicitation practices that do offend valid rules of professional conduct. See *Ohralik*. The manner of solicitation in this case certainly was no more likely to cause harmful consequences than the activity considered in *Button*. * * *

"The State's interests in preventing the 'stirring up' of frivolous or vexatious litigation and minimizing commercialization of the legal profession offer no further justification for the discipline administered in this case. * * *[31]

28. This record does not provide a constitutionally adequate basis for a finding, not made below, that appellant deliberately thrust her professional services on an individual who had communicated unambiguously a decision against litigation. Cf. Rowan v. Post Office Dept., 397 U.S. 728, 90 S.Ct. 1484, 25 L.Ed.2d 736 (1970). * * *

31. *Button* makes clear that "regulations which reflect hostility to stirring up litigation have been aimed chiefly at those who urge recourse to the courts for private gain, serving no public interest." * * * In recognition of the overarching obligation of the lawyer to serve the community, see Canon 2 of the ABA Code of Professional Responsibility, the ethical rules of the legal profession traditionally have recognized an exception from any general ban on solicitation for offers of representation, without charge, extended to individuals who may be unable to obtain legal assistance on their own. See e.g., In re Ades, 6 F.Supp. 467, 475–476 (Md.1934); Gunnels v. Atlanta Bar Assn., 191 Ga. 366, 12 S.E.2d 602 (1940); American Bar Association, Committee on Professional Ethics and Grievances, Formal Opinion 148 at 416–419 (1935).

"At bottom, the case against appellant rests on the proposition that a State may regulate in a prophylactic fashion all solicitation activities of lawyers because there may be some potential for overreaching, conflict of interest, or other substantive evils whenever a lawyer gives unsolicited advice and communicates an offer of representation to a layman. Under certain circumstances, that approach is appropriate in the case of speech that simply 'propose[s] a commercial transaction.' In the context of political expression and association, however, a State must regulate with significantly greater precision.[32]" [2]

**32.** Normally, the purpose or motive of the speaker is not central to First Amendment protection, but it does bear on the distinction between conduct that is "an associational aspect of 'expression'" and other activity subject to plenary regulation by government. *Button* recognized that certain forms of "cooperative, organizational activity," including litigation, are part of the "freedom to engage in association for the advancement of beliefs and ideas," and that this freedom is an implicit guarantee of the First Amendment. As shown above, appellant's speech—as part of associational activity—was expression intended to advance "beliefs and ideas." In *Ohralik*, the lawyer was not engaged in associational activity for the advancement of beliefs and ideas; his purpose was the advancement of his own commercial interests. The line, based in part on the motive of the speaker and the character of the expressive activity, will not always be easy to draw, but that is no reason for avoiding the undertaking.

2. The Court went on to add:

"The State is free to fashion reasonable restrictions with respect to the time, place and manner of solicitation by members of its Bar. The State's special interest in regulating members of a profession it licenses, and who serve as officers of its courts, amply justifies the application of narrowly drawn rules to proscribe solicitation that in fact is misleading, overbearing, or involves other features of deception or improper influence. [Footnote 33: "We have no occasion here to delineate the precise contours of permissible state regulation. Thus, for example, a different situation might be presented if an innocent or merely negligent misstatement were made by a lawyer on behalf of an organization engaged in furthering associational or political interests."] A State also may forbid in-person solicitation for pecuniary gain under circumstances likely to result in these evils. See *Ohralik*. And a State may insist that lawyers not solicit on behalf of lay organizations that exert control over the actual conduct of any ensuing litigation. See *Button* (White, J., concurring in part and dissenting in part). Accordingly, nothing in this opinion should be read to foreclose carefully tailored regulation that does not abridge unecessarily the associational freedom of nonprofit organizations, or their members, having characteristics like those of the NAACP or the ACLU."

Blackmun, J., concurred, saying:

"Although I join the opinion of the Court, my understanding of the [paragraph just quoted] requires further explanation. The dicta contained in that paragraph are unnecessary to the decision of this case and its First Amendment overtones. I for one, am not now able to delineate in the area of political solicitation the extent of state authority to proscribe misleading statements. Despite the positive language of the text, footnote 33 explains that the Court also has refused to draw a line regarding misrepresentation * * *."

Marshall, J., concurred in part and concurred in the judgment in an opinion portions of which are set forth above in connection with *Ohralik*. Justice Marshall's opinion also expressed agreement with Justice Blackmun's concerns just noted.

Rehnquist, J., dissented, decrying what he called "a jurisprudence of epithets and slogans * * * in which 'ambulance-chasers' suffer one fate and 'civil liberties lawyers' another" and saying:

"In distinguishing between Primus' protected solicitation and Ohralik's unprotected solicitation, the Court lamely declares, 'We have not discarded the "commonsense" distinction between speech proposing a commercial transaction, which occurs in an area traditionally subject to government regulation, and other varieties of speech.' Yet to the extent that this 'commonsense' distinction focuses on the content of the speech, it is at least suspect under many of this Court's First Amendment cases, and to the extent it focuses upon the motive of the speaker, it is subject to

*Primus* may be read narrowly as holding that lawyer solicitation is protected by the first amendment when it is—

(a) In writing,

(b) For free representation,

(c) By a nonprofit organization,

(d) Furthering ideological goals, and

(e) Not *in fact* deceptive or exerting undue influence.

But it seems that (b) and (e) are the only *crucial* elements, so that the holding may be read broadly to protect any *non-commercial* solicitation that is not *in fact* deceptive or exerting undue influence.[3]

(2) *Ohralik analysis.* Similarly, *Ohralik* may be read narrowly as holding that lawyer solicitation is not protected when it is—

(a) In person,

(b) For pecuniary gain, and

(c) Under circumstances likely to pose dangers the state has an "important" interest in preventing, such as:

(i) Overreaching and undue influence,

(ii) Invasion of individual privacy, or

(iii) The lawyer's professional judgment being clouded by pecuniary self-interest.

But it seems that (a), notwithstanding its repeated emphasis in the Court's opinion, is extraneous except as it bears upon (c), so that the holding may be read broadly to allow prohibition of *commercial* solicitation as long as it falls within (c).

(3) *R.M.J.* In In re R.M.J.,[4] a unanimous U.S. Supreme Court reversed a lawyer's reprimand for violating DR 2-102(A)(2)'s proscription on sending announcement cards to persons other than "lawyers, clients, former clients, personal friends, and relatives." The lawyer had sent cards announcing the opening of his office to a selected list of addressees. The Court, per Justice Powell, reasoned:

> "Mailings and handbills may be more difficult to supervise than newspapers. But * * * we deal with a silent record. There

manipulation by clever practitioners. If Albert Ohralik, like Edna Primus, viewed litigation ' "not [as] a technique of resolving private differences," ' but as ' "a form of political expression" and "political association," ' for all that appears he would be restored to his right to practice. And we may be sure that the next lawyer in Ohralik's shoes who is disciplined for similar conduct will come here cloaked in the prescribed mantle of 'political association' to assure that insurance companies do not take unfair advantage of policy holders. * * * "

Brennan, J., took no part.

3. Compare Note, In-Person Solicitation by Public Interest Law Firms: A Look at the A.B.A. Code Provisions in Light of *Primus* and *Ohralik*, 49 Geo.Wash.L.Rev. 309 (1981); Attorney Solicitation: The Scope of State Regulation after Primus and Ohralik, 12 U.Mich.J.L.Ref. 144, 157–63 (1978).

4. 455 U.S. 191, 102 S.Ct. 929, 71 L.Ed.2d 64 (1982).

is no indication that an inability to supervise is the reason the State restricts the potential audience of announcement cards. Nor is it clear that an absolute prohibition is the only solution. For example, by requiring a filing with the Advisory Committee of a copy of all general mailings, the State may be able to exercise reasonable supervision over such mailings.[19] There is no indication in the record of a failed effort to proceed along such a less restrictive path.[20] See Central Hudson Gas v. Public Service Comm'n, 447 U.S. 557, 566, 100 S.Ct., 2343, 2351, 65 L.Ed.2d 341 (1980) ('we must determine whether the regulation * * * is not more extensive than is necessary to serve' the governmental interest asserted)."

### *Questions*

(1) *Commercial solicitation by mail.* In addition to protecting the mailing of announcement cards, *R.M.J.* plainly undercuts state court decisions disciplining lawyers for circulating *general advertisments* by means of direct mail.[1] Does it allow for RPC 7.3's approach which prohibits *letters* soliciting professional employment except those addressed "to persons not known to need legal services of the kind provided by the lawyer in a particular matter, but who are so situated that they might in general find such services useful"?

RPC 7.3's Comment explains:

"[The] dangers [of undue influence, intimidation, and overreaching] attend direct solicitation whether in-person or by mail. Direct mail solicitation cannot be effectively regulated by means less drastic than outright prohibition. One proposed safeguard is to require that the designation 'Advertising' be stamped on any envelope containing a solicitation letter. This would do nothing

19. Rule 7.2(b) of the [RPC] requires that "A copy or recording of an advertisement or written communication shall be kept * * *."

[Eds.] See Foley v. Alabama State Bar, 481 F.Supp. 1308 (N.D.Ala.1979) (disciplinary rule may require sending ad to state bar within three days after publication), reversed on other grounds 648 F.2d 355 (5th Cir. 1981).

20. The Advisory Committee argues that a general mailing from a lawyer would be "frightening" to the public unaccustomed to receiving letters from law offices. If indeed this is likely, the lawyer could be required to stamp "This is an Advertisement" on the envelope. See Consolidated Edison v. Public Serv. Comm'n, 447 U.S. 530, 541–542 (1980) (billing insert is not a significant intrusion upon privacy, and privacy interest can be protected through means other than a general prohibition).

[Eds.] See also Gulf Oil Co. v. Bernard, 452 U.S. 89, 101 S.Ct. 2193, 68 L.Ed.2d 693 (1981), wherein the court, proceeding on the nonconstitutional basis that the district court had exceeded its authority under F.R.Civ.P. 23 to make "appropriate" orders in class actions, severely limited federal district courts' power to issue orders restricting communications with actual or potential class members in class actions.

1. *E.g.* Eaton v. Supreme Court, 270 Ark. 573, 607 S.W.2d 55 (1980), cert. denied, 450 U.S. 966, 101 S.Ct. 1483, 67 L.Ed.2d 615 (1981) (discipline for causing advertisement specifying $10 initial consultation fee and listing many areas of law to be included in mailed packet of local businesses' discount coupons).

Compare Bishop v. Committee on Professional Ethics, 521 F.Supp. 1219 (S.D. Iowa 1981) (state may not bar direct mailing of permissible advertisements), vacated as moot 686 F.2d 1278 (8th Cir. 1982); In re Madsen, 68 Ill.2d 472, 12 Ill.Dec. 576, 370 N.E.2d 199 (1977) (no discipline for mailing 2,090 clients communication entitled "Tips from your Lawyer for 1973" advising on many topics and indicating services firm could provide).

to assure the accuracy and reliability of the contents. Another suggestion is that solicitation letters be filed with a state regulatory agency. This would be ineffective as a practical matter. State lawyer discipline agencies struggle for resources to investigate specific complaints, much less for those necessary to screen lawyers' mail solicitation material. Even if they could examine such materials, agency staff members are unlikely to know anything about the lawyer or about the prospective client's underlying problem. Without such knowledge they cannot determine whether the lawyer's representations are misleading. In any event, such review would be after the fact, potentially too late to avert the undesirable consequences of disseminating false and misleading material.

"General mailings not speaking to a specific matter do not pose the same danger of abuse as targeted mailings, and therefore are not prohibited by this Rule. The representations made in such mailings are necessarily general rather than tailored, less importuning than informative. They are addressed to recipients unlikely to be specially vulnerable at the time, hence who are likely to be more skeptical about unsubstantiated claims. General mailings not addressed to recipients involved in a specific legal matter or incident, therefore, more closely resemble permissible advertising rather than prohibited solicitation."[2]

RPC 7.3 is sound in not prohibiting letters addressed "to persons not known to need legal services of the kind provided by the lawyer in a particular matter" albeit "so situated that they might in general find such services useful." A number of courts have found first amendment protection for such letters.[3]

But is it sound in prohibiting letters to persons "known to need legal services of the kind provided by the lawyer in a particular matter"? The Kansas Supreme Court's decision in State v. Moses[4] sup-

2. As indicated supra p. 537, the Comment goes on to state that the Rule would not prohibit a lawyer from contacting representatives of organizations that may be interested in establishing a group or prepaid legal plan, to inform them of the availability and details of the plan or arrangement the lawyer is willing to offer.

3. See Florida Bar v. Schreiber, 420 So.2d 599 (Fla.1982) (no discipline for sending international trade company letter recommending services for immigration and naturalization matters), vacating 407 So.2d 595 (Fla.1981); Kentucky Bar Association v. Stuart, 568 S.W.2d 933 (Ky.1978) (no discipline for letters to real estate agencies stating prices for routine real estate legal services); In re Appert, 315 N.W.2d 204 (Minn.1981) (no discipline for sending more than 150 letters to persons not known to have used IUD in question recommending contingent fee representation in litigation against IUD manufacturer).

But see Allison v. Louisiana State Bar Ass'n, 362 So.2d 489, 5 A.L.R. 4th 852 (La.1978) (no injunction against disciplining lawyers for sending letters to employers soliciting formation of prepaid legal service arrangements under which lawyers would serve). Cf. Adler, Barish, Daniels, Levin & Creskoff v. Epstein, 482 Pa. 416, 393 A.2d 1175, 1 A.L.R. 4th 1144 (1978), appeal dismissed 442 U.S. 907, 99 S.Ct. 2817, 61 L.Ed.2d 272 (1979) (injunction against associates who in person, by phone, and by mail told clients on whose cases they had worked that the clients could—using enclosed forms—discharge the law firm and retain a new firm the associates were forming).

4. 231 Kan. 243, 642 P.2d 1004 (1982).

ports this approach. The *Moses* court censured a lawyer for sending letters to 150 homeowners whose names the lawyer had gathered from the realtors multiple listing. The letters advised the homeowners that they could save thousands of dollars by terminating their real estate broker listing contract, selling "By Owner," and paying $300 for the lawyer's legal services. The Kansas court's rationale was that the *Ohralik* and *R.M.J.* opinions had recognized a distinction between advertising and direct solicitation. The Kansas court concluded:

> "The solicitation in the instant case, while not being of the nature of ambulance chasing and hospital room solicitation, nevertheless is directed to a segment of the public which, under present economic conditions, is extremely vulnerable to a suggestion of employment that may or may not be advantageous to the individual homeowner. We are of the opinion that the concept of the regulation and restriction of personal solicitation is one which is not only viable but works to the benefit of the general public and to the fair administration of justice." [5]

To the contrary is the decision of New York's highest court in Koffler v. Joint Bar Association.[6] There the court refused to discipline lawyers for sending letters soliciting real estate legal work from 7500 property owners the lawyers understood were selling their homes. The court reasoned:

> "We disagree * * * with the Appellate Division's conclusion that the solicitation that [the] provisions condemn can be differentiated from constitutionally protected commercial speech simply by categorizing the former as solicitation and the latter as advertising. The Supreme Court has said so in so many words, overruling in *Button* the contention that 'solicitation' is wholly outside the area of First Amendment protection, and declaring in Bigelow v. Virginia, 421 U.S. 809, 826, 95 S.Ct. 2222, 2235, 44 L.Ed.2d 600 [1975] that: 'Regardless of the particular label asserted by the State—whether it calls speech "commercial" or "commercial advertising" or "solicitation"—a court may not escape the task of assessing the First Amendment interest at stake and weighing it against the public interest allegedly served by the regulation.' * * *
>
> "Invasion of privacy and the possibility of overbearing persuasion, both of which were condemned in *Ohralik* and which could conceivably be present in telephone solicitation * * * are not sufficiently possible in mail solicitation to justify banning it. As the Supreme Court put it in Consolidated Edison Co. v. Public Serv. Comm., 447 U.S. 530, 542, 100 S.Ct. 2326, 2336, 65 L.Ed. 319 [1980], a recipient of a lawyer's letter 'may escape exposure to objection-

5. See In re Frank, — Ind. —, 440 N.E.2d 676 (1982) (lawyer agreed to public reprimand for solicitation letters to 20 persons court records indicated were unrepresented driving-under-the-influence defendants).

6. 51 N.Y.2d 140, 432 N.Y.S.2d 872, 412 N.E.2d 927 (1980), cert. denied 450 U.S. 1026, 101 S.Ct. 1733, 68 L.Ed.2d 221 (1981).

able material simply by transferring * * * [it] from envelope to wastebasket.' It is not enough to justify a ban that in some situations (marital discord, a death in the family) a solicitation letter may be offensive to the recipient, or that some people may fear receiving a lawyer's letter, or to suggest that there may be some who by reason of frequent receipt of lawyers' solicitation letters may discard without opening a mailed summons." [7]

(2) *Telephonic commercial solicitation.* Is RPC 7.3's prohibition of telephonic commercial solicitation valid?

As just noted, the *Koffler* court observed that "[i]nvasion of privacy and the possibility of overbearing persuasion * * * could conceivably be present in telephone solicitation." [8] In Greenberg v. Michigan Optometric Association,[9] a federal district court held that *optometrists* could be disciplined for hiring persons to engage in telephone solicitation of persons whose employer-provided insurance included optical benefits. Arguably telephonic solicitation by lawyers may be prohibited under *Ohralik* as likely to pose dangers of invasion of individal privacy and of overreaching and undue influence, and because its failure to produce a record impedes policing of solicitation restrictions.[10]

Contra it might be argued that some telephoning does not pose dangers of privacy invasion (e.g. calls to business location) or of overreaching and undue influence (e.g. calls to persons with knowledge of legal matters), and that the fact that telephoning produces no record is an insufficient reason to justify across the board prohibition.[11]

(3) *Face-to-face commercial solicitation.* Is RPC 7.3 sound in prohibiting face-to-face commercial solicitation without regard to whether it involves aggravating circumstances like those in *Ohralik*?

The U.S. Supreme Court apparently interprets *Ohralik* as permitting across the board prohibition of face-to-face commercial solic-

7. See Spencer v. Honorable Justices of the Supreme Court, 579 F.Supp. 880 (E.D.Pa.1984); Figa, Lawyer Solicitation Today and Under the Proposed Model Rules of Professional Conduct, 52 U.Colo.L.Rev. 393, 407 (1981).

8. Telephonic recommending of one's employment to a nonlawyer who has not sought advice regarding employment of a lawyer falls within DR 2–103(A)'s prohibition, but it is not at all clear that telephonic communication is reached by DR 2–104(A)'s restriction on accepting employment after "in-person" unsolicited advice to a nonlawyer recommending obtaining of counsel or taking of legal action.

Compare RPC 7.3 (" 'solicit' includes contact * * * by telephone").

9. 483 F.Supp. 142 (E.D.Mich.1980).

10. See Note, Attorney Solicitation of Clients: Proposed Solutions, 7 Hofstra L.Rev. 755, 775 (1979) ("[The potential] problem [of] invasion of privacy caused by the possible multitude of lawyers contacting potential clients * * * could be avoided only be permitting lawyers to solicit clients by sending one letter in the mail; personal or telephone contact would be prohibited until the client contacts the lawyer").

See generally Note, Give Me a Home Where No Salesmen Phone: Telephone Solicitation and the First Amendment, 7 Hastings Const.L.Q. 129 (1979).

11. See Note, Protection for Attorney Solicitation Slow in Coming, 33 U.Fla.L.Rev. 698, 718–19 (1981) (state should only prohibit telephone solicitation where lawyer of ordinary prudence should know the person is susceptible to pressure because of the person's emotional state).

itation by lawyers or their agents. In *R.M.J.* it said that the *Ohralik* Court had "held that the possibility of 'fraud, undue influence, intimidation, overreaching, and other forms of "vexatious conduct" ' was so likely in the context of in-person solicitation, that such solicitation could be prohibited."

Several post-*Ohralik* state court decisions have addressed the issue of face-to-face commercial solicitation by lawyers or their agents without indicating any first amendment qualms about *per se* prohibition.[12]

But in In re Teichner,[13] the Illinois Supreme Court held that in-person solicitation for pecuniary gain may not be prohibited "where associational values are * * * implicated." Accordingly, it refused to discipline Teichner for soliciting contingent fee representation of rail disaster victims in a Mississippi community. A black pastor who thought that the railroad claim agents were offering inadequate settlements and that local lawyers would not be satisfactory for the task invited Teichner and other lawyers to come into the community and helped them obtain victims' cases. However, the court did suspend Teichner for two years for soliciting in another disaster area where his acts "furthered the associational rights of no person or group."

Similarly, in Woll v. Kelley,[14] the Michigan Supreme Court, stating that some solicitation may be "too innocuous to prohibit consistent with *Ohralik*," indicated that the first amendment may limit the state's ability to prohibit even face-to-face commercial solicitation of potential clients by lawyers or their agents, and remanded the case to a lower court for further briefing and consideration of the issue.

A number of commentators have taken the position that some face-to-face commercial solicitation should be allowed.[15]

12. See In re Carroll, 124 Ariz. 80, 602 P.2d 461 (1979) (discipline for using and ratifying investigator's and client's conduct to solicit); Kitsis v. State Bar, 23 Cal.3d 857, 153 Cal.Rptr. 836, 592 P.2d 323 (1979) (disbarment for employing runners to solicit over 200 persons at accident scenes, hospitals and auto repair shops); Pace v. State, 368 So.2d 340 (Fla. 1979) (criminal conviction for instigating meeting with high school athlete who was prospective college football player which resulted in retainer agreement from student and his legal guardian); In re Perrello, 271 Ind. 560, 394 N.E.2d 127 (1979) (discipline for accepting employment after recommending obtaining of counsel and recommending own employment to traffic court defendants in courthouse). See generally Annot., 5 A.L.R. 4th 866 (1981).

13. 75 Ill.2d 88, 25 Ill.Dec. 609, 387 N.E.2d 265, cert. denied 444 U.S. 917, 100 S.Ct. 232, 62 L.Ed.2d 172 (1979).

14. 409 Mich. 500, 297 N.W.2d 578, 300 N.W.2d 171 (1980).

15. See, *e.g.*, Pulaski, In-Person Solicitation and the First Amendment: Was *Ohralik* Wrongly Decided? 1979 Ariz.St.L.J. 23, 65 (state should only prohibit misrepresentations, coercion, undue influence, and unduly intrusive forms of solicitation); Attorney Solicitation: The Scope of State Regulation after *Primus* and *Ohralik*, 12 U.Mich.J.L.Ref. 144, 180–83 (1981) (state should only (1) prohibit certain conduct such as deception, undue influence, intimidation, overreaching, promoting harassing litigation, and other types of vexatious conduct, (2) prohibit solicitation in settings where it would invade privacy, *viz.* hospitals, funerals, or accident scenes, (3) require soliciting lawyer to give potential client a list of other local lawyers who handle the same type of matter and an approximation of their fees, (4) require soliciting lawyer to give client notice of a cooling off period, e.g., 72 hours, during which client could rescind the retainer agreement without liability, and (5) bar solicitation of anyone who is apparently in a physical or mental condition which would make it unlikely that he or she could exercise reasonable, considerable judgment as to selection of a lawyer); Comment, Benign Solicitation of Clients by Attorneys, 54 Wash.L.Rev. 671, 688–92 (1979) (state should

(4) *Third party solicitation.* Should solicitation of third party referrals be treated differently than solicitation aimed directly at prospective clients?

Recent state court decisions have differed widely in their treatment of lawyer solicitation of third party referrals. Whereas several courts have attached no significance to the fact that the lawyer's solicitation was of a third party for a referral rather than directly to a prospective client,[16] the Michigan Supreme Court in In re Jaques,[17] relied upon the fact that the lawyer solicited a union's business agent to recommend the lawyer's employment to tunnel explosion victims as the basis for refusing to discipline, saying, "Under these circumstances, the union agent served as a buffer between the attorney and prospective clients thus alleviating the potential for overreaching and undue influence."

Contrariwise, in Greene v. Grievance Committee,[18] New York's highest court used the fact that the lawyer directed a *written* solicitation to real estate brokers seeking referrals rather than directly to prospective clients as the basis for imposing discipline, because of the dangers of *in-person* solicitation and the lawyer's judgment being affected by conflict of interest:

> "[S]ince the broker is in direct contact with his prospect (the lawyer's potential client), there is present * * * the in-person solicitation element which *Ohralik* found sufficient to sustain regulation against constitutional attack. * * *
>
> " * * * The possibility that the lawyer's view of marketability of title may be colored by his knowledge that the referring broker normally will receive no commission unless title closes, the improbability that the attorney will negotiate to the lowest possible

only (1) prohibit false, deceptive or misleading solicitation, (2) prohibit solicitation in situations that to an ordinarily prudent lawyer present a significant risk of undue influence, invasion of privacy, or overreaching, and (3) presume the impropriety of solicitation during a period in which judgment may be expected to be impaired, such as after an accidental injury or funeral unless a reasonable period for recovery has elapsed); Note, Protection for Attorney Solicitation Slow in Coming, 33 U.Fla.L.Rev. 698, 716, 728 (1981) (state should permit personal solicitation "if the lawyer knows, or it is reasonable to assume, that the person solicited is capable of rational decisonmaking"; it could forbid lawyer from taking an official action on behalf of client for a specified time during which client could rescind the employment agreement).

Compare American Medical Association v. FTC, 638 F.2d 443 (2d Cir. 1980), affirmed by equally divided court 455 U.S. 676, 102 S.Ct. 1744, 71 L.Ed.2d 546 (1982) (Blackmun, J., not participating) (FTC properly required AMA to cease and desist from promulgating, implementing and enforcing restraints on, *inter alia*, solicitation other than false or deceptive or "uninvited, in-person solicitation of actual or potential patients who, because of their particular circumstances, are vulnerable to undue influence").

**16.** See Kentucky Bar Association v. Stuart, 568 S.W.2d 933 (Ky.1978) (no discipline for letters to real estate brokers); Allison v. Louisiana State Bar Association, 362 So.2d 489, 5 A.L.R. 4th 852 (La.1978) (no injunction against discipline for letters to employers soliciting formation of prepaid legal service arrangements for employees).

**17.** 407 Mich. 26, 281 N.W.2d 469 (1979).

**18.** 54 N.Y.2d 118, 444 N.Y.S.2d 883, 429 N.E.2d 390 (1981), cert. denied 455 U.S. 1035, 102 S.Ct. 1738, 72 L.Ed.2d 153 (1982), reaffirmed after reconsideration in light of *R.M.J.*, in Alessi v. Committee on Professional Standards, 60 N.Y.2d 229, 469 N.Y.S.2d 577, 457 N.E.2d 682 (1983) cert. denied — U.S. —, 104 S.Ct. 1599, 80 L.Ed.2d 130 (1984).

level the commission to be paid to the broker who is an important source of business for him (or suggest to the client that he do so), the probability that the lawyer will not examine with the same independence that he otherwise would the puffery that the broker has indulged in to bring about the sale are examples of the conflict potential to be protected against."[19]

The Rules of Professional Conduct contain no provision like DR 2–103(C) prohibiting a lawyer's *requesting* a person to recommend or promote the lawyer's services,[20] as opposed to *compensating* the person for doing so.[21] Query whether such a request would violate RPC 8.4(a)'s prohibition of violating or attempting to violate the Rules of Professional Conduct "through the acts of another."[22]

**19.** Compare Blackmar, The Missouri Supreme Court and Lawyer Advertising: RMJ and its Aftermath, 47 Mo.L.Rev. 621, 656 (1982) (R.M.J.'s counsel calls *Greene* decision "absurd"); Note, Mail Advertising by Attorneys and the First Amendment, 46 Albany L.Rev. 250, 263–70 (1981) (third party mailings should not be prohibited, but only regulated to prevent conflict of interest, inadequate representation, and overreaching personal contacts).

**20.** Except as authorized in DR 2–101 regarding advertising in print and broadcast media and except that a lawyer may request referrals from and pay fees to a bar association lawyer referral service and may cooperate with the legal service activities of an organization enumerated in DR 2–103(D).

**21.** RPC 7.2(c) specifies:

"A lawyer shall not give anything of value to a person for recommending the lawyer's services, except that a lawyer may pay the reasonable cost of advertising or written communication permitted by this Rule [not involving solicitation as defined in Rule 7.3] and may pay the usual charges of a not-for-profit lawyer referral service or other legal service organization."

See DR 2–103(B) (lawyer shall not compensate person for recommending or securing lawyer's employment by a client, except lawyer may pay usual and reasonable fees or dues charged by organization listed in DR 2–103(D)).

**22.** Compare DR 1–102(A)(2) (lawyer shall not "[c]ircumvent a Disciplinary Rule through actions of another"); DR 2–103(E) ("A lawyer shall not accept employment when he knows or it is obvious that the person who seeks his services does so as a result of conduct prohibited under this Disciplinary Rule.").

*

# Index

**References are to Pages**

†